Dying

Dying
Facing the Facts

Second Edition

Edited by

HANNELORE WASS
University of Florida

FELIX M. BERARDO
University of Florida

ROBERT A. NEIMEYER
Memphis State University

HEMISPHERE PUBLISHING CORPORATION, Washington
A subsidiary of Harper & Row, Publishers, Inc.

Cambridge   New York   Philadelphia   San Francisco
London   Mexico City   São Paulo   Singapore   Sydney

DYING: Facing the Facts; Second Edition

2 3 4 5 6 7 8 9 0   B C B C   8 9 8

This book was set in Press Roman by Hemisphere Publishing Corporation. The editors were Eleana C. Villanueva and Janis K. Oppelt; the production supervisor was Peggy M. Rote; and the typesetter was Shirley J. McNett.
BookCrafters, Inc. was printer and binder.

Library of Congress Cataloging-in-Publication Data

Dying: facing the facts.

  (Series in death education, aging, and health care)
  Bibliography: p.
  Includes index.
  1. Death. 2. Thanatology. I. Wass, Hannelore.
II. Berardo, Felix M. III. Neimeyer, Robert A.,
    date. IV. Series. [DNLM: 1. Attitude to Death.
2. Death. BD 444.D94 D996]
HQ1073.D93   1987   306.9   87-8561
ISBN 0-89116-469-3 (cloth)
ISBN 0-89116-746-3 (pbk.)
ISSN 0275-3510

59,655

Contents

CONCLUSION

APPENDIXES

Contributors

Jeanne Quint Benoliel, RN, PhD, Professor and Chairperson, Department of Community Health Care Systems, University of Washington, Seattle, WA 98195

Felix M. Berardo, PhD, Professor and Chairperson, Department of Sociology, University of Florida, Gainesville, FL 32611

Donna Hodgkins Berardo, PhD, Assistant Professor of Pharmacy, University of Florida, Gainesville, FL 32611

Glen W. Davidson, PhD, Professor and Chairperson, Department of Medical Humanities, School of Medicine, Southern Illinois University, Springfield, IL 62708

Robert Fulton, PhD, Professor of Sociology and Director, Center for Death Education and Research, University of Minnesota, Minneapolis, MN 55455

Edward L. Kain, PhD, Associate Professor of Sociology, Southwestern University, Georgetown, TX 78626

Richard A. Kalish, PhD, Dean, External Degree Programs, Continuing and International Education, Antioch University, Yellow Springs, OH 45387

Anthony J. La Greca, PhD, Associate Professor of Sociology and Director, Urban Studies Center, University of Florida, Gainesville, FL 32611

John D. Morgan, PhD, Professor of Philosophy, King's College, Western Ontario University, London, Ontario N6A 2M3, Canada

Robert A. Neimeyer, PhD, Professor of Psychology, Memphis State University, Memphis, TN 38152

Lawrence C. Rainey, PhD, Behavioral Medicine Section, The Mason Clinic, Seattle, WA 98111-0900

Sheryl Schroeder Scheible, JD, School of Law, University of New Mexico, Albuquerque, NM 87131

Harry H. Sisler, Dean Emeritus of the Graduate School and Distinguished Service Professor of Chemistry, University of Florida, Gainesville, FL 32611

Judith M. Stillion, PhD, Professor of Psychology and Associate Vice Chancellor for Academic Affairs, Western Carolina University, Cullowhee, NC 28723

Robert M. Veatch, PhD, Professor of Medical Ethics, Georgetown University, Washington, DC 20057

Hannelore Wass, PhD, Professor of Educational Psychology, University of Florida, Gainesville, FL 32611

Arthur Zucker, Professor of Philosophy, Ohio University, Athens, OH 45701

Preface

Since the first edition of *Dying: Facing the Facts* was published, the field of thanatology has expanded and crystallized. In response to these changes, this second edition has also evolved, both in its editorship and its scope. Joining Hannelore Wass, an educational psychologist and editor of the original volume, is Felix M. Berardo, a sociologist, and Robert A. Neimeyer, a clinical psychologist. We have tried to contribute the unique expertise of our respective disciplines in our dual roles as authors and editors. We hope that our efforts, together with those of the other contributors, have resulted in a book that reflects the multidisciplinary character of thanatology, achieves scholarly rigor, and attains our goal of presenting state-of-the-art knowledge of the broad range of topics selected for inclusion in this volume. Of the 17 contributors to this edition, five are psychologists, five are sociologists, four are philosophers or medical ethicists, and the remaining three are specialists in nursing, law, and chemistry, respectively.

To meet our objectives, some changes in the range and organization of topics in the first edition were necessary. Of the 18 chapters in the current volume, 13 are newly written and the remaining five have been thoroughly revised. New chapters address topics that were omitted in the first edition, such as suicide, the experience of dying, death anxiety, and problems in studying death, as well as issues that have gained salience over the past several years, such as life preservation and global survival. Inevitably, the addition of these chapters required the deletion of others covered in the original edition. Most of these deletions were made reluctantly. Two highly literate introductory chapters providing an overview of the first edition have been replaced by a single, much briefer one. The chapter on the funeral industry has been deleted. Three other chapters, on death and the elderly, death education, and the physiology of dying, have been deleted with some regret, although whenever possible, related material has been assimilated into the reorganized chapters. Most notably, the material in the original chapter on social and psychological aspects of dying has been considerably expanded and is now discussed in three separate chapters. In spite of these changes, we have retained the organizational scheme of the first edition, combining the chapters into three major groupings: I. Problems and Perspectives; II. Data: The Facts of Dying and Death; and III. Challenge: Meeting the Issues of Death.

Finally, we should note that both the content and form of the book reflect our decision to produce a readable, but sophisticated, examination of thanatological issues suitable for the serious reader. For this reason, we have emphasized substance over style, omitting illustrations and other supplementary materials in the text proper in order to devote the space to a scholarly discussion of the various topics. Nonetheless, we have tried to avoid technical jargon as much as possible, in order to ensure the accessibility of the book to specialists and nonspecialists alike.

We have provided review questions at the end of each chapter and listed some suggested activities and a variety of additional resources, including selections from literature and the arts in the appendixes. We hope the reader will find these helpful and stimulating.

In conclusion, this second edition of *Dying: Facing the Facts* attempts to present up-to-date knowledge and current thinking in the field of thanatology. We hope that it will both inform and sensitize the reader to the complexities surrounding the human experience of death and dying in contemporary western societies.

Hannelore Wass
Felix M. Berardo
Robert A. Neimeyer

Preface
to the First Edition

Why add another book on death and dying to the many volumes that have already been written on the subject? This question must be asked today by anyone who thinks of writing in the field. The primary motivation to proceed with this book was the conviction that there is a need for a volume that focuses on the *basic facts of death* and that presents them comprehensively and in a systematic manner. Much information has emerged over the past few decades from the efforts of researchers, scholars, clinicians, and practitioners in various death-related disciplines and professional fields. This information can be found scattered in various journals and other publications but has not been brought together in one book. Nine chapters, almost two-thirds of this book, are devoted to the discussion of the facts of death.

A second objective was to provide a volume that is structured with *logic and cohesion,* leading from A to B to C. Such a structure is achieved, I believe, by using a simple basic assumption, namely, that we as individuals as well as a society have problems with death and dying, and if our aim is to solve them, we must first clearly identify these problems, then consider all the facts, and use this information in trying to find solutions. Therefore in designing the book, while keeping the discussion of the facts of death as the main focus, I recognized the need to offer a clear statement of the problems we have with respect to dying and death. Moreover, these problems had to be placed within a larger framework, that is, they had to be treated within a broad sociocultural and historical context to provide valid perspective. Thus in Part One the first two chapters introduce and define the problems of death-related attitudes and behaviors in our society and their manifestations and consequences. These chapters probe deeply and do not retreat from presenting complexities and ambivalence. They attempt to capture the problems in the process of change in a changing society. Oversimplification was avoided for the simple reason that it is of little value to those who seriously seek solutions. In Part Three, four chapters dealing with current issues and controversies are included. These chapters give an indication of the efforts by leaders on the field to grapple with contemporary controversies about death and dying. I feel they will stimulate thought as well as inform and thereby help the reader work through the problems and face the facts. In order to further unify the book, I have written a short introduction to each chapter, in which the chapter is discussed in the overall context of the book as a whole.

The contributors have made every effort to write in a straightforward manner, avoiding technical language whenever possible. I hope the reader will recognize that the simplicity of style did not interfere with maintaining high standards of scholarship. Contributors representing the broad spectrum of relevant fields (such as philosophy, psychology, psychiatry, medicine, nursing, sociology, anthropology, law, and education) have drawn upon existing knowledge and in many instances communicated new information and thought they generated in their respective areas.

In designing this volume, I envisioned it to become a comprehensive basic text for the serious student, whether he or she is an undergraduate student, a professional in the field, a parent, or simply an interested person. It should be mentioned that a number of the contributors to this volume have written their own books in the field of death and dying or are in the process of doing so. Their willingness to expend time and energy to write for this book is evidence that such a book is needed. Several contributors have written their chapters while carrying the burdens of personal tragedy, such as a terminally ill child or spouse, the death of a parent, or personal illness. Their dedication and commitment is deeply appreciated.

This book, then, delineates the problems related to dying and death that confront individuals and society as a whole. It presents in systematic fashion the facts of death as we now know them. I hope this book will stimulate the reader's interest and motivation to apply these facts toward achievement of solutions of the problems concerning dying in our society today and that this will be true for the reader who is a student or professional in regular contact with the dying and their families, as well as for the reader who seeks his or her own confrontation with death in an existential way in order to be better able to define life purposes and goals. It should help the reader achieve a clearer sense of self within a larger order. In sum, I hope the reader will find this a compact, comprehensive, and current volume of personal and professional value.

Hannelore Wass

Acknowledgments

We gratefully acknowledge the incalculable assistance rendered by the many unnamed students and colleagues who, through their interactions with the editors and authors of this volume, have helped in formulating the concepts and ideas that the editors and authors have tried to express. We are also grateful to those colleagues who anonymously urged us to prepare this second edition of *Dying: Facing the Facts*. The counsel and encouragement of many others are acknowledged. Herman Feifel, Don Irish, Darrell Crase, Galen Fletcher, Eugene Knott, Marylee Evans, Dana Cable, and Louis La Grand deserve special note. A number of people assisted us with specific portions of the manuscript. Special thanks for thoughtful help and encouragement go to Meredith Johnson. Donna Hall, Joyce Stechmiller, Diane Green, Jacqueline Allen, Cheryl Martin, Jana Raup, Elizabeth Ann Rider, Linda Shell, Lesa Hotary, Linda Logan, Susan Cliet, Deborah Porter, Donna Wheeler, and Betty Ann Franks also helped and we appreciate their efforts. Kate Roach of Hemisphere Publishing Corporation was invaluable for her unfailing support and patience.

H.W.
F.M.B.
R.A.N.

Introduction

An Overview of the Facts

Hannelore Wass, Robert A. Neimeyer,
and Felix M. Berardo

Many social observers are suggesting that a cultural revolution is under way in our society, bringing with it sweeping changes in our outlook and behaviors concerning death. According to these observers, we are undergoing a major transition in our death-related values and institutions. Technological advances in both the medical sciences and in the machinery of war are raising troubling new questions about the value and even the definition of human life. Legal disputes are examining whether a terminally ill individual's right to self-determination extends to the right to choose death rather than accept heroic life-extending measures. A new kind of institution, the hospice, has evolved to meet the needs of dying patients more humanely than treatment-oriented hospital settings. Scholars from a variety of disciplines have begun to examine such topics as the child's view of death, death anxiety, bereavement, and suicide. Taken together these trends have been interpreted as evidence that we are no longer a death-denying society but, instead, have begun to consider the complexity of death and the appropriateness of our traditional means of dealing with it.

We are not convinced that changes have been so pervasive. We do find that the study of death and dying has been expanding. Scholarly and empirical research on such topics has increased in both its quantity and quality. As a result, we now know more than we once did about the causes and effects of a broad range of death-related phenomena, such as maladaptive grieving, terminal illness, life-threatening behavior, and excessive risk taking. We have also become more acutely aware of the cultural and legal nuances of various institutions for dealing with death in contemporary society. However, with the answers generated by these inquiries have come new questions and problems that demand solutions in their own right. As the field of death studies has grown to address this blend of scholarly and practical concerns, it has begun to achieve the status of a specialty. In fact, many authors boldly proclaim we now have a new discipline of "thanatology." The term is already generally accepted among those active in the field and is beginning to be recognized by individuals in other disciplines as well. It seems to give a sense of coherence and respectability to this diverse and diffuse area of study and, at the same time, captures something of the mysterious that is certainly an essential part of our relationship with death. But while the term thanatology may help legitimize death studies, it may also help euphemize it by eliminating reference to the crude nakedness of the words death and dying. Thus, we consider it important to distinguish between the scientific productivity in this area and the posture of society at large in relation to death.

If the historians are correct, contemporary Americans do not confront death with the sort of equanimity and sense of "rightness" that their forebears did. In fact, they frequently consider death a scandal. Many seem to find it outrageous that in this day of astounding technological feats, medical science has as yet been unable to abolish death. We see no revolution in the general public's stance toward death except that the earlier taboo has finally been lifted, and the subject is open to discussion. The public is much more interested in the phenomena of death and dying than it was one or two decades ago. This widening interest is, in part, the consequence of the increasing publication of books about death—mostly personal accounts—that find their way into popular bookstores. Some of them have become bestsellers or are on their way. Television producers and filmmakers have begun to show greater psychological sophistication in their treatment of death themes in at least some movies, moving beyond the clichéd deaths that fill most action films. Televised interviews with experts on death have been more frequent. Both the print and broadcast media regularly report on legal questions concerning the right to die and other social, ethical, and medical issues as they come before our courts. In short, the public is increasingly becoming an informed consumer in matters of death and dying. Though it may fall short of being revolutionary, this development is an important step forward.

The current volume represents our attempt to further this trend toward growing public sophistication about the "facts" of death and dying. In keeping with the multiple implications that death has for our lives, the contributors examine these facts from the vantage point of numerous disciplines, including educational and clinical psychology, sociology, philosophy, medicine, nursing, law, and even chemistry. Each author has attempted both to present substantive knowledge concerning a particular topic and to consider the strengths and limitations of his or her own discipline in addressing thanatological issues.

PROBLEMS AND PERSPECTIVES

Part I, which consists of three chapters, presents some major problems that contemporary societies have with death and dying and offers perspectives on how they can be viewed. It thus lays the foundation of the book and defines its parameters.

In Chapter Two "Living Our Dying: Social and Cultural Considerations," John D. Morgan provides a broad cultural and historical foundation for understanding our orientation toward death. He offers conceptual tools for examining the meanings that we attribute to death and the strategies we use to cope with it in the context of twentieth-century North American culture. In particular, he introduces the concept of a "death system" and uses it to outline four historically distinct patterns of attitudes and behaviors toward death. Morgan guides the reader step by step to the conclusion that conflicting attitudes exist side by side in an uneasy partnership in our culture and that this basic ambivalence toward our mortality prevents us from effectively "living our dying."

Chapter Three, "The Definition of Death: Problems for Public Policy," by Robert M. Veatch deals with the fundamental question of When does death occur? This issue became critical in the 1960s when medical technology accomplished a milestone feat: the transplanting of a human heart from one individual to another. Never before in human history has the definition of life assumed such significance and caused such continuing debate, a debate that has so far spanned two decades.

At the crux of this debate is a cluster of technical issues with important practical and ethical implications. The first is the question of whether a person must suffer irreversible bodily loss in order to be considered dead. For example, should a patient who "died" on the operating table, but who was later resuscitated, be considered continuously alive? Second is the question of whether the definition of death should hinge on the loss of some critical function or structure. The case of an individual whose heartbeat has ceased, but whose heart remains anatomically intact, illustrates this problem. Finally, there is the matter of the level of bodily function at which life exists. This is problematic since some tissues or even organ systems may continue to show signs of life long after the human organism becomes incapable of organized activity. Veatch then discusses the growing advocacy for definitions of death based upon loss of brain function, rather than heart function, a viewpoint that generates new complexities. He then offers a recommendation that may startle some readers: The definition of death must be stipulated by public policy, since there is, in principle, no scientific basis for choosing one set of standards over another.

In Chapter Four, "The Study of Death: A Psychosocial Perspective," Richard A. Kalish focuses attention on problems inherent in a scientific approach to death studies. Kalish suggests three core concepts that encompass the subject matter addressed by most social scientists conducting thanatological research—namely, the meaning of death, the process of dying, and grief and bereavement. He then considers factors that limit the significance and practical utility of much of this research. Chief among these are the atheoretical nature of most studies, the limited generalizability of results, the confusion of nomothetic and applied research, and the shortcomings of commonly employed interview and questionnaire methods. As Kalish notes, psychosocial research on death is also constrained by the unique nature of the subject, particularly by ethical concerns about studying potentially vulnerable populations such as the seriously ill or the bereaved. Finally, he draws attention to a commonly ignored issue—the emotional demands on the sensitive investigator who risks becoming personally involved with such individuals and, as a consequence, comes to share a measure of their pain.

DATA: THE FACTS OF DYING AND DEATH

Death, or more accurately its prevention, has long been a primary concern of the medical profession. Death has also been central in every religious belief system. But the scientific exploration of dying and death is a twentieth century phenomenon. Seeking knowledge about all unexplained events and processes is characteristic of our era, and death and dying are not exempt. Surveying existing scientific and scholarly knowledge of death and its place in human life is the task of Part II. However, it is significant that even here, where the emphasis is on facts rather than controversies, the uncertainty and limitations of our knowledge become apparent. In part, this is a function of the very different disciplines that have contributed to our understanding of death. Some, like demography, deal with relatively objective, countable variables (e.g., death rates for different populations), whereas others, like psychology, must first create the means by which to gather reliable information about more abstract phenomena (e.g., death anxiety). Chapters also vary in the source of the knowledge they convey. Most derive their data from the systematic study of individuals and groups and try to distill the patterns in naturally occurring behavior, such as grieving or self-injury. Others literally manufacture their own "data," as in the chapter on death and the law, where the facts are established by legislation and arbitration within government and the legal system itself. Finally, chapters differ in their intent, with some being focused on scientific description and others having clear practical intent to humanize institutions that deal with the dying and their families (e.g., hospitals and the funeral industry). Together, these 10 diverse chapters provide a substantive overview of the data on death generated by thanatology and related disciplines.

In Chapter Five, "Trends in the Demography of Death," Edward L. Kain explores the implications of differential rates of mortality change in various social groups. The extremely rapid decline in mortality rates in modern developed nations has had a profound effect upon the experiences of people over the last century, a theme that Kain examines using life course theory and other concepts. He then turns to a consideration of mortality differentials by two crucial demographic variables—age and sex—and concludes that the latter result principally from sex differences in lifestyles, especially in cigarette and alcohol use. Finally, Kain examines mortality rates in relation to several other important social variables, including marital status, race, and social class, with special emphasis on experience in the United States. In combination, these data point to dramatic inequities in death rates for different social groups and suggest reasons for their existence.

In Chapter Six, Robert A. Neimeyer reviews the voluminous research conducted over the past decade on the topic of "Death Anxiety." He begins with a discussion of the meaning of death anxiety and the related concepts of death threat and fear, summarizing the evidence for the existence of unconscious as well as conscious levels of death concern. Neimeyer then evaluates several of the most commonly employed projective, experimental, interview and questionnaire methods for measuring death anxiety, with a particular emphasis on whether they assess death orientation as a unitary or multidimensional concept. In a large portion of the chapter, Neimeyer critically reviews data on the situational and personality correlates of death anxiety and their probable causes. Finally, he discusses the obvious improvements in the scientific quality of this literature over time and offers additional recommendations to further enhance its quality in the future.

The data analyzed in the previous chapter are based, for the most part, on the study of healthy populations for whom in most instances death appears to be an issue of the distant future. In Chapter Seven, "The Experience of Dying," Lawrence C. Rainey focuses on dying persons, exploring the psychological and social experiences in the terminal phase of life. He contrasts different models for explaining and understanding dying persons' responses to their impending death, notably the five-stages theory and the theories of phases and trajectories, and discusses the salient concepts of denial and awareness, including the social ritual of mutual pretense and open communications. Rainey notes the unique aspects of the dying experience. Finally, he examines various approaches to psychosocial support and therapeutic intervention for the dying. Of special interest is his analysis of the differences between therapy for dying and nondying patients. Throughout the chapter, case illustrations illuminate the discussion.

While the previous chapter deals primarily with individuals who are dying and how they cope with this reality, Chapter Eight is concerned with the institutions in which dying occurs. In "Institutional Dying: A Convergence of Cultural Values, Technology, and Social Organizations," Jeanne Quint Benoliel examines the unique cultural arrangements that typify dying in contemporary health care settings. Following a brief historical review, the author discusses "new forms of dying" resulting from increased life expectancy and life-prolonging procedures. She differentiates several major trajectories of hospital dying (e.g., sudden death in the emergency room vs. prolonged dying by cancer) and explains how information is exchanged and life-death decisions are made in each. Of special significance is her assessment of the primacy of the lifesaving ethic in our country's mainstream health care system and the value conflicts this engenders.

In Chapter Nine, "Hospice Care for the Dying," Glen W. Davidson describes the history of the hospice concept, an alternative to the traditional models of terminal care described in the previous chapter. He distinguishes five models of hospice care that have recently evolved in North America, including wholly volunteer programs, home-care services, freestanding institutions, hospital-based palliative care units, and continuum-of-care facilities. Yet, as Davidson points out, these developments have not been without their opponents. In particular, they have been opposed by the established medical and nursing professions and have been the center of controversies regarding appropriate standards for medical care. Despite the aim of the hospice movement to humanize terminal care, Davidson contends that it will survive only if it provides a competent alternative to standardized health care.

Chapter Ten deals with the special problems of "Death in the Lives of Children and Adolescents." In it, Hannelore Wass and Judith M. Stillion survey the accumulation of data on the development of children's understanding of death. They illustrate the cognitive progression in the child's views of death from preschool through the adolescent years and the general fit of this progression with cognitive developmental theory. They discuss how the child's views are influenced by societal attitudes and practices, whether inculcated directly or through the mechanism of television and other media. These considerations highlight the importance of sensitive parental guidance in shaping the child's understanding and attitudes toward death. Finally, special sections explore the needs and experiences of dying, bereaved or suicidal children and adolescents, and indicate the principles that should guide adult care giving in each case.

In Chapter 11, "Suicide: Prevalence, Theories, and Prevention," Anthony J. La Greca reviews the rates of suicide in relationship to demographic variables and points to the methodological limitations inherent in obtaining data on this subject. He then examines psychological and sociocultural theories of suicide considering their utility for explaining such behavior. La Greca gives special attention to the current issues of suicide among the elderly and the chronically ill and the newly arisen question of the right to commit suicide, organized efforts to legalize suicide, and assistance to suicide for the terminally ill. Finally, La Greca discusses approaches to prevention and provides a set of guidelines for identifying suicidal behaviors and for helping persons contemplating or attempting self-destruction.

Robert Fulton takes up the topic of "Death and the Funeral in Contemporary Society" in Chapter 12. In his opening reflections on the dramaturgy of death, he presents a historical account of the functions of the funeral—as a religious rite, as a ritual of disposal, and as a commemoration of a life. In addition, Fulton points out that the service also serves latent functions, such as the reaffirmation of the cohesiveness of the family, the extended kinship system, and the larger social order. Following this discussion, he analyzes both the beneficial and harmful aspects of contemporary funerals. He points to the fact that in the past few years the "average" American funeral has been charged with being pagan in origin, ostentatious in practice, and exploitative of the dead at the expense of the living. After analyzing these charges in detail, Fulton concludes that the contemporary funeral can be functional to the extent that it serves as a rite of separation and integration.

In Chapter 13, "Bereavement and Mourning," Donna Hodgkins Berardo discusses the various factors and conditions that affect how an individual copes with the loss of a loved one, including the intensity of the relationship to the deceased, the type of death, coping strategies of previous losses, social support, and sociodemographic and cultural factors. Berardo then describes the stages of grief that have been identified by a number of researchers and notes reactions to specific kinds of deaths such as suicide and the death of ex-spouses. The author also deals with the impact of bereavement on the survivor's health and on family structure and social status. Berardo concludes with suggestions for helping bereaved persons.

Sheryl Schroeder Scheible's chapter on "Death and the Law," Chapter 14, provides a detailed practical discussion of legal regulations concerning such death-related matters as body disposal and inheritance. With regard to the disposition of property, Scheible explains the probate process, the effects of dying intestate, state laws relating to the protection of family members from disinheritance, and wills and will substitutes. Similarly, she reviews legal considerations with respect to disposition of the body and examines one's power to determine one's own funeral and burial. Finally, Scheible discusses laws governing anatomical gifts, termination of treatment ("right to die"), police intervention in the case of death by violence or unnatural causes, and regulations of the funeral industry. Throughout, she stresses the importance of seeking professional consultation for legal matters associated with death and the dangers of proceeding without such counsel.

CHALLENGE: MEETING THE ISSUES OF DEATH

Part III consists of three "closing" chapters. Although they appear at the end of this volume, their aim is less to provide a sense of closure than to orient the reader to the most urgent issues that challenge us concerning death and dying. As we will see, these unresolved problems include both intensely personal and broadly social dimensions and carry direct implications for our existence as individuals and as a society.

One of the pressing problems of contemporary, industrialized Western societies concerns an individual's right to die in a natural manner. This issue is addressed by Arthur Zucker in Chapter 15, "The Right to Die: Ethical and Medical Issues." Zucker first argues the similarity between moral and scientific theory which he views as facilitating the application of ethics. He then analyzes the various approaches and often conflicting concepts and principles involved in the right-to-die issue, including the distinctions between voluntary and involuntary euthanasia, active and passive euthanasia, physicians' obligations, and patients' expectations. Illustrations from four specific medical settings highlight the moral dilemmas that exist when confronting principles of the sanctity of life vs. the quality of life, the quality of life vs. the quantity of life, and the distinction between ordinary and extraordinary treatment. The author gives special attention to euthanasia applied to infants and to adults and the question of paternalism. Appropriately, the chapter concludes with a question: "Is euthanasia a right?"

In "Life Preservation: Individual and Social Contexts," Chapter 16, Felix M. Berardo, Anthony J. La Greca, and Donna H. Berardo take up the subject of survivorship—"the other side of death and dying." They explore such questions as: What allows some people to live while others die in similar situations? What role do human relationships play in extending the length of life? What aspects of societal change promote or inhibit longevity? In regard to the individual context, the authors examine the implications of personal habits, attitudes, lifestyles, and nutrition in terms of their life-threatening potential, giving special attention to the linkage between stress and survivorship. The authors then present research findings indicating the importance of social relationships and networks for enhancing life. Finally, the authors examine the length and quality of life at the societal level, including demographic and regional trends in mortality differentials and survivorship relative to certain key changes in technology, cultural mores, and societal policies and goals. A number of strategies for strengthening survival capability are presented.

In their chapter on "Threats to Global Survival," Harry H. Sisler and Hannelore Wass provide a discussion of pervasive problems that carry the potential for catastrophic death. In particular, they concentrate on the twin dangers of destruction of the ecosystem on the one hand and of nuclear threat on the other. Thus, they describe the chemical processes brought about by increased industrial activity and their ecological consequences. These consequences are severe, including the devastation of forests by acid rain, the accumulation of wastes, and the depletion of the protective blanket of ozone in the upper atmosphere that shields living beings from excessive ultraviolet radiation. Perhaps even more urgently, they focus attention on the threat of nuclear war and the indirect danger of accidents that results from malfunctioning of nuclear power generators. Their aim in confronting the reader with these harsh realities is not to induce fatalism about the prospects for human survival but to encourage readers to take informed action toward the amelioration of these complex and interconnected problems.

Finally, in our closing editorial chapter, we attempt to draw together a few of the many strands woven through this volume. As in any scholarly discipline, there has been a tendency for the field-of-death studies to become increasingly specialized so that workers in one area become insulated from developments in another. Ironically, it was a similar tendency to compartmentalize death and insulate ourselves from its full reality that originally engendered the death-awareness movement. We hope that the multiple perspectives on thanatology represented in this book will work against this trend and help foster an informed and integrated view of the place of death in human life.

I

Problems and Perspectives

Living Our Dying: Social and Cultural Considerations

John D. Morgan

Death, the cessation of biological functions, is a fact. While age-specific death rates have changed over the centuries, the most elementary datum has not. Death is still one per customer and one for every customer. But, while death is a biological fact, something which *happens to us,* dying is a process in which a culture is involved. With the possible exception of those who die suddenly and without warning, dying is something *we do.*

While the physical fact of death exists outside of our minds, the idea of death exists only in each of our minds. Consequently, whenever we think of death, we think of it in terms of the meanings which each of us have attributed to it. The same is true of other death related terms such as tombstone, funeral, coffin, bereavement, dying, or death certificate. Even neutral terms such as doctor, hospital, nurse, or emergency exist only in our minds. We understand the physical reality in terms of the ideas by which we think of that reality. Since our conscious living takes place only in terms of our own ideas, we live our dying according to the meanings which we have learned. A culture, as the Spanish philosopher Jose Ortega y Gasset has said, consists of "the ideas by which we live" (1, p. 70). The purpose of this chapter is to examine and to criticize the death culture in North America in the latter part of the twentieth century. This critique shall take place first of all by an explanation of the concept of a death system and an indication of how death systems have varied through the centuries. Secondly, our own culture will be examined with special emphasis on the seeming contradiction between its preoccupation with achievement while at the same time speaking of the uniqueness and sanctity of life.

A DEATH SYSTEM

The term "death system" was coined by Kastenbaum (2) to describe the manner in which we comprehend our death or live our dying. Since there is a mutual causality between thought and action, the death system is more than a mere intellectual grasping; it refers to our whole "orientation toward death." It is:

> The total range of thought, feeling, and behavior that is directly or indirectly related to death. This includes conceptions of death, attitudes toward dying persons, funerary practices, and behaviours that have the effect of shortening or lengthening the individual's life-span. (pp. 191–192)

The twentieth-century North American death system includes the network of personal, social, religious, philosophical and psychological ways we have of handling death.

The death system is composed of the ideas with which we understand health and sickness, dependency and independency, life and death, bereavement, and the dying process. It encompasses the persons involved with dying such as the patient, family members, physicians and other health care professionals, clergypersons, funeral directors, police, lawyers, and cemetery personnel.

Places are a part of the death system as well because they play a specific role in the living of our dying, such as hospitals and hospices, morgues, funeral homes, and churches. While some places are more or less consistently identified with death (such as a funeral home), there are other places which may have a death purpose for only a few moments but will retain a death relatedness in a person's consciousness for a long time. Such a place might be an emergency room in a hospital, the neonatal and other intensive care units, operating rooms, or churches. They might be scenes of death only for a few of the hours in which they operate, but to those involved with a particular death which may have occurred in that place, the room may come to symbolize death perhaps more than any other place.

The traditions from which we think and act about death are perhaps the most important part of the death system. Our inability to speak of death without circumlocutions is part of the death system. The fact that death is not mentioned to children either at home or in school is part of the death system as is the use of professionals to prepare the body and arrange disposal. The sending of flowers, religious remembrances, and memorial gifts are traditions which shape our consciousness of death, as does the publishing of obituaries in the newspaper.

Roles also play an important part in the death system. Physicians and nurses have particular roles with respect to death as do the clergy and funeral directors. In some cultures, the dying person and the bereaved have had very well-defined roles. In sum, a death system is the totality of the persons, things, attitudes, and concepts with which we speak and think of death and dying and by which we understand them.

There is a mutual relationship between the death system and its constituting aspects. The death system not only changes attitudes but is itself changed by attitudes. For example, until fairly recently, although cigarette smoking was known as a cause of poor health, including heart disease and cancer, the prevalent attitude has been one of *laissez faire*. This was also the case for the tolerance given to automobile driving while alcohol impaired. The tolerance we have to these known causes of death was part of the attitudes of our culture and was indicative of our understanding about dying, death, and bereavement. As a result of the death awareness movement, as well as increased knowledge of the dangers, the attitudes have changed and we are no longer tolerating smoking in public places without complaint. We no longer think that it is funny or "macho" to drive when too drunk to control a car properly* (3). These are examples of death-related attitudes and behaviors that have changed in conjunction with changes in the total death system.

Death systems are not static. The North American death system changed from calm acceptance in the 1940s to denial in the 1970s and has changed again since then. Since death systems are cultural, they change as do key factors of the culture change. Specifically, a death system is shaped by two elements. The first is experiential; the second is theoretical (2, p. 193).

The experience of death and bereavement is the first element in its understanding. If we have little experience of the loss of significant others, our death attitudes will be limited by our inexperience. Funerals provide a good example. Many persons will speak of funerals as a waste of money, a rip-off. Usually, this critique is made by one who as yet has little experience of deaths. However, after one has received the support which comes from a tastefully planned and executed funeral, the attitude often changes. Thus, the death system for that individual has changed, or, more accurately, his/her experience now allows a fuller participation in the death system. The trend towards disposal without a funeral, or funerals without visitation, and the increasing use of cremation as a form of disposal will reshape our death system in the next few years.

Our exposure to death is related to life expectancy. A baby born in North America can be expected to live to his/her mid-seventies. Since relatives will also have (at least statistically) a similar life span, the probability is that the child will have little, or perhaps even no, exposure to the death of a significant other until his/her twenties or thirties.

On the theoretical level, our attitudes to death are shaped by our philosophy—specifically by our philosophy of the person and by our cosmology—our view of the world. In a culture which puts its emphasis on the uniqueness of the individual, persons will have a different orientation towards death than will a culture which perceives each individual as having meaning primarily as a part of the whole, whether that whole is religious or political. Our cosmology, or interpretation of the physical universe, is important in our death attitudes as well. If we believe that we are impotently subject to the laws of nature, then our death attitude will differ from those whose view is that we have significant control over the forces of nature.

In conclusion, our death system is shaped by our exposure to death and by life expectancy, by our view of what it is to be a person, and by our view of reality. Evidence for this can be seen if one examines the historical development of the western death system, a task that will be addressed before exploring our present culture in greater depth.

ATTITUDES TOWARD DEATH

As a result of his study of the literature of different periods as well as the examination of tombstones, Ariès postulated that attitudes to death over the centu-

---

*Perhaps a similar change will occur in our attitudes to disposal of waste, unguarded level railroad crossings, and violence on television.

ries are capable of being reduced to four periods (4). These he has titled "Tamed Death," "The Death of the Self," "The Death of the Other," and "Death Denied."

Tamed Death

The period which Ariès calls tamed death dates from the early Middle Ages but in reality "is the unchronicled death throughout the long ages of the most ancient history, and perhaps prehistory" (4, p. 5). The historical period is not as important as the attitude. This attitude has been held by some throughout all periods of history, even our own, but it dominated until the late Middle Ages. The characteristic of this period is first of all familiarity with death. Since life was, as Hobbes epitomized, "solitary, poor, nasty, brutish, and short," (5) one was constantly exposed to death. Death was a familiar, even if not always welcome, neighbor.

With the exception of a sudden death, death was calmly accepted. The dying man feels sadness about the loss of his life, but his sadness seemingly did not equal the depths of our own era (4). The dying person first of all was thought to be the best judge of his impending death (p. 6) and having said his farewells, calmly commended his soul to God (p. 17). Sudden death, which did not give one the opportunity to put one's physical and spiritual affairs in order, was considered a curse. The "litany of the saints," a prayer said often throughout the church year, had an invocation "to preserve us from a sudden death." This prayer seems less attractive to us in the light of the chronic debilitative diseases of the latter half of the twentieth century. To those of the tenth to fourteenth centuries, whose life span was already short, the prospect of a sudden death was more terrifying.

During this period, a death was public in the sense that the death of the individual was perceived as affecting the entire community; death diminished the community. Pascal's remark that one always dies alone referred to a psychological state rather than the literal truth (4, p. 19). A death disrupted a community which then had to reintegrate. The facility with which this happened was a test of the community (7, p. 195).

> Custom prescribed that death was to be marked by a ritual ceremony in which the priest would have his place, but as only one of many participants. The leading role went to the dying man himself. He presided over the affair with hardly a misstep, for he knew how to conduct himself, having witnessed so many similar scenes. (6, p. 55)

It is difficult for us in the West, in the latter half of the twentieth century, to comprehend the sense of community which existed previously and even exists today in other parts of the world. A Greek citizen of Socrates' time would think of himself/herself as an Atheanean first and as an individual second. The Christian of the Middle Ages would think of being a child of God first—a member of the communion of saints—and as an individual second. A Chinese or Japanese person today would have a different understanding of his or her relationship to the whole than we do.

Community integrity was stretched beyond the possibility of reintegration during the fourteenth century in Europe. The Black Death (or Bubonic Plague) killed one third of the population (8, p. 94). In Avignon, 400 died daily, in Paris—800, Pisa—400, Vienna—600. One gets a sense of the calamity by considering that

Paris had a population of only 100,000 (p. 95). Even in our well-structured society with hospitals, funeral directors, and well-run cemeteries, none of our cities of 100,000 could handle 800 deaths a day. Persons died without either religious solace (the last rites) or legal formalities (a will). Burials were haphazard and contributed to the spread of the disease:

> One man shunned another . . . Kinsfolk held aloof, brother was for-saken by brother, oftentimes husband by wife; nay what is more, and scarcely to be believed, fathers and mothers were found to abandon their children to their fate, untended, unvisited as if they had been strangers. (8, p. 97)

This is the period which Goldscheider called "uncontrolled mortality" (9). The disruption of the social order persisted for nearly a century. Land titles were meaningless as was royalty and government. One can readily see why the church chose the term "requiem" (rest) as the dominant prayer for the dead. Aside from the tragedy of the fourteenth century, the period was one of resignation in face of the inevitable. "This ancient attitude in which death is close and familiar yet diminished and desensitized is too different from our own view"; it is hard for us to understand (4).

The Death of the Self

Whereas in the earlier period the emphasis was on the community's ability to integrate the loss of a member, Ariès' second period is an emphasis on the death of the self—one's own death. At this period in history (approximately the twelfth to fifteenth centuries), the individual has become conscious of himself/herself (4). The recognition of one's individuality—distinct from that of the community—had its consequence in the death of that individual.

Death was less a public event. It was perceived as the last act of a very unique drama. It was the duty of the dying person to be master over one's own death and to create an appropriate scene. Cyrano de Bergerac's farewell to Rox-anne is an example of a death in which the central character has "staged" his death to be consistent with lifestyle and his values (10).

The concept of immortality was an important aspect of this period. One viewed oneself as a composite of soul and body (11). While this philosophical and theological position was held on a theoretical level, the hard fact was that the relationship between the soul and body was never a comfortable one (4, p. 606). The person, as perceived, is rendered apart at death to a fate known only by faith.

Wills regained predominance, especially wills which arranged for prayers for the deceased (4, p. 180). One believed that such arrangements brought merit before God which would guarantee salvation. Consciousness of one's own sinful-ness had the twofold effect of fear of hell (the Latin poem "Dies irae"—day of wrath—dates to this period) and emphasis on good works—even if they are posthu-mous. Dominant themes of the period are judgment, resurrection for the just and damnation for the wicked (p. 100). Elaborate tombs, often depicting praying fig-ures, became common and sometimes these were even placed in cathedrals (p. 266). Eleventh-hour conversions were prayed for both by the individual and his family. [A quotation of St. Augustine, Bishop of Hippo in the fourth century: "Lord, give me chastity—but not yet," is consistent with the period although he predates it. Dostoevsky's citing of an eleventh-hour conversion of a thief is consistent with this orientation (12).]

Death is no longer quite the welcomed friend as it was in the earlier period. The fear of hell and the sense of one's unworthiness made death a fearsome reality.

The Death of the Other

The nineteenth century saw the emphasis change again—away from death as a usual and common destiny (tame death) and away from a personal and specific act (one's own death) to an emphasis on the death of the other (4). This is the period of the "beautiful death." (p. 415). The art of the period reflects the sundering of relationships with a dominant hope of reintegration in the next life (p. 611). Privacy becomes important because it was the ingredient necessary for a relationship to develop.

Interestingly, few wills were written at the time as though it would be a breach of trust—or bad faith—to have a will when one had loved ones to carry out one's wishes.

> Thus when in the eighteenth century family affection triumphed over the traditional mistrust by the testator of his inheritors, the last will and testament lost its character of moral necessity and personal warm testimony. This was, on the contrary, replaced by such an absolute trust that there was no longer any need for written wills. (6, p. 56)

Public deathbed scenes no longer occurred. Rather, death was the last act of an intimate relationship. The death of the other is a dominant theme in opera. Perhaps the best example is the death of Mimi in *La Boheme*. The fourth act is dominated not by Mimi's slipping away but by Rudolfo's grief (13). Not all death idealizations were of romantic endings. This is also the period and philosophy of the French Revolution with public executions and Dickens' portrait thereof (14).

The above brief outline gives evidence for Kastenbaum's thesis that the death system—or a death attitude—is dependent upon the perception of longevity and exposure to death as well as the culture's predominate view of nature and the world. Until fairly recently the predominately held position was that persons were subject to the forces of nature and the will of God. One took one's self-definition from the view that one's life was a part of a larger, unified whole. In addition, the lack of clean drinking water and primitive agricultural methods kept life expectancy to a few years. We must now examine how these same elements create our own death system and indicate the adequacy of our culture's view of death. However, since the death system is consequent on philosophy, perhaps it would be useful to say something about philosophy and the closely related problem of religion.

PHILOSOPHY AND RELIGION

Philosophy has been classically defined as the art or science by which we understand things in their causes by reason alone. This definition is, as are most things classical, such to terrify the nonspecialist. However, if philosophy is taken to mean the basic understandings that each of us has concerning ourselves, those with whom we interact and the world around us, then philosophy has lost its terrifying aspect and is seen as something in which everyone engages from time to time and more often in situations in which we are forced to ask fundamental questions about our lives.

In spite of lessened church attendance, ours remains a religious culture. By religion is meant the sense that the individual is part of a larger whole and has a responsibility to that whole. The religious attitude also entails a sense that our present era is connected with the past and that we belong to a history which makes our individual lives more meaningful

> More than most other people in our society, the clergyman represents a tradition that has attempted over the centuries to provide an integral framework for man's total life experience. Not every person is inclined to think long and hard about the relationship between his own very personal life at the moment and all that has gone before him and all that is to come. (2, p. 227)

Finally, life is viewed as a gift. Some would even add that it is from a God who knows and loves each of us individually. In either case, the idea of life as a gift is important and is, unfortunately, often ignored in discussions of our culture. Obviously, life is a gift in the sense that no one ever earned it. There is, however, a deeper meaning which is far more important to thanatology.

Life is a gift in the sense in which we identify "gift" and "talent." When we speak of one having a gift for languages or for music, we mean that the development of this ability amplifies this person and all with whom he/she interacts. There is a sense of responsibility to acknowledge the gift, to develop it, and be thankful for it. The religious view is that life is a gift in this sense, the person has a special status in creation. The person is not a passive fragment of existence but amplifies or adds to it. If one believes that the universe came from the hand of a loving creator—as do all the great religious traditions, then one must ask, "Why is the world the way it is?" "Why do pain and evil exist?" In the words of Rabbi Harold S. Kushner (15), "Why do bad things happen to good people?" One answer is that the gift of life is not fully acknowledged. Consequently, our culture does not fully provide opportunities through which individuals can achieve all that they might. Life is precisely the gift by which the creative will of God—that all persons might be enhanced—is to be carried out.

What might be called the North American philosophy is ambivalent. We seem to hold conflicting views. On the one hand, we admire people who can get things done. As Cohen has stated, "American worship of business is not merely the worship of the dollar but rather worship of the active life" (16, p. 30). We are a continent of doers. This has given us one of the highest standards of living in the world. We transplant organs; we build malls and domed stadia to protect us from the elements; we repair satellites in space and land people on the moon. We emphasize this aspect of our culture even when there might be a high cost, even a high human cost. An examination of some of our cliches reveals this emphasis. "It's the bottom line that counts." "It's the cost of doing business." "You can't make an omelette without breaking a few eggs."

This orientation towards getting things done is what is known as "pragmatism." The word pragmatism comes from the Greek "pragma" which means action and stresses that an idea is meaningful only if it is useful (17, p. 142). Philosophical disputes are examined to see if the answer will make any concrete difference in a person's life. If not, then the answer, no matter what it is, is meaningless. The same criterion of practicality is applied to such questions as the existence of God, the existence of a soul or spiritual nature, and questions of life after death. Theoretical knowledge is valuable only to the extent that it has some possibility of application.

The pragmatists would distinguish between knowledge which is immediately useful and knowledge which may be useful at some other time in one's life. Thus, the question of the existence of a life after death may not be a question in which a healthy young person is interested. However, what one learns about a question such as immortality may at some time be useful. William James, who is perhaps the most readable of the pragmatists, speaks of the "cash value" of knowledge. What can I "buy" with this information? What use is it? Is it perhaps a deflated currency which does not allow me to get what I thought I might from it? However, just as we have two ways of handling our money—a checking account for immediate needs and a savings account for long term or "rainy day" needs—so James would admit that we may have two types of knowledge: information which we use daily to satisfy our immediate needs and information which we "store" to use in crises, etc. Thus, a position about immortality or that our lives are guided by a divine providence may not be information which an individual uses daily. It may, however, be part of the repertory of knowledge which he/she calls upon from time to time.

Our North American culture is a constant tension between these two aspects of the culture: the emphasis on efficient doing and expansive being. One the one hand, we look to achievement even if it means human cost; on the other, we look to the religious dimension of human existence even at the expense of achievement. There is no aspect of our lives which has not been touched by the engineering progress of North America. We transmit words and pictures instantaneously via radio, telegraph, television, and now via facsimile. Closed circuit television has allowed greater surveillance of both persons and property. Computer linkups have created enormous data bases which allow us to access information in a way never before imagined. At a push of a button, we can be aware of books, monographs, articles, and other references on almost any topic. We can check fingerprints and records. On the other hand, as a result primarily of labor contracts, the average worker today has health and other insurance programs which guarantee a standard of living undreamed of before. Dental care, prescriptions, and hospital care are taken today to be rights rather than privileges. The same is true of education and care of the aged. Old-age pensions such as social security provide a basic, if not always adequate, guarantee of a retirement period which is relatively free of care for the basic necessities.

THE SELF

All of us have had occasions to fill out resumes and application forms. This is standard practice in a complex and organized culture such as our own. We tell the reader our name, age, cultural and linguistic background, physical characteristics, our education and experience, perhaps our parentage, perhaps our medical history. Depending on the extent and complexity of the resume, the reader may know a great deal about us. Yet we would distinguish between knowing *about us* and knowing *us*. We believe that there is a self hidden within each of us which no resume or application blank captures.

This inadequacy of resume information is partly due to the fact that a resume is not an autobiography. There is much in each of our lives which cannot be captured on a resume. However, there is a more fundamental difficulty which we shall attempt to illustrate. Most of us can remember enough of our elementary school grammar lessons to distinguish between a subject and an object. A subject is the "doer"; the object is, more or less, what is done. This distinction is rooted in the philosophy of Aristotle which postulates a difference between what a thing is and what it does. A thing is a subject, a substance—a doer. An object is transitory, accidental in the sense that it could be otherwise.

Putting this in another way: A subject has a meaning in itself while an object has meaning only because of the subject. In the statement "John sees the red balloon," John is the subject. John exists whether the red balloon exists or not. But the "redness" of the balloon exists only because creatures capable of perceiving color recognize and categorize the characteristics of the balloon. In the statement "the candle is hot," "hot" is meaningful only because a conscious being perceives degrees of temperature.

The reason why we are uncomfortable with the idea that a resume can fully identify any of us is that resumes and applications by their very nature "objectify" something. A resume may tell the color of one's eyes or one's hair. In so doing, it describes the person in terms of something which the person is not. The person is not blue, rather the person is a person whose eyes happen to reflect light in a particular way. Persons are like subjects, that is, have an existence and a meaning in themselves.

Not only is the person a subject, but a person is a unique subject. Never before in the history of the universe did this person exist, never again will he/she do so. Several years ago, when the World's Fair was held in New York city, the Vatican gave permission for Michaelangelo's masterpiece, "the Pieta," to be brought for exhibit. There was general concern for the safety of the statue since boats and planes do have accidents. Luckily, no disaster occurred. However, Michaelangelo made several copies of the statue. The statue is, in that sense, replaceable. More fundamentally, the statue is a piece of marble which is replaceable although the accidental characteristics which the artist gave to it could only be replaced with difficulty. But the death of any individual person is a greater loss. There is no fundamental or accidental way of replacing the person. The person is a subject. The person is unique. The person is a once-in-the-lifetime-of-the-universe event.

There are moments in our lives in which we feel terribly alone, we may say that "no one really knows me." These moments usually come in depression or anxiety. Yet the Spanish philosopher Jose Ortega y Gassett would say that it is in precisely those moments that we have truly grasped what it is to be human. We are "radical solitudes" in the sense that there is something at the very root of us which is incommunicable (18, p. 130).

OUR DEATH SYSTEM

A comparison of our own life expectancies with that of previous generations would be helpful to understand our own culture. The earthquakes in Mexico, volcanic eruption in Central America, and chemical and nuclear disasters in India and Russia indicate that even our age is subject to uncontrolled mortality. However, these events create headlines precisely because they are unusual.

Today, we expect that we shall live to our early or mid-seventies. This is a relatively new phenomenon in history. Prehistoric man seemingly lived an average of 18 years. Living in a yet untamed world, violence, evidenced by skulls marked with blows, was the usual cause of death (19, p. 7).

> Survivorship in those days was very seldom beyond the age of 40. Persons who reached their mid-20s and more rarely their early 30s were *ipso facto* considered to have demonstrated their wisdom and were, as a result, often treated as sages. (p. 8)

Longevity progressed until our own century when it peaked in the United States in 1915 at 54.5 years. The great flu epidemic was a setback but following it, longevity returned and increased to 69.6 years in 1967 (p. 9). One can picture the variations in attitudes which were consequent on these data.

The data imply that, previously, not only was one's own life expectancy short but also the life expectancy of significant others. In Kastenbaum's terms, death was "a knife at our throat or a scourge at our child's bedside" (4, p. 206). There was, no doubt, great personal fear and bereavement involved in such a situation; however, death was expected. The almost continual presence of death seemingly did not raise a sense of injustice as it might today if our loved ones lived only an average of 18 years. In such a context of limited life expectancy and the great efforts necessary to provide the necessities, one did not dawdle in the transition from childhood to adult responsibility, given the prospect that the adult years would be so limited in number" (4, p. 192). There was no time for extended education and few learned to read or write. Courtships were short as were marriages themselves. Many women died in childbirth leaving widowers to care for the children who did survive.

Increased longevity has occurred because of better sanitation as well as improved asepsis and other medical care. The discoveries that contagious diseases could be prevented, indeed almost eliminated, through inoculation neutralized the diseases which killed most of the population in earlier times. Consequently, it is today reasonable to assume that mothers will not die from infections in childbirth and that the child will live to maturity. The discoveries of the sulfa drugs and penicillin in this century further wiped out the killers of the past (20, p. 39). Until the present time, the function of the medical practitioner was, as Ramsey stated, "to (only) care for the dying" (21). People live long enough today to die from chronic degenerative diseases. Cardiovascular diseases and cancer now account for the greatest number of deaths of persons over 60 years of age. In recent years, the incidence of Alzheimer's disease is increasing, and it is estimated that 90 percent of the population will have it if they do not succumb to other diseases first.

Women outlive men as they always have; however, the gap is closing. This seems to be due to the increased number of women holding jobs which previously were held only by men. These range from the dangers involved in construction work to military activity and the stress-related deaths of the executive. Interestingly, this ability to outlive men is found not only in humans but also in other animals. In cases of persons with relatively similar lifestyles, such as monks in a monastery and nuns in a convent—both leading lives of quiet prayer, the women still outlive men (22, p. 101).

One final note should be made about death and social status. It is a reprehensible fact of the North American culture that poverty classes, especially native persons, do not live as healthy or as long as do their fellow countrymen with higher socioeconomic status. This is as true in Canada with its socialized medicine as it is in the United States with entrepreneurial medicine. No doubt the causes are related to the sense of possibilities open to these persons. In better neighborhoods, persons accept the fact that they will see physicians. In higher classes, one is aware of nutritional needs and can afford to purchase vegetables, fruits, and protein substances. Finally, the incidence of alcoholism among the native people of North America is a high source of mortality.

> In general, the poverty population experiences relatively high mortality rates at younger ages and from communicable diseases while the white collar middle class, especially its male members, experiences relatively high mortality rates at mid-life and in the older ages, from the degenerative ages. The blue-collar working class, to the extent that it avoids both types of disabilities, appears for the moment at least to be experiencing the lowest mortality rates among the three strata. (19, p. 85)

In Canada, most recent evidence suggests a direct relationship between income and life expectancy at birth such that "the estimated disparity between the wealthiest 20 percent (fifth quintile) and the poorest (first quintile) is approximately 6.0 years for men and 3.0 years for women" (23, p. 95).

The increased life span and the change from diseases of childhood to diseases of longevity have had the effect of increasing the number of deaths which have occurred in hospitals. Hospitals have become increasingly more important as medicine has become more specialized. In earlier days, the physician's primary role was to be with the sick and to encourage life's own recuperative powers to regenerate the body. As medicine has specialized, it has become increasingly more difficult for one physician to do everything. He or she has had to specialize. As specialization occurred, the place of medicine changed. Medicine was no longer practiced in the doctor's office or in the patient's home but more and more in hospitals (24, p. 332).

As time has proceeded, this specialization has limited the physician's ability to see his role of supporting the patient's body's ability to cure itself, to cure as an end. Thus, death became defeat (25, p. 30). The medical profession has defined its roles as curing, researching, and teaching. Thus, the patient who can no longer be cured, and whose illness presents no particular research or teaching interest, no longer fits into the health care system.

Persons who become physicians could not have entered, much less completed, medical school without being bright, hard-working, and successful. The death of a patient may be the first time in the young physician's life when he/she meets a problem which will not respond to his/her enterprise. It is not surprising that the medical profession does not handle the dying patient easily, especially if Feifel is correct that medical doctors have a higher death anxiety than does the general population (26, p. 215).

Hospitals have existed for centuries in Europe, but the hospitals as we know them today began to develop after the Civil War to cope with the number of injured (24, p. 1). Today, at least 75 percent of the population dies in hospitals. Consequently, dying is seen by fewer people than it was previously. We do not have the mass deaths which once were viewed on streets nor do we have as many persons dying at home.

In addition, with the mobility of North American society, the aged are not seen by children or grandchildren. Few of us live within 500 miles of our place of birth. Consequently, we do not see the aging process taking place. The elderly, if still at home, are not visited on a regular basis. The elderly, more and more will be found in "homes" or retirement villages where they will be seen only by other elderly or by professionals (24, p. 1). Consequently, death for many of us is not a gradual process but, rather, a telephone call in the night. The dead are seen at funeral visitations, but dying is not seen. One consequence of this is that we have no role models either for our own dying process or for the grief we show at the time of another's death. However, it is not entirely true to say that we have no role models. There are many persons with physical disabilities or chronic degenerative illnesses who could teach us a great deal about accepting reality with graciousness and with faith—but our culture is not ready to listen to their lessons.

Modern societies control death through bureaucratization, our characteristic form of social structure. Max Weber has described how bureaucratization in the West proceeded by removing social functions from the family and the household and implanting them in specialized institutions autonomous of kinship considerations (27, p. 95). The increasing industrialization of the West as well as the mobility of our society has meant that we have turned our "death work" over to professionals (24, p. 1).

HOW EFFECTIVE IS OUR DEATH SYSTEM?

Do we, in Avery Weisman's terms, die an appropriate death?

Someone who dies an appropriate death must be helped in the following ways: He should be relatively pain-free, his suffering reduced, and emotional and social impoverishments kept to a minimum. Within the limits of disability, he should operate on as high a level as possible, even though only tokens of former fulfillments can be offered. He should also recognize and resolve residual conflicts, and satisfy whatever remaining wishes are consistent within his present plight and his own ego ideal. Finally, among his choices, he should be able to yield control to others in whom he has confidence. He also has the option of seeking or relinquishing significant key people. (28, p. 193)

In other words, an integrated death system would enable individuals "to think, feel and behave with respect to death in ways that they might consider to be effective and appropriate" (2, p. 193). A valuable death system is one which contributes to psychological growth as well as alleviates fears of death and bereavement so that one can get on with other aspects of living (p. 201).

Few cultures are as "progress" oriented as is ours. We are convinced that given enough time and money all problems can be solved. Few would openly espouse the position that we will eradicate death, but it is a hope in the back of the minds of many (25, p. 2). Today, death is viewed as something that does not have to happen when it does happen and "the idea is being entertained that it is remotely conceivable that for a very significant minority, that death eventually won't need to happen at all" (24, p. 11).

Ours is a society which speaks about the sanctity of life and death with dignity. However, the sanctity of life does not exist outside of the religious context of North American culture. Life is a gift from God which places on the individual the obligation to return the gift lovingly by the acceptance of our death (25, p. 5).

> In Christianity, the new note is that of love, with its evident relations to the theme of giving. The crucial gospel statement should perhaps be quoted in full: "For God so loved the world that he gave his only begotten son, that whosoever believeth in him should not perish, but would have everlasting life. For God sent not his son into the world to condemn the world, but that through Him the world might be saved." (John 3, 16–17)(25, p. 10)

Death ultimately is the proof that no matter what powers we as humans have or develop, we still are not gods (p. 7). Our nature is still fundamentally contingent. This does not mean that lives are without meaning; indeed, death gives meaning to our lives because it is the act by which we complete the task for which we were born (p. 16).

Once we have reached the age in which we can ignore our parents' wishes, each facet of our lives is controlled by the self. We decide when and what we eat. We decide whether or not we will go to school or work on a given day or whether we will resign from a job or quit school. We decide if we will go to church and which one if we decide to go. We decide if we shall marry, whom, and where. We can today decide with great accuracy whether we will have children or when. The day is not too distant when we will decide the sex of our children. We decide when to terminate a marriage. We decide if we shall smoke or engage in other life-threatening behavior. Death then is denied to us in the most fundamental sense that we do not control our own dying. For thousands of years, the person was lord and master of his/her death and the circumstances surrounding it. Today, this has ceased to be so (6, p. 53). Death has moved from the moral order—something which was an expression of our personal values—to the technological order (29, p. 121).

Death alone remains beyond personal control except for those who decide to terminate their own lives. Once a person is seriously ill, the decisions about the remaining aspects of his/her life and the decisions concerning the arrangements before and after death are made by someone else. The medical staff and the hospital organization tend to program deaths in keeping with their own organizational and professional needs. Thus, the modern hospital, devoted to the preservation of life and the reduction of pain, tends to become a "mass reduction" system, undermining the subjecthood of its dying patients (30, p. 97).

Our death is the last act of the drama. We find ourselves on the stage of life determining to be the person we want to be yet we are denied the last act.

It has been our intention to understand how we live our dying in the latter half of the twentieth century in North America. The death-awareness movement has made significant progress in bringing death back into our consciousness and, therefore, making it more human (31, p. 8–9), but in many ways, our life is no different from the peasant in the fourteenth century. Our forebear missed a fully human life because he/she was inundated with death. We do not live fully because we ignore death (2, p. 207). We accept the fact that to live fully in an economic manner we must budget—economize—our resources. Time is our most important—and most limited—resource, but we act as though no economy were necessary. Our fear of the human reality of death causes us to live not "as though there are no tomorrows" but as though there are always tomorrows. Consequently, we shirk from living fully.

REVIEW QUESTIONS

1. What is a death system? What are its constituting elements?
2. Discuss how changes in life expectancy and exposure to death over the centuries have affected our attitudes toward death.
3. In what sense can life be viewed as a gift? Explain usages of the term "gift" which might be attributed to human life.
4. How does pragmatism affect our understanding of what it is to be human?
5. What is meant by denying that the person is an object?
6. How do the chief causes of death today differ from those of previous times?
7. What effect does social status have on health and life expectancy?
8. In what sense is the twentieth century American or Canadian denied his/her death?

REFERENCES

1. Ortega y Gasset, J. (1944). *Mission of the university.* New York: Norton.
2. Kastenbaum, R., & Aisenberg, R. (1972). *The psychology of death.* New York: Springer.
3. Blackstone, W. T. (1980). The search for an environmental ethic. In T. Regan (Ed.), *Matters of life and death: New introductory essays in moral philosophy.* New York: Random House.
4. Aries, P. (1981). *The hour of our death.* New York: Knopf.
5. Hobbes, T. (1952). The leviathan. In *The great books of the Western world* (Vol. 23). Chicago: Encylopedia Britannica.
6. Aries, P. (1978). The reversal of death. In R. Fulton, E. Markusen, G. Owen, & J. L. Scheiber (Eds.), *Death and identity: Challenge and change.* Reading: Addison-Wesley.
7. Hertz, R. (1976). Death and the right hand. In R. Kastenbaum & R. Aisenberg. *The psychology of death.* New York: Springer.
8. Tuchman, B. W. (1984). *A distant mirror: The calamitous 14th century.* New York: Knopf.
9. Goldscheider, C. (1971). *Population, modernization and social structure.* Boston: Little, Brown.
10. Rostand, E. (1930). *Cyrano de Bergerac.* Paris: E. Sasquelle.
11. Aquinas, T. (1952). Summa theologiae. In *Great books of the Western world,* Part I, 76. Chicago: Encyclopedia Brittanica.
12. Dostoevsky, F. (1952). Rebellion. In *The brothers Karamazov.* Great books of the western world. Part II. Book V. Chicago: Encyclopedia Britannica.
13. Puccini, J. (1958). La boheme. In M. Cross (Ed.), *Complete stories of the great operas.* Garden City: Doubleday.
14. Dickens, C. (1983). *A tale of two cities.* New York: Bantam.

15. Kushner, H. S. (1981). *When bad things happen to good people.* New York: Schocken.
16. Cohen, M. R. (1962). *American thought: A critical sketch.* New York: Collier.
17. James, W. (1959). What pragmatism means. In A. Castell (Ed), *Williams James: Essays in pragmatism.* New York: Hafner.
18. Ortega y Gasset, J. (1956). In search of Goethe from within. In *Dehumanization of art and other writings on art and literature.* Garden City: Doubleday.
19. Lerner, M. (1970). When, why and where people die. In O. G. Brim, H. E. Freeman, S. Levine, & N. A. Scotch (Eds.), *The dying patient.* New York: Russell Sage.
20. Thomas, L. (1979). *The medusa and the snail.* Toronto: Bantam.
21. Ramsey, P. (1970). *The patient as person.* New Haven: Yale.
22. Goldscheider, C. (1978). The social inequality of death. In R. Fulton, E. Markusen, G. Owen, & J. L. Scheiber (Eds.), *Death and identity: Challenge and change.* Reading: Addison-Wesley.
23. Wilkins, R., & Adams, O. (1985). *Healthfulness of life.* Montreal: Institute for Research on Public Policy.
24. Fulton, R., Markusen, E., Owen, G., & Scheiber, J. L. (Eds.), *Death and identity: Challenge and change.* Reading: Addison-Wesley.
25. Parsons, T., Fox, R. C., & Lidz, V. M. (1973). The "gift of life" and its reciprocation. In Mack, A. (Ed)., *Death in american experience.* New York: Schocken.
26. Feifel, H., Hanson, S., Jones, R., & Edwards, L. (1972). Physicians consider death. In R. Kastenbaum & R. Aisenberg (Eds), *The psychology of death.* New York: Springer.
27. Blauner, R. (1978). Death and social structure. In R. Fulton, E. Markusen, G. Owen, & J. L. Scheiber (Eds.), *Death and identity: Challenge and change.* Reading: Addison-Wesley.
28. Weisman, A. (1978). An appropriate death. In R. Fulton, E. Markusen, G. Owen, & J. L. Scheiber (Eds.), *Death and identity: Challenge and Change.* Reading: Addison-Wesley.
29. Cassell, E. J. (1978). Dying in a technological society. In R. Fulton, E. Markusen, G. Owen, & J. L. Scheiber (Eds.), *Death and identity: Challenge and change.* Reading: Addison-Wesley.
30. Fulton, R. (1978). Epilogue. In R. Fulton, E. Markusen, G. Owen, & J. L. Scheiber (Eds.), *Death and identity: Challenge and change.* Reading: Addison-Wesley.
31. Feifel, H., & Morgan, J. D. (1985). Humanity has to be the model. *Death Studies, 10,*(1), 1-9.

3

The Definition of Death: Problems for Public Policy

Robert M. Veatch

At 5:41 a.m. on Sunday, November 10, 1985, Philadelphia Flyers' hockey star, Pelle Lindbergh, slammed his 1985 Porsche into a cement wall at a Somerdale, New Jersey, elementary school. The headline on the story in the newspaper the next day read, "Flyers' Goalie Is Declared Brain Dead." In spite of the claim that he was "brain dead," the story went on to say that Lindbergh was listed in "critical condition" in the intensive care unit of John F. Kennedy Hospital in Stratford, NJ.

Referring to his parents who were called from Sweden to be at his side, Vicki Santoro, nursing supervisor at the hospital, said, "They were just devastated." Flyers' team physician Edward Viner said that if Lindbergh's situation does not improve, the family will be left with a decision about how long to leave him on the respirator.

That was not the only decision they faced. If Lindbergh was dead, even though some of his vital functions remained, he would be an ideal candidate to be an organ donor. His intact heart and kidneys could provide life-saving help for three other people. Possibly even his liver, lungs, and corneas could benefit others. Suddenly, it becomes a very practical, life-saving matter to figure out whether Pelle Lindbergh is dead or alive. The headline writer says he is "brain dead," but then many people go on to speak as if he is nevertheless still alive. We used to believe that persons with beating hearts were alive even though their brain function was lost irreversibly. Now we are not so sure. The way Pelle Lindbergh is treated, the decisions his parents have to make, the behavior of the physicians and nurses, and the fate of several desperately ill human beings all hinge on figuring out whether Lindbergh is dead.

The public policy discussion of the definition of death began in earnest in the late 1960s. It began in the context of a world that had, in the previous decade, seen the first successful transplantation of an organ from one human being to another, including the December 1967 transplant of the human heart. It cannot be denied that this sudden infatuation with the usefulness of human organs was the stimulating context for the intense discussion of the real meaning of death. What many thought would be a rather short-lived problem, resolved by the combined wisdom of the health professionals and the nonscientists on the Harvard ad hoc committee, has lingered as an intractable morass of conflicting technical, legal, conceptual, and moral argument. I shall try to short circuit some of that argument by focusing exclusively on the problems for public policy remaining in the debate.

With this focus, I shall not perform a linguistic analysis of the term death. While that may be an important philosophical enterprise, and many have undertaken it (1–4), this analysis is only of indirect importance for public policy questions. Likewise, we need not provide a detailed theological account of the meaning of death. Those studies are numerous (5–8, 10–11) but not of immediate concern in the formation of secular public policy. Most significantly, we shall not be interested in a scientific description of the biological events in the brain at the time of death. That is of crucial importance for the science of neurology, and a vast literature is available giving such an account (13–15, 17, 19). The scientific, biological, or neurological description of precisely what takes place in the human body at the point of death is not a matter that need directly concern public policymakers.

THE PUBLIC POLICY QUESTION

What we are interested in is the public policy question that asks when we should begin treating an individual the way we treat the newly dead. Is it possible to identify a point in the course of human events where a new set of social behaviors becomes appropriate, where we may justifiably begin to treat human beings in a way that was not previously morally or legally appropriate? In short, what we are interested in is a social system of death behaviors.

Social and cultural changes take place when we label someone as dead. Some medical treatments may be stopped when a person is considered dead that would not be stopped if the person were alive—even if the living person were terminally ill. This, of course, does not imply that there are treatments that should not be stopped at other times, either before or after the time when we label somebody as dead. Many treatments are stopped before death for technical reasons. According to many, there are other treatments that may justifiably be stopped before death because the treatments are useless or too burdensome. In other cases, if the newly dead body is to be used for research, education, or transplant purposes, it is possible to continue certain interventions after death has been declared. Many have held that this is morally acceptable (7, 11). It appears, however, that, traditionally, at least, there have been some treatments that are stopped when and only when we decide that it is time to treat the person as dead.

Other behaviors also have traditionally taken place at the time we consider the person dead. We begin mourning in a pattern that is not appropriate in mere anticipatory mourning (20). We start several social processes that would not have been appropriately begun before the decision is made that death behavior is appropriate. We begin the process that will lead to reading a will, to burying or otherwise disposing of what we now take to be the mortal remains. We assume new social roles—for example, the role of widowhood. Normally, if the person who has been labeled as dead happens to have been the president of a country or an organization, the one who was formerly vice president will assume the role of president. Finally, and perhaps of most immediate relevance to the concern that generated the definition of death discussion, we change the procedures and justifications for obtaining organs from the body. Prior to death, organs can only be removed in the interests of the individual or, perhaps, in rare circumstances, with the consent of the individual or legal guardian (21–24). At the moment we decide to treat someone as dead, an entirely different set of procedures is called for—the procedures designated in the Uniform Anatomical Gift Act drawn up in 1968. At that point, if one has donated organs, they may be removed according to the terms of the donation without further consideration of the interest of the former person or the wishes of the family members. If the deceased has not so donated, and has not expressed opposition to donation, the next of kin or other legitimate guardian in possession of the body assumes both the right and the responsibility for the disposal of the remains. It is clear that in Anglo-American law, at least, the one with such a responsibility cannot merely dispose of the body capriciously in any way he sees fit but bears a responsibility for treating the new corpse with respect and dignity (27). This, however, has been taken both in law and in morality as permitting the justifiable donation of body parts by the one with this responsibility, except when there has been an explicit reservation expressed by the deceased during the time of his life.*

In short, traditionally, there has been a radical shift in moral, social, and political standing when someone has been labeled as dead. Until the 1960s, there was not a great deal of controversy over exactly when such a label should appropriately be applied. There were deviant philosophical and theological positions and substantial concerns about erroneous labeling of someone as dead but very little real controversy about what it meant to be dead in this public policy sense.

Now for the first time there are matters of real public policy significance in deciding precisely what we mean when we label someone dead. In an earlier day, all of the socially significant death-related behaviors were generated at the time of the death announcement, and very little was at stake in being less than precise in sorting various indicators of the time when this behavior was appropriate. Virtually all of the plausible candidates occurred in rapid succession, and none of the behaviors were really contingent upon any greater precision.

---

*In 1979, efforts surfaced in Britain to circumvent the requirement that next of kin give permission for removal of organs by means of the device of claiming that the health authorities are normally in possession of a dead body until such time as it is claimed by the person with the right to possession of it. This would, in principle, open the door for "donation" by health authorities. The British law requires that such a person must have no reason to believe that the spouse or any surviving relative objects, having made "reasonable enquiry as may be practicable." A British Working Party has implied that this may not be a serious restraint since they emphasize that "the designated person's duty is only to make such reasonable enquiry as may be practicable." They point out that "if a donor's relatives are found to be inaccessible it would be impracticable to ask them." The American discussion has not progressed to this point in looking for ways of excluding the next of kin and other family members from the decision to donate. Should the British recommendation be incorporated into law, Britain would have moved some distance away from the donation of organs in the direction of a policy based on salvaging (pp. 11, 25–26).

Now, matters have changed in two important regards. First, few technologies have greatly extended our capacity to prolong the dying process, making it possible to identify several different potential indicators of what we should take to be the death of the person as a whole and have separated these points dramatically in time. Second, the usefulness of human organs and tissues for transplantation, research, and education makes precision morally imperative. In an earlier day, the most that was at stake was that an individual could for a few seconds or moments be falsely treated as alive when in fact he should have been treated as dead or vice versa. Of course, it is important, out of our sense of respect for persons, that we not confuse living persons with their corpses, so in theory it has always been important that we be clear about whether someone is dead or alive. Yet, the greatly compressed time frame for the entire series of events meant that there was very little at stake as a matter of public policy. We could pronounce death based on the rapid succession of an inevitably linked series of bodily events.

As we extend this period of time, permitting much more precision in identifying what it is in the human body that signifies that it ought to be treated as dead, we must ask the question: Can we continue to identify a single definable point where all of these social death behaviors should begin? It may turn out that as the dying process is extended, all of these behaviors will find their own niches and that it really will cease to be important to label someone as dead at a precise moment in time. If so, death itself, as well as dying, may begin to be viewed as a process (28). However, it seems likely that this may not happen. Rather, we may want to continue to link many of these social events in time; we shall continue to say that there is a moment when it becomes appropriate to begin the entire series of death behaviors or at least many of them. If so, then death of the person as a whole will continue to be viewed as a single event, rather than a process (29). There are several plausible candidates for that critical point where we can say the person as a whole has died including the time when circulatory function ceases, the time when all brain functions cease, and the time when certain important brain functions (such as mental function) cease.

The question is, therefore, not precisely the same as the one the philosopher asks when he asks the question of the endpoint of personhood or personal identity (4, 30). Conceptual analyses of the concept of personhood or personal identity suggest that there may be an identifiable endpoint at which we should stop thinking of a human organism as a person. That analysis by itself, however, never tells us whether it is morally appropriate to begin treating that organism the way we have traditionally treated the dead unless personhood is simply defined with reference to death behavior, which it often is not. Under some formulations, such as those of Michael Green and Daniel Wikler (4), for example, it is conceptually possible to talk about a living body in cases where the person no longer exists. Logically, we would then be pressed to the moral and policy question of whether these living bodies that are no longer alive are to be treated differently from the way we are used to treating living persons.

Fortunately, for matters of public policy, if not for philosophical analysis, we need not take up the question of personhood but can confront directly the question of whether we can identify a point where this series of death behaviors is appropriate. In this way death comes to mean, for public policy purposes, nothing more than the condition of some group of human beings for whom death behavior is appropriate. This is, if you like, a reforming definition of death. We shall ask if we can identify a point where these behaviors are appropriate, and, for purposes of law and public policy, we shall label that point as the moment of death. The laws reformulating the definition of death do not go so far as to say they are defining death for all purposes theological, philosophical, and personal. Some explicitly limit the scope saying that the law defines death "for all *legal* purposes."

This policy-oriented formulation makes clear that when we talk about death, we are talking about death of the entity as a whole. It is with reference to the entire human organism that we want to determine appropriate behavior, not some particular body part.

Unfortunately, the term "brain death" has emerged in the debate. This is unfortunate, in part because we are not interested in the death of brains; we are interested in the death of organisms as integrated entities subject to particular kinds of public behavior and control. In contrast, the term brain death is systematically ambiguous. It has two potential meanings. The first is not controversial at all; it simply means the destruction of the brain, leaving open the question of whether people with destroyed brains should be treated as dead people. In my own work, I have consistently substituted the phrase "destruction of the brain" for brain death in this sense. It makes clear that we are referring only to the complete biological collapse of the organ or organs we call the brain. Exactly how that is measured is largely a neurological question.

Unfortunately, brain death has also taken on a second, very different, and much more controversial meaning. It can also mean the death of the individual as a whole, based on brain criteria. The problem is illustrated in the original report of the Harvard Ad Hoc Committee (17), which has become the most significant technical document in the American debate. The title of that 1968 document is "A Definition of Irreversible Coma." The article sets out to define "characteristics of irreversible coma" and produces a list of technical criteria that purport to predict this accurately. The name of the committee, however, is the "Ad Hoc Committee of the Harvard Medical School to Examine Brain Death." The presumption, apparently, was that irreversible coma and brain death were synonymous. We now realize that this is not precisely true. A person can apparently be in irreversible coma and still not have a completely dead brain. In any case, the title of the report and the name of the committee, taken in context of what the committee did, imply that the committee had as its objective to describe the empirical predictors of a destroyed brain.

The opening sentence of the report, however, says, "Our primary purpose is to define irreversible coma as a new criterion for death." It does not claim to be defining the destruction (death) of the brain, but death simpliciter by which everyone, including the committee members, meant death of the person for purposes of death behaviors, clinical practice, and public policy. Yet the report contains no argument that the destruction of the brain (measured by the characteristics of irreversible coma or by any other characteristics for that matter) should be taken as a justification for treating the person as a whole as dead. The members of the committee and many others believed that this should be so, possibly with good reason, but the reasons were not stated.

Since the term "brain death" has these two radically different meanings, there is often confusion in public and professional discussion of the issues. For instance, neurologists can claim that they have real expertise on brain death, meaning, of course, expertise in measuring the destruction of the brain, Others claim, however, that brain death is exclusively a matter for public policy consideration, meaning that the question of whether the death of the individual should be based on brain function criteria is really one outside the scope of neurological expertise. A far better course would be to abandon that language entirely, substituting precise and explicit language that either refers to the destruction of the brain or to the death of the individual as a whole based on brain criteria.

PRELIMINARY ISSUES TO PUBLIC POLICY DISCUSSION

1. *The difference between deciding to allow a living person to die and deciding that a person is dead.* In many cases, the public fascination with the definition of death discussion may be misplaced. There have been several cases where problems with the care of the critically ill have been addressed by attempting to resolve them using brain criteria for determining that a person has died. Efforts are sometimes made to resolve these critical problems in health care simply by defining the terminally ill patient as dead.

In the early phase of the discussion of the case of Karen Quinlan—the young woman in New Jersey who suffered irreversible brain damage and was sustained in a chronic vegetative state, the lawyer for her family, the judge, and many others initially cast their arguments in terms of the definition of death (31). It was much later in the case that everyone became convinced that Karen was not dead, according to brain criteria, but might be withdrawn from the respirator even though still alive. Likewise, when a Maryland nurse was prosecuted for disconnecting a respirator on a terminally ill cancer patient, her defense centered on the claim that her patient was dead according to brain criteria (32). The jury was sufficiently confused over the definition of death, and it was unable to reach a verdict; charges were eventually dropped.

Instead of insisting that we can resolve these problems of clinical care only by reformulating the definition of death, an alternative would be to recognize that it is possible that some persons are living but in such a condition that it would be appropriate to allow them to die. This, of course, raises moral questions of its own, but it does not force all of the complex problems of ethics concerning the terminally ill into the one potential solution of the redefinition of death. That prolonging life serves no purpose does not establish, by itself, that a person has died.

There are several unfortunate and tragic situations in which a patient may be stabilized indefinitely and still be considered living for public policy and legal purposes. One of these might turn out to be the condition known as persistent vegetative state (15, 33–34). This is the condition in which Karen Quinlan lived for 10 years (35–37). It is crucial to realize that in order to justify a treatment-stopping decision in a case such as Karen Quinlan's, it is not necessary to reach the judgment that she is dead. It is logically quite possible to decide simply that she should be allowed to die because there is no longer any appropriate justification for continuing treatment.

The same argument applies even more forcefully to patients who are terminally ill while perhaps senile or in a semi-comatose state but, nevertheless, retain some limited capacities for mental activity. Society will at some point have to address the very difficult questions of public policy related to the care of such individuals. This is not, however, an appropriate matter for the definition of death discussion. The definition of death problem is one small subset of the moral and legal issues related to death and dying.

2. *The difference between measurements to determine that the end of life has come and deciding what we mean by the end of life for public policy purposes.* One of the most crucial preliminary issues in public policy consideration of the definition of death grows out of the problem of the systematic ambiguity of the term brain death. Some of the questions related to the pronouncement of death based on brain-related criteria are clearly technical and scientific while others are questions of morality, politics, and law. It is crucial that the two be kept separate and the public role in each of these kinds of questions be identified (38).

Bodily structures and functions are generally assumed to deteriorate at different rates and times in all humans. Virtually no one holds that every body structure and function must be destroyed for the person as a whole to be considered dead for public policy purposes. That would mean that every cell in the body would have to be determined to be dead or at least every organ would have to be destroyed.

It is also generally held that those with appropriate medical skills are capable, in some cases, of developing tests, procedures, or criteria for precisely predicting that a particular bodily function or structure is irreversibly destroyed. For example, if heart function is determined to be important in deciding when to treat people as dead, certain measures—such as pulse and an electrocardiogram—are available to diagnose and predict the future status of heart function. If lower brain functions are determined to be critical, neurologists tell us that certain reflex pathways are good predictors of the status of the lower brain. If cerebral function is determined to be critical, different tests, based on the electroencephalogram (EEG) and cerebral angiography—which measures blood flow, can be useful.

It is now generally agreed that the tests, procedures, or criteria for determining that critical bodily structures or functions have been lost must be established by those with scientific skills in biology or medicine, that is, those with the appropriate knowledge and skill (26, 39–40). These tests, procedures, or criteria need not be incorporated into public policy or statutory law. In fact, since empirical measures of this sort are likely to change as the status of our scientific knowledge changes, many take the view that these tests should not be included in the statutory law. As a general rule, statutes that have been passed have not included any reference to any specific empirical measures.

Technically, it is not correct to treat even these criteria for measuring the death of the brain as a purely scientific problem completely lacking in evaluative or other public policy importance. For example, in applying tests to measure the destruction of the brain, a judgment must be made about how often these tests are to be applied and for how long a period of time they must be satisfied before pronouncing death. Different sets of criteria propose different lengths of time. The Harvard criteria (17) calls for 24 hours, the report of the medical consultants to the President's Commission (19) suggests 6 hours or 12 in the absence of confirmatory tests such as an EEG, and other groups have required 12 hours as the minimum time period to be satisfied (18). If the tests are not applied over a long period, some person may be declared to have irreversibly lost brain function when, in fact, such function could return. On the other hand, if the tests are applied for too long a period of time, some persons will be treated as if brain function has not irreversibly disappeared when, in fact, it has. Deciding on the correct length of time will depend on how one assesses the moral risks of falsely considering the brain to have stopped and falsely considering that the brain has not been shown to be irreversibly stopped. The best neurological science should be able to do is tell us the probabilities of each kind of error after different time periods. It cannot tell us how to trade off the two kinds of errors. That is fundamentally a moral or policy issue.

If neurologists' intuitions about the relative moral risks of these two kinds of error were the same as others in the society, then little would be at stake in asking the neurologists to pick the balance between the errors for the rest of us. There is reason to doubt, however, that neurologists balance the two kinds of errors the same way that other people do. If they differed significantly—if, for example, they worried more than most people about falsely treating people as alive and less about falsely treating people as dead, then they would systematically recommend the wrong time period for repeating tests. Logically, deciding the mix of the two kinds of errors is not a scientific question; it is a policy question for lay people to decide even though most of us do not treat it that way.

The more obvious policy question is just which structures or functions should be tested, that is to say, which changes in the body should signal the time when death-related behavior is appropriate? Should it be loss of heart function or brain function? We are attempting to determine when it is appropriate to treat the organism as a whole as dead. The loss of certain essential bodily structures or functions will almost certainly signal the time when such behavior is appropriate. These potential endpoints are normally called the concepts or standards of death.

For example, some people take the position that the organism as a whole should be considered dead if there is irreversible cessation of spontaneous respiratory and/or circulatory functions. Other people take the position that the organism should be considered dead if there is irreversible loss of all spontaneous brain functions. Still others maintain that the organism should be considered dead if there is irreversible loss of spontaneous cerebral functions.

Behind each of these formulations is some implicit view of what is essential in man's nature. While society might choose to specify precisely what that understanding is, it may not be either necessary or possible. It might turn out that different people would formulate the precise underlying concept somewhat differently but still be able to agree at the level of the standard of death that is to be specified in the law.

The selection of these basic standards of death is now generally agreed to be a matter of public policy, a task for the broader public. The only real question is the method that will be used to express public policy. Traditionally, there was such an overwhelming consensus on an apparent concept and standard of death that there was no need for explicit public policy formulation. We relied on the common law and saw very little dispute except perhaps in questions of inheritance in cases of almost simultaneous death. An example would be an inheritance following the death of spouses in an automobile accident, where a different pattern of inheritance would result if either spouse survives the other.

There is, in principle, no scientific basis for choosing one set of standards or underlying concepts over another, although once a particular concept or standard is chosen there may be good scientific reasons for selecting a set of criteria, tests, or measures that correspond to the standard or concept chosen. This does not necessarily mean, however, that the choice is entirely an arbitrary one. It is possible, in fact it is widely held, that such choices have foundations in objective reality. In deciding to make slavery or murder illegal, there is no scientific proof that either of these activities is wrong. It is not even clear what a scientific proof of such an evaluation would look like. Nevertheless, the society feels sufficiently sure that slavery and murder are wrong, and it chooses to make them illegal without any suggestion that such a decision is arbitrary or capricious. Thus, Henry Beecher, the Harvard physician and chairman of the Harvard Ad Hoc Committee, was not speaking precisely when he said that the choice of a definition of death is arbitrary. He probably meant that there is no basis in the natural sciences for making such a choice although he would, I believe, have conceded that some choices are better than others and some might be so persuasive that it is meaningful to call them the correct choices.

If this is correct, then selecting a point when it is appropriate to treat people as dead must be a matter of public policy. In an earlier time, the public judgment reflected such a wide consensus that common law was sufficient for expressing that policy judgment. Now, however, when many possible, plausible endpoints of life have been identified, the public policy question may have to be resolved more explicitly. For this reason, many hold that the policy question should be resolved legislatively (52, 58–59). Others see it as more appropriately derived from case law. The disadvantage is that many cases will potentially formulate the policy differently. Still others appear to believe that the policy question can be resolved without any formal expression of policy (50–51, 60–64). Some kind of resolution to the policy question must be reached, however. Deciding what changes in bodily structure or function justify treating a person as dead is logically prior to and independent of the question of what tests, measures, or criteria should be used for determining whether those structural and functional changes have taken place.

There is no need to resolve all of the philosophical problems pertaining to the definition of death in order to reach a public policy resolution of the question of when people are to be treated as dead. General agreements on the standards may be reached as a matter of public policy although the philosophical disagreement remains at the most abstract conceptual level.

3. *The reason for selecting a standard for death.* Some have suggested that a new standard for pronouncing death should be selected because if one is selected based on the use of brain criteria for death pronouncement, new organs will be available for transplantation and other worthwhile purposes (6). Upon reflection, however, others have questioned whether this constitutes an adequate reason for adopting a particular reformulation of the notion of death (65). Jonas (66) doubts that the interests of others in body parts can be a legitimate basis for deciding when someone has died. Paul Ramsey has expressed similar concern over using the usefulness of organs as a reason for choosing a new definition of death, arguing, "If no person's death should for this purpose be hastened, then the definition of death should not for this purpose be updated. . . . " (11, p. 103). Still others have countered, arguing that while it would be wrong to choose a new concept of death for this reason, the newfound potential usefulness to others of being clear on what we mean by being dead might justify the effort at clarification (26, pp. 33–34).

THE ISSUES OF THE DEBATE
PROPER

1. *The problem of irreversibility.* There are several questions that any public policy over the definition of death must resolve if that public policy is to be clear and complete. One is whether irreversibility is a requirement in the public policy related to the definition of death. The problem is whether we want to speak of people who have temporarily lost some critical body structure or function as dead, even though such functions or structures can be restored and, thus, the person will be alive at some point in the future. In the past, it has been common in folk discussion of death to talk about someone having died on the operating table, or in some other setting, who has been resuscitated and returned to life. This may simply be imprecise use of language, however. Many would hold that irreversibility is inherent in the notion of what it means to be dead. At least for public policy purposes, people who have temporarily lost a critical function like heart function really cannot be thought of as dead. Those mentioned in such a person's will do not inherit his possessions. The president of the United States would not have been removed from office because of such a temporary stoppage. The provisions of the Uniform Anatomical Gift Act, which gives next of kin authority over the use of organs, would not take effect. Irreversibility seems to be an essential requirement for public policies related to treating people as dead (67). If that is the case, then it is incorrect to talk about people dying temporarily and then coming back to life. Rather, in such cases we can say that the person continues to live but would have been dead at some point in the future had not certain critical features been recoverable.

2. *Is the critical bodily loss one of function or structure?* Some recent commentators have argued that the loss that is critical for treating people as dead is not necessarily a functional loss. It may be anatomical. That is, a person may continue to live until certain anatomical structures are destroyed (1, p. 343; 68).

There is no decisive argument for or against such a view. Should a society want to hold that the shape or form of the body is what is critical, rather than its activity, such a policy could be adopted. However, most continue to maintain that the critical loss is a functional one. It may be that those who talk as if the loss is anatomical, rather than functional, are really just seeking greater certainty of the irreversibility of the loss. Such persons might take the position that what is essential is irreversible functional loss, yet the only empirically certain way to demonstrate irreversible functional loss is by showing anatomical destruction. If so, the anatomical destruction is merely a test, measure, or criterion of irreversible functional loss and probably should not be incorporated into a formally articulated public policy. However, it is possible that some people actually believe that the critical loss is structural in which case that notion should be made a matter of the public policy formulation.

3. *Is the critical loss one at the cellular level or some higher level of function (or structure)?* The human organism operates at many levels, including cellular and supercellular levels of organization. It is possible to insist that each cell, or at least each cell of a critical organ, be destroyed. After all, as long as one cell remains alive it is possible to say there is life in the particular issue or organ. However, many would take the point of view that such a mere cellular level activity is of no significance when it comes to determining when people should be

treated as dead. If, for example, one is concerned about the irreversible loss of brain function, one may not really mean the firing of an isolated neuron within the brain but only the organ level integrated functioning at the supercellular level.

This has potential importance because certain tests or measures may actually indicate the presence of cellular life even though organ level functioning has irreversibly been lost. For instance, the technical literature pertaining to the use of the EEG for the measure of the loss of brain function makes clear that what is normally referred to as a flat EEG will, in fact, be one that shows very low microvolt levels of activity. To the uninitiated, it seems certain that if electrical activity is coming from the brain, it is not totally dead. If, however, neurologists are able to determine with certainty that certain low levels of activity are really only signs of cellular activity and not consistent with continued capacity for organ-level functioning, it is quite appropriate to exclude such activity (14) if one has adopted a policy of pronouncing death on the basis of the irreversible loss of total brain function at the supercellular level. This appears to be what the state of Wyoming had in mind when it passed a statute based on the Uniform Brain Death Act but added the sentence "Total brain function shall mean purposeful activities of the brain as distinguished from random activity." This still raises the question of what counts as purposeful activity but at least excludes random cellular level activity. Others make a similar distinction by talking of "integrated" (48) or "clinical" (69) functioning.

4. *Which functions (or structures) are critical for determining that a person should be considered dead?* We are still left with the most fundamental and important public policy question: Which functions or structures should be identified as critical for deciding that the person as a whole should be treated as dead? Several stages have taken place in the debate.

1. *The late 1960s period.* The first stage of the debate began in the late 1960s, especially with the preparation of the Harvard Ad Hoc Committee. At this point, virtually everyone formulated the question in terms of a struggle between two alternatives. One group believed that the critical activity that should be measured was the capacity of the heart and lungs (64; 70, pp. 243–45). This seems to be included in the early common law definition of death that says that a person shall be considered dead when there is "a total stoppage . . . of all animal and vital functions" (71, p. 488). Precisely what it was about heart and lung activity that was considered critical is not clear. It seems certain that it was not the functioning of the heart and lungs per se, but, rather, the activities they cause in the body that was thought to be critical. This is made apparent by the recognition that a person whose lungs have been destroyed but whose blood is oxygenated by a machine is obviously still alive. Likewise, a person whose heart had been destroyed, but whose blood was pumped by a machine, would also be considered alive. In fact, a person who might be maintained indefinitely on a heart/lung machine or artificial heart would obviously be alive according to this formulation. Thus, it seems probable that people taking this position hold a concept of death that emphasized the importance of the flowing of vital bodily fluids—that is, the blood and breath. According to this notion, then, a person should be considered dead when there is the irreversible loss of the capacity for the flowing of these vital fluids.

This is a rather vitalistic notion of the nature of the human being, one that sees the human as merely physicochemical forces. It totally excludes any concern for integrated functioning or for mental processes. Yet many have apparently held that anyone who has the capacity for the flowing of these fluids ought to be treated as alive.

During this period, the alternative position was that the critical loss which signaled the point at which people ought to be treated as dead was the loss of the capacities of the brain (6, 53, 55, 72–74). Defenders of this position were frequently not very precise about exactly what it was in the brain that was considered critical. The empirical measures that were performed implied that the critical functions were quite diverse and inclusive. They included a large number of integrating activities, including reflex pathways in the lower brain as well as the centers that control respiration. Thus, it has been suggested that holders of this view might have been taking the position at the conceptual level that people should be treated as dead when they have irreversibly lost the neurological capacity to integrate bodily activities. At this point, according to this view, the person no longer functions as a whole and can, therefore, legitimately be treated as dead.

Some people have continued to favor the use of heart- and lung-oriented standards for pronouncing death. Some even explicitly affirm such standards when they are given the alternative of pronouncing death based on the concepts underlying the use of brain-oriented standards (75). Nevertheless, the defenders of standards related to heart and lung function seem to have decreased substantially.

2. *The early 1970s period.* In the early 1970s, however, a new and more complicated question emerged: Which brain functions (or structures) are so critical that their loss ought to be considered the death of the person as a whole? Two major camps emerged in this debate. One held fast to the position that all brain function (at least at the supercellular level) must be lost (76, p. 399; 77–79). The second group took the view that some functions, even at the supercellular level, might remain intact, while it would still be appropriate to treat a person as dead (7, 42, 80–81). The choice was presented dramatically in two case reports by Brierley et al., in *The Lancet* (82).

The first case was that of a 58-year-old man who had suffered cardiac arrest related to bronchospasm. He was resuscitated with cardiac massage and placed on a respirator. The EEG was flat from the third day on. He maintained reflexes after the first day and respired without the aid of the respirator from day twenty on. He died (based on cardiac criteria) after five months.

The second case involved a 48-year-old man who suffered a massive allergic reaction. He was resuscitated with cardiac massage and mouth-to-mouth breathing. He also had reflexes after the first day but had a flat electroencephalogram from the second day onwards. He also died after five months (based on cardiac criteria). It was found in both cases, upon examination after death, that tissues in the higher brain (neocortex) were dead while lower brain centers were intact, showing slight to moderate neuronal loss. The patients at no time met the Harvard criteria purported to measure irreversible coma, yet clearly seemed to be irreversibly comatose (54).

Once these cases are presented, they reveal that there are at least two quite different positions, each reflecting a different concept of death. Those insisting on the destruction of total supercellular brain function would consider these patients alive. They breathed spontaneously. Defenders of this view probably hold fast to a concept that death is something like the irreversible loss of the capacity for bodily integration. They specifically recognize that integrated activities mediating through the lower brain, such as respiratory control mechanisms or the cough reflex, represent a level of bodily integration which would be taken as sufficient to justify treating the person as still alive. Others, however, have considered these patients dead. They have abandoned the whole-brain view, making it clear that a very different concept of death is operating. They focus on the activities of the higher brain centers, including such capacities as remembering, reasoning, feeling, thinking, and the like. One underlying concept of the human's nature that might be implied is that the human is essentially a combination of mental and physical activity, both of which must be present in order for the person to be alive. According to this view, probably any capacity for consciousness would be sufficient to treat the person as alive.

Closely related to this view is a notion having both Greek and Judeo-Christian roots, the notion that the human is essentially a social animal. According to this view, it might be appropriate to treat persons as dead whenever they have irreversibly lost the capacity for social interaction. It is important not to talk about a person being dead when there is merely the loss of social interaction. That would make being dead or alive dependent upon one's fellow human beings' willingness to interact. Rather, what is operating here is probably a concern for a capacity for such interaction. A standard might be chosen that focuses on higher brain function rather than total brain function. This standard is often articulated as the irreversible loss of total cerebral or neocortical function. The exact specification would depend upon exactly what functional loss was considered crucial and where that function was localized in the brain. There is substantial debate over whether there can be any exact identification between mental functions and brain functions (83–86). Probably we shall never be able to identify precisely which tissues are responsible for the functions often identified, such as consciousness, thinking, or feeling and interacting with one's fellow humans. There is general agreement, however, that without cerebral tissue, these functions are all impossible. To the extent that this is true empirically, the standard for death according to a holder of this position would be the irreversible loss of cerebral function. For holders of this view, in contrast with the whole-brain standard, a different set of empirical measures or tests would, quite clearly, be appropriate for confirming death.

3. *Since the late 1970s.* This reformulation of the question so as to ask which brain functions are critical has begun to raise additional questions. For instance, once one has moved to a concept of death based on higher brain function rather than total brain function, one might appropriately ask whether a person could be considered dead even though certain higher brain functions remain intact. If, for example, one retains motor capacities in certain brain centers but has no capacity to feel or think, should such a person be considered alive? There is no particular reason why this progressive narrowing of the criteria need stop at this point. For instance, one might ask whether a person could be considered dead solely on the basis of deterioration of mental function even though many higher brain centers remain intact. It is apparent that one of the dangers of the move from total brain function to higher brain function is that there may be no obvious and clear point to stop the progression to narrower and narrower formulations. Thus, there is the potential that gradually more and more people will literally be defined out of the category of human existence. Some critics of the move to higher brain function have opposed it. Their opposition does not come exclusively on the grounds that lower brain activity is an essential component of life, but more on the grounds that

once one moves beyond total brain activity it will be impossible to find a point for a public policy at which to stop the regression.

Defenders of the move to higher brain function notions of death reject this wedge argument. They maintain that it is possible to hold firmly to the notion that a person should be considered dead when there is loss of consciousness but insist that no compromise be made beyond that point.

Still others such as the President's Commission (40) may accept, in principle, the idea that death can be related to the irreversible loss of higher brain function but believe, empirically, that there are no solid grounds for measuring such loss. Logically, as a matter of public policy, such people should be willing to adopt a policy that people should be treated as dead when higher brain function has irreversibly ceased, leaving it to those with competent skills in the neurological sciences to determine whether there is any empirical way to measure the mere loss of a higher brain function. It might turn out that the only reliable test would be one that measures the loss of total brain function. That would seem to be the conceptually correct way to articulate public policy. However, policymakers may be made sufficiently uncomfortable by the possibility that some practitioners would prematurely attempt to measure the loss of merely higher brain function—uncomfortable enough that they would find it necessary to legally specify that death should be pronounced only when brain function is lost. However, in principle, they would be willing to accept death pronouncement even when certain lower brain functions remained intact—in cases where all higher function has irreversibly ceased.

With the attempt to move to a higher brain-oriented formulation, these practical concerns have characterized the debate since the later part of the 1970s. Advocates of higher brain standards have differed among themselves over exactly which tissues and functions are critical. Other concerns have also emerged, some of which have been mentioned previously. The difference between cellular level function and more complex function has become increasingly apparent. The tension between those who formulate a concept of death functionally and those who formulate it anatomically has also become recognized. The net effect has been that we have increasingly become aware that there are many different formulations that are plausible and seen as acceptable to different people. It is no longer a debate between two clearly contrasting camps as it was between the heart and the brain in the earliest days of the discussion or between the whole brain and higher brain as it was in the early part of the 1970s. It is clearly impossible to reach any consensus on the underlying theological and philosophical issues. It is probably even impossible to specify clearly what it is about the human that counts as a change so significant that we ought to begin treating that human as if he or she were dead. At best, we must come to a common understanding of some general area of bodily structure or function that is so significant that its destruction justifies treating the person as dead (45). We may be able to agree that a person is dead when, say, all brain function is lost even if we cannot agree on exactly what the critical function is.

The question is one that really cannot be reduced any further. We must determine what bodily conditions make treating a person as dead acceptable. It will probably be sufficient to express public policy in terms of general standards for death. Even though those standards have some concept implicit in them, it is clear that greater consensus can be reached on the standards than on the concepts themselves. The three primary candidates are those we have identified: the irreversible cessation of spontaneous respiratory and circulatory functions, the irre-versible loss of all spontaneous brain functions, and the irreversible loss of all spontaneous cerebral or higher brain functions.

SOME REMAINING ISSUES

1. *Should safer-course arguments prevail?* It is clear that there is, and will remain, controversy over which of the several plausible concepts or standards for pronouncing death ought to be adopted for public policy. Some standard or standards must be chosen at least for public policy purposes. This raises the question of whether, as a matter of public policy, we ought not to play it safe and choose the policy that will satisfy the most people. Some have argued that when we are in doubt about which of several public policies to adopt, we should take the safer course, especially in matters that are literally a matter of life and death. The safer-course argument is presumably the one that will avoid treating people as dead who ought to be considered alive (16; 70, p. 244). This safer-course argument might justify abandoning efforts to incorporate concepts or standards of death related exclusively to higher brain function since many people hold that a person can be alive even though higher brain function is lost. There is real doubt in our society over the use of such a standard for death pronouncement. Under a safer-course argument, we would move to the more conservative, now older, definition of death that requires that the whole brain be destroyed.

The problem with this safer-course argument is that we would be even safer and more inclusive were we to insist that not only the whole brain but also the heart and lung activity be irreversibly destroyed. In fact, we would be safer still if we were to insist that not only these functions be destroyed but the anatomical structures as well. If we adopted a position that all heart, lung, brain function, and structure must be destroyed, we would satisfy virtually everyone that a person is indeed dead before being treated as such.

There are difficulties that now become apparent with the safer-course arguments. If there were no practical or theoretical problems with treating people as alive who are in fact dead, we could safely continue a policy of erring on the side of treating people as alive, but it is clear there are good reasons not to do so. There are bad consequences from treating a dead person as alive. Some of these consequences are very practical. There are financial costs in medical care as well as human agony. There are organs and tissues that would be lost. None of these concerns about consequences would justify treating someone as dead who was really alive, but they do, at least, justify striving for precision in our social understanding of what it means to be dead. And they give us sufficient reason to avoid the extreme applications of the safer-course arguments. At the very least, this means that we can set some conservative limit on when people ought to be treated as dead. The majority of the population now seems prepared to move at least as far as the whole brain-oriented formulations, that is, treating people as dead when there has been total destruction of supercellular level brain function.

2. *Can there be variation in the public definition of death?* Since there is such disagreement among members of our society over a definition of death, many have speculated over the difficulties in reaching a policy consensus. In many cases in a pluralistic society, the resolution of this apparent problem is found in pluralism

by permitting individual variation based on personal or group preferences. However, the idea of permitting such a variation in the definition of death raises serious problems, each of which should be explored. Three kinds of variation have been considered.

The first is variation by the society. Society could endorse varying definitions of death, depending, in part, upon the anticipated use of the body. In fact, the law passed in the state of Kansas (87) appears to do just that. The Kansas statute includes two alternative definitions of death, one based on respiratory and cardiac function and the other based on brain function. There is no guidance for when either should be used, but the implication is that the latter should be used when transplantation or other use is anticipated for the body.

The criticism of such a variation has been that it seems that whether one is treated as dead or alive should not be contingent upon the anticipated use of the corpse. In fact, one could envision bizarre circumstances were alternative standards permitted. A transplant might be anticipated and death pronounced on that basis. But in the interim before the organ is removed from the newly deceased, if the planned recipient dies suddenly, there may no longer be an anticipated transplant. If so, there would be confusion over whether the person continued to be dead according to the original alternative or should suddenly have the other alternative applied to him in his new circumstance.

The second potential kind of variation is variation by physicians. The policy question is whether physicians should be permitted or required to use brain-oriented standards when pronouncing death. As a practical matter, this reduces to the question of whether laws should say that a physician *shall* pronounce death or that a physician *may* pronounce death. A model bill by the American Medical Association (AMA), dated January 1979, says, for example, "A physician, in the exercise of his professional judgment, may declare an individual dead in accordance with accepted medical standards. . . . " The immediate bizarre implication is that a physician need not declare an individual dead in accordance with accepted medical standards, that is to say, he might use his discretion and use some other standard. At the very least, this leads to policy confusion. Different physicians seeing the same patient may use different standards for pronouncing death. Thus, a physician who sees a patient at one point might decide not to use brain-oriented standards, while another physician, seeing the patient in exactly the same condition, decides to use them, exercises his option, and pronounces death.

In December 1979 at its Interim Meeting, the AMA amended its model bill removing the term "may." Possibly, it reintroduced another kind of variation, however, by proposing that "an individual who has sustained either (1) irreversible cessation or circulatory and respiratory functions, or (2) irreversible cessation of all functions of the entire brain, shall be considered dead." That is, alternative formulations are again introduced. Presumably, in this case, implying that if either condition is met, the person shall be considered dead even if the other is not met.

The Uniform Brain Death Act adopted in 1978 by the National Conference of Commissioners on Uniform State Laws avoided such a variation by specifying that "for all legal and medical purposes, an individual who has sustained irreversible cessation of all functioning of the brain, including the brain stem, is dead" (88). The ethics committee of the American Academy of Neurology follows a similar line. It praises the Uniform Brain Death Act because "it is written in such a way that the determination of death is mandatory, not permissive . . . " (69).

In an effort to overcome the ambiguity generated by having several different proposed statutes, the President's Commission worked with the AMA, the American Bar Association, and the National Conference of Commissioners on Uniform State Laws. They developed what is referred to as the Uniform Determination of Death Act, which all of these groups have endorsed in place of their previous proposals. It states that:

> An individual who has sustained either (1) irreversible cessation of circulatory and respiratory functions, or (2) irreversible cessation of all functions of the entire brain, including the brain stem, is dead. A determination of death must be made in accordance with accepted medical standards.

As long as this is interpreted as requiring that death must be pronounced if either of these conditions is met, there is no problem of variation from physician to physician. This formulation relies on "accepted medical standards," which could create a problem if the consensus of the profession about the relative significance of different types of errors is significantly different from the consensus of nonprofessionals.

The potential for difficulty, if variation by physician is permitted, is great. For example, if standards based on total supercellular brain function are adopted, but then physicians are given discretion as in the original AMA model bill, physicians could presumably opt either for more conservative or more liberal interpretations. Thus, a physician, at his discretion, could use traditional heart and lung standards, higher brain standards, or even more permissive criteria. It seems strange that citizens should be considered dead or alive depending upon the preferences of their physician. Many have concluded that such discretion is not acceptable, which leads to the conclusion that physicians should not have such discretion. They should not be permitted to refrain from pronouncing death in a state specifying brain criteria. By the same token, it is an even more serious offense if physicians in the jurisdictions that have not adopted such criteria take it upon themselves to pronounce death based on loss of brain function. There is some empirical evidence that physicians are, in fact, taking it upon themselves to use their own standards, pronouncing death based on brain criteria in states that have not authorized such pronouncement (89). In fact, in states with no legal authorization for death pronouncement based on brain criteria, persons with dead brains should be treated as still living. If a patient then really dies (based on heart and lung function appropriate in that jurisdiction) because treatment stopped following an erroneous death pronouncement based on brain criteria, a physician might appropriately be prosecuted for homicide.

There is a final kind of variation to be considered. This is variation by individual patients or their agents. There is overwhelming evidence that citizens differ over precisely what standards should be used for pronouncing death. These differences are rooted in underlying conceptual philosophical and theological differences over the definition of death having nothing to do with matters requiring knowledge of neurological science. It now seems clear that if any single policy is adopted, some citizens will have their personal convictions about something as basic as the meaning of life and death violated. Some have proposed that limited discretion be given to individuals to exercise conscientious objection to any policy adopted in this area.

In 1968, M. Martin Halley and William Harvey (90) proposed a very early version of a redefinition of death. It contained a provision for pronouncing death apparently using other than cardiac and respiratory standards in "special circumstances" provided that "valid consent" has been given by the appropriate relative or legal guardian. They were criticized for the consent requirement on the grounds that they had apparently confused making the state of being dead contingent upon consent when critics thought they must have intended to make the withholding of treatment from a dying person dependent upon consent (39).

It does appear that Halley and Harvey had confused two quite different questions. Certainly, it is more obvious that decisions to withhold treatment might be contingent on guardian consent. Yet a case can be made that even the choice of a standard for pronouncing death could incorporate discretion of the individual or his or her legal agent. What is at stake is not whether a person has experienced some bodily change—a fact that is, presumably, independent of the views of the individual or others. The question is when the person should be treated as dead, that is, when death behaviors become appropriate. Some limited discretion could logically be given to the individual or others in answering that question. Whether it should be given is, of course, another question.

In New York in the early 1970s, efforts to pass a bill redefining death met with opposition from certain minority groups who were strongly opposed to any change. These groups included some religious objectors and others who felt strongly that a person should be treated as alive as long as the heart beats regardless of the condition of the brain. In response, the governor proposed a bill in 1976 incorporating a standard based on "total and irreversible cessation of brain function." The proviso was added in the draft, however, that this brain-oriented standard would be used "unless the physician receives written notice from a parent, spouse, next of kin of such person that such pronouncement conflicts with such person's beliefs." It is not clear why written notice from the person himself written in advance while competent was not included. It is also not clear why parents were not given such veto power in cases where the person himself has not developed views on the subject (because of infancy or mental deficiency, for example). In any case, this bill has never passed, leaving New York without statutory authority to pronounce death in any cases based on brain standards (91, p. 60).

Recently, a New York State Task Force on Life and the Law was appointed to study and make recommendations concerning the ethical, legal, and medical issues related to the determination of death. In its 1986 proposed report, the Task Force recommends that "[b]oth the traditional standard cessation of heart and lung activity and the standard of total and irreversible cessation of brain function, including brain stem function, should be recognized as the legal standards for determining death in the State of New York" (92, p. 1). Although the 1984 New York Court of Appeals decision in *People v. Eulo* negates the necessity for legislation to adopt the brain death standard, the Task Force recommends the issuing of a Department of Health regulation to ensure that the brain death standard is uniformly applied throughout the state. The Task Force endorses a uniform determination of death standard although it " . . . believes that, where feasible, an effort should be made to respect the deeply held religious or moral beliefs of persons who object to the brain death standard for determining death" (92, p. 19).

Along these lines, one member of the Task Force, Rabbi J. David Bleich, rejects its recommendations. He suggests that the "[a]doption of a brain death statute is nothing other than a moral judgment to the effect that there is no human value which argues in favor of the preservation of the life of an irreversibly comatose patient or that there are other values which must be accorded priority" (92, p. 32). Bleich argues that, despite the apparent majority in favor of brain death standards, other individuals exist, especially within certain religious traditions. To impose brain-based criteria of determining death upon these persons would be a violation of their autonomy and, more legalistically, their religious and civil liberties. Bleich suggests, "The simplest, most expedient and most honest method of resolving the problem is not by redefining death, but by enacting a statute providing for the withholding of life support mechanisms from irreversibly comatose patients without at all disturbing the classical definition of death" (92, p. 34).

Because of such clear philosophical and theological disagreement underlying the debate and the absolute necessity of having some policy for initiating death behaviors, some have advocated limited discretion for individuals or their agents in selecting the standard of death to be used (26).

It is clear that there cannot be unlimited personal discretion that would permit individuals to choose to be pronounced dead and treated as dead when heart, lungs, lower brain, higher brain, and capacities for consciousness and thinking remain intact. No matter how strongly some deviant member of this society might think he is dead under such circumstances, we cannot, as a matter of public policy, permit death behaviors in such circumstances. Likewise, if some person holds the firm conviction that he is not dead until every cell in his body ceases to function, society probably cannot tolerate the justification of behaviors that would lead to treating such a person as alive.

It is logically possible, however, to adopt a public policy which would permit limited individual discretion. This could come in the form of adopting three or more alternative definitions from which each individual might choose. This, of course, would lead to severe problems in cases where people had not exercised such choice. For these and other reasons, it seems plausible that if any choice is to be tolerated at all, it would have to be in the context of a single definition being adopted. This definition would include the right of individuals to select from a limited range of alternatives in cases where they were motivated so strongly that they would go through the necessary procedures to reject the standard definition. Assuming that all people who had strong feelings on the matter would exercise such an option, it would make little difference which of the plausible definitions of death were adopted for public policy purposes. It would be efficient to adopt the policy that appeared to be held by the largest number of people. Alternatively, one might formulate policy under the assumption that many people would not take the initiative to exercise such judgment even if they did have rather strong feelings on the mater. In such a case, it might be a prudent policy option to adopt a rather conservative definition of death, perhaps even one based on irreversible loss of heart and lung function, then permit individuals to opt for formulations based on total brain function and possibly on higher brain function.

It seems bizarre that the definition of death should be left to such individual discretion. We have always considered death to be an objective fact. For policy purposes, however, we are not interested in biological, or even in philosophical or theological formulations. Rather, we want to know the much more practical question of when people ought to be treated as dead (67)—clearly an evaluative question where, traditionally, individual discretion has been tolerated within limits. The mechanics of tolerating such limited objections or basic philosophical concerns may make the option of permitting variations seem infeasible to some (93, pp. 169–70), yet the alternative of insisting that all operate under the same uniform definition of death regardless of their most deeply held religious and philosophical beliefs is also alien to our American tradition. While the President's Commission recommended the adoption of the Uniform Determination of Death Act in all jurisdictions in the United States and specifically rejected a "conscience clause" permitting an individual (or family member where the individual is incompetent) to specify the standard to be used for determining death, it also urged " . . . those acting under the statute to apply it with sensitivity to the emotional and religious needs of those for whom the new standards mark a departure from traditional practice," implying possible physician variation in selecting standards (40, pp. 43, 80).

Since its proposal, the Uniform Determination of Death Act has been endorsed by the American Academy of Neurology and the American Electroencephalographic Society and has been adopted in a number of states. Currently 36 states and the District of Columbia have adopted some statute endorsing the cessation of brain function as a standard for determining death. Additionally, in five other states the brain-based criteria have been established by judicial decision (92). Still no jurisdiction has seen fit to adopt a definition of death based on higher brain function. It is not clear whether that is because they disagree philosophically or simply believe that irreversible loss of higher brain function cannot be measured accurately. Still a growing consensus supports some kind of brain-oriented definition of death. Unfortunately, even with the growing consensus on what standards should be applied in determining the death of an individual, the problems or public policy for death and dying remain far from settled. Despite the President's Commission's 1983 report on Deciding to Forego Life-sustaining Treatment (94), attention still remains focused on public policy issues surrounding the care of those individuals determined to still be alive.

REVIEW QUESTIONS

1. Should an individual who has irreversibly lost consciousness, but who can still breathe on his or her own, be considered dead? If not, should the appropriate surrogate authorize stopping the treatment so that such a person may die?

2. Should an individual whose brain function has ceased irreversibly be considered dead if he or she is in a state that has not authorized death pronouncement based on brain criteria? If so, should physicians who pronounce death be able to choose any definition they want?

3. What would happen if individuals could, while still conscious, specify that they want some definition of death used other than the one favored by the state legislature? What policy problems would result from choosing a higher-brain-oriented formulation? What policy problems would result from choosing a heart-and-lung-oriented formulation?

4. Should the majority be able to impose their definition of death on other mem-

bers of the society? If so, should it be the majority of physicians, of neurologists, of heart specialists, or the majority of the entire population?

5. Suppose that the members of the society wanted to maintain a heart-and-lung-oriented definition of death but legalize certain behaviors (such as taking organs from people who would then still be living with dead brains). What policy changes would be required? Which of these changes would you favor?

6. How can one argue that the selection of the point at which a person is to be considered dead should be a matter of public policy rather than a medical concern?

7. Why don't statutes concerning the time of death have reference to specific empirical measures? Is this possible? Practical? Why or why not?

8. What are your personal concepts or standards of death? At what point do you believe a person is dead? At what point would you want your family members to consider you dead?

9. Should the donation of organs be a consideration in deciding the criteria for death? Why?

10. Discuss the notion of the irreversibility of death and the near-death experiences reported in the media. Compare and contrast the two concepts.

REFERENCES

1. Becker, L. C. (1975). Human being: The boundaries of the concept. *Philosophy and Public Affairs, 4,* 334–359.

2. Lamb, D. (1978). Diagnosing death. *Philosophy and Public Affairs, 7,* 144–153.

3. Mayo, D., & Wikler, D. I. (1979). Euthanasia and the transition from life to death. In W. Robinson & M. S. Pritchard (eds.), *Medical responsibility: Paternalism, informed consent, and euthanasia* (pp. 195–211). Clifton, NJ: The Humane Press.

4. Green, M. B., & Wilker, D. (1980). Brain death and personal identity. *Philosophy and Public Affairs, 9*(2), 105–133.

5. Bleich, J. D. (1979). Neurological criteria of death and time of death status. In J. D. Bleich & F. Rosner (eds.), *Jewish bioethics* (303–316). New York: Sanhedrin Press.

6. Fletcher, J. (1969). Our shameful waste of human tissue. In D. R. Cutler (Ed.), *Updating life and death* (pp. 1–27). Boston: Beacon Press.

7. Haring, B. (1973). *Medical ethics* (pp. 131–136). Notre Dame, IN: Fides Press.

8. Hauerwas, S. (1978). Religious concepts of brain death and associated problems. In J. Korein (Ed.), *Brain death: Interrelated medical and social issues* (pp. 329–338). New York: New York Academy of Sciences.

9. Kosnik, A. R. (1973). Theological reflections on criteria for defining the moment of death. *Hospital Progress,* December, pp. 64–69.

10. Pope Pius XII. (1958). The prolongation of life: An address of Pope Pius XII to an International Congress of Anesthesiologists. *The Pope Speaks, 4,* 393–398.

11. Ramsey, P. (1970). *The patient as person.* New Haven, CT: Yale University Press, 59–164.

12. Veith, F. J., Fein, J. M., Tendler, M. D., Veatch, R. M., Kleimen, M. A., & Kalkines, G. (1977). Brain death: I. A status report of medical and ethical considerations. *Journal of the American Medical Association, 238,* 1651–1655.

13. Black, P. M. (1978). Brain death. *New England Journal of Medicine, 299,* 338–44 and 393–401.

14. Collaborative Study. (1979). An appraisal of the criteria of cerebral death—A summary statement. *Journal of the American Medical Association, 237,* 982–986.

15. Cranford, R. B., & Smith, H. L. (1979). Some critical distinctions between brain death and the persistent vegetative state. *Ethics in Science and Medicine, 6*(4), 199–209.

16. Currie, B. (1978). The redefinition of death. In S. F. Spicker (Ed.), *Organism, medicine and metaphysics* (177–197). Boston: D. Reidel.

17. Harvard Medical School. (1968). A definition of irreversible coma. Report of the Ad Hoc Committee of the Harvard Medical School to examine the definition of brain death. *Journal of the American Medical Association, 205,* 337–340.

18. Mohandas, A., & Chou, S. N. (1971). Brain death: A clinical and pathological study. *Journal of Neurosurgery, 35,* 211–218.

19. "Report of the medical consultants on the diagnosis of death to the President's Commission for the Study of Ethical Problems in Medicine and Biomedical and Behavioral Research." President's Commission for the Study of Ethical Problems in Medicine and Biomedical and Behavioral Research. (1981). *Defining death: Medical, legal and ethical issues in the definition of death* (pp. 159–66). Washington, DC: U.S. Government Printing Office.

20. Fulton, R., & Fulton, J. (1972). Anticipatory grief: A psychosocial aspect of terminal care. In B. Schoenberg, A. C. Carr, D. Peretz, & A. H. Kutscher (Eds.), *Psychosocial aspects of terminal care* (pp. 227–242). New York: Columbia University Press.

21. Fellner, C. H. (1971). Selection of living kidney donors and the problem of informed consent. *Seminars in Psychiatry, 3,* 70–85.

22. Mahoney, J. (1975). Ethical aspects of donor consent in transplantation. *Journal of Medical Ethics, 1,* 67–70.

23. Robertson, J. A. (1976). Organ donations by incompetents and the substituted judgment doctrine. *Columbia Law Review, 76:* 48 ff.

24. Simmons, R. G., & Fulton, J. (1971). Ethical issues in kidney transplantation. *Omega, 2,* 179–190.

25. *Removal of cadaveric organs for transplantation: A code of practice.* Report of a Working Party set up by the United Kingdom Health Department under chairmanship of Lord Smith of Marlow, 1979.

26. Veatch, R. M. (1976). *Death, dying, and the biological revolution.* New Haven, CT: Yale University Press.

27. May, W. F. (1973). Attitudes toward the newly dead. *Hastings Center Studies, 1*(1), 3–13.

28. Morison, R. (1971). Death—Process of event? *Science, 173,* 694–698.

29. Kass, L. (1971). Death as an event: A commentary on Robert Morison. *Science, 173,* 698–702.

30. Tooley, M. (1979). Decisions to terminate life and the concept of person. In J. Ladd (Ed.), *Ethical issues relating to life and death* (pp. 62–93). New York: Oxford University Press.

31. Sullivan, J. F. (1975, October 3). Lawyer outlines arguments he'll use in coma case. *The New York Times,* p. 1.

32. Saperstein, S. (1979, March 22). Maryland law on brain death was unclear to jurors. *The Washington Post,* p. C1+.

33. Jennett, B., & Plum, F. (1972). Persistent vegetative state after brain damage. *Lancet, 1,* 734–737.

34. Levy, D. E., Knill-Jones, R. P., & Plum, F. (1978). The vegetative state and its prognosis following nontraumatic coma. In J. Korein (Ed.), *Brain death: Interrelated medical and social issues* (pp. 293–304). New York: New York Academy of Sciences.

35. *In re Quinlan,* 70 M.J. 10,355 A2d 647(1976).

36. Korein, J. (1978). Editor's comment. *Brain death: Interrelated medical and social issues* (320–321). New York: New York Academy of Sciences.

37. Korein, J. (1978). Terminology, definitions, and usage. *Brain death: Interrelated medical and social issues* (6–10). New York: New York Academy of Sciences.

38. Biorck, G. (1967). On the definition of death. *World Medical Journal, 14,* 137–139.

39. Capron, A. M., & Kass, L. (1972). A statutory definition of the standards for determining human death: An appraisal and a proposal. *University of Pennsylvania Law Review, 121,* 87–118.
40. President's Commission for the Study of Ethical Problems in Medicine and Biomedical and Behavioral Research. (1981). *Defining death: Medical, legal and ethical issues in the definition of death.* Washington, DC: U.S. Government Printing Office.
41. Veatch, R. M. (1972). Brain death: Welcome definition or dangerous judgment? *Hastings Center Report, 2,* 10–13.
42. Veatch, R. M. (1975). The whole-brain-oriented concept of death: An outmoded philosophical formulation. *Journal of Thanatology, 3,* 13–30.
43. Veatch, R. M. (1983). Definitions of life and death: Should there be consistency. In M. W. Shaw & A. E. Doudera (Eds.), *Defining human life* (pp. 99–113). Ann Arbor, MI: AUPHA Press.
44. Veatch, R. M. (1977). Considerations about the determination of death. In D. Self (Ed.), *Philosophy and Public Policy* (pp. 74–92). Norfolk, VA: Teagle and Little.
45. Veatch, R. M. (1978). The definition of death: Ethical, philosophical, and policy confusion. In J. Korein (Ed.), *Brain death: Interrelated medical and social issues* (pp. 307–321). New York: New York Academy of Sciences.
46. Devins, G. M., & Diamond, R. T. (1976–77). The determination of death. *Omega, 7,* 277–296.
47. Foster, H. H. (1976). Time of death. *New York State Journal of Medicine,* 2187–2197.
48. Grenvik, A., Pawner, D. J., Snyder, J. V., Jastremski, M. S., Babcock, R. A., Loughhead, M. G. (1978). Cessation of therapy in terminal illness and brain death. *Critical Care Medicine, 6,* 284–291.
49. Kennedy, I. M. (1973). The legal definition of death. *Medico-Legal Journal, 41,* 36–41.
50. Kennedy, I. M. (1975). A legal perspective on determining death. *The Month, 8,* 46–51.
51. Kennedy, I. M. (1977). The definition of death. *Journal of Medical Ethics, 3,* 5–6.
52. Skegg, P. D. G. (1976). Case for a statutory "definition of death." *Journal of Medical Ethics, 2,* 190–192.
53. Toole, J. F. (1971). The neurologist and the concept of brain death. *Perspectives in Biology and Medicine, 14,* 599–607.
54. Van Till-D'Aulnis de Bourouill, A. (1975). How dead can you be? *Medical Science Law, 15,* 133–147.
55. Task Force on Death and Dying, Institute of Society, Ethics and the Life Sciences. (1972). Refinements in criteria for the determination of death: An appraisal. *Journal of the American Medical Association, 221,* 48–53.
56. Roelofs, R. (1978). Some preliminary remarks on brain death. In J. Korein (Ed.), *Brain death: Interrelated medical and social issues* (pp. 39–44). New York: New York Academy of Sciences.
57. Veatch, R. M. (1979). Defining death: The role of brain function. *Journal of the American Medical Association, 242,* 2001–2002.
58. Mills, D. H. (1971). The Kansas death statute: Bold and innovative. *New England Journal of Medicine, 285,* 968–969.
59. Richardson, D. R. (1976). A matter of life and death: A definition of death: Judicial resolution of a medical responsibility. *Harvard Law Journal, 19,* 138–148.
60. Frenkel, D. A. (1978). Establishing the cessation of life. *Legal Medical Quarterly, 2*(3), 162–168.
61. Friloux, C. A. (1975). Death? When does it occur? *Baylor Law Review, 27,* 10–21.
62. Kennedy, I. M. (1971). The Kansas state statute on death—An appraisal. *New England Journal of Medicine, 285*(17), 946–949.
63. Mackert, J. F. (1979). Should the law define brain death? *Hospital Progress, 60*(3), 6ff.
64. Potter, R. B. (1968). The paradoxical preservation of a principle. *Villanova Law Review, 13,* 784–792.

65. Forrester, A. C. (1976). Brain death and the donation of cadaver kidneys. *Health Bulletin, 34*, 199–204.
66. Jonas, H. (1974). Against the stream: Comments on the definition and redefinition of death. In *Philosophical essays: From ancient creed to technological man* (pp. 132–140). Englewood Cliffs, NJ: Prentice-Hall.
67. Ladd, J. (1979). The definition of death and the right to die. In J. Ladd (Ed.), *Ethical issues relating to life and death* (pp. 118–145). New York: Oxford University Press.
68. Byrne, P. A., O'Reilley, S., & Quay, P. M. (1979). Brain death: An opposing viewpoint. *Journal of the American Medical Association, 242*, 1985–1990.
69. Cranford, R., et al. (1979). Uniform brain death act. *Neurology, 29*, 417–418.
70. Jonas, H. (1969, Spring). Philosophical reflections on experimenting with human subjects. *Daedalus, 98*, 219–247.
71. *Black's Law Dictionary* (4th ed., rev.), p. 488. St. Paul: West Publishing Co.
72. Beecher, H. K. (1970). *The new definition of death, some opposing views.* Paper presented at the meeting of the American Association for the Advancement of Science.
73. Collins, V. (1971). Considerations in defining death. *Linacre Quarterly, 38*, 94–101.
74. Wasmuth, C. E. (1969). The concept of death. *Ohio State Law Journal, 30*, 32–60.
75. Charron, W. C. (1975). Death: A philosophical perspective on the legal definitions. *Washington University Law Quarterly, 4*, 979–1008.
76. Black, P. M. (1977). Three definitions of death. *The Monist, 60*(1), 136–146.
77. Diagnosis of death. (1979). *Lancet, 1*, 261–262.
78. Horan, D. J. (1978). Euthanasia and brain death: Ethical and legal considerations. *Linacre Quarterly, 45*(3), 284–296.
79. Stickel, D. L. (1979). The brain death criterion of human death. *Ethics in Science and Medicine, 6*, 177–197.
80. Olinger, S. D. (1975). Medical death. *Baylor Law Review, 27*, 22–26.
81. Sweet, W. H. (1978). Brain death. *New England Journal of Medicine, 299*, 410–411.
82. Brierley, J. B., Adam, J. A. H., Graham, D. I., & Simpson, J. A. (1971). Neocortical death after cardiac arrest. *Lancet, 2*, 560–565.
83. Burnham, J. C. (1977). The mind-body problem in the early twentieth century. *Perspectives in Biology and Medicine, 20*(2), 271–284.
84. Feigl, H. (1967). The "mental" and the "physical." Minneapolis, MN: University of Minnesota Press.
85. Globus, G. G. (1973). Consciousness and brain I: The identity thesis. *Archives of General Psychiatry, 29*, 153 ff.
86. Wilson, D. L. (1976). On the nature of consciousness and of physical reality. *Perspectives in Biology and Medicine, 19*, 569ff.
87. Kansas State Ann. 77-202 (Supp. 1974).
88. National Conference of Commissioners on Uniform State Laws (1978). *Uniform Brain Death Act.* Chicago, IL.
89. Black, P. M., & Zervas, N. T. (1984). Declaration of brain death in neurosurgical and neurological practice. *Neurosurgery, 15*, 170–174.
90. Halley, M. M., & Harvey, W. F. (1968). Medical and legal definitions of death. *Journal of the American Medical Association, 204*, 423–425.
91. Guthrie, L. B. (1979). Brain death and criminal liability. *Criminal Law Bulletin, 15*, 40–61.

92. New York State Task Force on Life and the Law. (1986, February). *The Determination of Death: Proposed Report.*

93. Ramsey, P. (1978). *Ethics at the edges of life.* New Haven, CT: Yale University Press.

94. President's Commission for the Study of Ethical Problems in Medicine and Biomedical and Behavioral Research. (1983). *Deciding to forego life-sustaining treatment: Ethical, medical, and legal issues in treatment decisions.* Washington, DC: U.S. Government Printing Office.

4

The Study of Death:
A Psychosocial Perspective

Richard A. Kalish

Death and taxes may share the quality of being life's two constants, but they share little else. Poets and painters rarely represent taxes in their art, and the cost of one good study of taxes is probably greater than the cost of the entire world's expenditures for research on death and grief.

The reasons for studying taxes are sufficiently obvious to entice governments and corporations to fund the research. But why study death anyway? After all, we can alter the tax structure, but death . . . ?

This chapter will begin with a discussion of the three core concepts of the study of death, followed by the reasons for studying death. There will then be two brief sections, one on methodological decisions that require attention and the other on ethical issues in death-related research. Following these will be the major focus of the chapter: a discussion of some of the major concerns and limitations of death-related research, including selection of the research question, issues in terminology, development of scales, program evaluation, interpreting results, and difficulties generated by the affect-laden nature of the topic of death. A brief final statement attempts to provide a conclusion.

STUDYING DEATH

The Three Core Concepts

Before discussing the study of death, it seems important to know that we are all talking about the same concept. What does it mean to "study death"? First, I believe we need to examine the parameters of what is encompassed by "death." If

Although parts of this chapter appear to address only quantitative research, most of the comments are equally applicable to qualitative research.

we were to examine the two major journals in the field, *Omega* and *Death Studies*, we would find that death includes homicide, stages of dying, death anxiety, funeral directors, bereavement, customs of the Bororo Indians of Brazil, reactions to catastrophic death, death education, and legal and ethical issues. These are from just one issue of each journal.

The study of death appears to encompass three core concepts: death itself and its meanings, the process of dying, and grief and bereavement. In relationship to each of these core concepts, we can study attitudes and values, caring relationships, family relationships, professional training, cultural differences, legal aspects, ethical concerns, health concerns, theology, institutional treatment, age and gender differences, research methodologies, children's literature, folklore and myth, involvement in psychotherapeutic processes, changes over time under stipulated circumstances, relevant professional roles—the list is truly limitless.

To complicate matters further, the study of death has significant overlap with the study of other concerns, each related in one way or another. These include suicide, chronic illness, medical education, disasters, violence, homicide, and euthanasia. Whether these issues should be subsumed under "death" or remain separate entities appears to be a function of individual preference and the context in which the question arises.

All in all, therefore, I am not personally persuaded that the "study of death" is a field or a discipline, nor that applying the term *thanatology* changes anything. I view death as a topic, an issue, a concern, aspects of which can be studied in innumerable disciplines: psychology, sociology, clinical medicine, social work, religion/theology, anthropology, economics, demography, philosophy, biology, chemistry, geography, epidemiology, law. Again, the list is extensive, albeit not limitless, in this instance.

Sometimes, of course, the study of death emerges indirectly through the study of something else. Those who study how to improve biomedical treatment for cancer are not studying death, but those who study psychological factors in the care of cancer patients may be studying death since one very significant factor influencing the affective responses people display to having cancer is its lethality. Similarly, a study of counseling older adults may gather information on how people deal with the death of a spouse or the eventual death of self.

We don't need to define the study of death with precision—virtually all abstract concepts become blurred around the perimeter. Clearly, evaluating changes in expressed death-related attitudes as a function of a death-education course is a study of death; clearly a comparable study of attitudes toward older people is not a study of death, even though one item on the questionnaire might allude to death. But where the study of death becomes the study of other-than-death requires individual definitions and decisions.

Let me return to the core concepts: death, dying, grief. The closer our research is to these concepts, the more readily we can ascertain that we are, indeed, studying death; the farther we drift from this core, the less likely we are truly to be studying death.

Whys and Wherefores

There was a time when those working with death-related issues could claim that their efforts were too recent to be based on sound research. That time is over.

To provide an overview of the field: Herman Feifel's early work is now over 30 years old (1, 2); university courses on death and grief have been taught for over 20 years; and it is over 20 years since Hinton's paperback *Dying* appeared in its first edition (3). If the death-awareness movement is not yet well into adolescence, it is certainly no longer in its infancy.

And, therefore, the continued dependence on intuition, good intentions, and the prevailing fashion (or fad) is no longer sufficient. It is no longer appropriate to maintain the platitudes that have guided the field, simply because they contradicted earlier platitudes that violated our developing sense of propriety.

A few examples of operating without adequate information should be sufficient. Do most people bargain with God or fate for prolonged life as a stage in their dying process, as Kübler-Ross (4) contends? Is bargaining, when it does occur, expressed as a stage or as an irregular, ongoing phenomenon? Who bargains? Does bargaining facilitate death acceptance? If so, for whom and under what conditions? Should we consider intervening to encourage its use?

Or consider the role of religious beliefs in death attitudes. Are religious people more or less fearful of their own eventual death, or imminent death, than nonreligious people, or is that a nonsensical question without a clear statement as to the definition of *religious* or without indicating the content of the religious belief system? What kinds of religious values would lead to a less fearful dying process and death? Is it the specific content of the religious belief system, the extent to which it is intrinsic or extrinsic, or the way in which it interacts with the circumstances existing for the individual that determines its impact on the anticipation of death? Research does exist on this topic, especially on the first question, but it hasn't begun to answer even the basic questions (5, 6).

Finally, consider another example, *healthy* grieving. Is it more effective to grieve openly immediately after the death of a loved person than to hold back from grieving at that time? Some evidence supports this stance (7). Or do different people have different grieving trajectories that "work for them"? Therefore, is it appropriate to intervene to encourage early expression of grief, or is this approach likely to be counterproductive because each person has his or her own optimum grieving trajectory?

All of the above are researchable questions. All would provide information that would be simultaneously interesting and useful and would also contribute to the development of theory. And in each instance, the death-awareness movement has created its own mythology, albeit a mythology that is not universally held. Nonetheless, we continue to make decisions that affect the well-being of innumerable individuals based more on supposition, mythology, and fashion than on empirically developed information.

We study death for many reasons, some deeply personal, some motivated by financial gain or professional advancement, some to improve competence in caring for others. Although the reasons to pursue the scientific study of death overlap with these, they differ somewhat. One way to view the bases for the scientific study of death is in terms of theories/models, substance/knowledge, and practice/applications. Another classification system could be based on the nature of those whom the research benefits: the dying, the survivors, relevant professionals, everyone else; or we could consider it topically: death, the process of dying, grief; or by discipline: medical, psychological, sociological, economic, geographical; or by nature of events: health, family, community, services, legal aspects, theology, postdeath ceremonies and rituals, related professionals. There are undoubtedly other possibilities.

For present purposes, however, the theory/substance/practice classification of death research seems most appropriate.

Developing Theories and Models

An aggressive doctoral student, perhaps trying to impress his professors with his erudition, once asked me to discuss my "theory of death." When I tried to determine what aspects of death concerned him, he simply reiterated his initial question as though my probes did not merit a response. Finally, frustrated and, perhaps, not thinking too clearly myself, I said that we didn't need a theory of death and that people just died. The student sat back smugly in his chair and grinned, as though he had just beaten Ivan Lendl in straight sets.

It was only later that I realized the full complexity of "a theory of death" and why I became too flustered to answer intelligently. We could, for example, have a theory on why we die: because we are not gods; to permit improvement of the species; to eliminate the ill and decaying; to avoid overcrowding; because we are simply one of several experimental groups being manipulated by psychologists on another solar system; because when we were created, we were created imperfectly either on purpose or by accident; and so forth.

We could develop a biologically based theory as to how we age and, from this, create a theory on why we die, although it might not include deaths from accidents, wars, and suicides. That the heart stops beating or the lungs stop taking in oxygen or that the brain stops functioning do not seem to be adequate theories of death.

We could also have other kinds of theories about death: a theory regarding why (or why and if) people fear death, a theory regarding attitudinal/affective stages of the dying process, a theory regarding near-death experiences and their effects, a theory regarding the grief trajectory, a theory differentiating normal and abnormal grieving, a theory concerning how to intervene in the dying or grieving processes in order to effect a stipulated improvement, and countless more theories. In fact, although I cannot comprehend that there can be a theory of death, I can accept the likelihood that there are endless theories and models about various aspects of death, the dying process, and grief.

Why bother with theories of death-related issues? For the same reasons that we bother with any theories at all. Because theories provide a cohesive way to integrate isolated pieces of information and to understand better the phenomenon under consideration. Because when we lack a theory, even an implicit and unstated theory, we are compelled to make a new decision every time we are confronted with a new circumstance; with a theory, we can view the new circumstance in a theoretical context, and we can use research to test theories, then confirm, alter, or discard the theory based on the research findings.

Although there may be no "theory of death," there are ample theories and models that exist and are often accepted at face value, without adequate scientific testing. For example, do people really die in five stages and is acceptance of death adaptive for the dying person, as Kübler-Ross' (4) well-known system would indicate, or is dying at home really contributing to an "appropriate" death and, since evidence does support this assumption (9), what are the characteristics of dying at home that make it preferable? Does touching a dying person improve the mental health and spiritual well-being of that person and, if so, under what circumstances might it be counterproductive? In each of the above examples, an initial theoretical statement is given, followed by a second clause that extends and broadens the theory. However, scientific, replicable research is, for the most part, lacking in these theories, although we continue to function as though the theories were established.

In effect, a theory gives us basis for action and, if well-stated and open, it is amenable to improvement. Research promotes this improvement.

Substance

Research also provides us with information to help us understand "the human phenomenon." It improves our understanding of ourselves, of others, of our social institutions, of differences and similarities among people and groups. It is true that much of the substance of death-related research is both time-bound and place-bound, i.e., we are not creating universal principles but, rather, principles that are restricted to our era (a decade? a century?) and to our region (a town? a state? a nation? a culture?). Nonetheless, as long as we recognize the limitations of research, we can gain much from it.

Unfortunately, but not surprisingly, the substance of research frequently appears inconsistent, and we often turn to literature reviews to help us sort out the inconsistencies. One good example is Rando's (8) integration and analysis of research findings on anticipatory bereavement and its effects. She points out that some investigators simply assumed that anticipatory grieving had occurred because the bereaved person had advance knowledge of the death, while other researchers required supporting evidence that the bereaved person actually did grieve prior to the death. In making this differentiation, Rando provides a clearer picture of what anticipatory bereavement is and what it is not (it is *not* simply duration prior to death of a loved person), as well as its apparent effects. We do not know whether this phenomenon cuts across cultures nor whether it will occur in the same fashion a century from now or had occurred a century ago, but we are developing a fairly good idea of its nature and how it works here and now.

Some studies are obviously time-bound and place-bound, e.g., an analysis of how much people know about hospices and how they view the movement. Other studies might or might not be time-bound and place-bound: the relationship between various measures of religiousness and various death attitudes. A few studies at least offer the possibility of providing information that is neither time-bound nor place-bound: the relationship between views of immortality and proximity to one's own death, next-of-kin responses to anticipated versus unanticipated death.

Practice/Application

Although it has been stated that nothing is more practical than a good theory, we are often unable or unwilling to wait for that good theory to be developed, and there is an ongoing need to utilize research to improve practice. If one of your parents was dying and you were considering hospice care, you would be much more interested in how well a hospice might work for your parent than in a theoretical base for its effects.

And the ways in which we can apply research to improve practice are beyond counting: improving training programs for hospice volunteers, evaluating the leaderless group structure of self-help groups such as Compassionate Friends (10), determining whether funeral directors can provide a meaningful service by contacting grieving persons a month or so after the death, tracking students two or three years after completing a death-education course to see what long-term effects are found, and on and on and on.

Such studies are very likely to be time-bound and place-bound, with valid generalizations being limited to other times and places (and populations) that share significant characteristics with the time, place, and population studied. But research of this nature is important, which brings up the issue of the value of dissemination of findings. The usual assumption is that a study worth doing is a study worth publishing. However, some research into practice is so limited to one group of people with one organization in one community at one time that the generalizability is too limited to merit publication. Perhaps one of the journals in the field, presumably *Omega* or *Death Studies,* would offer space for a special section permitting brief reports (and addresses to which to write for elaborations) of this kind of applied research.

Put Them All Together

The three kinds of research—theory-building, substantive, and practical or highly applied—enrich each other. It is not unusual for a theoretician to incorporate applied-research findings into his or her theory or for an applied researcher to find that the data on which a theoretical advance is based have relevance to his or her particular program. Therefore, not only do all three kinds deserve encouragement and, when appropriate, publication, but even the applied research that has virtually no generalizability and will probably never be considered for publication requires thoughtfulness and care in its planning, conceptualization, and conduct.

METHODOLOGICAL DECISIONS

In theory, and according to textbooks, decisions about the research methodologies to be used must be based on the research question that is asked. In practice, most researchers have their preferred methodological approaches and only occasionally venture into unexplored methodological procedures. Nonetheless, the research available on death-related issues utilizes an immense variety of methodologies, and each has made a contribution.

For example, the issue of qualitative versus quantitative research always arises, yet this need not be an issue. Thus, Kalish and Reynolds (9) used both simultaneously and integrated the findings, although the lack of sufficient planning by the senior author led to an emphasis on the quantitative findings. Early in the history of the death-awareness movement, three of the most frequently cited sources were qualitative studies based on grounded theory, and the impact of these studies is still evident (11, 12, 13). On the other hand, Feifel's early studies on attitudes toward death (1, 2, 14), were all carefully quantified, although the author brought his clinical sensitivities to their interpretation.

Another question relates to the extent to which research needs to probe below the level of immediate conscious awareness. Again we turn to Feifel (15, 5) who has conducted studies on various levels of awareness with the same respondents. An early series of studies by Irving Alexander and his associates (16, 17) investigated nonaware reactions to death-related stimuli, such as galvanic-skin-response change when presented with death-associated words. Nonetheless, it is probably safe to state that at least 99 percent of relevant research is based on consciously motivated responses.

A third methodological consideration is whether to focus on intrapsychic phenomena, on the individual within a social context or system, or on the social context or system itself. Do we examine the feelings and perceived experiences of hospice nurses, the effects on hospice nurses of working in differing organizational structures, or the various kinds of hospice organizational structures that exist and how each relates to staffing patterns?

Sources for research data extend virtually without limit. It is obvious that we can study death in fairy tales, but how about death in comic strips? We have examined the experience of near-fatal falls, but have done relatively little with near-fatal drownings (a much more common experience), which could utilize interviews, questionnaires, checklists, recounting feelings and perceptions, and so forth. We can observe our own experiences and report on them, and we can observe what others seem to be experiencing; we can use experimental and comparison groups with systematic interventions and analysis-of-covariance designs; we can collect and content-analyze dreams and relate these to feelings, experiences, and demographic variables; we can examine Freudian symbolism, Jungian symbolism, or games people play; we can look at health records, psychotherapy outcomes, church attendance, or workshop registration; we can compare death-related measures (or nonmeasures) to personality characteristics, coping mechanisms, family supports, physical health, and MMPI scores; we can allow for unconscious distortions in responses, measure these distortions, or assume for research purposes that they do not exist.

This discussion raises questions that researchers must deal with each time they develop a research project. Sometimes the decision is forced upon the researcher by circumstances; sometimes the decision is influenced by time, money, energy, and the creativity of the researcher; sometimes the decision can be based on what will lead to the most meaningful findings.

In each instance, however, the specific decision made seems much less important than developing a study that is well conceived, well planned, well conducted, and well interpreted. A good case history, a good factor-analytic study, and a good grounded-theory investigation can all make important contributions; a poor case history, factor-analytic study, or grounded-theory investigation can be useless or misleading.

The theme of the previous paragraph will emerge frequently in this chapter. It is a concept that everyone knows and agrees with, yet it is a concept that is ignored more often than followed.

ETHICS OF RESEARCH

Ethical issues arise in any kind of research involving human beings or other forms of animal life, and discussions of these issues are well-chronicled in numerous sources. In this chapter, our concerns will be limited to those pertaining to death-related issues.

The evaluation of research ethics is not simply a variant of hedonic calculus, in which the benefits are compared to the deleterious effects and the higher number is considered "the winner." The more serious issue is whether the benefits of the research merit endangering the physical or mental health of any participant: For whom may this research be harmful; how extensive might be the harm; what might be the nature of the harm? This is not to contend that any suggestion of harm should be sufficient to cancel the research. Rather, it is an attempt to evaluate carefully all such research in relationship to the effects on the participants and then to make every effort to reduce or eliminate all hazards. There does seem to be some irony in that researchers have, with few or no exceptions, ignored research into the impact on participants of their research.

There are, of course, the usual ethical issues in research: not overgeneralizing from the data; reporting procedures and respondent characteristics accurately; being sensitive to ethnicity, age, gender, linguistics, and related matters; avoiding interventions that cause stress; working diligently to ascertain that helpful interventions, such as counseling or improved care, are a) maintained beyond the termination of the project and b) provided in some fashion to the control/comparison groups as well; not intruding unnecessarily into privacy and retaining all confidences with rigid adherence to guidelines; offering, as appropriate, to provide participants with a summary of findings at the completion of the research and following through on the offer; and many others.

Those ethical issues for which death-related research provides special salience appear to be relatively few, relatively obvious, and relatively important. And they arise when the well-being of the research participant might be affected in ways in which the well-being of a participant in research on rote learning, employee selection, success in psychotherapy, or visual perception would not be affected.

The kinds of ethical concerns that appear to require special attention include hazards arising from interviews and questionnaires and hazards arising from interventions.

Hazards of Interviews and Questionnaires

When Herman Feifel submitted his first grant proposal to study the feelings of dying persons, it was rejected, at least in part on the grounds that asking dying persons about their feelings was potentially hazardous to their well-being (Feifel, personal communication, circa 1960). When Feifel was finally permitted to conduct the study, he learned that just the opposite was true—that the participants indicated many benefits from participating in the study, including the opportunity to talk to someone about what was important to them and about which forms of conversation were restrained by the milieu. In my own community-interview study of death attitudes, conducted with David Reynolds (9), 44 percent of the respondents said that the one-hour interview had a beneficial effect, 45 percent said that the effect was essentially neutral, and just slightly over 10 percent indicated that their participation had negative effects.

However, the interviews in Feifel's research were conducted by skilled clinicians, and the questionnaire in our research was constructed to avoid probing too deeply into feelings.

Nonetheless, 44 respondents in the Kalish-Reynolds study and, we might surmise, at least a handful from Feifel's initial study were displeased with having participated. For the former, this does not include those few persons who began the interview then decided against completing it. While Reynolds and I did have the courtesy—or was it curiosity?—to ask about the effects of participation, we did not have the compassion—or the funds—to provide any kind of follow-up with those respondents who might have been upset. Today, of course, we would need to incorporate into a federally funded project some way of being responsive to this particular matter, but many, perhaps most, studies of death that utilize interview and/or questionnaires are not government-sponsored and are not so constrained.

Most interview and questionnaire studies are conducted with individuals who are not listed as vulnerable populations and who will not have more than momentary upset in responding to a question. Nor is it likely that such questions will be an invasion of privacy in any fashion that the respondent cannot handle easily for himself or herself. But this is not always the case. Assume that a researcher is attempting to correlate a questionnaire on death-related matters to two or three personality tests: Will participating in this study be particularly upsetting for a respondent who has just learned that her mother is dying? For someone whose infant daughter was a homicide victim? For someone whose experiences and resulting feelings in Vietnam have never been adequately resolved?

If the answer to any of the above questions is in the affirmative, what responsibilities do I, as the person who constructed or is administering the questionnaire, have in the situation? If I felt so constrained in topics for teaching, I might never be able to teach social psychology or child psychology or—most certainly—the psychology of death. It would seem, then, that the ethical question is not whether or not to administer the questionnaire, but how I, as the person who administers it, can take relevant, but not obsessive, precautions to see that anyone who is upset has some way, with or without my help, to handle the upset. If possible, the event can be turned into an opportunity for learning, for personal insight, and—on rare occasion—for developing support for the individual and a learning opportunity for other research participants.

When we move from questionnaire to interview research, the hazards increase slightly but so do the options for overcoming the hazards. The more the interview probes into feelings and experiences, the more the hazards for being upset mount, while the greater the chance the interviewer has for perceiving the upset and responding to it, the greater the chance for the interview to provide positive benefits, consonant with Feifel's experiences.

Death-related concerns, as is well known, are emotionally charged in many ways. They are often denied, repressed, and displaced. It is not difficult to assume that a certain percentage of individuals who respond to questionnaires or interviews, even those who begin their task in a lighthearted fashion, will find that their defenses are punctured, and strong feelings may be aroused. Since we cannot protect all people from all conceivable stresses, since we need to assume that nonvulnerable populations can make decisions for themselves, and since death research has value both for workers in the field and for research participants, the previous paragraphs are in no way a demand that such research be stopped.

Rather, I wish to raise this as a legitimate ethical concern that requires close attention of all who conduct research on these issues.

The Hazards of Intervention Studies

In order to improve the well-being of the dying, the grieving, relevant professionals, and institutional systems, we normally wish to try new kinds of services, programs, or interventions or to modify those we are using. In order to determine whether the new or modified programs are "better"—in terms of efficiency, effectiveness, cost, or whatever criteria we select—we need to conduct research of some sort.

Often the research consists of nothing more than the program director's examining reports and deciding that an improvement has occurred, frequently verifying what he or she had assumed in the first place. More cautious decision makers will require more systematic research, and some of these may properly be designated as intervention research or program evaluation research.

Once again we confront the usual ethical issues: With the need for services being so great, why not simply use the perceptions of service providers as to the effects of the intervention and apply the research funds to improved services? Since program evaluation is so error-prone, aren't the results likely to be misleading? By the time we get results from program evaluation, we are usually working on a different program, so why bother? There are good answers to each of these questions, but they are not presently at issue. They are being raised only as familiar ethical issues that need to be addressed in any intervention/programmatic study.

When we explore ethical issues of intervention studies with the dying and the grieving, we immediately become aware that we are considering people who form what has been termed a "vulnerable population." This requires, legally, and certainly morally, special consideration. For example, researchers often solicit participants for research on the basis that the investigation will help others in the future, but does a researcher have the right to ask a dying person or a grieving person to participate in research on that basis? Or, with many studies, a comparison group can receive no treatment initially but is subsequently given the same treatment condition as the experimental group as a courtesy or in appreciation for participation. However, if we are concerned with dying persons, members of the comparison group may not remain alert or even alive long enough for such a reward to be meaningful. Or, dying persons are sufficiently dependent on health caretakers that, in perceiving the researcher as a health caretaker, they may believe refusal to participate in the research would jeopardize their care, even though we assure them, orally and in writing, that such is not the case. Are we justified in conducting research with people who may be this vulnerable? We can take a leaf from Phyllis Silverman's widow-to-widow program evaluation: not only was she turned down by 39 percent of the widows approached, but the greatest number of these claimed that they were unable to participate because they were too busy with job, family, or setting affairs in order (18). Given a research study with individuals who are either suffering emotionally or who find themselves in tight financial circumstances, an ethical issue arises: Do we as researchers have the right to ask them to help us without providing something concrete—therapy or money—in return? (Silverman, of course, provided the opportunity to be in her widow-to-widow program.)

The questions outlined above are not rhetorical questions that I have answered to my own satisfaction and now wait for you, as reader, to catch up. These are ethical concerns that I personally believe call for consideration as to the general principle and also to each individual instance.

Although researchers often discuss research ethics among themselves, the topic rarely surfaces at professional meetings or in journals. The demands of the federal apparatus in the late 1960s and early 1970s led to guidelines and committees to protect human research participants, albeit sometimes with what appeared as overkill. Since professionals working with death and grief have established a bill of rights for dying persons, they might consider a comparable bill of rights for research participants.

CONCERNS AND LIMITATIONS IN DEATH-RELATED RESEARCH

Each topic for research has its own unique problems and each topic shares certain problems with other topics. Research on death-related matters is no exception. This section will not review the more general research limitations and concerns but will examine those that are either unique to the study of death, are applied in a unique fashion to the study of death, or are shared with relatively few other research topics.

Selection of Research Questions

It is generally axiomatic that the research questions most frequently asked are those for whom someone else will pay. Funding, and not need or academic interest, is the guiding hand for selection of research topics. However, as this is written, the only death-related concern that seems to have significant financial support is the mental health of the bereaved. This appears a fortunate choice, since the topic has theoretical, substantive, and practical implications, but it does limit the extent to which other important issues can be examined.

If outside funding is close to nonexistent, the second compelling factor in developing research is access to established measurement instruments or, at the very least, to concepts that are readily amenable to measurement. This criterion has led to an abundance of studies in which some measure of death attitudes is utilized as documented by Neimeyer (19). One major difficulty with measures of death attitudes will be discussed in the next section, but other difficulties exist.

Undoubtedly, the above two paragraphs are unnecessarily cynical and only represent a partial truth. However, it does often appear that the more demanding research questions seldom get asked. For example, there has been only very limited research on the extent to which and the conditions under which Kübler-Ross's stages occur. Nor have we examined what phenomenon is represented by the various concepts of death and dying, when individuals respond to questionnaires based on those terms. Few, if any, investigations have been conducted into how the living will is utilized and the characteristics of those who complete it, into the characteristics of persons who wish to die at home and their bases for this choice, into the variety of forms attributed to immortality or continuity of self after death and how knowledge of one's eventual death guides one during life, or into ethnic and gender by age differences on almost anything.

Perhaps the issue is not so much the selection of a specific research question as the development of a research program. The questions listed above cannot be settled with an individual study but require a series of studies that can eventually be integrated. When all is said and done—and again with the exception of work on grief and mental health—it appears that research questions are not being given much consideration, perhaps because research programs are seldom being conducted. It is one thing to develop an interesting and feasible dissertation project; it is a very different thing to develop an extended and comprehensive research plan.

Issues in Terminology

Even a casual reading of the literature, both research writings and nonresearch writings, would indicate that terms having clearly defined differences, known to all, are frequently used as though they were interchangeable. And perhaps the worst of all is the way the word "death" is used. Sometimes it appears that death refers to the sum of being dead, dying, being in pain, being buried, and interacting with funeral directors. Just examine some of the death-attitude scales or the ways in which educators and counselors decide what a person's feelings are regarding death.

Three triads of terms seem to offer consistent difficulty and are often responsible for obscuring even minimal clarity: 1) death, dying, and dead; 2) grief, bereavement, and mourning; and 3) anxiety, fear, and dislike/hate/avoidance (20).

DEATH, DYING, DEAD

Few people, in normal conversation, have difficulty differentiating between the process of dying and being dead. While each of these concepts has its own sources of confusion, e.g., "being dead" for those with a strong intrinsic belief in reincarnation may differ from the meaning of "being dead" for those who believe in total extinction. There is little likelihood that we would use either term for the other.

The concept of *death* can be more confusing. It has been defined as the transition between being alive and being dead (21); however, it is also used almost synonymously with being dead, a position supported in some dictionaries. However, if you use one term in a sentence, then substitute the other term, you will realize that they are not really interchangeable. For example, "When we arrived there, he was already dead." Or "Her death was announced in the morning newspaper." The concept of death emerges as more transitory, more a passage from one state or status to another. Consider the parallels with *born* and *birth*. Once birth has occurred or you have been born, you are alive—the transition is over, one term implies status and the other implies transition.

If we have so little difficulty conceptualizing these terms, why do we have so much difficulty in applying them accurately? For example, a death attitude questionnaire might state, "One of the reasons I'm afraid of death is because of the physical pain involved." There is no pain in death nor, in fact, need there be pain in the dying process. Being afraid of pain is certainly a legitimate response to knowing one is going to die, but neither is necessarily an inevitable component of the other. Although many suffer great pain during the dying process, others suffer very little or none at all; much, perhaps most, physical pain and discomfort are experienced when we are *not* dying. Certainly, pain and suffering while dying may have special, unique meaning, but that is a surmise, not an established fact.

"I am afraid of dying." "I am afraid of death." "I am afraid of being dead." Each of these statements conjures up different sources of fear with some obvious overlap. The first suggests the likelihood that the individual fears the discomfort, the emotional stresses, the anticipations of loss, and the eventual conclusion: death itself. Dying is a process, and the fear would be in regard to what occurs during that process. If a person contemplates instant death through a massive coronary, with no prior history of heart problem, he or she is unlikely to indicate fear of dying.

Fear of death connotes fear of the unknown, of judgment, of both the transition and what occurs afterward. It is, in a way, a mystical fear, since it is fear of an event or passage that we seldom view with the kinds of imagery that we view the dying process. Develop a visual image of dying and write it down. Do the same for death. They may convey very different kinds of images. Of course, if you personified death—and there have been studies of this form of imagery—then, perhaps, both dying and death would include human forms. However, if you tried to imagine death as a transition, your image might well have been a blur, a shining light, a distorted religious symbol, but lacking the clarity of your image of dying.

Fear of being dead differs from both the other concepts. It may include fear of hell and damnation, of suffering and torment, of being enclosed in a coffin and buried in the cold ground, prey to rot and worms. In order to fear being dead, one has to have some notion of what occurs to the self or the soul after death, unless, of course, one focuses on the physical body without regard to what made that body human.

The point is that good research, good research reporting, and good teaching and counseling all require that care be taken to report accurately the concept that is being considered. Neither the clinician nor the student nor the researcher is helped if we refer to fear of death when the issue is clearly fear of the dying process.

GRIEF, BEREAVEMENT, MOURNING

These terms provide a much less serious, although equally confusing, issue. Grief essentially refers to feelings; bereavement addresses one's status in relationship to the dead person; and mourning describes behavior. With justification, these terms are sometimes used interchangeably, and we often assume that a bereaved person is feeling grief and displaying mourning.

Although it is probable that little damage is done—clinically, educationally, or regarding research—from the misuse of these terms, applying them with greater care would serve to enhance rigor in research, teaching, and counseling. If we are truly studying grief, rather than mourning, it is necessary that we determine what the individual is feeling, rather than how he or she is behaving. Technically, crying at a funeral is mourning behavior, although the chances are that it is also a real expression of grief.

ANXIETY, FEAR, DISLIKE/HATE/AVOIDANCE

Labels take on their own reality. When a psychological test claims to measure something called "death anxiety," people assume that it is a measure of the extent to which the respondent experiences feelings of anxiety in response to thoughts of or other forms of confrontation with death. A scale called "fear of death" is similarly assumed to measure what the title outlines. Seldom will individuals look at the specific items on the scale and ask themselves whether these items combine to define the construct described by the label. And sometimes, of course, it is difficult or impossible to learn what items did constitute the scale or the measure.

Anxiety is one of the most difficult terms in the behavioral sciences to define, although it carries the implications of vague feelings, anticipation of future unpleasantness, and lack of specific object. Fear is more concrete. "I am afraid when a lion charges at me," but "I experience anxiety when I walk past the lion's cage in the zoo." When the feelings experienced resemble fear, but are out of keeping with the objective reality, it is often said that it is anxiety that is experienced (T. Mehler, 1986, personal communication). For example, an individual may claim to be unafraid of being dead, fearful about aspects of the dying process such as pain and loss but fully capable of expressing explicitly the source of those fears, and yet indicate some kind of fear of death that is unrelated to being dead or to the dying process. It would seem as though anxiety, rather than fear, is the proper term for this latter feeling of apprehension.

In discussing an existential view of anxiety, one author stated that "anxiety is the experience of the threat of imminent nonbeing" (Hunter, 1986, personal communication). This statement seems to come as close as any to what is often implied by death-anxiety scales when they add up scores for only moderately related items. It also seems related to Becker's (22) "morbid-minded" position that death anxiety is an inevitability, not a learned response. Thus, although the case for assuming that the label *death anxiety* can be measured by adding together reactions to fear of pain, not liking to attend funerals, and so forth can be made, it would appear from the literature that extremely few who use such scales have developed their thinking to this point.

A valid measurement of anxiety in general is extremely difficult to design; a valid measurement of death anxiety that is not equally applicable to fear of death is at least as difficult, probably more so.

We can develop concrete images of the dying process and describe the bases for our fears of this process; we can develop images of being dead, perhaps with less precision, but we can, nonetheless, usually state what concerns us about being dead. With death itself, the images are often vague and blurry, and our ability to explicate the source of our fears and avoidance is considerably less in most instances. Since the concept *death* is in the future, is frequently an unknown in many ways, and is usually seen as negative, unpleasant, or evil, it seems more likely to elicit anxiety than is either the dying process or being dead. We can, therefore, explain what it is about the dying process or being dead that concerns us, but we are often at a loss to say what there is about the transition, death, that concerns us. Perhaps it is the gateway to nonbeing, but, if so, why does nonbeing arouse so much anxiety? If it is viewed as the gateway to judgment, we must then assume that a great many people see themselves as having violated the standards by which they felt certain of admission to heaven. It reminds me of a comment that Professor Chatterjee (I first heard this in 1949) would often make: "What sin has thou committed that heaven and hell concern you so?"

Differences between fear and anxiety are probably not serious, since the differences in meaning are slight. What can be misleading is to include statements such as "I don't like to go to funerals" or "I don't want to die" to measure fear of death or death anxiety. It requires a conceptual leap to go from not liking funerals to fearing death. Perhaps the person who avoids funerals does so because he finds them boring; she is disturbed by so much expression of deep emotion; he is distressed by being immersed in sadness; she resents religious or even secular rituals.

It seems important to differentiate not wanting to die or not wanting to be involved in death-related ceremonies from fear and anxiety. Sometimes the more innocuous, but probably more accurate, term of *death avoidance* is applied.

A FEW MORE COMMENTS

When research on death is already beset by so much error variance and other forms of bias, it may seem unimportant to haggle over terminology. However, it appears as though this misapplied terminology occurs in our basic research articles and dissertations and, therefore, becomes incorporated into the "givens" of the field. When someone reading a secondary source learns that those who score high on death anxiety also score high on a particular personality measure, the reader will assume that a score on death anxiety is what it claims to be and not a potpourri of matters—some of which have only tangential relationships to death itself and others that have little to do with anxiety.

While we need to continue to develop statistically-tested scales, it is also important that these scales be conceptually accurate and that the scale title represent the scale contents as precisely as words permit.

Scale Development

Even when the researcher has decided what research question he or she wishes to answer and has the meaning of terms clearly in mind, valid and reliable scales are extremely difficult to construct.

For one major concern, we need to return to problems in terminology. What do you do, for example, when you are confronted with a Likert-type item, inquiring into the extent to which you fear death? Where do you put your "x"? Does this refer to fear of your death? Of the death of others? Of death if it were imminent now? Of death that is inevitable but far from imminent? Collett and Lester (23), long ago, differentiated some of these factors, but relatively few studies have followed in their footsteps. So, in reading an item, it is easy to respond to one interpretation of the question while someone else responds to an entirely different interpretation of the question. When your scores are then compared or used as an independent or dependent variable, it is truly apples and alligators that are being compared, not the same meaning of *fear of death*.

To complicate matters further, these scales assume that the individual is capable of assessing accurately his or her fear of death and, equally important, chooses to do so at this moment. Does *fear of death* mean that my heart must beat more rapidly than usual when I hear the word *death* or when I drive past a cemetery? What would happen if the researcher developed a guided fantasy which ended with *my death:* Would I then display physiological changes that do not arise when I simply look at a sentence on a piece of paper? Which is the more valid measure?

Again, I need to refer back to the study that Reynolds and I conducted nearly 20 years ago (9). Although based primarily on one-hour interviews with 434 respondents, we also used the highly structured interview form as the basis for a limited number of in-depth interviews. In these instances, we learned to our fascination, and sometimes chagrin, that identical responses to such questions as "Some people say they are afraid to die and others say they are not. How do you feel?" represented totally unrelated underlying phenomena. This does not serve to invalidate the quantitative approach, but it certainly signifies the need for extreme caution in interpreting results.

And we also need to consider the issue of unidimensionality which was alluded to earlier. What research investigations often do is to select a number of death-related items, assume they all are measuring "death anxiety" or whatever variable name they select, and add the item scores together to attain that end. Combining items that ask about fear of pain, fear of being buried, anxiety concerning the future well-being of one's survivors, and not wanting to die into one scale is dubious, although the researcher might contend that each item represents a different aspect of death and, therefore, the accumulation of items represents the totality of the concept *death*. If the scale is carefully developed to have high construct validity, this position can be defended, but construct validity is often either ignored or determined in a haphazard fashion.

As a result, we have scale scores that are not measures of one dimension or factor but that combine a variety of factors in unknown, albeit varying, degrees. And little research has gone into differentiating the various factors or concepts that are thereby combined.

Having said this, it becomes important to modify it: Not all studies ignore these differences. Thus, there are several factor analytic studies that provide factorial constructs matching, in varying extents, the constructs of death, dying, and dead (discussed above). Sometimes, of course, the results of the factor analysis propose new, occasionally unanticipated, factors. It would appear from the factor analytic studies that there is no G-factor (i.e., general factor) of "death," which can effectively be measured in isolation from the S-factors (i.e., specific factors) that emerge from the statistical analysis.

To complicate matters further, factorial validity is not construct validity; each has its place in research, but these places are not identical. In a very early study of death-related attitudes (24), a factor analysis of items showed that attitudes toward birth control and attitudes toward abortion were one factor—an understandable result; in fact, one item measuring attitudes toward birth control correlated more highly with one item measuring attitudes toward abortion than either item correlated with any other item or any other predetermined variable on the entire questionnaire of some 70 + Likert-type items. These results (not previously published) do not require us to view birth control and abortion as conceptually the same, regardless of how many replications support the initial findings.

In these last few paragraphs, we have attempted to address some significant conceptual issues in scale development: the phenomenon "in the head" of the respondent that is used to correspond to the terms presented in the questionnaire; the ability of a respondent to represent his or her view on an issue without significant distortion; the development of unidimensional scales; the relationship between factorial validity and conceptual adequacy. Other possibilities undoubtedly occur to you, and there has been no attempt to discuss such methodological issues as the assumption of ratio scales where they probably do not exist or the contribution of any given item to the variance of the total scale. Any general text on scaling techniques can present these concerns more effectively than we can accomplish here. (See also 25, for an excellent analysis of relevant instruments.)

Program Evaluation

There are, I believe, simultaneously too many and too few evaluations of educational and other programs. There are too many because the temptation to conduct a simple before-and-after study of a college course or church-based workshop is too great to pass up; there are too few because most such studies are meaningless at best (except as feedback to the planners and presenters, who usually find this appropriately valuable) and misleading at worst.

Here are some of the more important limitations:

- During a course or a workshop, students/participants learn the "right answer," even though they are repeatedly told there is no right answer. When they retake the questionnaire at the end of the program, they respond in terms of this "right answer," which may, in fact, be internalized as what they see themselves as believing but has no resemblance to real change.
- Following the above point, educational program evaluations seldom include any measures of behavior.
- Program participants, whether educational or service, want to believe that their time, money, and energy have been well spent, and, therefore, they are capable of orienting their responses to justify their participation.
- Those who conduct program evaluations do not always have a clear picture of their goals, e.g., new knowledge, attitude change, professional skills, human relationships skills, behavior change. For example, they may want behavior change but are limited to providing for and measuring improved knowledge. Without a clear relationship between goals and measures, the evaluators may end up with either a Type I error (the data show that a relationship or a difference exists, when it actually does not exist) or a Type II error (the data show no relationship or difference exists when it actually does exist).
- Most program evaluations are one shots, i.e., they are conducted for one course or workshop but not repeated. What is needed is a cohesive set of program evaluations to permit comparisons across groups so that we may begin to tease out what matters and what doesn't matter, what is idiosyncratic and what is generalizable. Right now we don't even have a patchwork; all we have are unconnected patches.

Hospice programs are now undergoing scrutiny, and analysis of comparative costs seem to display little difference between hospice programs and traditional care programs (26). A hospice may be less expensive than dying in a private room of a proprietary or community hospital but more expensive than dying at home without extensive professional care. A good hospice program costs good money. However, when the preferences of the service recipients (patient and family members) are considered, the evaluation favors hospice (27).

Other care programs are also being evaluated, with varying results. The widow-to-widow program gets fairly high marks in a systematic study (18), but many programs either avoid research as a matter of policy or have neither the time nor the inclination for such studies.

Good program evaluation can be conducted with modest cost but not with haphazard planning, late starts, and sloppy record keeping. It is neither the statistical analysis nor the experimental design that destroys the value of so many of these evaluations. Rather, it is lack of proper conceptualization of the legitimate purposes and goals of the program, along with inappropriately conceived instruments.

Interpreting Results

Even the most competent and honest of research investigators find themselves motivated to interpret their research findings to support their own initial hypotheses or, if lacking hypotheses, their own initial suppositions. Once again, we are not concerned with the familiar, nonspecific concerns in interpreting results: What do you do with .07 level of significance with a one-tailed test? How do you take observer bias into account in a phenomenological study? To what extent can you generalize from responses or observations of 42 university freshmen?

Most certainly one of the greatest hazards in interpreting research results of death-related studies is the extent to which generalization is possible. If the investigator reports procedures and respondent samples accurately and adequately, each reader can make his or her own interpretations and generalizations. However, the tendency remains to leap much too quickly from the research population to all of humanity.

One cause of overgeneralizing is ignoring the self-selection of research participants. It does, in fact, matter whether they participate in the study because they are taking a course on death and grief, because they are hospice volunteers, or because they happened to be at the checkout counter of the local Safeway. We need to examine very carefully the nature of the respondents, the nature of the instruments, and the purpose of the study. For some purposes, a hospice-volunteer sample is totally inappropriate; for other purposes, all that is required is that we generalize from the results with caution.

Other hazards include being confounded by age, ethnicity, gender, and locale. A recent study of mine was conducted at Brooklyn College in two undergraduate classes on death and grief (27). The topic of the study was the frequency of visits to cemeteries. The ethnic distribution included Irish, Italians, Jews, and Blacks, almost all of whom were at least second- or third-generation Americans, although a small number of Asian-Americans and of "whites" who belonged to none of the above ethnicities were included. An estimated 35 percent of the black students who participated had been born outside the United States, primarily in the West Indies. Almost all the students had roots in Brooklyn, often with large extended families living within a 45-minute drive. To generalize from the results of this study to undergraduates in courses on death at San Diego State University would require extreme caution not only because of ethnic differences but because of regional differences within ethnicities.

The dangers of overgeneralizing increase as one gets farther from the original source. Those who read the original study and know Brooklyn College in the 1980s can evaluate the findings better than those who know little about Brooklyn or Brooklyn College; those who read a discussion of the article in a well-done literature review have less basis for a critical evaluation; and those who read two

sentences that report only the findings without regard to the respondent characteristics are very likely to err in whatever generalizing they choose to do. In addition
to ethnicity and locale, age and gender were also relevant factors, but those were
described in the study and more closely approximate the experiences of individuals
who have been students at large public universities.

Looking at Death Is Like Looking into the Sun

The subject of our studies is death, along with the dying process and grief.
Studying death is impossible; studying the dying process directly is difficult because of the capacity of the dying to respond and because they are vulnerable in
every sense of the term; studying grief requires extreme sensitivity. And as the
subject of our studies ranges from impossible to difficult to investigate, the subjects in our studies reflect these conditions.

It is not that dying persons or grieving persons are unwilling to participate in
research; in fact, they usually seem most amenable to such participation. But they
are confronted with obvious priorities and demands that interfere with their participation. The realities of their lives can be such that they must be given complete
and explicit permission to forego their participation as other eventualities arise.
This is similarly true for their caretakers, both family and professional.

This can create a new reality for the researcher as well. Distributing a questionnaire to 200 undergraduates may produce half a dozen office visits from students who want to discuss some personal concerns, but these can be worked
around the research itself. Conducting a study of the dying process or the grieving
process may bring the researcher into much closer proximity with suffering people. Under these circumstances, the researcher may be pressed into providing
information, counseling, or personal care and even affection in such a way that the
care-provider role interferes with the research itself.

Closely related to this is the possibility that intense personal involvement
with the dying and the grieving might be emotionally upsetting for the researcher.
Again, it is one thing to field questions about chronic illness or near-death experiences in a classroom or workshop; it is quite another matter to be repeatedly
exposed to persons who have become incapacitated or who have died between
scheduled interviews. Death researchers can shield themselves from the affective
impact of their work only up to a point. The mere fact that they selected this topic
for research or the mere fact that they selected research rather than other careers
may speak to their capacity for handling continued emotional onslaughts. These
comments are highly speculative, since there is no data base as to who studies
death and the dying, and there is little information about those who minister to
these individuals.

Even without personal contacts with the dying and the grieving, being immersed in studying death-related matters can become upsetting to the investigators.
Depersonalizing the meaning of the data by emphasizing philosophical, methodological, or statistical matters may not always protect the researcher from feeling
the impact personally. Conducting death-related research could be stressful for the
researcher, although there appears to be no literature on this possibility.

Thus, in studies related to death, we find that a variety of circumstances may
lead the research participants to remove themselves or be removed from the pro-

ject (including their own incapacitation and death), and there is also a variety of circumstances that may lead the researcher to find the research affectively difficult to conduct. Relevant conditions may change over time, such as worsening health for a dying person or the death of a family member of the researcher.

We need to keep in mind that we are studying a topic with immense affective impact and that the closer we come personally to those we are studying, the greater this impact is likely to be. Yet to hide behind our desks places us, like the familiar absentee landlord, in a context that substantially reduces our effective grasp of what is taking place.

REVIEW QUESTIONS

1. Different approaches to the scientific study of death have been identified by topics or disciplines, among others. In your opinion, which approach is most appropriate? Why?
2. Why is it important to develop theories and models for the study of death?
3. Identify two major ethical issues in intervention studies in thanatology.
4. What safeguards can the researcher take in addressing the ethical issue of "a vulnerable population"?
5. How do problems in definition and conceptualization interfere with carrying out "good" research in dying, death, and bereavement?
6. Discuss major limitations of program evaluation studies in death education and care.
7. In what ways do researchers tend to overinterpret results? Why is this a pronounced problem in the study of death?
8. In your opinion, can a researcher who intensively studies dying or bereaved persons, maintain emotional distance? Defend your answer. Should he or she provide counseling or care even if it compromises the research design and may alter the findings?

REFERENCES

1. Feifel, H. (1955). Attitudes of mentally ill patients toward death. *Journal of Nervous and Mental Diseases, 122,* 375–380.
2. Feifel, H. (1956). Older persons look at death. *Geriatrics, 11,* 127–130.
3. Hinton, J. (1967). *Dying.* Baltimore: Penguin Books.
4. Kübler-Ross, E. (1979). *On death and dying.* New York: Macmillan.
5. Feifel, H., & Nagy, V. T. (1981). Another look at fear of death. *Journal of Consulting and Clinical Psychology, 49,* 278–286.
6. Florian, V., & Har-Even, D. (1983–84). Fear of personal death: The effects of sex and religious beliefs. *Omega, 14,* 83–91.
7. Parkes, C. M. (1972). *Bereavement.* New York.: International Universities Press.
8. Rando, T. A. (Ed.). (1986). *Loss and anticipatory grief.* Lexington, MA: D. C. Heath.
9. Kalish, R. A., & Reynolds, D. K. (1981). *Death and ethnicity: A psychocultural study.* Farmingdale, NY: Baywood. Originally published by the University of Southern California Press, 1976.

10. Klass, D. (1982). Self-help groups for the bereaved: Theory, theology, and practice. *Journal of Religion and Health, 21,* 307–324.
11. Glaser, B. G., & Strauss, A. L. (1965). *Awareness of dying.* Chicago: Aldine.
12. Glaser, B. G., & Strauss, A. L. (1967). *The discovery of grounded theory.* Chicago: Aldine.
13. Sudnow, D. (1967). *Passing on: The social organization of dying.* Englewood Cliffs, NJ: Prentice-Hall.
14. Feifel, H. (1959). Attitudes toward death in some normal and mentally ill populations. In H. Feifel (Ed.), *The meaning of death.* New York: McGraw-Hill.
15. Feifel, H., & Branscomb, A. B. (1973). Who's afraid of death? *Journal of Abnormal Psychology, 81,* 282–288.
16. Alexander, I. E., & Adlerstein, A. M. (1960). Studies in the psychology of death. In H. P. David & J. C. Brenglemann (Eds.), *Perspectives in personality research.* New York: Springer.
17. Alexander, I. E., Colley, R. S., & Adlerstein, A. M. (1957). Is death a matter of indifference? *Journal of Psychology, 43,* 277–283.
18. Silverman, P. R. (1986). *Widow-to-widow.* New York: Springer.
19. Neimeyer, R. A. (1987). Death anxiety. In H. Wass, F. Berardo, & R. A. Neimeyer (Eds.), *Dying: Facing the facts* (2nd ed.). Washington, DC: Hemisphere.
20. Kalish, R. A. (1985). *Death, grief, and caring relationships,* (2nd ed.). Monterey, CA: Brooks/Cole.
21. Kass, L. R. (1971). Death as an event: A commentary on Robert Morison. *Science, 173,* 698–702.
22. Becker, E. (1973). *The denial of death.* New York: Free Press.
23. Collett, L. J., & Lester, D. (1969). The fear of death and the fear of dying. *Journal of Psychology, 72,* 179–181.
24. Kalish, R. A. (1963). An approach to death attitudes. *American Behavioral Scientist, 6,* 68–70.
25. Marshall, V. W. (1982). Death and dying. In D. J. Mangen & W. A. Peterson (Eds.), *Research instruments in social gerontology: Volume 1, Clinical and social psychology.* Minneapolis: University of Minnesota Press.
26. Kane, R. L., Wales, J., Bernstein, L., Leibowitz, A., & Kaplan, S. (1984). A randomized controlled trial of hospice care. *Lancet,* 890–894.
27. Kalish, R. A. (1986). Cemetery visits. *Death Studies, 10,* 55–58.

II

Data: The Facts
of Dying and Death

5

Trends in the Demography of Death

Edward L. Kain

One of the most fundamental elements of social change affecting human life in the past century has been the rapid decline in mortality throughout much of the world. In Western developed countries the radical transformation of life chances since the turn of the century, combined with decreases in the fertility rate, have led to an "aging" of the population—larger proportions of the population are over the age of 65. Census data for the United States clearly illustrate this shift. Only 2 percent of the population was 65 years or older when the first national census was taken in 1790. By 1980, this group comprised 11.3 percent of the population, and it is projected that by 2030, 20.9 percent of the population will be age 65 or older (1). This changing age structure has had a major impact upon almost every institution in society—including the family, medicine, education, politics, and the world cf work and retirement.

In developing countries, the decline in mortality has preceded declines in fertility, leading to rapid population growth and serious strains upon the food supply as well as upon the economic system. Indeed, many of the central concerns of demographers in recent decades have been related to problems of population growth and the limitation of fertility in countries where mortality declines have not been followed by concomitant shifts in fertility (2).

This chapter examines a number of trends in the demography of death and explores some of the implications of differential rates of mortality change in various social groups. The discussion is divided into three sections. The first section outlines a number of important concepts and terms used by demographers in studying mortality. Two theoretical frameworks are also reviewed which will help to structure the analysis of continuity and change in mortality patterns. The second section concentrates upon patterns and change in mortality differentials by two crucial demographic variables—age and sex. The concluding section turns to the patterning of mortality in relation to several other important social variables, including marital status, race, and social class. Particular emphasis is given to the experience of the United States. This final section concludes with an exploration of some of the implications of these changes in death by using a life course perspective to examine historical changes in race differences in mortality.

THE DEMOGRAPHY
OF DEATH—SOME DEFINITIONS
AND TOOLS

Within the broader field of population studies, formal demography is concerned with the structure, distribution, size, and change of populations. (For a fuller discussion of the scope and content of demography, see reference 3.) Change in a population can occur in three ways—births, deaths, and migration. Individual members enter a population either by birth or migration and exit the population by death or migration. These three components of population change are clearly interrelated, and the relative rates of births, deaths, and migrations have a profound effect upon life in any society. This chapter focuses upon some of the data on change in mortality patterns and how these changes have affected social life in the twentieth century.

Demographic Measures

One of the central tools used in the study of mortality is the *life table*. While a life table includes a number of types of information, its basic purpose is to measure the expectation of life at various ages. The opening of the next section of this chapter clearly illustrates that mortality rates vary considerably by age. A life table can be used to determine the age-specific mortality rates for different age groups. A common measure employed by demographers is the *expectation of life at birth*, which combines all of the age-specific mortality rates for a group or a population into a summary measure.

Demographers typically summarize information about mortality using a wide range of statistics. This chapter will attempt to place some of these statistics in social, historical, and cultural context. Without some understanding of these broader contexts, most measures (such as the expectation of life at birth noted above) have little meaning. It is only by exploring the patterning of mortality statistics and how they vary among social groups, across historical time, and between cultures that we can begin to appreciate the significance of mortality declines upon social life.

A useful way to place mortality rates in context is to use the concept of a *cohort*. At the broadest level, a cohort is any group which experiences something at the same time. Demographers usually employ a more specific use of the concept of a cohort—the birth cohort—which includes everyone who is born in the same year. While the advantages of using cohort analysis to study social change and mortality have long been recognized (e.g., 4), it is Ryder's article (5) which first outlined the strengths of taking a cohort analytic approach to study social change. Ryder suggests that analyses of differences between cohorts can be employed to study social change, and differences within cohorts can be used to study social variation.

Cohort analysis provides many of the conceptual and methodological tools necessary for thinking about mortality change. Two theoretical frameworks help to structure how we think about applying the techniques of cohort analysis. At the macro level, neoevolutionary theory (6) points to the importance of shifts in the technological level of a society in predicting demographic trends such as the decline in mortality. At a more microanalytic level, life course theory (7) provides a structure for thinking about how broader social changes, such as the decline in death rates, have an impact upon the lives of individuals as they move through their lives from birth to death.

Neoevolutionary Theory and Long-term Shifts in Mortality

Neoevolutionary theory suggests that a key element in understanding the differences and similarities between societies is the overall level of technological development. Many elements of population and social structure vary considerably between hunting and gathering, agricultural, and industrial societies. When a long-term perspective is taken to human populations, it is clear that technological development is a crucial factor in understanding mortality change and population growth (8). While the initial appearance of humanity may be placed at approximately 1 million years ago, most of the growth of the human population has been relatively recent. The first 99 percent of human history consisted of very slow population growth, while the very brief period since the introduction of agriculture (in approximately 8000 B.C.) has seen rapid population growth, which has accelerated with the mortality declines of the past century (9).

In both hunting and gathering societies and in agricultural societies, fertility and mortality rates tend to fluctuate in response to environmental shifts. There is some disagreement as to whether the transition to agriculture increased or decreased mortality and fertility rates. Coale (9) suggests that the Neolithic revolution actually increased mortality since agricultural technology led to larger villages with a greater susceptibility to disease. Changes in climate or crop failures would also have a more pronounced impact upon agricultural societies than upon hunting and gathering societies. The higher mortality was offset by an even larger increase in fertility rates, however, and population growth began at a rate faster than had occurred throughout most of human history.

While there may be some debate concerning the impact of the rise of agriculture upon death rates, more recent changes with the transition to industrial technology are much more clear. The patterned shift from high birth and death rates to low birth and death rates has come to be called the *demographic transition.* Throughout the developed countries since the eighteenth century, this transition has involved a doubling of the expectation of life at birth and a halving of the total fertility rate. In most cases, the fertility decline came after the mortality decline, and a period of population growth occurred during the interim. Before this demographic shift, birth rates were high and relatively constant. Death rates were high but fluctuated with famines and epidemics. After this shift, death rates are relatively stable, while birth rates are subject to more variation (as evidenced by the postwar baby boom in the United States) (9).

The experience of developing nations is quite different. The importation of medical and agricultural technology from the West has meant that mortality rates have declined much more rapidly than was the case for most of the developed nations. Fertility rates in most of these countries have remained high, resulting in a world which is demographically divided. The developed countries, or the First World, have low rates of both fertility and mortality. Death is something which is largely associated with old age. In developing countries of the Third World, death still occurs in all age groups, despite decreases resulting from Western medicine. Because fertility rates remain high, these developing countries have rapid rates of population growth (10). Problems of overpopulation are intimately linked to mortality trends and could easily become the focus of any chapter on the demography of death. The focus in this chapter, however, is largely upon the United States and other developed countries where both mortality and fertility rates are very low compared to those experienced throughout most of human history.

Life Course Theory and More Recent Declines in Mortality

The extremely rapid declines in mortality over the past century have meant that different cohorts have had widely diverse experiences with death. While neoevolutionary theory is useful in outlining the long-term shifts in mortality, life course theory provides a framework for understanding how rapid changes in death rates have an impact upon individual lives. At several points throughout this chapter, a life course perspective will be used to illustrate how changes in death have had a profound impact upon the life experiences of individuals and families during the past century.

PATTERNS AND CHANGE IN MORTALITY DIFFERENTIALS— AGE AND SEX

Even though there have been large general declines in mortality over the past century, these reductions have not been shared equally by all segments of the population. Unfortunately, detailed records on historical changes in mortality and how these are related to variables such as age, sex, race, and social class are often not readily available even in the developed countries. In the United States, for example, central death records were only kept in 14 states before the turn of the century. The death registration area did not include the entire United States until 1933 (11). As a result, it was not until 1973 that Kitagawa and Hauser published their study (11) which carefully examined how mortality rates vary by social group in the United States. They found significant differences in life chances by a large number of variables, including educational level, income, occupation, race, sex, and marital status. The rest of this chapter is devoted to an examination of some of the relationships described by Kitagawa and Hauser and other researchers who have examined the patterning and change in mortality rates over the past century. Both the structuring of mortality and changes in that structure will be examined for each variable.

Age and sex are the two variables for which the most data are available concerning mortality differentials. This section concentrates upon mortality patterns and changes in relation to these two variables. The next section turns to a discussion of mortality differentials by marital status, social class, and race. When possible, the data will be presented in a cumulative manner, so that the discussion of sex will incorporate information about age, and the discussion of marital status will look at both age and sex as well.

Age

As noted earlier, mortality rates vary considerably by age. No matter what the overall level of mortality in a population, the general relationships between age-specific mortality rates are relatively similar. The highest chances of mortality are in the first hours of life. After that point, age-specific mortality decreases dramatically until the teen years, where it again begins to rise. This increase in age-specific mortality becomes successively more rapid with age (12).

While the general shape of a curve which plots age-specific mortality rates is the same in populations with different levels of overall mortality, the decline we have seen in mortality, particularly since the turn of the century, has meant that death has become more and more concentrated in the later years of life. This is clearly illustrated if we examine one commonly used measure of age-specific mortality, the infant mortality rate.

INFANT MORTALITY

The infant mortality rate is the number of children out of every 1,000 live births who die during the first year of life. Life table values for 1900 indicate an age-specific mortality rate of 162.4 under the age of one (13). Quite simply interpreted, this means that at the turn of the century, more than 16 out of every 100 babies did not survive the first year of life. Death at a very early age was a common experience. By 1983, the infant mortality rate had fallen to 10.9, meaning that only about one in every hundred babies does not survive the first year of life (14).

Another way to think about this dramatic decline in infant deaths is to look at the cumulative percentage of the population which has died by a certain age. It was noted above that age-specific death rates decline rapidly after the first few hours of life, and do not begin to rise again until the later teen years. In fact, age-specific death rates remain low throughout most of the adult years, and do not begin to increase rapidly until the ages of 50 and above. This age patterning of mortality combined with historical declines in the death rates of infants means that death has been radically transformed in this century. U.S. life table values indicate that by 1970, a significantly smaller proportion of the population died before reaching the age of 75 than died before reaching the age of one in 1900 (13)!

This movement of the majority of deaths to older ages has led some researchers to talk of a rectangularization of the mortality curve. This simply refers to the fact that if the number of people still surviving in any birth cohort is displayed graphically, historical declines in mortality have led to a curve which approximates a rectangular shape, with very few deaths occurring in early ages, and most mortality happening near the end of life (15).

A LIFE COURSE PERSPECTIVE
ON THESE CHANGES

The full implications of this rapid decline in the infant mortality rate become even more clear when shifts in fertility are also taken into account. In 1900, fertility rates in the United States were considerably higher than they are today. At that time the average number of children per mother was approximately four. The average completed fertility for a woman today has dropped below replacement level (less than two children per couple). Taking a life course perspective, Uhlenberg (16) has illustrated that these combined changes have radically altered the experience of childhood deaths within the family. Comparing the experience of three different cohorts—1900, 1940, and 1976—Uhlenberg shows that the probability of one or more children dying out of the average number of births was .62 in 1900. It was, thus, the normal course of events for a typical family to experience the death of at least one of its children before they reached the age of 15. This probability had dropped to .04 for the 1976 cohort. This means that the chances of a family losing one of its children to death have dropped from approximately two out of three to less than one in 20 in the brief span of time since the turn of the century. Childhood death has become the exception rather than the rule.

Uhlenberg goes on to illustrate other changes which have occurred as a result of the mortality declines of this century. Because adult death rates have also dropped, the incidence of orphanhood has declined considerably. He estimates that at the turn of the century, the chances were approximately one in four that before reaching the age of 15, a child would lose at least one parent. By 1976, this probability had fallen to one in 20. The increase of the average life expectancy has also significantly improved the probability that grandchildren will have the opportunity to know their grandparents. As the turn of the century, less than one in five teenagers still had three or four grandparents alive. By 1976, this was the case for over half of the 15-year-olds in this country.

Uhlenberg goes on to trace the impacts of mortality declines upon individual lives throughout the life course, from young adulthood through old age. He points out that the decline in mortality means that recent cohorts are more likely to have long marriages than earlier cohorts. Declines in mortality have more than offset increases in the divorce rate, so that fewer couples experience a marital disruption before their fortieth anniversary than was the case at the turn of the century. When these couples reach middle age, they are also more likely to have their parents alive. In 1900, over half of middle-aged couples did not have any of their parents alive, and only about one in ten had two or more of their four parents alive. By 1976, the balance had shifted so that nearly half of middle-aged couples had two or more of their parents alive (16).

CHANGES IN THE CAUSES OF DEATH

The changing age structure of mortality can also be viewed in terms of the changes in the most typical causes of death. Changes in nutrition, sanitation, and medical technology have meant that deaths from infectious and parasitic diseases have declined drastically over time. Using death certificates collected from 43 nations over the past century, Preston (17) estimates that declines in deaths caused by influenza, pneumonia, and bronchitis account for one quarter of the mortality reductions of the past century. Another 15 percent of the reduction is accounted for by "other infectious and parasitic diseases," while diarrheal diseases and tuberculosis account for another 10 percent each.

Over time a smaller and smaller contribution of overall mortality in modern populations is attributable to the specific infectious diseases. Medical progress against these causes of death has been much more rapid than for other causes. When the life expectancy at birth is 25, nearly two thirds of those born in a cohort will eventually die of an infectious or parasitic disease. When the life expectancy has reached 75 or 80, only one tenth of that amount will die from those same causes (17).

While the infectious and parasitic diseases have declined over time in their overall contribution to mortality, cardiovascular disease and neoplasms have become the major causes of death in a population with longer life expectations. Using the same comparison (the change from a life expectation of 25 to 75), Preston shows that the chances of dying from these two categories increase fivefold (17).

Sex

While age is the most important social characteristic which predicts mortality differentials in all human populations, sex is the variable which has received the second largest amount of attention. Contrary to the popular conception of women constituting "the weaker sex," the average life expectancy of women is longer than that of men in almost every country in the world (14). The excess of male mortality indeed seems almost universal throughout most animal species (18).

LONG-TERM CHANGE

When examining the whole of human history, the excess of male mortality appears to be a relatively recent phenomenon. Most studies of skeletal remains in early settled populations indicate that the average age at death for males is older than that for females. This difference is usually attributed to extremely high rates of maternal mortality in early human populations. In all recorded life tables, however, the general rule has been an excess of male mortality. This difference was noted as early as 1662 in the demographic work of John Graunt (19) and is currently the case in developed and developing countries alike (20).

CHANGE OVER THE LIFE
COURSE AND EXPLANATIONS
OF THE DIFFERENTIAL

Sex differentials in mortality operate even before birth. The sex ratio (the number of males per 100 females) is approximately 124 at conception but drops to approximately 104 for full-term births. Among premature babies, the probability of being male goes up the more premature the baby (21). Three general explanations are usually given for the very consistent finding that male mortality is higher than female mortality—biological differences in males and females, lifestyle variations between the sexes, and differential health care (22). While all three may indeed play a role in sex differentials in mortality (and the contribution of the latter two may vary considerably between historical eras and across cultures), most evidence seems to suggest that differences in lifestyle—particularly alcohol and cigarette consumption in developed countries—contribute to the differences in adult mortality between the sexes. If the use of alcohol and cigarettes by women continues to increase while consumption rates by males decline (a pattern indicated by current data), the sex differential in mortality may narrow in the future.

Current international data indicate that the excess of male mortality does not hold true for all age groups, however. A female excess in mortality is most common in ages one to four, and there is sometimes an excess during the ages of childbearing as well. In fact, in developing countries, an excess of female mortality during the early childhood years is the rule, rather than the exception. This pattern only disappears when the overall expectation of life at birth exceeds 70 years of age (23).

Why is there an excess of female mortality during early childhood in many developing countries? A central reason is that nutritional levels have a major impact upon childhood mortality both directly and indirectly through the increased incidence of infectious diseases in cases of poor nutrition. A number of studies have shown that female children in developing countries may receive less food than their male siblings, which shows up in higher mortality rates during early childhood (23). This differential treatment is particularly important in South Asia. While it is noted above that the expectation of life at birth is higher for women than men in almost every country in the world, one consistent exception to this rule is the Indian subcontinent. Shushum Bhatia has clearly demonstrated the role of social status differentials and cultural practices, such as differential nutrition and access to medical care, which lead to higher overall mortality among women in these cultures (24).

RECENT CHANGES
AND FUTURE PREDICTIONS

As life expectations have increased in the developed countries, the mortality differences between the sexes have increased. This changing pattern has been the focus of a number of investigations (e.g., 20, 25). The general conclusion is that this widening gap has been a result of an increased disparity in death from cancers, motor vehicle accidents, the cardiovascular diseases, and the virtual elimination of maternal mortality. The health and living habits of men, particularly the higher rates of cigarette smoking, have been singled out as central to the increasing disparity in mortality rates by sex. Indeed, Retherford's data on the United States indicate that three quarters of the increase in the sex differential in mortality after the age of 50 is accounted for by smoking habits and how they have changed over time (25). This is corroborated by Preston's work which showed that when stress, diet, exercise, and smoking are all examined, it is smoking which has the major impact upon changes in the sex mortality differential (26). It is possible that this trend may be somewhat reversed as the smoking rates of women and men become more alike. (As noted earlier, recent data indicate an increase in smoking among women—especially in the younger ages.)

Retherford quite surprisingly shows that the decline in maternal mortality has added very little, if any, to the increased disparity in life expectation between the sexes. Reductions in the rates of industrial accidents among males in the same age groups have been more than equaled the declines in female mortality related to childbirth. In fact, it is declines in mortality near the end of the life course—from ages 60-79—which have had the most impact upon increasing the differences in the life expectancy of men and women. Since medical advances in the past several decades have consistently had the greatest impact upon lowering mortality in the older years (27), it may be that the sex differential in mortality will continue to increase at least in the near future.

THE IMPACT OF OTHER SOCIAL VARIABLES—MARITAL STATUS, CLASS, AND RACE

While the majority of the research on mortality differentials has focused upon the two basic demographic variables of age and sex, significant numbers of studies have also examined the impact of other social variables such as marital status, class, and race. This section of the paper turns to these variables and how they interact to produce significant differences in the life chances of different social groups.

Marital Status

SUICIDE

There is a long research tradition within sociology which has examined the impact of marital status upon mortality rates. Research on marital status and one particular cause of death—suicide—has a research tradition over a century old. Halbwachs (28) notes that in 1879 a researcher named Morselli pointed to a number of social variables such as age, sex, marital status, and religion in predicting differences in suicide rates. It was the classic analysis of suicide by Durkheim in 1897 (29), however, which first systematically organized data on suicide and various social factors, including marital status. This groundbreaking work of Durkheim provides the foundation for much of the subsequent research which has been done not only on marital status and suicide but in the more general area of marital status and mortality.

The comprehensive analysis of Durkheim raises most of the important issues involved in the analysis of marital status as a predictor of differential mortality. It is one of the central variables in his analysis of suicide. When age is controlled, marriage "reduces the danger of suicide" considerably (29).

Using data from several countries, Durkheim constructs what he calls a *coefficient of preservation,* which is "the number showing how many times less frequent suicide is in one group than in anther at the same age." This coefficient is obtained by examining the ratio of age-specific rates for the two comparison groups. When this number falls below unity, Durkheim calls it a coefficient of aggravation. Overall, Durkheim found that while early marriages tend to increase suicide, after age 20, both sexes of a married couple are less likely to commit suicide than their unmarried counterparts. Widowhood decreases the advantage of married persons over the never-married, but it seldom eliminates it entirely.

CAUSAL MECHANISMS

Durkheim suggests that there are two possible causal explanations for the patterning of suicide by marital status. The first may be labelled a protection hypothesis—married persons commit suicide less because marriage itself alters the tendency toward suicide. The second is a selection argument—the causal direction is reversed, and it is argued that the tendency to suicide itself acts as a screening device which sorts persons with high suicidal tendencies out of the marriage market and decreases their chances of getting married in the first place.

For a number of reasons, Durkheim argues against the selection hypothesis and for the protection hypothesis. For example, he points out that if selection were operating, it should be equal for both sexes. The data, however, point out that women benefit less from marriage than do men. A number of researchers have expanded upon the classic work in subsequent years, and his basic assertions are, in general, supported (30). For a more detailed examination of suicide, see Chapter 10.

MARITAL STATUS, SEX, AND OTHER TYPES OF MORTALITY

Gove (31) has used the coefficient of preservation to move beyond the study of suicide to a more careful examination of the relationships between marital status, sex, and different types of mortality. Like Durkheim's findings on suicide, Gove illustrates that, with age controlled, the married have lower mortality rates than the never-married, divorced, and widowed. Further, these differences are greater for men than for women. Gove argues that selective processes do not appear to account for the variation in rates. Rather, he proposes a role explanation which can account for the way the patterns vary with age. By examining mortality patterns by specific causes of death, Gove illustrates that the pattern of sex and marital status differences is primarily a characteristic of the types of mortality which can be affected by one's psychological or social situation—deaths which result from overt social acts, the use of socially approved drugs, or diseases which require prolonged care.

Gove shows that for a variety of causes of death, the married are at an advantage when compared to the unmarried. Divorced men, for example, are almost eight times as likely as married men to die of homicide and almost nine times as likely to die of cirrhosis of the liver. They are over nine times as likely to die of tuberculosis and over four times as likely to die of diabetes. The rates for divorced women are also higher than for married women, but the difference is not nearly as large as for men. Indeed, throughout his analysis, Gove finds that the shift from being single to being married is more favorable for men, and the shift from being married to being formerly married is more *un*favorable for men. This disparity between the unmarried and the married tends to decrease with age. These patterns hold true for mortality due to overt social acts (suicide, homicide, motor accident deaths, pedestrian deaths, accidental deaths), mortality related to the use of alcohol and tobacco (cirrhosis of the liver and lung cancer), and mortality from diseases which require prolonged care (tuberculosis and diabetes) (31).

When Gove's analysis turns, however, to mortality which is largely unaffected by social and psychological factors—(leukemia and aleukemia), there is little difference in the rates by marital status and sex. This further supports his position of social causation rather than selection.

PROBLEMS WITH DATA AND MEASUREMENT

One problem in determining the cause of the differences in mortality between marital statuses is the lack of good data on the topic. The pattern described above sems to hold cross-culturally, but data cross-classified by sex, marital status, age, and cause of death are available for only a few countries at one or two points in time (25). Early research on the topic (32) determined that the causes of death most responsible for the excess in mortality among the unmarried were tuberculosis and syphilis, followed by influenza, pneumonia, suicide, homicide, accidents, and cirrhosis of the liver. Later work by Shurtleff (33) found a similar pattern but also singled out heart diseases for analysis and noted a decline over time in the importance of tuberculosis and syphilis in contributing to the marital status differentials.

Durkheim's pioneering work set out two hypotheses to explain the marital status differentials—selection and protection. Subsequent research has added a third possible explanation—measurement error. Retherford (25) concentrates upon two types of measurement problems in the data, misreporting and underenumeration. Incorrect reporting of marital status is most likely to occur among individuals living alone. If a person is not home during a survey, neighbors may be used by an enumerator to gather information. Divorced persons are often misreported as being single, thus inflating the mortality rates of the never-married, and underestimating the rates for the divorced. Kitagawa and Hauser (11) note that there are large discrepancies between reports of marital status on the census and on death certificates, again particularly in the case of the divorced. Thus, it appears that all three explanations—selection, protection, and measurement error—may play some role in the patterns of mortality differentials by marital status and sex.

Social Class

Another variable which the work of Kitagawa and Hauser found to be important in predicting mortality rates is social class. Indeed, their research suggests that all three standard measures of social class (income, education, and occupation) are related to mortality differences in the United States. As education and income go up, mortality goes down. The relationship between education and mortality is stronger for women than for men and is also stronger below the age of 65. Both education and income remain important when the other is controlled. Most of the differences by specific occupation are usually attributed to variations in the risks and occupational hazards associated with different types of jobs (11).

Social class differences in mortality are not unique to the United States. Using English and Welsh data, Antonovsky (34) documents differences between mortality rates between social classes. He notes, however, a decline in these differences over time, particularly between the middle and upper classes. It is the lowest class which remains much worse off than other classes. Data from the United Nations indicate that socioeconomic differentials in mortality are the rule throughout the industrialized world (35), clearly pointing to inequalities in access to medical care as well as an adequate diet and environment for people at the lower end of the economic spectrum within society.

Race

Another variable which the work of Kitagawa and Hauser found to be important in predicting mortality rates is race (11). Their work on the U.S. population indicated that Japanese had the lowest mortality rate and blacks had the highest. The second highest rates were among native Americans, and the Chinese and whites fell between them and the Japanese. The patterns in the relationships between race and mortality are consistent with the research reviewed above showing that social class is related to the probabilities of death. Blacks and other minorities in the United States are much more likely to live in poverty than the white population, and lower levels of income predict higher levels of mortality. Kitagawa and Hauser conclude their work on differential mortality by arguing that:

Perhaps the most important next gain in mortality reduction is to be achieved through improved socio-economic conditions rather than through increments to and application of medical knowledge . . . If the United States is to demonstrate that she is indeed a land of equal opportunity, she must do considerably more to increase equality of opportunity on all those fronts which affect the most significant index of effective egalitarianism—the ability to survive—duration of life itself. (11, p. 180)

There is one interesting exception to the patterning of mortality by race. Several studies indicate that the age-specific mortality rates of blacks are *lower* than whites after the age 75 (11, 36, 37). This consistent pattern has been labeled the black/white *mortality crossover.* Several theories have been proposed to explain this unusual mortality pattern—including selection and measurement error approaches similar to the explanations found for mortality differences by marital status. Analysis of mortality by specific cause of death indicates that the overall pattern is a result of race differences in the age pattern of death from various diseases. Blacks have a much more rapid increase in mortality rates from circulatory diseases in middle age which produces the overall excess of early mortality. The rapid increase in deaths from circulatory diseases occurs at a later age for whites and, eventually, passes the rate for the black population (73).

Thus far, this chapter has outlined a number of issues related to the demography of death. It has reviewed some of the basic data on patterning and change in mortality as well as suggesting the importance of placing these data within broader historical, cultural, and social contexts. Now that the tools of mortality analysis have been reviewed, the conclusion will use the final variable which has been discussed—race—as an illustration of how a life course framework using cohort analysis can help us to begin to understand the significance of historical change in mortality rates.

Up to this point, data have not been presented in tabular form. As noted at the outset, until the context of various demographic measures is understood, they have little meaning. Now that the context has been provided, our illustration of race differences in mortality in the United States can gain new significance.

CHANGES IN VARIOUS
MEASURES OF MORTALITY

Standard measures of mortality illustrate the rapid rate of mortality decline in the United States and how it has varied by both race and sex (13, 38). If we examine three cohorts, 1900, 1940, and 1980, it is clear that the expectation of life at birth has increased significantly. Table 1 illustrates that race differences at the turn of the century painted strikingly different pictures for the life chances of blacks and whites. In 1900, the expectation of life at birth was 48.2 years for white men and 51.1 for white women. The corresponding figures for the black population were 32.5 and 35.0 respectively. In 1980, whites continue to have a longer life expectation, but the race difference is now approximately six years, compared to 16 years at the turn of the century (see Table 2).

These first two tables reflect patterns which have been discussed earlier in this chapter. In all three cohorts, the expectation of life at birth is higher for whites than nonwhites, and within racial group, it is higher for women than for men.

TABLE 1   Expectation of Life at Birth by Race and Sex, U.S.: 1900, 1940, 1980

Year	White		Black and other	
	Male	Female	Male	Female
1900	48.2	51.1	32.5	35.0
1940	62.8	67.3	52.3	55.5
1980	70.7	78.1	63.7	72.3

Data for the first two cohorts are from the *Historical Statistics of the United States*. 1980 data are from *The Statistical Abstract of the United States* and compare only blacks and whites.

(Because national data on mortality vary from year to year, the categorization by race is not consistent. In some years, blacks are tabulated separately, and in other years, all nonwhite groups are tabulated together. While the term "nonwhite" is an unfortunate choice, it will be used to ease readability.) Table 2 indicates that the historical trend in mortality differences has been in opposite directions for sex and race. While sex differences in mortality have increased over time, the differences by race have declined.

Age-specific measures of mortality also illustrate race differences in changing life chances since the turn of the century. The infant mortality rate and the maternal mortality rate have improved for both racial groups. Despite improvements for both races, significant differences between the groups remain (see Table 3). In addition, the maternal mortality rate has declined faster for whites than blacks, but this is not true of the infant mortality rate.

Life table data on race differences in the United States (39) provide information which is rich enough for an analysis that takes a life course perspective, much in the same manner as that noted by Uhlenberg near the beginning of this chapter. The implications of mortality shifts could be traced throughout the individual life course, from birth to death. For illustration, two points—one at each end of the life course—will be used. Further illustrations can be found in Kain (40).

CHILDHOOD LIFE CHANCES

The review of age differences in mortality in the opening of the chapter noted that age-specific mortality is highest during infancy and early childhood. During the demographic revolution in the West, medical technology, sanitation, and nutrition combined to decrease mortality in these early years by virtually

TABLE 2   Race and Sex Differentials in the Expectation of Life at Birth, U.S.: 1900, 1940, 1980

Year	Sex difference (F-M)		Race difference (W-B&O)	
	White	Black and other	Male	Female
1900	2.9	2.5	15.7	16.1
1940	4.5	3.2	10.5	11.8
1980	7.4	8.6	7	5.8

Data for the first two cohorts are from the *Historical Statistics of the United States*. 1980 data are from the *Statistical Abstract of the United States* and compare only blacks and whites.

TABLE 3   Race Differences in Maternal and Infant Mortality Rates, U.S.: 1915, 1940, 1980

Year	Maternal mortality rate*			Infant mortality rate**		
	White	Black and other	NW/W	White	Black and other	NW/W
1915	60.1	105.6	1.76	98.6	181.2	1.84
1940	32.0	77.4	2.42	43.2	73.8	1.71
1980	.7	2	2.86	11.1	19.1	1.72

*The maternal mortality rate = deaths per 10,000 live births.
**Infant mortality rate = deaths per 1,000 live births.

eliminating infant deaths during childbirth and significantly reducing mortality from early childhood diseases. While many of these shifts occurred throughout the eighteenth and nineteenth centuries, they continued well into this century. Table 4 shows the major differences in childhood life chances between three cohorts in this century. The probability of survival for the 1900 cohort was well below that of later cohorts.

The race and sex differences in the probabilities of a child surviving to adolescence are just as striking within the three cohorts as is the overall level of social change in early age-specific mortality. The strongest comparison would contrast a black male to a white female. In 1900, the probability of a black male surviving to adolescence was only slightly better than three out of five. A white female's chances were better than four out of five. A comparison of intercohort differences (social change) and intracohort differences (social diversity by race and sex) shows that the difference between blacks and whites in 1900 is of the same magnitude as the difference between white cohorts spaced 40 years apart (1900 and 1940)!

THE CHANCES OF SURVIVAL
TO OLD AGE

The impact of race and sex differences in mortality is just as evident at the other end of the life course. Table 5 uses life table values to estimate the chances of

TABLE 4   Race and Sex Differences in the Probability of Death to Children:
1900, 1940, 1978

Year	Probability of surviving from 0–15			
	White		Black and other	
	Male	Female	Male	Female
1900	.78	.83	.64	.68
1940	.93	.95	.90	.92
1978	.98	.99	.97	.98

These probabilities are calculated from life table values, *Vital Statistics of the United States, 1978, Vol. II, Part A.* (DHHS Pub. No. 83-1101) Washington, D.C.: U.S. Government Printing Office, 1982, Table 5-4. Data for 1900 are for death registration states and include only blacks in the "black and other" category. Data for 1940 and 1978 are for the full United States. Blacks always comprise at least 95 percent of the "black and other" group.

TABLE 5   Race and Sex Differences in the Probability of Reaching Old Age (the "Older Old") by Yourself and with Your Spouse:* 1900, 1940, 1978

	Probability of survival to age 75[a]					
	Male		Female		Both	
Year	White	Black and other	White	Black and other	White	Black and other
1900	.29	.17	.33	.20	.10	.03
1940	.37	.24	.48	.29	.18	.07
1978	.48	.36	.69	.56	.33	.20
	Probability of survival to age 85[a]					
1900	.07	.04	.09	.06	.006	.002
1940	.10	.08	.16	.12	.02	.01
1978	.18	.15	.37	.29	.07	.04

Note. This table assumes that both spouses marry at age 25.
[a]These probabilities of survival are calculated from age 25, not from birth.

survival to both the ages of 75 and 85. The table also presents calculations of the chances of surviving to these ages with your spouse still alive. Because there are differences in mortality by marital status, this table may underestimate the chances of surviving to old age, since the life tables do not include marital status differential in mortality.

The "older old"—those over the age of 75—comprise the part of our population which is growing most rapidly. This is reflected in Table 5. Race and sex differences in the probability of survival to this latest stage in the life course are again evident. In both race groups, women are more likely to reach both the age of 75 and 85. This sex difference has increased over time, so that by 1978, women in both race groups are twice as likely as men to reach the age of 85.

The final columns of the table reflect a very significant aspect of mortality change in the last century. In 1900, it was an extreme rarity for both spouses to survive to the age of 85 in either racial group. The chances were only six in 1,000 for a white couple and two in 1,000 for a black couple. While this is still an unusual occurrence, by 1978 such couples were more than 10 times as likely. The decline in mortality has meant that survival into very old age is now more than a statistical rarity for individuals as well as couples.

CONCLUDING COMMENTS

While death is an inevitable part of life, the nature of mortality has changed radically in recent centuries of human history. Dramatic declines in age-specific mortality in the early years of life have meant that death is now an experience which usually occurs when individuals are quite old. This experience of mortality varies cross-culturally and historically, but it is only in developed countries during the last century that death has become a rarity during the early stages of the life course.

These declines in mortality have not been evenly distributed among various social groups, however, and demographic measures of death indicate significant differences in the experience of mortality by a number of variables. Declines in mortality have been particularly large during the very early periods of life as well as at the end of life. This change in the age-specific rates of mortality is related to changes in medical technology, nutrition, and public health, which in turn have led to a decline in infectious diseases.

In recent human history, women tend to live longer than men, and this sex difference in life expectation has increased over time. Mortality rates are lower for married people than for various nonmarried groups, and a variety of measures of social class shows that mortality is higher in groups which are lower in the class structure of a society. Finally, there are also significant variations in mortality rates by race.

Demographic statistics comparing these various social groups gain more meaning when they are placed within historical, social, and cultural context. At the broadest level, neoevolutionary theory points to the importance of technological change in predicting overall levels of mortality in a society. At a more micro level, a life course framework which examines the implications of mortality differences within a cohort as well as social change between cohorts helps to illustrate the meaning of some of the trends which have been occurring in the demography of death.

REVIEW QUESTIONS

1. How can the concept of a cohort be used to study mortality?
2. How are mortality and fertility rates linked to technological development? Describe the changes in these two variables as technology changes.
3. Describe the relationship between mortality rates and age. How has the shape of the mortality curve changed since the turn of the century in this country? How is this related to changes in the cause of death over time?
4. What is the relationship between mortality rates and sex? Describe this pattern for different age groups. How does the pattern vary cross-culturally? How has it varied over time within Western countries?
5. How is mortality linked to marital status? What explanations have been used to account for this pattern?
6. Briefly describe changes in the expectation of life at birth, infant mortality, and maternal mortality since the turn of the century. How have race and sex differences in these variables changed over time?
7. What changes in the most common cause of death occur as medical technology in a society raises the expectation of life at birth?
8. What is the relationship of socioeconomic differences to mortality rates in industrialized countries?
9. What are the key elements suggested by neoevolutionary theory for understanding differences and similarities between societies?
10. What is your prediction concerning the life expectancies of a black male child, a white male child, a black female child, a white female child? Explain the basis for your prediction.

REFERENCES

1. Atchley, R. C. (1985). *Social forces and aging* (4th ed.). Belmont, CA: Wadsworth.
2. Reining, P., & Tinker, I. (Eds.). (1975). *Population: Dynamics, ethics and policy.* Washington, DC: American Association for the Advancement of Science.
3. Shryock, H. S., Siegel, J. S., & Associates. (1975). *The methods and materials of demography* (3rd. ed.). Washington, DC: U.S. Government Printing Office, U.S. Bureau of the Census.
4. Frost, W. H. (1940). The age selection of mortality from tuberculosis in successive decades. *The Milbank Memorial Fund Quarterly, 18,* 61–66.
5. Ryder, N. B. (1965). The cohort as a concept in the study of social charge. *American Sociological Review, 30,* 843–861.
6. Lenski, G., & Lenski, J. (1982). *Human societies, an introduction to macrosociology* (4th ed.). New York: McGraw-Hill.
7. Elder, G. H., Jr. (1985). Perspectives on the life course. In G. H. Elder, Jr. (Ed.), *Life course dynamics* (pp. 23–49). Ithaca, NY: Cornell University Press.
8. Heer, D. M. (1975). *Society and population* (2nd ed.). Englewood Cliffs, NJ: Prentice-Hall.
9. Coale, A. J. (1974). The history of the human population. In a Scientific American book, *The human population* (pp. 14–25). San Francisco: W. H. Freeman.
10. Freedman, R., & Berelson, B. (1974). The human population. In a Scientific American book, *The human population* (pp. 3–11). San Francisco: W. H. Freeman.
11. Kitagawa, E. M., & Hauser, P. M. (1973). *Differential mortality in the United States.* Cambridge, MA: Harvard University Press.
12. Wrigley, E. A. (1969). *Population and history.* New York: McGraw-Hill.
13. United States Bureau of the Census. (1975). *Historical statistics of the United States, colonial times to 1970, bicentennial edition.* Washington, DC: U.S. Government Printing Office.
14. United Nations. (1985). *Demographic yearbook, 1983.* New York: United Nations.
15. Comfort, A. (1956). *The biology of senescence.* London: Routledge & Kegan Paul.
16. Uhlenberg, P. (1980). Death and the family. *Journal of Family History, 5,* 313–320.
17. Preston, S. H. (1976). *Mortality patterns in national populations: With special reference to recorded causes of death.* New York: Academic Press.
18. Hamilton, J. B. (1948). The role of testicular secretions as indicated by the effects of castration in man and by studies of pathological conditions and the short lifespan associated with maleness. *Recent Progress in Hormone Research, 3,* 257–324.
19. Wood, C. S. (1979). *Human sickness and health: A biocultural view.* Palo Alto, CA: Mayfield.
20. Lopez, A. D., & Ruzicka, L. T. (Eds.). (1981). *Sex differentials in mortality: Trends, determinants and consequences.* Canberra, Australia: Misc. Series No. 4, Department of Demography, Australian National University.
21. Rossi, A. (1985). Introduction. In Rossi, A. (Ed.), *Gender and the life course* (pp. xiii–xvii). New York: Aldine.
22. Hetzel, B. S. (1983). Life style factors is sex differentials in mortality in developed countries. In A. D. Lopez & L. T. Ruzicka (Eds.), *Sex differentials in mortality: trends, determinants, and consequences.* Canberra, Australia: Miscellaneous Series No. 4, Department of Demography, Australian National University.
23. Lopez, A. D., & Ruzicka (Eds.), *Sex differentials in mortality: Trends, determinants and consequences* (pp. 1–5). Canberra, Australia: Miscellaneous Series no. 4, Department of Demography, Australian National University.
24. Bhatia, S. (1981). Traditional practices affecting female health and survival: Evidence from countries of South Asia. In A. D. Lopez, & L. T. Ruzicka (Eds.), *Sex differentials in mortality: Trends,*

determinants and consequences (pp. 165–177). Canberra, Australia: Miscellaneous Series no. 4, Department of Demography, Australian National University.

25. Retherford, R. D. (1975). The changing sex differential in mortality. Westport, CT: Greenwood Press.

26. Preston, S. H. (1968). Analysis of a change in western mortality patterns. Unpublished doctoral dissertation, Princeton University, Princeton.

27. Preston, S. H. (1984). Children and the elderly in the U.S. Scientific American, 251, 44–49.

28. Halbwachs, M. (1978). The causes of suicide. (H. Goldblatt, Trans.). New York: The Free Press. (Original work published 1930)

29. Durkheim, E. (1897). Suicide. New York: The Free Press, 1951.

30. Danigelis, N., & Pope, W. (1979). Durkheim's theory of suicide as applied to the family: An empirical test. Social Forces, 57, 1081–1106.

31. Gove, W. (1973). Sex, marital status, and mortality. American Journal of Sociology, 79, 45–67.

32. Dublin, L. I., Lotka, A. J., & Spiegelman, M. (1949). Length of life. New York: Ronald Press.

33. Shurtleff, D. (1956). Mortality among the married. Journal of the American Geriatrics Society, 4, 654–666.

34. Antonovsky, A. (1967). Social class, life expectancy and overall mortality. The Milbank Memorial Fund Quarterly, 45, 31–73.

35. United Nations Population Division. (1981). Socio-economic differential mortality in industrialized societies. New York: United Nations Population Division.

36. Thornton, R. G., & Nam, C. B. (1972). The lower mortality rates of nonwhites at the older ages: An enigma in demographic analysis. Research Reports in Social Science, 11, 1–8.

37. Manton, K. G., Poss, S. S., & Wing. S. (1979). The black/white mortality crossover: Investigation from the perspective of the components of aging. The Gerontologist, 19, 291–300.

38. United State Bureau of the Census. (1985). Statistical Abstract of the United States, 1986, (106th ed.). Washington, DC: U.S. Government Printing Office.

39. United States Government Printing Office. (1982). Vital statistics of the United States, 1978, Vol. II, Part A (DHHS Publication No. 31-1101). Washington, D.C.: U.S. Government Printing Office.

40. Kain, E. L. (1985, November). Race, mortality, and families. Paper presented at the meeting of the National Council on Family Relations, Dallas, Texas.

6

Death Anxiety

Robert A. Neimeyer

. . . Of all things that move man, one of the principal ones is his terror
of death.

Ernest Becker (1)

Traditionally, when poets, philosophers, and scientists have contemplated the
human encounter with death, they have taken for granted that it is an encounter
marked by fear, terror, or uneasiness (2). While this assumption of the universality
of death fear is not itself universal, it has clearly been a dominant motif in Western
culture. Thus, with the emergence of the new "death-awareness movement" in the
1950s (3), it was not surprising that the study of *death anxiety* would come to
occupy a prominent place in the literature generated by the movement.

My aim in this chapter is to survey this now voluminous literature in an
attempt to winnow out of the profusion of reports those reliable "facts" about
death anxiety that have been fairly well established. To place this effort in perspective, I will begin with a few remarks on the growth of this literature over the last
30 years and will briefly sketch the methods commonly used to study death attitudes. As we will see, even this brief examination will point up certain crucial
conceptual and methodological problems that have limited our ability to study the
human encounter with death. Is death anxiety conscious or unconscious? Is it a
single, global fear or a multifaceted concept, encompassing such distinctive reactions as the fear of nonexistence, the fear of eternal punishment, and the fear of
experiencing the painful death of oneself or another? A consideration of these
questions will lead to a critical appraisal of the validity of the instruments and
techniques used to operationalize the concept of death anxiety.

The next and longest section of the chapter will focus on the results of
empirical research on the correlates of fear of death. For the sake of clarity, these
will be organized under two general headings, including demographic and situational factors on the one hand, and personality characteristics on the other. To
counterbalance this general emphasis on the "trait" of death anxiety, I will also
consider its modifiability, particularly through death education. I will conclude by

summarizing the main themes of this review and offering recommendations that, if followed, could help make future research more progressive.

OVERVIEW OF THE LITERATURE

From its inception, thanatology has been a multidisciplinary field. This is illustrated in the diverse authorship of leading textbooks in the area, from Feifel's 1959 book entitled *The Meaning of Death* (4) to the present volume. In keeping with the pervasive implications that death carries for various aspects of human activity, these source books routinely feature contributions by philosophers, sociologists, physicians, psychologists, anthropologists, lawyers, educators, theologians, and even art historians.

In sharp contrast to this trend, research on death anxiety has been conducted mainly by psychologists, with occasional contributions from other social scientists and medical professionals. Perhaps for this reason, the resulting literature has shown an increasing concern with methodological issues, often at the expense of broader social, cultural, philosophical, and applied perspectives that might enhance the pertinence of the findings. But at least if assessed in quantitative terms, this concentration of effort has also been fertile: to date, some 528 published articles have appeared that focus on death anxiety or the closely related constructs of death fear, threat, and concern. Taken together, this growing body of research represents the largest empirical literature in the field of thanatology—and one that continues to attract new investigators.

Figure 1 depicts the growth in this literature over the last three decades. As the figure suggests, death anxiety became a topic of consistent psychological interest in the mid-1950s, although a handful of pioneering studies appeared before that time. Methodologically, these early studies tended to rely upon projective methods (e.g., the tabulation of death themes in Thematic Apperception Test (TAT) stories)

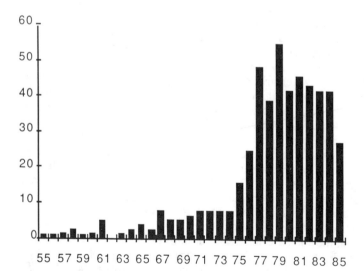

FIG 1 Number of publications on death anxiety by year, 1955–1985 (total n = 528).

and simple face valid questionnaires (5). By the mid-1960s, the volume of reports began to increase, coincident with the rising popular interest in the topic of death, as reflected in the appearance of Kübler-Ross' bestseller, *On Death and Dying* (6). But a "publication explosion" in this literature did not occur until the mid-1970s, when the number of articles began increasing geometrically, peaking at over 50 articles per year in 1979. Interestingly, the explosion of this literature appeared to be ushered in by the development a few years earlier of the first validated and widely available instruments designed specifically for the direct assessment of death fear (7, 8), threat (9), and anxiety (10). Both in the shape of the growth curve and in the apparently facilitative role played by methodological advances, the evolution of the death anxiety literature closely parallels the development of other specialty areas in psychology (e.g., 11) and science more generally (12).

At the high point of interest in death attitudes in the late 1970s, several review articles appeared in order to integrate (13), criticize (14), and give direction (3) to the burgeoning literature. Together, they provide an adequate overview of the methodological limitations and substantive findings of the research through 1977, and to make the present review more manageable, I will rely on them for coverage of this older literature. But the rate of publication on death anxiety over the last decade has remained so high that these reviews, although once comprehensive, are now seriously dated. Moreover, their current value is limited by the fact that they were written just as research in the field was beginning to burgeon, making it difficult for their authors to discern the difference between consistent findings on the one hand and anomalous results on the other. As we shall see, recent years have produced at least a few lines of programmatic research on certain instruments, populations, and issues that were only dimly foreshadowed a decade ago.

Finally, as death anxiety research moved into the 1980s, there was a plateauing of interest, followed by an apparent decline. Whether this represents a simple year-to-year variation in publication or forecasts a gradual shifting of empirical interest to new or different topics is difficult to assess at this time. What is clear is that despite its volume, the literature on death fear remains remarkably diffuse in its publication outlets as well as in its content. For example, the top three publishers of death anxiety research, *Omega, Psychological Reports,* and *Death Education/Death Studies* (in that order) have published, collectively, only 146 articles on the topic or approximately 28 percent of this literature. The remainder is scattered through literally dozens of journals, the majority of which are not read widely by thanatologists. This wide dispersion in publication tends to delimit the impact of the conceptual and methodological advances that do occur in the field, thereby helping perpetuate the theoretical and empirical problems discussed in the next two sections.

DEATH ANXIETY: THE PROBLEM OF DEFINITION

It might seem obvious that the study of any topic must start with a clear definition of what is to be investigated. Yet in spite of this, definitional problems have plagued the field of death anxiety from the beginning. The first, and most persistent, of these difficulties concerns the term "death anxiety" itself. For over

20 years, prominent thanatologists have argued that death *fear* and death *anxiety* are logically distinct concepts that are not interchangeable, despite their being frequently treated as equivalent in the published literature. For example, in what may be the earliest and still the most sophisticated discussion of this issue, Choron (2) argued that fear represents a more realistic reaction to a specific danger, whereas anxiety refers to a more neurotic response that is out of proportion to any actual external hazard. This same distinction continues to be made by current writers such as Kalish (15), who point out that whereas fear may have a concrete object, anxiety does not. In the opinion of reviewers like Kastenbaum and Costa (3), much of the confusion in the literature on death attitudes can be traced to this "careless interchange of 'fear' and 'anxiety,' each of which implies different approaches to measurement" (3, p. 233). For example, a questionnaire regarding fear of death might contain questions about the pain of dying or one's reactions to witnessing the death of another, while an instrument measuring death anxiety might inquire about reactions to more abstract factors, such as apprehension about the state of nonbeing that death may represent.

As persuasive as these arguments may be, I believe that a distinction between fear and anxiety is no longer compelling on conceptual or practical grounds. Theoretically, the distinction has always received its strongest support from the psychoanalytic camp, who link the experience of anxiety with the expression of unconscious conflicts in the anxious person (2). As the influence of the psychodynamic model has continued to wane since mid-century, this theoretical grounding for the distinction has become less secure. More importantly, the fact that anxiety and fear have seldom been differentiated in the construction of instruments assessing apprehension about death means that the concepts have become equivalent in practice, the objections of purists notwithstanding.

But this argument should not be taken to imply that no theoretical distinctions can be made among different types of death concern. Indeed, at least one such distinction between death *threat* on the one hand and anxiety or fear on the other has been fairly well established in the literature over the last decade. In contrast to the negative emotional reactions to death denoted as fear or anxiety, death threat refers to a more "cognitive" predisposition to view one's own death as fundamentally incompatible with one's identity as a living being (9). Unlike the fear/anxiety literature, the numerous studies of death threat have used a consistent and validated assessment technique (16, 17) grounded in a well-researched general theory of personality (18). Thus, the concept of death threat is more clearly defined at both the theoretical and empirical levels than are most other death attitudes (see below). The general point here is that terminological distinctions may indeed be valid, but only if suitably and consistently operationalized.

LEVELS OF DEATH ANXIETY AND THE PROBLEM OF MEASUREMENT

The Denial of Death?

It has become almost a cliche within the death-awareness movement that ours is a death-denying society (e.g., 6). As applied to the individual, this assertion carries the strong implication that however much we may profess to accept the reality of our death at a conscious level, at an unconscious level we remain terrified of its occurrence (1). Obviously, if this contention could be supported, it would have important implications for the assessment of death anxiety. At the very least, it would require that, to be comprehensive, our measurement strategies would have to tap death fears at conscious and nonconscious levels. Indeed, some investigators—notably Feifel and his coworkers (19–21)—have attempted to do just this, and their efforts will be reviewed below. But while there may be important senses in which we do deny the psychological reality of our deaths, direct evidence for the ubiquitous denial of death *anxiety* is remarkably sparse.

A large scale study conducted by Warren and Chopra (22) provides an interesting perspective on this question. Administering a face-valid survey on death attitudes to 749 Australian respondents, they discovered that although only 9 percent of their sample described themselves as specifically "fearful" when reflecting on their own death, fully 30 percent reported some variety of negative emotional reaction (e.g., discouragement, depression, purposelessness). Perhaps the most reasonable conclusions to draw from such findings are that a) a substantial percentage of individuals in Western society do not deny feeling apprehensive about death, and that b) the determinants of denial, when it does occur, deserve further study. The few recent studies of denial of death fear that have been conducted support this view. For example, in study that is notable for the sophistication of its sampling procedures, Nelson (23) found a modest negative correlation between death anxiety denial and occupational and educational status among 699 Virginia residents. Similarly, professional and well-educated respondents tended to report less avoidance of death-related situations than their lower SES counterparts. But while such studies indicate that denial does exist and is associated with certain personal or social factors, they do not necessarily establish that it masks a "deeper" level of unconscious death anxiety. Nor should we assume too quickly that individuals who deny that they fear death are simply trying to present themselves in a socially favorable light. In fact, one recent study (24) demonstrated precisely the reverse: Denial of death anxiety was actually inversely correlated with a test of social desirability.

In sum, the little research that is available raises more questions than it answers about the nature and extent of death anxiety denial. Certainly, it remains possible that the denial of death anxiety may sometimes be linked to repression, as will be discussed in the section on personality factors below. But in order to understand more clearly the results of this broader literature, it is first necessary to review the various direct and indirect means of assessing death orientation that have been employed to date.

Indirect Methods

One of the important consequences of assuming denial of death fear was that investigators began to devise *indirect* methods for assessing death anxiety. Thus, by studying fantasies, reaction times, or physiological responses to death stimuli, some researchers have attempted to circumvent subjects' tendencies to deny or otherwise distort their "true," possibly unconscious, emotional reactions. Two fairly distinct kinds of indirect assessment have resulted, the first based upon projective testing, the second upon experimental reaction time and word association tasks.

PROJECTIVE METHODS

One of the most influential early traditions in personality assessment was based on the *projective hypothesis,* the assumption that individuals project their own conflicts by seeing in ambiguous stimuli those emotional issues that are most central to their own personalities (25). Thus, in telling a story that contained frequent allusions to death in response to the vague drawings presented in Murray's Thematic Apperception Test (TAT), a subject was assumed to indirectly reveal his or her anxious preoccupation with death issues.

Although such projective methods were relatively common in the early years of death anxiety research (e.g., 26), they have since fallen into disfavor because of their dubious reliability and validity (27). One of the few remaining examples of this approach to assessment in contemporary research occurs in the work of Feifel and Nagy (20, 21). These authors employed a battery of tests in an attempt to measure three different "levels" of death anxiety experienced by over 600 persons who varied in their level of "life-threatening" behavior (e.g., drug abusers, deputy sheriffs, government employees). At a "conscious" level, subjects were simply asked to rate their personal fear of death on a five-point scale. At a "fantasy" level, they were instructed to select an image that best represented their view of death. These projective images were then classed as positive (e.g., a soft pillow) or negative (e.g., a devouring tiger). It was assumed that this fantasy task circumvented the respondents' defensive or intellectualized conception of death. Finally, as a "below the level of awareness" measure, they administered a color/word interference task that will be described more fully in the next section.

Results, however, did not clearly support the independence of these three levels. Instead, conscious and fantasy measures were found to be significantly more correlated with one another than either was with the nonconscious measure (21), a result that has been replicated by Epting, Rainey, and Weiss (28). In fact, Rigdon (29) has provided evidence that direct fear ratings and imagery measures actually form a single factor, which he terms "conscious death fear." Thus, the key assumption of projective methods, that they disclose emotional conflicts of which the respondent is unaware, does not seem to be clearly supported by present data.

While the case for unconscious death denial and the rationale for projective methods have both weakened in recent years, it may still prove to be interesting to investigate death fantasies as phenomena in their own right, irrespective of whether or not they offer us glimpses of unconscious death anxiety. Lonetto's work (30) is a case in point. Asking a sample of over 300 students in death education, nursing, and funeral studies to describe their fantasy image of death in human terms, he found that responses tended to cluster into five separable groups. Interestingly, the most common cluster contained images of death as a "gay seducer," attractive and beguiling. The second most frequent depicted death in active terms, such as beckoning or stalking its victim. Other personifications included the image of death as a gentle comforter, an automaton, and a macabre spectre. Moreover, these various personifications were linked to different facets of death anxiety. For example, students who fantasized of death as a gay deceiver also reported more frequent and anxiety-producing thoughts of death, while those who viewed it as an active pursuer experienced more concern over the physical alterations it caused. Lonetto (30, p. 407) concluded that "imagination may serve to heighten or diminish components of death anxiety."

EXPERIMENTAL TASKS

A second set of indirect measures of death anxiety has been derived from laboratory tasks administered under highly controlled circumstances. In such tasks, subjects are presented both death-related words and neutral words and are asked to either read them aloud, associate to them, or identify the color of ink in which they are printed. The number of errors made, the time require to react, or the degree of physiological arousal displayed in responding to the death words as opposed to the neutral words supposedly reflects the degree of "perceptual defensiveness" or anxiety that the former arouse in the subject (e.g., 31).

As with projective methods, these indirect experimental methods have largely been abandoned in the last decade, mainly because of their failure to demonstrate sufficient reliability or validity (3). Again, the only exception to this general rule can be found in the work of Feifel (20, 21) who has continued to employ the color/word interference task and related measures to assess a "below awareness" level of death anxiety. While further refinement of these measures may indeed be worth pursuing, available data do not support the conclusion that they tap a theoretically consistent "nonconscious" level of death fear. Rigdon (29), for example, analyzed the responses of 60 high school and college students to Feifel's multilevel assessment, and discovered that the five "nonconscious" measures, while independent of the conscious and fantasy measures of death anxiety, were also poorly related to one another. This raises the distinct possibility that the variations in response to them reflect idiosyncratic method variance rather than a theoretically distinct level of death orientation.

Direct Measures

Although death anxiety has been conceptualized by some authors as a multilevel phenomenon requiring a multilevel assessment, this has clearly been a minority position among empirically oriented thanatologists. As Wass and her colleagues note, most "authors of death scales . . . have assumed, as least implicitly, that death anxiety, like death fear, is a conscious experience" (32, p. 188). In keeping with this assumption, most work in the area has employed fairly direct measures of death attitudes, ranging from the occasional interview to the ubiquitous questionnaire.

INTERVIEWS

The use of interviews to assess death anxiety, while still infrequent, has gained in popularity over the last decade. Yet unlike indirect methods, whose development was motivated by the common assumption of unconscious death denial, interview methods have been devised for a host of practical and theoretical reasons. As a result, they vary widely in their format, length, structure, and demonstrated validity. Perhaps the simplest "interview" method consists in simply reading aloud a brief, forced choice questionnaire and asking the interviewee to respond verbally rather than in writing. This method has been employed when Templer's Death Anxiety Scale (10) has been administered to populations requiring special assistance, such as the elderly (33, 34). At the opposite extreme, some investigators have coded unstructured verbalizations to open-ended prompts on the rationale that death concern can best be assessed by simply encouraging people to talk freely and then listening carefully to their responses. A good example of this approach is the recent work of Viney (35), who compared the death attitudes of 496 severely ill people with 297 healthy controls. In the course of an interview about lifespan transitions experienced by her respondents, she invited them to "talk with her for a few minutes about what their lives were like at the moment—the good things and the bad—what it was like for them." She then categorized their responses using the Death Anxiety Subscale of the Gottschalk content analysis system in order to compare the incidence of death concerns as a function of age, sex, health status, and other medical factors (results reviewed under appropriate headings below). Such an approach clearly possesses distinctive advantages over a more constrained, forced choice questionnaire, although the usefulness of the responses obviously hinges on the establishment of trust and rapport between the interviewer and interviewee.

A second example of sophisticated research that takes these interpersonal factors into account has been provided by Kalish (36). In a study designed to examine the impact of age and ethnicity on death concern, Kalish first constructed a carefully stratified sample of over 400 Los Angeles residents, reflecting a broad range of ages and four contrasting subcultural groups: whites, blacks, Mexican-Americans, and Japanese-Americans. His effort to solicit candid replies to potentially delicate questions was reflected in the fact that the hour-long interview was conducted in the first language of the interviewee by a research assistant of the same ethnic background. This degree of sensitivity paired with a strong research design has been rare in this literature.

Finally, it is noteworthy that, with the exception of research using the Gottschalk scale, the validity and reliability of interview procedures have seldom been considered. Indeed, it is curious that although previous reviewers have been sharply critical of questionnaires whose psychometric properties are poorly researched (e.g., 3, 5, 14), they remain generally silent concerning the use of interview techniques that are no better established. Yet there is no apparent reason for believing that *spoken* responses to questions about death anxiety are any more exempt from concerns about their consistency or accuracy than are *written* answers to the same questions. Indeed, one can easily enough imagine interview situations that could subtly influence the respondent's answers, a topic that has been entirely unresearched in the death anxiety area.

The one interview method whose validity and reliability have been extensively scrutinized is the Threat Index (TI), a measure originally introduced by Krieger, Epting, and Leitner in 1974 (9). Of the major techniques for assessing death attitudes, the TI is the only instrument to be explicitly derived from an overarching theory of personality. Founded in Kelly's personal construct theory (20), it represents an attempt to measure the degree of threat implied by one's idiosyncratic concept of death. From a construct theory perspective, threat occurs when a "person's identity and understanding of the world is challenged" (9, p. 301). The TI procedure operationalizes this concept by measuring respondents' tendencies to define their own identities as living beings and their own death in incompatible terms on a sample of personal constructs. These constructs are elicited in a structured interview in which respondents are first asked to compare and contrast such situations as "your father dying while trying to save someone from drowning," "three children dying when a tornado hits their school," and "your own death, if it were to occur at this time in your life." For example, an interviewee might respond that the first situation is "purposeful," whereas the last two are "meaningless." In a second step, he or she is asked to describe himself or herself and his/her own death in these terms. Instances in which self is described by one construct pole (e.g., as purposeful) and death by the opposite (e.g., meaningless) are taken to indicate threat. The higher the number of such "splits," the more threatened the subject is assumed to be by the prospect of his own mortality. A detailed description of this structured interview procedure has recently been provided by Neimeyer, Epting, and Rigdon (17).

Considerable evidence now supports the validity of this index of death threat. For example, individuals who score low in threat report that they are more able to accept death and to conceive of their personal mortality (9). Moreover, the death constructs elicited by this interview procedure appear to be more meaningful to respondents than a standard list of semantic differential dimensions (37), and the score on the instrument seems to be free of social desirability bias (38). In addition, if the investigator wishes to study the idiosyncratic meanings attributed to death by the subject, the content of the elicited constructs can be coded using a reliable system of 25 categories devised by Neimeyer, Fontana, and Gold (39), a system that can also be applied to the content of conventional interviews. Further data on the validity and reliability of the TI have been provided elsewhere (16).

In summary, a variety of interview methods of assessing death orientation have been explored over the last decade, which have the advantage of adding breadth, detail, and flexibility to the study of death anxiety (27). Particularly if used in conjunction with either of the two established content coding schemes, such methods deserve to be utilized more frequently.

QUESTIONNAIRES

While alternative methods continue to be used, the dramatic increase in research on death anxiety over the last decade owes almost entirely to the broader use of questionnaire measures of death orientation. In fact, over 95 percent of published studies to date rely upon some form of direct questionnaire. Because the study of death anxiety has become almost synonymous with the use of a relatively small number of instruments, it is crucial to consider precisely what these instruments measure. As we will see in the next section, this is a matter of some dispute. At issue is the fundamental question of whether it is even meaningful to speak of "death anxiety" as a unitary concept or whether it consists of a cluster of distinguishable fears that cannot be treated as interchangeable. Before considering the correlates of death anxiety, then, it is important to clarify both the meaning of this potentially multifaceted concept and the adequacy with which each of the most commonly used scales assess it.

DEATH ANXIETY OR DEATH ANXIETIES?

Exactly what do we fear if we experience "fear of death?" From quite early in the death-awareness movement it was recognized that this was a complex question. Choron (2), for example, argued for a tripartite distinction among varieties of death fear. Grounding his discussion in Western philosophy and theology, he distinguished between fear of what happens after death (e.g., eternal punishment), fear of the "event" of dying (e.g., the pain and indignity involved), and fear of ceasing to be (e.g., extinction and loss of the activities that comprise life). He went on to speculate that the apparently selfless fear of the impact of one's death on others may be designed to hide a more basic fear of one's own annihilation. Thus, at a theoretical level, Choron believed death anxiety to be *multidimensional,* consisting of at least three interacting concerns. Contemporary theorists have refocused attention the various dimensions of death anxiety. Some, like Kalish (15), have essentially echoed Choron's distinctions, while others have proposed somewhat different dimensions. Mount (40), for example, has put forward the most elaborate of these taxonomies, differentiating between three separate triads of fears: a) fear of pain, indignity, and being a burden; b) fear for the fate of one's body after death, of judgment, and of the unknown; and c) fear of loss of mastery, a chance to complete one's projects, and of relatedness to others.

While all of the above represent plausible components of death anxiety, it is not clear on the basis of theory alone which of these dimensions (if any) are being measured by particular death attitude questionnaires. It therefore becomes essential to distinguish between the *theoretical dimensionality* of a given questionnaire and its *empirical dimensionality.* The former refers to what it purports to measure the latter to what it actually does. For example, many death orientation questionnaires that were assumed by their originators to measure a single construct (general death anxiety) appear, on closer scrutiny, to tap a number of distinct dimensions. Moreover, it is clarifying to distinguish between the empirical dimensionality of a single instrument and that which emerges across instruments. For instance, a particular questionnaire may measure two related aspects of personal death anxiety (e.g., fear of extinction and concerns about a painful death), but the use of additional instruments may disclose additional facets of death concern (e.g., fear of the loss of loved ones). In the following section, I will discuss the dimensionality of four of the more commonly used death attitude questionnaires to illustrate these issues and to pave the way for a more refined discussion of the impact of situational and personality variables on death anxiety.

Four Approaches to Measurement of Death Anxiety

Concern about the empirical dimensionality of death anxiety instruments dates from the first review of the literature, published 20 years ago (5). After surveying the assortment of scales used in the early research, Lester voiced the suspicion that "different techniques used in the studies may not be measuring the same dimension" (5, p. 34). His difficulty in interpreting the nascent literature was compounded by the fact that, at that point, only three studies had considered the validity or reliability of the questionnaires they employed.

Pointed criticism of the failure of investigators to establish the psychometric soundness of their instruments continued for the next decade (e.g., 3, 13, 15, 41). Perhaps the bluntest of these criticisms was voiced by Simpson (14, p. 139), who concluded that "research on death . . . is often logically and methodologically shoddy and has produced discrepant and contradictory results. This has been due to . . . the appalling lack of critical rigor that allowed too much indifferent or sloppy work to be published too easily." This critical sentiment typically has been counterbalanced by general optimism that inconsistencies in the literature will be clarified as greater attention is paid to the various components of death anxiety (5, 13, 42).

A close examination of the current literature suggests that these mounting criticisms have had an effect. A much smaller proportion of recent articles relies upon unvalidated instruments—although other design problems persist in these studies and will be addressed below. Moreover, as the field has progressed, early instruments such as Boyar's (43), Lester's (7), and Dickstein's (44) that treated death anxiety as a unidimensional concept have been supplemented by others, such as Nelson's (23, 45), that are explicitly multidimensional. An extremely useful discussion of nine of these instruments has been provided by Wass and her colleagues (32).

Although numerous questionnaires continue to be used occasionally in the current death anxiety literature, there has been a gradual winnowing of measures, leaving only a handful of instruments accounting for most of the empirical literature of the last decade. I will briefly consider four of these, with an emphasis on the dimensions of death anxiety that each assesses both in theory and practice.

THE DEATH ANXIETY SCALE

Developed by Templer in 1970 (10), the Death Anxiety Scale (DAS) has become by far the most commonly used measure of death orientation. In fact, it has been employed in over 60 percent of the studies published in the last 10 years. Much of the reason for the scale's popularity lies in its simplicity. The DAS consists of 15 short statements (e.g., "I am very much afraid to die"; "I am often distressed by the way time flies so very rapidly") which the respondent simply endorses as true or false. The number of responses indicative of a negative reaction is taken as a straightforward measure of death anxiety.

A certain degree of construct validation for the DAS has been provided by its moderate correlations with other measures of death fear (see 32 for review), as well as its responsivity to a film selected to provoke death anxiety (37). Reliability estimates on the DAS have also been moderately high (.8) over periods of three weeks (10, 46). Estimates of its internal consistency, on the other hand, have been more equivocal. For example, Warren and Chopra (47) reported a Chronbach's alpha of only .65 for the DAS administered to 159 Australian respondents and Schell and Zinger (48) found it to have a split-half reliability of only .43 for a Canadian sample of 577. In a successful attempt to improve the internal consistency and precision of the instrument, McMordie (46) revised the DAS to include seven-point scales on which to indicate extent of agreement with each item, replacing the true-false format of the original. Unfortunately, only four subsequent studies have employed this psychometrically improved form of the Templer scale (49–52).

These low estimates of internal consistency for the DAS strongly suggest that the instrument is measuring more than a single dimension of death attitude. A number of recent studies using factor analysis, a statistical method for determining the underlying dimensions in a set of data, tend to support this claim (24, 33, 47, 53, 54). Across these studies, which collectively include over 2,500 subjects, the DAS tends to produce three to five distinguishable factors. Typically, these include: a) a general death anxiety dimension, b) a factor focusing on thoughts and talk of death, c) a cluster of items bearing on the subjective proximity of death, and d) a factor suggesting fear of pain and suffering. Less consistently, they also have yielded factors concerned with fear of physical alterations or of the unknown. Thus, although the DAS was proposed as a theoretically unidimensional questionnaire, it is clearly empirically multidimensional. This state of affairs has led Durlak (55) to recommend that the use of the instrument be discontinued, since the scores it yields are uninterpretable. For example, a group of retirees and teenagers might obtain the same mean score on the DAS, but the former might do so by scoring high on the "subjective proximity to death" factor, whereas the latter might score higher on the "fear of physical alterations" dimension. In this case, the conclusion that the two groups have similar death anxieties would clearly be unwarranted. In recognition of this problem, Gilliland and Templer (54) have recently recommended that factor scores, rather than total scores, be used in future research employing the DAS. Unfortunately, the small number of items that load on each of the factors is likely to result in meager reliability coefficients for the resulting scores. Whether researchers will respond to these concerns by further revising the scale remains to be determined.

THE THREAT INDEX

Originally introduced in a structured interview format by Krieger, Epting, and Leitner (9) in 1974, the Threat Index (TI) was eventually adapted to a paper and pencil format to promote its more widespread use in research (37, 38). In this form it has become the second most popular instrument in recent death-orientation research, being employed in 23 percent of the studies published in the last decade.

Like the interview format of the TI, the paper and pencil version of the instrument assesses threat by measuring the subject's tendency to construe self and death on contrasting poles of a sample of constructs (e.g., sick vs. healthy, static vs. changing). Unlike the interview form, it circumvents the need to elicit constructs from the subject by providing a standardized set of dimensions used most frequently by subjects in the early studies. As a result, it is easily administered in group settings and requires far less time to administer than its predecessor. Complete instructions for the instrument have been provided by Neimeyer, Epting, and Rigdon (17).

Although the interpretation of the threat score derived from the index has been questioned (56), the developers of the TI have defended its validity on both logical and empirical grounds (38, 57). For example, Krieger, Epting, and Hays (38) found that respondents showed a strong tendency to rate something they found very "comfortable" as they would rate themselves and to contrast both with ratings of a personally "terrifying" event. This finding supports the construct validity of the "split" configuration as a measure of threat. Further evidence of the construct validity of the TI has been provided by Rainey and Epting (58), who found that death education students and persons who had made arrangements for the disposal of their bodies after death had lower threat scores than relevant control groups. Other studies have demonstrated the convergence of the TI with established death anxiety instruments (e.g., 28, 59, 60), providing some evidence of the concurrent validity of the measure. Moreover, the paper and pencil version of the TI appears to have high test-retest reliability, with estimates of .8 to .9 being reported over periods of up to three months (37, 38, 58). Unlike the DAS, it also displays internal consistency coefficients above .9 (38, 61, 62). While consistency estimates of this magnitude suggest that the TI is more uniform and hence more interpretable than the DAS, it should be noted that a factor analytic assessment of its empirical dimensionality has yet to be reported. Even with this limitation, however, the TI seems to be the best researched instrument for the assessment of death attitudes available in the current literature, leading independent reviewers to consider it as a model for future research (3, 14).

THE COLLETT-LESTER FEAR OF DEATH SCALE (CL)

Developed by Collett and Lester in 1969 (8), the CL is unique in being the only theoretically multidimensional questionnaire in wide use. In fact, it is the third most frequently employed measure in the death anxiety literature of the past 10 years, appearing in 18 percent of all published studies. Its 36 items were written to assess four conceptually distinct dimensions of death fear. The *death of self* (DS) subscale contains items like "The idea of never thinking or experiencing again after I die does not make me anxious," thereby assessing concerns about the state of death. In contrast, the *dying of self* (DyS) subscale focuses on the passage from life to death, with items such as "I am disturbed by the physical degeneration involved in a slow death." Similarly, the *death of others* (DO) subscale taps reactions to known or unknown others who have died (e.g., "I would not mind having to identify the corpse of someone I knew."). Finally, the *dying of others* (DyO) subscale deals with discomfort regarding others in life-threatening situations (e.g., "If a friend were dying, I would not want to be told."). Respondents indicate their agreement or disagreement with each item on a six-point Likert scale.

The primary validational evidence for the CL comes from its moderate convergence with the DAS (60, 64) and TI (57). But compared with those instruments, it is less reliable, with test-retest correlations for various subscales seldom exceeding .6 over a six- to seven-week period (62, 65). The one available study reporting the internal consistency estimates of its subscales (66) suggests that they are only modestly cohesive, raising the possibility that the empirical factor structure of the CL departs from theoretical expectations.

A recent study by Livneh (67) suggests that this is the case. Cluster analyzing 200 CLs completed by a student group, Livneh found that the questionnaire yielded five item clusters rather than four and that these bore only slight resemblance to the theoretical dimensions it was designed to tap. From largest to smallest, these clusters addressed a) general fear of one's own death and dying, b) discomfort over interaction with dying friends, c) negative reactions to the death of a friend, d) actual avoidance of friends who are dying, and e) rationalization of one's own death. A subsequent principal components analysis tended to reinforce this interpretation. Thus, of the aspects of death anxiety the instrument was designed to measure, only DO clearly retained its structure, DS and DyO each split into two separate clusters, and DyS virtually disintegrated, dispersing its items over four of the five empirically derived dimensions. At minimum, these results indicate that revision of the CL is needed to improve its reliability and to clarify its empirical dimensionality.

THE HOELTER MULTIDIMENSIONAL FEAR OF DEATH SCALE

As a comparatively new scale, the Hoelter MFODS (68) has been used in only 4 percent of the literature published since 1977. But it deserves mention here because it represents the best current attempt to construct a genuinely multidimensional measure of death anxiety on empirical grounds. It consists of eight independent subscales, each of which contains six items on which the respondent indicates extent of agreement. Factors and representative items are as follows: I *Fear of dying* ("I am afraid of dying very slowly."); II *Fear of the dead* ("I dread visiting a funeral home."); III *Fear of being destroyed* ("I do not want to donate my eyes after I die."); IV *Fear for significant others* ("I sometimes get upset when acquaintances die."); V *Fear of the unknown* ("No one can say for sure what will happen after death."); VI *Fear of conscious death* ("I am afraid of being buried alive."); VII *Fear for body after death* ("The thought of my body decaying after I die scares me."); VIII *Fear of premature death* ("I am afraid I will not have time to experience everything I want to."). In Hoelter's original study, these dimensions emerged from a factor analysis of a larger sample of items administered to 395 American students. They have, however, been largely replicated in a subsequent study by Walkey (69), who administered the scale to 256 Australian adults. In fact, he found that five of the eight factors almost perfectly reproduced (Factors I, II, III, IV, and V) and that only Factor VIII seriously departed from the American structure reported by Hoelter.

But other data reported by Long (70) limit the generalizability of these findings. Translating the original MFODS into Arabic, Long administered the scale to 84 Saudi Arabian men temporarily living in the United States. In contrast to the previous studies, he found that the best factor solution produced only three dimensions of death anxiety, including a general fear of dying and the dead, a fear for significant others, and a fear of premature death. The extremely high religious orthodoxy scores obtained by the sample suggested that several of the fear dimensions posited by Hoelter (e.g., fear of being destroyed, fear of conscious death) may be entirely inapplicable to a devout Islamic respondent. These studies serve as a useful reminder that death anxiety (or its absence) is embedded in larger cultural and philosophical contexts that are typically ignored in this (primarily American) literature. At a methodological level, they also remind us that we should not simply assume the generalizability of even empirically constructed instruments to cultures that contrast sharply with those on which they were based.

Finally, in the specific case of the MFODS, it is worth noting that, while it remains a promising instrument, it is not yet adequately established at a psychometric level. Acceptable levels of internal consistency (averaging .75) for the various subscales have been reported by both Hoelter and Walkey (68, 69), but to date, no published study has examined the questionnaire's test-retest reliability. Even more seriously, essentially no validational evidence for the MFODS or its component factors has been reported, although the correlations of some of its subscales with measures of religiosity (see below) could be interpreted as supporting their construct validity (68). In summary, the MFODS deserves to be employed in future research, but this research should first focus upon establishing its reliability and validity.

Dimensions of Death Anxiety
Across Instruments

Finally, before leaving behind methodological concerns and progressing to a discussion of the correlates of death anxiety, it is worthwhile to consider briefly the multidimensionality of death attitudes *across*, rather than *within*, instruments. This is important because it permits us to detect both common and unique aspects of death fear assessed by different measures. The best existing study on this question has been reported by Durlak and Kass (66), who administered 15 different measures of death orientation to 350 college students. Subjecting the results to a commonly used method of factor analysis to determine the empirical clustering of the instruments, they found the following five factors: I *Negative evaluation of personal death*, II *Reluctance to interact with the dying*, III *Negative reaction to pain*, IV *Reaction to reminders of death*, and V *Preoccupation with thoughts of death*. Each of these dimensions was defined by two to nine measures that loaded significantly on that factor. Moreover, while a few of the measures were factorially "pure" (e.g., the Death of Self subscale of the Collett-Lester loaded only on Factor I), many loaded highly on more than one dimension. This led the authors to recommend that more attention be paid by future investigators to the actual constructs that their scales appeared to be measuring.

However, a reanalysis of these data by Rigdon and Epting (71) calls the specific conclusions of Durlak and Kass into question. In particular, they question the latter researchers' choice of (a varimax) rotation method, since it minimizes the possibility of a larger general factor emerging, which might be expected if one believed that death orientation were somewhat more global. Instead, they employed alternative (quartimax) rotational procedures and reported a three-factor solution, which included only a general negative reaction to death, an avoidance of the dying and death reminders, and a preoccupation with thoughts of death. Although in this alternative solution death concern could still be considered multidimensional, the interpretation of several established inventories was clarified, with only the Death Anxiety Scale continuing to show multiple high factor loadings. At present, which of these two alternative views on the empirical dimensionality of death anxiety instruments is preferable remains very much a live issue (72). But this series of reports does illustrate a point that is too often ignored in the death anxiety literature: Methodological decisions powerfully influence results, and competent investigators may differ among themselves in their preferred approach to an empirical problem. Considered somewhat more broadly, the burgeoning interest in the dimensionality of death anxiety also illustrates the complexity of the human encounter with death. Some of the demographic and personal factors that color that encounter are discussed in the remainder of this chapter.

EMPIRICAL CORRELATES OF DEATH ANXIETY

Demographic and Situational Factors

A great deal of research in the last 10 years has focused on the relationship between demographic variables and death anxiety, owing largely to the ease with which such variables as age and sex can be measured. But ironically, relatively few of these studies have been designed primarily to test demographic hypotheses. Instead, most simply report differences between demographic groups in passing, while pursuing other questions of greater interest to the investigator. As a consequence, a diffuse and largely atheoretical literature has grown up in the area, leaving many important questions about the impact of such variables on death anxiety unanswered. This is less true of the recent research on such situational variables as health status and experiences with death, where *a priori* hypothesis testing is more common. In reviewing this research, I will try to emphasize consistencies in results where they exist and suggest more useful strategies for finding such consistencies where none can presently be identified.

SEX

In his review of the death anxiety literature through 1977, Pollack (13) noted that the majority of the earlier work indicated that females reported more death fear than males, with virtually all of the remaining studies demonstrating no differences between the sexes. Research conducted over the last decade reinforces this conclusion and provides a slightly more refined view of this possible sex difference than was available at that time.

Not surprisingly, the most commonly used instrument employed in these studies is the Death Anxiety Scale, and the most commonly studied subject group consists of college students. Much of the work using this measure with this population supports the conclusion that females are more death anxious than males (46, 64, 73–76). Moreover, there is some indication that this is not simply an American phenomenon, since Lonetto and his associates have found the same trend in a study of 570 Irish and Canadian students (77). Other studies using the DAS have found similar sex differences in demographically varied samples, ranging from rural southern high school students (78) to husbands and wives in military families (79), and rural elderly responding to the DAS in interview form (34). Occasional reports using the Lester fear of death scale (37), the Templer-McMordie version of the DAS (46), and the Threat Index (62) also corroborate this view.

However, the literature is far from unequivocal regarding the more negative death attitudes of females. For example, Neimeyer and his associates found no differences between men and women in death threat as measured by the TI, in either college student (37) or adult samples (60, 79), and Eggerman and Dustin have reported similar negative results with the TI in a study of first-year medical students and physicians (80). Some studies with the DAS also fail to show a gender difference (47, 81), particularly for more mature, professional samples (60, 83–85) and in one study of elderly nursing home residents (86). Two additional studies using rather different methods also have yielded a "no difference" conclusion. Conte, Weiner, and Plutchick (87) found that males and females scored similarly on their Death Anxiety Questionnaire, a new instrument for which they provide some preliminary validational evidence. Similarly, Viney was unable to detect any sex differences in her interview-based study of nearly 800 ill and healthy adults (35). Although these conflicting studies call into question the robustness of a sex difference in death concern, they are quite clear in indicating the direction of this difference when it does occur. In fact, only two recent reports counter the general trend, by finding that men, rather than women, experience higher death threat (91) and anxiety (88).

In keeping with the above discussion of the multidimensionality of death anxiety, a few investigators have tried to establish more specifically on what aspects of death concern males and females differ. For example, Neimeyer, Bagley, and Moore (64) found that women enrolled in death education courses tended to outscore men on the Dying of Self subscale of the Collett-Lester inventory but not on Death of Self or Death or Dying of Others subscales. This tendency for females to have higher DyS scores has been found in other studies as well (62, 89). Keller and his associates (42) have also provided support for the specificity of gender differences using a 12-item death questionnaire of their own design. They found that in a heterogeneous group of 874 respondents, females scored higher than males on negative evaluation of death and anxiety regarding personal death but did not differ from them in concerns about an afterlife. Taken together, these studies point toward a female tendency to report more anxiety about death in general and especially about their own dying. Moreover, this tendency may be stronger among adolescents and young adults than among middle-aged subjects.

Although the existence of a gender difference in death anxiety measures is fairly clear, its explanation and significance are not. One hypothesis would be that the discrepancy in death anxiety scores simply reflects the greater female tendency to admit troubling feelings that males would be less likely to share openly (c.f. Stillion, 90). This "emotional expressiveness" hypothesis receives indirect support from the fact that studies reporting sex differences tend to utilize the DAS or similar "feeling-oriented" questionnaires, whereas those that find no such differences often use more "cognitive" measures, such as the Threat Index or Lonetto's death personification procedure (30). However, this hypothesis has yet to be systematically evaluated by statistically or experimentally controlling for discrepancies in general emotional expressiveness between men and women and then determining whether sex differences in death anxiety still emerge. A second hypothesis might relate women's tendency toward greater death anxiety to their comparatively smaller sense of control over the events of their lives, a factor that will be discussed further in the section on personality factors below. Both of these potential explanations could refer to the contrasting socialization experiences of males and females to account for these dispositional differences. But whatever explanation is put forward, it seems clear that it would have to be quite general, since recent evidence suggests that the greater death anxiety of females may extend to Eastern as well as Western cultures (50).

Finally, it should be emphasized that the sex differences that are detected in these studies are typically subtle, if statistically reliable. The substantial overlap in male and female distributions on fear of death is illustrated by Lonetto's (77) finding that sex of subject, although significant, accounted for only 2 percent of the variance in death anxiety. With the remaining 98 percent of the variance unaccounted for, it is clear that a more comprehensive understanding of death orientation will need to be multivariate as well as multidimensional.

AGE

Curiously, the effect of age on the death anxiety of adults has been ignored until relatively recently. In large part, this stemmed from the early assumption that aging had little effect on death attitudes once "mental development" was complete (5). As a result, as recently as the late 1970s Pollack (13) was unable to find a single study that addressed the relationship between age and fear of death in adult subjects. In the past 10 years, this situation has changed dramatically. While much remains to be learned about the maturation of death attitudes beyond adolescence, an outline of major shifts in death concern across the lifespan has begun to emerge.

Kalish's elegant study of over 400 California residents provides a point of departure for this literature (36). Conducting door-to-door surveys of white, black, Mexican-American, and Japanese-American communities, he found that the elderly of all ethnic groups thought about death more often but were less anxious about it than respondents at earlier stages in the life cycle. Across ethnic categories, approximately 10 percent of the elderly reported fearing death compared to 25 percent of the middle-aged, and 40 percent of the young. This general pattern has been replicated in a sophisticated sociological study of 699 Virginia residents conducted by Nelson (23), which found that age was negatively correlated with death avoidance, fear, and reluctance to interact with the dying as measured by a multidimensional inventory. The greater death anxiety of younger respondents has also been demonstrated in other studies (e.g., 83), including investigations of more specific populations such as rehabilitation clients (85) and medical students (80).

Research on death threat within the personal construct tradition has reinforced the above conclusions. For example, Robinson and Wood (91) studied the death threat and anxiety displayed by 100 subjects who varied considerably in age and health status. They discovered that older subjects scored lower on the TI, as well as the DAS and the Death of Self subscale of the Collett-Lester inventory. Moreover, age accounted for up to 16 percent of the variance in these measures, confirming that it was a nontrivial predictor of death attitudes. These results were partially replicated by Neimeyer (92), who found that older subjects did indeed show less fear of personal death but did not differ from younger respondents on the TI or other dimensions of death fear assessed by the CL or DAS.

Results are not entirely consistent, however. For example, Keller (42) has reported that the middle-aged, rather than the elderly, rank lowest in general death fear. This latter position is at variance with a carefully conducted study by Gesser, Wong, and Reker (93). These authors began by constructing a multidimensional Death Attitude Profile to meet both rational and empirical criteria and then administered it to 50 respondents in each of three age groups: the young (18–25), the middle-aged (35–50), and the elderly (60+). As predicted, general fear of death and dying displayed a curvilinear relationship with age such that death anxiety was relatively high in the young, peaked in middle adulthood, and was minimal in old age. Moreover, various aspects of death acceptance were also endorsed more frequently by the elderly than by other groups. Future use of multidimensional inventories like the DAP could help clarify discrepancies in findings that arise from the use of theoretically unidimensional scales with diverse populations.

Finally, it must be acknowledged that a handful of studies (21, 35, 94–96) have failed to find the expected negative relationship between age and death anxiety. For the most part, however, these represent studies that employ subjects of a restricted age range or that rely on less conventional measures of death concern. Thus, although recent research is not entirely uniform in its conclusions, the majority of published work now supports the view that death anxiety tends to decrease with age.

As with sex differences in death anxiety, the negative correlation of age with death fear is more obvious than its explanation. For example, the more positive attitude toward death and dying in the elderly could reflect the diminished quality of their health and lives, their greater religiosity, their more extensive experience in having "worked through" the deaths of parents, peers, and partners or the fact that their expectation to live a certain number of years has been met (c.f.36). As yet, which of these reasons (if any) is most appropriate is a matter of speculation.

A second topic that deserves research attention concerns variations in death anxiety *within* the elderly population. For example, while nursing home residents may generally experience less fear of dying than younger persons (33), there is some evidence that the "old-old" (75 +) in such institutions may become more death anxious than their "young-old" (60–75) fellow residents (86). This resurgence of fear of death as assessed by the DAS may reflect an exacerbation of anxieties about the pain involved in dying or about the subjective proximity of death, however, rather than fear of the state of death per se. This would seem to be a plausible hypothesis, given that death anxiety in this group was heightened for residents within diminished functional ability or subjective health. But a definitive answer to such questions requires a multidimensional assessment of death orientation that has not yet been attempted with subjects of this advanced age. Investigators who wish to study such age effects across the life span would do well to consider the use of interview as well as questionnaire techniques, as Wass and Forfar (27) suggest.

OCCUPATION

When he first surveyed the literature on occupational differences in death attitudes 20 years ago, Lester (5) could find little sense in investigators' choice of vocational categories for comparison. In contrast, the recent research in the area is much more focused, studying mainly those workers who in some way encounter death or its possibility as part of their professional roles.

Much of the current research extends that of Feifel and his colleagues (97), who reported in the late 1960s that physicians and medical students, relative to other groups, tend to display exaggerated death anxiety. However, attempts to replicate this finding have produced negative or equivocal results (c.f. 13). For example, Howells and Field (89) administered simple Likert ratings of fear of personal death and dying and apprehension about the dying of others to 178 medical students and a comparable number of social science students. They reported no significant differences between the groups. Similarly, Neimeyer, Bagley, and Moore (64) could detect no differences between allied health professionals enrolled in death education courses and their classmates, on either the DAS or the subscales of the Collett-Lester. Thus, current data do not support the earlier contention that medical professionals are significantly more apprehensive about death and dying than relevant comparison groups.

Of course, the fact that the *average* health care worker is not unusually death anxious does not negate the possibility that at least some facets of death are distressing to many such individuals. A second study by Field and Howells (98) reinforces this view. Surveying 98 medical students on what aspects of death they found most disturbing, they found that fully 84 percent expressed worries about dying themselves, especially fears of pain and loss. Worries about someone close to them dying, with an emphasis on the emotional impact that such bereavement would have on them, affected 91 percent. Concerns about interacting with terminal patients, particularly in terms of their own awkwardness in communicating with the dying, were shared by 76 percent. Across domains, it was striking that most of the fears expressed by these students referred more to their own reactions than to those of others who would be affected. This finding might reflect their stage of life rather than their chosen profession, however, since others have found that one of the more distasteful aspects of death for older physicians is their inability to provide for their dependents (99).

Of course, these analyses for the death attitudes of health care workers leave unanswered the more critical question of how such personal concerns might influence their professional behavior. A handful of recent studies have addressed this issue, and it is beginning to appear that the impact may be significant. Neimeyer, Behnke, and Reiss (100) for example, administered the TI, along with a questionnaire soliciting probable reactions to hypothetical patient deaths, to a group of neonatal physicians. They discovered that highly threatened physicians were more likely to respond to patient death with "avoidance strategies," such as attempting to lose themselves in their work. In contrast, less threatened doctors were more likely to acknowledge personal psychophysiological distress caused by the death of a patient and reported that they would be more likely to attend the patient's funeral. Methodologically divergent work by Kane and Hogan (101) tends to support the view that a more repressive stance may be adopted by highly death anxious physicians.

Perhaps the most critical question of all concerns the effect of a health care professional's death attitudes on his or her direct patient care. Although Momeyer (102) has argued that it is death denial, rather than anxiety per se, that determines a caregiver's treatment of a patient nearing death, emerging evidence indicates that death fear is also a relevant variable. For instance, Eakes (94) gave the DAS to 159 nursing home personnel and found that those who were more death anxious also held more negative attitudes toward the aged. It remains to be established whether such attitudinal negativity is subtly expressed in nurse/patient interaction. In the case of physicians, data are even more provocative. Eggerman and Dustin (80), for example, have reported that medical students who are highly threatened by the prospect of their own death are likely to consider more factors before deciding whether to inform terminal patients of their diagnoses. But the clearest indication of the behavioral impact of death anxiety comes from the research of Schulz and Aderman (103), who assessed the death attitudes of 24 physicians and then surreptitiously examined hospital records of dying patients treated by each. As they predicted, the average final hospital stay of patients treated by the more death anxious physicians was five days longer than that of terminal patients treated by their less anxious colleagues. Given the emotional and financial cost of prolonged heroic measures on the one hand, and their potential for saving lives on the other, the results of this study deserve careful replication.

A more limited literature has begun to address the death attitudes of other occupational groups outside the medical professions. Amenta and Weiner (104) have administered the DAS to 100 hospice volunteers and found it to be correlated with several indices of psychological maladjustment. Amenta (105) also compared the death anxiety scores of volunteers who withdrew from the program before serving one year with those who continued to work with the dying patients. As predicted, these dropouts were found to have significantly higher DAS scores than the persisters, suggesting one possible criterion for future volunteer selection.

Neimeyer and Dingemans (60) have examined the death orientation of another paraprofessional group—suicide prevention volunteers. Administering a full battery of death attitude measures to 54 workers at a crisis center and 62 nonvolunteer controls, they found the suicide interventionists to be higher on the DS and DyS subscales of the Collett-Lester, on the TI, and on Lester's Fear of Death Scale (7). This pattern of results clearly implied that suicide workers experienced heightened anxieties about their own deaths but not about the deaths of others. Moreover, this appeared to represent a self-selection effect, since novice and veteran interventionists did not differ on any of these dimensions. However, a subsequent attempt by Neimeyer and Neimeyer (79) to replicate this finding using the DAS actually produced the opposite results, with suicide interventionists scoring *lower* than demographically similar controls. Thus, there is no clear evidence that volunteers who work with life-threatening callers are more death anxious than comparison groups. Moreover, it is questionable whether those interventionists who are more fearful of death are less skillful than those who are less fearful, since data from the latter study (79) found no correlation between the DAS and a validated and reliable test of suicide counseling skills (106).

Findings are also equivocal concerning the distinctive death attitudes of funeral directors relative to other professionals. Rockwell (84) presented evidence that funeral directors and psychiatrists may have lower DAS scores than psychologists and suicidologists, but these results failed to attain statistical significance. Similarly, Schell and Zinger (48) reported that practicing funeral directors, while comparable to funeral service students in death anxiety, scored lower on the DAS than a group of university students. However, a reexamination of their data suggests that the apparently lower scores of the funeral directors may principally reflect the much lower percentage of women in that sample compared to in the student group, a confound that the authors did not acknowledge. One of the few clear-cut occupational differences reported in the recent literature occurs between firefighters and police officers on the one hand and college faculty and business students on the other (107). The former groups seem to show more apprehension about their own dying than the latter (as measured by the DS and DyS subscales of the CL) but do not differ in their concern about the deaths of others. This finding, however, stands in need of replication.

In summary, a good deal of research has now been conducted on the death attitudes of people employed in various death-relevant work settings. However, in reviewing this literature, I would argue for a distinction between *death exposure* occupations and *death risk* occupations in future research. The former would refer to professions such as medicine, nursing, and funeral services which may entail contact with the deaths of others, whereas the latter represent careers such as law enforcement, firefighting, and active military service, in which one's own life may be in jeopardy. Current evidence indicates that while workers in death risk occupations may experience elevated death anxiety, members of death exposure professions do not. However, it remains true that a certain percentage of the latter do express heightened fear of death, and data are beginning to suggest that this may adversely affect the quality of care they provide to patients. This issue may rank as the most important area for further research in vocational studies of death attitudes.

HEALTH STATUS

Despite the intuitive importance of the topic, relatively little research has been conducted on the relationship between physical illness and death anxiety. This relationship has been studied by Mullins and Lopez (86), however, who found that nursing home patients reported worse health and diminished functional ability scored higher on the DAS, regardless of their age. Other work by Kureshi and Husain (108) has reported that smokers outscore nonsmokers on the DAS, indirectly reinforcing the conclusion that perceived health has an impact on death concern. But two additional studies qualify the interpretation of this research. The first (91) compared 100 subjects, divided equally among the following groups: a) healthy individuals, b) persons having routine medical checkups, c) rheumatoid arthritics, d) diabetics, and e) cancer patients. In contrast to the above studies, the investigators could detect no differences among the various subject groups on the TI, DAS, or CL. However, they did find a significant relationship between various dimensions of death anxiety and personality variables, as will be discussed below. The second study (35) compared large numbers of patients and nonpatients using the Gottschalk interview-based measure of death anxiety. It was found that a) ill persons displayed higher death concern than the well, b) surgical patients were more death anxious than other patients, c) acutely ill patients were more fearful of death than chronically ill patients, and d) those persons receiving treatment in their own homes were less apprehensive than those treated in hospital settings. But still more interesting was the finding that the expression of death anxiety in patients may be adaptive, insofar as it was associated with positive affect and mastery as well as a certain amount of anger and uncertainty. In nonpatient groups, on the other hand, it was related only to anger and negative effect. Thus, while this study reinforces (and refines) previous reports of a connection between death anxiety and health status, it also helps reinterpret their significance.

Geilen and Roche (109) have made a valuable contribution to this literature by studying the death anxiety of a small group of Huntington's disease patients in some detail. They found that as the illness progressed, patients showed an increasing level of depression and concern for physical and emotional care. But death anxiety was widely dispersed, with a consensus only emerging that death represented a relief—to the point that over one-third of the patients considered suicide an option to continuing to live with the illness. Studies of this kind imply that much could be learned about the fluctuating death anxiety that characterizes different "illness trajectories" if more investigators adopted a longitudinal perspective in their work.

BIRTH ORDER

Two recent studies have examined the impact of birth order on death orientation, with similar results. Eckstein and Tobacyk (110) administered the Threat Index to 118 college students and found that first-borns, as predicted, displayed greater death threat than later born siblings. These results have been conceptually replicated by McDonald and Carroll using the DAS (111). Thus, although the data are scant, they are consistent in pointing up the greater death apprehension of first-born and only children. Although Eckstein and Tobacyk's Adlerian interpretation of this finding in terms of birth-order effects on lifestyle is plausible, no empirically tested explanation of these differences is currently available.

EDUCATION

The relationship between educational background and death attitudes has been another curiously neglected topic over the last decade. Nelson's large scale survey study (23) provides the strongest argument that education serves as a buffer against death anxiety, with years of schooling correlating negatively with both the death denial and death avoidance factors of his multidimensional inventory. However, Viney (35) has reported conflicting results using an interview-based measure with an equally large Australian sample. Whether this discrepancy in results reflects the tenuousness of the relationship between education and death concern or methodological or cultural confounds cannot be determined at this time. However, Neimeyer and his colleagues (64) have recently reported that education, while unrelated to either the DAS or CL in their more modest sample of community college students, was associated with several aspects of cognitive structure regarding the meaning of death. For example, more educated respondents tended to have more coherent, flexible, and certain systems for construing death, as measured by an adaptation of repertory grid technique (18). Thus, while these rather divergent studies do not permit generalization, they do suggest that education might be included as a variable in future death attitude research.

EXPERIENCE WITH DEATH

Tokunuga (112) has provided a recent review of the relatively small empirical literature on the effect of bereavement on death attitudes. He concluded that "with varying degrees of certainty these studies reach the same conclusion: suffering the death of a close friend or relative has little or no effect upon survivors' feelings about their own impending mortality" (p. 272). In line with this conclusion, Neimeyer, Dingemans, and Epting (37) were unable to discover any relationship between previous personal experience with death or bereavement, on the one hand, and death concern as measured by the TI, Lester Scale, or direct self-report of death fear on the other. Similarly, Pratt, Hare, and Wright (113) found death of a friend or relative to have no impact on death anxiety as measured by the DAS. While more positive findings might be yielded by systematic studies that would take into consideration the temporal and emotional context of these death encounters (e.g., age at which a family member was lost), this area currently seems less pressing than others in the death anxiety literature.

CULTURAL AND SUBCULTURAL FACTORS

The consideration of cultural influences on death anxiety is of comparatively recent origin. For the most part, this work consists of fairly large scale administrations of the DAS to broadly similar samples of different nationalities. This approach is exemplified by the work of Mercer, Bunting, and Snook (114), who asked 315 university students from conflict-torn Northern Ireland and 302 from the much more tranquil Republic of Ireland to respond to the instrument. As expected, the Northern Ireland students obtained higher DAS scores, and this exaggerated death anxiety was especially evident for those who had experienced the country's civil unrest firsthand. Lonetto and his coworkers (77) failed to conceptually replicate this finding, however, in a comparison of similarly large samples of students from Canada and Northern Ireland. But they did discover distinctive dimensions of death fear in the two cultures—Canadians reported more frequent thoughts of death, and the Irish showed greater concern for the shortness of life and fear of viewing a corpse.

Comparisons of Eastern and Western cultures have also been conducted, though with mixed results. McMordie and Kumar (50) have reviewed a number of unpublished cross-cultural studies using the McMordie revision of the DAS and concluded that, on the average, Western samples (e.g., Australia, Canada) score higher than Eastern (e.g., India). This finding is at variance with a more modest study conducted by Beshai and Templer (115), who were unable to detect any average differences between 45 Egyptian printers and 100 American public health workers on the DAS.

Subcultural or ethnic differences in death anxiety have also begun to be addressed in this country. Three separate studies have reported that in samples ranging in age from the late teens (78, 116) to old age (34), blacks tend to report greater fears than whites. Although subcultural differences in subjective sense of control over one's life may help account for this finding (115; see below), a satisfactory explanation of this effect has yet to be established.

In summary, while the recent interest in cultural and subcultural correlates of death anxiety is commendable, it is also fairly unfocused and preliminary. Much more attention needs to be paid to the potential mechanisms that mediate the development of death attitudes in various cultural or ethnic groups. It is perhaps in this area, more than any other, that the disciplinary limitations of psychology have tended to constrict the range of topics studied and methods employed. Since the cultural factors that inculcate particular attitudes toward death clearly seem to transcend the processes at work in individuals and even small groups, multidisciplinary efforts that involve sociologists and anthropologists in addition to psychologists clearly will be required in the future.

Personality Factors

While psychologists have generated a good deal of data concerning the relationship between situational factors and death attitudes, the study of personality has unquestionably been closer to their traditional area of concern. For this reason, the literature that has emerged concerning the relationship between personality factors and death anxiety, while not necessarily more extensive than that on demographic correlates, tends to be somewhat more systematic. For convenience, I have interpreted "personality" broadly to include factors ranging from religious orientation through psychopathology to general lifestyle. No commitment to an individualistic conception of these variables is implied by this classification.

SOCIAL DESIRABILITY

Reviewing the research on the psychology of death conducted through the late 1970s, Kastenbaum and Costa (3) observed that study of the influence of a social desirability set on reports of death anxiety had been neglected. They strongly recommended that future investigators examine whether respondents to their questionnaires were modifying their answers in what they believed to be a socially approved direction. This examination has now been conducted for each of the major instruments used in the area. For example, Krieger and his associates (38) found no relationship between the Marlowe-Crowne Social Desirability Scale and the Threat Index in either its interview or paper and pencil forms. Similarly, Loo (117) found the Collett-Lester to be unrelated to the Lie Scale of the Eysenck Personality Inventory. Only the DAS appears to be susceptible to a social desirability bias in both its original (24) and revised versions (46). To the extent that future investigators continue to rely upon the DAS, these findings suggest that they pair it with a social desirability measure and control the influence of this extraneous variable through covariance methods before interpreting their results.

RELIGIOUS BELIEF

In his earlier review, Pollack (13) chose to ignore what he termed "the whole confusing area of death anxiety as it relates to religious attitudes and beliefs" (p. 97). Fortunately, the increasing attention to this area over the last decade permits a somewhat clearer view of this domain. As with situational correlates of fear of death, attempts to study the relationship of religion to death concern began with attempts to establish simple group differences between subjects classed according to religious belief. In general, less focused studies which include only a simple face-valid measure of religiosity have produced equivocal results. For example, Krieger and his associates (9) could detect no differences on the TI between students who did and did not believe in an afterlife, and McMordie (46) found no correlation between his version of the DAS and self-rated religiosity in a group of over 300 undergraduates. Similar negative results have been reported by Pratt and her colleagues (113), who found the DAS to be unrelated to a simple rating of "the importance of religion" in the perspectives of 96 early childhood educators. On the other hand, relatively unsophisticated indices of religious belief have yielded positive results in a few studies. For example, Neimeyer and his collaborators (37) found Jews to score higher than Protestants on the TI, and Wagner and Lorion (96) discovered a negative correlation between death anxiety and frequency of church attendance in a group of 40 institutionalized elderly. Nonetheless, the relationship between these direct, unidimensional assessments of religiosity and death fear are seldom robust, even when they attain statistical significance (c.f. 77, 78).

Investigators who adopt a more refined view of religiosity report more complex results. Rigdon and Epting (62), for instance, administered the TI and CL to 95 college students and learned that those who experienced less death fear and threat were more likely to express a stronger belief in an afterlife, report more frequent church attendance, and engage in more religious reading. But work by Downey (118) suggests that the relationship between religious belief and death anxiety may not be a simple linear one. She administered a well-constructed religiosity scale along with Boyar's Fear of Death Scale to a sample of 237 middle class men and found no significant relationship between death fear and either religious affiliation or self-rated religiosity. Instead, she discovered a *curvilinear* relationship, such that men who were moderately religious were more death anxious than either those who were clear believers or nonbelievers. This implies that ambivalence of belief, rather than religiosity per se, is the critical variable affecting one's apprehension about dying.

A recent study by Tobacyk (119) further clarifies the components of belief that are effective in reducing death threat. Administering the TI and a multidimensional Paranormal Belief Scale to an undergraduate sample, he found that only traditional religious belief was negatively correlated with death threat. In contrast, other varieties of nonscientific belief (e.g., in witchcraft, ESP, and superstitions) were associated with increased thoughts of death and dying. He interpreted these findings as indicative of the greater institutional and social support given to the former as opposed to the latter.

But even belief in traditional religious systems may have its drawbacks, as suggested by Florian and Kravetz (120). These investigators gave a well-designed Fear of Personal Death Scale to 178 Israeli Jews, along with an established measure of religious practice. Results indicated that although moderately religious respondents scored higher on some dimensions of death fear (e.g., concern over the consequences of one's death on family and friends), highly religious subjects scored higher on others (e.g., fear of punishment in the afterlife). Thus, it appears that more and less religious persons may have qualitatively different, as well as quantitatively different, anxieties about death.

Even if a stable relationship between strength of religious conviction and death fear is beginning to be identified, its meaning is open to interpretation. For example, while religious belief may genuinely assuage death anxieties, it may also simply help repress them, since they may be incompatible with one's verbalized belief in a benign god. A fascinating study by Kunzendorf (121) has recently examined this issue. Kunzendorf administered a series of face-valid questions concerning fear of death to 50 college students under two conditions—when they were in a normal state of consciousness and when they were in a hypnotically induced trance. In the trance state, students were instructed to let their "subconscious minds" "automatically" write true answers to the same death anxiety questions. As predicted by the repression hypothesis, one dimension of death fear—fear of inexistence—was greater under hypnosis, an effect that was especially pronounced among students who professed a conscious belief in an afterlife. This raises the possibility that some varieties of religious belief may merely suppress, rather than extinguish, deeper level fears about one's mortality.

Finally, it should be mentioned that religion may have other effects on one's death attitudes, aside from affecting their simple positivity or negativity. For example, Feifel and Nagy (21) found that religious members of a diverse group of men displayed more *consistent* attitudes toward death, as measured by their multilevel assessment of death fear. This finding is reinforced by the work of Neimeyer, Bagley, and Moore (64), who found that believers in an afterlife may have more coherent and less uncertain understandings of death-related situations, irrespective of their positivity. Thus, future work on the psychology of religion could include more sophisticated assessments of the structure of belief systems about death, which may vary considerably within, as well as between, members of particular denominations.

MALADJUSTMENT

Since death fear, threat, and anxiety are typically conceived to be distressing, it is logical to raise the question of whether they are related in any systematic way to other forms of psychological distress. A good deal of research has focused on this topic in the last 10 years, and the resulting evidence strongly suggests a relationship between conscious death anxiety and broader maladjustment.

At a general level, Howells and Field (89) administered a neuroticism scale to over 300 medical and social science students along with a measure of death anxiety and discovered a low, but positive, correlation between the two. These findings are reinforced by Loo's (117) similar results with an undergraduate sample. Moreover, Vargo and Black (122) found that the DAS correlated negatively with personality measures assessing well-being, self-control, and tolerance in a group of first-year medical students. Thus, these studies point to an association between death anxiety and neurotic symptoms, a finding that is compatible with the older literature in this area (13).

Recent research has also attempted to establish the connection between death concerns and more specific expressions of psychopathology. Not surprisingly, given the term "death anxiety" itself, much of this work has concentrated on a possible link to state and trait anxiety. In general, this research has indicated that subjects with exaggerated death anxiety (37, 54, 77, 87, 104), fear (117), and threat (59) also obtain higher scores on traditional anxiety scales, particularly those assessing its more enduring, characterological forms. Multidimensional investigation of this relationship using the Hoelter scale has suggested that the link between general and death-specific anxiety is a global one, since both trait and state anxiety are significantly correlated with seven out of eight of the MFODS subscales (123).

Nor do recent studies indicate that the link between maladjustment and death concern is accounted for only by its relationship to anxiety per se. For example, Amenta and Weiner (104) found that more death anxious hospice workers displayed not only greater generalized anxiety but also more frustration, suspiciousness, and guilt proneness. But it is noteworthy that the pattern of association between fear of death and other psychological disorders may vary with the population being studied. This is illustrated by the factor analytic work of Gilliland and Templer (54), who found that general and death anxiety both loaded on the same factor in a normal population but were sharply distinguished in a psychiatric comparison group. In the latter group, where maladjustment was much more significant, death anxiety was clearly separable from depression and anxiety, but it accounted for only 5 percent of the variation in this more disturbed group.

The fact that death anxiety has been found to correlate with depression (54, 87), one of the more serious and potentially lethal forms of psychological disturbance, raises the question of whether death concern should be a separate focus of treatment for depressive patients. Preliminary data provided by Templer, Ruff, and Simpson (123) suggest that the answer is no. Administering the DAS and a depression scale to psychiatric inpatients on admission and discharge, they found that when depressive symptoms were accompanied by elevated death anxiety, the latter subsided with symptomatic treatment of the depression alone. This implies that fear of death tends to form part of a constellation of problems in more disturbed populations and need not be a direct target of intervention. Of course, this generalization is unlikely to hold for particular psychiatric subgroups (e.g., the psychotic individual with delusions about slowly dying), who may require that psychotherapy focus on their death fears more directly.

Finally, the link between death anxiety and depression raises the possibility that death attitudes may play a role in promoting or inhibiting suicidal behavior. To date, researchers have failed to find any connection between death threat and suicide ideation (9), but this has remained a badly underinvestigated area. However, Rigdon (124) has reported a suggestive case study of a young man who was administered the Threat Index several weeks before and shortly after making a serious attempt on his life. His death threat score fell dramatically from the first to second testing, reflecting more a devaluation of himself than a more favorable evaluation of death per se. Since suicide represents an often tragic form of elective death, elucidating the relationship between death attitudes and self-destruction should be given greater priority in future work.

SELF-ACTUALIZATION

Just as interest has increased in the connection between death anxiety and maladjustment, interest has also grown in the possible link between minimal death anxiety and optimal functioning. The occasional studies that had addressed this issue prior to the late 1970s generally supported the view that more competent individuals who experienced a greater sense of purpose in life also experienced less death anxiety (13).

More recent research adds considerable weight to this conclusion. Several studies have been consistent in pointing to a negative correlation between measures of death fear and anxiety and such indices of self-actualization as the Purpose In Life Test (27, 125), self-esteem scales (73, 76), and various subscales of the Personal Orientation Inventory (126, 127). Similar findings have emerged even when investigators initiated the study with contrary hypotheses. For example, Aronow and his associates (81) administered the DAS and seven self-relevant measures to 117 college students to test the prediction that individuals who highly value themselves would be more afraid of death. In contrast, results indicated that subjects who reported greater subjective well-being scored *lower* on the DAS than more self-devaluing subjects. Thus, the tendency of more actualized individuals to express minimal fear of death is one of the more extensively replicated findings in the literature.

One coherent line of research to arise in this area stems from the work of Neimeyer and Chapman (128). Basing their argument on existential philosophy, they hypothesized that individuals whose life projects were incomplete, whose current identities were discrepant with their ideals, would show greater fear of death than would their more actualized peers. To test this, they derived a self-ideal discrepancy measure from the Threat Index and compared it to scores on the CL and DAS taken by 101 noncollege adults. As predicted, they found that subjects with less self-ideal discrepancy (i.e., those who were more actualized) reported less general death anxiety on the DAS and less fear of Death of Self and Death and Dying of Others on the CL. The only dimension of death concern on which more and less actualized respondents did not differ was fear of Dying of Self, an aspect of death anxiety that might be more related to other factors, such as apprehension about the pain that dying might entail.

An interesting replication of this study was subsequently performed by Wood and Robinson (129). Administering the same questionnaires to an undergraduate sample, they found that highly actualized respondents scored lower on the CL but not on the DAS. Moreover, of the CL subscales, only DyS failed to correlate with level of actualization, again fitting the Neimeyer and Chapman pattern. But Wood and Robinson also found that *within* the high actualization group, subjects who were also more "integrated" (i.e., showed more compatibility or less "threat" in their construing of self and death) scored even lower on the CL and DAS than the equally actualized, but less integrated, comparison group. This suggested to them an "additive hypothesis," with both factors contributing to the prediction of the individual's level of death anxiety. A follow-up test of this hypothesis seemed to provide support for this view (130).

In a dramatic test of the robustness of the effect of actualization on death concern, Robinson and Wood (91) then tested a group of 100 adult subjects, who varied in health status from quite healthy to seriously ill (e.g., diabetics and cancer patients). Perhaps counterintuitively, they found that health status was unrelated to level of death fear or anxiety. Actualization, on the other hand, correlated with scores on the DAS, as well as both self-relevant subscales of the CL. However, they were unable to demonstrate an additive effect between actualization and integration, contrary to their previous findings. A subsequent test of the additive hypothesis conducted by Neimeyer (92) also failed to uncover any interaction between the two variables in predicting death anxiety, although each was significantly related to different aspects of death fear. In combination, these studies reinforce the relationship between actualization and minimal death concerns, but questions remain about how psychological adjustment interplays with other factors in predicting death attitudes.

TEMPORAL ORIENTATION

In contrast to the relatively well-researched areas of religiosity, maladjustment, and self-actualization, other personality factors have received less attention in the thanatology literature. This is exemplified by the work on the relationship between temporal orientation and death anxiety. Reviewing the older literature in this area, Pollack (13) concluded that anxious preoccupation with death was linked to a tendency to live in the past rather than the future, to eschew experimentation and change, and, in general, to choose safety over novelty in life. The few relevant studies that have been conducted in the last decade add little by way of elaboration or qualification to this picture. Vargo and Batsel (126) replicated the finding that less death-anxious subjects adopt a more present orientation than those with greater death fears, and Neimeyer and his associates (64) reported that individuals with a greater personal fear of death and dying on the CL tended to cognitively "postpone" death by projecting a longer life expectancy. On the other hand, Joubert (131) could establish no relationship between subjective acceleration of time and death anxiety as measured by the DAS. Thus, the relatively scant evidence that has accumulated suggests that death anxiety may be more related to broader temporal orientation to past, present and future than to one's moment-to-moment sense of time passing, although this conclusion clearly stands in need of more empirical support.

LOCUS OF CONTROL

Pollack's earlier review (13) found inconclusive evidence for a connection between fear of death and locus of control, a person's sense of whether the ability to determine one's life resides with oneself or with external forces. Although only a few studies have concentrated on this issue in recent years, they help consolidate and flesh out our understanding of this relationship. Vargo and Black (95) found that medical students having a more internal locus of control experienced less death anxiety, reinforcing the majority opinion among previous investigators. Moreover, Peterson (132) discovered that the DAS showed a weak, but significant, correlation with mistrust of government, and a negative correlation with one's own sense of political efficacy. This finding is interesting, since it establishes a link between one's attitudes toward death and government, both of which are certainly important external loci of control over our lives.

Two additional studies provide a somewhat more refined view of the association between locus of control and death concern. The first, by Hunt and his coworkers (107), found that a belief in control by chance was related only to fear of personal death and dying on the CL, whereas belief in control by powerful others had more pervasive links to all four facets of death fear indexed by the instrument. The second, by Sadowski, Davis, and Loftus-Vergari (74), clarifies the interaction between locus of control and gender in determining death anxiety. These authors administered the DAS and a three-factor, locus-of-control scale to 375 college students, and learned that females were generally both more death anxious and more external, a finding that may help explain the sex differences in death orientation reviewed above. Still more interesting, however, was their finding that for men, greater death anxiety correlated with a pervasive sense of fatalism, whereas for women, it was related more to a sense of control by the larger social system. For both sexes, however, death anxiety was minimal for persons who experienced heightened feelings of self-control in their lives. Thus, these studies are reasonably consistent in suggesting that, at least within Western societies, death anxiety is associated with the feeling of being at the mercy of external forces beyond one's control. Whether this more passive, resigned posture might be associated with death acceptance in particular personal or cultural contexts has yet to be examined.

REPRESSION

Thanatological interest in repression has waned somewhat since direct questionnaires have attained virtual methodological hegemony in the death-anxiety literature. But in line with the older literature (13), there remains a lingering suspicion among researchers that low scores on death anxiety questionnaires may be obtained by subjects with repressive or defensive personality styles. This possibility has been given credence by a handful of recent studies. Tobacyk and Eckstein (59) for example, administered the Threat Index and a repression-sensitization scale to over 100 students and found that those with lower threat scores also scored as more extreme repressors. Kane and Hogan have reported similar results in a physician group using the DAS (101). Both of these studies offer at least correlational support for the proposition that reduced death anxiety may be a function of a defensive personality style aimed at avoiding, rather than confronting, threatening stimuli.

Two experimental studies also have examined the repression-death anxiety link. The first, by Handal (133), involved 159 female college students in a hypothetical life-or-death problem solving task under group and individual conditions. He discovered that low death-anxiety subjects performed better in the latter, but not the former, condition and interpreted this as evidence that they effectively repressed extraneous stimuli under the "simpler" instructional set. The more parsimonious interpretation—that the poorer showing of the highly death-anxious group reflected the disruptive effects of anxiety—was not entertained. Consequently, the conclusion that low scorers were repressors remains dubious, although the study does represent one of the few attempts to employ a genuine experimental design in this area.

The second experiment, by Kunzendorf (121), yields clearer conclusions. As noted above under the review of religiosity on death concern, Kunzendorf used hypnotic suggestion to instruct subjects to "automatically" write their true reactions to death-anxiety questions, and discovered that such responses were greater than for the same subjects under a normal test-taking set. To the extent that the trance state permitted Kunzendorf to circumvent his subjects' usual defenses in responding to questions about fears of inexistence, this study raises important questions about the interpretation of scores on face-valid questionnaires. Among other things, it suggests the need for future researchers to distinguish between individuals who express little death anxiety as a result of repressing their actual death fears and those who are more genuinely unafraid of their mortality.

CHANGES IN DEATH ANXIETY RESULTING FROM DEATH EDUCATION

With few exceptions, the studies reviewed in this chapter have treated death anxiety as a stable individual trait and have examined its relationship to a host of situational and personality factors. In contrast, the studies reviewed in this final section have considered death orientation to be a more malleable state that can be altered by relatively brief educational interventions. As we will see, these intervention studies have produced mixed results.

As Warren (134) observed, many death education programs have at least implicitly adopted the reduction of death anxiety as a primary goal, one which has occasionally been met. Tobacyk and Eckstein (59), for instance, were able to demonstrate that a semester-long undergraduate thanatology course produced a greater decrease in death threat than did unrelated course work, even though death education students had lower TI scores than controls at the outset. But even in studies in which an antianxiety effect has been found, it does not necessarily generalize across instruments. For example, Rosenthal (135) administered both the DAS and Nelson's three-factor scale to a class of death education students and controls before and after their five-week courses. She found that thanatology students showed reduced death avoidance, disengagement, and death fear on the Nelson inventory across time, but no comparable changes on the DAS. This suggests that when changes in death anxiety result from educational experiences, they may be limited in their generality.

Perhaps a more common finding is that such interventions have no predictable impact on death attitudes at all. Several studies of interventions as diverse as brief death-awareness exercises (62), professional workshops (136), hypnosis (137), counseling groups (138), and behavior therapy (149) have failed to produce any mean change in death threat and anxiety in their experimental groups. But the failure to detect a mean effect in these studies cannot be taken as evidence that they have no effect. This point was vividly illustrated in a study by Rainey and Epting (58), who found that although students' average scores on the TI did not change across the course of a semester of death education, the variance of their scores increased threefold. No such change occurred in a control group subjects. In other words, death education seemed to destabilize students' construing of themselves in relation to death, but whether this resulted in their experiencing increased or decreased death threat was a highly individual matter. The reality of "negative" (i.e., anxiety-provoking) outcomes should be taken seriously, in light of the fact that some studies have actually reported that death fears were aggravated by death education (139), especially in sensitive medical contexts (140, 141).

A well-designed study by Durlak (82) sheds some light on the anxiety-provoking and anxiety-alleviating aspects of these interventions. The intervention consisted of an eight-hour workshop covering emotional reactions to grief and death and communication with the terminally ill, which was offered to a broad spectrum of hospital personnel. However, this same material was presented in one condition in purely didactic form (through lectures and films) and in a second condition with a more experiential component (using role plays and death-awareness exercises). When he compared the outcome of both groups with a no-intervention control group, Durlak discovered that DAS scores increased over time for all groups, suggesting a sensitization effect that may have been attributable to serial completion of the DAS itself. In contrast, scores on the Lester fear of death score rose for subjects in the didactic and control conditions but dropped for those in the more experiential workshop. Thus, it appears that heavily didactic forms of death education may be most at risk for provoking greater death fear.

The variability of these findings underscores Warren's (134) caveat that the anxiety-reduction model of death education may be inadequate to deal with the complex personal meanings with which different students shroud death. Examined from a different angle, they also remind us of the limits of our understanding of death anxiety and the factors that influence it. Although much has been learned about death anxiety and its correlates, perhaps the most important lessons of the above review concern the limitations of the research conducted to date. As a constructive response to these shortcomings, I will conclude with a few observations to guide future research in this area.

CONCLUSIONS

A fair evaluation of the current state of death anxiety research yields a more optimistic conclusion than did similar evaluations written a decade ago (3, 13, 14). Although this research has proceeded somewhat haphazardly, it has nonetheless addressed and partially surmounted many of the shortcomings of the earlier literature. Among the more tangible signs of progress in the area is the development of improved methodology, as reflected in the much greater concern of investigators with the psychometric precision of the instruments they use to assess death attitudes. Coupled with growing methodological sophistication has been a clearer recognition of the multidimensionality of death attitudes, leading to the refinement of older scales and the construction of new, more comprehensive instruments. The generalizability of research findings has also been bolstered, as investigators have sought larger and more diverse samples on which to base their conclusions. Finally, at least a few research groups have begun to conduct sustained lines of programmatic research which take greater cognizance of previously conducted studies.

As a result of the increase in both the quality and sheer volume of this literature, we now know more than we once did about the demographic and situational correlates of death anxiety. There now exists ample evidence for concluding that women express more fear of personal death than men, although the explanation of this sex difference is less clearly established. We are beginning to realize that death orientation is anything but stable across the course of adult development, showing instead subtle structural shifts and increased comfort with mortality in later life, at least among relatively healthy respondents. There are also data indicating that while pursuit of death exposure professions such as medicine does not necessarily predict high levels of death fear, individuals with exaggerated anxieties concerning death may enact their professional roles differently than their less anxious coworkers—perhaps to the detriment of their patients. Fear of death may be enhanced in other occupations, however, especially those that entail actual death risk to the worker (e.g., law enforcement, firefighting). How this affects job performance in these careers has yet to be examined.

Interestingly, health status does not seem to be the potent predictor of death anxiety that one might expect, perhaps due to the highly individualized ways in which individuals adapt to their illness. Other sociodemographic variables such as birth order, education, and acculturation display suggestive relationships to death anxiety, although work in these areas remains more germinal.

Substantial numbers of studies have also established connections between personality factors and attitudes toward death. In general, individuals with strong traditional religious beliefs or with the need to respond in a socially desirable fashion tend to report less death anxiety, though the extent to which this is the result of repression is difficult to estimate. Good evidence now supports the view that fear of death is often associated with other forms of psychological maladjustment, particularly anxiety and depression. Conversely, individuals who are more self-actualized appear more comfortable with their mortality. The literature also hints that apprehension about one's eventual death is associated with a tendency to cognitively "postpone" its occurrence and to focus instead on past events that may be subjectively safer to contemplate. In addition, there is general support for the contention that death anxiety is greatest for individuals who adopt an external locus of control in their lives, whereas persons with a greater sense of self-control view their deaths with greater equanimity.

Finally, we are starting to recognize that one's fears of death are not easily altered by even well-intentioned educational interventions. In fact, there is at least as much evidence that death education may arouse death anxiety as dampen it. This outcome should sensitize us to the complex and poorly understood processes by which we develop and revise our personal philosophies of life and death in response to relevant life experiences.

But despite this admittedly substantial literature, many of even the best researched areas contain unanswered questions. To a large degree, this reflects certain persistent conceptual and methodological inadequacies in the study of death anxiety. For example, although methodological advances have indeed occurred, they have typically had only a local impact, with the majority of investigators continuing to rely on simply administered but psychometrically ambiguous instruments devised in the early days of this literature. On the other hand, even those investigators who have devised new and more revealing assessment techniques typically have been too impatient in their use, rushing into application of their scales before undertaking the often arduous work of establishing their reliability and validity. As a consequence of these two trends, the death anxiety literature too often resembles a gray mosaic of randomly assembled studies, embellished by an occasionally brilliant, but fragile and isolated, investigation. On the conceptual side, the corpus of research on death attitudes is impoverished by its simplistic approach to the concept of "attitude" itself. As social psychologists remind us (142), attitudes can be identified as having affective, cognitive, and behavioral components. Yet thanatologists have operationally defined death attitudes in almost exclusively affective terms (hence the focus on fear and anxiety), leaving crucial cognitive and especially behavioral features of these attitudes virtually ignored. Since it is self-evident that human beings have the capacity to *think* about their mortality and to *act* on that basis, a thanatology that examines only their *feelings* about death is destined to remain fragmentary and disappointing. At a still more general level, far too much of the research on death orientation is atheoretical and opportunistic, addressing easily investigated issues rather than pursuing more scientifically incisive questions. When this is compounded by a heavy reliance on correlational, rather than genuinely experimental designs, the result is a body of knowledge that is vaguely suggestive, rather than clearly authoritative.

As scientific research on the psychology of death enters its fourth decade, we are presented with the opportunity to base our future work not only on the findings of these accumulated studies but also on a keener appreciation of their limitations. In this chapter, I have tried to highlight both the substance and the shortcomings of studies conducted to date in the hope that the fourth decade of research will be stronger than the preceding three. Understanding our relation to death is one of the most ancient and persistent questions that human beings have framed. If reasking the question in the context of current psychological research is to yield fresh answers, then we owe it to ourselves to be as systematic and articulate in our questioning as possible.

REVIEW QUESTIONS

1. Define death anxiety. In your view, to what extent do existing methods adequately capture the concept? How could you improve on the definitions of death anxiety used by psychologists?
2. Ninety-five percent of the research on death anxiety has involved the use of direct questionnaires. Do you believe that this approach is adequate? What is the basis for your belief? If you were to use nonquestionnaire measures of death anxiety, which measures would you choose and why?
3. Complete one of the questionnaires commonly used to study death anxiety (e.g., Templer's Death Anxiety Scale, the Threat Index, or the Collett-Lester Fear-of-Death Scale). What problems did you have filling out this questionnaire? How well do you feel it measured your personal fears of death?
4. Which aspects of Hoelter's Multidimensional Fear-of-Death Scale are most anxiety-provoking to you? Which are least anxiety-provoking? What life experiences do you think did most to shape your attitude toward these aspects of death?
5. Much research suggests that death anxiety changes as a function of age. How have your feelings toward death changed with the years?
6. What factors do you think account for the sex differences in death anxiety found in many studies? How might these differences change with the changing role of women in our society?
7. Research indicates that traditional religious views reduce one's fear of death but leaves open the question of whether this reflects genuine death acceptance or simply repression of unacceptable death anxiety. How do your own philosophy and theology of death influence your death attitudes?
8. Many studies indicate that death anxiety is higher in people who are maladjusted or less self-actualized. What relationship do you think exists between fear of death and psychological health? If there is a "psychologically healthy" way of viewing death, what do you think it would be?

REFERENCES

1. Becker, E. (1973). *The denial of death.* New York: Macmillan.
2. Choron, J. (1974). *Death and modern man.* New York: Macmillan.

3. Kastenbaum, R., & Costa, P. T. (1977). Psychological perspectives on death. *Annual Review of Psychology, 28,* 225-249.

4. Feifel, H. (Ed.). (1959). *The meaning of death.* New York: McGraw-Hill.

5. Lester, D. (1967). Experimental and correlational studies of the fear of death. *Psychological Bulletin, 67,* 27-36.

6. Kubler-Ross, E. (1969). *On death and dying.* New York: Macmillan.

7. Lester, D. (1967). Fear of death of suicidal persons. *Psychological Reports, 20,* 1077-1078.

8. Collett, L. J., & Lester, D. (1969). The fear of death and the fear of dying. *Journal of Psychology, 72,* 179-181.

9. Krieger, S. R., Epting, F. R., & Leitner, L. M. (1974). Personal constructs, threat, and attitudes toward death. *Omega, 5,* 299-310.

10. Templer, D. I. (1970). The construction and validation of a death anxiety scale. *Journal of General Psychology, 82,* 165-177.

11. Neimeyer, R. A. (1985). *The development of personal construct psychology.* Lincoln: Nebraska Press.

12. Mulkay, M. (1980). The sociology of science in east and west. *Current Sociology, 28,* 1-184.

13. Pollack, J. M. (1979). Correlates of death anxiety: A review of empirical studies. *Omega, 10,* 97-121.

14. Simpson, M. A. (1980). Studying death: Problems of methodology. *Death Education, 4,* 139-148.

15. Kalish, R. A. (1987). The study of death: A psychosocial perspective. In H. Wass, F. Berardo, & R. A. Neimeyer (Eds.), *Dying: Facing the facts* (2nd ed.). Washington, DC: Hemisphere.

16. Rigdon, M. A., Epting, F. R., Neimeyer, R. A., & Krieger, S. R. (1979). The Threat Index: A research report. *Death Education, 3,* 245-270.

17. Neimeyer, R. A., Epting, F. R., & Rigdon, M. A. (1984). A procedure manual for the Threat Index. In F. R. Epting & R. A. Neimeyer (Eds.), *Personal meanings of death* (235-242). Washington, DC: Hemisphere.

18. Kelly, G. A. (1955). *The psychology of personal constructs.* New York: Norton.

19. Feifel, H., & Branscomb, A. B. (1973). Who's afraid of death? *Journal of Abnormal Psychology, 81,* 282-288.

20. Feifel, H., & Nagy, V. T. (1980). Death orientation and life-threatening behavior. *Journal of Abnormal Psychology, 89,* 38-45.

21. Feifel, H., & Nagy, V. T. (1981). Another look at fear of death. *Journal of Consulting and Clinical Psychology, 49,* 278-286.

22. Warren, W. G., & Chopra, P. N. (1979a). An Australian survey of attitudes to death. *Australian Journal of Social Issues, 14,* 134-142.

23. Nelson, L. D. (1979). Structural conduciveness, personality characteristics and death anxiety. *Omega, 10,* 123-133.

24. Martin T. O. (1982). Death anxiety and social desirability among nurses. *Omega, 13,* 51-58.

25. Henry, W. E. (1973). *The analysis of fantasy.* Huntington, NY: Krieger.

26. Rhudick, P. J., & Dibner, A. S. (1961). Age, personality and health correlates of death concern in normal aged individuals. *Journal of Gerontology, 16,* 44-49.

27. Wass, H., & Forfar, C. S. (1982). Assessment of attitudes toward death: Techniques and instruments for use with older persons. *Measurement and Evaluation in Guidance, 15,* 210-220.

28. Epting, F. R., Rainey, L. C., & Weiss, M. J. (1979). Constructions of death and levels of death fear. *Death Education, 3,* 21-30.

29. Rigdon, M. A. (1983). Levels of death fear: A factor analysis. *Death Education, 6,* 365-373.

30. Lonetto, R. (1982). Personification of death and death anxiety. *Journal of Personality Assessment, 36,* 404-408.

31. Alexander, I. E., & Alderstein, A. M. (1958). Affective responses to the concept of death in a population of children and early adolescents. *Journal of Genetic Psychology, 93,* 167-177.

32. Wass, H., Corr, C. A., Pacholski, R. A., & Forfar, C. S. (1985). *Death Education II: An annotated resource guide.* Washington, DC: Hemisphere.

33. Devins, G. M. (1979). Death anxiety and voluntary passive euthanasia. *Journal of Consulting and Clinical Psychology, 47,* 301-309.

34. Sanders, J. F., Poole, T. E., & Rivero, W. T. (1980). Death anxiety among the elderly. *Psychological Reports, 46,* 53-56.

35. Viney, L. L. (1984). Concerns about death among severely ill people. In F. R. Epting & R. A. Neimeyer (Eds.), *Personal meanings of death* (143-158). Washington, DC: Hemisphere.

36. Kalish, R. A. (1977). The role of age in death attitudes. *Death Education, 1,* 205-230.

37. Neimeyer, R. A., Dingemans, P., & Epting, F. R. (1977). Convergent validity, situational stability and meaningfulness of the Threat Index. *Omega, 8,* 251-265.

38. Krieger, S. R., Epting, F. R., & Hays, L. H. (1979). Validity and reliability of provided constructs in assessing death threat. *Omega, 10,* 87-95.

39. Neimeyer, R. A., Fontana, D. J., & Gold, K. (1984). A manual for content analysis of death constructs. In F. R. Epting & R. A. Neimeyer (Eds.), *Personal meanings of death* (213-234). Washington, DC: Hemisphere.

40. Mount, E. (1983). Individualism and our fears of death. *Death Education, 7,* 25-31.

41. Kurlychek, R. T. (1978). Assessment of attitudes toward death and dying: A critical review of some available methods. *Omega, 9,* 37-47.

42. Keller, J. W., Sherry, D., & Piotrowski, D. (1984). Perspectives in death: A developmental study. *Journal of Psychology, 116,* 137-142.

43. Boyar, J. I. (1964). The construction and partial validation of a scale for the measurement of the fear of death. *Dissertation Abstracts, 25,* 2041.

44. Dickstein, L. (1972). Death concern: Measurement and correlates. *Psychological Reports, 30,* 563-571.

45. Nelson, L. D. (1978). The multidimensional measurement of death attitudes: Construction and validation of a three-factor instrument. *Psychological Record, 28,* 525-533.

46. McMordie, W. R. (1978). Improving measurement of death anxiety. *Psychological Reports, 44,* 975-980.

47. Warren, W. G., & Chopra, P. N. (1978). Some reliability and validity considerations on Australian data from the Death Anxiety Scale. *Omega, 9,* 293-299.

48. Schell, B. H., & Zinger, J. T. (1984). Death anxiety scale means and standard deviations for Ontario undergraduates and funeral directors. *Psychological Reports, 54,* 439-446.

49. Testa, J. (1981). Group systematic desensitization and implosive therapy for death anxiety. *Psychological Reports, 48,* 376-378.

50. McMordie, W. R., & Kumar, A. (1984). Cross-cultural research on the Templer/McMordie Death Anxiety Scale. *Psychological Reports, 54,* 959-963.

51. McMordie, W. R. (1982). Concurrent validity of Templer and Templer/McMordie Death Anxiety Scale. *Psychological Reports, 51,* 265-266.

52. Kumar, A., Vaidya, A. K., & Dwivedi, C. D. (1982). Death anxiety as a personality dimension of alcoholics and non-alcoholics. *Psychological Reports, 51,* 634.

53. Lonetto, R., Fleming, S., & Mercer, G. W. (1979). The structure of death anxiety: A factor analytic study. *Journal of Personality Assessment, 43,* 388-392.

54. Gilliland, J. C., & Templer, D. I. (1985). Relationship of death anxiety scale factors to subjective states. *Omega, 16,* 155-167.

55. Durlak, J. A. (1982). Using the Templer scale to assess "death anxiety": A cautionary note. *Psychological Reports, 50,* 1257-1258.

56. Chambers, W. V. (1986). Inconsistencies in the theory of death threat. *Death Studies, 10,* 165–175.
57. Neimeyer, R. A. (1986). The threat hypothesis: A conceptual and empirical defense. *Death Studies, 10,* 177–190.
58. Rainey, L. C., & Epting, F. R. (1977). Death threat constructions in the student and the prudent. *Omega, 8,* 19–28.
59. Tobacyk, J., & Eckstein, D. (1980). Death threat and death concerns in the college student. *Omega, 11,* 139–155.
60. Neimeyer, R. A., & Dingemans, P. (1980). Death orientation in the suicide intervention worker. *Omega, 11,* 15–23.
61. MacInnes, W. D., & Neimeyer, R. A. (1980). Internal consistency of the Threat Index. *Death Education, 4,* 193–194.
62. Rigdon, M. A., & Epting, F. R. (1985). Reduction in death threat as a basis for optimal functioning. *Death Studies, 9,* 427–448.
63. Vargo, M. (1980). Relationship between the Templer Death Anxiety Scale and the Collett-Lester Fear of Death Scale. *Psychological Reports, 46,* 561–562.
64. Neimeyer, R. A., Bagley, K. J., & Moore, M. K. (1986). Cognitive structure and death anxiety. *Death Studies, 10,* 273–288.
65. Larabee, M. (1978). Measuring fear of death: A reliability study. *Journal of Psychology, 100,* 33–37.
66. Durlak, J. A., & Kass, R. A. (1981). Clarifying the measurement of death attitudes: A factor analytic evaluation of fifteen self-report death scales. *Omega, 12,* 129–141.
67. Livneh, H. (1985). Brief note on the structure of the Collett-Lester Fear of Death Scale. *Psychological Reports, 56,* 136–138.
68. Hoelter, J. W. (1979). Multidimensional treatment of fear of death. *Journal of Consulting and Clinical Psychology, 47,* 996–999.
69. Walkey, F. W. (1982). The Multidimensional Fear of Death Scale: An independent analysis. *Journal of Consulting and Clinical Psychology, 50,* 466–467.
70. Long, D. D. (1985). A cross-cultural examination of fears of death among Saudi Arabians. *Omega, 16,* 43–50.
71. Rigdon, M. A., & Epting, F. R. (1981). Reclarifying the measurement of death attitudes. *Omega, 12,* 143–146.
72. Kass, R. A., & Durlak, J. A. (1981). Clarifying and reclarifying the measurement of death attitudes: A comment. *Omega, 12,* 147–149.
73. Davis, S. F., Bremer, S. A., Anderson, B. J., & Tramill, J. L. (1983). The interrelationships of ego strength, self-esteem, death anxiety and gender in undergraduate college students. *Journal of General Psychology, 108,* 55–59.
74. Sadowski, C. J., Davis, S. F., & Loftus-Vergari, M. C. (1979). Locus of control and death anxiety: A reexamination. *Omega, 10,* 203–210.
75. McDonald, G. W. (1976). Sex, religion, and risk-taking behavior as correlates of death anxiety. *Omega, 7,* 35–44.
76. Davis, S. F., Martin, D. A., Wilee, C. T., & Voorhees, J. W. (1978). Relationship of fear of death and level of self-esteem in college students. *Psychological Reports, 42,* 419–422.
77. Lonetto, R., Mercer, G. W., Fleming, S., Bunting, B., & Clare, M. (1980). Death anxiety among university students in Northern Ireland and Canada. *Journal of Psychology, 104,* 75–82.
78. Young, M., & Daniels, S. (1980). Born again status as a factor in death anxiety. *Psychological Reports, 47,* 367–370.
79. Neimeyer, R. A., & Neimeyer, G. J. (1984). Death anxiety and counseling skill in the suicide interventionist. *Suicide and Life-Threatening Behavior, 14,* 126–131.

80. Eggerman, S., & Dustin, D. (1985). Death orientation and communication with the terminally ill. *Omega, 16,* 255-265.

81. Aronow, E., Rauchway, A., Peller, M., & DeVito, A. (1980). The value of the self in relation to fear of death. *Omega, 11,* 37-44.

82. Durlak, J. A. (1978). Comparison between experiential and didactic methods of death education. *Omega, 9,* 57-66.

83. Stevens, S. J., Cooper, P. E., & Thomas, L. E. (1980). Age norms for Templer's Death Anxiety Scale. *Psychological Reports, 46,* 205-206.

84. Rockwell, F. P. A. (1981). Death anxiety: Comparison of psychiatrists, psychologists, suicidologists and funeral directors. *Psychological Reports, 49,* 979-982.

85. Johnson, J. C. (1980). Death anxiety of rehabilitation counselors and clients. *Psychological Reports, 46,* 325-326.

86. Mullins, L. C., & Lopez, M. A. (1982). Death anxiety among nursing home residents: A comparison of the young-old and old-old. *Death Education, 6,* 75-86.

87. Conte, H. R., Weiner, M. B., & Plutchik, R. (1982). Measuring death anxiety: Conceptual, psychometric and factor analytic aspects. *Journal of Personality and Social Psychology, 43,* 775-785.

88. Cole, M. A. (1978). Sex and marital status differences in death anxiety. *Omega, 9,* 139-147.

89. Howells, K., & Field, D. (1982). Fear of death and dying among medical students. *Social Science and Medicine, 16,* 1421-1424.

90. Stillion, J. M. (1985). *Death and the sexes.* Washington, DC: Hemisphere.

91. Robinson, P. J., & Wood, K. (1984). Fear of death and physical illness. A personal construct approach. In F. Epting & R. A. Neimeyer (Eds.), *Personal meanings of death* (127-142). Washington, DC: Hemisphere.

92. Neimeyer, R. A. (1985). Actualization, integration and fear of death: A test of the additive model. *Death Studies, 9,* 235-250.

93. Gesser, G., Wong, P. T. P., & Recker, G. T. (in press). Death attitudes across the life-span: The development and validation of the Death Attitude Profile. *Omega,* (in press).

94. Eakes, G. G. (1985). The relationship between death anxiety and attitudes toward the elderly among nursing staff. *Death Studies, 9,* 163-172.

95. Vargo, M. E., & Black, F. W. (1984). Attribution of control and the fear of death among first year medical students. *Journal of Clinical Psychology, 40,* 1525-1528.

96. Wagner, K. D., & Lorion, R. P. (1984). Correlates of death anxiety in elderly persons. *Journal of Clinical Psychology, 40,* 1235-1241.

97. Feifel, H., Hanson, S., Jones, R., & Edwards, L. (1967). Physicians consider death. *Proceedings of the 75th Annual Convention of the American Psychological Association,* 201-202.

98. Field, D., & Howells, K. (1985). Medical students' self-reported worries about aspects of death and dying. *Death Studies, 10,* 147-154.

99. Warren, W., & Chopra, P. (1979b). Physicians and death: Some Australian data. *Medical Journal of Australia,* March, 191-193.

100. Neimeyer, G. J., Behnke, M., & Reiss, J. (1984). Constructs and coping: Physicians' responses to patient death. In F. R. Epting & R. A. Neimeyer (Eds.), *Personal meanings of death* (159-180). Washington, DC: Hemisphere.

101. Kane, A. C., & Hogan, J. D. (1985). Death anxiety in physicians: Defensive style, medical specialty and exposure to death. *Omega, 16,* 11-22.

102. Momeyer, R. W. (1985). Fearing death and caring for the dying. *Omega, 16,* 1-9.

103. Schulz, R., & Aderman, D. (1979). Physicians' death anxiety and patient outcomes. *Omega, 9,* 327-332.

104. Amenta, M. M., & Weiner, A. W. (1981b). Death anxiety and general anxiety in hospice workers. *Psychological Reports, 49,* 962.
105. Amenta, M. M. (1984). Death anxiety, purpose in life and duration of service in hospice volunteers. *Psychological Reports, 54,* 979–984.
106. Neimeyer, R. A., & MacInnes, W. D. (1981). Assessing paraprofessional competence with the Suicide Intervention Response Inventory. *Journal of Counseling Psychology, 28,* 176–179.
107. Hunt, D. M., Lester, D., & Ashton, N. (1983). Fear of death, locus of control and occupation. *Psychological Reports, 53,* 1022.
108. Kureshi, A., & Husain, A. (1981). Death anxiety and intrapunitiveness among smokers and nonsmokers: A comparative study. *Journal of Psychological Research, 25,* 42–45.
109. Gielen, A. C., & Roche, K. A. (1979). Death anxiety and psychometric studies in Huntington's disease. *Omega, 10,* 135–145.
110. Eckstein, D., & Tobacyk, J. (1979). Ordinal position and death concerns. *Psychological Reports, 44,* 967–971.
111. McDonald, R. T., & Carroll, J. D. (1981). Three measures of death anxiety: Birth order effects and concurrent validity. *Journal of Clinical Psychology, 37,* 574–576.
112. Tokunaga, H. T. (1985). The effect of bereavement upon death related attitudes and fears. *Omega, 16,* 267–380.
113. Pratt, C. C., Hare, J., & Wright, C. (1985). Death anxiety and comfort in teaching about death among preschool teachers. *Death Studies, 9,* 417–425.
114. Mercer, G. W., Bunting, B., & Snook, S. (1979). The effects of location, experiences with the civil disturbances and religion on death anxiety and manifest anxiety in a sample of Northern Ireland university students. *British Journal of Social and Clinical Psychology, 18,* 151–158.
115. Beshai, J. A., & Templer, D. I. (1978). American and Egyptian attitudes toward death. *Essence, 2,* 155–158.
116. Dodd, D. K., & Mills, L. L. (1985). FADIS: A measure of the fear of accidental death and injury. *Psychological Record, 35,* 269–275.
117. Loo, R. (1984). Personality correlates of the Fear of Death and Dying Scale. *Journal of Clinical Psychology, 40,* 120–122.
118. Downey, A. M. (1984). Relationship of religiosity to death anxiety in middle aged males. *Psychological Reports, 54,* 811–822.
119. Tobacyk, J. (1984). Death threat, death concerns, and paranormal belief. In F. R. Epting & R. A. Neimeyer (Eds.), *Personal meanings of death* (29–40). Washington, DC: Hemisphere.
120. Florian, V., & Kravetz, S. (1983). Fear of personal death: Attribution, structure and relation to religious belief. *Journal of Personality and Social Psychology, 44,* 600–607.
121. Kunzendorf, R. G. (1985). Repressed fear of inexistence and its hypnotic recovery in religious students. *Omega, 16,* 23–33.
122. Vargo, M. E., & Black, W. F. (1984). Psychosocial correlates of death anxiety in a population of medical students. *Psychological Reports, 54,* 737–738.
123. Templer, D. I., Ruff, C. F., & Simpson, K. (1974). Alleviation of high death anxiety with symptomatic treatment of depression. *Psychological Reports, 35,* 216.
124. Rigdon, M. A. (1984). Death threat before and after attempted suicide: A clinical investigation. In F. R. Epting & R. A. Neimeyer (Eds.), *Personal meanings of death.* Washington, DC: Hemisphere.
125. Amenta, M. M., & Weiner, A. W. (1981a). Death anxiety and purpose in life in hospice workers. *Psychological Reports, 49,* 920.
126. Vargo, M. E., & Batsel, W. M. (1981). Relationship between death anxiety and components of the self-actualization process. *Psychological Reports, 48,* 89–90.

127. Lester, D., & Colvin, L. M. (1977). Fear of death, alienation and self-actualization. *Psychological Reports, 41,* 526.

128. Neimeyer, R. A., & Chapman, K. M. (1980). Self/ideal discrepancy and fear of death: The test of an existential hypothesis. *Omega, 11,* 233–240.

129. Wood, K., & Robinson, P. J. (1982). Actualization and the fear of death: Retesting an existential hypothesis. *Essence, 5,* 235–243.

130. Robinson, P. J., & Wood, K. (1983). The Threat Index: An additive approach. *Omega, 14,* 139–144.

131. Joubert, C. E. (1983). Subjective acceleration of time: Death anxiety and sex differences. *Psychological Reports, 57,* 49–50.

132. Peterson, S. A. (1985). Death anxiety and politics. *Omega, 16,* 169–174.

133. Handal, P. J. (1980). Individual and group problem solving and type of orientation as a function of high, moderate and low death anxiety. *Omega, 10,* 365–377.

134. Warren, W. G. (1982). Personal construction of death and death education. *Death Education, 6,* 17–28.

135. Rosenthal, N. R. (1983). Death education and suicide potentiality. *Death Education, 7,* 39–51.

136. McClam, T. (1980). Death anxiety before and after death education: Negative results. *Psychological Reports, 46,* 513–514.

137. Pettigrew, C. G., & Dawson, J. G. (1979). Death anxiety: State or trait? *Journal of Clinical Psychology, 35,* 154–158.

138. Bohart, J., & Bergland, B. W. (1979). The impact of death and dying counseling groups on death anxiety in college students. *Death Education, 2,* 381–391.

139. Wittmaier, B. C. (1980). Some unexpected attitudinal consequences of a short course on death. *Omega, 10,* 271–275.

140. Mullins, L. C., & Merriam, S. (1983). The effects of a short-term death training program on nursing home staff. *Death Education, 7,* 353–368.

141. Hayslip, B., & Walling, M. L. (1985). Impact of hospice volunteer training on death anxiety and locus of control. *Omega, 16,* 243–254.

142. Berscheid, E. (1985). Interpersonal attraction. In G. Lindzey and E. Aronson (Eds.), *Handbook of Social Psychology* (413–484). New York: Random House.

7

The Experience of Dying

Lawrence C. Rainey

Man has a symbolic identity that brings him sharply out of nature. He is a symbolic self, a creature with a name, a life history. He is a creator with a mind that soars out to speculate about atoms and infinity, who can place himself imaginatively at a point in space and contemplate bemusedly his own planet . . .

Yet, at the same time, as the Eastern sages also knew, man is a worm and food for worms. This is the paradox: he is out of nature and hopelessly in it; he is dual, up in the stars and yet housed in a heart-pumping, breath-gasping body that once belonged to a fish and still carries the gill-marks to prove it. His body is a material fleshing casing that is alien to him in many ways—the strangest and most repugnant way being that it aches and bleeds and will decay and die. Man is literally split in two: he has an awareness of his own splendid unique-ness and that he sticks out of nature with a towering majesty, and yet he goes back into the ground a few feet in order blindly and dumbly to rot and disappear forever. It is a terrifying dilemma to be in and to have to live with. (1, p. 26)

It is this dialectic—finding ourselves "in" nature, yet "above" it; finite, yet aware of our finitude—that gives rise to "the experience of dying." Existentialist thinkers would have us all more aware of this plight, regardless of how young and healthy we might be. They are impressed with the fact that, despite advanced technological gains, the death rate hovers at 100 percent. Personal appropriation of this basic reality (if done with a measure of steadfastness and authenticity) is said to have a bracing effect—if not endowing us with "the courage to be" (theologian Paul Tillich's phrase), perhaps at least enabling us to shed a few of our more annoying neuroticisms. But with the press of taxes to be filed, classes to attend, football games to be won, dinners to be made, deadlines to be met, and other distractions of daily life, most mortals live blithely untroubled, thank you, with mortality.

A few among us at any given time are not so distracted, however: These are individuals who are caught acutely in the dialectic of alive now/going to die, the period Mansell Pattison (2) has called the "living-dying phase." Not all would be "terminal" patients, in the medical sense, for physicians tend to save this descriptor for those who are truly moribund. It would, however, be comprised of those who, by dint of advanced age or the presence of incurable illness, know that death awaits them, not as an intellectualized abstraction but as a very real threat in the not-so-distant future.

Individuals caught in the living-dying phase, including their families and close friends, are the focus of this chapter. It should be noted that this excludes many who die from *sudden* death—victims of homicides and fatal accidents to name but two examples—situations wherein there is no extended trajectory of dying but instead an abrupt and unexpected termination of life. The experience of those who take their own lives will also not be considered here, deserving, as it is, of special treatment. Understanding the experience of dying children and adolescents, as well as helping them in this process, is not entirely different than addressing these concerns in an adult population, but in the pediatric context, special attention must be given to an array of important developmental issues. Our concern here will be primarily with adult patients. With reference, then, to this group, two basic issues will be discussed. First, we shall consider several important psychosocial factors that characterize the experience of dying. We will then consider the nature of psychosocial interventions with dying patients and their families.

PSYCHOSOCIAL PERSPECTIVES ON THE EXPERIENCE OF DYING

Over the last two decades, there has been an outpouring of treatises on dying. Books for health care professionals, educators, clergy, and other "helping professions" abound as do first-person accounts and guidebooks for the afflicted themselves. Specialized journals—for example, *Omega, Death Studies,* and *The Hospice Journal*—are devoted to the topic. Even television and movie script writers seem to be "into" thanatologic themes. Discussion of the historical and sociological bases for this surge in discussion of death would take us too far afield. It should be noted, however, that commentary on the experience of dying has, to a large extent, been skewed toward *psychosocial* perspectives—i.e., the cognitive, affective, behavioral, and interpersonal dimensions of dying. Other very important perspectives—for instance, medical, economic, demographic, and anthropologic (cultural) facets of dying—have not had as much attention in the thanatology literature. Of course, all of these factors are interactive. Matters such as the availability and nature of medical intervention, the staggering costs of end-stage care, and cultural norms about appropriate behavior will impinge directly and, in many cases, quite dramatically on the psychological and interpersonal experiences of the dying patient. The interrelatedness of these concerns affects not only how one theoretically conceptualizes the experience of dying but the way in which services for the dying are pragmatically organized (e.g., the multidisciplinary approach of hospices, palliative care facilities, and hospitals serving the terminally ill). Important as these other dimensions are in shaping the experience of the dying patient, this chapter will deal primarily with psychosocial issues.

Stages of Dying

Construing the experiences of dying in terms of a series of "stages" or "phases" has widespread appeal. Of course, stage concepts have long held sway in childhood development theories (e.g., Piaget's stages of intellectual development, Erikson's stages of personality development, Kohlberg's stages of moral development, etc.). If broad realms of unfolding human experience can be so conceptualized at the beginning of life, why not at the end? There is, after all, a certain intellectual appeal to an orderly process with one stage building on the foregoing stage(s), leading to a final resolution. Dr. Elizabeth Kübler-Ross' influential book, *On Death and Dying* (3), presented just such a conception of the dying process. Based on interviews with over 200 terminal patients, Kübler-Ross postulated five stages in the process of psychological response to dying: 1) denial and isolation, 2) anger, 3) bargaining, 4) depression, and 5) acceptance. Let us look at these a bit more closely.

Denial and isolation—A very common initial reaction to the diagnosis of terminal illness: "No, not me. It can't be true." Though total denial of the reality of illness is rare, at least a temporary and partial denial is nearly universal.

Anger—Shock, denial, and disbelief are soon battered down by the realities of disease. Quick on the heels of denial are feelings of anger, rage, envy, and resentment. Medical staff and family may become inappropriate targets of anger as the patient struggles with the bitter question, "Why me?"

Bargaining—Kübler-Ross felt that the stage of anger was not usually sustained but, instead, gave way to a form of bargaining to help forestall the inevitable from happening. Patients would begin formulating their plight in these terms, "If you'll . . . , then I'll . . . ." A bargain might be struck with the doctor, the family, or, for the religious patient, God. It is as if the patient regressively believes good behavior will buy more time.

Depression—The losses associated with illness and treatment mount—body parts, time, money, independence, social status, and much more may all be sacrificed—with the specter of ultimate loss of life itself lurking in the future. Depression (in the sense of a normal human reaction to the loss, not a full-blown affective disorder) is a common and understandable response in these circumstances.

Acceptance—Given enough time and appropriate help in working through the previous stages, the patient will, Kübler-Ross believes, reach a stage when he or she is neither depressed nor angry nor trying to leverage more time but, instead, accepting of his or her fate. This stage, says Kübler-Ross, "should not be mistaken for a happy stage. It is almost void of feelings. It is as if the pain had gone, the struggle is over, and there comes a time for the final rest before the long journey" (3, p. 113).

Kübler-Ross was careful to make clear that dying patients do not always march through these stages precisely in the order she described. However, many health care workers, patients, and families of patients have read her that way and have tried to force their understanding of terminal process into a procrustean mold. It has not been uncommon, in my experience, to hear nurses and doctors, for instance, complain that "this patient will be dying soon and he simply hasn't 'accepted' what is happening to him. Why does he seem to be stuck in denial?" The implication of their complaint is, or course, that one should move "through" denial to some other mode of coping.

Kübler-Ross' pioneering work did a great deal to direct attention to the emotional needs of dying patients and their families. However, the stage formulation came in for much critical commentary in subsequent years. There has been, in fact, very little, if any, empirical evidence to support the notion that patients proceed through any sort of discernible series of stages (4, 5). Summarizing his clinical experience, psychologist Edwin Shneidman wrote:

> Indeed, while I have seen in dying persons isolation, envy, bargaining, depression, and acceptance, I do not believe that these are necessarily "stages" of the dying process, and I am not at all convinced that they are lived through in that order, or, for that matter, in any universal order. What I do see is complicated clustering of intellectual and affective states, some fleeting, lasting for a moment or a day or week, set not unexpectedly against the backdrop of that person's total personality, his "philosophy of life. . . . " (6, p. 6)

In similar fashion, thanatologist Mansell Pattison states:

> I find *no* evidence . . . to support specific stages of dying. Rather, dying patients demonstrate a wide variety of emotions that ebb and flow throughout our entire life as we face conflicts and crises. It does seem misleading, then, to search for and determine stages of dying. Rather, I suggest that our task is to determine the stresses and crises at a specific time, to respond to the emotions generated by that issue, and, in essence, to *respond to where the patient is at* in his or her living-dying. We do not make the patient conform to our idealized concept of dying but respond to the patient's actual dying experience. (2, p. 141)

Dying Trajectories and Phases

Though an ineluctable series of psychological stages may be disputed, few would argue the contention that there are discernible phases in the process of dying. For instance, Pattison (2) simply divides this process into three clinical phases: 1) the acute crisis phase in which one learns of terminal illness, 2) the chronic living-dying phase, and 3) the terminal phase. The nature of one's affliction and a variety of other factors will dictate, however, the path or trajectory one takes through these phases. Furthermore, different psychological responses tend to be elicited by each trajectory.

For instance, Martocchio (7) describes four patterns. Illnesses such as leukemia or lymphoma, in which there may be dramatic remissions and then recurrences of the illness, fall into a pattern he calls "peaks and valleys." After the hope and excitement generated by the initial remission, resignation or fatalism may set in as recurrent crises occur. "Descending plateaus" is the phrase used by

Martocchio to describe diseases such as multiple sclerosis wherein there tends to be a stepwise decline in functioning. Anger, depression, and futility are typical, and the patient is apt to spend a good deal of time in nursing homes or chronic care facilities. The "downward slope," a process of inexorable decline, is typical of a wide variety of illnesses wherein there is no effective treatment even for a period of remission. Patient and family often have a sense of urgency and acute anxiety, particularly if the downward course is steep. Finally, there are an increasing number of chronic conditions wherein the patient has an essentially incurable disease but dying can be forestalled for lengthy periods of time, yielding a very gradual, almost imperceptible decline toward death. In these instances, issues of patience and endurance confront the patient and family and a host of ethical issues about sustaining the patient must be addressed.

Glaser and Strauss (8) have discussed dying trajectories with regard to expectations about the process of dying. One common clinical phenomenon is the situation in which different individuals (e.g., members of the treatment team, family members, friends, employers, etc.) are at different points on their respective psychological trajectories. Consider the following example:

> Mrs. G., a 44-year-old married mother of two teenagers, had had her initial bout with breast cancer over 10 years ago. She was hospitalized now with widespread metastatic disease. Her 46-year-old husband of 20 years had been referred because of what had been perceived as "his difficulty accepting the fact that his wife is dying."
>
> After two psychotherapy sessions, he confided that he was involved romantically with another woman. Though guilty and ashamed of this, he felt he had "broken his ties emotionally" with his wife over a year ago when she had nearly died from a lung metastasis. Indeed, he had gone through much anticipatory grieving then, fully expecting her to die and now was unprepared to deal with her current emotional needs. He was still quite attentive and involved in her physical care but had long ago withdrawn his emotional involvement.

Many times family members will not have "reinvested" their emotional energies in such dramatic fashion but, nonetheless, will find themselves "out of step" with the patient. For instance, a family member may want the patient to "let go," while the patient is still at the point of "fighting." This can also be reversed, leading to situations in which the family has difficulty giving the patient "permission to die."

> Mrs. B., a 67-year-old retired department store clerk, was hospitalized with widely disseminated, recurrent lymphoma. By her own account, she was "tired" and wanted to be "with the Lord." She was not clinically depressed, but she was (appropriately) "ready to die." Her 42-year-old daughter, a social worker, brought her audiotapes about "holistic healing." When the patient quietly refused the "holistic" intervention, the daughter requested psychological consultation *for her mother*, pleading, "Doctor, make Mother take responsibility for herself and fight."

As illustrated in this example, the caregiver must be attuned not only to the *content* of the expressed concerns but also to where each individual is in the *process* of dealing with impending death.

Levels of Awareness

It would be an understatement to say that thanatologists have been preoccupied with the degree to which dying patients and their families are aware of the fact that death is in the offing. As we have already seen, Kübler-Ross started her stage sequence with "denial" and ended with "acceptance." (It is as if the Alpha and Omega of psychological experiences of the dying revolve on the denial-acceptance continuum.) At clinical case conferences in which dying patients are discussed, the concept of "denial" will be bandied about freely, often with little clarification as to what is being denied and in what sense. Perhaps most troubling has been the tendency to view "openness" and "acceptance" in very positive terms, while assuming that "denial" is invariably pathologic and counterproductive. This has led to unnecessary and often unfortunate confrontations with patients, tactless disclosure, and battering of sorely needed psychological defenses.

The definition of denial is fraught with difficulties. It can be used to describe a process (e.g., "The patient is using denial to deal with his illness") or to describe a fact (e.g., "The patient's denial is impeding his care"). Dr. Avery Weisman, who has written extensively on terminal illness, coping processes, and denial (9), distinguishes first-, second-, and third-order denial. First-order denial involves unequivocal disavowal of the primary facts of illness. For instance, a woman with a six-year history of untreated breast cancer was recently referred to me for psychological evaluation. According to her husband's report, she had steadfastly denied the fact that she was ill, despite repeated pleas from her physician and others that she receive medical care. Second-order denial refers to the inferences that a patient draws about the implications of his or her illness. For instance, exacerbations and complications of illness might be explained away in a fog of rationalizations. Patients may accept their diagnosis with its complications and hazards but still not acknowledge that they have an incurable illness that results in death. For instance, a 42-year-old man with pancreatic cancer (who, in fact, died eight months after his diagnosis) would openly discuss his diagnosis and even chronicle the grim downward course he had suffered in recent months; but, in the same breath, he would discuss his long-term career advancement plans.

"Middle knowledge" is a term Weisman has used to describe a very common state, "somewhere between open acknowledgment of death and its repudiation" (9, p. 65). This state of fluctuating acceptance and denial is illustrated by the following case.

Mr. G., a 31-year-old urban planner, had frank AIDS diagnosed ten months ago. In psychotherapy sessions shortly after this diagnosis, he had directly discussed the fact that patients with his diagnosis and with his clinical course had, on average, very short life expectancies. He had updated his will, made provisions for his funeral, and contacted a local hospice organization to provide services at his home when necessary. In these regards, he appeared to have resigned himself to the fact of his death. Yet, when faced with a brief delay in the arrival of an experimental drug that he has scheduled to take, he reacted with intense anxiety and anger. "How can they do this to me? I *need that medication!*"

Psychologically astute observers have often noted that denial is *not* invariably dysfunctional. For instance, Lazarus and Folkman (10) have discussed denial within the context of active coping strategies. "What is needed," they state, "are principles that specify the conditions under which denial and denial-like forms of coping might have favorable or unfavorable outcomes" (10, p. 136). Denial may be quite adaptive, for instance, when there is nothing that the individual can do to overcome the threat. In these situations, denial or denial-like processes can help alleviate psychological distress. Certain facets of the situation, if not the whole, may be adaptively denied. For example, the diabetic patient might adaptively deny the probability of future renal disease, loss of limbs, or blindness, if still giving needed attention to diet, activity level, and insulin. The *timing* of denial can also be quite important. For instance, denial during the onset of heart attack symptoms could obviously be very destructive in leading the patient to delay necessary treatment. But the same psychological process could be very helpful by facilitating recovery during the rehabilitation phase.

Certainly, denial cannot be thought of in black and white terms. It is neither an all-or-nothing process, nor is it uniformly helpful or harmful.

Contexts of Awareness

Of course, it is not just intrapsychic processes (e.g., defense mechanisms or coping styles) that will dictate the exchange of information around the dying individual but also the social context. Sociologists Barney Glaser and Anselm Strauss in their early book *Awareness of Dying* (11) report on interactions between hospital staff members and patients with life-threatening illness. Four "contexts of awareness" are described: closed awareness, suspicion, mutual pretense, and open awareness.

When staff members are aware of the patient's unfortunate diagnosis but do not share this information with the patient, a "closed awareness" context exists. Twenty-five years ago, when Glaser and Strauss conducted their research, this was a very common management strategy for dying patients. Direct conversations about the patient's prognosis would be avoided. Nurses and doctors would "manage" conversations, directing them to "safe" areas of information exchange. Outright lies may have been avoided, but every effort would be taken to avoid disclosing the painful truths about the patient's terminal condition. It is to be understood that much, if not all, of this maneuvering and avoidance would be done unconsciously. In fact, staff members might not construe their withholding information as "protecting the patient" but simply do it unreflectively as a matter of propriety, common sense, or benevolent care. Today, with a great deal more emphasis on "full disclosure" to "consumers" in many fields, including, of course, health care, maintaining a closed awareness context is much less common.

There are many sources of information in a hospital context. Kalish (12) has listed a variety of information inputs that may be available to the patient: a) direct statements from the physician; b) overheard comments by the physician to others; c) direct statements from other personnel (aides, nurses, technologists, social workers, etc.); d) overheard comments by staff to each other; e) direct statements from family, friends, clergy, lawyer; f) changes in the behavior of others toward the patient; g) changes in medical care routines, procedures, medications; h) changes in physical location; i) self-diagnosis including reading of medical books, records, and charts; j) signals from the body and changes in physical status; k) altered responses by others toward the future. Though the physician, for instance, might attempt to maintain a "closed context of awareness," discrepancies may arises from other sources, leaving the patient to feel that he or she has not been dealt with directly. A "confusion of fictions" may arise in which the staff is aware of the patient's true condition, but the patient only suspects this.

> Mr. Q., a 56-year-old furniture salesman with metastatic lung cancer, was transferred from a semiprivate to a private room on the cancer ward. Shortly after this seemingly innocuous change in rooms, his behavior changed from cooperative and quiet to belligerent and argumentative. Indeed, when I saw him, he was quite angry initially, but this affect soon gave way to frightened tears. At the bequest of his family, the staff had been quite "upbeat" with him, stressing short-term objectives such as increased nutritional intake, regaining self-care skills, possibly a discharge from the hospital soon, but they had been instructed (by the family) to avoid any intimation that he might be dying. However, a transfer to a private room and a coincidental visit by the hospital chaplain had signaled to the patient that he was "a goner."

Glaser and Strauss point out that suspicion is inherently unstable and will usually yield to one of two possibilities—mutual pretense or open awareness.

Mutual pretense is perhaps the most interesting and psychologically complex of the four contexts of awareness. The following example describes a situation in which both patient and staff are quite cognizant that the patient is dying but pretend that this is not so. Though at first this may sound bizarre, it is actually common and, in certain instances, very useful. The grim, awful facts of terminal illness may be all too apparent to all concerned, but in mutual pretense, participants choose to act, at least in some regards, as if that reality were not there. In order to maintain a modicum of emotional stability, the pretense must be maintained. Sometimes these rituals become quite elaborate.

> Mr. C., a 32-year-old married truck driver and father of two young children had recently been diagnosed with a fast-growing malignant brain tumor. There was no known effective treatment to arrest the disease. The patient had a history of drug abuse, so the psychologist was consulted to "provide assistance in preventing a relapse in addictive behavior." The patient, in fact, had had that problem controlled for many years, and it was, of course, quite irrelevant to his immediate needs. Nonetheless, in the six remaining months of his life, he spent much time and energy "winning the battle" (against a relapse of his drug problem). Ironically, while the patient was focused on this "ghost from the past," his oncologist proceeded with an aggressive course of futile chemotherapy treatment, lasting until a few days before the patient's death.

Glaser and Strauss point out that mutual pretense sometimes helps the staff to do their jobs better, keeping a safe emotional distance from the dying patient. The pretense context may actually give some patients more dignity and privacy, a sense that there is something left in life that he or she controls. (It was essentially this ploy that was going on in the case above, at least from the patient's perspective, and it would have been less than clinically astute to have undermined this unwitting defense.) The danger in mutual pretense, however, is the possibility of alienation, with the patient left without any authentic relationships.

Open awareness, the final context described by Glaser and Strauss, is a situation in which both patient and staff are aware of the patient's true condition and openly acknowledge it. Some details of prognosis may be spared, but the essential facts are openly discussed. Obviously, this facilitates practical matters such as having the patient prepare a will, make arrangements for children, say "good-bye" to important persons, and in other ways prepare for death. This context may put considerable emotional strain on hospital staff who work constantly with dying individuals, but, at the same time, it frees them from the careful scripting that is needed for closed awareness or mutual pretense.

Undoubtedly, open communications about dying are becoming more the norm today than they were a few years ago. Patients frequently request to be fully informed about their conditions, treatments, and prognoses, and they also often want to be involved in decision making about their care. However, it would be a gross mistake to think that this posture describes all patients or that it is always the superior way of dealing with dying. Most clinicians are sensitive enough to know, for instance, that not every expectant father has the psychological wherewithal to be present during a cesarean section on his wife. If such a straightforward surgical procedure is too threatening for some, how could one reasonably expect that all patients would be prepared to stare at the reality of their own annihilation and talk about it unreservedly. We have all encountered individuals who have not been able, for instance, to address openly their sexual needs or to deal forthrightly with feelings of anger or resentment. Yet one finds health professionals still who expect everyone to muster the courage and flexibility necessary to countenance their own dying. Of course, this doesn't happen! We have already discussed the value of denial. Some patients cope best with threatening situations, including dying, by using minimization, avoidance, suppression, and other denial-like coping processes. Unless these strategies severely affect the patient's or the family's welfare in a clearly adverse way, they are probably best left in place.

"Personologic" Perspectives

There has always been a strong idiographic tradition within psychology—that is, an appreciation of individual differences. This tradition has found its expression in the thanatologic domain, as well. In contrast to those who are impressed with perceived stages, phases, trajectories, or context, which apply across individuals, the more person-centered (personologic) perspective takes as its starting point the individual's needs, traits, coping mechanisms, and other individual characteristics.

The notion of "appropriate death" as articulated by psychiatrist Avery Weisman is representative of this perspective. He writes:

Many years ago, while trying to understand patients who, without qualms or questions, fully expected and accepted their own demise, I realized that not only some deaths were better than others, but that certain deaths were so fitting that they could be called *appropriate*. These were not, of course, ideal deaths, nor particularly propitious, but they did share characteristics that were consistent with good coping and sustained morale. Appropriate death, in brief, was the opposite of suicidal death, in which an unhappy person appropriates death. (13, p. 80)

Weisman has discussed appropriate death as having the following characteristics: a) conflict is reduced; b) compatibility with the individual's ego ideal is obtained; c) continuity of important relationships is preserved or restored; d) consummation of basic instincts and wishes of fantasy reemerge and are fulfilled. What is "appropriate" for one person will not necessarily be so for another, but a death is appropriate if it is consistent with what the person has been, with what is meaningful and important to him or her, and if it maintains important relationships. This describes a desired condition that, obviously, is not always met, but it clearly guides the caregiver to different ends than would, for instance, the notion of progression through a set of sequential stages.

Another spokesman, firmly in this tradition, has been Edwin Shneidman. To understand terminally ill individuals or respond to the challenges associated with dying we must, according to Shneidman, understand how they have lived during stressful periods of their lives. "The life of a person who is dying pragmatically mirrors the times of his life when he has been threatened and upset. . . . One sees in dying persons the vast array (not all of it in each person) of stoicism, rage, guilt, terror, cringing, surrender, heroism, dependency, ennui, fight for autonomy and dignity, ad infinitum" (14, p. 31). How individuals behaved during periods of stress, crisis, or loss earlier in life will give significant clues to the predicted pattern of response to dying.

Mr. C., a 62-year-old electrician with metastatic lung cancer, was referred for psychological assistance by his oncologist. The physician was troubled by the patient's extreme fretfulness (illustrated for instance by long lists of minor physical complaints about which he often needed reassurance), and by the patient's dour, uncommunicative style. Furthermore, as his oncologist put it, "The patient isn't dealing with the real issue, the fact that he is dying." Among other factors uncovered at the initial consultation was the fact that the patient's son had been murdered several years ago. The patient's wife reported that her husband had had little to say about that and had, in fact, declined the opportunity to attend the trial of the murderer. He had not shown any open overt grief response. Indeed, his approach to his cancer mirrored in many ways the way he had dealt with the earlier traumatic loss of his son.

Less traumatic but similar examples are encountered every day in my practice. For instance, it is very common for me to be asked to see couples who "aren't communicating" about the presence of a life-threatening illness in one or the other.

When I entered the room of Mr. P., a 68-year-old gentleman dying of progressive colon cancer, I found him reading his newspaper and his wife knitting silently at his side. After just a brief interview, it became clear that, like many couples, they had not made it a habit to talk about anything of deep emotional significance during the 45 years of their marriage. They talked *to* each other *about* a number of *things*, but seldom, if ever, did they talk *with* each other, especially about emotionally laden topics. Having contracted colon cancer, of course, did not endow Mr. P. nor his wife with the requisite communication skills nor the emotional empathy to have such interchange now.

Thus, we could summarize this position by saying that to appreciate the experience of dying, it is not death per se we need to ponder so much as the interaction between situational factors (e.g., constraints imposed by the patient's disease, social factors inherent in the treatment setting, etc.) and individual factors (e.g., coping history, personality traits, etc.). The situation may be extraordinary, but it is populated with quite ordinary folks. One dies but once, says an old axiom, but the individual's behavior and affect and thoughts are not apt to be entirely novel when viewed against the backdrop of the patient's personal history. To the contrary, they are apt to manifest long-established personality traits and coping mechanisms.

PSYCHOLOGICAL SUPPORT FOR TERMINAL PATIENTS

The perspectives outlined above give important guidance to those who provide psychological assistance to terminal patients and their families. This help will be less than optimal if a savvy appreciation for the special circumstances of the terminally ill patient is not balanced with a broad insight into the *individual patient's* coping capacities.

Psychosocial support to seriously ill patients used to fall within the purview of the primary physician caring for the patient. However, for a host of technological, economical, and social-historical reasons, the physician caring for the dying patient today is not apt to devote the time required for this aspect of patient care nor have the necessary understanding and sensitivity to fulfill this role. Not only in large university medical centers, but also increasingly in community hospitals and clinics, there are specialists from psychology, social work, psychiatry, pastoral care, and nursing who are charged with providing psychological support. This division of labor is far from ideal but, perhaps, a necessity. However, for this multidisciplinary model to have a chance to operate effectively, it is necessary that those who focus on providing psychological support are closely integrated with other caregivers on the treatment team.

Psychological care of the *terminal* patient is not radically different than psychological care for other medically ill patients. There is no need for counselors who "specialize" in death. Rather, what is needed are well-trained psychologists, nurses, social workers, etc., who appreciate the special challenges faced by those who are dying and by their families.

Meeting Basic Needs

I recall an instructive encounter I had with one of the first cancer patients I counseled. Shortly after I introduced myself to the unfortunate gentleman who lay before me (he had a fast-growing brain tumor), my attention was drawn to the distracted and pained expression on his face. "Anxiety about our meeting?" I wondered to myself or "is he about to cry, perhaps already responding to this opportunity to explore his feelings." Before I could inquire further, he relieved my confusion. "Doctor," he said, "right now, understanding is not what I need. Could you please get me a bedpan!" Though, as the passage quoted at the beginning of this chapter put it, we "transcend" nature, nonetheless, we are firmly rooted in it. Psychological services for the terminally ill are only meaningful if, first, basic physical care issues are addressed.

Take end-stage cancer management for example. There are a host of important, sometimes quite complicated medical care issues to address, even though curative therapy may no longer be possible. These include appetite disturbance, fever, dysphagia (swallowing problems), persistent constipation, infections, dyspnea (difficulty breathing), various hematologic complications, bladder dysfunction and incontinence, and metabolic disturbances (many of which can affect, sometimes quite dramatically, the patient's mental status) (15). No amount of empathy is helpful, for instance, for the delusional, hypercalcemic patient. Of special importance for the terminal patient is adequate management of pain, a multifactored problem that is finally receiving increased clinical and research attention (16). The patient who is sleep-deprived from poorly controlled pain is not in a position to benefit from even the most exquisite structural family therapy maneuver. If the patient does not have adequate respiratory support and is literally gasping for every breath, he or she is not apt to be impressed by a discussion of anticipatory grieving. Those who are there to provide psychological ministrations to the terminally afflicted are advised to ponder their own professional contributions the next time they, themselves, suffer from the common flu. Multiply the nausea and gastric distress by a large factor, then try to focus, for instance, on children's reactions to a parent's illness, working through feelings of unresolved guilt, dealing assertively with health care providers, or any of a number of common psychological issues for the terminally ill. "The spirit" may be willing, but "the flesh" has a certain primacy.

Careful diagnostic workup of all the many medical complications that might occur in the terminal patient is, of course, very important. No right-thinking physician ever tells a patient suffering from incurable disease that "there is nothing more we can do" for there is always much to be attended to and, quite often, palliative intervention to be made. Sometimes fairly aggressive intervention—e.g., chemotherapy, radiation, or even surgery—must be pursued for palliative purposes. It has been popular in thanatology circles to decry aggressive medical treatment (with curative intent) of incurable diseases, but, at the same time, we must recognize that concerted medical intervention, with all of its technological trappings, can be vitally important in sustaining a meaningful quality of life.

In addition to medical care, however, a host of other disciplines contribute to meeting what we are here calling basic needs. In the moderately sized community hospital in which I work, a multidisciplinary team meets weekly to discuss support services for selected oncologic patients. In addition to clinical psychology, there are representatives from occupational and physical therapy, dietary services, clinical pharmacology, discharge planning and home health care services, pastoral care, and, the linchpin of the whole system, nursing. To my mind, addressing the patient's psychological well-being without first providing adequate care in these other dimensions is foolhardy.

Who Needs Psychological Support?

If, by "psychological support," we simply mean empathic understanding, appreciation of individual differences, acknowledgment of the patient's feelings, awareness of the patient's family, and other such rudimentary aspects of caring, then *everyone* needs psychological support. Patients, their families, and staff can all benefit from liberal doses of empathy, tolerance, clear communication, and social support. In the crucible of terminal patient care, such basic human qualities are vitally important, but all too often are woefully lacking. Clearly, however, fostering basic human virtues of maturity, graciousness, and empathy for the needs of others is not the exclusive province of mental health professionals nor of any other select group. It is as much the responsibility of the surgeon, internist, and nurse to foster this atmosphere as it is that of the psychologist, pastoral counselor, or social worker.

Unfortunately, direct observations of doctor's and nurse's interactions with dying patients suggest that distancing tactics are very frequently used. These include false reassurance and selective inattention to communication about psychosocial concerns (17). Training programs designed to alert the medical caregiver to common psychological concerns and to enhance basic communication skills can be helpful in addressing these deficits (18).

Psychological support can have a more focused meaning, however, referring to more intensive, structured interventions aimed at alleviating emotional distress, behavioral problems, or interpersonal conflict. Such treatment can, at times, be complex, very time consuming, and require special training and skill. Usually, psychosocial intervention of this sort is administered (or at least coordinated and directed) by mental health professionals (social workers, psychiatrists, and psychologists).

There are a variety of psychosocial interventions, ranging from informal peer support groups to formal psychotherapy directed at identified behavioral, attitudinal, affective, or interpersonal problems. Psychotherapy may be structured as individual, family, or group treatment.

If the question about "who needs psychological support" refers to these more specialized psychosocial interventions, then the answer is quite different. Certainly, not all patients need formal psychological assistance. The fact is that only a small fraction of patients with life-threatening conditions would consider themselves candidates for psychological help and even a smaller fraction will receive it, in fact.

Data regarding the incidence rate of psychological disturbance among those with life-threatening illness is just beginning to be collected. However, one relatively large-scale study of cancer patients found that, overall, 46 percent of the patients manifested a psychiatric disturbance (according to the criteria of the *Psychiatric Diagnostic and Statistical Manual*) and the incidence rate rose considerably in those patients with more advanced disease (19). Unfortunately, recognition rates of psychological disturbance by physicians (and they are the primary gate-keepers for such referrals) are very low.

This situation could be roughly summarized by stating that a sizable proportion of terminally ill patients, but by no means all patients, will manifest marked emotional dysphoria, changes in mental status, characterologic problems, or severe interpersonal conflict. This distress is apt to be recognized only in a small percentage of cases, and there is limited availability of professional services to address these needs in any well-organized formal sense. Depending on the hospital, nursing home, clinic, or community in which the patient resides, services may range from ample to nonexistent. The following section describes a) several types of psychosocial services that have relevance to dying patients and b) significant clinical issues that arise in the context of providing such services.

Support Groups

Support groups for individuals facing a wide variety of special life circumstances have become very popular in recent years. This phenomenon can certainly be observed in the arena of caring for patients with life-threatening illness. Examples include organizations such as Candlelighters (support groups for parents of children with cancer), Make Today Count (support groups for individuals with life-threatening conditions), and I Can Cope (support and educational groups for individuals with cancer). In addition, many hospitals and clinics now offer their own patient and family support groups tailored for patients with a variety of serious afflictions. The format will vary from group to group, but an essential component of all these groups is the opportunity for patients and/or their families to share concerns in a supportive atmosphere as well as receive validation for their feelings ("It's good to know I'm not all alone with this problem"). As needed, information and guidance about specific disease management issues, availability of other resources in the community, and practical steps that might ease the patient's or family's plight are also discussed. Input from a variety of patients and families helps the individual put the problems he or she faces in perspective, drawing attention perhaps to issues that may have been previously ignored or, in other instances, highlighting strengths and assets that had not been previously appreciated ("I thought I wasn't doing so well, but then I heard about the problems faced by so and so").

Although many professionals worry about the possible demoralizing effect of having patients exposed to the suffering of others, group leaders consistently report that the usual effect is quite the contrary—i.e., patients and families more often than not seem to be bolstered by the testimony of others who are struggling with similar issues (20).

Researchers have noted, however, that women, Caucasians, and upper socio-economic groups tend to be overrepresented in such support groups, including groups for persons with cancer or other life-threatening conditions (21). The bases for this phenomenon need to be better understood, but there is a clear and immediate need to make support groups more attractive and available to men, poor people, and members of various ethnic and racial minority groups.

Individual and Family Psychotherapy

When active psychotherapeutic intervention is indicated, the need is recognized by physician and/or patient, and such services are available (a not-too-frequent confluence of events, as noted above), the content and process of psycho-therapy take on characteristics that in several ways differentiate it from psychotherapy with those whose life expectancy is not an issue. Psychologist Edwin Shneidman has written about the special characteristics that mark clinical thanatology (22). Some of these differences are listed and briefly discussed below.

1. The goals are different. In psychological care of the terminally ill, in which the overriding goal is the psychological comfort of the individual, the thera-pist may forego the uncovering of previously hidden material, a mainstay of traditional psychotherapy. As Shneidman expresses it, "The goal, as one fights the clock and the lethal illness, is *to will the obligatory;* to make a chilling and ugly scene go as well as possible; to give psychological succor; to permit the tying up of loose ends; to lend as much stability to the person as it is possible to give" (22, p. 210).

2. The rules are different. Many of the "rules" of the therapist's conduct—prevalent in traditional psychotherapy (e.g., the therapist's reserve, patience in letting the patient work out his or her own solutions, etc.)—may be sus-pended in working with the terminally ill patient. The intensity of transference and countertransference feelings and the rapidity with which these "connec-tions" between therapist and patient develop can be quite different.

3. It may not be psychotherapy. Shneidman means that the process between ther-apist and patient may be sufficiently different to warrant another label. "Psy-chotherapy with a dying person incorporates elements of traditional psycho-therapy, but it also is characterized by other genres of human interaction, including rapport building, interview, conversation, history taking, just plain talk, and communicative silences. There is no movement toward goals such as termination of therapy; there is rather a process that goes on until it is inter-rupted by death" (22, p. 211).

4. The focus is on benign intervention. Active intervention on the therapist's part conducted in the patient's interest is the rule rather than the exception in thanatology work. A therapist may serve as a liaison with other members of the treatment team, with the family, and with others. Whereas the therapist in traditional psychotherapy would certainly shun this role, the psychotherapist in the thanatological situation often takes on a role somewhat akin to an om-budsman.

5. No one has to die in a state of psychological grace. Good psychotherapists—whatever the setting—appreciate that seldom, if ever, do patients work through all their complexes and maladaptive patterns. This pertains, all the more, when working psychotherapeutically with someone who is dying. There may not be time nor energy remaining for the patient to "work through" many shortcomings, blind spots, inhibitions, interpersonal conflicts, and other problems.

6. "Working through" is a luxury for those who have time to live. This follows from the above. Weisman's "appropriate death" would be the more fitting goal—to be "relatively pain-free, suffering reduced, emotional and social im-poverishments kept at a minimum . . . resolving residual conflicts, and satis-fying whatever remaining wishes are consistent with the patient's present plight and ego ideal" (22, p. 212).

7. The dying person sets the pace. The helper's task is to be present but not to

force any particular roles. In particular, no patient need be compelled to "confront" his or her terminal state.

8. Denial will be present. Denial in one form or another is ubiquitous in this situation. Denial-like mechanisms, as we have discussed above, may indeed be helpful, and only on rare occasions must they be directly challenged. Even moments of frank denial by the patient can and usually should be tolerated. As Shneidman observes, "If the therapist will only go along with this transient denial, the dying person will, as abruptly as he began it, abandon it and return to the reality of the present moment."

9. Just as the role of transference is paramount, the place of countertransference bears careful watching. Good psychotherapists are always attuned to their own feelings toward the patient and attempt to understand the origins and meanings of these reactions. In terminal patient care, wherein emotions are so raw and the stress is so severe, this principle obtains all the more. Working in a grim situation, which inevitably becomes grimmer, the therapist is constantly confronted with his or her own impotence. The therapist allows her- or himself to become intertwined in the lives of individuals who die. Though careful to differentiate empathy from identification, the therapist is, nonetheless, subject to issues of bereavement and loss. A good support system, including peer consultants and an active, well-developed, extra-vocational life, is vital.

10. The survivor is the victim and, eventually, the patient: the concept of postvention. From the beginning of working with the dying patient, the psychotherapist ought to become acquainted and, if possible, clinically involved with the survivor(s) to be. During the period of caring for the dying patient, rapport with the patient's family can be built. The psychotherapist should make it clear that he or she will be available to the survivor(s) following the death of the patient. Widows and widowers, as well as children and parents of dying patients, are at risk for physical and psychological complications following the loss of a loved one. They should be offered, and will often need, follow-up supportive counseling. If a relationship has been created with the family member(s) during the period of their loved one's terminal illness, "postvention work" can proceed more easily and probably much more efficaciously.

The last point regarding therapy involvement with the patient's family bears further emphasis. A basic clinical dictum, in my opinion, is that life-threatening illness presents a serious challenge to the integrity and continued functioning of the family system. Only rarely is formal family therapy indicated (though the concepts and perspectives of family therapists can be invaluable). However, if the family is ignored and the patient is worked with exclusively, the psychotherapist is needlessly hampered. Family members can be important sources of information about the patient, and, of course, they can be, and often are, the primary caregivers and social supports for the patient. Their role, even under the best of circumstances, is very challenging. They too are in need of understanding, encouragement, support, and various forms of active assistance from the psychotherapist. When psychotherapeutic inventions are implemented with the patient, family members can also serve as valuable allies in reaching behavioral goals.

A special set of considerations that must always be addressed in working with terminal patients and their families is that of "anticipatory grief" (23). Grief work does not begin at the time of death but long before it, particularly when there is an extended or slowly declining "death trajectory." The patient and family, recognizing (at whatever level) that death is approaching, begin to mourn during the illness period. Commonly, there are "little deaths" along the course of terminal illness (i.e., sacrifices or compromises of physical function, social status, work roles, economic resources, etc.) that trigger anticipatory grieving. In mourning these partial losses, the patient and family are, in fact, doing the work of grieving. It is not just death per se, but all that is lost in the process of dying that must be grieved. If the patient and family are invested in maintaining a "positive perspective" or "fighting the disease," the psychotherapist must often "give permission" to engage in anticipatory grieving, making clear to all concerned that an optimistic spirit is not inconsistent with acknowledgment of the emotional pain associated with very real and present losses.

The following case illustrates just a few of the many losses that a family will sustain when a member is dying. It also illustrates the important role that developmental factors can play; individuals within the family at varying points in their psychosocial development will react to the same events with different needs, preoccupations, and projections. The helper must be attuned to not only each individual's dynamics but must also consider the family's overall style of communication and coping.

Mrs. A., 38-year-old mother of three (ages 7, 9, and 12), had recently been informed (one year following the diagnosis of breast cancer) that she now had widespread bone metastases and liver involvement. Well informed about her disease, she fully appreciated the gravity of her situation. Her husband had just been transferred to another city, their second move in just two years. She was at home alone now, being charged with selling the home and managing the move to a new city. A fast-talking, almost frenetic woman by nature, she saw the news of her recurrent disease as "just one more complication in the whole mess." She sought psychological consultation herself to "plan how I should break the news to the children." As she put it, "I know I am going to die of this disease, but I don't want to lay the whole thing on them at once." She quickly decided that she would frame her announcement in simple terms, emphasizing what must be done presently. "I will tell them that things aren't going well with my cancer and that I need more treatment from the doctors." We discussed some questions she might anticipate and issues to be attuned to for each of the three children. She went home, gathered her children, made her agreed-upon statement, and a week later reported these results. "My seven year old looked me in the eye and said 'Mommy, does that mean you are going to die?' The nine year old, always a quiet and pensive child, had nothing to say but just looked at her shoes. My twelve-going-on-twenty-year-old listened to my announcement, put her hands on her hips, shook her head, and said 'Mom, does this mean we can't go to the shopping mall this afternoon to buy my new swimming suit?' "

Obviously, each member of this family manifested a different style of coping and, at this point in time, each was at a different point in working through his or her feelings about the impending loss of the mother. If this family were to be seen as a unit in psychotherapy, the therapist would have to be attuned to each of these widely divergent reactions. It isn't the mother's disease per se that dictates the psychological response, it is but a stimulus that elicits feelings, attitudes, and behavior reflecting each family member's developmental stage, personal history, characterological traits, and family roles.

Hospice Care

The primary mission of hospitals is to diagnose and treat disease. They are, for the most part, acute care facilities, armed with impressive technology and staffed by highly trained professionals prepared to carry out the institution's mission. This orientation makes the acute care hospital setting, as it is usually structured, less than ideal for end-stage care of persons dying of chronic, incurable conditions. And yet the fact is that relatively few patients die at home today but, instead, rely upon hospitals to provide end-stage care. One response to this dilemma, gaining increasing popularity over the past 15 years, has been the hospice concept of care.* The National Hospice Organization estimated that in 1984 that there were over 1,000 hospice programs currently operating in the United States. Additional momentum was added in 1983 by federal legislation providing at least partial reimbursement for hospice services to Medicare recipients. Many private insurance carriers have also increased hospice benefit packages in the mid-eighties.

The National Hospice Organization defines hospice care as "a specialized health care program emphasizing the management of pain and other symptoms associated with terminal illness while providing care for the family as well as the patient. The aim of hospice is to improve the quality of life remaining for dying patients and support for the family through the bereavement period. Hospice care is provided by physicians, nurses, social workers, therapists, clergy, and specially trained volunteers and is given in the home whenever possible, with inpatient care provided when necessary" (24).

Several different models for providing hospice care have emerged (25). Freestanding units, which provide beds for inpatient care as well as services for home care, have received the most attention in the popular press. Because of costs, reimbursement problems, and a host of other practical matters, this model has not been too popular in North America. Other models include "palliative care units" within general acute care hospitals. These are special sections set aside for terminal care. The patients assigned to such units would not be receiving curative therapy, and the usual array of diagnostic workups typical of patient care in other units would be suspended. However, comfort care—e.g., pain control, controlling nausea and vomiting, nutritional support, psychological and spiritual care, and other ancillary services—would be actively pursued. Some large medical centers have organized hospice consultation teams which provide assistance to physicians and health care providers throughout the hospital with regard to terminal care. The advantage of this model is that the philosophy and modus operandi of hospice can be extended throughout the entire medical center. The potential problem in this

---

*Though hospice care is discussed extensively elsewhere in this volume (see Chapter Nine), it deserves at least brief mention here to illustrate how psychotherapeutic services for the terminally ill can be integrated into a comprehensive care model.

model is that since there is no defined location, nor a core staff, actual implementation of hospice care principles could be diluted. Perhaps the most common model in this country is community-based home care programs. These rely heavily on volunteer efforts but attempt to provide a range of supportive services for terminal patients and their families in the home. Many of the community-based programs contract with area hospitals to provide inpatient beds when necessary.

In the foregoing, it is obvious that the term "hospice" refers to a philosophy of care for the terminally ill not to the location of such care nor to one particular service delivery model. In individuals who have fatal diagnoses and curative therapies have failed, active treatment is no longer warranted. However, maintaining at least a modicum of control over their remaining lives and helping their families deal with the impending loss is a challenge that requires active medical and nursing management, as well as an array of other support services.

Recent surveys of cancer patients (26) and of health care professionals (27) show a high degree of acceptance of the importance of hospice services. Both professional and patient respondents ranked medical consultation for symptom control, home nursing care, and psychological counseling for patients and families as the three highest priorities. However, cancer patients themselves also reported a high likelihood of using other hospice services, where they readily available (e.g., nutritional evaluation, respite care for family members, spiritual guidance, home support services, legal and financial advice, occupational and physical therapy, and bereavement care).

A well-organized hospice service offers the advantage of integrating medical, nursing, psychological, and other support services, an ideal often touted but seldom achieved in the care of the terminally ill in traditional hospitals, nursing homes, or outpatient settings. However, despite impressive gains in recent years, many communities still have no hospice services available. Where they are available, many patients find that they have no insurance benefit for hospice services, or the benefit provided by Medicare or their private insurance is less than adequate in relation to actual costs. Many outpatients accustomed to technologically based medicine simply demand that their physicians "do something!" (i.e., continue curative attempts) even though they have an incurable disease. There are also, of course, some physicians who would be reluctant to refer patients to a palliative care setting.

REVIEW QUESTIONS

1. Compare the model of the stages of dying with that of the dying trajectories and phases. What are the major differences between these models? Which model, in your opinion, is more useful in explaining an individual's experience of dying?

2. Describe the levels of denial postulated by Weisman. Under what circumstances would you consider first-order denial as appropriate? In what ways can the timing of denial be important to the patient?

3. The phrase "mutual pretense" has been used to describe the situation in which the terminal patient, his/her family, and health professionals all act as if the patient were not dying. Under what circumstances would you consider mutual

pretense as desirable? Under what circumstances would it be harmful to the patient? In this context, what is the relevance of the patient's rights?
4. What are the characteristics of an "appropriate death?" How do these differ from an "idealized death?"
5. Distinguish between informal, general psychosocial support and formal, specialized psychosocial interventions for terminally ill patients.
6. Describe some of the support groups listed in this chapter. How do you account for the finding that the poor and ethnic and racial minority members do not participate in these groups? How would you go about making support groups more available to these minorities?
7. Describe major differences between psychotherapy for terminally ill persons and those not terminally ill.
8. Describe ways in which family members can be of critical importance in assisting their dying loved ones directly and indirectly through the psychotherapist.
9. What are the major needs of family members of a dying patient? Who, in your opinion, should provide this help: members of the health care system, hospital or hospice volunteers, community agencies, or a self-help support group? Give your reasons.

REFERENCES

1. Becker, E. (1973). *The denial of death.* New York: The Free Press.
2. Pattison, E. M. (1978). The living-dying process. In C. A. Garfield (Ed.), *Psychosocial care of the dying patient* (pp. 133–168). New York: McGraw-Hill.
3. Kübler-Ross, E. (1969). *On death and dying.* New York: MacMillan.
4. Schulz, R., & Aderman, D. (1974). Clinical research and the stages of dying. *Omega, 5,* 137–143.
5. Rodabough, T. (1980). Alternatives to the stages model of the dying process. *Death Education, 4,* 1–19.
6. Shneidman, E. S. (1973). *Deaths of man.* Baltimore: Penguin Books.
7. Martocchio, B. C. (1982). *Living while dying.* Bowie, MD: Robert J. Brady.
8. Glaser, B. G., & Strauss, A. L. (Eds.). (1968). *Time for dying.* Chicago: Aldine.
9. Weisman, A. (1972). *On dying and denying.* New York: Behavioral Publications.
10. Lazarus, R. S., & Folkman, S. (1984). *Stress appraisal and coping.* New York: Springer.
11. Glaser, B., & Strauss, A. (1965). *Awareness of dying.* Chicago: Aldine.
12. Kalish, R. A. (1970). The onset of the dying process. *Omega, 1,* 57–69.
13. Weisman, A. D. (1984). *The coping capacity: On the nature of being mortal.* New York: Human Sciences Press.
14. Shneidman, E. S. (1977). Aspects of the dying process. *Psychiatric Annals, 8,* 25–40.
15. Doyle, D. (Ed.). (1984). *Palliative care: The management of far advanced illness.* Philadelphia: Charles Press.
16. Twycross, R. G., & Lack, S. A. (1983). *Symptom control in far advanced cancer: Pain relief.* Baltimore: Urban & Schwarzenberg.
17. Maguire, P. (1985). Barriers to psychological care of the dying. *British Medical Journal, 241,* 1711–1713.
18. Rainey, L. C., Wellisch, D. K., Fawzy, F., Wolcott, D., & Pasnau, R. (1983). Training health professionals in psychiatric aspects of cancer. *Journal of Psychosocial Oncology, 1,* 41–59.

19. Derogatis, L. R., Morrow, G. R., & Fetting, J., et al. (1983). The prevalence of psychiatric disorders among cancer patients, *JAMA, 249,* 751–757.

20. Yalom, I. D. (1980). *Existential psychotherapy.* New York: Basic Books.

21. Taylor, S. E., Falke, R. L., Shoptaw, S. J., & Lichtman, R. R. (1986). Social support groups and the cancer patient. *Journal of Consulting and Clinical Psychology, 54,* 608–615.

22. Shneidman, E. S. (1978). Some aspects of psychotherapy with dying persons. In C. A. Garfield (Ed.), *Psychological care of the dying patient* (pp. 201–218). New York: McGraw-Hill.

23. Rando, T. A. (Ed.). (1986). *Loss and anticipatory grief.* Lexington, MA: D.C. Heath.

24. National Hospice Organization. (1984). Fact sheet. Arlington, VA: Author.

25. Buckingham, R. W., & Lupu, D. (1982). A comparative study of hospice services in the United States. *American Journal of Public Health, 72,* 455–463.

26. Rainey, L., Crane, L., Breslow, D., & Ganz, P. (1984). Cancer patients' attitudes toward hospice services. *Ca—A Journal for Clinicians, 34,* 191–201.

27. Ganz, P., Breslow, D., Crane, L., & Rainey, L. (1986). Professional attitudes toward hospice care. *The Hospice Journal, 1,* 1–15.

8

Institutional Dying: A Convergence of Cultural Values, Technology, and Social Organization

Jeanne Quint Benoliel

Death and dying are experiences known in all human societies. How people manage these important social transitions is determined by a composite of the values and beliefs that govern their society, the level of technology available, and the types of death most commonly encountered. Sudden death has always been a part of the human condition. Prolonged dying by large numbers of people is a phenomenon of the twentieth century closely related to the appearance of urban industrial systems of existence and prolonged life expectancy.

In any society, cultural belief systems determine the procedures and rituals established for handling the transition of dying, the settings in which it takes place, and the persons likely to be present during its passage. These institutionalized practices also reflect the complexity of lifestyle required of a people as well as the meaning and frequency of death in everyday experience. The procedures and practices related to death and dying in hunting and gathering societies reflect this interplay among cultural values, technologies, and daily life demands.

DEATH, CULTURE, AND CAREGIVING PRACTICES

In the hunting and gathering societies of earlier times, human beings moved about in small bands exploiting the surroundings for food and sustenance. Their relatively simple technology was used primarily for survival, and their social organization and social relationships were organized around the achievement of that goal. Life expectancy was short, and death was a commonplace event in the daily lives of the people. Not uncommonly, people in such societies surrounded the dead with an aura of terror, buried them quickly, and utilized procedures that erased their names quickly from the memories of survivors (1).

Cross-cultural studies of societal practices for coping with death reveal several commonly observed customs: use of priests or special functionaries at the funeral ceremonies; isolation or separation of the bereaved from other members of society; and final ceremonies that bring the mourning period to an end after a culturally prescribed period of weeks, months, or sometimes years (2). Cultural configurations also determine the customs to be used for the care of the sick, including the places set aside for ill persons and those about to die. In hunting and gathering societies, the role of shaman or witch doctor—responsible for driving out the demons or other causes of illness—was commonly filled by a man and the role of caregiver of the sick filled by a woman (1).

Special institutions for the care of sick persons probably did not appear until agriculture replaced hunting and gathering as the major style of human living. This major change in lifestyle set the stage for the emergence of civilization, complex social and hierarchical institutions, and specialized occupations of many kinds. The evidence available suggests that the earliest hospitals—whether in ancient Egypt, Buddhist India, or Judaic Palestine—were associated with temples or other institutions concerned with religious beliefs and practices. Military operations also fostered the appearance of hospitals, as is shown in historical documents describing the Roman Empire (3).

INSTITUTIONS FOR DYING: A PRODUCT OF CIVILIZATION

In Western society, both religious and social considerations contributed to the growth of care-providing facilities. Following the fall of Rome, Christianity became increasingly influential through the activities of Paul and other teachers of the new religion. By the fourth century the Christian values of faith, hope, and charity were translated into religious obligations such that care for the sick became not only a Christian duty but beneficial for the salvation of the soul. On order of religious authority, hospitals were constructed in every cathedral city, and services were provided to a variety of persons in need—travelers, the infirm, the elderly, and the indigent. As time went by, support for these institutions came from many benefactors, including kings, lords, merchants, and guilds; yet the hospitals continued to be managed and run by members of religious communities. Closely tied to the development of Christian monasticism, the hospital in medieval times existed not as a place solely devoted to the care of sick people but rather as a center committed to medical care, philanthropy, and spirituality (3).

The Impact of Industrialization

With the development of specialized crafts, mercantilism, and trade came the appearance of a middle class. Industries began to appear, and small villages were replaced by towns and cities to house the workers in these new systems of work. As agricultural lands were taken for industrial and other uses, the conditions of the poor worsened. Increased numbers of sick and poor people placed a heavy strain on charity-providing institutions since the society at the time had no mechanisms for helping to better the condition of those in need.

The Catholic church was pressured to change, and by the late Middle Ages, differences in religious interpretations precipitated the Reformation and a movement toward secularization of Western society. Powers once held by church authorities were taken over by secular leaders, and in due time, the state replaced the church as the primary controlling influence over peoples' lives. Responsibilities once assumed to be religious became the province of the community. Under the influence of a new set of values, public assistance and welfare appeared as societal approaches for responding to the needs of the sick and the poor.

The changing times put heavy pressures on established caregiving institutions and created a need for new kinds of services. The old philanthropic institution sponsored by the church gave way to hospitals and institutions designed for special purposes—venereal disease, smallpox, mental illness, and many others. Physicians began to be associated with hospitals on a regular basis, and public institutions were created for care of the sick and the poor. From the seventeenth century on, hospitals came more and more to be seen as places specifically for the treatment of disease. It also should be noted that the death-preventing capabilities of medical treatments were negligible, and mortality rates in hospitals were high rather than low with infection and cross-contamination contributing heavily to these outcomes (4). Regardless of the development of hospitals, the majority of deaths occurred outside of these establishments for many centuries—taking place in private homes and on the streets, close to the daily lives of the people.

Influence of Science on Medical Care

The ties between physicians and hospitals were strengthened by the emergence of science and the application of the scientific method to the study of the human body and its ills. As knowledge relevant to medicine accumulated, hospitals came to be places for the study and teaching of medicine as well as for the treatment of the sick. The decline in religious involvement in running hospitals affected the availability of human power to provide direct care to an expanding population in need, and the focus on hospital use was increasingly limited to sick patients with treatable diseases. Persons with chronic, incurable, and terminal diseases were relegated to almshouses, poorhouses, and other forms of public institutions. These settings came to be known as undesirable places set aside for the dying of persons with limited means (4).

THE NEW CULTURE OF THE TWENTIETH CENTURY

In the twentieth century, a combination of changing societal values, expanding technology, and population pressures altered the nature of living and dying in profound ways. Attitudes and behaviors in relation to death and dying were affected by the secularization of society, the dominance of science over medical practice, and the demands of an expanding population.

Separation of Dying from Human Existence

As the culture of Western society changed from a religious orientation toward life and death to a perspective dominated by the values of science, trade, and business, the act of dying underwent changes such that control over its management shifted progressively from the dying person to the family and eventually to the physician and the hospital team (5, 6). The rise of science was accompanied by a progressive spread of religious disbelief, and, over time, fear of death emerged as *the* pervasive attitude (7). Direct experience with death and dying disappeared for many members of society as new occupations appeared to take care of the many death-related tasks associated with an expanding population. Management of dying as a social process shifted from the family to the larger society, and the necessary services associated with death became bureaucratized as was also true for many other activities essential to the ongoing flow of human affairs.

Under the influence of science, death changed from being defined as a supernatural phenomenon to a natural one—an event capable of being conquered by human ingenuity and the application of societal resources for all classes of society (8). With this shift in values, ordinary people were increasingly removed from direct experience with death and dying as human transitions and, therefore, had little opportunity to learn how to handle themselves in these situations. The pattern of "protecting" the dying person by not talking about the fatal disease replaced the traditional religious obligation of informing the dying person so that preparation for death could be completed. Eventually, changes in attitudes and practices led to patterns of withholding information about diagnosis and prognosis of disease from the individual with the terminal illness.

Influence of Science and Applied Technology

The influence of science and technology on Western societal attitudes and practices increased progressively between 1700 and 1900, paving the way for a takeover of applied technology in the twentieth century. By the turn of the century, human existence had already been altered by secularization, urbanization, and industrialization as these affected work, family, and lifestyle possibilities. However, these changes were minor compared to what the next 85 years would bring. The creation of mass transportation brought a shift to a mobile society. The development of mass communication radically changed the flow of information and knowledge, facilitating thereby a movement toward industrialization of the world.

Contributing to these changes in the United States was the creation of an assembly-line model of work production that operationalized the historical values of hard work, pragmatism, control over nature, and active doing and, eventually, made the products of technology readily accessible to ordinary members of society. On the other side of the coin, the assembly-line model encouraged a depersonalization of work through fragmentation of the tasks to be done, leading thereby to monotony of daily effort for many people. In time, the model came to be applied to service agencies as well as to factories, and the one-to-one, provider-client relationship gave way to the emergence of social, educational, and health care services provided by multiple workers (9).

Population Changes and Social Control

Science and technology also contributed to a growth of population on a worldwide scale. This change resulted from a progressive increase in the general standard of living and the application of public health measures to problems of food, water, and waste disposal. Population expansion increased the number of groups with special needs and introduced a requirement for special institutions to regulate and control the social problems created by these groups. Thus, the growth in numbers of young people and the need to educate them for work in an industrial society led to the phenomenon of mass education and the public school system. Increases in the number of persons breaking the laws of society expanded the need for prisons and similar institutions to isolate such lawbreakers form regular contact with other members of society.

Population expansion brought increased numbers of people with various illnesses, but the nature of illness changed as people lived longer, and infectious diseases came under medical control. At the turn of the century, science and technology had already altered the practice of medicine as a result of such discoveries as bacteriology, anesthesia, and prevention of disease through public health measures (10). Yet at the same time the life-saving capabilities of physicians were relatively limited, and the primary killers of people continued to be infectious diseases. By the 1950s relative control of the communicable diseases had been achieved by a combination of improved sanitation, immunization, and specific drug therapies (11). In the second half of the century, chronic disease became the major contributor to morbidity and mortality statistics, and the hospital came to play a central part in the treatment of these disorders.

The character of hospitals in the twentieth century was as much influenced by changes affecting the practice of medicine as by the needs of sick patients. After the Flexner report on medical education in 1910, the apprentice model of training was replaced by university teaching of medical students, and the hospital came to play a major part in the education of students (12). To provide an arena for practice, the teaching hospital was created as a site for internship and residency programs; historically, these hospitals were places to treat the indigent (13). The increasing application of science and technology to the diagnosis and treatment of disease led to the development of scientific medicine, but the full effect of this historical movement on the hospital as a caregiving institution came into being following World War II (4, 9).

Dominance of Science over Medical Practice

The influence of science on medicine came in two ways. Scientific discoveries, such as x-ray and radiation, led to the direct application of technology to methods of diagnosis and treatment. The creation of a scientific method, known as the *biomedical model* of disease, for applying the reductionist principles of the physical sciences to the study of disease led to an objectification of the doctor-patient relationship and a disregard for social and behavioral factors affecting illness. Expansion of knowledge led to the rapid development of specialized fields of medical practice, often centered in hospitals. For patients, this change meant receiving services from many doctors instead of one. The movement of medical schools into universities brought increased control over medical education by the scientific community, and the hospital became as much a medical laboratory for the study of disease as a setting for patient care (12).

By 1945, the biomedical model of disease had become the dominant influence in the practice of medicine and the education of new practitioners. In this model, disease is defined as physical and biochemical deviations from established norms, and the body is treated as a breakdown of machinery subject to recovery through replacement or repair of defective body parts. In Engel's view, this belief system has become a cultural imperative on the American scene—that is, all members of society are influenced to a greater or lesser extent by these beliefs (14). Within such a framework, an expansion of the life-saving ethic and a deployment of resources into life-prolonging activities can be understood as socially adaptive mechanisms to resolve the uncertainties surrounding disease and to control death, now defined as the enemy. More and more, hospitals came to be places designed and organized for the purpose of controlling death (9).

The industrialization of disease management and death control moved rapidly after the end of World War II, and the hospital became in short order a technical life-saving establishment. In the United States, this change was facilitated by the government's active movement into financial support for biomedical research and social legislation expanding the availability of health care services to certain high-need members of society. Out of medical research came a variety of life-sustaining and supporting procedures and machines, and new paramedical occupations were developed to implement the new and specialized functions created by the new technology. More and more the medical school was dominated by governmental influences over biomedical research funds and directions, including the use of the university-affiliated hospital as the most favorable environment for biomedical research (12).

Responding to the pressures imposed by the discovery of kidney dialysis machines, respirators, transplant surgeries, and other life-prolonging techniques, administrators of hospitals reorganized the use of staff and space to accommodate these many changes (4, 12, 13). Between 1960 and 1970 came the development of a variety of kinds of critical care settings all emphasizing medical control over death (15). By 1981, there were intensive care units in 95 percent of acute care hospitals in the United States, providing an estimated 66,000 beds for adults and 8,000 beds for pediatrics and neonatal intensive care (16). Training programs were developed to prepare nurses and other workers for coping with the demands of this highly technical work, and nurses in hospitals increasingly found their daily activities dominated by the pressures and stresses of life-saving medical activities (17). Over a very short span of years, the hospital became a setting in which dying became a technologized experience, and the influence of science led to new forms of dying.

NEW FORMS OF DYING

For much of the history of humankind, the deaths of children have been commonplace events. At the beginning of the twentieth century, the loss of one or more children in a family was not unusual, and much of the time these deaths occurred at home. Progressive control over the communicable diseases resulted in a sharp decline in childhood deaths such that around 1960, the death of a child, especially from an infectious disease, was a rare occurrence that carried a special kind of poignancy. Although children do die today of cancer, poisons, and accidental injuries, their numbers are small compared to adult deaths, and peoples' reactions of loss are disproportionately intense.

Effects of Increased Life Expectancy

Over the same span of 60 years, increased life expectancy in the adult population created a new social phenomenon—large numbers of people living to be 70 years of age and older. This rise in the numbers of elderly persons changed the model character of dying by making chronic illness and the deteriorations of aging the primary causes of death in Western societies. As a result of this change, the relatively short time periods formerly taken for dying from acute infectious processes were replaced by a new norm—that of prolonged dying over a period of weeks, months, or sometimes years.

In the 1970s, a social problem of serious dimensions was identified when it became clear that the number of elderly over the age of 80 years was rising faster than those over 65 in general. This old-old group contains proportionately large numbers of "frail elderly" with limited capacities to take care of themselves, and society faced a growing need for caregiving services for these partially or completely socially disabled human beings. Improvements in the life-saving capabilities of modern medicine meant that for many older people dying, rather than living, was the stage being prolonged. Thus, the technical advances capable of postponing death brought negative as well as positive consequences to the quality of living for many people—perhaps especially to the elderly. With the advent of antibiotics and other chemotherapeutic agents, pneumonia, once known as the old man's friend, could no longer function easily as a "friend" of those who were ready to die (18).

Effects of Life-saving Medical Procedures

The use of new life-saving techniques and procedures also kept alive persons who in years gone by would have died at an early age. New populations in need of special services and institutional care appeared. For example, children with Down's syndrome (mongolism), long known to have a high susceptibility to respiratory infection, have shown an increase in life expectancy greater than that of the general population. This outcome resulted from the application of medical techniques to physical defects formerly leading to death in the first year of life. For the first time in human history, Western society must plan for the special needs of a population of elderly mongoloid people, a situation unheard of prior to 1950. In a more general sense, the prevalence rate of severely retarded people is growing rapidly, bringing with it a demand for special institutions capable of providing services to those with limited capabilities to care for themselves (18).

In a similar way, the products of medical technology were found capable of keeping alive many newborn infants with severe congenital deformities or other physical problems as well as prematures whose vulnerability to early death has always been high. Special settings for the intensive treatment of these and other high-risk infants and children are commonplace in many medical center hospitals. Physicians and nurses in these settings find themselves faced with the tensions and strains of work in constant contact with dying babies as well as living ones (17).

Medical technology also made possible the prolongation of life with chronic diseases that in days gone by would have led to early death. The discovery of insulin by Banting and Best in 1922, for example, meant that children with insulin-dependent diabetes mellitus no longer were subject to childhood dying due to ketoacidosis and an inability to control the metabolism of carbohydrates and fats. Instead they could live into adulthood only to die from the vascular complications of diabetes prone to appear in the middle and later years (18). People with chronic kidney failure were able to have their lives extended by spending part of their time attached to kidney dialysis machines, but their living styles were radically altered by the requirements of this time-consuming medical regimen.

Although advances in medical technology made it possible for many people with these and other forms of chronic disease to live longer, they often had to spend part of that time in the hospital because of complications and acute exacerbations of illness (19). In many cases, prolongation of life with chronic disease brought periods of near-death and institutional dying, not just an extension of time. Although defined by general beliefs as places for sustaining life, hospitals are also places in which people die and other people are caregivers during the process of dying.

INSTITUTIONAL DYING: NURSING HOMES AND HOSPITALS

Statistics on the location of dying are difficult to obtain. Mortality statistics for 1980 in the United States show 60.5 percent of deaths occurring in hospitals or medical centers, 13.5 percent in other institutions, 8.4 percent classified as dead-on-arrival, 17.5 percent occurring in other places, and 0.1 percent as unknown (20, p. 304). These results suggest that the final period of living for the majority of those who die takes place in hospitals, but the length of time involved and the setting for dying is not completely clear.

It is clear that many people who are dying in institutions are not defined as dying by the personnel providing care. It is also clear that institutional dying takes many different forms with particular types of dying associated with different types of settings. Each pattern of dying is determined by an interplay among several interacting factors: a) the physical state of the person who is dying; b) the social and spatial arrangements of the settings; c) the patterns of social interaction around and with the dying person; d) the patient's defined state; e) the methods of treatment and caregiving provided; f) the availability of advocates or allies for the dying person; and g) the number and types of caregiving personnel involved.

Dying in a Nursing Home: The Forgotten Ones

In the United States, the nursing home industry expanded rapidly after World War II to meet a growing demand for institutional services for the incapacitated elderly. These and other custodial institutions became places for the prolonged dying of individuals with low social value, and they effectively served to remove these "reminders of death" from open visibility by other members of society. This segregation of the elderly can be viewed as a direct reflection of the youth-oriented, death-denying value ascribed to American society.

The allocation of resources to these institutions appears to coincide with the low value accorded its occupants and, according to Vladek, the failure of public policy to provide mechanisms for caregiving to an aging population (21). The typical nursing home resident is an 80-year-old white widow or spinster of relatively limited means and with three to four chronic ailments; the average length of stay is 2.6 years with 30 percent of discharges due to death (21). Often the people hired for positions of direct patient care are both poorly trained and poorly paid, and the work itself is hard (22). In some instances, the situation is one that encourages practices of patient abuse, sometimes contributing to a patient's death (23).

Although many people sent to nursing homes are undergoing a prolonged process of dying, observations in the 1960s of the staff in interaction with their elderly clients gave evidence of very little open discussion about death (24). When the institution must provide services for large numbers of confused and physically disabled elderly patients, the work of keeping them bathed and fed and mobile is organized in regimented ways, removing many of the personal touches enjoyed by elderly people. In a study of one nursing home, Kayser-Jones observed that staff members used a variety of depersonalizing practices with the patients: a) scolding and calling by first names; b) routinizing care and preventing personal choices; c) providing little protection against theft of personal belongings or personal harm; and d) showing insensitivity to patients' feelings and a lack of compassion and kindness (22).

Cultural Values and Long-Term Care

In the United States, the organization of work and the typical patterns of communication in nursing homes create nonstimulating and depersonalized living environments in which elderly persons, who are unable to negotiate other living arrangements for themselves, undergo a prolonged process of impersonal dying. Assuming that institutional dying is a social process defined and influenced by the perceptions of those involved—the recipients of services, their families, the providers of care, and those who allocate resources—people who die in nursing homes might be viewed as socially dead long before they reach the point of biological death.

Even in its organization the nursing home tends to be a model of the larger society. The sick elderly are segregated from those who are physically well. Often patients who become critically ill are sent to the hospital for active medical treatment. For others, the final period of dying means placement in a room alone so that the event of death will not be disturbing to other patients, and the staff keeps quiet watch hoping to prevent the end from taking place without another's presence. Although dying is an ever-present phenomenon in the nursing home, its existence, in many, is seldom acknowledged openly; activities around the elderly dying patient are managed by the staff to keep the possibility of emotional disruption under control.

In contrast to the United States, the government of Great Britain made geriatric care an integral part of health care services in the late 1940s. As a result, the care of the chronic long-term patient occurs in the mainstream of medical care. Well-developed supportive services exist to help elderly persons stay at home. Government-owned, long-term care institutions were developed to provide care for those unable to do so on their own, and careful geriatric assessment is performed prior to entry into such an institution (22).

Comparing a long-term facility in Scotland and a proprietary nursing home in the United States, Kayser-Jones found the former organized to offer home-like services that emphasized good food, planned and regular social activities, and regular attention to personal care. Further, she noted that family members, including children, came for lengthy visits with their elderly relatives who appeared to be comfortable and pleased with the care they received. In contrast, the latter institution was observed to provide food that was displeasing, no outdoor activities, and little attention to modesty or personal wishes. Children were not permitted to visit their elderly relatives, and family members who came stayed for only a short time (22). These variations reflect basic cultural differences in attitudes toward the elderly as manifested in both family behaviors and social policies governing the allocation of governmental resources for elder care.

Hospital Dying: Complexity and Variability

In previous centuries, the treatments available to patients in hospitals were the symptomatic and comfort activities commonly classed as nursing care. In the twentieth century, highly specialized and technical medical procedures became the dominant form of therapy, and hospital services were altered to accommodate this change. During the 20 years immediately following the end of World War II, urban hospitals not only increased in size but also became intricate multipurpose social structures to accommodate the pressures of three interrelated goals: research, instruction, and patient services. During the immediate postwar period in the United States, government support of hospital construction contributed to an increase in acute care general hospitals and a decline in long-term care hospitals (4).

Dominated by the continually growing power of the biomedical model of disease, the practice of medicine came to be structured and organized around the primacy of the cure ethic. Life-saving procedures and machines became increasingly important in the daily activities of physicians, and the solo practice of general practitioners rapidly gave way to group practice provided by specialists. Heavily influenced by these changes in the practice of medicine, the work in hospitals came to be organized around the diagnosis and treatment of disease. The focus of nursing work was altered by the pressures of medical technology and the demands for attention to activities for maintaining control over death. As the day-to-day activities of physicians, nurses, and other hospital workers came to center on the primacy of life-saving tasks, services to meet the human needs of patients and families came to be tangential and secondary processes. These changes appeared not because the various professional groups lacked concern but, rather, because the work to be done was organized for the purpose of saving lives, and the dying patient represented failure. -

The primacy of the *cure goal* over the *goal of care* institutionalized the secular value of control over death and facilitated the objectification of the practitioner-provider relationship (14). Despite the appearance of mental health concepts and knowledge about the psychological needs of patients and families, the education of new practitioners in nursing was strongly influenced by the power of death control and was relatively ineffective in preparing them for the psychosocial aspects of implementing care to dying patients and their families (25). Yet the work in hospitals brought them face-to-face with the dilemmas of care and cure, and sometimes they found themselves faced with choices involving conflicts between personal and professional values. The technologizing of death in the hospital increased dehumanizing outcomes for dying patients, but it also added greatly to the stresses and strains of hospital work.

The stresses and strains associated with death and dying are not the same in all parts of the hospital, however. Some units may have very few dying patients, and others may have many. Medical specialization set the stage for different kinds of treatment arenas and different forms of death-related work.

Hospital Work, Dying Patients, and Caregiving

A major outcome of specialization in medicine was the appearance of special purpose hospital units organized specifically for the medical treatment of particular groups of patients. Reaching its peak in 1965, this influence was most powerfully experienced in university-affiliated teaching hospitals through the ready availability of federal research monies (12). It shifted the focus of hospital services away from a concept of generalized medical-surgical care toward treatment settings geared for highly specialized treatments of special groups—patients with heart attacks, burns, cancer, trauma, or birth defects (9, 15). Although centrally concerned with life-saving activity, the staff in these settings must also provide services for patients who die there. The "death work" in different settings in the hospital becomes regularized around several interrelated elements in the situation: a) the types of dying most characteristically found there; b) the types of death-related tasks expected of the workers; c) the primary emphasis attached to the work to be done; d) the frequency of death and dying; and e) the staffs' preparation for and experience in the tasks they must perform.

Specialization and new technology have complicated the business of caregiving by increasing the numbers of people required to get the work done. Strauss and his associates described the social organization of medical work in hospitals as requiring five kinds of work that shape the characteristics of illness trajectories and the essential tasks to be done (26). Machine work relates to the inventing, servicing, and using of various technologies for the medical diagnosis and treatment of diseases and other ailments. In some settings—such as coronary care—a great deal of time and effort must be given to monitoring both the machines and the patients.

Safety work is closely related to machine work in that attention must be given to judging whether or not a given technology is harmful to patients, but safety work also involves attention to the effects of medical treatments and other procedures on the well-being of patients. It also means assessing and monitoring clinical hazards in the work environment, including the competency of various personnel, and developing safety measures and routines (26).

Comfort work is centrally concerned with activities and measures for the relief of pain and discomfort. Sentimental work refers to a variety of interpersonal activities having to do with interacting with patients, building trust, maintaining composure, supporting identities, and controlling patients' awareness of their illness states. Articulation work relates to the coordination of all other forms of work in the best interests of the patient, but it is highly susceptible to disruption for a variety of personal, interpersonal, and organizational reasons. Patients can suffer harm when articulation work is impossible to achieve, but all patients suffer some disarticulation in today's complex hospitals because of the number of people involved (26).

Communication with patients, family members, and other providers is a central component of caregiving in hospitals. In the 1960s, investigators of dying in hospitals reported some common problems in social relationships and personal experiences of staff regardless of differences in the characteristics of the settings. These common problems included: a) a tendency for the staff to avoid open conversations with dying patients about their dying; b) communication difficulties among the staff associated with differences in expectations and failures in the flow of information; and c) strong emotional reactions to difficult choices and decisions (27). Depending on how the work of death was organized, these problems might or might not lead to explicit role conflicts and interpersonal difficulties involving patients, families, and members of the unit involved. These observers noted that the more that death work was routinized and regularized the more were the disruptive effects of death minimized and controlled (27, 28).

Hospital Care: The 1970s

In the 1960s, a death-awareness movement appeared in the United States as something of a counterculture against the death-avoiding practices of the twentieth century (9). Professional and lay literature dealing with many complex issues related to death and dying proliferated in the 1970s. Public interest in finding alternatives to hospitalization was demonstrated in the creation of hospices for terminal care, demands for new legislation permitting consumer participation in decisions about the use of life-prolonging methods, and an outpouring of voluntary groups devoted to helping people with various life-threatening disorders and situations. Professional interest in creating alternative forms of care for dying people commonly took the form of federally funded demonstration projects such as the Minnesota home care program for children with leukemia (29).

In the 1970s, the death-awareness movement influenced hospital practices in several ways. It legitimized medical care of the dying patient and permitted the introduction of palliative care services and hospice units into established hospitals (30). It stimulated a variety of workshops and other educational activities to prepare physicians, nurses, and other health care providers for work that involved them with dying patients and their families (31). These teaching efforts did not refocus the goals of the health care system, but they did sensitize a number of providers to the complexities of interpersonal collaboration in death work.

Others attempted to bring about changes in the institutions themselves. One way that organized nursing attempted to counteract the depersonalizing influences of institutional routines in hospitals was to introduce well-prepared nurses to assist patients and families with the situationally derived stresses and strains that hospitalization often brings. These nurses were known by a variety of different names, such as *clinical specialist* or *nurse practitioner*, and their achievements were variable depending on whether their activities were perceived as nonthreatening or threatening by physicians, other nurses, and other members of the institutional staff (32). In some settings, the introduction of clinical nurse specialists led to discord between the medical and nursing staffs, but in other settings, it paved the way for the creation of new services—for example, a protocol and procedure for providing regular support to grieving spouses of patients hospitalized in a coronary care unit (33).

In the 1970s, the work of caregiving in hospitals was greatly influenced by a range of ethical and legal problems associated with the utilization of advanced biomedical technology. Serving as a kind of exemplar of the problem was the case of Karen Quinlan and the question of parental rights to discontinue active medical treatments as surrogates for a daughter (34). These ethical and legal concerns added to the complexity of decision making in terminal care and to the tensions of decision makers. Legal questions, in particular, put pressure on physicians to do everything possible in the way of treatment to avoid the possibility of being sued for malpractice. Analysis of records of patients who died in one teaching hospital showed the majority as having been designated no code (nonuse of active cardio-pulmonary resuscitation) and as having conditions labeled by their physicians as grim or terminal prognosis. Yet the medical treatment orientation was overwhelmingly toward the use of life support maintenance and active cardiopulmonary resuscitation (CPR) (35).

Hospital Care: The 1980s

By the 1980s, ethical and legal questions about treatment decisions expanded to include the appropriateness of discontinuing fluids and nutrition for terminal patients and/or those who requested it, and Elizabeth Bouvia became the exemplar case for these considerations (36). In addition, the cost of hospitalization became a major political issue, and the appearance of acquired immune deficiency syndrome (AIDS) created a variety of personal, social, and political problems.

In 1950, the average cost of hospital care was about $15.62 a day and $126.52 for the total hospital stay. By 1982, the average cost per day had increased to $327.37, and the average cost for hospital stay to $2,500.52 (13). This change was directly related to an overall increase in health care expenditures in the United States: the proportion of the gross national product accounted for by health expenditures shifted from 4.4 percent in 1950 to 10.5 percent in 1982. Also of importance, the government assumed increased responsibility for payment of health care expenditures, and beginning in 1965, an increased proportion of these funds were spent on personal health services (37). Using data for 1968, Mushkin and DiScullio estimated that about one-fourth of all Medicare hospital costs were spent for the care of aged dying patients, and they argued that terminal illness claimed a significant share of hospital resources (38). Using secondary analysis of cost data from several studies, Scitovsky argued that the large proportion of costs at the end of life was not so much due to intensive treatment of terminal patients as to the cost of ordinary medical care for very sick patients (39).

In an effort to contain Medicare costs of hospitalization, the Health Care Financing Administration (HCFA) initiated a prospective payment system based on 467 Diagnosis Related Groups (DRGs) to control the amount of funds available to hospitals for different types of medical cases. The DRG system does not take account of variations in severity of illness within groups, and hospitals that treat a disproportionately large share of severely ill patients can be disadvantaged financially when DRGs are not adjusted for severity for illness (40). In a prospective payment system with a fixed schedule of rates, the hospital must bear the costs of outlier cases (13, 40). Just how these cost-containment strategies will affect hospital care, including that provided for the dying, is not completely clear. It is probably fair to say that the situation will be most difficult for those persons with low incomes and limited resources.

In 1981, AIDS was identified as an HTLV-III viral infection that increased the vulnerability of young infected adults to fatal opportunistic diseases and an early death (41). The shift from a few diagnosed persons in 1981 to 10,000 in 1985 and the association of spread with sexual activity (particularly homosexual) created almost a panic state among groups at high risk for exposure and others who were frightened (42). This epidemic of the 1980s has created a form of dying that involves much suffering and frequent hospitalizations in young men in particular. It has created problems for insurance companies which must bear the burden of hospital costs—estimated to be $140,000 for the average AIDS case (43). It has created tensions for the providers of care to victims of AIDS and concerns about their safety when in contact with AIDS victims.

DIFFERENT TYPES OF HOSPITAL DYING

The concept of dying trajectory was coined by Glaser and Strauss to refer to dying as a social process created and modified by the decisions and actions of the various people involved (44). According to this definition, dying is a process that takes time—sometimes only a few minutes but more often measured in days and weeks. As a social process, dying can be described by the pattern of events that serve as markers of the dying patient's movement toward death. These events function as indicators of the certainty (or uncertainty) that death is forthcoming at a predictable (or unpredictable) time.

In its simplest form, the dying trajectory is one in which all persons involved have the same perceptions about the speed and certainty of death's arrival and share a common perspective on the proper activities to perform during the final period of life. In reality, however, the process of dying is often much more complicated because the people involved have different expectations about whether or not the patient is actually dying. Many communication difficulties associated with dying are directly tied to these different perceptions on what is taking place (27, 44).

Among the common types of dying trajectory observed in hospitals are three: 1) a lingering pattern of dying; 2) a quick trajectory leading to expected death; and 3) a sudden trajectory leading to unexpected death. The different types are characteristically associated with particular types of hospital units, and they typically produce different types of staff activity. The actual social process of dying in any one situation, however, reflects a convergence of cultural values and individual choices as well as organizational structure, available technology, and medical treatment goals.

The Emergency Room: DOA and Sudden Death

Emergency rooms are settings designed and organized for the rapid treatment of accidental injury and sudden critical illness. The problems brought in for treatment range from simple cuts and bruises in one person to massive and extensive injuries involving large numbers of people. Workers in emergency rooms in large metropolitan areas often are exposed to death and near-death in its most unpleasant forms. The work requires them to offer help to victims of homicide, fire, hit-and-run, child abuse, suicide, and other forms of violence and destruction. The quick trajectory leading to expected death is a common pattern in these settings.

When patients are admitted in critical condition, emergency room work requires rapid evaluation of the problem and rapid initiation of action in a context of incomplete information and uncertainty. The work is organized to implement immediate life-saving activity and to meet the challenge of preventing death. Because of the intense focus on medical treatment activities during an emergency situation, little time is available for contacts between staff members and waiting family members. The nature of emergency work in combination with the limited time for contacts between families and the staff contributes to communication difficulties between them and stressful circumstances for both (32).

Using observations of family members' reported experiences in an emergency room in relation to the sudden death of a relative or friend, Jones identified the sequence of their experiences as follows: a) arrival and the search for information; b) waiting; c) notification of death; d) viewing the body; e) signing papers; and f) concluding process (45). About half of the respondents reported the experience to have been well handled because staff members took time to provide explanations, notified them of the death in a warm and concerned manner, and remained with them when viewing the body. The others reported feelings of anger, frustration, confusion, and emptiness as remnants of their unsatisfactory contacts with emergency staff.

Traditionally, emergency rooms were structurally organized to offer emergency medical treatments but not the crisis-intervention services needed to assist patients, families, and staff to cope with the psychosocial crises associated with sudden death. Hess observed that the staff behaviors that appeared to be "callous" to the outside observer came in time to be understood as necessary "coping mechanisms" for dealing with difficult choices, decisions, and patient situations (46). The need for crisis-intervention services in emergency settings and/or emotional support training for emergency staffs has been recognized and implemented in several hospitals (45–47).

Hooked to Machines: Dying in Intensive Care

Critical care settings are typically organized to prevent the occurrence of death in patients whose physical conditions can suddenly worsen thereby moving them rapidly onto the trajectory toward sudden death. Some of these settings deal only with special problems such as coronary care or extensive burns. Others provide services for a range of medical and surgical conditions, and the patients can be children as well as adults. Some settings offer care for only a few patients; others are available to large numbers of critically ill patients.

Regardless of size and established purpose, critical care settings are structurally and spatially organized to maximize the application of life-sustaining medical technology. Nurses in such settings tend to be highly committed to life-saving goals, and their activities are organized around the primacy of preventing death. Often their work involves tending the machines that monitor the patients' conditions or assisting them to maintain their vital functions (26). Nurses in these settings must maintain constant vigilance to pick up early cues that something must be wrong, and they must be ever ready to move into rapid action when an emergency takes place. Their situation has been compared to that of soldiers serving in an elite combat team for they are never able to remove themselves from the stresses of battle (48).

Because these settings are organized to prevent death, they are spatially arranged so that the doctors and nurses can easily maintain observation of all the patients assigned there. To accomplish this goal, privacy for the patients gives way to the need for constant vigilance, and contacts with patients are done mainly for the implementation of technical tasks and the performance of medical procedures. Relationships between patients and providers are centered around the life-saving activities of the setting, and contacts are frequently short because the staff carry responsibility for many patients. The unit regulations are commonly designed to minimize disruption of staff activities by controlling the family's presence at the bedside, and disclosure of information to the family by members of the staff is more likely than not to be minimal and controlled.

These structural and organizational conditions create a depersonalizing situation for many patients. Those who recover from their critical states ordinarily remain in intensive care for only short periods of time. Others who remain in serious condition may be kept there for prolonged spans of time. Those who die there generally end their lives attached to all manner of life-prolonging apparatus, and often death occurs following intensive heroic activity by the staff. Dying in intensive care is one of the new rituals of transition in a technologically sophisticated society, and it makes the central participant something of an object.

Although outsiders tend to view the doctors and nurses in intensive care as detached and unfeeling people, the reality is that work in these settings results in many situational and psychological stresses. Staff members are faced with frequent exposure to death and dying, daily contact with unsightly patients, heavy workloads, intricate machinery, and many communication difficulties involving physicians, nurses, patients, and families (17). The work is easiest when patients are comatose. It increases in complexity when patients are alert and young, have likeable personalities, or stay long enough for the staff to become attached to them. Among the coping mechanisms used by doctors and nurses for adapting to the pressures of work in settings devoted to critical care are detachment, increased activity, and humor (49). Yet even these adaptive mechanisms cannot protect them completely from feelings of sadness, anger, and frustration as they confront the daily uncertainties of their work, nor can they eliminate feelings of negligence associated with errors in judgment or lack of needed supplies at a time of emergency.

The context of critical care is one of recurring crises involving patients, families, and members of the hospital staff in complicated and tension-producing interactions and decisions. Often mechanisms evolve for attempting to maintain a sentimental order of composure and constraint in the face of these difficulties. Yet the people involved cannot help but be personally affected by the stresses of the situation and the difficult task of maintaining composure in the face of conflicting pulls and pressures (27).

In and Out: The Prolonged Dying of Cancer

Although patients with cancer occasionally end their days on an intensive care ward, they are much more likely to die on a general medical-surgical unit or one designed specifically for the care of cancer patients. Typically, patients dying of cancer have been undergoing treatment for some time, and many have been in and out of the hospital several times before arriving for the final stay. This history of several hospitalizations means that dying cancer patients and hospital staff have already established a pattern of involvement such that efforts at detachment are difficult to maintain.

Sometimes the end of a lingering trajectory lasts only one or two days. The patient is brought to the hospital to die usually because the family is unable to manage the situation at home. Sometimes the dying cancer patient is sent from a nursing home unable to provide care during the final period of dying. In either case, the patient is clearly known to be dying, and, usually, the treatment consists of comfort measures and symptomatic support. The situation for the staff is usually one of watchful waiting and is easiest to perform when the patient is comatose and not a social being. Far more difficult for all concerned is the situation of a fully alert dying cancer patient who is capable of initiating conversation that may be awkward or unsettling. Equally upsetting is the family that has not come to terms with the forthcoming death and insists on active life-saving treatment even though its use is to no avail.

Very difficult for the patient and staff alike is the prolonged hospital dying of a person with far advanced cancer, particularly when the patient is not to know the diagnosis and prognosis (27, 32). When either the physician or the family makes this kind of judgment, the nurses feel trapped by an unrealistic situation that they frequently handle by minimizing their contacts with the dying patient. The problem for the patient is social isolation, often brought into being by well-intentioned relatives who believe they are offering "protection" through preventing dissemination of bad news about forthcoming death. The consequence is that the person facing death is effectively barred from bringing closure to life by communicating openly about personal wishes and by participating in decisions about the context of dying.

Cancer is notably a tension-producing disease, and many of the difficulties encountered in the hospital are tied to problems in communication associated with the progression of disease. Patients with advanced cancer have high levels of anxiety associated with fears of painful dying and abandonment by other people, and they often reach out for opportunities to express their fears and concerns. The problem is that other people experience difficulty in listening to these expressions of concern for the situation of the cancer patient triggers a variety of strong and difficult feelings including helplessness, anger, guilt, sadness, and depression. Family members and staff alike protect themselves by using many behaviors designed to maintain control over strong emotional reactions (26, 27).

These problems of communication can be compounded by the physical changes associated with advancing cancer and the difficulties encountered in helping the patient achieve a comfortable death. One of the most difficult problems encountered on a cancer unit is the patient whose pain is not amenable to control, and situations of this nature exacerbate tensions and interpersonal conflicts among the staff. Feelings of helplessness are intense when little can be done to help the patient, and the tensions can sometimes permeate the entire atmosphere of the ward.

The problem for the staff working on cancer wards is that they are functioning in settings in which dying is an ever-present process even though not explicitly acknowledged. Cancer units typically have patients at different stages of living with cancer and undergoing different kinds of oncologic treatments, and the doctors and nurses constantly interact with patients and families at different points on the living-dying timetable. It is a context in which uncertainty about the future and tension about the present are constant themes affecting patient and staff alike and molding their interactions so as to control the underlying stresses.

The Patient Whose Family Cannot Let Go

One of the most tension-producing problems encountered by nurses in the hospital is the situation of the patient whose family insists on active life-saving activity when the patient is clearly on the trajectory toward death. This situation happens most commonly when the trajectory has been precipitated suddenly—as with an accident or heart attack—and the members of the family are not prepared for the shocking possibility of death. Often the physicians and nurses are aware of the seriousness of the person's condition soon after arrival at the hospital, but the actual decision to discontinue active medical treatment may be delayed until the family has had time to agree with the medical recommendation.

Much of the time the trajectory of dying in these situations is one or two days at most. The process of dying can be extended, however, if the patient is attached to life-support machines that keep the vital physiological systems functioning, and the family cannot agree to discontinue the treatment. Both family and staff are faced with the interpersonal complexities of maintaining composure and control in a context of uncertainty and tension. When this form of dying extends for a long period of time, the nursing staff carries the burden of care—a task made additionally burdensome if members of the family withdraw from contact with the patient.

There are also occasions when a member of the family, most commonly a spouse, cannot face up to the possibility of death during prolonged dying and insists on the patient's receiving active medical treatment. If the patient is young, the staff are often in sympathy with the fight for life, and active participation in treatment provides a mechanism for counteracting prevailing feelings of helplessness. If the patient is elderly, the nurses are likely to view the choice as somewhat inappropriate, particularly if the patient has indicated on previous occasions a personal wish not to have life prolonged.

The undercurrent of unspoken and unresolved feelings and tensions associated with this type of dying makes it one of the most problematic in hospital work. Yet it also is evidence of the lack, in many hospitals, of effective services for helping families cope with the complex personal and social problems that the process of dying brings into being.

The Special Poignancy of Dying Children

In some hospitals, the dying of a child is a rare occurrence, and staff members are unprepared for the stresses and strong feelings that this difficult problem provokes.

In other hospitals, the dying of children is fairly commonplace, and staff must cope with these same feelings on a regular basis. In the first instance, staff members react in a manner very similar to people in general, and they frequently cope by recounting the history of the events of dying over and over again. In the second case, staff members are likely to have developed a number of routines for distancing themselves from the stresses.

As is also true when adults are dying, nurses and doctors are better able to keep themselves detached from involvement when the child is in a coma. When the child is alert and capable of social interactions, contacts include conversation as well as treatment, and withdrawal from involvement is difficult to achieve. The care of dying children is always affected by the reactions and behaviors of parents, and many of the difficulties described by hospital staff are associated with the problem of relating with parents living under continuing stress. Bluebond-Langner found that terminally ill children learned that they were dying before death became imminent, but the majority participated in a game of mutual pretense with parents and staff. This dominant mode of interaction allowed parents and caregivers to play their reciprocal roles and maintained the sentimental and social order without disruption, but the children came to see their roles as supporting others (50).

Hospital settings providing services for multiple numbers of dying or potentially dying children carry their own special poignancy since on units such as these, children cannot help but be aware of the deaths of other children. In fact, Bluebond-Langner observed that dying children learned to define themselves as dying through watching what happened to children who died before them (50).

Some kinds of dying are distressing to be around because of their effects on the body, as in the case of massive burns (51, 52). Others are distressing because they drag on and on or serve as reminders of certain tragic aspects of the human condition. Providing care for dying children is a difficult task for, probably, the majority of physicians and nurses. It triggers a sense of professional failure along with strong personal reactions associated with the loss of a child (53).

NEGOTIATIONS, DECISIONS, AND ADAPTATIONS TO DYING

Just as styles of living have been diversified in the twentieth century, so too have styles of dying. For the most part, dying has been removed from public visibility into the private realm of institutions. At the same time its characteristics as a social and interpersonal process have become more variable. Medical technology and cultural values have interacted with new causes of dying to create new rituals of transition. Under the influence of industrialization, dying has moved from being a tribal or familial ritual to becoming an organizational procedure governed by bureaucratic rules and dominated by the influence of health care providers.

Death Information and Communication

Many patients who enter the hospital are not defined as dying. The labels used by staff for defining patients are based on their perceptions of the stability of the illness process: a) well, b) acutely ill, c) chronically ill, d) high risk of dying, e) dying, and f) dead (54). Assignment of these labels by doctors and nurses is a process—not a single event, and a new label is given when the illness process is perceived to have changed. In a study of adult patients on medical and surgical wards, Martocchio observed four patterns of living-dying that culminated in death: 1) peaks and valleys, referring to a swing back and forth between apparently well and high risk of dying; 2) descending plateaus, referring to periods of relative stability of illness interspersed with periods of apparent deterioration; 3) downward slopes, meaning a fairly rapid downward movement toward death; and 4) gradual slants, referring to a gradual, rather than a rapid, movement toward the end. Different labels were assigned to patients at different points during the various dying trajectories, and these labels influenced the patterns of communication among patients, family members, and health care providers (54).

The shift from the label *high-risk-of-dying* patient to *dying* patient took place through processes of negotiation by which different interactants became aware of a change in status. Although patients were infrequently told directly "you are going to die," they picked up cues about their futures from changes in the actions and behaviors of others (54). On a cancer ward, McIntosh noted that patients who wanted confirmation about their conditions had to take the offensive in seeking information from physicians (55). On a burn unit, Mannon observed that patients picked up a lot of information about their futures from physicians' comments during weekly grand rounds (52). He also noted that when the staff began to be certain that death was forthcoming, they made efforts to predict the length of the trajectory and to prepare families for what was forthcoming.

Information Exchange and Life-Death Decisions

Hospital staff also sought confirmation of the dying label through negotiations with others. Doctors and nurses exchanged information through face-to-face interaction or through written comments on the patients' records. Sometimes disagreements arose among staff because the nurses wanted clear messages about the dying state, but the physicians continued to function in terms of high risk of dying. Sometimes physicians were loath to make a clear designation because they were waiting for new information on which to make a decision (56). Often the context was one of uncertainty, rather than certainty, about the patient's condition. Reaching a point of labeling a patient as dying is not a light decision, given the life-saving values of medical practitioners. Degner and Beaton observed that processes of decision making by physicians relative to life-death situations involved calculations of the pros and cons of various alternatives: a) risks and benefits of treatment; b) getting better or getting worse in relation to the patient's condition; c) advantages and disadvantages of a treatment in relation to the work order on the ward; d) disruptive or nondisruptive effects of a treatment choice on the sentimental order; e) costs and benefits of a given treatment; and f) quality of life considerations (56).

It is clear that treatment decisions are affected by a variety of personal, social, and organizational factors. All participants in the situation engage in their own calculations relative to whether or not a patient is dying, but clear information from physicians can make an important difference in the dying experience of patients and families and the caregiving practices of other providers. Acknowledgment of the dying label is clear to nurses when the physician writes a no code order and palliative care only. One problem is that in many settings there are many physicians involved. In hospital units with large numbers of physicians, disagreements among them can lead to conflicting orders being given and problems for the nurses in communicating with families about the reality of what is happening. Such actions have been found to contribute to confusion for families and to make it difficult for them to give up active medical treatment (52).

Movement to considering the patient as dying requires some consensus among the various people involved and working agreements among them about boundary rules and subject matter appropriate for discussion. Once consensus has been reached, the rules related to getting well are relaxed, and the rules relating to dying are accepted. The latter usually includes a relaxation of visiting hours, permission for families to sleep over, and minimal attention to therapeutic medical regimens (54). This shift in focus permits the patient and family to adapt to the experience of dying.

Patient and Family Adaptations to Dying

Martocchio found that dying patients in the hospital indicated their personal awareness of dying in a number of ways. Some turned to religion and its special meaning for them. Others described and interpreted their dreams. Others talked about particular symbols that signified the meaning of life and death to them. The patterns of patients' adaptations to the dying label were twofold. *Relief from uncertainty* was a response characterized by a searching for closure either through religion or coming to terms with the universe. It was observed most commonly following a lingering illness. *Escape* was a response characterized by an attitude of resignation and efforts to get away from loneliness and despair. It was most often observed in the downward slope trajectory (54).

Families also make changes in adaptive patterns once the dying trajectory is clear, according to Martocchio. *Permission to die* is a pattern of adaptation characterized by the family openly offering consolation to the dying person and giving the message that continuing to fight to live is no longer necessary. *Invitation to die* is an acknowledgment to the dying person, usually following a long and debilitating illness, that giving up and letting go is all right. *Relabel as nonperson* is an adaptive pattern in which the family members no longer perceive the dying patient as a person. This pattern was observed under these conditions. The patient was no longer able to communicate. The noncommunicative state was persistent and consistent. The timetable for dying was unpredictable (54).

Although, initially, the physician has great power over information and other factors affecting the social experience of hospital dying, the ongoing processes of living, working, and dying are shaped by the actions and transactions of all participants in the experience. The interpersonal negotiations among them are intricate and subject to change. The outcomes for dying patients as persons are quite variable and greatly dependent on the choices and actions of physicians, nurses, and members of their families.

INSTITUTIONAL DYING: A CHANGING SOCIAL PROBLEM

The changed nature of dying in the 1980s is quite understandable when viewed simply as another reflection of the secularization and technologization of Western societies. Yet with it has come a range of complex problems including the allocation of scarce resources to the living and the dying and the dehumanizing effects of applied technology on the experiences of people whose lives are ending.

Values in Conflict

Even though dying has become a phenomenon largely organized and controlled by organizational goals, it also continues to be a singular experience in the personal and interpersonal lives of those for whom forthcoming death carries significant meaning. The problematic nature of some types of institutional dying can be explained, at least in part, as a collision between two systems of values.

For the organization and its workers, services for dying people comprise a portion of the work to be done and the tasks to be accomplished. These tasks associated with dying need to be regularized and routinized to maximize efficiency and to assist the staff in the maintenance of sentimental and social control (27, 28). The problem is that dying is also a human transition with significant meanings in the cultural, social, and personal sense. The tasks associated with this definition of dying have to do with bringing closure to life in an acceptable manner and completing unfinished business with persons who are important. The values at issue here are particularistic, having much to do with the relationships of the dying person to nature, other people, and the community.

The institutions for patient care in the United States have been organized around the primacy of the life-saving ethic, and the value accorded to control over death has impeded the development of person-oriented services (9). The bulk of health care resources has been allocated to high technology and biomedical research centered on the diagnosis and treatment of disease. Also, Medicare coverage is designed to support the biomedical model and provides coverage for hospitalization but little for nursing home care (37). Societal investment in high technology medical care has fostered a public attitude of expecting too much from technology—an oversimplified expectation that early diagnosis of *any* disease can lead to cure (57). To date, investment in caregiving services for an aging population at risk has been comparatively minimal.

Costs, Technology, and Aging

Current evidence suggests that high technology in health care produces burdens as well as benefits and is very expensive. Knaus, Draper, and Wagner performed a prospective study of 1,987 consecutive ICU admissions over a 30-month period and identified 74 patients with severe acute and chronic problems who represented 40 percent of the ICU admissions but received 80 percent of the resources (16). Of this group, 80 percent were dead before leaving the hospital, and 92 percent of the 74 were dead by six months posthospitalization. Based on this and other analyses, Knaus and associates argued that there is little evidence that ICU has improved survival or the quality of life for many patients and, further, is a highly inefficient use of medical resources (16).

A marker of the 1980s is growing public awareness of finite resources and high costs for medical care. In 1984, about 11 percent of the GNP in the United States was spent on health, and, roughly, one-third went to the care of those over 65 years. Elderly persons make more use of hospitals and nursing homes than younger persons, and the cost is greater. In 1981, the average annual per capita expenditures for the hospitalized aged were $1,381 compared to $392 for the hospitalized nonaged (58).

Many questions have been raised as to the effect of high-technology medicine on living and dying. Verbrugge made a case that mortality rates have fallen with one consequence being that elderly persons are living longer with the progressive disabilities of chronic disease (59). Avorn believes there is a need for rethinking the relationship of medical therapy to death and questions whether additional medical care is necessarily in the best interests of the patient (60). Callahan argues that the high cost of medical care in combination with an aging population has created a serious moral problem vis-à-vis the allocation of health resources disproportionately to the illness needs of the elderly (61).

Over the past 40 years, institutional dying in the United States has been shaped by two societal forces: 1) the powerful influence of high-technology medicine on the characteristics of hospitals as places for dying; and 2) the paucity of attention to the social as well as health needs of an aging population. The care needs of elderly persons require different kinds of services than intensive medical care and/or custodial placement without concern for personal wishes.

Efforts to change societal policies to reflect a concern with basic human values is demonstrated in the rise of the hospice movement. Yet the power of scientific medicine and a worship of technology permeate the society in a way that makes the introduction of change very difficult. People still look to physicians for miraculous ways of curing them from their ills, and this image is perpetuated through the influence of the mass media. The push for cost containment means that fewer, rather than more, governmental resources will be available for the caregiving needs of vulnerable groups, and cost containment will, undoubtedly, influence the characteristics of hospital dying in the future. What the future will bring in the balance between technology and humanism remains to be seen, but whatever the outcome, it will show in the services available to those who are dying.

REVIEW QUESTIONS

1. Describe and discuss the influence of religion, industrialization, and science on the development of European hospitals as caregiving institutions.
2. Discuss the nature of the relationship between changing demographic patterns and medical technology in this century. What impact does the interrelationship of these factors have on health care delivery systems?
3. Compare and contrast long-term institutional care for the elderly in Great Britain and the United States in terms of cultural values, allocation of resources for geriatric services, and characteristics of long-term care institutions.
4. Compare the characteristics of death and dying on emergency and cancer wards with particular attention to types of dying trajectories, staff-family relationships, and difficulties commonly experienced by doctors and nurses who work there.
5. When patients are hospitalized with life-threatening illnesses, decision-making

processes used by physicians include calculations of the pros and cons of different alternatives available to them. Identify and discuss three ways in which physicians use these calculations in practice.

6. In the 1970s, the death-awareness movement influenced hospitals in several ways. Describe two specific effects of this movement on caregiving practices in relation to dying patients.

7. What is meant by "new forms of dying?" What are the positive and the negative implications (and repercussions) of these "new" forms?

8. What are the implications of the adoption of the biomedical model, along with the prevalence of acute care facilities, for the terminally ill?

9. How is medical technology utilized in ways that fail to meet the needs of our society; how do institutional goals fail to meet the needs of the family? Can you offer a solution?

REFERENCES

1. Downs, J. F. (1971). *Cultures in crisis.* Beverly Hills: Glencoe Press.
2. Rosenblatt, P. D., Walsh, R. P., & Jackson, D. A. (1976). *Grief and mourning in cross-cultural perspective.* Minneapolis: HRAF Press.
3. Rosen, G. (1963). The hospital: Historical sociology of a community institution. In E. Freidson (Ed.), *The hospital in modern society* (pp. 1–36). New York: Free Press.
4. Knowles, J. H. (1973). The hospital. In *Life and death and medicine* (pp. 91–100). San Francisco: Freeman.
5. Aries, P. (1974). *Western attitudes toward death.* Baltimore: Johns Hopkins Press.
6. Aries, P. (1981). *The hour of our death.* New York: Knopf.
7. Toynbee, A. (1968). Traditional attitudes toward death. In A. Toynbee, A. K. Mant, N. Smart, J. Hinton, S. Yudkin, E. Rhode, R. Heywood, & H. H. Price (Eds.), *Man's concern with death* (pp. 59–94). London: Hodder and Stoughton.
8. Illich, I. (1976). *Medical nemesis.* New York: Random House.
9. Benoliel, J. Q. (1978). The changing social context for life and death decisions. *Essence, 2*(2), 5–14.
10. Wilcocks, C. (1965). *Medical advance, public health and social evolution.* New York: Pergamon Press.
11. Morison, R. S. (1973). *Dying: Life and death and medicine* (pp. 39–45). San Francisco: Freeman.
12. Ebert, R. H. (1986). Medical education at the peak of the era of experimental medicine. *Daedalus, 115,* 55–81.
13. Raffel, M. W. (1984). *The U.S. health system: Origins and functions* (2nd ed.). New York: John Wiley & Sons.
14. Engel, G. L. (1977). The need for a new medical model: A challenge for biomedicine. *Science, 196,* 129–136.
15. Hilberman, M. (1975). The evolution of intensive care units. *Critical Care Medicine, 3,* 159–165.
16. Knaus, W. A., Draper, E. A., & Wagner, D. P. (1983). The use of intensive care: New research initiatives and their implications for national health policy. *Milbank Memorial Fund Quarterly, 61,* 561–583.
17. Benoliel, J. Q. (1975). The realities of work. In J. Howard & A. L. Strauss (Eds.), *Humanizing health care* (pp. 175–183). New York: John Wiley & Sons.
18. Gruenberg, E. M. (1977). The failures of success. *Milbank Memorial Fund Quarterly, 55,* 3–24.

19. Strauss, A. L., Corbin, J., Fagerhaugh, S., Glaser, G. B., Maines, D., Suczek, B., & Wiener C. L. (1984). *Chronic illness and the quality of life* (2nd ed.). St. Louis: Mosby.

20. National Center for Health Statistics. (1985). *Vital statistics of the United States, 1980, Vol. II, Mortality, Part A* (DHHS Publication No. PHS 85-1101). Washington, DC: U.S. Government Printing Office.

21. Vladek, B. C. (1980). *Unloving care: The nursing home tragedy.* New York: Basic Books.

22. Kayser-Jones, J. S. (1981). *Old, alone and neglected.* Berkeley: University of California Press.

23. Stannard, C. I. (1973). Old folks and dirty work: The social conditions for patient abuse in a nursing home. *Social Problems, 20,* 329–342.

24. McGinity, P. J., & Stotsky, B. A. (1967). The patient in the nursing home. *Nursing Forum, 6,* 238–261.

25. Quint, J. C. (1967). *The nurse and the dying patient.* New York: Macmillan.

26. Strauss, A., Fagerhaugh, S., Suczek, B., & Wiener, C. (1985). *Social organization of medical work.* Chicago: University of Chicago Press.

27. Glaser, B. G., & Strauss, A. L. (1965). *Awareness of dying.* Chicago: Aldine.

28. Sudnow, D. (1967). *Passing on: The social organization of dying.* Englewood Cliffs, NJ: Prentice-Hall.

29. Martinson, I. M., Armstrong, G. D., Geis, D. P., Anglim, M. A., Gronseth, E. C., MacInnis, H., Kersey, J. H., & Nesbitt, M. E. (1978). Home care for children dying of cancer. *Pediatrics, 62,* 106–113.

30. Wilson, D. C., Ajemian, I., & Mount, B. M. (1978). Montreal (1975)—The Royal Victoria Hospital palliative care service. *Death Education, 2,* 3–19.

31. Benoliel, J. Q. (Ed.). (1982). *Death education for the health professional.* Washington, DC: Hemisphere.

32. Benoliel, J. Q. (1977). Nurses and the human experience of dying. In H. Feifel (Ed.), *New meanings of death* (pp. 124–142). New York: McGraw-Hill.

33. Dracup, K. A., & Breu, C. S. (1977). Strengthening practice through research utilization. In *Communicating nursing research, Vol. 10* (pp. 339–353). Boulder, CO: Western Interstate Commission for Higher Education.

34. Regan, T. (Ed.). (1980). *Matters of life and death.* Philadelphia: Temple University Press.

35. Mumma, C. M., & Benoliel, J. Q. (1984–85). Care, cure, and hospital dying trajectories. *Omega, 15,* 275–288.

36. Kane, F. I. (1985). Keeping Elizabeth Bouvia alive for the public good. *Hastings Center Report, 12*(6), 5–8.

37. Benoliel, J. Q., & Packard, N. (1986). Nurses and health policy. *Nursing Administration Quarterly, 10*(3), 1–14.

38. Mushkin, S. J., & DiScuillo, A. (1974). Terminal illness and incentives for health care usage. In S. J. Mushkin (Ed.), *Consumer incentives for health care* (pp. 183–216). New York: PRODIST.

39. Scitovsky, A. A. (1984). The high cost of dying: What do the data show? *Milbank Memorial Fund Quarterly, 4,* 591–608.

40. Horn, S. D., Sharkey, P. D., Chamber, A. F., & Horn, R. A. (1985). Severity of illness within DRGs: Impact on prospective payment. *American Journal of Public Health, 75,* 1195–1199.

41. Centers for Disease Control. (1985, May 10). Update: Acquired immunodeficiency syndrome—United States. *Morbidity and Mortality Weekly Report, 34,* 245–248.

42. Bennett, J. A. (1985). AIDS: Epidemiology update. *American Journal of Nursing, 85,* 968–972.

43. AIDS costs: Employers and insurers have reasons to fear expensive epidemic. (1985, October 18) *The Wall Street Journal,* pp. 1, 10.

44. Glaser, B. G., & Strauss, A. L. (1968). *Time for dying.* Chicago: Aldine.

45. Jones, W. H. (1978). Emergency room sudden death: What can be done for the survivors? *Death Education, 2,* 231–248.

46. Hess, G. (1970). Health care needs inherent in emergency services—Can they be met? *Nursing Clinics of North America, 5*, 243-249.

47. Jensen, D. (1973). Crisis resolved: Impact through planned change. *Nursing Clinics of North America, 8*, 735-742.

48. Hay, D., & Oken, D. (1972). The psychological stresses of intensive care nursing. *Psychosomatic Medicine, 34*, 109.

49. Swanson, T. R., & Swanson, M. J. (1977). Acute uncertainty: The intensive care unit. In E. M. Pattison (Ed.), *The experience of dying* (pp. 119-137). Englewood Cliffs, NJ: Prentice-Hall.

50. Bluebond-Langer, M. (1978). *The private worlds of dying children.* Princeton, NJ: Princeton University Press.

51. Seligman, R. (1977). The burned child. In E. M. Pattison (Ed.), *The experience of dying* (pp. 245-251). Englewood Cliffs, NJ: Prentice-Hall.

52. Mannon, J. M. (1985). *Caring for the burned: Life and death in a hospital burn center.* Springfield, IL: Charles C Thomas.

53. Suarez, M., & Benoliel, J. Q. (1976). Coping with failure: The case of death in childhood. *Issues in comprehensive pediatric nursing* (pp. 3-15). New York: McGraw-Hill.

54. Martocchio, B. C. (1980). *Living while dying.* Bowie, MD: Robert J. Brady.

55. McIntosh, J. (1977). *Communication and awareness in a cancer ward.* New York: PRODIST.

56. Degner, L. F., & Beaton, J. I. (1987). *Life-death decisions in health care.* Washington, DC: Hemisphere.

57. Jennett, B. (1985). High technology medicine: How defined and how regarded. *Milbank Memorial Fund Quarterly, 63*, 141-173.

58. Davis, K. (1986). Aging and the health-care system: Economics and structural issues. *Daedalus, 115*, 227-246.

59. Verbrugge, L. M. (1984). Longer life but worsening health? Trends in health and mortality of middle-aged and older persons. *Milbank Memorial Fund Quarterly, 62*, 475-519.

60. Avorn, J. L. (1986). Medicine, health, and the geriatric transformation. *Daedaelus, 115*, 221-225.

61. Callahan, D. (1986). Adequate health care and an aging society: Are they morally compatible? *Daedalus, 115*, 247-267.

9

Hospice Care for the Dying

Glen W. Davidson

What is hospice care? *Hospice* is a medieval term that refers to the wayside inns for pilgrims and other travelers, particularly at those places of greatest vulnerability and hardship. The hospice movement represents the development of a variety of programs designed to better assist terminally ill patients for whom aggressive medical treatment is no longer deemed appropriate in travel through life.

Care of the dying is not new. Concern about what constitutes appropriate care is found in mythic and symbolic dimensions of language and tradition. Whether it is the ritualistic storytelling of a Navajo in modern-day Arizona or the 3,000-year-old Vedic texts of ancient India, we can see that humankind is concerned universally about dying. Care of the dying is one of life's major responsibilities in most faith traditions.

Like other aspects of living in mass society, patterns of health care delivery, even while offering better and more widespread services, have so disrupted traditional rituals of care known by our grandparents that this generation has had to radically reexamine how best to preserve human dignity in the closing moments of life. Advocates of the hospice movement have argued that we not only have the opportunity to bring to the terminally ill new medications, new skills, and new understandings but also the obligation to restore value-sensitive and humane approaches to terminal care in a more cost-effective manner.

In this chapter, I will sketch the historical context for care of the dying, including the rise of the "new" hospice; define the role of terminally ill patients in modern health care as an attempt to explain why these patients are so often neglected; describe the models of various hospice organizations which attempt to meet the needs of the dying; and set forth what I see as the pressing challenges for the hospice movement.

We can find the antecedents for the hospice movement as early as the time of Emperor Asoka in India (d. 238 B.C.). Hindu pilgrims came to the River Ganges at Varanasi (Banaras) in hopes of dying there so that their ashes could be spread upon the most holy of waters and thereby escape, according to Hindu belief, the trials of rebirth and reincarnation. Sometimes the pilgrims would wait until they were infirm or too ill to complete their journey and would, therefore, be stranded in midjourney. Other pilgrims were felled upon by bandits and others who took advantage of their vulnerabilities. Asoka established shelters for the pilgrims and their families. These hospices are believed to be the earliest evidence of institutional care in human history.

Later building of shelters for pilgrims between Europe and the Middle East suggests Asokan influence and cultural exchange along the trading routes of Asia Minor. A good example is the early Christian Monastic Hospice in Turmanin (A.D. 475) located in what today is Syria. Turmanin architecture suggests a facility used as an inn for pilgrims as well as wards for the sick and dying. Such inns were founded upon the biblical mandate: "For when I was hungry, you gave me food; when thirsty you gave me drink; when I was a stranger you took me into your home; when naked you clothed me; when I was ill you came to my help; when in prison you visited me" (Matt. 25:35–36, *The New English Bible*). To these injunctions a seventh work of mercy was identified: burying the dead (see Tobit, 1:16–17).

The earliest hospitals did not specialize; specialization is a modern concept. As Thompson and Goldin (1) explain: "Since in the guiding text all categories of social assistance were jumbled together, Christian charitable foundations might cater to one, some, or all of the victims of wretchedness: aged, infirm, dying, diseased, wounded, blind, crippled, idiot, insane, orphans, paupers, wanderers, pilgrims" (p. 6). At Turmanin, travelers would receive the monks' hospitality overnight or for as long as they required. Almost by definition a traveler was a pilgrim who would be more or less sick, having undertaken the journey as a form of penance. The metaphor of the pilgrim or wanderer is used extensively in modern hospice literature. Unlike the ancient hospices, however, no modern facility provides space for graves.

From the monastic model in the Mediterranean, we can trace both the architectural and organizational influence to North America where the first institutions for the sick were also concerned for both the traveler and the settler. Some of the first monasteries established in sixteenth-century New Spain and seventeenth-century New France and New England had "hospitals" that provided multiple services, but all had in common care for the dying. In the nineteenth and twentieth centuries, various religious communities in both Canada and the United States have long maintained palliative care facilities, of which the most famous still in existence is probably Calvary Hospital in the Bronx, New York.

HOSPICE CARE IN NORTH AMERICA

Much of the inspiration for the hospice movement in North America comes from Dr. Cicely Saunders who founded St. Christopher's Hospice in London. Dr. Saunders is an exceptionally trained person. She earned an Oxford degree in philosophy, politics, and economics, and holds diplomas or degrees in the fields of nursing, social work, and medicine. While she was a Fellow in the Department of Pharmacology at St. Mary's Medical School, she carried out research on analgesics and other drugs that could be more effective in controlling intractable pain of patients with terminal illness.

St. Christopher's Hospice was developed outside of the National Health System through the philanthropic generosity of a large number of people. The specialized facility was built in Sydenham, London in 1967. Today there are more than 30 hospices throughout Great Britain (some are referred to as Marie Curie Homes).

While some of the hospices offer unique services and are organized differently, they have in common a philosophy of compassion in terminal care. As institutions, the hospices attempt to raise the nursing process to its greatest height. They dispense a knowledge of pharmacological control of pain and organize a team that involves the patient, and, usually, members of the family, or close friends.

Contrary to many visitors' expectations, St. Christopher's Hospice does not convey an environment of a "death house" where patients are bedridden, narcotized, depressed, or obtunded. One hears the sound of laughter, sees a variety of creative activities including that of the children of staff and patients, and perceives a home-like environment. Each patient brings some personal belongings and is encouraged to maintain as much self-care as possible.

St. Christopher's dedication to "total care of the dying patient" refers not only to the medical-symptomatic management but, also, as importantly, to the concept that anything that produces distress or pain for the patient or the family is a concern for hospice staff. The total psychosocial impact on the dying patient and the family is addressed, including the grief reaction of the family subsequent to the patient's death.

Dr. Saunders' philosophy is not restricted by the principles of quality nursing, home care, and medicine. She frequently refers to the "spiritual dimension" of care. Her increasingly sophisticated way of articulating what that means is symbolized by the one architectural change made to St. Christopher's Hospice since its opening. It has been necessary to expand the chapel, which is centrally located in the facility.

While prototypes for North American health care institutions can be found throughout a long and honorable history, the unique needs and values of people on this continent have reshaped, reorganized, and reapplied European institutions. A reshaping of Dr. Saunders' vision has been inevitable. With rare exceptions, the people trying to organize hospices in North America have been inspired by, but have not tried to duplicate, St.Christopher's Hospice in London.

Until the 1950s, most needs of the sick and dying in North American were taken care of in the home. Rituals of care among the general population must be seen in that context. However, by the 1950s, a majority of acute diseases were cared for in hospitals. Care of chronically ill patients and convalescent care began to be provided in what evolved as nursing homes. By 1970, over 70 percent of Canadians and Americans dying would do so in one of these two types of institutions. When one controls these generalized statistics to a given state like California or Florida, more than 80 percent die in hospitals or nursing homes. And in specific metropolitan cities in both countries, as many as 90 percent of the people who die spend their last days in hospitals or nursing homes.

The earliest of hospitals and nursing homes in North America provided a variety of services. However, since the implementation of national health care in

Canada and Medicare funding for health services in the United States, utilization of hospitals has become more and more confined to curing acute diseases, and nursing homes have been restricted to care for the chronically ill or those needing rehabilitation. This is not to ignore the fact that as many as 30 percent of all nursing home patients die in a year. Rather, it is to make the point that the objectives for the institutions and the protocols of care are organized for cure or rehabilitation, not for palliative care and symptom relief.

THE DYING ROLE:
A SOCIOLOGICAL PERSPECTIVE

Where people die and how well they are cared for may be explained in part by the way the dying role is understood by the patients, their families, and the staff who serve them. Parsons first described the sick role from a sociological perspective (2). Like other roles in society, the ill person has both rights and obligations. Those who are ill are excused from their usual responsibilities and obligations but only for a limited time. They take on the obligation to will themselves back to health.

The ill person also has the right to be cared for, with primary obligation falling to the next of kin. But the patient is obligated, in turn, to seek competent medical help in an effort to regain health and to demonstrate good intentions. A further right of the patient is to avoid conditions that might aggravate being ill. In turn, the patient is obligated to cooperate with treatment modalities prescribed by health care authorities, even if that means being subservient and dependent on caregivers.

What Parsons described, without being explicit, is the sick role for the acutely ill. Acute illness strikes quickly and, it is popularly assumed, occurs through no fault of the patient. Such notions are the products of the impact made on human memory by the great epidemics when fear of infectious diseases symbolized illness.

The primary institution for caring for the acutely ill is the hospital, particularly as accrediting boards and statutory bodies define institutional authority by narrower expectations. Since the adoption of Medicare in the United States and the national health scheme in Canada, hospitals, by definition, are acute-care facilities. Consequently, the authority, responsibilities, and roles of competence that hospital health care staff have exclude the needs of patients who do not fit the roles of the acutely ill.

The chronically ill, by contrast, have received primary attention only in recent times. Preventive and rehabilitative medicine are still looked upon in many schools of medicine as luxuries and are suspect as appropriate within the science of medicine. Confusion abounds over whether to treat cancer patients as having acute or chronic pathologies.

Chronic illnesses refer to acute situations that persist over a lifetime, such as heart disease consequent to infarct; degenerative processes, such as arthritis, diabetes, and hypertension; and injuries that cannot be totally rehabilitated, particularly traumas to the central nervous system.

Using Parson's typologies to describe the rights and obligations of the chronically ill, we can see that patients are exempt from the responsibilities of their usual social roles but only insofar as they are impaired. Unlike acutely ill patients, the chronically ill have no time limit placed on their impairments. But the patients do have the obligation to will to be rehabilitated as soon as possible.

In order to obtain rehabilitative services, the patient has the right of access to both appropriate information and therapy. In turn, the patient is obligated to maintain rehabilitative regimes. It is not enough for a patient to be fitted with a prosthesis; he or she must use it. It is not enough for the diabetic to lose weight through some therapeutic process; he or she must maintain weight control.

Like the acutely ill, the person with chronic illness has a right to be cared for when disabled, particularly by the family. But unlike the acutely ill, the person with chronic illness must avoid dependence so as not to be any more of a burden on the caregiver and society than the disability necessitates. Necessary dependency will be tolerated; evidence of independence will be rewarded.

The primary institution providing care for the chronically ill in North American society is the convalescent center or nursing home. As hospitals were being forced to define their authority and responsibility for caring more narrowly, so too were nursing homes being forced to define and limit their services to chronic care. Hospitals could and can be accredited without rehabilitative services. However, many states now refuse to accredit a nursing home that cannot offer such expertise. And the staffs of nursing home and convalescent facilities are trained and evaluated on their abilities to provide the kind of care that the chronically ill have a right to expect.

Nursing home facilities, even more than hospitals, have failed to meet the needs of the terminally ill despite the fact that 30 percent of patients in nursing homes in the United States die every year. With accountability based on meeting definitions of chronic care, it is perhaps understandable—if no less regrettable—that nursing home personnel are not trained to meet the needs of the terminally ill except insofar as they risk their defined competence by assuming unique roles of caring for the terminally ill.

Governmental and accrediting definitions of institutional authority account, in part, for the scenes of terminally ill patients being transferred back and forth between hospital and nursing home because "this patient doesn't belong here." The reason such facilities as Calvary Hospital exist at all is to provide patients and their families options of care that otherwise are not available to them. It is by design, not by accident, that some of the private hospitals in Manhattan and the Bronx in New York City can claim that no patient has died in their facilities. When the patient's diagnosis changes from that of acute or chronic illness to terminally ill, the patient is "referred out." When a patient appears about to die, it is not an uncommon practice for nursing homes to rush the person to an acute care center's intensive care facility because, in words used so frequently as to be a cliché, "we're not equipped to handle this emergency here."

Russell Noyes and John Clancy (3), psychiatrists at the University of Iowa, have used Parson's typologies to explore the unique roles of the terminally ill. They note that, like the acutely ill, the terminally ill patient is time-limited; only now, rather than being limited by restoration to health, death limits time and health. Even so, the terminally ill are under the obligation to desire to live as long as possible so that they are without responsibility for their dying.

Being without responsibility affords the terminally ill patient the right to be taken care of, particularly by the family. But the patient is, in turn, obligated to take advantage of all supports necessary for sustaining life and to cooperate with those giving the support so as not to be any more of a burden than necessary. Recognizing the burden that terminal illness is, Noyes and Clancy believe, is the reason society relieves most of the physician's obligation to the patient—except that of overseeing supportive and palliative treatments—when a patient's role changes from being sick (acute or chronic) to dying. "Society reserves the physician's role for the more important restorative function and, in so doing, jealously guards against inroads upon the physician's time and energy" (p. 42).

To be terminally ill is to be exempt from social roles of responsibility and commitments, but the patient is under the obligation to transfer to others, in orderly ways, property and authority. Unlike the acutely ill, terminally ill persons are expected to maintain as much independence as their declining resources will permit. And having done so, those persons have the right to be given continuing respect and status as a human being despite the loss of health and life.

The typology of roles of the sick is useful for understanding why, in contrast to our grandparents' era, care of the dying has become less humane. By definition, both hospitals and nursing homes function to provide care for the acutely and chronically ill, not for the terminally ill. Rather than care of the dying being a universal obligation, as it is in the ethics of most faith traditions, modern health care delivery restricts such care.

With the change of options for care of the dying, a "new" institution became necessary—the hospice, where the definitions of care, the standards of staff competencies, and the protocols of behavior directly address the needs of the terminally ill.

MODELS FOR HOSPICE CARE

As with other European ideas and institutions adopted in North America, the hospice has been reshaped, reorganized, and reapplied according to the unique needs and values of a specific locale. Although most organizers of hospices prefer to operate as comprehensive a program as possible, local needs and impediments have led to the development of at least five different models (4): the wholly volunteer programs; home care programs; freestanding, full-service, autonomous institutions; hospital-based palliative care units, and continuum-of-care subacute units.

Wholly Volunteer Programs

Wholly volunteer programs have developed because of the unavailability of financial backing for institutional care and because of opposition from established health care personnel, institutions, or organizations. In many rural areas of the continent, this program model is the sole option because of sparse population and resources. As part of the mutual-help group phenomenon, however, which reached major proportions in the 1970s, care for the terminally ill became the focus for citizen action to: provide such things as equipment needed for home care; serve as a clearing-house of information between those citizens who have already experienced the crises of terminal care for a loved one and those newly in need of community services; function as patient and family advocates with the medical community; and initiate bereavement support services for survivors. Interestingly, hospice volunteer programs also have provided opportunities for many health care personnel who have been frustrated by organizational barriers in their usual work settings for delivery of competent care for the terminally ill.

Some of the more established hospice units began as wholly volunteer programs and many programs registered with The National Hospice Organization operate at this level. Typical of citizen initiative, there is evidence of a great deal of creativity and innovation for meeting community needs. In some locales, the program planners focus on stimulating other voluntary and service organizations to provide expanded coverage. Still others focus on generating financial support for individuals or existing institutions, organizing telephone support networks, or fostering volunteer training. As many families testify, when there had been little or no help in care for the terminally ill before, the wholly volunteer programs have brought improved support into their communities. The main disadvantage, however, is that this model often cannot function adequately for meeting the spectrum of needs faced by the terminally ill and their families.

Home Care Programs

Home care programs usually provide all of the services of wholly volunteer programs plus skilled nursing care in the patient's home. The first program was started in 1974 as Hospice, Inc. (now the Connecticut Hospice, Inc.) in New Haven when their organizers were prevented—by medical and institutional politics and lack of financing—from establishing a freestanding, full-service, autonomous facility.

Coordinated home care by members of the local Visiting Nurses' Association, skilled symptom control under the direction of hospice physicians and nurses, and psychosocial support for patients and families by hospice social workers, chaplains, and volunteers allowed significant numbers of terminally ill patients to spend their final days in a familiar environment. Assessing the Connecticut program after its first three years, the then medical director, Sylvia Lack, found that 65 percent of hospice patients were allowed to die at home in contrast to the national average of 70 percent dying in hospitals or nursing homes (5, p. 43). Advantages of this model over the wholly volunteer program are coverage by a trained interdisciplinary team, availability of service around the clock, and coordinated care with medical services. Disadvantages of the model are that it is often difficult to coordinate patient transfer when inpatient care is needed, managing those symptoms of pain which cannot be controlled at home without hospital-based equipment for pain control, and the inability of some families to cope with the demands of home care.

Freestanding, Full-service, Autonomous Institutions

Freestanding, full-service, autonomous institutions are a third model for hospice care and come the closest to duplicating the services provided by St. Christopher's Hospice in London. Hillhaven Hospice of Tucson was the first hospice to follow this model and was opened in 1977. The Connecticut Hospice, Inc. became a freestanding facility in 1979.

While allowing terminally ill patients to remain at home is often the primary objective of the hospice, a significant number of patients need the back-up of inpatient care and also inpatient day care for patients who can be cared for at home by relatives or friends at night. Supportive services of physical and occupational therapy, dietetics, and pharmacy are more accessible.

The freestanding facility has certain advantages over the two models described above, including the staff's ability to control all levels of care, isolating the actual needs of patients from the expectations associated with acute and chronic care, and focusing in-service training for staff on needs for palliative care. Two major disadvantages prevent many communities from adopting this model. The first is that if no administrative authority exists between the separate facility and other health care institutions in the community, coordination of care depends solely on maintaining good will between the hospice and other facilities. Second, funding for this type of program requires development of new financial sources, a process that usually takes several generations to develop in a particular community. It is noteworthy that Hillhaven Hospice functioned as a freestanding facility only for the three years when federal funds were available. Its program is now under the shelter of St. Mary's Hospital and is known as the St. Mary's Hospice.

Hospital-based Palliative Care Units

Hospital-based units are a fourth model for hospice care. They obviate the need to create new referral and funding sources or to build new facilities. The palliative care unit of the Royal Victoria Hospital in Montreal is the oldest, having been opened in 1975, and best-studied facility of this type. Use of laboratories for better diagnosis, technology such as radiation for better pain control, and established financial resources allow for the widest spectrum of care. In addition, staff at the Royal Victoria Hospital have discovered that the close proximity of both palliative and acute care units separately staffed tend to stimulate improved care in both.

The hospital-based unit is not easily duplicated in the United States, however. Utilization guidelines of individual hospitals which restrict what kinds of care can be provided in the facility and reimbursement standards of Medicare and Medicaid discourage administrators from pursuing development of this model. At best, American hospitals such as St. Luke's Hospital in New York City have used a specially trained consultation/liaison team which circulates throughout the hospital on an as-needed basis to assist with palliative care. The team specializes in pain control and management of symptoms such as nausea and in providing emotional and spiritual support to patients and their families whether in the hospital or at home, as well as support to the acute care staff.

Besides the difficulty in blending the utilization guidelines for the acutely ill and the terminally ill, another major difficulty with this model in the United States is conflict between staff trained to follow acute care protocols versus palliative care protocols. Staff in acute care areas often fail to understand why their ways of caring for patients are inadequate or inappropriate for the terminally ill, and, given the staffing patterns by which many nurses rotate between these areas, it is extremely difficult to train them to adequately assess the need for a change in care let alone to master the ability to do so.

Continuum-of-care
Subacute Units

The continuum-of-care concept is the fifth model for providing care for the terminally ill. As with the hospital-based unit, the continuum-of-care model is operated under the authority of an established hospital. Unlike the hospital-based unit, however, space and staff are separate from acute care units. Such an arrangement permits explicit, coordinated treatment goals—both inpatient and outpatient—and staff training for meeting the needs of the terminally ill. At the same time, acute care resources are available if necessary.

A major advantage of this model is the relative ease with which coordinated care can be provided for the full spectrum of services. Investigators have found that patient stress caused by transferral from one health care facility to another—for example, from a convalescent to an acute care facility or even to different levels of care within the same facility—contributes to and, in some cases, causes morbidity and mortality, especially among terminally ill elderly patients (6). Transfer between home care or a freestanding facility to an acute care hospital for the purposes of bringing pain under control with the use of radiation takes between eighteen hours and three days. Transfer in hospital-based units or continuum-of-care facilities can be accomplished in a few hours.

An example of a continuum-of-care facility is St. John's Hospital in Springfield, Illinois. Currently a 670-bed community acute care hospital, St. John's administrators purchased a nearby 170-bed subacute care facility to hold patient care services such as skilled and intermediate nursing and adult day care which could be combined with the acute care facility. Hospice services were opened in 1979. The advantages to patients are a wide spectrum of coordinated patterns of access and referral to and from any unit in the hospital, centralized administrative control and auditing, and specialized care at a cost lower than in an acute care setting.

The major advantage is also the major disadvantage of this model. While this model has the security of established referral and funding sources, it is also vulnerable to the competition for resources within the institution. The rhetorical question of a hospital administrator captures this conflict: "When you need half a million dollars to buy a new piece of diagnostic equipment which will return your investment quickly or half a million dollars for a hospice unit in which you will be lucky to get much return at all, which do you think I'll favor?" Finally, an additional problem with this model is the trend to turn health care delivery into a shareholder-owned, business-like, manager-controlled, for-profit industry. It is clear that, in some communities, established acute and convalescent centers are trying to control hospice care so as to prevent competition but without providing appropriate palliative care.

CHALLENGES FOR THE HOSPICE
MOVEMENT

No matter how scandalized the citizenry may be by the rejection or abandonment of patients when prognoses are terminal nor how good the intentions of well-meaning individuals to provide care for their loved ones, consistent palliative therapy requires skilled care and effective organization. In some communities a citizen-initiated movement has been received as a threat to professionally defined services. In other communities, provision for specialized palliative care is perceived as condemnation of the dominant health care delivery system. In still other communities, hospice facilities, providing volunteer services in patients' homes with relatively inexpensive costs, are seen as a rejection of the free-enterprise, for-profit, economic system. All of these fears have some justifiable basis. All of these fears bespeak vested interests in health care delivery. What the expressed fears cannot mask, however, is the fact that the terminally ill were not, and could not, be cared for consistently and effectively before the hospice movement gave channel for expressing scandal over the inability of the terminally ill and their families to have access to palliative care.

The hospice movement has, from time to time, become the object of opposition from powerful economic and political forces, first from established medicine and nursing and later from the for-profit health care corporations. The hospice movement needed vigorous advocacy. To promote the hospice concept in the United States, the National Hospice Organization (NHO) was formally established in 1978. Setting standards for hospice care became the organization's top priority.

From the beginning of the hospice movement, whether it was Dr. Saunders' definition or North America's, the desirable characteristics of hospice care would include: support for the autonomy of the patient, provision of skilled symptom control, care by an interdisciplinary team, regard for the patient/family as the unit of care, use of volunteers as part of the interdisciplinary team/family unit of care, and offering of bereavement support for family and caregivers. With the founding of NHO, *Standards of a Hospice Program of Care* was adopted and is summarized as follows: Hospice should improve patients' quality of life; improve patients'/families' bereavement outcomes; and reduce inpatient care by making home care available without increasing total costs (7).

There were those who argued that palliative care could be regulated under existing standards for home care, nursing home, or hospital services. Both because hospice philosophy calls for some unique services—medical and psychosocial— and because it was feared that control of existing regulations by already-established health care providers would be used to impede and even thwart palliative care, NHO pushed for adoption of its *Standards* and for specific regulation of hospice services. As Roberta Rakov pointed out, though, the "final determination of standards rests with state and local health planning and regulating bodies, which operate in accordance with certificate of need legislation" (8). In many states, the NHO *Standards* have been used as models.

Tensions between voluntary, citizen-initiated health care and standardized, regulated health care delivery by licensed professionals has always been part of a paradox in the American republic. On the one hand, the initiative of the citizen to organize in voluntary associations is part of the very fabric of our society. On the other hand, the same citizenry rejected the Jacksonian laissez-faire notions as applied to health care which had dominated the nineteenth century in favor of a regulated and licensed group of practitioners who were under oaths, codes, and statutes to provide care according to standards. By the turn of the century, most states had adopted acts regulating physician and nurse behavior (9). By 1965, even the courts, in application of principles first set forth in medical practice acts, held hospitals accountable for standards of care by all clinicians practicing within the facility (10). The paradox of citizen initiative versus health care standards is not something that can either be digested or regurgitated philosophically in this republic. In tension—some say with indigestion, the opposites must be tolerated.

There seems to have been two motivations for promoting NHO's *Standards:* to protect the quality of care given to terminally ill patients and their families in the name of hospice and to promote financial support for hospice care.

In large part, financing of the first hospice programs came philanthropically. But by the 1970s, the overwhelming majority of Americans, and all Canadians, expected some part of costs of health care to be covered by either government or private insurance. Accordingly, health care professionals and institutions reorganized to receive reimbursement through third-party payment. In the United States, few health insurance policies covered care of the terminally ill, only those problems which were defined as acute or chronic. Some hospice leaders promoted inclusion of terminal care coverage with the large corporations and labor unions but without much success. Corporate purchasers of health care insurance as well as governmental leaders were becoming alarmed over escalating costs of health care. Those costs, over the last 10 years, far outdistanced inflation rates and were consuming 10 percent of the gross national product.

By 1979, NHO leaders had adopted the strategy to focus on amending the Medicare Act to include coverage of hospice services for approximately 100,000 Medicare-eligible patients a year. Through the efforts of Rep. Leon E. Panetta, D-CA, who introduced the proposed hospice bill in the House, and Sen. Robert Dole, R-KS, who introduced a similar bill in the Senate, enough interest was generated to justify hearings on the bills. *Hospice Letter,* a monthly report for hospice personnel, quoted Rep. Panetta as having said that the biggest selling point was "the significant savings that would result from encouraging the availability of hospice care" (11). During the hearings, two reports were cited: One funded by the Warner-Lambert Foundation and the other conducted by the Congressional Budget Office in which Medicare savings over a five-year period were predicted to range between $30 to $130 million and $100 million respectively. The legislation was passed as part of the Tax Equity and Fiscal Responsibility Act of 1982.

Medicare coverage, like other third-party payments, requires setting standards and accrediting hospice care. For the rest of 1982, political maneuvering and negotiations dominated the scene in attempts to influence the shape of the federal regulations. In the meantime, the number of hospices continued to grow, from less than 50 in 1978 to over 1,000 by the end of the year.

Management rather than care issues dominated the hospice movement during 1983, leaving a number of hospice directors uncertain whether to pursue Medicare recognition of their services when the regulations were published in September. Among the problems was the level of reimbursement. When the legislation had passed on the cost-savings argument, the NHO leaders had hoped for a $7,000 maximum level of funding for each patient—a cap; but the first proposal of the federal Health Care Financing Administration proposed only $4,332. A cap of $6,500 was finally adopted but only after HCFA was mandated by the Congress to do better. Regulations required that each accredited hospice must have both an administrative manager and a medical director. Some of the regulations included the hospice principles such as recognition of volunteer staff who may provide up to 5 percent of total patient care, and bereavement services which must be offered at no cost to patients. But, by and large, most hospice leaders remained skeptical that the Medicare legislation would allow their programs to function according to perceived principles or meet their financial obligations. They were caught in a dilemma over operations. Unstable financial situations jeopardized their freedom of operation, even their survival, but the federal regulations seemed to distort their very reason to exist by altruistic principles.

Harry S. Shanis found that in Missouri, hospices most likely to apply for Medicare coverage were those already organized along the more conventional models of health care (12). Regulations required a hospice staff to provide direct "core services," which included nursing, social work, management of medications and bereavement, and dietary and spiritual counseling. Other types of services that must be provided can be contracted to others, such as homemaker services, short-term inpatient care, and inpatient respite care. These regulations would not support the wholly volunteer and most of the home care models of hospice programs described above. Only the major endowment of autonomous programs or those affiliated with hospitals which could provide alternative funding would seem to be options for Medicare funding. Few, if any, of the former are known to exist, and the latter are unlikely as hospitals have been forced under Diagnosis Related Groupings (DRGs) (standards for reimbursement prospectively for acute and chronic care services) to maximize revenue. They are likely to support hospice services only if consistent with the more traditional hospital methods of health care delivery (13). As a consequence, Shanis believes hospice managers are at the mercy of Medicare restrictions, hospital domination, or corporate takeover. "Unfortunately, the costs of finding a secure niche in the health care delivery system may eliminate the unique grassroots community quality that has made hospice care special" (12, p. 381).

Even the strategy for Medicare reimbursement received an almost immediate blow. In March 1984, preliminary results of the federally funded national Hospice Study conducted by Brown University, which examined care of 26 hospices receiving Medicare funding, concluded that hospice care was not appreciably less costly than conventional care. And from the perspective of caregivers in the study, the patient's quality of life was slightly better with conventional care. Strategies, rationales, and methods of research took over management issues as the dominating concerns of the movement. A number of studies of both cost and quality of patient care have now been published with inconclusive, contradictory, or controversial findings (14–21). Yet, despite these findings, the number of hospice programs registered with NHO continued to grow, exceeding 2,000 by 1986!

Perhaps economics of health care is in such flux that prognostication should be suspended for awhile. Whatever the financial implications of the cost-savings controversy, Vincent Mor, Director of the Brown University National Hospice Study, concludes that all of the studies still have one common finding: "a consistently positive picture of hospice care." Further, "findings relevant to hospice cost effectiveness are positive because hospice at least does not appear to have cost any more than nonhospice under the very different scenarios examined in these studies" (22).

While strategies for funding hospice services dominated the NHO between 1979 and 1984, an undercurrent of concern about quality of care was palpable at state and regional meetings of hospice leaders. Were the two strategies being pushed by NHO antithetical: Could there be governmental regulation compatible with hospice principles? Rather than care based on altruistic principles, would hospice care become driven by commercial interests? Many thought their worst fears were confirmed when the leader of the two-strategy effort announced (in April 1984) that he and a partner would establish a new for-profit hospice corporation. Together with investors headquartered in Miami, Florida, they formed a $5 million corporation called Hospice Care, Inc., with the stated intention of managing 12 to 15 hospices across the country. The chief advocate of the two-strategy effort was also chairman of the board of NHO in 1984 and had spearheaded the Medicare reimbursement strategy. One of the services to be offered by Hospice Care, Inc. was consultation "to help other hospices quality for Medicare benefits." The uproar from hospice leaders across the country forced him to offer his resignation from the board. Many had entered the hospice movement in reaction to the profit-motivated, crass commercialism of health care and "feeding upon the vulnerable." The shades of Asoka! And the movement continued to grow and expand.

Other issues have been explored: How to care for terminally ill children, use of music and art therapy, improved pain control, better nursing techniques, the nature of bereavement, and what to do to care for AIDS victims are but examples. NHO not only survived the powerful internal tensions but also survived competition from others, particularly for-profit home care organizations, by offering a wide range of services to hospice personnel regardless of their institutions' models of care.

Of the many challenges to the hospice movement probably none is more pervasive or more important than how to bridge the tensions between values and competent care. *Hospice,* in its modern usage, is meant to distinguish a kind of care an institution can provide and the kind of patient needs its staff will address. It is meant to be a contrast to acute care (hospitals) and chronic care (nursing homes) institutions. But to define unique service of three kinds of health-related institutions does not identify the major challenge to any of the three.

It is ironic that popular usage makes a distinction between *hospice* and *hospital.* Both words were synonymous in Western history for a place where the pilgrim/patient could find compassion and shelter. It is only in our time that health care services have been defined more precisely and separate institutions have been provided for specialized care. Even as recently as the 1950s, many hospitals in the United States and Canada provided, to the best of their resources and abilities, all three levels of service—acute, chronic, and terminal care. However, with the development of costly technological sophistication, the rise of the medical specialties, and the implementation of third-party payers—all designed to correct major problems in health care delivery, the functions of health care institutions became more restricted and staff roles more uniform. The primary focus for intervention in health crises shifted from the patient suffering to the clinician diagnosing, from the patient as person to the person as diseased organ. It was a shift in the history of ideas which Foucault (23) calls the "clinical gaze" or perspective. It is to look at a human being and see primarily what is diseased, to respond to that individual as though one were addressing an object, and to assess that object as a statistic. What the hospice movement has done, along with other humanely influencing forces driven by other issues in health care delivery, is to provide the kind of contrast that allows us to see otherwise hidden values. Even to articulate the contrasts forces us to define what is presumed about human beings when acutely ill, chronically ill, or terminally ill.

The hospice movement is, itself, a moral concept. Defining *hospice* in competition with other modes of health care has allowed values to emerge which may have been present in our cultures in the past but had become hidden until the present. Five such values are central to the concept of hospice and, according to Churchill (24), need to be basic commitments about the care of the dying. Stating these values declaratively they are:

- Dying is a human experience.
- Dying persons are ends in themselves.
- Dying persons are self-determining.
- Dependence and need are not demeaning.
- The basic unit of care is the community (p. 164).

These five values are not exhaustive, but they are definitive. Without them, hospice care would be adrift and hospice caregivers would be without guidance. Then, the hospice movement truly would be at the mercy of market forces, political ideologies, and vested interests. We are in the debt of the hospice movement for forcing these values to emerge.

But values are only one side of the primary tension in health care. The other side emerges as we try to define what competence means for the acutely, chronically, and terminally ill. Malpractice controversies, an international phenomenon that has been a prominent part of recent health care, is at least a reflection of society's demand for professional accountability in the health fields. They must be seen as part of the same historical and sociopolitical context in which we understand the changing functions of health care institutions. Professional accountability, or competence, is possible only if roles of the professions can be knowledgeably reviewed and tested. Health care training then has emphasized standards, health care institutions have functioned according to protocols, and health care staff tend to behave according to standards of accountability. Patients are expected to behave according to patterns compatible with standards of accountability. For acute care institutions, the persuasive outcome that standards are designed to foster and against which evaluations are measured is cure. For chronic care institutions, the outcome is rehabilitation. Staff performance that leads to cure or rehabilitation is, by definition, competent.

In reaction to the objective, scientific, and fragmented competencies of modern health care, of which abandonment or mistreatment of the terminally ill are but parts, there are efforts to make all health care delivery more humane. Certainly as a corrective to historical developments in health care institutions, and as a complement to services already available, the hospice movement is making a distinct contribution. But it will be tolerated by the same society which now encourages it only if it provides competent alternatives. What will define competence for the people serving the terminally ill? Will it be behavior that will foster a specific style of dying? Will it be behavior that will foster a specific style of living? Or will it provide a new understanding of competence, based not on the "clinical gaze" but on the patient's sense of values? If it is this last one, then the resolutions to the tension between the values and the competencies of health care delivery, particularly as they apply to care of the terminally ill, will lie more with the arts and theology than has yet been identified. Compassionate care is not glibly defined nor easily practiced.

REVIEW QUESTIONS

1. Describe the ways in which Talcott Parsons' conceptualization of the "sick role" is both appropriate and inappropriate as it is applied to the terminal patient.
2. What are the factors that inhibit hospital systems from delivering appropriate care to the terminal patient?
3. What advantages and services does hospice care offer the terminal patient and his/her family as compared with the services offered by hospital care?
4. In what ways does terminal illness fail to conform to either the definition of acute illness or chronic illness? What problems does this failure to fit either category pose for the terminal patient?
5. Define, compare, and contrast the five different hospice models.
6. Describe the major factors that challenge the hospice movement. What positive changes may be made to deal with these challenges?
7. What are the central issues concerning reimbursement for terminal care?
8. In your opinion, what are the ethical issues raised by the hospice movement?

REFERENCES

1. Thompson, J. D., & Goldin, G. (1975). *The hospital: A social and architectural history.* New Haven: Yale University Press.
2. Parsons, T. (1951). *The social system.* New York: Free Press.
3. Noyes, R., Jr., & Clancy, J. (1977). The dying role: Its relevance to improved patient care. *Psychiatry, 40,* 41–47.
4. Davidson, G. W. (Ed.). (1985). *The hospice: Development and administration* (2nd ed.). Washington: Hemisphere.
5. Lack, S. A. (1978). New Haven (1974). Characteristics of a hospice program of care. In G. W. Davidson (Ed.), *The hospice: Development and administration* (1st ed.). Washington: Hemisphere.
6. National League of Nursing. (1966). Statement on continuity of nursing care. New York: Division of Nursing Services, National League of Nursing.
7. National Hospice Organization (1979). *Standards of a Hospice Program of Care* (6th ed.). McLean, VA: National Hospice Organization.
8. Rakov, R. (1979). Hospice care: A planning perspective. *Quality Review Bulletin, 5,* 11.
9. Shyrock, R. H. (1967). *Medical licensing in America, 1650–1965.* Baltimore: Johns Hopkins.
10. *Darling vs. Charleston Memorial Hospital,* 33 Ill 2d 326, 211 NE 2d 253 (1965).
11. *Hospice Letter,* (1982 December), 4:1.
12. Shanis, H. S. (1985). Impact of Medicare certification on the hospice movement. *Death Studies, 9,* 365–382.
13. Paradis, L. F. (1984). Hospice program integration: An issue for policy-makers. *Death Education, 8,* 383–398.
14. Greer, D. S., Mor, V., Morris, J. N., Sherwood, S., Kidder, D., & Birnbaum, H. (1984). An alternative in terminal care: Results of the National Hospice Study. In L. H. Aiken and B. H. Kehrer (Eds.), *Evaluation Studies Review Annual* (Vol. 10) (pp. 146–158). Beverly Hills: Sage.
15. Birnbaum, H. G., & Kidder, D. (1984). What does hospice cost? *American Journal of Public Health, 74,* 689–697.
16. Kane, R. L., Bernstein, L., Wales, J., Leibowitz, A., & Kaplan, S. (1984). A randomized controlled trial of hospice care. *The Lancet, 1,* 890–894.

17. Holden, C. (1983). Hospices compared with conventional care. *Science, 222*, 601.
18. Bloom, B. S., & Kissick, P. D. (1980). Home and hospital cost of terminal illness. *Med-Care 18*, 560–564.
19. Morgan, N. C. (1984). An analysis of selected hospice programs. *Journal of Risk Insurance, 51*, 99–114.
20. Brooks, C. H., & Smyth-Staruch, K. (1984). Hospice home care cost savings to third-party insurers. *Med-Care, 22*.
21. Brooks, C. H. (1983). The potential cost savings of hospice care: A review of the literature. *Health Matrix, 1*, 49–53.
22. Mor, V. (1985). Commentary: Results of hospice evaluations: A view from the National Hospice Study. *Quality of care for the terminally ill: An examination of the issues* (pp. 80–85). Chicago: Joint Commission on Accreditation of Hospitals.
23. Foucault, M. (1973). *The birth of the clinic.* (A. M. Sheridan Smith, trans. First American edition) New York: Pantheon.
24. Churchill, L. (1985). The ethics of hospice care. In G. W. Davidson (Ed.), *The hospice: Development and administration* (2nd ed.) (pp. 163–179). Washington: Hemisphere.

10

Death in the Lives of Children and Adolescents

Hannelore Wass and Judith M. Stillion

Many adults are ill at ease and reluctant to discuss the subject of death with the young. This may stem from the desire to spare children the fears and anxieties that the topic could provoke, from the misconception that children are unaware of death and uninterested in the subject, and from a host of other factors. Whatever the reason, such hesitancy is unhelpful according to professionals who are knowledgeable about the young and sensitive to their needs.

Interestingly, adult denial and avoidance of death have not always been present. Death was an integral part of everyday human experience throughout most of history. The average life expectancy of humans in the Middle Ages was 33 years. Women gave birth every 18 months on the average. The rates of infant and maternal mortality were very high, disease was rampant, nutrition and medical technology were inadequate, and everyday life was a hazardous affair. Even as late as 1900 the average life expectancy in the United States was only slightly more than 47 years and infant mortality was still high. Until the early part of this century, children were intimately acquainted with death. It was not unusual for a child to lose one or more siblings as well as a parent before reaching adulthood. Death occurred most often in the home, and children helped with the care of the dying family member, were present at the moment of death, participated in the preparations for the funeral, and attended it. Today the average life expectancy in the United States has increased to 76 years. Over 70 percent of the individuals who will die in 1986 will be 65 years old or older, over 70 percent of their deaths will occur in an institution rather than in the home, and parents today often exclude their children from the funeral. Only 4 percent of all deaths occur among children under the age of 15 years (Chapter 11); thus, Fulton's suggestion that contemporary youth may be called the first "death-free" generation in the history of the world. This does not mean, however, that today's young have no contacts and experiences with death.

In this chapter, we will discuss common types of death experiences of children, the evolution of mature understandings of death, children's and adolescents' reactions and attempts to cope with the demise of a loved one or with their own impending deaths. We will also examine suicidal behavior, including symptoms and approaches to prevention, and provide some guidelines and suggestions for helping children cope with death.

UNDERSTANDING DEATH

Most studies of children's understanding of death report an orderly progression from immature to mature concepts. These findings hold across several generations (from the 1920s to the 1980s), several cultures (England, Germany, Hungary, Canada, the United States), and divergent methodologies (interviews, questionnaires, observation, projective techniques) (1-8). Many authors have used Piaget's model of cognitive development as the theoretical basis for their investigations or as an explanation of their findings (e.g., 4, 5, 7, 9-11).

Piaget's Periods of Cognitive Development

Piaget developed one of the most comprehensive, complex, and widely recognized theories of intellectual development to date. For our purposes, a much abbreviated review of this theory will suffice. Piaget views cognitive development as a progression from undifferentiated to differentiated, simple to complex, ego-centered to ego-decentered, concrete to abstract, nonlogical to logical. The first fundamental component of his theory is that of organic growth or *maturation,* which determines the sequence of the child's intellectual development. However, Piaget recognizes the importance of the social and physical environment and views *experience* as the second major factor necessary for mental development (12). Thus, cognitive development happens in constant and close interaction between child and environment. Piaget himself focused primarily on cognitive development in an *optimum, constant* environment, ignoring effects of environmental variations on cognitive processes. From studies of his own children and public school students, he identified three major periods of cognitive development including two subperiods or stages (13). In the first, the *sensorimotor period,* in infancy, sensory and motor actions through repetition become established as behavioral and perceptual sequences or schemes that form the basis for later cognition. Infants can form images of objects found in their immediate environment and learn to remember them when they are not present. However, Piaget believes that no actual conceptualization occurs during this period. The second period is one of *preparation and organization* consisting of two stages (Table 1). The first stage is that of preoperational thought in early childhood (ages 2-7 years). (An "operation" refers to a cognitive act.) At this stage, children understand events only from the perspective of their limited experiences which are dominated by their basic egocentric orientation. That is, the child views him/herself as the center of the universe. The child's reasoning is based on animistic, magical, artificialistic, and psychological thinking. In animistic thinking, the child attributes life to inanimate objects. In magical thinking, the child ascribes superhuman power to others, him/herself, and objects thereby providing "reasonable" explanations for otherwise incomprehensible occurrences. In artificialistic thinking, the child believes that objects, people, plants,

TABLE 1   Children's and Adolescents' Concepts of Death

Piaget's periods and stages	Concepts	Developmental/ educational status
II. Preparation and Organization		
1. Preoperational thought (2–7 yrs)	Reversibility External causation (violence, accidents) Revival by various means	Preschool years
2. Concrete operations (7–11/12 yrs)	Irreversibility Cessation of functions Internal causation Universality Simple beliefs about life after death	Early school years Middle childhood years/ preadolescence
III. Formal operations (11/12 yrs and over)	Religious and philosophical theories about the nature of death and existence after death	Adolescence

the sun, the moon, etc., are manufactured for our convenience and pleasure. In psychological thinking, the child perceives a personal motive as the cause of certain events. For example, contracting an illness may be understood as a punishment for misbehavior. At no time during cognitive development is a young child's thinking more qualitatively different from that of an older child or an adult than at this stage.

The second stage, concrete operations (Table 1), occurs in the early school years, in middle childhood and preadolescence. This period in cognitive development is characterized by the child's ability to recognize his/her subjective orientation and to begin the process of decentering, that is, understanding that his own thoughts and thinking are distinct from those of other people. Operations or cognitive activities are now based on observation of concrete events and on the laws that govern them. The child also discovers simple rules of logic such as geometric, arithmetic, temporal, and mechanical. During the third period, formal operations (Table 1), which begins in adolescence, previous cognitive functions and structures are integrated and expanded. The adolescent now is capable of formulating generalizations far beyond what is based on experience or can be experienced. The child now can hypothesize, theorize, and, in general, effectively manipulate abstract ideas (14).

What are the research findings on children's and adolescents' concepts of death, and how well do they fit Piaget's model of conceptual development in general?

Acquisition of Concepts of Death

To our knowledge, no systematic studies of infants concerning death-related concepts have been reported. Thus, at present, it has not been demonstrated that infants conceptualize about death. At most, it can be assumed from infants' negative reactions to separation (15) and from casual observations (16) that infants possess some sort of "awareness" of death. Major findings of studies investigating the concepts of death of children ages three years to 18 years are summarized in

Table 1. There is a striking consistency among these studies showing that, generally, children in the preschool years have no realistic comprehension of death. They understand death as a temporary restriction, sleep, or departure. They believe that the "dead" can be brought back to life, spontaneously, by administering food, medical treatment, or magic (1, 2, 5, 17).

> One little boy explained: "Boys don't die unless they get run over. If they go to a hospital, I think they come out living" (3, p. 421).

> Another said: "The nurse gives out a pill. Then he is all better." A preschool girl responded to the question "What happens when people die?"
> Girl: They get shot.
> Q: What happens then?
> Girl: Their mama has to come and get them.
> Q: Then what happens?
> Girl: They eat.

Young children view death as caused externally by acts of violence such as shooting or stabbing, by accidents such as car crashes or falls from heights, or by self-indulgence as through alcoholism or overeating (2-5, 18-19).

> Some of the causes of death young children give are bizarre:

> Boy, age 4: Big birds come and eat you.
> Boy, age 6: They get attacked by a tiger.
> Girl, age 7: They get killed by rat poison.

These results indicate a close correspondence to the stage of preoperational thought in Piaget's model of cognitive development.

During the school years, children generally come to understand the concepts of *irreversibility, cessation of functions,* and *universality* of death (20) (Table 1). The concept of the cessation of functions apparently is more difficult to grasp than that of irreversibility. Although children may understand that death is a permanent state, they only later recognize that the dead no longer have physical needs, feelings, or thoughts (2, 5). One study suggests that children understand first that the dead do not move, eat, or speak and only later that cognitive and affective functions also cease (6). Closely related to the concepts of irreversibility and cessation is the concept of *internal causation.* During the school years, children report illness and old age as causes of death in addition to external ones (2-7, 17, 21).

The concept of universality also seems more difficult to grasp than irreversibility and also seems to be attained in steps. Children apparently recognize the mortality of others, especially strangers, before they recognize the mortality of the members of their families (3, 19) or their personal mortality (5, 6, 11). It is probable that children understand the idea of universality of death or personal mortality intellectually in the middle childhood and preadolescent years and in some cases even earlier, but children and adolescents (in fact, many adults) do not readily acknowledge that death can happen to them at any time.

> One 11-year-old wrote this about her own death: "I think when someone knows they are going to die they are very scared. I would. I think

after someone dies they just lie there forever and disintegrate. I hope I never die." (21, p. 12)

And a 12-year-old wrote: "When you die, you lie there wondering if you will go to Heaven or Hell. I get scared and I don't want to die. I don't know about *you*, but *I'm* going to Heaven." (2, p. 12)

Children and adolescents may defend against unacceptable levels of fear and anxiety by denying the possibility of their own deaths except as an abstract event in a remote future (16). This buffer against anxiety may contribute to the illusion of invulnerability that many adolescents experience. For example, adolescents often drive faster than safe road conditions allow, experiment with drugs, and otherwise exhibit a lack of concern for the potentially fatal outcomes of their behavior.

Mature concepts of death such as irreversibility, cessation of functions, and universality are acquired over a period of years at a developmental level approximately corresponding to Piaget's theory (Table 1) but with *one* difference: Many children apparently attain these these understandings at younger ages than Piaget suggested. Speece and Brent (20) analyzed over 40 studies on children's acquisition of the concepts of irreversibility, cessation of functions, and universality. The data show large variations among findings in the chronological ages at which children comprehend these concepts. For example, the understanding of the concept of the universality of death ranged from four years of age in some studies to 10 years and older in others. This variability can be viewed as consistent with the wide range of individual differences found in other aspects of children's development. These differences may tend to obscure any sequence in the development of these concepts. Alternately, there may be no sequence. Instead, these concepts may be obtained in fluid and uneven patterns of development.

During the childhood and preadolescent years, children also adopt simple beliefs about life after death, primarily the Christian belief in heaven or hell or, less frequently, the absence of an afterlife (5, 17, 21) (Table 1). These beliefs seem to be relatively nonspecific. At least children's responses to researchers' questions are laconic and stereotypical. When asked what they would do in heaven, children in one study said, "Praise the Lord" or "fly around as an angel." Only after some prodding did children admit that they "have no idea what heaven or hell are like" or express doubts about heaven being much fun (22).

In contrast, adolescents formulate abstract ideas about the nature of death. For example, adolescents describe death as darkness, light, transition, or nothingness (18, 23). They also formulate their own theologies about life after death which include belief in reincarnation, transmigration of souls, spiritual survival on earth, and spiritual survival at another level in a state of indescribable peace and beauty, in addition to beliefs about heaven and hell or total annihilation at death (5, 18, 22, 24) (Table 1). These findings are consistent with Piaget's period of formal operations. Thus, research with healthy children and adolescents despite an array of methodological problems (20) seems to suggest that concepts of death develop generally in accordance with the Piagetian model of cognitive development.

Part of the age variation in attaining mature understandings of death may be attributed to demographic variables. In one study, children from families of low socioeconomic status were found to comprehend the concept of the irreversibility of death at an earlier age than those from high socioeconomic backgrounds (25). In another study, early adolescents with college-educated parents more frequently formulated theories about life after death than did those whose parents completed only high school (21). The Cross-cultural comparisons involving Brazilian, Greek, Swedish, and American children and adolescents, however, suggest that there are more similarities than differences, especially in younger children (18, 26, 27).

The most striking variation in findings comes from studies involving special populations of children. Children who have lost a family member through death exhibited mature understandings of death at younger ages than did nonbereaved children (6, 11, 25). Similarly, studies of terminally ill children revealed amazingly accurate understanding of the threat to their lives among children as young as four years of age (28–30). It is clear that extreme circumstances and close personal encounters with death have a powerful impact on children and bring about mature death-related perceptions and cognition far beyond their years.

SOCIALIZATION

Children learn the ideas, beliefs, values, patterns, and norms of their culture through a variety of experiences and interactions. Many things contribute to their socialization into adult members of society: their parents, peers, and day-to-day experiences; the television shows and movies they watch, the music the listen to, and the books they read. Certainly this is true of death-related beliefs, values, and behaviors. Because of the complex and contradictory nature of our society's stance toward death, our children are subjected to many conflicts and contradictions.

Television and Films

Today's children do not experience death directly as often as did children in previous eras. Nonetheless, death is an intimate part of most children's lives—on film, video, and television. Through television, the most violent and unnatural deaths are brought daily into the homes of the vast majority of Americans. It is estimated that three- and four-year-olds spend an average of four hours per day viewing television. This figure increases with increasing age. It is suggested that children, in fact, spend more time in front of the television set than they do in school and perhaps in interaction with their parents (31). Children's cartoons contain about six times as many violent episodes per hour as do adult programs (32). In the Roadrunner, for example, the coyote is smashed by a locomotive, falls off a cliff, or is blown up by a rocket; the next scene shows him, only slightly battered, moving on to the next death-defying scheme. There are, on the average, five acts of violence per hour on prime-time commercial television drama (33). In a recent analysis of over 1,500 commercial television drama programs nearly 80 percent of all deaths were caused by violence, less than 10 percent of the characters expressed intense grief, and only nine funerals were depicted (34).

The Surgeon General's Report (35) and the more recent report of the National Institute of Mental Health (36) have concluded that televised violence has negative effects on young people's behavior, especially on aggression. Televised violence seems to convey the idea that life is cheap and violence is a common solution to problems. Psychologists have begun to focus research attention on the effects of television's violence and distorted depiction of death on children's perception of social reality (37). We do not yet have empirical data on the total effect such violence and distortion have on children's views of death and life, but we are beginning to discover part of its impact. In a study of academically gifted children and adolescents, it was found that 90 percent of the students overestimated the number of murders committed in the United States each year. About 75 percent overestimated it by more than four times and approximately 33 percent by more than 200 times (38). If bright students have such unrealistic ideas about deadly violence in our society, perhaps all children do. If so, how does this affect their feelings and attitudes toward others, and how does it influence their behavior? Research is needed to clarify these questions.

Among an array of ever more violent films that are top box office draws in movie theaters across the United States and abroad are the Rambo series directed by Sylvester Stallone who is also their hero. The latest of his productions has been banned for its violence by the government of Brazil. Similarly, the Star Wars movies have captured the interest and imagination of millions, young and old. In these films, entire galactic systems—though evil ones, of course—are destroyed for the entertainment of the audiences. It is not surprising that young people and adults become desensitized and begin to accept massive destruction as commonplace if only in fantasy.

Television also introduces children to the grim reality of real death through the nightly news. Frequently, accounts of deaths by accidents, starvation, natural disasters, terrorist acts, wars, as well as the ever present threat of nuclear destruction are reported by newscasters. Many accounts of death are accompanied by scenes of the victims' mutilated bodies. Except in the homes of very wise parents, children rarely find opportunities to express and relieve the shock, outrage, or dread that accompany their increasing knowledge of violent death. It should not surprise us that denial of the subject of death is pervasive and that children should overestimate the amount of killing that occurs.

It is futile to attempt to screen out all that is of potential harm in the child's environment. This does not mean we can do nothing. Parents can monitor the television programs their children watch regularly and preview films as well. It is helpful to counterbalance adverse material by guiding children toward programs with prosocial models and benign content.

Adolescent Rock Music

Music is an important part of children's and adolescents' experience. Although its forms vary, rock music is by far the most popular genre among the young (39). Records are believed to have a wider public than any other medium because they are not limited by considerations of literacy or language and cross, as they do, all national and cultural boundaries (39). Anglo-American mass-produced rock music seems, thus far, to have dominated the world. In addition to records, audiotapes of rock music are available, and rock music, like other music, is aired by a large number of radio stations. Rock music is also mass-produced as short video-vignettes that can be rented for viewing on home video recorders or on television as, for example, on MTV channels. Several thousand new rock singles and albums are released annually. Some of these have sales in seven digits. In 1980, rock music records were released under nearly 200 different labels (40). Successful rock musicians play concerts before large audiences in arenas and stadiums all over this country and abroad. Rock music is big business.

There are wide variations within the genre of rock music, notably between "soft" rock (such as jazz rock, blues rock, and pop rock), and "hard" rock, which includes punk, heavy metal, glitter, and avant-garde (41). Sociologists and other students of rock music agree that its evolution began some 30 years ago as an expression of "counterculture" ideas and values and tends to continue this function today (41, 42). Pielke (41) described rock music as revolutionary art and suggested a typology beginning with the 1950s that includes periods of negation, affirmation, and dormancy. He characterizes contemporary soft rock as absorbed in the mainstream of popular music, and hard rock, in general, as expressions of negative attitudes with emphasis on images of sex, pornography, satanism, dismemberment, and the grotesque. Religious groups, the National PTA, and particularly a group of parents who founded the Parents' Music Resource Center have spoken out sharply against explicit sex, violence, satanism, and other negative themes in rock music. As a result of the efforts of these pressure groups, a Congressional Committee held hearings in 1985 on the subject of the contents of music and the lyrics of records (43). The question before the committee was that of record labeling. The following system for labeling albums was proposed: X for sexually explicit lyrics, D/A for lyrics condoning drug and alcohol abuse, V for those with violent themes, and O for lyrics dealing with the occult. Such labeling has not been adopted by many record companies, nor has the demand by some groups that the lyrics of the songs be printed on the album covers. Some self-regulatory measures have, however, been adopted by distributors and some segments of the industry. For example, the record division of CBS has established guidelines for monitoring the lyrics of their records (44). The Walmart discount chain, with more than 900 retail outlets, has recently removed a number of rock albums from their shelves (45). Radio rock stations apparently are responding to some degree by airing controversial material late at night rather than during daytime or evening hours. Even MTV presents objectionable programming only intermittently and most frequently late at night.

Attig (46) has provided a useful list of categories for death-related themes in rock music that includes immortality, grief and bereavement, suicide, war, apocalyptic music, drugs and death, violence, murder, and death in the ghetto. No systematic attempt has been made, to our knowledge, to list all singles and albums by contemporary bands and individual singers that contain these themes in their lyrics. Such a list would be an important step in exploring the frequency of these themes as well as their popularity. New records are released at a rapid pace. Therefore, such a list would need frequent updating. With the limited space available here we can give only a small sample of the bands considered popular based on the sales of albums, concert tours, and ratings and write-ups in a variety of rock magazines such as *Circus, Hit Parader, Metal,* and *Rock Scene.* Similarly, we will list only a small number of the songs and sample lines from their lyrics that deal with themes of suicide, deadly violence, and war/nuclear holocaust. One of the songs by the Twisted Sister (who performed in New York's Radio City Music Hall) is called "Under the Blade" (1985). It deals with murder, as illustrated by the following lines from its lyrics:

Now here it comes that glistening light.
It goes into your side.
The blackness comes.
Tonight's the night.
The blade is gonna ride.

A song by the Mötley Crüe called "Shout at the Devil" (in a double platinum album, 1983) contains these lines:

Not a woman but a whore.
I can taste the hate.
Well, now I'm killing you . . .
Watch your face turning blue . . .

The lyrics of another song by the same band called "Bastard" (1983) read as follows:

Out goes the light,
In goes my knife,
Pull out his life.
Consider the bastard dead.

Other examples in the context of killing are "Shoot to Thrill" (1980), "Squealer" (1983) (by the band AC/DC), "The Torture Never Stops" (by W.A.S.P., 1984), "Whiplash" (by Metallica, 1983), and "Piece by Piece" (by Slayer, 1986).

The same bands and others also speak out against war, the threat of nuclear destruction, and capital punishment. These lines are from the song "Disposable Heroes" (Metallica, 1986).

Bodies fill the fields I see, hungry heroes end.
No one to play soldier now, no one to pretend,
Running blind through killing fields,
Bred to kill them all.
Victim of what said should be,
A servant till I fall.

Among other songs that speak out against war and destruction are "Peace Sells—But Who's Buying?" (Megadeth, 1981), "Before the Storm" (Megadeth, 1983), and "Another One Bites the Bullet" (Queen, 1980).

Among recent rock songs about suicide, one by Ozzy Osbourne, "Suicide Solution" (1981) has been cited in the Congressional Hearings as promoting suicide, although the singer himself protests this interpretation. We find the lyrics clearly promotive of suicide. The song includes these lines:

Suicide is the only way out.
Take a dive to drown your sorrows.
Let it flush away tomorrows.

On the other hand, the song by Queen titled "Don't Try Suicide" (1980) clearly discourages the act. Some lines follow:

Don't do it!
Don't try suicide!
Don't, Don't, Don't, Don't do that!
You've got a good thing goin' now!

One hard rock band, Stryper, calls itself Christian rockers and is receiving wide media recognition. One of the band's videocassettes is rated in the top 10 nationally (47).

The major problem with contemporary rock music and the young is the absence of any research on adolescents' perceptions and understandings of this music and its lyrics and on the effect of both of these on young persons' attitudes and behavior. If it can be demonstrated, for instance, that under certain conditions, teenagers who are heavy consumers of violent rock music are more likely to commit suicide or to kill someone, then the record industry could be persuaded to refrain from publishing such songs. Perhaps even many of the writers would turn to more constructive lyrics.

Toys and Games

A casual observation of a toy store or the toy section of a department store in the United States demonstrates the striking number and variety of toys and games manufactured for playful imitation of individual aggression as well as war. The range extends from more than a dozen types of weapons to the sophisticated video games popular among teenagers. According to Ms. Levin, a spokeswoman for the Toy Manufacturers' Association of America, the G. I. Joe line of soldiers and accessories now ranks first in toy sales in the nation's stores (48). An article by Haessli published in *Sharing Space* (*8*, 3, 1985) lists war toys as the leading category of toys sold, making up five of the six best-selling toys in the United States. On playgrounds, front and back yards, and in the streets of our towns and cities, some of the most common sights and sounds are young boys playing "cops and robbers," "cowboys and Indians," or "soldiers" with the typical cry of "bang, bang, you're dead." The child, thus "killed," follows the rules of the game, falls down, and remains motionless on the ground "playing dead" for a short period of time. Older children plan and carry on more elaborate war games, often with entire toy armies, fleets of warships, including nuclear submarines, and with missile-carrying war planes and other sophisticated toy weapons.

An article in *Newsweek* (49), reports that two computer geniuses have invented Tech Force, an army of robot soldiers that can be directed by audiosignals encoded in the soundtracks of television programs (or audiocassettes). A child can pit his/her robot against one responding to TV signals. The robots move, make sound, and fire infrared beams at each other on command. The biggest toy fad, according to *Fortune* magazine, is a $40 kit, Laser Tag, that includes a light-emitting pistol, belt and holster, and a sensor that automatically records each "hit," (*Gainesville Sun*, November 20, 1986). Commercials for Laser Tag on MTV channels show a man as the target, and there is no doubt that Laser Tag is a "killing" toy. Playing with such toys familiarizes children with the many ways people can kill each other. It also makes such action appear easy, painless, and without consequence. Furthermore, children learn, albeit through play, the role of attacker and killer (and less often that of the victim). Thus, lethal violence in imaginative play and for amusement is a common aspect of children's, especially boys', socialization in our society. It would be naive to assume that such cultural practice has no influence on the child's attitudes, values, and beliefs.

The Printed Word

Death along with warnings of hell and damnation was part of most children's stories in the eighteenth and nineteenth centuries and was often portrayed in a frightening manner. The popular McGuffey readers used in elementary schools until the 1930s contained many such stories and poems. They were intended as lessons for building morality. Fairy tales, nursery rhymes, and games contained explicit descriptions of sadistic violent death (50, 51). Some psychologists, particularly those of Freudian persuasion, believe that cruel death in literature is good for children's healthy personality development. Bettelheim (52) has made the case for the therapeutic value of the original Grimm's fairy tales suggesting that not only do the bad always receive cruel punishment by death (thus justice, even though primitive, is done) but that through identification with the punisher the child can "work through" his or her own unconscious destructive impulses, wishes, and anxieties.

In the early part of this century, however, most of this early material, including the Central European fairy tales, was "purged" of specific references to cruel death. Even so, a number of gruesome rhymes were retained in *The Oxford Nursery Rhyme Book* as late as the 1960 edition (Oxford: Clarendon Press) as this sample illustrates:

> Giant Bonaparte
> (Verses 3 and 4)
> Baby, baby, if he hears you,
> As he gallops past the house,
> Limb from limb at once he'll tear you,
> Just as pussy tears a mouse.
> And he'll beat you, beat you, beat you,
> And he'll beat you all to pap,
> And he'll eat you, eat you, eat you,
> Every morsel, snap, snap, snap (p. 20).

Fortunately, a new genre of children's literature by professional writers, who portray death in a benign and sensitive manner and as a natural part of the life cycle, have been written in the recent past (50). Research has demonstrated that reading about the feelings and behavior of others is strikingly potent in altering attitudes and behaviors (53). It is not known how widely read these more recent books are but they may, to a degree, counteract the negative effect of the distorted portrayal of death in the electronic media.

Humor

Each generation of children apparently has its own tradition concerning death-related humor. Whereas many of the cruel nursery rhymes of the previous centuries are believed to have originated from less than loving and devoted servants employed to care for young children, children also create their own death humor. Wolfenstein cites the following jokes made up by a six-year-old: "My name is East River. Why don't you drop in some time" (54, p. 88). And a 12-year-old, "inspired" by "Custer's Last Stand," drew a picture of a man with a fruit stand thus converting the bloody deaths of Custer's men into innocent, colorful fruit (54, p. 28). Several generations ago, humor about body decomposition was popular ("The worms crawl out, the worms crawl in, they crawl all over your mouth and chin"). The same type of humor is popular today except that these earlier jokes seem to "pale" in comparison to the "dead baby" jokes in circulation today. It is difficult for adults even to learn of these current jokes. Most recently, following the space shuttle Challenger's disaster, a number of gruesome jokes related to this tragedy have surfaced and are circulating among older children and adolescents. It is easy for adults to condemn these jokes as the products of calloused, sick, and sadistic juvenile minds (if indeed they are made up by young people). But why are they repeated by others and passed along? There are other explanations for the popularity of these jokes. A number of psychologists believe that children ward off or release anxiety through such humor (54, 55). It seems reasonable to claim that "death" or "gallows" humor is not the prerogative solely of morticians, medical students, police personnel, and other adults who have to deal with death on a regular basis.

Animals and Pets

For many children, the earliest and only direct experience with death throughout childhood and adolescence is with animals and pets. Children frequently are confronted with animal death. They see dead insects, worms, toads, birds, and larger animals. Many families keep animals as pets. Children often form very close and tender relationships with pets, not only with dogs and cats but also with turtles, goldfish, mice, snakes, and even beetles. Psychologists and educators suggest that keeping animals as pets is beneficial to the growing child for a number of reasons. One of them is that it gives the child an opportunity for direct experience with the life cycle, including dying and death and the feelings of pain and grief associated with loss through death. When a pet dies, parents frequently have problems dealing with the death. Parents often try to conceal the animal remains and avoid any and all discussion (56). This, of course, creates additional difficulties for the child. The death of a pet can be a valuable learning experience provided that the parents are able to offer sensitive help and guidance, including open confrontation and communication about the event and the feelings it engenders (57). The death of a pet affords a natural occasion for broaching the subject with children. Some believe that experiencing the death of a pet prepares the child for coping more effectively with the loss of a close person (56, p. 29).

Talking About Death

Most parents feel uncomfortable talking about death with their children. McNeil reports that over 80 percent of a large group of parents she interviewed felt uneasy abut discussing death with their children and that over 70 percent rarely or only occasionally talked about death with other adults. Most of the mothers could recall no discussion about the subject occurring in their homes when they were children (58). Furman found that, even when a member of the family dies, discussion of the subject is minimal. Over 40 percent of the parents in one of her studies told their children under age 16 little about the death of the other parent (59). Others report similar findings of parental avoidance of the topic of death (38, 56, 60, 61). In a study of gifted children and adolescents, it was found that children rarely talk about death with parents or friends. Adolescents, on the other hand, more often reported talking about death with their friends (38).

To help parents in dealing with the topic of death with their children, some general guidelines have been suggested (50, 51, 56, 57, 60–62).

Confront your own death and clarify your own thoughts, feelings, values, and beliefs. Parents must decide what messages about death they want to convey to their children. They must be prepared to address such questions as "Does the reality of death have positive implications for the way we live our lives? What are they? Is there an existence after death, or is death the end? What is an appropriate death?"

Provide an atmosphere of love and acceptance. Of course, this is an ideal for all families in all circumstances. It is of particular significance when sensitive and potentially anxiety-arousing subjects are discussed. Emotional support (e.g., holding, hugging) often ensures that the child is not unnecessarily alarmed by some given information.

Be open and honest in your communication with the child. Ideally, parents should be able to respond to children's inquiries about death calmly, straightforwardly, and with correct information when factual matters are under question. Skillful parents encourage their children to ask questions without fear of ridicule or rebuke. It is helpful when parents share their beliefs and values, as well as their uncertainties, about this complex issue.

Recognize that learning about complex matters such as death is an extended process. It cannot be accomplished in one sitting, nor can parents teach it in one easy lesson. Parents should be prepared to discuss the topic from the perspective appropriate to their child's developmental level. It is important to find out how much of what the parent said the child actually "heard." Children frequently pick up partial or confused messages from parents, share them with other fragmentally informed children and, thus, build up a mass of half-truths which they then use to organize new "information" about death.

Deal with the affective as well as the cognitive aspects of the subject of death. Recognizing that very young children are likely to be frightened by the separation aspects of death while older children are more likely to fear mutilation and decomposition of the body will help parents in addressing these issues. Understanding that adolescents are concerned with achieving independence and suffer illusions of invulnerability may assist parents in structuring their discussions in such a way as to allow their teenage children to air their own beliefs and concerns while gently guiding them toward a more realistic acknowledgment of death and a more emotionally mature way of managing death-related fears.

Respond to your children's questions and concerns when they arise. The time may be inconvenient for you but immediate answers may be essential for the child. It is all too easy to postpone a discussion one finds difficult to begin with and then hope that the child will forget. When discussions must be delayed (e.g., the parent has to leave for work, has guests for dinner), parents should set a definite time for the discussion to take place and then be sure to follow through.

Use "teachable moments." Children are surrounded by death in their everyday lives; however, they react to different stimuli at the various developmental levels. Alert parents will use occurrences in a child's experience—the death of a pet, a dead animal discovered on the highway, television programs, films, news clips, books, conversations overheard—as entrees into the expansion of their child's cognitive understanding of death and their emotional coping with its reality.

INTIMATE ENCOUNTERS
WITH DEATH

Personal experience with death has a powerful effect on children's perceptions, cognitions, and emotions related to themselves, significant others, and their futures.

Terminally Ill Children
and Adolescents

We indicated in a previous section that children with a terminal disease understand death at a younger age than their healthy peers. In an extensive study of leukemic children ages three to nine years of age, Bluebond-Langner (30) has shown that such children move through a series of five stages of knowledge about their condition despite attempts by parents and medical staff to conceal the fact of these children's impending death. She also observed concomitant changes in children's self-concepts at each stage. Table 2 shows that children become sequentially more informed about their illness and catastrophic prognosis. They derive this knowledge and understanding from the cumulative events that occur in their day-to-day experience.

Waechter (28) notes that several studies have found young children to be knowledgeable about the seriousness of their illnesses. It is irrelevant, therefore, to argue whether children should be informed that their disease is fatal although many parents and health professionals still do.

Waechter (28) and Spinetta and Maloney (29) reported that anxiety levels in terminally ill children were almost double those of other hospitalized children and three times those of healthy children. In a recent study, Waechter interviewed the parents of 56 four- to ten-year-old leukemic outpatients and found that all reported discussing aspects of treatment with their children. Although the parents of the youngest children said they were guarded in their talks, no parent refused to answer questions their children raised. Most of the children in this particular study were under medical care that espouses the open approach (63). Waechter and others have found that children who know about and understand their condition, and whose family communicates openly with them, experience lower stress and anxiety levels, express relief at being allowed to discuss their concerns, and show improved ability to cope with their illness (28, 30, 64, 65).

Terminally ill children do, however, frequently distance themselves psychologically from adults as they approach the terminal phase of their illness. This withdrawal may be for specific reasons related to the child's prior experience (66)

TABLE 2   Acquisition of Information and Concomitant Self-concept Changes
in Terminally Ill Children

Information	Self-concept
"It" is a serious illness	Seriously ill
Names of drugs and side effects	Seriously ill but will get better
Purposes of treatment and procedures	Always ill but will get better
Disease as a series of relapses and remissions minus death	Always ill and will never get better
Disease as a series of relapses and remissions plus death	Dying

or may be a natural part of the depression many dying patients experience when realizing that their condition is growing graver. A number of practitioners have suggested that children in this way attempt to protect their parents and others from the overwhelming grief they will experience at the death. The research literature clearly indicates that dying children generally know that they have a terminal illness (28–30, 63–66). Developmental level, social support, and coping skills become powerful mediating variables as to how children cope with such knowledge.

Very young children who have no understanding of death suffer primarily from separation anxiety. Indeed, separation anxiety may be equivalent to death anxiety for the very young since the absence from the mother figure is a threat to the child's fundamental safety and eventually to his/her life. Spitz (15) described fatalities occurring among infants as a consequence of being separated from their mothers and placed in orphanages. These children responded first with anger expressed by crying which was replaced by a quiet resigned despair. Some children refused nourishment and eventually died. "Hospitalism" as this phenomenon is termed was not learned behavior. It was a natural response of children who suffered an overwhelming loss. Dying children are experiencing multiple losses. They are separated from their families for long periods of time, find themselves in an unfamiliar or at least unhomelike environment, and, in addition, have to endure often painful medical procedures the purpose of which they may not understand (63).

School-age children frequently replace separation anxiety with mutilation anxiety. By now they have fairly well-developed self-concepts and, therefore, often react with anxiety, anger, and depression to threats to their body integrity inherent in medical treatments. School-age children and even adolescents sometimes seem to suffer more from the loss of hair or disfiguring surgery than they do from the threat of death itself (63).

Terminally ill adolescents have achieved a mature understanding of death and begin to deal with their condition much as terminally ill adults do. While school-age children begin to have the cognitive capacity to grieve the loss of the future, terminally ill adolescents understand the full implications of this loss (63). It is difficult for young people as well as adults to make sense of such an apparently unfair situation. As young people become aware of the likely outcome of their condition, they experience a torrent of emotions, including denial ("This can't be happening to me"), anger ("How can you let this happen to me?"), resentment ("Why me? Why not you?"), fear ("What will dying be like? Will I suffer? Will I be alone? What will happen after I die?"), and guilt ("I must have been very bad to deserve this. I should have been more obedient, cheerful, diligent"). Preparatory grief can be debilitating. In dying, the child loses everything: possessions, friends, family, personality, and self. It is right to grieve then, if he or she realizes even a bit of this loss. Caregivers can facilitate the grieving process in many ways. When communications between dying children and their parents are closed instead of open, these children often cannot share their grief, in fact, they often protect their parents in an unusual role reversal. A 15-year-old cancer patient said to her confidant: "My chances on the six months or one year chemotherapy aren't good at all. Also, he wants to start right away so I can't go home. . . . I'm just gonna have to be brave and not feel sorry for myself. . . . Dad was upset again today. I could tell. I think if I try to keep a good attitude, it'll be a whole lot easier on Mom and Dad."

Caring for the Dying Child

In caring for the dying child, the natural core conflict between compassion and nurturance, on the one hand, and repulsion against the impending loss, on the other, is heightened. The death of a child evokes greater depths of anger, guilt, and frustration than adult deaths do. Parents often feel an additional burden of guilt, feeling that they have failed in the most basic parental task, namely, to protect their children and keep them healthy (64, 67). Furthermore, medical personnel often feel great frustration and stress since their primary goal of restoring health is denied when a child dies (68). Poorly managed stress on the part of the caregiver affects treatment of the dying child, perhaps leading to overprotection and overindulgence or to isolating the child emotionally and caring only for his or her physical needs (67, 68).

Quality care of a dying child begins with the diagnosis of the terminal illness. A positive climate for communication with a dying child is often established at that point. For example, a physician, with the parents' permission and in their presence, might give the following explanation to a leukemic child: "You have a serious blood disease, leukemia. Years ago, there was no treatment for leukemia, and many people died. Now there are a number of drugs which can be used to treat leukemia. There are several types of leukemia, and the type that you have is the one for which there are the most drugs. Treatment to keep the leukemia cells away will last three years. You'll miss at least one month of school. The main problem right now is infection. If you stay free of infection, you will be out of the hospital in about five days. If an infection occurs, you'll be hospitalized for at least two weeks" (69, pp. 1115–1116).

Such an explanation, offered at a pace that the child can understand, and after basic rapport is built, sets the stage for continued honest communication. The child should be encouraged to ask questions and share feelings at any time during the illness in order to create the setting of mutual trust necessary and to decrease the sense of isolation during the final period of life. Lack of open discussion of the seriousness of the illness causes the child to face a worsening disease process without the support of caring family members and professionals. It is important that hope for recovery always be expressed explicitly as long as such hope has any basis in reality.

Martinson and her associates have pioneered a program of home care for dying children as a way of alleviating many of the problems discussed (59). Pediatric hospices based in the home are similar in principles and practice. All the goals of adult hospice care apply to the care of dying children; only the emphases are different (71). Pediatric home-based care has advantages over hospital care. The child is in the familiar surroundings of the home. The family is in active control of the care of their child which may alleviate some guilt and lessen the sense of helplessness. On the other hand, caring for the dying child at home may place too great a strain on the family physically and emotionally. Decisions about terminal care require careful consideration of the family's resources.

Bereaved Children and Adolescents

Next to the child's own death, the most hurtful loss to a child is the death of a parent. About 6 percent of the child population under 18 experiences the death of one or both parent(s). For this group, the death of a father is twice as probable as that of a mother (72). Most of these early parental deaths are sudden, allowing little time for preparation on the part of the children. Frequently, the remaining parent is in a state of shock after the death, making it difficult to help the child deal with his/her grief. The death of a parent is a shattering event for the child, evoking a host of emotions. It stuns, shocks, bewilders, overwhelms, and frightens a child. It leaves the child feeling lonely, abandoned, and helpless, as well as angry and guilty. Behaviorally, children often respond with aggression, hostility, noncooperation or, on the other hand, withdrawal (62).

Some early studies suggest that the trauma of losing a parent may have long-lasting effects on the mental health of a child. In one such study, 27 percent of adult patients in a highly depressed group reported the loss of a parent before the age of 16 as compared with 12 percent of adults in a nondepressed group (73). A more recent analysis of medical doctors who developed cancer found some evidence that cancer in adulthood may be causally related to trauma, especially parental and sibling death, in childhood (74). The death of a parent in childhood has also been identified as an etiological factor in schizophrenia (75). Another investigation followed 105 children between the ages of 2 and 17 over a 13-month time period (76). The children were interviewed at one month after the parent's death and again 12 months later. The researchers found significant increases in three symptoms. The first was an increase in dysphoric mood, which was shown by sadness, crying, and irritability. The second was an increase in depression-related behaviors such as sleeping and eating difficulties, withdrawn behavior, etc. Finally, regressive behaviors such as bed-wetting and a significant drop in school performance were found. However, most parental deaths do not necessarily lead to psychiatric problems and disturbances. Children are naturally resilient. With the caring support of adults and otherwise optimal conditions such as physical and emotional health, the child may resolve his/her grief without prolonged difficulties (59, 77).

Another traumatic loss during childhood is the death of a sibling. Balk (78) conducted interviews with 33 bereaved adolescents whose siblings had died from four to eighty-four months prior to the interview. Teenagers reported immediate emotional responses to the death including shock, confusion, numbness, depression, loneliness, and anger. Behavioral disturbances included problems with eating and sleeping. Many reported thinking about the dead sibling continually. All but two reported experiencing anniversary reactions. Eleven of the 33 had thoughts of suicide and one-half had hallucinations in which the dead sibling appeared or spoke to them. Twenty-three said that the death had bad effects on their schoolwork. These teens said that parents and friends were important sources of help to them. Some of them felt that talking about the death and finding support in their religion were also helpful. They wanted other bereaved teens to know that the pain will go away, that they must accept the death as a fact, and that it is vital to confide in others (79).

Other researchers have documented negative consequences of sibling deaths on children and adolescents. One researcher has reported that adolescent siblings frequently feel anger and guilt for being survivors, are unable to share the emotions, and, thus, feel isolated and neglected (81). A clinical study of bereaved children and adolescent siblings observed similar reactions as well as a strong sense of responsibility for the death of the sibling, various forms of regressive behaviors, and lowered academic performance (81). Unfortunately, since parents themselves are trying to cope with the death of a child, they may have little energy left to supporting the surviving siblings. Indeed, children often report feeling protective toward their parents, and, therefore, they deny their own grief in an attempt not to add to the parents' problems (82). It is not uncommon for a role reversal to occur in which children attempt to help their grieving parents and, thus, postpone their own grieving process.

A 12-year-old boy who recently lost a brother said this to one of the authors: "My Dad doesn't talk about it, and my Mom cries a lot. I just stay in my room so I won't be a bother."

The evidence is impressive that loss by death in childhood is a traumatic event that may have lifelong repercussions. However, some have suggested that such a loss may also have positive consequences. Children often emerge from bereavement with better coping skills, a higher level of maturity, and a new determination to live their lives wisely and well (56, 77, 79, 82).

In helping a young child cope with the death of a parent, sibling, or much-loved grandparent, the following suggestions are offered (83).

Reassure the child that he/she will be taken care of, loved, and cherished as before. Reassure the child that he/she is not in danger of death. Touch, hold, and hug the child. Explain that the loved one did not intend or want to die. Explain that the death was not the child's fault, that the dead person loved the child very much but can never come back, and that, like the child, many people are sad and will be for a long time. Encourage the child to ask questions and answer the questions simply, directly, and honestly. Encourage the child to express his or her feelings and thoughts. It is normal for a child confronting a major crisis to regress to levels of behavior below the child's present maturational level. Be tolerant. If the child withdraws for an extended period of time, look for behavioral clues to feelings such as anxiety, anger, or loneliness. Then initiate conversation about such feelings and how they are common in times of loss. For older children and adolescents, these suggestions need to be modified to correspond to their levels of maturity.

Child and Adolescent Suicide

Until recently, most professionals believed that since young children did not have a mature view of the finality and irreversibility of death, they could not commit suicide. When young children died by their own hand, therefore, it was thought to be a miscalculation or accident. Within the past decade, however, researchers have documented that children experience the same type of depression, hopelessness, and cognitive rigidity that lead to suicidal behavior in adults (84). Children's suicidal actions most frequently fall into the category of surcease suicide; that is, the suicide attempt is carried out with the goal of removing oneself from a psychologically or physically painful life situation (85). Orbach, Glaubman, and Gross have proposed that children are most likely to commit suicide when their experience of the world is one of being rejected, being confronted with unsolvable problems, suffering multiple losses, and in other ways developing a generalized negative attitude known as "repulsion by life" (86). When this attitude is accompanied by an immature glorification of death as a condition which will meet more of the children's needs, result in their rejoining a dead loved one or result in less psychological pain and frustration, the child develops an "attraction to death," and the inclination toward suicide is increased (86). Other theorists point to disturbed family systems, multiple losses, and/or genetically inherited biological imbalances as causal factors in child and adolescent suicide. Regardless of the reasons why children attempt and commit suicide, it is clear that it is a growing phenomenon in American culture and one which increases during late childhood and adolescence.

In 1983, the suicide rate among children aged 5 to 14 was 0.6 per 100,000 (87). While this is a very small figure, it is noteworthy since it represents official recognition that children as young as five may commit suicide. Pfeffer has pointed out that the rate of suicide among children under 12 years old increased threefold in the years from 1955 to 1975 (88). In addition, the incidence of suicidal threats and attempts has also risen. One study reported that 72 percent of children admitted to a city hospital's psychiatric ward showed suicidal ideas, threats, or attempts (89). Another study showed that of 100 children referred to a psychiatric hospital unit, 33 percent evidenced suicidal behavior (90).

Suicide among adolescents has also increased dramatically. Government statistics show that since 1961, the suicide rate in the 5–24 year age group has increased 132 percent (91). It is currently the third leading cause of death among adolescents, preceded only by accidents and homicides (92). In 1983, the male death rate in this age group was 20.0 per 100,000 compared to a female death rate of 4.7 per 100,000 (93). It has been estimated that by the year 2000 there will be a 94 percent increase in suicide among the 15- to 19-year-old age group (94).

Given the evidence of increasing suicide and the gloomy future predictions, it is important to develop a working knowledge about child and adolescent suicide. Most suicide attempts are prefaced by some kind of change in behavior. These changes can be grouped into four main categories: physical, cognitive, affective, and behavioral. Physical changes include increased frequency of somatic symptoms such as headaches and digestive upsets, self-neglect, a general slowing down of movement, and a general appearance of unhappiness and disinterest. Cognitive changes encompass increased rigidity and negativeness of thoughts, loss of interest in surroundings and activities, preoccupation with suicidal thoughts, and formulation of suicide plans. Affective changes include increased feelings of hopelessness, helplessness, guilt, shame, and remorse, as well as an overall decrease in self-esteem and a general loss of pleasure in life manifested in sadness, crying, and increased irritability. Behavioral changes may be seen in appetite disturbances, sleep difficulties, giving away possessions, increased use of alcohol or drugs, discussion of suicide, and increased social isolation. Since late childhood and adolescence are characterized by turbulent change, it is often difficult to distinguish between the painful process of maturing within normal limits and the changes which signal the beginning of suicidal thoughts.

Recent developments in the area of suicide intervention have focused on illuminating the breadth and specificity of young people's suicidal thoughts. The old caution against discussing suicide with troubled youth because it might give them ideas is being replaced by an emphasis on discovering their existence. Posing specific questions to a young person exhibiting signs of suicidal thinking is now a prescribed approach. Although the questions should be asked in a supportive, nonjudgmental manner, they should be direct enough to shed light on the specificity of the suicidal ideas. Questions should be asked about the method under consideration and the availability of the method as well as about the time frame under consideration. A young person who has decided to attempt suicide but has no real plan is less at risk than one who has decided to attempt suicide by taking pills, has collected the pills, and has placed them under the mattress. The persistence of the suicidal thoughts and the ability or inability of the young person to control the thoughts should also be ascertained. An occasional suicidal thought or fantasy is far less serious than being flooded with suicidal ideas which will not go away and which leave the young person feeling vulnerable and helpless. Feelings should also be examined. Young people who are feeling ashamed of their suicidal thoughts or who admit being ambivalent are far easier to work with than those who feel resignation or anticipation when thinking about suicide. Determining whether the young person wants help and what sources of support and help are available to him/her may also result in alleviating a suicidal situation. Finally, it is important to see if the young person can visualize a personal future. Those who can are less at risk than those who express hopelessness about the future and feel helpless in the present. Obviously, working with suicidal young people requires patience, the ability to listen and be supportive, and the willingness to engage the help of other professionals in the treatment process.

Fortunately, a great deal of progress has been made in treatment of suicidal young people. Such psychological approaches as cognitive restructuring and behavioral strategies have been used with good results. Cognitive restructuring involves identifying the persistent thoughts that cause feelings of depression, training the young person to recognize that such thoughts are distortions of reality, and learning to neutralize their intensity by disputing them rationally (95). Behavioral strategies frequently involve homework such as exercise or the monitoring of diet to help ensure change between therapy sessions. Biological treatments for depression such as the tricyclic antidepressants, the monoamine oxidase inhibitors, and the new limited electroconvulsive shock therapies offer promise to severely depressed people who do not respond to psychological approaches (96). A combination of biological and psychological approaches may well prove to be the most effective approach to reaching suicidal youth.

While treatment for suicidal young people has been improving, another area of research has begun which may lead to new understandings of the way in which children and young people view suicide. Stillion and her associates have normed a suicide attitude scale that is designed to measure the extent to which young people sympathize, empathize, and agree with suicidal target figures in a variety of problem situations. The results of the norming study—carried out with 198 twelfth-grade students enrolled in a public high school in a southern city—indicated that females expressed more sympathy toward suicidal target figures than did males. Females also sympathized, empathized, and agreed more with female target figures than they did with male target figures. In addition, agreement scores correlated positively with depression scores and negatively with self-esteem scores, indicating that people who agree with suicidal behaviors are more depressed and value themselves less than do people who do not agree with suicidal behavior (97). A second study compared attitudes toward suicide among ninth- and twelfth-grade students and sophomores in college. This study once again documented higher levels of sympathy among female students, but the major finding was that the older the adolescent, the less agreement there was with suicidal actions (98). Other investigations have shown that females with higher IQs agree less with suicidal actions than do females with lower IQs and males, regardless of IQ (98). Females with mental health problems severe enough to require institutionalization agree more with suicidal behavior than do institutionalized males, or than do males and females in a noninstitutionalized group (99). Finally, students who scored higher on a measure of self-actualization agreed less with suicidal behavior than did students who scored lower on the same measure (16). The overall pattern emerging from this work supports the idea that older, intellectually brighter, mentally healthy people view suicidal actions more negatively than do younger, less intellectually gifted, and less mentally healthy people; and that females, more than males, sympathize with suicidal actions.

Although much has been written on the topic of suicide, it remains a subject obscured by myth and misunderstanding. However, since the rate of child and adolescent suicide is increasing in our society, it seems important to develop education and prevention programs for use in both the home and school. Such programs must recognize that suicidal people generally give warnings about their state of mind and intended actions, that suicide threats must be taken seriously and dealt with forthrightly, that intervention in suicide plans is often an effective permanent treatment, and that suicidal young people can frequently be helped by a combination of physical and psychological treatment. Parents and educators dealing with young people can immunize them against suicide by teaching them specific techniques for coping with the inevitable painful and negative experiences of life. Stress reduction and cognitive restructuring techniques are relatively easy to learn. Promoting the use of humor as an aid for maintaining objectivity is another approach which can be taught both in the home and school. Encouraging young people to share their frustrations and concerns with supportive, understanding adults who will listen to them and help them explore options, is perhaps the most important method of reaching out to suicidal youth.

SUMMARY

Most studies show that children's understandings of death develop in an orderly progression from immature to mature concepts. Many leaders in the field have found Piaget's model of cognitive development to be a useful theoretical framework for understanding the maturation of children's concepts of death. They have found that changes in children's understandings of death are generally consonant with Piaget's periods and stages of cognitive development. Thus far, it has not been demonstrated that infants conceptualize about death, and, generally, children in preschool years have no realistic comprehension of death, understanding it as a temporary restriction, sleep, or departure, corresponding closely to Piaget's stage of preoperational thought. During the school years, children generally come to understand the concepts of irreversibility, cessation of functions, and universality of death in approximate correspondence to Piaget's stage of concrete operations. During childhood and preadolescence, children adopt simple beliefs about life after death. In adolescence, they formulate abstract ideas concerning the nature of death and life after death, basically in accordance with Piaget's period of formal operations.

Though children in the United States today do not have the direct experience with death that their grandparents had, they do have contacts with death and acquire understandings and attitudes from these contacts. Frequently, children's experiences with death are indirect.

Violence is the major cause of death portrayed on television programs and motion pictures. Its effects on children and adolescents, particularly on their conception of the role of violence in contemporary society, is a matter of mounting concern. The relative frequency of violent death themes in some types of today's popular rock music is also of great concern. Children are also introduced to the grim reality of death through the visual reporting of news on television. A relatively large proportion of children's toys and games are associated with violence, particularly toy weapons, toy soldiers, and video games.

Keeping animals as pets provides an opportunity for direct experience with the life cycle, including death and the feelings of grief associated with the loss of a pet. With sensitive parental guidance, the death of a pet can be a valuable learning and emotional growth experience.

Terminally ill children develop understandings of death at younger ages than their healthy peers and derive knowledge of their condition from their cumulative day-to-day experience despite attempts by parents and medical staff to shield to them from the fact of their impending death. Very young children who do not understand death experience separation anxiety when hospitalized. School-age children frequently replace separation anxiety with mutilation anxiety, stemming from threats to and actual invasion of their body integrity. Adolescents experience emotions similar to those of adults because they fully comprehend the extent of their impending loss.

The death of a child evokes anger, guilt, frustration, and anxiety in parents and caregivers alike. These emotions often interfere with helpful interaction. Nevertheless, open communication with terminally ill children is a requisite of quality care. There is evidence that honest discussion with terminally ill children about their condition lowers their stress and anxiety levels and improves their ability to cope with their illnesses, but it is important that such communication not exclude explicit expression of hope.

Other than the child's own death, the most hurtful loss to a child is the death of a parent. It stuns, overwhelms, and frightens the child and evokes feelings of abandonment and helplessness, as well as anger and guilt. Bereaved children often are aggressive, destructive, and noncooperative or respond by withdrawal. The trauma accompanying such a loss may have long-lasting effects on the child's mental health. Studies of effects of parental death on the child during the first year of bereavement show three types of symptoms: increase in dysphoric mood (crying, irritability, and sadness), increase in depression-related behaviors (sleeping and eating difficulties, withdrawal), and regressive behaviors (significant drop in school performance, bed-wetting). Children, however, are naturally resilient; with the support of adults and otherwise optimal conditions, most parental deaths do not lead to psychiatric disturbance.

Sibling death during childhood is a major loss for the surviving child, and investigators have identified a variety of psychological and physical reactions, some of them severe. Similar to those of a parent's death, emotional responses include shock, confusion, numbness, depression, loneliness, anger, and even contemplations of suicide. Feelings of guilt, death phobias, identifications, and misidentifications with the dead sibling as well as losses of concentration and memory are also reported. A strong sense of responsibility for the death of the sibling and various types of regressive behavior on the part of the surviving child sometimes result.

Adolescent and child suicide is a growing phenomenon in the United States. Suicide has been reported for children as young as 5 years. The suicide rate for children under 12 years of age tripled from 1955 to 1975. Suicide is the third leading cause of death among adolescents. A dramatic increase is estimated during the next decade. Most suicide attempts are prefaced by types of changes. Among physical changes that preface child and adolescent suicide are increases in somatic symptoms such as headaches and digestive upset, self-neglect, slowing down of movement, and general unhappiness and disinterest. Cognitive changes encompass increased rigidity and negative thinking, loss of interest in surroundings and activities, and preoccupation with suicidal thoughts and plans. Affective changes include attitudes of hopelessness, helplessness, guilt, shame, remorse, decrease in self-esteem, and general loss of pleasure in life. Behavioral changes such as loss of appetite, insomnia, giving away possessions, increased use of alcohol or drugs, discussion of suicide, and decrease in social interaction may be observed. Because late childhood and adolescence are characterized by turbulent change, it is often difficult to identify behavior that signals suicidal tendency.

Progress has been made in the treatment of suicidal young people by using cognitive restructuring of the young person's thought patterns and by various behavioral strategies. These are sometimes combined with biological treatments for severe cases of depression. It is important to recognize that suicidal young people generally give warnings about their state of mind and intended actions, so suicidal threats must be taken seriously and forthright action taken.

CONCLUDING STATEMENT

Several aspects related to death and the young are not discussed, or are only briefly mentioned, in this chapter. Research on the effects of the nuclear threat on children and adolescents and some implications for socialization are presented in Chapter 17. The subject of homicide is omitted. Although children and adolescents are only infrequently the victims of homicide, it is significant that children *are* murdered. Mass murders of children and adolescents, such as the Atlanta murders, fortunately occur rarely, but when they do, they are widely publicized and terrify children and their families in the region but also, albeit to a lesser degree, in the entire country. It is important for appropriate community agencies to develop guidelines for assisting in safeguarding as well as in coping during the stressful period before the murderer is apprehended. Young children are also murdered by their parents. This occurs infrequently, also. Nevertheless, early detection and reporting of child abuse, as well as parent education, are essential elements of prevention.

Finally, from the data presented in this chapter it seems to us that today's young children could benefit greatly from improved adult assistance with the whole subject of natural, accidental, or violent death; the death of pets, relatives, peers, and acquaintances; and the prospect of their own death. Helping children cope with death is certainly a fundamental task of parents. A good case can be made for providing help through death education in the schools as well. This can be accomplished both by making death education an integral part of the school curriculum and through informal educational processes in which "teachable moments" are used to bring about significant learning and assistance with coping.

REVIEW QUESTIONS

1. Describe children's concepts of death at different developmental levels. To what extent is Piaget's theory of cognitive development useful in explaining these differences? What alternative theories would you propose?
2. What do you think is the effect of violence in television drama and films on children's perceptions of violence in the real world?
3. Describe ways in which parents can help their children to cope with death. In retrospect, have your parents helped you to cope with death in any of these ways? How would (do) you help your child with problems concerning death?
4. Describe the function humor may play in reducing death-related anxieties among children and adolescents. Give several examples from your own experience.
5. Terminally ill children appear to acquire information about their illnesses and impending deaths in steps. How, in your opinion, do children come by their knowledge, even when not told?
6. The care of dying children is difficult for health professionals. Identify reasons for this difficulty and describe how such difficulty might affect the experience of a dying child. What do you think should be done to alleviate this problem?
7. Identify emotional and behavioral responses of children and adolescents to the death of a parent or sibling. What are some ways of providing emotional support for bereaved children and adolescents?
8. Discuss the physical, cognitive, affective, and behavioral changes that commonly precede suicidal attempts by adolescents.
9. What factors have contributed to the significant increase in suicidal behavior among children and youth in the United States?

REFERENCES

1. Von Hug-Hellmuth, H. (1965). The child's concept of death. *The Psychoanalytic Quarterly, 34,* 499–516. (Originally published as Das Kind und Seine Vorstellungen vom Tode, 1912, *Imago, 1,* 286–298.)
2. Nagy, M. (1948). The child's theories concerning death. *The Journal of Genetic Psychology, 73,* 3–27. (First published in Hungarian in *The child and death,* 1936, Budapest.)
3. Schilder, P., & Wechsler, D. (1934). The attitudes of children toward death. *Journal of Genetic Psychology, 45,* 406–451.
4. Anthony, S. (1940). *The child's discovery of death.* New York: Harcourt, Brace.
5. Koocher, G. P. (1973). Childhood, death, and cognitive development. *Developmental Psychology, 9,* 369–375.
6. Kane, B. (1979). Children's concepts of death. *Journal of Genetic Psychology, 134,* 141–153.
7. White, E., Elsom, B., & Pravat, R. (1978). Children's conceptions of death. *Child Development, 49,* 307–320.
8. Wass, H. (1984). Concepts of death: A developmental perspective. In H. Wass & C. A. Corr (Eds.), *Childhood and death* (pp. 3–24). Washington, DC: Hemisphere.
9. Townley, K., & Thornburg, K. R. (1980). Maturation of the concept of death in elementary school children. *Educational Research Quarterly, 5,* 17–24.
10. Jenkins, R. A., & Cavanaugh, J. C. (1985). Examining the relationship between the development of the concept of death and overall cognitive development. *Omega, 16,* 193–199.

11. Reilly, T. P., Hasazi, J. E., & Bond, L. A. (1983). Children's conceptions of death and personal mortality. *Journal of Pediatric Psychology, 8,* 21–31.

12. Piaget, J., & Inhelder, B. (1969). *The psychology of the child.* New York: Basic Books.

13. Piaget, J. (1973). *The child and reality-problems of genetic psychology.* New York: Grossman.

14. Piaget, J. (1965). *The child's conceptions of the world.* C. K. Ogden (Ed.). Totowa, NJ: Littlefield, Adams.

15. Spitz, R. A. (1945). *Hospitalism: An inquiry into the genesis of psychiatric conditions in early childhood. The psychoanalytic study of the child, Volume I.* New York: International Press.

16. Kastenbaum, R., & Aisenberg, R. (1972). *The psychology of death.* New York: Springer.

17. Lonetto, R. (1980). *Children's conceptions of death.* New York: Springer.

18. Wenestam, C. G., & Wass, H. (1987). Swedish and U.S. children's thinking about death: A qualitative study and cross-cultural comparison. *Death Studies, 11,* 99–121.

19. Swain, H. L. (1979). Childhood views of death. *Death Education, 2,* 341–358.

20. Speece, M. W., & Brent, S. B. (1984). Children's understanding of death: A review of three components of a death concept. *Child Development, 55,* 1671–1686.

21. Wass, H., & Scott, M. (1978). Middle school students' death concepts and concerns. *Middle School Journal, 9,* 10–12.

22. Gartley, W., & Bernasconi, M. (1967). The concept of death in children. *Journal of Genetic Psychology, 110,* 71–85.

23. DeMuth, B. (1979). Life and death drawings in adolescence. *School Arts, 79,* 42–44.

24. McIntire, M. S., Angle, C. R., & Struempler, L. J. (1972). The concept of death in midwestern children and youth. *American Journal of Diseases of Children, 123,* 527–532.

25. Tallmer, M., Formanek, R., & Tallmer, J. (1974). Factors influencing children's concepts of death. *Journal of Clinical Child Psychology, 3,* 17–19.

26. Wass, H., Guenther, A. C., & Towry, B. J. (1979). United States and Brazilian children's concepts of death. *Death Education, 3,* 41–55.

27. Wenestam, C. G., & Wass, H. (1986, July). *Qualitative differences in thinking about death: A cross-cultural exploration of American, Greek and Swedish adolescents.* Paper presented at the Eighth International Conference on Cross-Cultural Psychology, Istanbul, Turkey.

28. Waechter, E. H. (1971). Children's awareness of fatal illness. *American Journal of Nursing, 71,* 1168–1172.

29. Spinetta, J. J., & Maloney, L. J. (1975). Death anxiety in the outpatient leukemic child. *Pediatrics, 56,* 1034–1037.

30. Bluebond-Langner, M. (1978). *The private worlds of dying children.* Princeton: Princeton University Press.

31. Singer, D. G. (1983). A time to reexamine the role of television in our lives. *American Psychologist, 38,* 815–816.

32. Gerbner, G., Gross, L., Elee, M., Jackson-Beeck, M., Jeffries-Fox, S., & Signorielli, N. (1977). *Violence profile No. 8: Trends in network television drama and viewer conceptions of social reality 1967-1976.* Annenberg School of Communications, University of Pennsylvania.

33. Gerbner, G., Morgan, M., & Signorielli, N. (1982). Programming health portrayals: What viewers see, say, and do. In D. Pearl, L. Bouthilet, & J. Lazar (Eds.), *Television and behavior: Ten years of scientific progress and implications for the eighties* (pp. 291–307). Washington, DC: U.S. Government Printing Office.

34. Wass, H. (1985). Depiction of death, grief, and funerals on national television. *Research Record* (National Research Information Center), *2,* 81–92.

35. Surgeon General's Scientific Advisory Committee Report on Television and Social Behavior. (1972). *Television and growing up: The impact of televised violence.* Washington, DC: U.S. Government Printing Office.

36. National Institute of Mental Health. (1982). *Television and behavior: Ten years of scientific progress and implications for the eighties, Vol. 2: Technical reviews.* Washington, DC: U.S. Government Printing Office.

37. Singer, J. L. Cognitive and affective aspects of television: Introductory comments. In D. Pearl, L. Bouthilet, & J. Lazar (Eds.). *Television and behavior: Ten years of scientific progress and implications for the eighties* (pp. 2–8). Washington, DC: U.S. Government Printing Office.

38. Wass, H., Stillion, J. M., & Fattah, A. F. (1986, April). *Exploding images: Gifted children's views of violence and death on television.* Paper presented at the National Conference of the Forum (Association for Death Education and Counseling), Atlanta, Georgia.

39. Frith, S. (1981). *Sound effects: Youth, leisure, and the politics of rock 'n' roll.* New York: Pantheon.

40. Macken, B., Fornatale, P., & Ayers, B. (1980). *The rock music source book.* New York: Doubleday.

41. Pielke, R. G. (1986). *You say you want a revolution: Rock music in American culture.* Chicago: Nelson Hall.

42. Denisoff, R. S., & Peterson, R. A. (Eds.). (1972). *The sounds of social change.* Chicago: Rand McNally.

43. Committee on Commerce, Science, and Transportation, United States Senate, Ninety-Ninth Congress. (1985). Hearing, *Record Labeling.* S. Hrg. 99-529. Washington, DC: U.S. Government Printing Office.

44. *Rolling Stone,* April 24, 1986, p. 13.

45. *Rolling Stone,* September 11, 1986, p. 15.

46. Attig, T. (1986). Death themes in adolescent music: The classic years. In C. A. Corr & J. N. McNeil (Eds.), *Adolescence and death* (pp. 32–56). New York: Springer.

47. *Circus,* January 31, 1987, p. 26.

48. *Denton Record-Chronicle,* December 4, 1986.

49. Toy soldiers go high-tech. *Newsweek,* 1986, May 5, p. 54.

50. Wass, H. (1984). Books for children. In H. Wass & C. A. Corr (Eds.), *Helping children cope with death: Guidelines and resources* (2nd ed.) (pp. 151–207). Washington, DC: Hemisphere.

51. Wass, H., & Cason, L. (1984). Fears and anxieties about death. In H. Wass & C. A. Corr (Eds.), *Childhood and death* (pp. 25–45). Washington, DC: Hemisphere.

52. Bettelheim, B. (1977). *The uses of enchantment—The meaning and importance of fairy tales.* New York: Vintage Books.

53. Bandura, A., & Mischel, M. (1965). Modification of self-imposed delay of reward through exposure to live and symbolic models. *Journal of Personality and Social Psychology, 2,* 698–705.

54. Wolfenstein, M. (1954). *Children's humor.* Glencoe, IL: The Free Press.

55. Anthony, S. (1972). *The discovery of death in childhood and after.* New York: Basic Books.

56. Rudolph, M. (1978). *Should the children know? Encounters with death in the lives of children.* New York: Schocken Books.

57. Carson, U. (1980). A child loses a pet. *Death Education, 3,* 399–404.

58. McNeil, J. N. (1984). Death education in the home: Parents talk with their children. In H. Wass, & C. A. Corr (Eds.), *Childhood and death* (pp. 293–313). Washington, DC: Hemisphere.

59. Furman, E. (1974). *A child's parent dies: Studies in childhood bereavement.* New Haven: Yale University Press.

60. Stillion, J., & Wass, H. (1979). Children and death. In H. Wass (Ed.), *Dying: facing the facts* (pp. 208–235). Washington, DC: Hemisphere.

61. Wass, H. (1986). Death education for children in the home and at school. In R. Turnbull (Ed.), *Terminal care* (pp. 215–228). Washington, DC: Hemisphere.

62. Wass, H. (1984). Parents, teachers, and professionals as helpers. In H. Wass & C. A. Corr (Eds.),

Helping children cope with death: Guidelines and resources (2nd ed.) (pp. 90–103). Washington, DC: Hemisphere.

63. Waechter, E. H. (1984). Dying children: Patterns of coping. In H. Wass and C. A. Corr (Eds.), *Childhood and death* (pp. 51–68). Washington, DC: Hemisphere.

64. Spinetta, J. J. (1978). Communication patterns in families dealing with life-threatening illness. In O. J. Sahler (Ed.), *The child and death* (pp. 43–46). St. Louis: Mosby.

65. Vernick, J., & Karon, M. (1965). Who's afraid of death in the leukemia ward? *American Journal of Diseases of Children, 109,* 393–397.

66. Spinetta, J. J., Rigler, D., & Karon, M. (1974). Personal space as a measure of a dying child's sense of isolation. *Journal of Consulting and Clinical Psychology, 42,* 751–756.

67. Adams, D. W. (1984). Helping the dying child: Practical approaches for nonphysicians. In H. Wass & C. A. Corr (Eds.), *Childhood and death* (pp. 95–112). Washington, DC: Hemisphere.

68. Vachon, M. L. S., & Pakes, E. (1984). Staff stress in the care of the critically ill and dying child. In H. Wass & C. A. Corr (Eds.), *Childhood and death* (pp. 151–182). Washington, DC: Hemisphere.

69. Foley, G. V., & McCarthy, A. M. (1976). The child with leukemia in a special hematology clinic. *American Journal of Nursing, 76,* 1115–1119.

70. Martinson, I. M. et al. (1978). Home care for children dying of cancer. *Pediatrics, 62,* 106–113.

71. Wilson, D. C. (1982). The viability of pediatric hospices: A case study. *Death Education, 6,* 205–212.

72. Palombo, J. (1981). Parent loss and childhood bereavement: Some theoretical considerations. *Clinical Social Work Journal, 9,* 3–33.

73. Beck, A. T., Sethi, B. B., & Tuthill, R. (1963). Childhood bereavement and adult depression. *Archives of General Psychiatry, 9,* 129–136.

74. Duszynski, K. R., Shaffer, J. W., & Thomas, C. B. (1981). Neoplasm and traumatic events in childhood: Are they related? *Archives of General Psychiatry, 38,* 327–331.

75. Watt, N. F., & Nicholi, A. (1979). Early death of a parent as an etiological factor in schizophrenia. *American Journal of Orthopsychiatry, 49,* 465–473.

76. Van Eerdewegh, M. M., Bieri, M. D., Parilla, R. H., & Clayton, P. J. (1982). The bereaved child. *American Journal of Psychiatry, 140,* 23–29.

77. LeShan, E. (1976). *Learning to say good-by: When a parent dies.* New York: Macmillan.

78. Balk, D. (1983). Effects of sibling death on teenagers. *The Journal of School Health, 53,* 14–18.

79. Balk, D. (1983). How teenagers cope with sibling death: Some implications for school counselors. *The School Counselor, 31,* 150–158.

80. Rosen, H. (1986). *Unspoken grief.* Lexington, MA: D. C. Heath.

81. Coleman, F. W., & Coleman, W. S. (1984). Helping siblings and other peers cope with dying. In H. Wass & C. A. Corr (Eds.), *Childhood and death* (pp. 129–150). Washington, DC: Hemisphere.

82. Fulton, R., Gottesman, D. J., & Owen, G. M. (1982). Loss, social change, and the prospect of mourning. *Death Education, 6,* 137–153.

83. Wass, H. (1985). Helping a young child cope with the death of a parent. *Thanatos, 10,* 5–7.

84. Orbach, I. (1984). Personality characteristics, life circumstances, and dynamics of suicidal children. *Death Education,* Supplement, Suicide: Practical, developmental and speculative issues, *8,* 37–52.

85. Shneidman, E. S., & Farberow, N. L. (1957). The logic of suicide. In E. S. Shneidman and N. L. Farberow (Eds.), *Clues to suicide,* New York: McGraw-Hill.

86. Orbach, I., Glaubman, H., & Gross, Y. (1981). Some common characteristics of latency age suicidal children. *Suicide and Life Threatening Behavior, 11,* 180–190.

87. Advance Report of Final Mortality Statistics, 1983, National Center for Health Statistics, *34*(6), Supplement (2), September, 1985.

88. Pfeffer, C. R. (1984). Death preoccupation and suicidal behavior in children. In H. Wass and C. A. Corr (Eds.), *Childhood and death* (pp. 261–278). Washngton, DC: Hemisphere.

89. Pfeffer, C. R., Conte, H. R., Plutchik, R., & Jerret, I. (1980). Suicidal behavior in latency-age children: An empirical study. *Journal of the American Academy of Child Psychiatry, 18,* 703–710.

90. Lomonoco, S., & Pfeffer, C. R. (1974). *Suicidal and self-destructive behavior in latency-age children.* Paper presented at the American Academy of Child Psychiatry Annual Meeting, San Francisco, CA.

91. Holinger, P. C. (1978). Adolescent suicide: An epidemiological study of recent trends. *American Journal of Psychology, 135,* 754–756.

92. Peck, M. (1984). Youth suicide. In H. Wass and C. A. Corr (Eds.), *Childhood and death* (pp. 279–290). Washington, DC: Hemisphere.

93. National Center for Health Statistics. (1983). *Monthly Vital Statistics Report, 32,* (7).

94. Frederick, C. J. (1981). The suicide-prone depressive: The widening circle. In *Depression in the 80's:* A Lederle Laboratory Symposium. New York: Science and Medicine.

95. Beck, A. T. (1970). Cognitive therapy: Nature and relation to behavior therapy. *Behavior Therapy, 1,* 184–200.

96. Beck, A. T. (1967). *Depression: Causes and treatment.* Philadelphia: University of Pennsylvania Press.

97. Stillion, J. M., McDowell, E. E., & Shamblin, J. R. (1984). The suicide attitude vignette experience: A method for measuring adolescent attitudes toward suicide. *Death Education,* Supplement, Suicide: Practical developmental and speculative issues, *8,* 65–79.

98. Stillion, J. M., McDowell, E. E., & May, J. H. (1984). Developmental trends and sex differences in adolescent attitudes toward suicide. *Death Education,* Supplement, Suicide: Practical, developmental and speculative issues, *8,* 81–90.

99. Stillion, J. M., McDowell, E. E., Smith, R. T., & McCoy, P. A. (1986). Relationships between suicide attitudes and indicators of mental health among adolescents. *Death Studies, 10,* 289–296.

11

Suicide: Prevalence, Theories, and Prevention

Anthony J. La Greca

We are all familiar with the many different scenarios of suicide. These range from the noble acts of Socrates taking hemlock, to the "star-crossed" lovers' death of Romeo and Juliet, to the driver of a car bomb that crashed into an embassy in Lebanon. All of these seem somehow removed from our daily lives, yet each has a tie-in to some of the basic explanations given to the "why" of suicide. In this chapter, we will look at suicide from varying perspectives, ranging from demographic rates, to theories of suicide, to ways to prevent suicide.

Since adolescent suicide is discussed elsewhere in this volume, I shall focus attention on adult suicides. Admittedly, each of you reading this chapter comes with your own outlook, moral evaluation, and thoughts about suicide. So, toward the end of the chapter I shall briefly present some of the controversial concerns that our society is discussing today regarding the moral and legal ramifications of suicide in contemporary America. We are fortunate to live at a time when open discussion and research can be devoted to a topic that at one time was so forbidden that no one was allowed to theorize on its nature or consequence. As recently as the early part of the last century, the "enlightened" society of England buried "perpetrators" of the "crime of suicide" at crossroads with a stake through the heart. Such a burial deprived a person of eternal rest in consecrated ground since, it was thought, the person had taken on the power of God by taking their own life. Also, the goods and property of the deceased were confiscated by the government (1). It has been only 30 years since certain mainstream Christian religions have allowed formal church services for suicides.

Although we are now more open to the study of suicide, many of us still have some misunderstandings about what it is and how it can even be studied. Suicide is the conscious, intentional taking of one's own life through an identifiable, discrete act. This means that truly accidental deaths are not included. This definition also excludes those series of behavior that may result in death but were not intended to do so. The person who habitually drinks too much and drives may have self-destructive tendencies but is not considered a suicide unless he/she actually intentionally sought to drive the car off the road. Similarly excluded from this definition are those with negative habits (e.g., smoking) that may mean a hastened death. Therefore, when we speak of "suicide," we are talking of a focused consideration of how one dies by their own direct action.

RATES OF SUICIDE

As one might expect, it is very difficult to get accurate data on suicides or suicide attempts:

> Many genuine suicide deaths are hidden, or masked, often by survivors, or misreported by the authorities, and very few *attempts* are recorded at all. (2, p. 1)

This lack of accurate data means that figures reported do not actually reflect the complete picture. Also, it is common knowledge that some single vehicle accidents and some drownings are, in fact, suicides; therefore, even efficient data collecting agencies misclassify suicides as accidents.

Officially, there are almost 30,000 suicides in the United States each year. Some estimate that the actual incidence of suicide in America is closer to 100,000 (3). Table 1 shows the suicide rate for the United States from 1970 to 1984. These official statistics show a general rise in suicides but do not reflect the strength of what many experts contend is a trend toward the highest suicide rate in over three decades (2, p. 1). These experts base their assessment on evidence they consider to be more reflective of the actual situation than do official statistics. Before making some general conclusions about suicide rates in the United States, it is interesting to compare the official data of our country with those of other countries.

Table 2 shows official rates of suicide for selected countries from 1975 to 1978, the latest year for which most of these data are available. Although data from these countries also suffer from some element of underreporting, we can still make some overall comparisons. The suicide rate for American males is not as high as many other countries. Austria, Denmark, West Germany (German Federal Republic), Sweden, and Switzerland have male suicide rates quite a bit higher than those in America. Greece, Ireland, Israel, Spain, and Northern Ireland have male suicide rates far below that of the United States. The female suicide rate in America is appreciably higher than Greece, Ireland, Poland, Spain, and Northern Ireland. We can see, therefore, that the suicide rate for America is not as high as several industrialized nations, but it is higher than nations whose economic/industrial development is not as far along as the United States.

In looking again at only the United States, I want to present some general conclusions and considerations about American suicides. I emphasize that some of these are based on data and research that go beyond official reports, so there will be some discrepancy with studies I cite versus data in Table 1. In regard to rates of suicide, I shall focus on the key demographic considerations of age, gender, and race. Later in the chapter, some possible explanations for demographic differences of suicide will be considered.

Age. Suicides and suicide attempts increase with age. Historically, older

TABLE 1 Suicide Rates, by Sex, Race, and Age Group: 1970 to 1984 (Rates per 100,000 in Specified Group)

Age (years)	Total[a]					Male White					Male Black					Female White					Female Black				
	1970	1980	1982	1983	1984	1970	1980	1982	1983	1984	1970	1980	1982	1983	1984	1970	1980	1982	1983	1984	1970	1980	1982	1983	1984
All ages[b]	11.6	11.9	12.2	11.4	11.6	18.0	19.9	20.7	19.3	—	8.0	10.3	10.1	10.5	—	7.1	5.9	6.1	5.6	—	2.6	2.2	2.1	2.1	—
5–14	.3	.4	.6	.6	.6	.5	.7	.9	.9	—	.1	.3	.8	.5	—	.1	.2	.3	.3	—	.2	.1	.1	.6	—
15–24	8.8	12.3	12.1	11.9	12.2	13.9	21.4	21.2	20.6	—	10.5	12.3	11.0	11.5	—	4.2	4.6	4.5	4.6	—	3.8	2.3	2.2	2.7	—
25–34	14.1	16.0	16.0	15.8	16.1	19.9	25.6	26.1	26.2	—	19.2	21.8	20.3	19.1	—	9.0	7.5	7.5	7.2	—	5.7	4.1	3.7	2.9	—
35–44	16.9	15.4	15.3	14.6	14.3	23.3	23.5	23.6	23.2	—	12.6	15.6	15.6	14.0	—	13.0	9.1	9.2	8.2	—	3.7	4.6	4.0	3.5	—
45–54	20.0	15.9	16.6	16.2	16.9	29.5	24.2	25.8	25.5	—	13.8	12.0	11.8	12.1	—	13.5	10.2	10.4	9.9	—	3.7	2.8	3.1	3.0	—
55–64	21.4	15.9	16.9	16.5	16.3	35.0	25.8	27.9	27.4	—	10.6	11.7	11.9	11.6	—	12.3	9.1	9.5	9.1	—	2.0	2.3	2.2	1.7	—
65+	20.8	17.8	18.3	—	—	41.1	37.5	38.9	—	—	8.7	11.4	12.4	—	—	8.5	6.5	6.6	—	—	2.6	1.4	1.8	—	—

[a]Total also includes races and age groups not shown separately.
[b]Source for 1983 and 1984 is *Health: United States, 1985.* U.S. Department of Health and Human Services, December, 1985, page 62.
Source: Statistical Abstract of the United States, 1986. U.S. Government: Bureau of the Census, 106 Edition, page 78.

TABLE 2   Suicide Rates by Selected Countries

Country	Male					Female				
	1975	1976	1977	1978	1981	1975	1976	1977	1978	1981
U.S.	25.5	24.9	26.5	—	18.0	8.9	8.6	8.8	—	5.7
Australia	20.9	21.7	21.9	—	16.4	9.5	7.9	8.4	—	5.6
Austria	47.4	43.6	45.3	47.2	42.1	17.6	17.0	18.8	17.8	14.5
Belgium	27.4	28.4	—	—	—	14.6	14.4	—	—	—
Canada	24.5	—	28.3	—	—	9.2	—	9.6	—	—
Denmark	38.8	39.2	39.9	36.0	38.9	23.6	22.6	22.6	23.7	21.3
Finland	52.6	—	—	—	—	13.2	—	—	—	—
France	30.0	29.8	—	—	28.5	11.5	11.5	—	—	11.1
Germany, Fed. Rep.	35.8	37.2	38.3	37.7	29.6	18.2	18.5	19.5	18.4	14.4
Greece	4.6	5.0	6.2	5.5	—	2.6	2.3	2.6	2.0	—
Ireland	9.7	—	—	—	8.6	4.1	—	—	—	2.9
Israel	13.8	14.9	12.5	9.9	8.1	10.0	8.8	7.0	6.9	3.8
Japan	28.5	28.2	29.3	29.2	22.0	18.9	18.3	17.9	17.3	12.4
Netherlands	14.5	15.8	15.2	14.5	12.2	9.3	9.3	9.0	10.7	7.9
Norway	18.6	21.1	22.2	22.7	19.1	7.2	7.3	7.6	7.7	6.5
Philippines	1.7	—	—	—	—	1.4	—	—	—	—
Poland	25.6	27.1	27.8	30.0	21.8	4.8	5.2	5.2	5.4	4.0
Portugal	18.9	—	—	—	—	5.5	—	—	—	—
Puerto Rico	20.7	—	—	—	—	3.6	—	—	—	—
Spain	8.3	—	—	—	—	2.7	—	—	—	—
Sweden	35.2	33.6	35.6	33.1	24.6	13.8	14.1	13.9	14.7	10.6
Switzerland	42.3	41.4	43.5	43.5	33.6	16.4	15.9	17.9	17.8	14.4
United Kingdom:										
England	12.0	12.8	12.9	—	—	7.6	7.5	7.9	—	—
Northern Ireland	6.8	7.9	7.1	—	—	3.6	4.6	5.6	—	—
Scotland	12.1	13.3	13.1	14.5	—	9.6	8.7	8.4	7.8	—

Source: *Statistical Abstract of the U.S., 1980.* National Data Book and Guide to Sources. Bureau of the Census, 101 edition, pages 187–188.

persons have had the highest rate of suicide and young people have had the lowest. Recent trends show a drop in the suicide rate for the elderly and a sharp increase for adolescents (4). Most of the decrease for elderly suicide is concentrated in males. This relationship between suicide and age has been found in cross-cultural analyses of both industrial and traditional societies (5). Haas and Hendin (6) projected suicide rates for the American elderly to the year 2020. They base this projection on the aging of present cohorts (e.g., those between 15–24), and they conclude that the dip in elderly suicide may only be temporary. By the year 2020, as the percentage of elderly increases dramatically in America, Haas and Hendin speculate there may also be a dramatic rise in elderly suicides.

   Gender. One of the clearest conclusions about suicide is that males commit suicide 2–3 times more frequently than females. Females, on the other hand, attempt suicide 3–5 times more than males. Such trends have led to the axiom that " . . . women and the young attempt and men and older people complete suicide" (7, p. 133). There are about 10 times more attempts than completed female suicides (8). Although female rates are lower than those of males, some speculate that the gap is narrowing over time (9).

Race. Whites have a suicide rate 2–3 times higher than that of blacks. Whereas suicides for whites increase with age, suicides for blacks decrease with age. Beginning with the age range of 35–40, the black rate begins a descent while that of whites continues to increase. For those age 60 and over, the differences in racial suicide rates reaches its maximum with whites killing themselves at least three times as often as blacks (10). This discrepancy holds true for both females and males. Also, this racial discrepancy holds true for nonwhite Hispanic and American Indians (10); however, Chinese Americans appear to have a suicide rate similar to that of white Americans (10).

SOME METHODOLOGICAL CONSIDERATIONS

There are three things to keep in mind about how suicide is studied. First, many studies seek simply to describe patterns of suicide based on certain possible correlates such as age, sex, race, as well as certain key SES (social-economic status) variables such as income. While the patterns that emerge are very illuminating, these studies are often limited by the fact that there are other variables that may be affecting suicide rates but are not taken into account.

Second, much of the research on suicide is limited by collecting and analyzing data that are "aggregated." The use of aggregate level data is based on the strong tradition of using ecological correlations. This means that a given behavior is studied for a given geographic area, and this behavior is correlated to selected characteristics of that area. One could, for example, get the suicide rates for 20 cities. One could also gather data on each city for: a) the average income of families, b) the number of divorces, c) the percentage of black, and d) average age. From such a study, one could then find which of these four independent variables is significantly related to suicide rates. However, such relationships are not necessarily the same as one would find if *individual* cases of suicide were studied where the researcher gathered data on the dead person's income, marital status, race, and age. To generalize aggregate data to individuals is an "ecological fallacy" (11). That is, it is incorrect to make inferences about significant relationships for individual suicides when that data is totally based on this aggregate level.

However, a great deal of research is still done on aggregate data since it is oftentimes the only available data. Therefore, there are ways to offset the possibility of ecological fallacy. One procedure is to make sure that the independent variables are inclusive of as many relevant factors as possible. A second procedure is to make certain that the relationship between the dependent variable (suicide) and the independent variable is linear (that is, suicide rates do not vary systematically with the independent variable). When these precautions are taken, there is a stronger, but still not conclusive, basis for making inferences.

A third methodological consideration concerns studies of individual suicides. Such studies can include gathering a rich array of background information on a large number of cases. Since such data gathering is expensive, time consuming, and hard to obtain, most research on individual suicides is concerned with a rather limited number of case studies.

Lethality of Method

Suicide takes a more poignant dimension when one actually scrutinizes not so much the "why" as the "how" of self-annihilation. Some means to kill oneself are active and include hanging, shooting, jumping off a building, and impacting a vehicle. Other means are more passive and include gas poisoning (e.g., carbon monoxide), taking a drug overdose, and swallowing poison. Some means have both active and passive characteristics and include cutting one's wrists, drowning, placing a plastic bag over one's head, and self-immolation (12, 13). Lethality refers to the probability that one will die from using a given method. Generally speaking, high lethality methods include use of firearms, hanging, carbon monoxide poisoning, jumping, and drowning. The lesser lethal means include drug and alcohol ingestion, poison, and cutting or piercing oneself. In a study of over a thousand suicides, Card (12, p. 40) found the following rank of method based on the percentage of incidents ending in death:

1.	Gunshot	91.60
2.	Carbon monoxide	78.00
3.	Hanging	77.53
4.	Drowning	66.67
5.	Plastic bag	54.76
6.	Impact	41.63
7.	Fire	34.62
8.	Poison	23.16
9.	Drugs	11.38
10.	Gas fumes	8.51
11.	Cutting	4.10

The leading means of suicide for those who actually die are firearms and explosives, poisoning and gassing oneself, and hanging/strangulation. Table 3 shows the distribution of suicide methods on a national level. The expected tendency for male suicides to choose the very lethal means of firearms is apparent. Women tend to choose the less lethal means of poisoning. Many researchers specu-

TABLE 3   Suicide by Type of Method Used (1980)

Method	Total	Male	Female
Gunshot and explosion	15,404	12,945	2,459
Gases	2,418	1,672	746
Hanging	3,401	2,836	565
Drowning	547	326	221
Plastic bag	177	84	93
Impact	41	32	9
Fire	148	88	60
Drugs and poisons	3,035	1,325	1,710

Note. Totals do not equal 1980 totals reported elsewhere because smaller incidences for other methods are not reported. Also, some other sources' compilation for total suicides are not based on data where method can be determined.

Source: *Vital Statistics of the United States: 1980.* U.S. Department of Health and Human Services, 1985.

late that this shows females to be less intent on their desire to die (14). While this may be true, it certainly does not hold true for the lives represented in this table. Therefore, one should not be too quick to accept the idea that lethality of method is a direct assessment of degree of intent to die for a particular person (15).

If one were to look at the method of suicide for attempters only, the distributions are quite dissimilar from those in Table 3. There is an inverse pattern for methods of attempted suicide compared to those who actually kill themselves. In a study of 246 attempted suicides, Lester and Beck (13) found only one had used a firearm. In fact, only 10 percent used a highly lethal means of trying to commit suicide.

Lester and Beck (13) studied attempted suicides by comparing those who cut or pierced themselves (called "cutters" in suicide research) versus those who took coma-producing drugs. Both methods are considered to be low lethality. Their analysis shows that cutters are more apt to be male and single than those ingesting drugs. Also, cutters were more likely to be psychotic (as opposed to neurotic) and were more likely to have problems with alcohol. Since they investigated attempted suicide, Lester and Beck were able to administer a variety of psychological tests and scales to the respondents. They found that cutters seemed to have less suicidal intent than those who took drugs. This correlates to the fact that the cutters were discovered sooner and were more likely to be conscious than those who ingested drugs. However, it is difficult to know what kind of inferences one can make from these differences. Future research will help establish whether or not cutters view their self-infliction more as a possible cry for help than as an actual path to self-destruction.

Communication of Intent

A popular myth has been that people who talk about committing suicide are not likely to actually complete the act. In fact, the opposite is true; when someone talks about killing themselves, they are waving a red flag for help and are warning that they may not be far from the act of suicide itself. It has been over 25 years since this myth was corrected by empirical research (16). Unfortunately, the general public frequently misunderstands this link of communicating an intent to kill oneself and actually going through with it.

There are some methodological difficulties in studying the link between communication and suicide. For example, if someone tries to kill himself and "fails," some researchers view this as an attempt to communicate. Also, some researchers look at both direct (telling someone) and indirect (putting financial records together) forms of communication for completed suicide and for attempted suicide. Since communication can be viewed so differently, my comments will be confined to those who actually committed suicide and whether they actually verbally or in writing communicated their intent.

Research has shown that for those who commit suicide, there is a clear link between suicide and communicating the desire to kill oneself. In a study of Los Angeles suicides, Rudestam (17) found that eight out of ten had communicated their intent before actually killing themselves. Other research shows that from half to over 80 percent of suicides studied had communicated their intent (18).

Unfortunately, we cannot say much about the characteristics of those who communicate intent versus those who do not. Studies have found no significant differences between communicators and noncommunicators in regard to sex, age, marital status, education, religion, income, or occupational status (18). Nor can we say much about the characteristics of those who leave suicide notes. This is especially true regarding communication since a suicide note is found after the fact and cannot be categorized as an attempt to communicate a need for help.

There is, of course, much public attention given to the content of suicide notes. Yet, not that many people leave such notes. One study of 742 suicides showed that only 24 percent left notes (19); in a 10-year study of Los Angeles, each year saw only a range of 12 to 15 percent doing so. There are other problems with studying such notes. The researcher must develop a satisfactory classifying scheme for the notes. In addition to basic demographic factors, notes can be classified according to some psychiatric category (e.g., mental illness), a social relationship category (e.g., loss of a girlfriend, death of a child, divorce), or a more environmental category (e.g., harsh economic times).

Given these dilemmas, however, there is still something to be gained from analyzing such notes. As Jacobs (20) observes, there is some advantage to actually having confidence in what a suicide victim writes as opposed to trying to offer too many subjective interpretations to that note:

> I believe it is necessary to take seriously what the suicide writes in attempting to explain to the survivor, as a reasonable person, why he is committing suicide. . . . (20)

In his study of notes of young people, Jacobs found that one of the more common underlying themes was that of "necessity"—the person felt that his/her options in life had been reduced to only one choice: suicide. Also, this choice is clearly and calmly in full view of the suicidal person even though they recognize that the people reading the note may not be able to appreciate the "fact" that suicide was the only way out. Also, except for those suffering from an incurable disease (a more "legitimate" reason for suicide), many suicides asked that the survivors forgive them. Less than 10 percent accused someone else as being the reason for suicide.

MODELS EXPLAINING SUICIDE

Although suicide is the ultimate, most personally individualistic act, there *are* patterns to such behavior. These patterns reveal that no suicide is done in isolation; each was someone influenced by the social world around him/her. Given these patterns, we are able to formulate theories on suicide. These theories range from those which are almost atomistic in nature and focus on psychotic individuals in very idiosyncratic situations to theories that concentrate on entire societal structures and changes. No complete accounting of these theories can be given here but there are excellent sources for future study (21–23). I discuss, briefly, some of the psychiatric and psychological frameworks for explaining suicide. However, I give greater attention to the sociocultural models since these best place an understanding of suicide in the context of societal factors. In this sense, I agree heartily with those researchers who contend that suicide is best understood from a social and social-psychological framework (24).

Psychiatric and Psychological Models

The psychiatric model of suicide assumes that most people who kill themselves suffer from a mental or emotional disorder. Chief among these are psychotic disorders, extreme neuroses, personality disorders, and depression with the latter being the dominant explanation for suicide (3). Psychosis is seen as an extreme impairment of mental functioning such that a person is grossly unable to correctly process and deal with the ordinary stimuli of life. Psychoses can range from an almost complete state of hallucination to one of extreme inability to perceive what is occurring in any given situation. The most common psychoses are schizophrenia, affective disorders, and paranoid states. Most neuroses, on the other hand, are not associated with gross distortions of external reality. Rather, they deal more with a subjective distress felt by an individual in trying to cope with life. Common neuroses include extreme anxiety, hysteria, phobias, and obsessive-compulsiveness. Personality disorders are ingrained, usually lifelong maladaptive patterns of behavior. These disorders include such behaviors as sexual deviance, drug dependency, and alcoholism. I shall not explore these models in detail since they are too technical for our discussion here. I shall, however, briefly discuss the personality disorder of alcoholism as it relates to suicide, and I shall discuss the link of depression to suicide.

The latest estimate is that 15 to 25 percent of all suicides are alcoholics (3). While alcoholism may be linked to other factors such as depression, some hold that alcoholism itself can be a direct influence for suicide. Alcoholics who commit suicide tend to be males over the age of 30. Most of these have usually experienced the major trauma of a significant life event such as spousal separation, arrest, or being fired from work. Some commit suicide after binge drinking when inhibitions toward self-destruction are reduced (3).

For those who hold that alcoholism is linked to some factor for inducing suicidal behavior, it is stressed that this other factor is usually hopelessness (a part of depression discussed below). Hopelessness, when accompanied by intoxication, can intensify suicidal feelings. While intoxicated, a person may be so much more impulsive that he/she will commit suicide even if the intent to do so were not so dramatically there before consumption (25). What is more, alcohol can actually increase the effect of certain less-lethal methods of suicide (e.g., drug overdose) so as to enhance their effect to kill. Health practitioners are widening their awareness of the negative effects of alcoholism to include attention to its relationship to suicide.

Depression is an encompassing concept that is understood to refer to:

> . . . a sad despairing mood or profound, painful dejection; loss of spontaneity; decrease in mental productivity, reduction of drive, and inability to accept responsibility; retardation or excitation of expressive motor responses; diminished ability to give gratification or love; loss of self-esteem, self-contempt, disintegration of ego; and pathological, narcissistic aspirations or ideals. (22, p. 212–213)

People suffering from psychoses or neuroses can also be depressives. Most of us, however, are familiar with depression that is neither but stems, rather, from a reaction to a given event or series of events in life. Almost all of us get depressed.

Most of us at one point or another will even be acutely depressed for a given time period.

The depression that leads to suicide, however, is an engulfing sense of hopelessness. It is a total exhaustion or depletion of any ability to cope: "Suicide is the ultimate coping mechanism because it rids one of the need to cope further" (7, p. 133). Not all depression is characterized by such hopelessness. When it is, however, it can lead to suicide especially if: a) the person does not seek help and b) the person is not so immobile from depression that he/she does not have the mental and physical energy to complete the act of suicide.

The genesis of the link between depression and suicide goes back to the early days of psychiatry. The classic psychoanalytical formulation for suicide comes from Freud who published two key works in the early part of this century (26, 27). Freud saw suicide as proceeding from a highly intense feeling of depression which is often triggered by the loss of a relationship. In many cases, Freud argued, a person becomes so enraged that they want to kill the person who is responsible for the loss. However, almost no one acts on the urge to kill another. Some, however, turn this deeply experienced rage on themselves in the form of suicide. All of this is on an unconscious level, and the person is not really aware of the dynamic that overcomes and destroys the desire to live. The later work of Menninger (28) continued this early framework pioneered by Freud. For theorists/practitioners like Freud and Menninger, suicide does not result from social pathology or personal disorganization. Rather, they viewed suicide " . . . as an act of displaced murder, as much as murder in the 180th degree" (29, p. xxxvii). In this sense, according to Menninger, suicide contains the three wishes: the wish to kill, to be killed, to die (29). Inherent in the work of both Freud and Menninger is the "instinct toward death," dominating the "instinct toward life." Both felt that suicide was most likely during times of strong psychological tension and inner conflict.

While some contemporary psychiatrists still hold to the Freudian view, others lean toward a more multivariate approach of linking depression to suicide (22). There are other factors related to this hopelessness that influence some to kill themselves. Alienation from society, lack of interpersonal support, isolation from strong normative structures are some possible accompanying influences.

The evaluation of the utility of the psychiatric model is a matter of considerable and intense debate. There are those who see the mental illness model as too all encompassing and too narrow of a model. Yet, those who support the psychiatric model feel that it accounts for at least 90 percent of all suicides in America (3). We cannot settle this debate here.

However, we can look at a major psychological model of suicide that seeks to "fill in the gaps" which some feel are present in the psychiatric model. A major emphasis on the psychological study of suicide is to look at the cognitive processes that predispose one to depression as well as mediate between depression and suicide (30). A major branch of this cognitive school is that of construct theory. Construct theory is predicated on the idea that all individuals "hypothesize about the meanings of events, and assess, refine and elaborate these hypotheses on the basis of their subsequent behavior" (30, p. 133). That is, individuals look at the world through their own personal unit of meaning or theory. They construct a system of understanding how X and Y are related to each and how they are distinct from a third factor. For example, a person may see their spouse and friends as being traitors to fidelity and commitment of love and friendship. But they view their mother as the epitome of faithful concern. This person may then take this construct of "infidelity versus faithfulness" as the main rubric for evaluating everything in life. As time progresses, they may begin to apply this construct in such a pronounced manner so as to constrict any other interpretation. An ever-narrowing constriction leaves one with few options for interpreting events around them. As options lessen, depression can set in as one sees fewer and fewer situations in life that can be successfully managed by their narrow construct.

This link between depression and suicide is under the general rubrics of "fatalism" and anxiety (31). Fatalism refers to the situation where a person sees no possibility of a bad situation getting better. When the outcome is inevitably despised, a person turns to the only "obvious" choice of not being passive to await that outcome—the choice of suicide. Suicide provoked by extreme anxiety occurs when a person sees reality so unpredictable, so uncertain, that suicide is the only sure course to take. In such severely depressive situations as those prompted by fatalism or anxiety, a state of mind is so constricted that one moves toward the deliberate, planned act of self-inflicted death (30).

Ringel (32) saw this idea of constriction as one of the three aspects of a "presuicidal syndrome" which refers to a specific psychic state of mind that leads to suicidal acts. Constriction is so pronounced that a person feels helpless to see any way out except self-destruction. In the presuicidal syndrome, this constriction is accompanied by the two other factors of autoaggression and suicidal fantasies. Autoaggression parallels Freud's idea of turning violence and aggression on oneself. A person has completely assimilated the idea that all expressions of aggression and anger toward others are always wrong. Hence, there is no outlet for this aggression except to turn it inward. Although suicidal fantasy occurs among many of us, for some people these fantasies take on a compulsive, compelling dynamic. The thought of the relief from psychic pain by being dead turns to the fantasy of suicide in general, and, finally, to the planning of specific means to kill oneself. Such fantasy can prove to be lethal when occurring with constriction and autoaggression. When combined with each other these three components lead to the "fatal teamwork" designated as the presuicidal syndrome.

Yet, all of this is not to say that mainstream psychological models focus exclusively on the individual. Even Kelly, the author of the classic work on construct theory, gave mention of the social and interpersonal dimensions of suicide. More recent psychologists have expanded on Kelly's work to emphasize that depressives see themselves as being isolated from others (30, 33). It is an interpersonal isolation that severely limits the quantity and quality of close relationships. Some depressives keep people at such a distance that they do not allow themselves to internalize the positive feedback and support of significant others. They have only their own evaluation of themselves, and this evaluation is negatively colored by depression and isolation. Of course, interpersonal relationships represent a broad subject since how a person relates to others is emphatically impacted by how they relate to society. In the next section, we look at those theories of suicide that focus on this concern.

Sociocultural Models

Some theories of suicide encompass an array of considerations that take into account the cultural context of the individual and how the individual relates to that context. These models lay varying emphasis on the individual's adjustment to the social order and the strength of that social order to influence suicide.

The classic study of suicide was done by the sociologist Emile Durkheim. His seminal book *Suicide (Le Suicide)* first appeared in France at the end of the nineteenth century. It was translated into English in 1951 (34) and has been the major theoretical background for all sociological research on suicide. Durkheim's framework has also strongly influenced psychological and economic theories of suicide. The basic tenets of Durkheim can be reduced to three: 1) suicide is not due to extra social influences such as the demographics of race, the presence of mental illness, imitative forces, nor heredity; 2) rather, suicide is due to the strength or weakness of the bond between an individual and the social groups they belong to; 3) the prevalence and rate of suicide in a society is a basic fact *sui generis* that can be studied on its own in relation to group cohesiveness.

Durkheim went to extensive lengths to substantiate his claim that suicide is not due to extrasocial factors. He looked at psychopathic states, climate, race, heredity, and an array of other extrasocial factors to conclude that the key to understanding suicide was not found in considerations of individual factors since people who commit suicide:

> . . . do not form a natural group, and are not in communication with one another, the stable number of suicides can only be due to the influence of a common cause which dominates and survives the individual persons involved. (34, p. 313)

This "common cause" Durkheim postulates is that of the collective life (social structure) of a society. This collective life, as we shall see shortly, is best understood in the context of "group belonging." I must, however, point out here that no matter how much I and others admire Durkheim's formulation and have gained from it, he did, in retrospect, pay too little attention to the psychotic dimensions of suicide. This is mostly due, of course, to the fact that not much was really understood about these dimensions and other psychological pathologies in the nineteenth century. Durkheim was too often exposed to people being called insane even though they were not. Also, Durkheim was able to show that the rate of insanity and alcoholism did not explain the suicide rate once group cohesion was introduced as a factor. Still, we now know that psychoses and other pathologies do play a role, for some, in influencing suicidal behavior. We realize that at times the psychopathological explanations of suicide are not always at variance to social factors and may, in fact, be highly intertwined with social factors.

For Durkheim, the dominant factor is that of social cohesion and integration gained through group structure. All of us belong to groups and all of us are part of a larger society. We are members of a family; we are all affected by the normative structure of our society; many of us belong to some religion, and all of us have some opinion regarding the strength of our own religious beliefs even if such beliefs revolve around no acceptance of the existence of God or religious order. Durkheim felt that such considerations affected suicide stronger than any other factors, thereby leading to his three famous hypotheses:

1. Suicide varies inversely with the degree of integration of religious society.
2. Suicide varies inversely with the degree of integration of domestic society.

3. Suicide varies inversely with the degree of integration of political society (34, p. 209).

These hypotheses stem from the importance of the strength of social groups so that " . . . suicide varies inversely with the degree of integration of the social groups of which the individual forms a part" (34, p. 209). Yet, there are times when the reverse is true—the hold that society has on people may be so strong that people see it as their duty or obligation to commit suicide. Also, Durkheim recognized that for some, society does not provide clear rules and regulations thereby leading them to kill themselves. With all these considerations in mind, he analyzed aggregate suicide data from European countries (and the United States in some cases). From this analysis, he concluded that suicide can be categorized into three major types: egoistic, altruistic, and anomic.

Egoistic suicide refers to a lack of integration that leads to suicide. Integration in a group or society is best seen as shared beliefs and practices. One has a sense of belonging and is able to gain support from that feeling. To Durkheim, this meant that religions with stated rules and tightly bound structures would help lessen the chance of suicide for its members. He felt that Protestantism was more open to free inquiry and had fewer common beliefs and practices than Catholicism and Judaism. Therefore, he felt that data supported egoistic suicide reflecting a higher suicide rate for Protestants than Catholics or Jews, with Jews having the lowest rate.

This notion of Protestants having a higher suicide rate has been so intrenched that it has even been referred to as "sociology's one law" (35). But is it? When looking only at the religious dimension of egoistic suicide, Pope and Danigelis (35) found no support for this religious differentiation in the twentieth century. However, Maris (22) found support for the religion variable in a study of suicides in Chicago. But this latter study points toward the need to reassess the link between religion and suicide. What may be important is not religious affiliation as such but rather the degree of participation people have in religion and the degree of social integration that they gain from that participation.

Egoistic suicide also posits that domestic integration is inversely related to suicide. Durkheim found that married people with children commit suicide less than married people without children; he also found that married people without children committed suicide less than single people. He even developed a "coefficient of preservation" which showed that egoistic suicide decreased with marriage and the presence of children. Recent research has tended to support this marital status/family correlation of suicide (36). Later in this chapter, it will be shown that there are other aspects of family life that also affect suicide.

Egoistic suicide also suggests that at times of great political turmoil and crisis in a society, suicides decrease. Durkheim attributed this decrease to the idea that at times of crises, societies demand greater activity and allegiance of its members. A war forces citizens to close ranks, share a common cause, face a common threat. Collective sentiment and patriotic fervor increase social integration and lessen egoistic suicide. Most twentieth century research has supported Durkheim's original conclusion of the inverse relationship between political integration and suicide. However, recent research suggests that economic factors (e.g., full employment during war) are more influential than political integration resulting from a national crisis such as war (37).

In some ways, *altruistic* suicide proceeds from the opposite dynamics of egoistic suicide. The hold that a group or society has on an individual can be so strong that a person is willing to kill himself for the sake of the group. The ego of the individual is no longer under its tutelage. Durkheim saw altruistic suicide ranging from obligatory altruism to a more optional altruism. The kamikaze pilots of Japan during World War II are examples of obligatory altruism while a soldier throwing himself on a grenade is a more optional altruism.

It is true that some people do choose to kill themselves from altruistic motives. Perhaps the most common example of dutiful altruism today is found in terrorism. When a Moslem of deep religious fervor drives a truck-bomb into an embassy or marine compound, he is seen by his peers as fulfilling the ultimate commitment to his faith and his people—a self-directed martyr who gives his life to his belief and country by taking the lives of the enemy with his own certain death.

In 1986, during a large protest, a young Korean student publicly set himself on fire and then leaped from a building. A meaningless death? From the student's viewpoint, it was a means of showing the Korean government the strength and depth of his beliefs and of those who supported him. Buddhist monks were making similar statements when they burnt themselves to death in the streets of Viet Nam to protest the escalation of the war there.

For Durkheim and the Europeans, such voluntary self-destruction was almost mystifying. Durkheim was intrigued by the Hindu practice where women were obliged to kill themselves on the death of their husbands or warriors were obliged to kill themselves on the death of their leader. Sharma (38) has argued that the Hindu Suttee women killed themselves as a form of sanctifying sacrifice to insure a long dwelling with their husband in a next life. Although the motivation of Suttee suicides may be based on Hindu scripture, it still does not argue against the power of the group or society to influence one to kill themselves. Durkheim's attempt to distinguish a range of altruism (e.g., obligatory, optional) may be too speculative. However, his formulation of altruistic suicide is still a powerful and pertinent explanation of some suicides.

Durkheim was also intrigued by the explosive rate of change that had taken (and was taking) place in the world. Societies were changing from tightly knit normative structures to societies constantly in flux where one's function (tasks) was more important than one's sense of belonging. Durkheim felt that industrial and commercial change fueled suicides by leaving many with an unclear understanding of the normative structure they were to follow. Times of intense change can produce, for some, a sense of *anomie,* a sense of normlessness. People no longer know what rules to follow and no longer know where they fit in with the groups they belong to and the society in which they live. For some, this anomic state is so painful and long-suffering that they escape through self-inflicted death. Durkheim also felt that anomie can occur at times of widowhood and divorce thereby leading to higher rates of suicide compared to those still married.

In regard to anomie resulting from economic change, Durkheim felt that anomie is precipitated by both positive and negative change. A type of economic anomie (39) appears to elevate the suicide rate. Marshall and Hodge (40), however, did not find an empirical basis for a general direct correlation between economic change and suicide. Rather, they found that suicides are more likely to show an increase during times of economic hardship rather than general economic change. Later on in this chapter, I shall discuss more fully this relationship between economic conditions and suicide.

Durkheim's formulation on suicide carries a degree of profound perspective and analytical thinking. However, his writings were after-the-fact explanations of behavior. He was, therefore, able to create rather tight, neat categories to fit the data at hand. These categories deserve a final summary from Durkheim himself:

> Egoistic suicide results from man's no longer finding a basis for existence in life; altruistic suicide, because the basis for existence appears to man situated beyond life itself . . . [anomic suicide] results from man's activity's lacking regulation and his consequent sufferings. (34, p. 258)

If we look closely at these three types, we can conclude that they all, in fact, revolve around the issue of social integration. Egoism, altruism, and anomie all reflect the degree to which a person is understood by, belongs to, and is appreciated by some group or referent of society.

Economic and Political Context

Recall that Durkheim postulated that economic and political change—be it positive or negative—produced an increase in suicides. And recall that research tends to be leaning toward the conclusion that negative economic change is really the important change factor to increase suicides rather than positive change. Platt (41) found that there was a relationship between unemployment and suicide. Poor employment conditions produce an increase in suicides. This relationship between unemployment and suicide is one of the few conclusions about suicide that is supported by studies of both individual and aggregate level data.

Another form of economic change occurs during a labor dispute. If one follows through on Durkheim's ideas on political integration, then labor strikes should see a lowering of suicides. Strikes are both an economic and a political phenomenon so striking workers would have activities that unite them in a common action. This unity should, according to Durkheim, offset any negative consequences of the economic turmoil that can result from a strike. Therefore, strikes should have a strong integrative impact on all participants thereby lowering the suicide rate.

Stack (42) did a cross-national study of 31 nations to assess this relationship between strikes and suicides. He looked at the magnitude/size of the striking force as well as the duration of the strike with the latter measure helping to evaluate the notion that short strikes may actually be divisive. He found that for males the size of the strike was significantly related to a lower suicide rate but duration was not. However, there was a significant negative relationship between the female suicide rate and strike duration. Stack speculates that suicides would decrease even more dramatically at times of national strikes such as those in Poland, the Philippines, and other countries struggling with national labor and political problems.

Durkheim also postulated that wars tend to unite people and achieve a lower suicide rate by increasing social integration. However, as noted earlier, much of the research on this subject has ignored the confounding influence of economic changes during war times. Marshall (37) stresses that the relationship between war, integration, and suicide is profoundly influenced by economic changes occurring during a war. He studied suicides in the United States from 1933–1976 and found that the Durkheim position did not hold true for Americans during World War II, Korea, and Viet Nam. Suicides did not go down significantly during times of war because of war *per se*. If there is going to be a decrease in wartime suicides it may be more a factor of less unemployment than uniting to fight a common enemy.

Suicide Career

While suicide is one discrete consequence of a specified behavior, the journey for some to that behavior is often times composed of a series of steppingstones along the road to suicide:

> Suicide is one product of a gradual loss of hope and the will and resources to live, a kind of running down and out of life energies, a bankruptcy of psychic defenses against death and decay. (22, p. 69)

When looked at in this light, one can speak of a suicide career (43), the ongoing development of a person's movement toward self-destruction. It has commonly been thought that such careers have their origin in early losses (e.g., loss of parent at a young age) and/or a preponderance of family problems while growing up (e.g., sexual abuse, alcohol problems).

It has been suggested that children who, at a young age, lose a parent through death or divorce are more prone toward suicide than those who did not suffer such a loss. It has also been suggested that children from homes characterized by an abusive parent or criminal activities of siblings or similar familial pathologies are more likely to be suicidal than those not being reared in such backgrounds. These two lines of thinking focus on the overall biography of suicide. Each person's story in life is strongly influenced by their most formative years of growing up and moving through adolescence. For some who suffer early parental loss and familial distress, their story line is thought to be headed toward a self-inflicted death.

Research by Maris (22) points toward partial support of the familial origin of a suicide career. He compared suicide completers with suicide attempters and those dying a natural death. He found that the early loss factor was highest for nonfatal suicide attempters. He also found that the early loss occurred earlier in life for suicide completers than for the other two groups. However, Maris concludes that the early loss hypothesis as a general predictor for the origin of the suicide career is not supported by his research although it may prove to be of help in understanding the origins of nonfatal attempts.

However, his research does point toward the need to look at the origins of a suicide career in the context of familial problems during one's most formative years. He found that nonfatal attempters scored highest on "multiproblem family of origin" followed by suicide completers and natural deaths. This is especially revealing since Maris' measurement of a "multiproblem family" entailed a person's family being characterized by three or more of the following: drug abuse, sexual deviance, alcoholism, emotional illness, physical illness, or foster home problems. Most of us might see the occurrence of even one of these as being problematic let alone three. Also, Maris found that suicides and their families of procreation suffered from the same pathologies as their parents and siblings.

Stephens (44) found support for this family problem hypothesis as the origin of suicide careers in her study of 50 female suicide attempters. Two out of three of these women had parents who did not express affection and were often "relentlessly critical" of them. They lived a childhood of depression, social isolation, and fearful of punishment or abandonment. One-third of these women grew up in broken homes, and those reared in foster homes were especially negatively affected by the foster home placement. One pathology was often accompanied by another: 30 percent of the women had been sexually and/or physically abused by their parents; 26 percent had at least one family member suffering from mental illness; 22 percent had one or both parents who were alcoholics. This evidence provides strong support for hypothesizing that, for many people, the suicide process begins with a childhood in a problem family.

There even is a relationship between domestic integration and suicide on both an aggregate as well as a cross-cultural level (45). Also, Stack (46) discussed a strong relationship between marital dissolution and suicide in his aggregate data study of all 50 American states. He found that divorce was related to suicide on such a magnitude that a 1 percent increase in divorce meant an additional 127 suicides. This relationship held true even when controlling for economic factors, age, race, and migration patterns: "Our results suggest that the social isolation, hurt, guilt, and other characteristics of many of the divorced population affect suicide . . ." (46, p. 89).

OTHER CONSIDERATIONS

Imitative Suicide

A psychiatrist once told me that too much publicity on suicide can be harmful. He told me that many psychiatrists and psychologists feel that when the topic of suicide becomes too much of a "news item," suicides actually increase. This line of thinking is often given by people on television after a series of adolescent suicides in a given area. There have been times when I noticed in the local news that one person would commit suicide only three or four days after someone else. In looking into this matter, I came across the concept of "imitative suicide." Phillips (47) postulated that: a) suicides increase as publicity (news reporting) increases (e.g., front-page coverage) and b) this increase occurs in a geographic area affected by the publicity.

Research on imitative suicide is very complex since there are a variety of factors one must take into account, including the effect of national economic trends, unemployment rates, and other factors that might be affecting suicide rather than imitation. One piece of research that has taken these factors into account is that done by Bollen and Phillips (48) who used the national evening news programs of the three major commercial networks. They looked at stories of specific suicides (not general stories) that were covered on at least two of the three networks. By using national networks, they were able to conduct a nationwide study of imitative suicide.

Bollen and Phillips found strong support for the imitative hypothesis. They were even able to plot the number of days in an imitative cycle when suicide increased:

The first peak occurs on the day of the publicized story and the day after . . . and the second peak occurs on the sixth and seventh days after the story . . . (48, p. 806)

They speculate that those who kill themselves in the first peak are impulsive suicides of people who had already thought of killing themselves. The second peak consists of people who have made a "more considered" response to the nationally publicized story.

Elderly Suicide

One area of suicide research that is not given a great deal of public attention is that of elderly suicide. Since it is in this age group that suicide rates are the highest, I thought I would discuss this issue separately from our general considerations of suicide. Earlier in this chapter, I noted that the elderly (65 or over) have the highest suicide rate for any age group. The most vulnerable group is elderly white males. Also, the difference between white and black suicide rates is highest in this age group. As our society ages, there is great concern that the temporary lessening of the high rate for the aged (older adults) will disappear and future suicide rates for this age group will be even higher.

Explanations for the high elderly suicide rate revolve around the intense and accelerated rate of changes experienced as they age. Significant life events—e.g., retirement, loss of spouse, change in health, lessening of income—are thought to be related to a high degree of stress taxing the coping skills of the older adults. Even the daily hassles of life and the swing from good to negative events in a given day are seen as stress provoking. However, we also know that the aged go through life with a history of developed coping skills. Therefore, an encompassing rationale for elderly suicide is not easy to formulate.

We do know, however, that the loss of spouse can affect suicide rates. This is especially true for the elderly widower who often experiences this loss with a much greater sense of isolation and adjustment than an elderly widow (49). Durkheim (34) saw the widower more at risk for suicide than the widow because males rely more on the domestic normative environment than do females. With the death of his wife, the widower can experience a type of domestic anomie stemming from not understanding how to regulate daily life and to maintain everyday chores and household duties. If this is true, it will be interesting to see if widowers from the dual-career families of today have a lower suicide rate because of an enhanced understanding of everyday domestic life.

Also, Durkheim saw a trend toward egoistic suicide among the elderly. As older adults retire and withdraw more and more from lifelong goals and roles, they can experience a lessening of integration into society as a whole. This can be especially true for the elderly male who saw his work world as the pivotal center for status and role relationships. The symbolic meaning of life alters to such a degree that some elderly experience a loss of self-esteem and meaning. At an extreme level, this experience can lead to a retreatist response of suicide.

Some argue that the status and role loss for the elderly is endemic in our society. Rosow (50) points out that the aged reach the only stage in the life cycle where status loss occurs. Not only are careers ended and children gone from home, but the knowledge and abilities of the elderly are often not widely appreciated or even recognized by society at large. Many view the elderly as a burden—a cohort of people consuming public money through social security and making heavy demands on our national health care delivery system. The youth orientation of our society pitches fade creams to lighten those "ugly age spots." Television advertisements abound with celebrities endorsing insurance policies aimed at lessening the stress of health costs—done while the siren of an ambulance is heard in the background. Our society finds very little to exalt about old age while it heightens individual fears about the consequences of growing old. Stress, when accompanied by low self-esteem and hopelessness, makes for a potent factor in elderly suicides.

One of the more provocative areas receiving more attention is that of the relationship between elderly suicide and the ability for intimacy in relationships. The sexual dimension of one's social self is an integral part of that identity. Leviton (51) has hypothesized that the sexuality of the aged is directly related to the desire for death in general, and suicide in particular. That is, when one feels they have lost the ability or capacity to have loving, sexual relationships, they also lose a certain desire to live. Such thinking makes sense given the intrinsic rewards of intimacy, along with the fact that the elderly do not lose the desire for intimacy as a result of aging. Leviton proposes that counselors and medical personnel take this matter of sexuality into account when seeking to help older adults.

Elderly suicide is also related to changes in one's health. Illness can be debilitating and can induce long suffering. Heart disease, strokes, cancer, Parkinson's disease, and other diseases can cause body disfigurement and extreme changes in mood (29). People used to a life of mobility and challenge may suddenly find the simplest daily activity to be a major chore. People used to a life of independence may now find themselves dependent on total strangers to bring them meals or care for them. For some elderly, this "illness factor" is a strong motivator to end the pain and low quality of life through suicide (29).

However, we all know of older adults who, through a whole series of losses and setbacks, continue to have a sense of vitality and relatedness to life. Being old is not pathological *per se* any more than being young can be thought to guarantee happiness. Yet, we must recognize that not all elderly enter this life stage with equal coping skills. For some, the combination of role loss, health changes, and kinship/friendship deaths is too much to bear. The passivity of waiting for natural death is too slow a solution to their heartbreak and suffering. For some of these people, suicide becomes an option. Osgood (29) presents over two dozen strategies for reducing the suicide rate of the aged. Underlying all these strategies is the assumption that the aged will not opt for suicide if society made it clear to them that they were still wanted and appreciated.

Prolonged Illness

Everything in our culture and traditional value system points toward trying to prolong life. But those with a terminal illness can, at times, desire to die, to be freed from their suffering. The play and movie *Whose Life Is It Anyway?* portrays the drama of a quadriplegic's wanting to be allowed to die with dignity. There have also been recent court cases where people have sued the hospital and physician for the right to die with dignity rather than live a life of prolonged suffering. Terminally ill patients may become suicidal after realizing that a cure is not to be found or after concluding that any improvement they experience will only be modest or short-lived (52).

In settings where health care givers seek to help a person to live longer and not be suicidal, certain factors must be given close attention. Foremost is the relationship between the patient and those medical personnel and family members who are significantly involved (53). Even when the patient feels "like a burden" on everyone's shoulders, health care givers, family, and friends must not falter in their attention and concern. The patient must not be allowed to feel abandoned, unimportant, or isolated.

This can be difficult to do since patients who express suicidal thoughts and intent are sometimes viewed negatively by the medical staff (53). In such cases, it is necessary for the staff to redefine the problem—it is not that the patient should be viewed negatively but rather that the staff must do more to positively reach out to the patient. The staff might, for example, get to know the patient more as a person than as a patient. The staff can seek to know what the patient did in his/her career, hobbies, and the like. If the patient becomes too manipulative, a single nurse may be assigned to help filter communication and understanding between the patient and staff.

Family, friends, and staff can also help reduce suicidal inclinations by assisting a patient to be as active as possible. This may include merely moving a bed to a window view. Also, as taxing as it might become, patients should be encouraged to ventilate their negative feelings about their illness and/or care. Such ventilation reduces isolation and can profoundly mitigate a patient's internalizing these negative feelings and turning such feelings against themselves. Many health care facilities now develop a plan, under the supervision of a psychiatrist, that helps to implement an overall program toward lessening the suicidal drift in terminally ill patients.

The "Right to Suicide"

However, what if a person is so ill that they want someone to help them die to end their suffering? The controversy over one's right to take one's own life is not recent. Over 50 years ago in England a formal organization was established to promote the recognition of suicide as a reasonable alternative to enduring suffering from a terminal illness. Exit—the Right to Die with Dignity has extended its organizational efforts to providing guidelines on "how to do it." In 1980, Exit published *A Guide to Self-Deliverance* that discusses five major at-home methods for killing oneself (these methods concentrate on drug ingestion). The pamphlet also tells one to avoid violent means of self-destruction, and it cautions people not to combine alcohol with an aspirin overdose because of the hours of agony of internal bleeding before death. The Hemlock Society goes one step further by trying to get states to decriminalize the act of helping a terminally ill person to die. Both Exit and the Hemlock Society show how far society has come from the days when suicides were buried at the crossroads. However, present society appears most unwilling in extending the "right to die" too far.

Moral, legal, and social issues abound in the debate over the notion of a right to suicide. This debate is not directly congruent with the issue of euthanasia, but there is overlap. The Roman Catholic Church has the most clearly stated position (of organized religions) on euthanasia in that it permits an end to treatment that serves only to " . . . secure a precarious and burdensome prolongation of life" (54). This applies, however, only to formal medical treatments and procedures such as taking a person off a respirator when there is no chance of ever having a healthy, normal life where death is not imminent. Some argue that if the Catholic Church permits cessation of treatment, why not permit forced starvation or liquid deprivation to induce death for those who are terminally ill and wish to die? Also, can the family make a decision to terminate life when a person is not capable of deciding?

A case in point is that of Clarence Herbert, a 55-year-old Californian who slipped into a coma after surgery. Doctors told his family that he was clinically dead, and the family then allowed doctors to terminate food and water intake. After Herbert's death, Los Angeles authorities tried, unsuccessfully, to prosecute the doctors for murder. Herbert's family now feels misinformed by the doctors and are suing them for malpractice. With such legal machinations on the increase, the right-to-suicide movement must contend with the possibility of having attorneys arguing over one's bedside before a judge. Both the medical and legal professions are hesitant to take the matter of life and death out of the hands of health care deliverers and put them under control of the courts.

But it is in the courtroom that the most celebrated right to suicide case of the '80s is being pursued. Elizabeth Bouvia, in her mid-20s, went to court to get a legal injunction against being force-fed and to get a court order to place her on medication to lessen the agony of starving to death while conscious. The Bouvia case is especially poignant in that she is not terminally ill. She is a cerebral palsy quadriplegic who feels the quality of her life entails unbearable hardships. Yet, some of her hardships (a miscarriage and dissolution of her marriage) are not germane only to cerebral palsy victims. Still, her illness has deteriorated her condition to the point where she wants to die. Her case is winding through the courts with the most recent ruling favoring her starvation plea.

The Bouvia and similar cases have heightened our pubic awareness about suicide. At least part of American society appears to be evolving toward some approval of a right to die for the terminally ill, but the "right-to-suicide" notion has not taken substantial hold. Some have speculated that the correlation of religious affiliation and attitudes against suicide is declining (55). This same research shows that males tend to be more accepting of suicide and euthanasia than are females. However, the matter of the "right to suicide" will be settled in the same political-economic arena that is debating abortion and euthanasia. It is impossible to predict what will transpire in such an arena of conflicting ideologies, values, and power. For now, our society is moving slowly and, some would argue, with due caution on the matter of the "right to suicide." Over a dozen states now allow for living wills whereby people can specify limits and durations of extreme medical treatment to prolong life when death is certain. Over 40 states allow a legal proxy to act on behalf of a comatose or incompetent patient. However, all states forbid anyone's assisting another's direct suicide.

SUICIDE PREVENTION

It is a testimony to the complexity of the issue of suicide to move from discussing the "right to suicide" to a discussion of suicide prevention. I shall discuss this topic from two considerations: 1) the community/societal response to prevent suicide through Prevention Centers; and 2) how an individual can be aware of the warning signs of suicide in others.

Suicide Prevention/Crisis Intervention Centers

Societal concern over suicide was highly formalized in the 1960s. The National Institute of Mental Health founded a national coordinating effort on suicide prevention. In that same decade, the government began issuing the federally sponsored *Bulletin of Suicidology*. The American Association of Suicidology was founded, and communities began to form Suicide Prevention Centers. These were local community helping centers that allowed anonymous "call-ins" by people who sought help to prevent their own suicide. It was soon thought that the scope of the centers should not only be to prevent suicide but also to handle other psychological and emotional problems of a crisis nature. So, most centers changed their names to Crisis Intervention Center to broaden the emphasis on helping people in need of any counseling.

In the past decade, more attention has been directed toward evaluating the success of such centers with respect to the reduction of suicide. This assessment is almost impossible to make. Societal emphasis on suicide prevention led to better reporting of suicide, so rates appeared to remain the same or increase "in spite of" such crisis centers. Also, these centers have had to struggle for financial resources to get a share of dwindling public funds. At times of budget cutbacks, evaluation and assessment of programs are two of the first budget items cut. However, the staying power of these centers is affirmation enough that they are meeting a critical need.

It is best to view such centers as being able to *intervene* at times of an acute emotional emergency. Optimally, they could expand their efforts whereby trained personnel could go throughout the community with a suicide prevention education program. This program could help people to develop coping resources before a crisis occurs. It could also help people to recognize the signs of a potential suicide in others. This is important since the person who calls a crisis center is not always the same type as those completing the suicide act (24).

While it is difficult to imagine that the difference between life and death may only be the dialing of a phone, crisis centers give proof every day that such is the case. The centers have trained people (mostly volunteers) who are there to:

1. Answer the phone and engage in communication to assess why the person is calling
2. Try to find out what particular problem initiated the call
3. Determine the lethality of the suicide situation
4. Discuss other solutions
5. Help the person to get additional counseling
6. Send help; if immediate face-to-face contact is essential, a "CARE team" (two volunteers) can be sent to help the person.

These six steps have helped to save lives by virtue of the presence of crisis centers. However, each of us can be educated to help prevent suicide.

Individual Suicide Prevention

Many of us know someone who has tried to kill himself/herself or has talked seriously about doing so. In such situations, the statistics and theories of suicide may not come readily to mind, and they may not be immediately relevant. There are signs and indications that someone is suicidal and knowing them can be lifesaving:

1. *Take threats seriously.* Someone who says they might kill themselves are already at risk. Between 60–70 percent of all suicides told someone they were suicidal before killing themselves. It is a myth to believe that people who talk about suicide do not commit suicide.
2. *Evaluate support systems.* Some people feel they are going to commit suicide as a result of negative forces in their support network while others can benefit from such networks. Therefore, one's family can help to lessen the suicide risk if they are seen as supportive.
3. *Evaluate psychodynamic issues.* Each event in our lives carries with it our evaluation, feeling, and associations about that event. Some people see the loss of a job as a deep scar on their intrapersonal self-image. Some see the breakup of a dating arrangement as a strongly negative indicator of their ability to maintain interpersonal relationships. Even if such a loss is not considered a real tragedy by most people, there are those who will give a strongly negative symbolic meaning to that event. Some people are especially at risk when they perceive a loss to have both interpersonal and intrapersonal consequences.
4. *Is substance abuse present?* People who are thinking of committing suicide increase their risk with the use of drugs or alcohol. These substances greatly distort the intensity of any situation let alone the extreme one of self-inflicted injury or death.
5. *Ask the right questions.* Ask a person if he/she is actually thinking of committing suicide. While we may think this asking may be a precipitating suggestion, this is not true. The experience of crisis prevention centers proves otherwise. Guggenheim (56) reports that at the Los Angeles Suicide Prevention Center no person was harmed when this question was asked in a thoughtful, concerned manner. But do not try to analyze motives or argue with the person.
6. *Try to assess feelings.* A person at risk for suicide is usually in the throes of experiencing helplessness, exhaustion, feelings of deep inadequacy and failure, and hopelessness. Some real cues are expressions such as "I can't stand it any longer, I just want out"; "I'm so tired of struggling, I need a way out"; "I'm in pain so much, I hurt so deeply, I've got to do something to end this pain." These expressions, when coupled with some of the other considerations listed here, are a strong sign that the person needs caring help. Also, look at cues to what is called a "presuicidal syndrome": does a person see life as a useless, no-win situation, where values and interpersonal relationships are empty and useless? Does the person see everything in an either/or, black/white dichotomy with the "solution" of suicide as being the best way out?
7. *Determine presence of suicide plans.* A strong marker of suicide can be found in how thought out one has planned taking his/her life. If someone inserts statements such as "I've bought a gun," or "I know where by dad keeps his gun," or "I remember last year when that coed jumped from the top floor of the dorm" then you can well assume that the person is giving serious consider-

ation of a lethal means to take their life. If the means are not extremely lethal (e.g., "I'll try to get a prescription for sleeping pills") or if a person talks about the impact of their suicide on loved ones, then the risk factor is not as strong, but the person still needs help.

8. *Ask about the past.* If a person has previously attempted suicide, they are at much greater risk to try again. If they have put their affairs in order or have spent the recent past withdrawn and isolated, they are at increased risk of suicide.

9. *Be vigilant.* Some people can be assessed as being so suicidal that they literally cannot be left alone. In certain situations, this will mean calling someone to help oversee the person's behavior even if the person resents calling, for example, the police.

Each of the above is something we should be mindful of so that we can be prepared to deal with a possible suicide. If you are confronted with someone who is suicidal, do not feel overly perplexed about having to make some tough decisions. The situation is inherently difficult since there are so many factors operative at a time of crisis. Psychiatrists in a psychiatric emergency room even find it difficult to adequately assess the potential for suicide (56). The important thing is not to be passive. Confront the situation, tell the person you care, and, if necessary, call a Crisis Intervention Center or get other professional help.

SUMMARY

Suicide cannot be viewed merely as a topic characterized by certain demographic variables. Each suicide is a life-taking event, an action by a human being, for whatever reason, to leave this world. The discussion on lethality of method provides a clue to the forceful dynamics of this action. The "why" of suicide can be explained for a variety of social, psychological, and cultural reasons. However, even these reasons lose some of their clarity compared to reflection on the life gone because of suicide. For some terminally ill people, perhaps the "right to suicide" is one of many options to consider. Yet, society and the individual have much to gain by seeking to help an individual move from crisis . . . to change . . . to wanting to live.

REVIEW QUESTIONS

1. Give a summary of the main demographic and socioeconomic correlates of suicide in the United States. How does the overall rate of suicide in the United States compare with the rates in other countries? What might be some possible explanations for these relationships and differences?

2. Describe the relationship between lethality of method for suicide and suicidal intent.

3. What are the methodological difficulties in studying the relationship between communication of intent and completed suicide?

4. Define the concept of "suicidal career" and explain its possible importance in understanding suicide.

5. Some psychologists feel that the shortcomings of the psychiatric model for

explaining suicide can be overcome, in part, by considering depression and suicidal ideas as cognitive processes. Discuss this .contention. Do you agree with it? Why, or why not?

6. In what way can the comparatively high suicide rate among the elderly cause more severe problems in our society in the future? How might we as a society decrease this rate? Should we? Why or why not?

7. Three classic types of suicide and explanatory models offered by Durkheim are anomie, egoism, and altruism. In your opinion, are these models useful in explaining suicidal behavior in contemporary societies? Explain.

8. The "right-to-suicide" movement presents society with some very complex and serious issues. What is your evaluation of society's allowing and/or helping someone to commit suicide? Would you be willing to assist someone to commit suicide? Why, or why not?

9. You are asked to address a civic organization of adults on how they might help to prevent suicide. What are the major points you would present in your talk? Consider both what an individual can do as well as what a community can do to help prevent suicide.

REFERENCES

1. Gates, B. T. (1980). Suicide and the Victorian physicians. *Journal of the History of the Behavioral Sciences, 16,* 164–174.
2. Thanatology Today (1980). *Newsletter, 1,* 1.
3. Suicide: Part I. (1986). *Harvard Mental Health Letter, 2,* 1–4.
4. Seiden, R. H., & Freitas, R. P. (1980). Shifting patterns of deadly violence. *Suicide and Life-Threatening Behavior, 10,* 195–209.
5. Stack, S. (1980). The effects of age composition on suicide in traditional and industrial societies. *The Journal of Social Psychology, 111,* 143–144.
6. Haas, A. P., & Hendin, H. (1983). Suicide among older people: Projections for the future. *Suicide and Life-Threatening Behavior, 13,* 147–154.
7. Wilson, M. (1981). Suicidal behavior: Toward an explanation of differences in female and male rates. *Suicide and Life-Threatening Behavior, 11,* 131–140.
8. Heshusisus, L. (1980). Female self-injury and suicide attempts: Culturally reinforced techniques in human relations. *Sex Roles, 6,* 843–857.
9. Bourque, L. B., Kraus, J. F., & Cosand, B. J. (1983). Attributes of suicide in females. *Suicide and Life-Threatening Behavior, 13,* 123–138.
10. Seiden, R. H. (1981). Mellowing with age: Factors influencing the nonwhite suicide rate. *International Journal on Aging and Human Development, 13,* 265–284.
11. Robinson, W. S. (1950). Ecological correlations and the behavior of individuals. *American Sociologial Review, 15,* 351–357.
12. Card, J. J. (1974). Lethality of suicidal methods and suicide risk: Two distinct concepts. *Omega, 5,* 37–45.
13. Lester, D., & Beck, A. T. (1980–81). What the suicide's choice of method signifies. *Omega, 11,* 271–277.
14. Seiden, R. H. (1977). Suicide prevention: A public health/public policy approach. *Omega, 8,* 267–276.
15. Peck, D. L. (1985–86). Completed suicides: Correlates of choice method. *Omega, 16,* 309–323.
16. Robins, E., Gassner, S., Kayes, J., Wilkinson, R., & Murphy, G. (1959). The communication of suicidal intent. *American Journal of Psychiatry, 115,* 724–733.

17. Rudestam, K. E. (1971). Stockholm and Los Angeles: A cross-cultural study of the communication of suicide intent. *Journal of Consulting and Clinical Psychology, 36,* 82–90.

18. Bernstein, M. (1978–79). The communication of suicidal intent by completed suicides. *Omega, 9,* 175–182.

19. Tuckman, J., Kleiner, R., & Lavell, M. (1959). Emotional content of suicide notes. *American Journal of Psychology.*

20. Jacobs, J. (1982). *The moral justification of suicide.* Springfield, IL: Thomas.

21. Hendin, H. (1982). *Suicide in America.* New York: Norton.

22. Maris, R. W. (1981). *Pathways to suicide.* Baltimore: Johns Hopkins University Press.

23. Reynolds, D. K., & Farberow, N. L. (1981). *The family shadow: Sources of suicide and schizophrenia.* Berkeley: University of California Press.

24. Selkin, J. (1983). The legacy of Emile Durkheim. *Suicide and Life-Threatening Behavior, 13,* 3–14.

25. Beck, A. T., Weissman, M. A., & Kovacs, M. (1976). Alcoholism, hopelessness, and suicidal behavior. *Journal of Studies on Alcohol, 37,* 66–77.

26. Freud, S. (1955). Mourning and meloncholea. In J. Strachy (Ed.), *The Standard Edition of the Complete Works of Sigmund Freud* (247–252). London: Hogarth.

27. Freud, S. (1955). Beyond the pleasure principle. In J. Strachy (Ed.), *The Standard Edition of the Complete Works of Sigmund Freud* London: Hogarth.

28. Menninger, K. (1985). *Man against himself.* New York: Harcourt, Brace & World.

29. Osgood, N. J. (1985). *Suicide in the elderly: A practitioner's guide to diagnosis and mental health intervention.* Rockville, MD: Aspen.

30. Neimeyer, R. A. (1984). Toward a personal construct conceptualization of depression and suicide. In F. R. Epting & R. A. Neimeyer (Eds.), *Personal Meanings of Death* (127–173). Washington, DC: Hemisphere.

31. Kelly, G. A. (1955). *The psychology of personal constructs.* New York: Norton.

32. Ringel, E. (1976). The presuicidal syndrome. *Suicide and Life-Threatening Behavior, 6,* 131–149.

33. Rowe, D. (1978). *The experience of depression.* New York: Wiley.

34. Durkheim, E. (1951). *Suicide.* New York: The Free Press.

35. Pope, W., & Danigelis, N. (1981). Sociology's "one law." *Social Forces, 60,* 495–516.

36. Stack, S. (1982). Suicide: A decade review of the sociological literature. *Deviant Behavior: An Interdisciplinary Journal, 4,* 41–66.

37. Marshall, J. R. (1981). Political integration and the effect of war on suicide: United States, 1933–76. *Social Forces, 59,* 771–785.

38. Sharma, A. (1978). Emile Durkheim on suttee as suicide. *International Journal of Contemporary Sociology, 15,* 283–291.

39. Pierce, A. (1967). The economic cycle and the social suicide rate. *American Sociological Review, 32,* 457–463.

40. Marshall, J. R., & Hodge, R. W. (1981). Durkheim and Pierce on suicide and economic change. *Social Science Research, 10,* 101–114.

41. Platt, S. (1984). Unemployment and suicidal behavior: A review of the literature. *Sociological Sciences & Medicine, 19,* 93–115.

42. Stack, S. (1982). The effect of strikes on suicide: A cross-national analysis. *Sociological Focus, 15,* 135–146.

43. Lester, D. (1972). *Why people kill themselves.* Springfield, IL: Thomas.

44. Stephens, B. J. (1985–86). Suicidal women and their relationship with their parents. *Omega, 16,* 289–300.

45. Stack, S. (1980). Domestic integration and the rate of suicide: A comparative study. *Journal of Comparative Family Studies, 11,* 249–260.

46. Stack, S. (1980). The effects of marital dissolution on suicide. *Journal of Marriage and the Family, 42*, 83–92.

47. Phillips, D. P. (1974). The influence of suggestion on suicide: Substantive and theoretical implications of the Werther effect. *American Sociological Review, 39*, 340–354.

48. Bollen, K. A., & Phillips, D. P. (1982). Imitative suicides: A national study of the effects of television news stories. *American Sociological Review, 47*, 802–809.

49. Berardo, F. M. (1970). Survivorship and social isolation: The case of aged widowers. *Family Coordinator, 19*, 11–25.

50. Rosow, I. (1967). *Social integration of the aged.* New York: Free Press.

51. Leviton, D. (1973). The significance of sexuality as a deterrent to suicide among the aged. *Omega, 4*, 163–174.

52. Suicide: Risk factors. (1981). *Thanatology Today, 3*, 3–4.

53. Peterson, L. G. (1984). The hopeless, suicide-prone medical patient. In F. G. Guggenheim & M. F. Weiner (Eds.), *Manual of psychiatric consultation and emergency care* (173–181). New York: Aronson.

54. Debate on the boundary of life. (1983, April 11). *Time*, 68–70.

55. Johnson, D., Fitch, S. D., Alston, J. P., & McIntosh, W. A. (1980). Acceptance of conditional suicide and euthanasia among adult Americans. *Suicide and Life-Threatening Behavior, 10*, 157–166.

56. Guggenheim, F. G. (1984). Management of suicide risk in the psychiatric emergency room. In F. G. Guggenheim and M. F. Weiner (Eds.), *Manual of psychiatric consultation and emergency care* (23–32). New York: Aronson.

12

The Funeral in Contemporary Society

Robert Fulton

THE DRAMATURGY OF DEATH

Burial of the dead is an ancient practice among humans. From paleolithic times to the present, human beings have responded to the death of their fellow humans with solemnity and ceremony. Not only has the event of death evoked a religious awe, but its threat to the survival of communal life has engendered fear, while its disruption of family life has aroused sorrow. The vehicle through which these reactions to death have been expressed has been the funeral. The funeral traditionally has served as a ceremony acknowledging a death; a religious rite; an occasion to reassure and reestablish the social group; a commemoration of a life; and a ritual of disposal.

The dramaturgical celebration of death and its significance for the individual and society have long attracted the interest of scholars. Several authors (1–10) have emphasized the function of ritualized behavior in promoting and maintaining the emotional well-being of the individual as well as the social cohesion and structural integration of the group.

Malinowski (11), for instance, viewed ceremonies associated with death as a part of the sacrilizing institution of religion which bestowed upon individuals the gift of mental integrity, a function, he believed, that was also fulfilled with regard to the whole group. He saw funerary customs as powerful counteracts to the centrifugal forces of fear, dismay, and demoralization. He believed they possessed the potential for providing the most powerful means of reintegrating a group's weakened solidarity and reestablishing their shaken morale.

Radcliffe-Brown (2) and Durkheim (12) emphasized the role of ritualized behavior in promoting and maintaining social forms. Durkheim, for example, spoke of ceremony as being a collective expression of sentiment and interpreted certain attitudes and rituals as "objectified sentiments." On the other hand, Van Gennep (1) assigned the greatest importance to the rituals associated with death because he found that funeral rites, which had as their express purpose the incorporation of the deceased into the "world of the dead," were characteristically the most extensively elaborate.

More recently, Mandelbaum (7) has examined death rites in five widely separated cultures. His research has not only contributed new insights into our understanding of the role of death rituals and ceremonies, but it also permits us to comprehend more clearly their place and meaning in our changing world. Mandelbaum concludes that funeral customs serve "manifest" as well as "latent" functions. Manifest functions refer to those activities associated with mortuary rites that are most readily apparent, such as the disposal of the body, assistance to the bereaved, the public acknowledgment of the death, and assertions and demonstrations of the continued viability of the group.

Less readily perceived or understood, but nonetheless important, however, are the latent functions that funeral practices serve, including the economic and reciprocal social obligations that are remembered and reenacted at the time of a death. In this way, he observes, the role taken by a participant in a funeral not only reflects his or her position in society but also reaffirms the social order. A second latent function is found in the obligations and restrictions placed upon all members of the deceased's family with regard to such things as dress, demeanor, food, and social intercourse. Such observances, he notes, serve to identify as well as to demonstrate family cohesion. A third latent function of the funeral is the acknowledgement and affirmation of the extended kinship system. Members of the larger family console the survivors and frequently share in the expenses of the ceremony.

Mandelbaum argues that participation in the funeral ceremony, the procession, the partaking of food and other social exchanges, as well as the mourning and keening, all add to the sense of being a part of a larger social whole, just as the order of precedence in the conduct of the ceremony reminds one that there is structure and order in the social system. Finally, he regards the funeral as a "rite of passage." It not only marks the end of life and separation of the dead from the living, but it also reaffirms the belief in the immortal character of human existence.

CEREMONY: FUNCTIONAL AND DYSFUNCTIONAL

The question for us, however, is whether or not the funeral (as described by Mandelbaum and others and based, as their analyses have been, on non-Western or preindustrial societies) is relevant for modern Western society. Is the funeral a functional ceremony in the urban, industrial world of today? Does it meet the needs of our citizens? These are not new questions; yet, they are still being asked. Indeed, they still need to be asked—perhaps now more than at any time in our history.

Ritual can be dysfunctional. Geertz (13) cites the case of a funeral in Java in which the insistence on traditional practices served to disrupt, rather than restore, the sense of community. He reports that traditional rites which were suited to an agricultural village and folk milieu served to be inappropriate and caused much dissension and confusion among villagers transplanted to town life where the economic, social, and political orientations were different from those of the village.

Mandelbaum (7), too, gives us the example of the Kota where, typically, the traditional funeral ceremony actually aggravates the sorrow of the mourner and serves to provoke social discord. At one stage of the Kota funeral, at what is termed the "dry funeral," there is a juncture when all Kotas who are present at the ceremony come forward one by one to give a parting bow of respect to the relics of the deceased. This becomes a time of great tension and conflict. Mandelbaum describes the situation as follows:

> Around this gesture of social unity, violent quarrels often rage. When kinsmen of a deceased Kota are fervent supporters of one of the two opposing factions in Kota society, they may try to prevent a person of the other faction from making this gesture of respect and solidarity. This is tantamount to declaring that those of the other faction are not Kotas at all—a declaration which neither side will quietly accept. Thus a ritual action which symbolizes concord has frequently triggered a good deal of discord. Yet among the Kotas, as in other societies, neutral people try to bring about a compromise—the ceremony is somehow completed with as much show of social unity as can be managed—especially for funerals of the great men of the tribe. (p. 213)

In this instance, however, Kota mourning ceremonies appear to be "rituals of rebellion" rather than an illustration of ritually inspired discord and disunity *per se* (14).

There is still a further point to consider: the level of social organization under analysis. We have come to learn that what may be operative and functional at one level of social life (for example, the family or community) may not be functional for, or congruent with, the aims and purposes of the broader social system.

Let me illustrate. In 1969, the Minister of Defense for Kenya, Mr. Tom Mboya, was assassinated. His death resulted in the subsequent deaths of more than a dozen fellow citizens among the Luo and Kikuyu tribes of that nation, and the destruction of hundreds of thousands of dollars worth of property. The English journal, *The Economist,* reported at the time that never in the history of Nairobi had there been such disturbance and loss of life as that which followed the memorial service that was held in his honor in Nairobi.*

In Kenya, it is a family obligation to see that the deceased is returned to his village and buried on his father's land with only members of the tribal community in attendance. Mr. Mboya was killed by a member of the Kikuyu tribe. The Kikuyu were excluded from taking part in his funeral—not only by virtue of the fact that they had been held responsible for his death but, also, because it is

---

*The Economist, in the July 12 issue (1969) also expressed concern over the assassination of Mr. Mboya by a Kikuyu member from the Kenya African National Union youth movement. It reported that the rioting that followed the Requiem Mass that was said for Mr. Mboya was the worst that Nairobi had ever seen. *The Economist* observed that his death provoked a return to tribal politics as the Luo, convinced that the murder was a political ploy, showed signs of forming a united tribal front against Kikuyu domination of the government and its agencies. In return, it was reported that President Kenyatta moved to reinforce old tribal alliances with the Kalenjin and Kamba in order to forestall any attempt to isolate the Kikuyu. (p. 239)

traditional for the tribes to exclude all but their own. Therefore, there was the possibility that when Jomo Kenyatta, the then prime minister of Kenya, died, there would be civil strife in Kenya—strife of such magnitude that the national aspirations of Kenya could well have been threatened. Mr. Kenyatta was a Kikuyu. It was highly possible that his mourners would exclude the Luo (who represent the second strongest political party as well as the second largest tribal group in Kenya) from participation in the ceremonies. Indeed, they may have held the Luo responsible for the death itself. If the national state of Kenya survived President Kenyatta's death, it would only be because the Kikuyu and the Luo recognized that the state must take precedence over tribal ambitions and traditions if it is to endure.*

By way of contrast, let me recall to mind our own society's experience with death in recent years. The sudden and unexpected assassinations of President John F. Kennedy, Senator Robert Kennedy, and Dr. Martin Luther King came as successive shocks to the American body politic and were sorely felt.

To review the events following the assassination of President Kennedy is to recall a period of social and political turmoil unparalleled in this country since the assassination of President Lincoln a century earlier. At that time, the country bordered on panic as rumors of conspiracy and intrigue swept through Washington and across the nation. The attempted assassination of other members of Lincoln's cabinet gave substance to those fears and placed Washington, D.C., on a war emergency alert.

A sequel to that episode in our history was re-enacted in the hours and days following President Kennedy's death. At the same time that the nation was plunged into grief and mourned his death, the country was alive to reports and rumors of conspiracies both from the political left and right. The assassination of Lee Harvey Oswald, President Kennedy's alleged assassin, by Jack Ruby, before a nationwide television audience, only aggravated the anxiety and compounded the fears of the entire nation as it added to the sense of tragedy.

The state funeral that was held for President Kennedy was the most widely viewed ceremony in history. It is estimated that one-half billion people throughout the world watched the funeral proceedings on television (15). In attendance were, in addition to President Kennedy's immediate family, personal friends, colleagues, dignitaries from all branches of the government, representatives from the various political parties, and the heads of state or their personal representatives of all nonbelligerent countries.

The wedding of President Kennedy's daughter, Caroline, served to remind us of that profound occasion. Those of us who witnessed the funeral of the President on national television experienced what almost amounted to a *deja vu* as we watched Mrs. Jacqueline Kennedy and her son, John, along with other members of the Kennedy family "in procession" once again—albeit celebrating a much happier event.

President Kennedy's funeral served to declare not only that he was dead but

---

*In 1978, Prime Minister Kenyatta died a natural death. His funeral took place amid great mourning but without incident. This was mainly due to the fact that precautions were taken to make his funeral as public and as symbolic of the nation as possible. The British government helped to arrange the funeral and provided the use of Winston Churchill's funeral carriage in order to emphasize the international significance of the event (*The Economist*, August 9, 1969, p. 240).

also that order had been restored to the country and that the nation was secure in its relations with most other nations of the world.

The state funeral of President Kennedy was followed in quick succession by the funeral of his brother, Senator Robert Kennedy and that of Dr. Martin Luther King. As before, their deaths threatened social and political disruption throughout the nation. As one of the leading spokesmen for the peaceful integration of white and black America, Dr. King's sudden and violent death, particularly, was little short of cataclysmic in its import. It precipitated racial disturbances across the country, resulting in the deaths of more than a score of citizens, both black and white, as well as the destruction of millions of dollars worth of property (16).

Dr. King's death removed the strongest voice of moderation from our racially antagonistic society. Despite this fact, however, and the fact that his assassin was a white man, his funeral included many prominent political and social leaders from the white community. In effect, his funeral announced to the nation as well as to the world that, regardless of his death and the friction between the black and white races in America, the followers of Dr. King were determined to remain true to his philosophy of nonviolence and to his dream of a nation free from bigotry.

Death evokes powerful emotions within us that need to be vented or calmed. This was made evident with the assassinations of President Kennedy, his brother Robert, and Dr. King. The country grieved their deaths; the nation mourned openly not only as solitary citizens but also together as a society. As a society, it observed public as well as private expressions of grief; it participated in three funerals to which the whole world paid heed.

Public evidence of the private reactions to President Kennedy's death is available. At least 39 different surveys (19) were conducted at varying intervals following his assassination. While the studies were manifestly different in design and intent, certain common reactions were discernible. These reactions are best shown by the study of the National Opinion Research Center in Chicago (20) which polled a representative national sample of 1,400 adults within a week of the assassination. The study showed the following results:

1. Preoccupation with the death was almost total.
2. Nine out of ten people reported experiencing one or more physical symptoms such as headache, upset stomach, tiredness, dizziness, or loss of appetite.
3. Two-thirds of the respondents felt very nervous and tense during the four days.
4. A majority of the respondents confessed to feeling dazed and numb.
5. Most people—men and women—cried at some period during this time.
6. The event was compared most often to the death of a parent, close friend, or relative.
7. There was a tendency to react to the assassination in terms of personal grief and loss rather than in terms of political or ideological concern or anxiety about the future.

As the researchers described it, reactions of the American people during the four days following the death of President Kennedy appeared to have followed a well-defined pattern of grief familiar to medical practice. The funeral of the President channeled that grief and gave it poignant expression.

Moreover, the relatively peaceful association of white and black in this country is to some extent made possible today by virtue of the fact that in his funeral

Dr. King's survivors saw an opportunity to bind the wound that his death had caused to the body politic. The funerals of President Kennedy, Senator Kennedy, and Dr. King were functional in that they served the formal structural needs of our society and, at the same time, provided a vehicle for the utterance of private grief.

A funeral, then, is a functional or a dysfunctional set of activities depending upon place and circumstance. In the case of Kenya, the funeral of President Kenyatta had the potential to do the state profound injury, given Kikuyu philosophy and tribal tradition. But for the United States, I would contend that the national funerals of the Kennedys and of Dr. King have been functional with respect to the social order.

But what of the "average" American funeral, the funeral of the ordinary man or woman? Is it also beneficial? The question is more than an academic one in view of the fact that, in the past few years, criticism of the funeral, funeral practices, and the funeral director has become increasingly strident as well as extensive. The funeral has been charged with being pagan in origin and ostentatious in practice, while the funeral director has been characterized as one who exploits the dead at the expense of the living (21).

FUNERAL PRACTICES AND ATTITUDES

Over the past 25 years, I have conducted three nationwide surveys (24–27) dealing with the issues surrounding mortality in America. Let me highlight the major findings from these studies.

The first study (24), conducted in 1959, surveyed the attitudes of clergymen toward funerals and funeral directors in the United States. It showed that clerical criticism of the funeral director and of funeral practices was both widespread and intensive. Among the different reasons the clergy gave for their negative appraisal, two stand out. First, the funeral director was charged with dramatizing the presence of the body while ignoring spiritual matters, and, second, the funeral director was charged with taking undue advantage of the bereaved. A third factor was left unstated but was, nevertheless, implicit in the clergy's criticism: The funeral director makes his services available to people of different faiths and relates all funerals past and present. By such a relative attitude toward the religious aspects of funeral rites, he appears to leave himself open to the charge of paganism.

Specifically, the study showed that the Protestant clergyman, more so than his Catholic colleague, was troubled by contemporary funeral rites and practices and by the emerging role of the funeral director in connection with these rites and practices. Inasmuch as the religious service for Protestants is most often held in the chapel of the funeral home, the relative change of function of the Protestant clergyman vis-à-vis the funeral director appears to be troublesome for many clerics, both professionally and personally.

These factors, as well as others, have led some members of the clergy to charge the contemporary funeral with paganism and to view the expense associated with it as conspicuous waste. Such concern has also led to active promotion of what is called the "simplified" funeral to the advocacy of cremation and to the recommendation that monies normally spent on funerals be diverted to scientific research and public charities.

The second study (26), conducted in 1962, surveyed the attitudes of the American public toward death, funerals, and funeral directors. Included in the study was a cross-section of those persons who were members of the funeral reform or memorial society movement. As with the clergy study, the survey showed that negative and critical attitudes toward contemporary funeral rites and practices are held by some segments of the public. However, the survey showed that these attitudes are not shared equally by the public but, rather, that criticism of the contemporary funeral varies by geographical region as well as by religious affiliation, education, occupation, and income.

It was found that a majority of the American public surveyed was favorably disposed toward present-day funeral practices and the funeral director. The majority of respondents also viewed the funeral as providing a meaningful emotional experience for the survivors. Moreover, more than half of the respondents viewed the funeral director as a professional person or as one who combined a professional service with a business function.

Members of the memorial societies, however, expressed views strongly divergent from those of the general public. They believed the funeral director was primarily a businessman offering the public no professional service whatsoever. The majority of them expressed an unfavorable opinion of both funeral costs and funeral directors. In addition, a majority of these respondents did not believe that the purposes of the funeral were, in fact, served by the funeral ceremony. Only 25 percent of the memorial society respondents believed that the funeral served the emotional needs of the family in any way, while 16 percent perceived the traditional funeral as performing no useful function at all. Consistent with these findings, the study further showed that the memorial society members were the strongest advocates for cremation, for the donation of the body to medical programs and scientific research, and for recommending that the ritual and ceremony of the funeral be simplified or avoided.

Of interest here is the social profile of the average memorial group. The study showed that the members of a memorial society group reported educational attainments significantly higher than nongroup members as well as the highest percentage of professional occupations and an average annual income twice that of the typical American family. On the other hand, they reported the lowest percentage of traditional religious affiliation.

As a whole, the study showed that favorable responses toward funerals and funeral directors varied with religious affiliation. Religious affiliation, or its absence, was the pivotal factor around which the various attitudes expressed in the study revolved. Simply stated, Catholics most often reported being favorably disposed toward the funeral and the funeral director, followed by Protestants, Jews, nonaffiliated respondents, and Unitarians. The order was reversed with respect to critical attitudes. The Unitarians were the most critical, followed by Jews, nonaffiliated, Protestants, and, finally, Catholics. Regionally, the most favorable attitudes toward the funeral and the funeral director were expressed by residents from central sections of the country, while the least favorable views were expressed by respondents residing along the Atlantic and Pacific coasts.

In the third study (27), it was sought to determine the character of contemporary funeral practices in the United States. A questionnaire was prepared and mailed to the 1967 membership of the National Funeral Directors Association as well as to the membership of the Jewish Funeral Directors Association. In all, 14,144 questionnaires were mailed. One out of every four (24.6 percent) of the funeral directors polled returned the questionnaire for a total of 3,474 replies.

In many important aspects, the results of the third study complemented the findings of the two previous studies. The 1967 study, however, went beyond mere confirmation. It showed that the funeral in contemporary America is a different thing to different people: While what might be called the "traditional" funeral (a public service with a public viewing and a public committal service) is almost totally characteristic of the great central portion of the United States and the predominant mode of behavior everywhere else, it is nevertheless subject to modification and change. New rites and practices for coping with death and for disposing of the dead are emerging. Emergent variability is a fact in funeral dramaturgy as it is a fact throughout all of society. Change is at work not only in the mode of disposal of the dead but also in every sphere of funeralization as well—from the type of funeral establishment constructed to the emotional climate in which the funeral is conducted to the meaning imputed to death itself.

In order to grasp the significance and implications of the findings of the third study, as well as the two that preceded it, they must be placed within the larger context of American life. A funeral does not take place in a vacuum. Rather, these three studies can be understood to mirror, albeit in a small way, what society as a whole has been experiencing by way of a shift in its beliefs and values as they relate to death and dying since at least the time of World War I.

First, let us be reminded of a cultural baseline, as it were. According to religious doctrine, we are creatures of God and have been formed in His image. Due to our fall from grace, however, we are born in sin and, therefore, spiritually flawed. Death is the consequence of that sin and is a necessary experience for each one of us if we are to be restored to our prior state of perfection. In our society, the funeral has been the instrument of such a theology, and its ritual has served to dramatize such beliefs for the living at the same time that it effected a liturgy for the dead.

However, this sacerdotal image of man is not shared by everyone in the United States today. Rather, the idea being entertained by a growing number of persons is that death is not the wages of sin nor need it be as certain as taxes. And also it is no longer an unquestioned belief that life is the gift of God. The papal Encyclical on birth control in 1968, *Humanae Vitae,* created a storm of continuing debate in this country that has had almost no precedent (28). Protests, petitions, and pronouncements by clergy and laity of all religious faiths strongly questioned or opposed the papal edict. Moreover, the same year saw the first successful heart transplant in the United States, the continued progress toward kidney and other organ transplants, and increased speculation regarding the unlimited possibilities being opened by medical science technology. The religious, moral, and legal arguments surrounding such operations and their future implications are only now beginning to take definite form. One thing appears increasingly clear: Humankind persists in its refusal to accept the inevitability of death and with death, as well as with birth, seeks to be the final judge.

DEMOGRAPHIC FACTORS

A second point to consider is the demographic one. This year approximately 1 percent of the United States' population, or more than 2 million persons, will die (32). Over 70 percent of these deaths will occur among persons 65 years of age or older (33). In excess of 70 percent of these deaths, moreover, will now take place outside the home either in hospitals or in a nursing home.* The number of persons over the age of 65 is now over 28 million—11 percent of the population (33). In contrast, 80 million, or approximately one-third of the population, are children under 15 years of age (33). Children, however, account for only 4 percent of all deaths (32). This is a dramatic reversal in mortality statistics as compared to the 1920s when the mortality rate was highest for children (34). As a matter of fact, contemporary American youth could be called the first "death-free" generation in the history of the world. That is, statistically, a family in the United States can expect not to have a death occur among its immediate members for 20 years or one generation. The implications of these statistics cannot be overlooked. Our conception of death as well as our view of what constitutes an appropriate response to it are colored by these basic demographic facts.

INFLATIONARY ECONOMY

A third factor that must be considered among the myriad of social and cultural changes that could be mentioned is the seemingly relentless inflationary character of the American economy. Inflation seriously threatens the private household economies of literally millions of American families. Over 10 million households today are headed by a widow who, in the majority of cases, lives on a fixed income consisting of social security or other retirement benefits (35). Regardless of the provisions made beforehand, death expenses cannot help but be a source of anxiety and concern to them. Moreover, such concern is deepened by a fourth factor: the changing character of the United States' family.

CHANGING FAMILY

Over the past several generations, the United States' family has been transformed from a large, extended family into a small, nuclear group. It is more mobile, socially as well as geographically, than ever before. It is child oriented rather than adult oriented; it is more individualized than integrated. The young, contemporary family is less a part of a rural community or a neighborhood-enclosed group than before, while, increasingly, it tends toward being singular in an anonymous urban environment. As it has been pointed out, death is increasingly an experience of the aged, most of whom are retired from work, free of parental obligations, and frequently outside of, or absent from, the main current of family life. The extension of medical service and the advances in medical science research, moreover, make possible not only the prolonging of life of the elderly

---

*This figure is an extrapolation of data gathered from indirect and diverse sources. See Table 67 for the most direct reference to place of death in the United States: Public Health Service. (1960). Vital statistics of the United States (vol. 2). Washington, DC: U.S. Government Printing Office.

but often cause those hospitalized to be further separated from their families. Familial and friendship commitments are made fewer by such separations, and emotional and societal bonds are often loosened by time and distance. Not the least consequence of this development is the fact that great numbers of the elderly must not only live alone but, as a survey of ours shows, they die alone as well (36). Therefore, the disengagement of the aged from society prior to their deaths means that their dying has little effect on the round of life.

As we have noted, the death of a leader such as President Kennedy, Senator Robert Kennedy, or Dr. King can seriously disrupt the functioning of modern society. The vacuum they left in the social and political life of the United States has been sorely felt. For the common man or woman and for the average family, it is the death of someone either in the middle productive years of life or someone young and unfulfilled that will have a comparable effect upon the social or familial group. Because the elderly are less relevant to the functional working of our modern secular society, their deaths do not compel such attention. Like the late General MacArthur's "old soldier," they do not die but seemingly "fade away."

CHANGE IN VALUES

Changing attitudes toward the funeral as a meaningful rite for the dead have led to criticism and attacks on it in recent years. In a society where only half of the population is church-affiliated and the social and spatial mobility of its citizens is one of its more remarkable characteristics, the religious, emotional, and economic obligations that a funeral has traditionally imposed on a family are often seen as inappropriate today. Increasingly, the funeral is for that member of the family who is least functionally relevant to it. He or she has been, as I have suggested, often physically and socially removed from the family, perhaps by a long confinement. In our society which has a strong bent towards the youth generation as well as a need to economize, the expenses of the funeral strike the utility-minded citizen where he is most sensitive.

Advocacy of memorial services with the body absent and cremation are attempts within the context of emerging contemporary values to resolve the different problems associated with the traditional disposal of the dead.

What of the funeral, then, in the face of these trends and developments? Sixty thousand years ago, as recent archaeological discoveries at Shanidar, Iraq show, humans buried their dead with ceremony (37). They did so in a particular way and presumably for very specific ideological or religious reasons, given the manner of burial recorded. We must ask ourselves: Are paleolithic funeral practices still relevant and functional for contemporary humans?

While entombment is not universal, it has been practiced in many different societies far back into archaeological time and has served to express the idea of immortality through the symbolism of the funeral as a rite of incorporation. The concept of immortality implies another world, a world in which the "dead" live. As Van Gennep (1) observed, this corollary belief has meant that, historically, a primary focus of the funeral has been the "physical" incorporation of the dead with all their attributes, possessions, and effects into the "next world."

Today, such beliefs and practices are contrary to the religious, philosophical and ideological commitment of many people in American society. They do not believe in a "world of the dead," nor do they believe that it is necessary or felicitous to consume the resources of the living for the doubtful benefit it may have for the dead. For some, the most desirable procedure is also the simplest— one that involves as little material expense as possible and few people in atten- dance at the funeral. For a growing number of persons, this means immediate disposition of the body with no public ceremony (27).

But, as we have noted, anthropologists have recognized that there are impor- tant aspects of the funeral other than the symbolic expression of a theological belief in immortality or the dramaturgical incorporation of the dead into an after- life. I think it is important for us to consider what these aspects are and what their place and function may be for our contemporary world.

THE FUNERAL AS A RITE OF INTEGRATION AND SEPARATION

Besides being a rite of incorporation (that is, burial or entombment for rea- sons of resurrection or rebirth), the funeral is a rite of separation and integration. The funerals of President Kennedy, Dr. King, and Senator Kennedy, as well as that of Mr. Mboya, were rites of integration. The dramaturgy of those funerals de- clared that the world goes on, that we, the survivors, still live, that the social order prevails, and that we continue to have faith in the justice and mercy of God. But the funeral is also a drama that tells us that we have lost someone through death. As such, it focuses attention upon the survivors and to the degree that it does so is a rite of separation as well.

Psychologically, the loss of a significant person by death is a crisis situation. Medical and behavioral science experts have taught us in recent years that such loss evokes powerful emotions which need to be given proper expression (38–50).

Several authors (51–56) inform us, however, that the acceptance of separa- tion or permanent loss is an exceedingly difficult task to achieve. Many persons never do recover from permanent loss or ever wholly accept, or indeed ever admit to, the death of a loved one. "How do we get people to accept permanent loss?" is the question.

Two leading British psychiatrists, John Bowlby and C. Murray Parkes (57), have pointed out that a major element in acute grief is the denial that the death or the separation has occurred. As they describe it:

> There is a restless searching for the lost person, a constant wandering from room to room as if seeking for the loved individual, often calling his or her name. The necessary tasks and rituals, whether they are religious or not, which surround death, serve, however, to bring home gradually to the bereaved person the reality of the loss they have sus- tained and the knowledge that life will never be quite the same again. Drawing the blinds, viewing the body, attending the funeral service, lowering the coffin into the grave all serve to emphasize the finality and the absoluteness of death, and make denial more difficult.

When it is responsive to the psychological needs of the survivors, the ritual of the funeral can aid in the ventilation of profound emotions and help facilitate the normal dissolution of grief. Viewing the dead potentially allows this dissolution to take place.

It is true, as critics charge, that there are elements of disguise in the preparation of the body for the funeral. But such disguise is no more the basis of the funeral ceremony than the use of cosmetics or a veil is the basis for the wedding. I am led to propose that slight disguise of death is functional because it helps to move the grieving survivors along from a shocked denial of the death to a final acceptance of it. As Emily Dickinson would have us remember, "The truth must dazzle gradually, or else every man be blinded."

The events leading up to the actual internment or cremation of the body are those in which the survivors are invited to gather together, acknowledge the death, share in the grief, participate in the mourning rites, and witness the final disposition of the body. The funeral must be understood in terms of this dramaturgical denouement: The deceased has been removed forever from the living community.

STIGMA AND CALLOUSNESS

The work of Geoffrey Gorer (58) has shown that the problems of the recently bereaved are not limited to the United States. Gorer reports that there is the same repudiation and denial of death in Great Britain as in America. He hypothesizes a link between this stigmatization and public callousness. It is his contention that the present preoccupation with death and cruelty, coupled as it is with an excessive squeamishness concerning it, displays the modern irrational attitude toward this inevitable event. Gorer argues that such an attitude toward death makes it something obscene or pornographic and, ultimately, invites the maladaptive and neurotic behavior observed in his study.

In this regard, it is my belief that the observation he made several years ago regarding the denigration of grief and mourning in Great Britain now finds its counterpart emerging in this country. Such movies as *The Rocky Horror Picture Show* and *The Night of the Living Dead,* which commanded attention just a few years ago, were mild precursors of poor taste compared to the blatant and gross assault on our sensibilities that is presented by some mass media "entertainments" today.

IS THE FUNERAL BENEFICIAL?

The question before us still is: If the funeral is a rite of integration and separation, is it beneficial? The answer to that question is a contingent one. Ultimately, it is one that depends upon the individual survivor and the circumstances surrounding a death. For some survivors, the loss of an elderly relative is an occasion for the barest acknowledgment of the death and the most expeditious disposal of the body. In such an instance of what could be described as a "low-grief" death, loss can be slight and grief muted. The sudden, unexpected death of a child or of a young husband on the other hand may be perceived as premature and unjust and/or denied or resented by the survivors. Such a death could be termed a "high-grief" loss. The social and emotional needs of family, friends, and community in such instances are infinitely greater and the potential problems of the survivors more extensive than in the case of what has been termed a "low-grief'' loss. On the other hand "no grief" may be felt by a relative who is privately relieved or pleased at a death while "improper grief" may be experienced by a person who is not allowed to mourn publicly. Care has to be taken, therefore, not to define too narrowly what funeral rites or behaviors are appropriate for the bereaved. Insensitivity and poor social management of the intensity or absence of grief and the social expectations of the bereaved can only intensify their difficulties. For instance, when members of the clergy perceive the funeral as a rite of passage only and describe death as a joyful spiritual victory, they ignore the fact that death is also separation (of say a husband from a wife or a father from a daughter) and as with any irrevocable separation, the survivor may experience a profound sense of loss.

Mourning is the intersection of grief (a psychological drama) and bereavement (a social drama) where loss through death may find harmonious expression. The proper orchestration of this human event can permit social therapy to take place or at least begin so that private grief may be expressed and the process of mourning facilitated.

The funeral provides a setting in which both private sorrow and public loss can be expressed and shared. It is a ceremony that can facilitate the mourner's expression of grief. It is Fulcomer's (59) conclusion, based on his case studies of 72 bereaved subjects, that there is a definite indication that the bereaved person's responses are positively affected if he realizes or imagines that other persons are also mourning. In other words, "Sorrows tend to be diminished by the knowledge that another sorrows with us" (60). Likewise, it is the conclusion of Glick, Weiss, and Parkes (61), following their recent four-year case analysis of 68 bereaved persons, that even though the survivor is frequently mixed in his or her feelings, the tasks and activities associated with the ceremonies of leave-taking meet profound human needs. It was their observation, however, that many survivors found it difficult to view the corpse. But as they and Elisabeth Kübler-Ross (53), and others have observed, viewing is a way for many to confront the death of their loved one. Glick et al. (61) quote one widow who remarked, "I didn't believe he was dead until I saw him in the casket" (p. 110).

Loss through death can be a crisis situation. Studies show, however, that survivors display a wide range of responses and demonstrate varying capacities to adjust to a death. Prolonged maladjustment, however, as characterized by mental and physical ailments as well as the increased consumption of alcohol and sedatives, is all too common. On the other hand, preliminary findings from a study at the University of Minnesota (36) as well as the results from the studies of Mole (62) and Glick et al. (61) show that, apart from family and friends, relatively few health care persons are in contact with a survivor following a death. Yet, the evidence strongly suggests that many persons are in need of much more than the good will and concern of their closest family members or friends. The Minnesota study shows, for example, that only 15 percent of the survivors out of a sample of 558 widows and widowers reported professional health care contact or support following the death of the spouse.

The funeral, as a rite of separation and integration, requires of funeral directors that they too be cognizant of, and sensitive to, the social and emotional needs of the families that they serve. They must believe (as must the survivors) that the funerals they conduct and in which they participate are something more than commercial transactions.

In this connection, it is important to note that, in addition to this author's own previously cited work, both the study by Binger (63) and his colleagues at Langley-Porter Institute and the Harvard Bereavement Study conducted by Glick et al. (61) found the funeral director played a valuable social role in the discharge of his responsibilities. Binger et al. reported, for instance, that 15 of the 20 families interviewed "expressed positive feelings toward the mortician or funeral director." They observed that "experience with grief reactions makes them skilled in offering solace to grieving families" (p. 417).

Since this chapter was first written in 1978, there has appeared an increasing amount of research to support the contention of Binger and Glick and others that bereaved individuals typically find their interaction with funeral directors to be a supportive and helpful experience. Kheif's (64) study of some general populations and the studies of widows and widowers by Winn (66), Carey (67), and Lieberman and Borman (68) as well as the studies of bereaved parents by Cook (69, 70) and Anglim (71) show that the majority of respondents rated their funeral directors as somewhat or very helpful and/or supportive. Two studies of the widowed, moreover, found that the majority described their spouse's funeral as helpful to their adjustment (66, 68).

I think the different studies now available to us show that the contemporary funeral can be functional to the extent that it recognizes the separation and integration issues associated with a death. I would argue, given our new-found understanding of the social and psychological dimension of loss and grief, that we should put greater emphasis upon the funeral as a rite of separation and integration and less emphasis upon the funeral as a rite of incorporation. To do so is not only to recognize the social and personal values to be derived from such an orientation, but it is to recognize also the decreasing relevancy of the funeral as a rite of incorporation. I would think that in appreciating this subtle but, nevertheless, significant shift in emphasis, we will do ourselves and our fellow citizens a considerable service.

Of course, our citizens must not only be competently and adequately served; they must also be protected from malpractice. They must have freedom of choice as well. Ultimately, a client's relationship with the funeral director must be based on trust.

There is increasing scholarly evidence today that can stand beside social custom for the belief that a funeral is a ceremony of value for the mourner, just as skilled funeral directors can be and are of assistance to the bereaved—socially and emotionally.

Our society is experiencing rapid social change, particularly with regard to death and death customs. We are presently in the process of defining and redefining grief, bereavement, and loss to say nothing of death itself. Comparable issues face us with respect to the elderly and the dying. The role of the funeral director is an emergent one.

It would be beneficial if the funeral director would come to be seen as a participant in a community's mental health network. This view would not only support those practices which historically have served human needs, but it would also strengthen the movement within the funeral service itself and play a positive part in helping with the burdens of bereavement. Perhaps, most of all, by treating funeral service people as one would normally treat other professional and paraprofessional health care givers, trust in the good intentions of others is expressed. To do so might be to remove, finally, the admonition: *Caveat Emptor* (let the buyer beware) that has been held over the funeral director's head. I would hope to see that warning replaced by the historic medical directive, *Primum non Nocere* (above all, do no harm)—an admonition to which we might all pay more heed.

The ceremonialization of death compels the recognition that a death has occurred. In a society where there is a strong tendency for many to respond to the death of another by turning away, the funeral is a vehicle through which recovery from the crisis of bereavement can be initiated. The funeral, importantly, is also a ceremony that recognizes the integral worth and dignity of a human being. It is not only a sociological statement that a death has occurred, it also proclaims that a life has been lived.

CONCLUSION

What of the future of the funeral? The funeral, as well as every other social practice invented by human beings, is subject to change. Mourning rites and funeral customs have not been carved in concrete nor do they exist in a vacuum. Rather, they are contained within a cultural context which they help delineate as well as reflect. American funeral customs and practices have continued to evolve, since colonial days, from both internal and external social forces. Following World War II, for instance, the black hearse, the black tie, the black armband, the wreath on the door, and other public signs of death, loss, and grief disappeared from public view.

In the last two decades, however, we have not only observed appreciable changes within traditional mourning ceremonies—the white pall of the Catholic funeral mass and the emergence of the humanistic funeral, but we have also witnessed extensive public criticism of funeral practices from without. Such criticism provoked direct intervention of the government through the instrumentality of the Federal Trade Commission which ultimately effected a bill requiring funeral directors to abide by rules of conduct and business procedures designed to protect the public's interest.

Change can also be observed in the public's behavior as well. In San Francisco, Los Angeles, New York, and other major cities across the United States, upwards of 25 percent of the deaths annually go unreported in the obituary columns of the daily newspaper (72).

In San Diego County, a contemporary scenario for the disposition of the dead that is now practiced in almost one-sixth of all deaths in that area is as follows. Upon the declaration of a patient's death, the body is removed to the hospital morgue; an organization called Telephase is notified; the body is picked up at the morgue and enclosed in a rubberized bag; it is transported in an unmarked station wagon to a crematorium; the body is cremated, and the ashes are placed in a cardboard or plastic container for storage, dispersal, or delivery to a designated recipient; the legal survivor is later billed. Similar services are now appearing in other cities across the country. Indeed, cremation in particular as an alternate form of disposition to earth burial is on the increase all across the country. While the practice still varies considerably— from approximately 10 percent of all deaths in Minnesota to 20–30 percent on the Pacific and Atlantic coasts, there is little doubt that with the Catholic church conditionally lifting its ban on cremation that it can be expected to continue to gain in acceptance.

But another more serendipitous factor may come in to play—AIDS—a new, aggressive, incurable illness. While AIDS is not contagious in the normal course of human interaction, it may, nevertheless, by reason of the fear that it is generating among the American public, result in mandatory changes not only in our funeral customs but in many other social practices as well. Only time will tell whether AIDS will have the same relative impact on contemporary society and on the funeral that the Plague did during the successive centuries that it ravaged the populations of Europe.

Talcott Parsons, the late distinguished American sociologist, believed that the emergent changes that have been observed in contemporary funeral practices are the result of the convergence of the social, industrial, and medical trends that have characterized the United States since the turn of the century. Advocacy of change in funeral practices, he argued, was natural and to be expected in a society that strives to achieve order, practicality, efficiency, and economy in all facets of life. Robert Blauner, another American sociologist, is even more direct in his analysis and prognosis. He argues that the dramatic changes that have occurred in society, particularly the piofound demographic shifts, have resulted in a situation in which the majority of persons who die are those who, for the most part, are no longer central to the stream of life. Their deaths have little consequence for the social order. Under such circumstances, Blauner argues, we should expect the American funeral not only to continue to change significantly—to continue to be diminished—but eventually to "wither away."

There is some evidence to support Blauner's contention that funeral customs, as presently practiced in the United States, could, rather than just "change," "wither away." A study of 558 bereaved persons conducted recently by the Center for Death Education and Research at the University of Minnesota showed that the death of an elderly parent is appreciably less disruptive emotionally, less debilitating, and socially less significant than is the death of either a spouse or a child. To be sure, adult children of the study (average age of 48) did mourn the loss of their parent—in some instances profoundly—but as a group the responses of the adult children were markedly different from the other two groups.

The study showed, for instance, that, compared to the bereaved parents and spouses, a significant proportion of the adult children reported the least amount of change in regard to such postdeath measures of adjustment as crying, depression, anorexia, insomnia, smoking, drinking, and hallucinations. They also reported the least amount of illness following their bereavement. Additionally, the surviving adult children not only reported being the least affected of the three groups on the different behavioral and physiological measures employed but also were found to be the least socially expressive of their respective losses. That is, they were least likely to conduct traditional funeral rites, least likely to view the body, and least likely to observe the anniversary of their parent's death.

The study showed further that of the three groups, the adult children were least affected by memories of the death of the deceased and least likely to be preoccupied with that memory. Finally, the adult children were least likely to be more appreciative of life following the death of their parents, to be helpful toward others, to enjoy life or their families more, or to be warm toward other persons. On the other hand, the adult children reported more personal guilt and more hostility toward others following the death than did the other two groups of survivors (73).

The constellation of feelings and behaviors demonstrated by the adult children of the study following the death of an elderly parent was characterized by diminished or transitory grief followed by limited postdeath activities. While the sample of adult children in the study is admittedly small, we may be witness to a potential for diminished interpersonal relationships that promises to grow more pronounced in the years ahead. Like the tip of an iceberg, the responses of the adult children suggest the magnitude of the changes that lie hidden below the surface of social practices. Although the tip in no way tells us of the iceberg's actual proportions, it does inform us of the iceberg's presence.

It is important to recognize that the mature adult child need not experience the grief reaction or the profound sense of loss that characterized the responses of the parents and spouses of the study. In modern society, the elderly are oftentimes defined differently from other age groups. They "have had their life." It is seen only as normal and natural that they die.

The following cases taken from the study (73) are illustrative:

Case A. The respondent, a 45-year-old male construction worker had the primary responsibility of attending to the death of his 79-year-old father after a long bout with emphysema. The father had planned in advance that his body should be cremated with no service of any kind. The son complied with his wishes. The respondent and one brother took "the last ride" with his father from the funeral home to the crematorium. At one point he looked into the furnace, which he regretted for a time. Later he distributed the ashes in a nearby lake, taking the ride alone with his father's ashes. At one point in the interview, after the respondent had denied experiencing any of the ordinary grief symptoms, the interviewer asked him what had helped him adjust to his loss. He replied by saying, "There was no adjustment required. I don't consider myself bereaved." When the interviewer asked him why he had chosen not to view the body, he said that he would have, "had the person been especially close, like a wife or a child." (pp. 31–32)

Case B. The respondent, a 42-year-old banker, described his feelings following the death of his 81-year-old mother after she had developed pneumonia, 5 months following nursing home confinement. He acknowledged no symptoms of grief but did note that he felt angry with his mother's physician. He felt that the doctor had gone to "extreme efforts to maintain her life after she developed pneumonia." (p. 32)

Case C. The respondent, a 51-year-old life insurance agent, was interviewed six months following the death of his 87-year-old father. The interviewer observed: "there was no evidence that the son was experiencing any of the ordinary grief symptoms." Both he and his father were members of memorial societies and the disposition of the body was by cremation. The respondent indicated that his father was nearly blind and had been declining in health. He could not think of any way in which his father's death had affected his life or the life of his family. He felt it was most important to "work out details in advance to spare the survivors." When the respondent was asked what had helped him adjust to his loss, he responded that, "there really wasn't any adjustment necessary, after all, he was 87 and we all have to go sometime." (p. 33)

The minimal ceremonialization following the death of a socially disengaged, elderly person may make sense at the personal level. Funerals, it is said, are for the living, and if the living are not seriously affected by the death of a family member, the need for traditional rites of passage may be little felt. A funeral, however, has traditionally had other functions besides disposing of a corpse or publicly acknowledging a death. As a social ceremony, it serves to bring together not only the members of a family but friends and representatives of the larger community as well. As it does so, it provides a socializing experience for the participants, particularly the young. As such, it serves as an important vehicle of cultural transmission.

The contemporary impulse to preclude funerals from society or to exclude children from funerals can have unintended consequences. In addition to cutting children off from direct expressions of love, affection, concern, and support at the time of a family crisis, it may also deprive them of the opportunity to learn about one of life's basic facts—death. The social meaning and intrinsic value of human life itself, moreover, may be implicitly denied by the failure to acknowledge our mortality.

REVIEW QUESTIONS

1. Describe the "manifest" and "latent" social functions of funeral rituals.
2. In what ways can funeral ceremonies be dysfunctional?
3. Identify factors that have contributed to negative views of the traditional funeral in the United States.
4. Describe the beneficial effects of the funeral for surviving family members and friends. In your opinion, is the viewing of the cosmetically prepared body necessary for the acceptance of death?
5. What is meant by "low grief" and "high grief?" Do you agree that these concepts can be related to the type of funeral the survivors arrange and hold?
6. Define the concepts of the funeral as a "rite of separation and integration" and as a "rite of incorporation." Given the research evidence to date, which type of rite seems more functional today? How would you explain this?
7. It is suggested that the funeral director be viewed as a participant in the network of services and support for the bereaved. In your experience, have funeral directors functioned in such a role? What kinds of factors would enhance such a role?
8. It is predicted that the traditional funeral practice in the United States will not only diminish but will disappear altogether. What basis is provided for this projection? Do you agree or disagree with this prediction?

REFERENCES

1. Van Gennep, A. (1961). *The rites of passage* (M. B. Vizedom & G. L. Caffee, Trans.). Chicago: The University of Chicago Press.
2. Radcliffe-Brown, A. R. (1952). Taboo. In *Structure and function in primitive society* (pp. 131–152). London: Cohen and West.
3. Evans-Pritchard, E. E. (1965). *Theories of primitive religion*. Oxford: Clarendon Press.
4. Hertz, R. (1960). *Death and the right hand* (R. Needham & C. Needham, Trans.). Glenco, IL: The Free Press.
5. Goody, J. (1962). *Death, property and the ancestors: A study of the mortuary customs of the Lo Dagaa of West Africa*. Palo Alto, CA: Stanford University Press.
6. Goody, J. (1962). Religion and ritual: The definitional problem. *British Journal of Sociology, 12*, 142–164.
7. Mandelbaum, D. (1959). Social uses of funeral rites. In H. Feifel (Ed.), *The meaning of death* (pp. 189–217). New York: McGraw-Hill.
8. Habenstein, R. W., & Lamers, W. M. (1963). *Funeral customs the world over*. Milwaukee: Bulfin.
9. Puckle, B. S. (1926). *Funeral customs: Their origin and development*. London: Laurie.
10. Bendann, E. (1930). *Death customs: An analytical study of burial rites*. New York: Knopf.
11. Malinowski, B. (1954). Death and the reintegration of the group. In B. Malinowski (Ed.), *Magic, science, and religion and other essays* (pp. 31 ff.). New York: Doubleday.
12. Durkheim, E. (1954). *The elementary forms of religious life* (J. Swaine, Trans.). London: Allen and Unwin.
13. Geertz, C. (1957). Ritual and social change: A Javanese example. *American Anthropologist, 59*, 32–54.
14. Gluckman, M. (1962). Rituals of rebellion in South-East Africa. In M. Gluckman (Ed.), *Essays on the ritual of social relations* (pp. 1–35). New York: The Humanities Press.
15. Kennedy is laid to rest on an open slope in Arlington National Cemetery. (1963, November 26). *The New York Times*, p. 2.
16. They came to mourn. (1968, April 19). *Time*, pp. 18–19.
17. Wolfenstein, M., & Kliman, G. (Eds.). (1965). *Children and the death of a president*. Garden City, NY: Doubleday.
18. Greenberg, B. S., & Parker, E. B. (Eds.). (1965). *The Kennedy assassination and the American public: Social communication in crisis*. Stanford, CA: Stanford University Press.
19. Bureau of Social Science Research. (1966). Studies of Kennedy's assassination. Washington, DC: Author.
20. Sheatsley, P. B., & Feldman, J. J. (1964). The assassination of President Kennedy: A preliminary report on public relations and behavior. *Public Opinion Quarterly, 28*, 189–215.
21. Mitford, J. (1963). *The American way of death*. New York: Simon and Schuster.
22. Harmer, R. M. (1971). Funerals, fantasy and flight. *Omega, 2*, 127–135.
23. Bowman, L. E. (1959). *The American funeral: A study in guilt, extravagance and sublimity*. Washington, DC: Public Affairs Press.
24. Fulton, R. (1961). The clergyman and the funeral director: A study in role conflict. *Social Forces, 39*, 317–323.
25. Fulton, R. (1965). The sacred and the secular. In R. Fulton (Ed.), *Death and identity* (pp. 89–105). New York: Wiley.
26. Center for Death Education and Research. (1971). *A compilation of studies of attitudes toward death, funerals and funeral directors*. Minneapolis: University of Minnesota.
27. Fulton, R. (1971). Contemporary funeral practices. In H. C. Raether (Ed.), *Successful funeral service practice* (pp. 216–235). New York: Prentice-Hall.

28. Humanae vitae. (1968, July 30). *The New York Times*, pp. 1, 20.
29. Pope speaks on birth control. (1968, August 2). *Time*, p. 54.
30. Particular criticism reported on birth control. (1968, August 9): *Time*, p. 40.
31. Particular criticism reported on birth control: 1968, October 4, *Time*, p. 57.
32. U. S. Bureau of the Census. (1986). Statistical abstracts of the US (106th ed.) (p. 106, Table 70). Washington, DC: U.S. Government Printing Office.
33. Monthly vital statistics report U.S. Bureau of the Census (Vol. 34[3]), (1985).
34. U.S. Bureau of the Census. (1960). Historical statistics of the University States, colonial times to 1957. Washington, DC: U.S. Government Printing Office.
35. Berardo, F. (1968). Widowhood status in the United States: Perspectives on a neglected aspect of the family life cycle. *The Family Coordinator, 17,* 191–203.
36. Fulton, R., & Gupta, V. (1974). *Psychological adjustment to loss.* Unpublished manuscript, Center for Death Education and Research, University of Minnesota, Minneapolis.
37. Solecki, R. S. (1971). *Shanidar.* New York: Knopf.
38. Ciocco, A. (1940). On the mortality in husbands and wives. *Human Biology, 12,* 508–531.
39. Cox, P., & Ford, J. R. (1964). The mortality of widows shortly after widowhood. *The Lancet, 1,* 163–164.
40. Frederick, J. F. (1961). The physiology of grief. *Dodge Magazine, 63,* 8–10.
41. Holmes, T. H., & Rahe, R. H. (1967). The social readjustment rating scale. *Journal of Psychosomatic Research, 11,* 213–218.
42. Kraus, A., & Lilienfeld, A. (1959). Some epidemiologic aspects of the high mortality rate in the young widowed group. *Journal of Chronic Diseases, 10,* 207–217.
43. Parkes, C. M. (1965). Bereavement and mental illness (part I): A clinical study of the grief of bereaved psychiatric patients. *British Journal of Medical Psychology, 38,* 1–12.
44. Parkes, C. M. (1964). Effects of bereavement on physical and mental health—a study of the medical records of widows. *British Medical Journal, 2,* 274–279.
45. Rahe, R., McKean, J., & Arthur, R. J. (1967). A longitudinal study of life-change and illness patterns. *Journal of Psychosomatic Research, 10,* 365.
46. Rahe, R., Meyer, M., et al. (1964). Social stress and illness onset. *Journal of Psychosomatic Research, 8,* 35–43.
47. Rees, D. W., & Lutkins, S. (1967). Mortality of bereavement. *British Medical Journal, 4,* 13–26.
48. Stern, G. et al. (1961). Alterations in physiological measures during experimentally induced attitudes. *Journal of Psychosomatic Research, 5,* 73–82.
49. Wretmark, G. (1959). A study of grief reactions. *Acta Psychiatrica Neurologica Scandinavica* (Supplement 136), 292.
50. Fulton, R. (Ed.). (1973). *Bibliography on death, grief and bereavement (1945–1973)* (3rd ed.). Minneapolis: Center for Death Education and Research, University of Minnesota.
51. Lindemann, E. (1944). Symptomatology and management of acute grief. *American Journal of Psychiatry, 101,* 141–148.
52. Weisman, A. (1972). *On dying and denying.* New York: Behavioral Publications.
53. Kübler-Ross, E. (1969). *On death and dying.* New York: Macmillan.
54. Bowlby, J. (1963). Childhood mourning and its implications for psychiatry. *Journal of the American Psychoanalytic Association, 11,* 500–541.
55. Bowlby, J. (1953). Some pathological processes engendered by early mother-child separation. *British Journal of Psychiatry, 99,* 265–272.
56. Young, M. et al. (1963). The mortality of widowers. *The Lancet, 2,* 254–256.
57. Bowlby, J., & Parkes, C. M. (1970). In E. J. Anthony & C. Koupernik (Eds.), *The child in his family* (p. 198). New York: Wiley.
58. Gorer, G. (1965). *Death, grief and mourning.* New York: Doubleday.

59. Fulcomer, D. M. (1942). *The adjustive behavior of some recently bereaved spouses: A psychosociological study.* Unpublished doctoral dissertation, Northwestern University, Evanston, IL.
60. Shand, A. F. (1914). *The foundations of character.* London: MacMillan.
61. Glick, I. O., Weiss, R. S., & Parkes, C. M. (1974). *The first year of bereavement.* New York: Wiley.
62. Mole, R. L. (1974). *Next of kin: A study of bereavement, grief and mourning.* Unpublished doctoral dissertation, Howard University, Washington, DC.
63. Binger, C. M. et al. (1969). Childhood leukemia: Emotional impact on patient and family. *The New England Journal of Medicine, 208,* 414–18.
64. Khleif, B. (1975). The sociology of the mortuary: Attitudes to the funeral, funeral director and funeral arrangements. In O. Margolis et al. (Eds.), *Grief and the meaning of the funeral* (pp. 37–46). New York: MSS Information.
65. Khleif, B. (1976). The sociology of the mortuary. In V. Pine et al. (Eds.), *Acute grief and the funeral.* (pp. 55–91). Springfield, IL: Thomas.
66. Winn, R. L. (1981). Perceptions of the funeral service and post-bereavement adjustment in widowed individuals. *National Reporter, 4,* 1–8.
67. Carey, R. G. (1979). Weathering widowhood: Problems and adjustment of the widowed during the first year. *National Reporter, 2,* 1–5.
68. Lieberman, M. A., & Borman, L. D. (1982). Widows view the helpfulness of the funeral service. *National Reporter, 5,* 2–4.
69. Cook, J. A. (1981). Children's funerals and their effect on familiar grief adjustment. *National Reporter, 4,* 1–2.
70. Cook, J. A. (1983). A death in the family: Parental bereavement in the first year. *Suicide and Life-threatening Behavior, 13,* 42–61.
71. Anglim, M. A. (1976). Reintegration of the family after the death of a child. In I. Martinson (Ed.), *Home care for the dying child: Professional and family perspectives* (pp. 144–167). New York: Appleton-Century-Crofts.
72. McReavy, J. (1980). N.F.D.A. paid obituary notice survey. Milwaukee: National Funeral Directors Association.
73. Owen, G., Fulton, R., & Markusen, E. (1982). Death at a distance. *Omega, 13,* 191–226.

Bereavement and Mourning

Donna Hodgkins Berardo

INTRODUCTION

Bereavement may be viewed as a state of loss of a significant other through death or as a process which individuals must work through or recover from. Grieving, the emotional response to bereavement, has been defined as a disease at worst (1) and as an important aspect of the process of adjustment to the loss. Several variables impact on the reactions that we have to the death of those we love: previous losses and coping strategies we learned from them, the intensity of the relationship we had with those who died, the type of death they experienced, the response of our own social support network, concurrent stressors during bereavement, as well as a variety of sociodemographic and cultural factors such as age, sex, religion, culture, and economic resources. This chapter explores and summarizes the research on these variables related to bereavement.

Preparatory Losses and Anticipatory Grief

How do we anticipate the changes associated with the death of significant others? If we daydream or logically consider the death of loved ones, we are likely to feel guilty or even afraid that thinking about it may cause it to happen (2, pp. 285–305). We may, however, partially prepare for the loss of an important person by considering various losses in our lives as a way to learn. Each of life's disappointments or failures can teach us coping strategies for succeeding to live with ourselves and balance our desired goals with actual achievements. There are normal losses associated with living that prepare us for the kind of grief that comes with the loss of people who are most special to us. One of these usual losses is the aging of one's physical self. Changes in appearance, physical activity, or endurance are a source of loss that can be grieved. Loss of more distant others can prepare us for the loss of someone close. Terminal illness can also prepare us by giving us a longer time to consider the loss before it actually happens. However, in caring for the terminally ill relative, caregivers must deal with their own anticipatory grief as well as the patient's.

Intensity of Relationship to the Deceased

Reaction to the death of another is intensified by the closeness of the relationship to the survivor. Fulton (3) distinguishes this reaction by his discussion of "high-grief" and "low-grief" experiences. High grief may be felt when one's child dies—at a point when many years of fruitful living were awaiting to be discovered. In contrast, low grief may be experienced upon the death of an older relative who has had a long and productive life. The more attached we are to those who die, the more intense is our feeling of loss. In this respect, grieving is an individual experience; hence, what constitutes low grief for one may be the major trauma of a lifetime for another. Likewise, an unresolved conflict between the deceased and the survivor may produce an especially anguished bereavement response (4). Bereavement studies appear to focus on the most intimate relationships. The least research appears to be on the grief responses to the deaths of siblings while the most often studied grief response is that of the bereaved spouse.

Major Role Changes Associated with Death

The assumption of most life roles is usually preceded by some degree of **anticipatory socialization** relative to those roles. We often have the time, the training, and the models to assist us in taking over the responsibilities associated with these roles. Widowhood or no longer having a spouse, however, are major role changes for which many arrive totally unprepared. A role exit associated with the death of a spouse or child is especially difficult when one is unprepared. To no longer perform the tasks associated with being a wife, or a parent, or a daughter who was a caregiver, can shake one's identity and create major adjustment problems. In addition, the individual may have to deal with the feeling of the total inappropriateness of the death of a young spouse or child. Because life is known to be finite, our expectations for ourselves and our loved ones not unexpectedly include living out the majority of the potential years of our species. Death of an aged parent is viewed as more appropriate and often with less shock than the death of a young individual. It is the sudden and unexpected death that requires special adjustment. For example, younger widows appear to have more difficulty adapting and are likely to need more psychiatric counseling (5) than older widows. When a number of friends' spouses have died, the older widow has a cohort of widows to help socialize her into the new role of widowhood (6). This same group of older widows also "help" new widowers adjust by bringing them casseroles and inviting them to group events. The widowers, in turn, can enjoy the attention associated with the imbalanced sex ratio, that is, the fact that there are more women than men over age 65, a factor which may facilitate their role transitions. In contrast, there is not a large cohort of experienced bereaved parents who can help newly bereaved parents deal with the loss of a child. Role changes are more dramatic with losses of younger people and are more likely to be associated with sudden unexpected deaths.

Sudden, Unexpected Death

While few people are actually prepared for the death of a person close to them, we know that sudden, unexpected death produces the most severe reactions (2, 7). Accidents are the major cause of death in the United States for people prior to age 44 (8). The sudden and unexpected loss of a loved one in an accident can cause a debilitating shock to survivors. One of the earliest modern death and dying investigators was Lindemann (9), a psychiatrist, who followed the bereavement experiences of the few survivors of a devastating fire in Coconut Grove in Boston in 1942. His detailed discussions of the reactions of the survivors to the unexpected death of their spouses and children provided recognizable symptoms which could be utilized in future research. Early investigations suggested that under such circumstances the bereaved usually recovered within six months to a year. More recent sudden-death survivor research has suggested that the bereavement reaction may last longer than had been previously assumed. For example, in a retrospective study (8) of survivors who had lost a spouse or child in a motor vehicle accident four to seven years ago, findings indicated that psychological distress continued for these people for years after the accident. The results suggest that the psychological impact of sudden loss remains evident for much longer than previously suspected. Depressed reactions to the loss of a child were significant for respondents on two out of three scales utilized by the researchers. Bereaved parents showed several coping difficulties including less ability to talk with their relatives about their loss. Over a third noted that they had felt depressed or sad all of the time for at least two of the years since the accident and almost a third reported depression for three or four days of the previous week.

Even higher figures of depression were measured for bereaved spouses (8). Over half said that they had experienced sadness or depression for at least two years since the accident; and one-third for three or four days of the past week. Bereaved spouses' general psychological well-being was similar to that of psychiatric outpatients. They felt much less optimistic about their future, not as confident about their own coping abilities to handle serious problems, and more worried about bad things that might happen to them.

The most important aspect of these results is that survivors were still actively dealing with their loss four to seven years later. Two-thirds of them had talked with someone about the loss in the past month. These findings suggest that long-term bereavement is a normal part of sudden loss and not as had been previously thought, an indication of failure of some individuals to cope. Parkes and Weiss (10) called this phenomenon the unexpected grief syndrome. They point out that people who do not have the opportunity to prepare for an unexpected loss may respond with disbelief and intense anxiety both initially and for a continued period of time.

The financial impact of sudden bereavement is also evident. For both grieving parents and surviving spouses, sudden death may be associated with a decrease in financial status. Bereaved parents and spouses in one study had a greater tendency to change jobs and experience a financial loss (8). Divorce—with all its resulting financial reductions—is higher among bereaved parents. For both parents and spouses, bereavement is often associated with a decreased financial status (8, 11). Younger adult survivors, especially those with some work skills and experience, are less likely to experience poverty.

GRIEVING AS A PROCESS

Bereavement for most survivors is experienced as a process. There are numerous viewpoints from which to examine the sequence and tasks of grief work. Researchers have identified various stages as markers for progress (10, 12-14). As the word "process" implies, there is a somewhat clear beginning: the death of the important other or the notice of terminal illness. The end of the process is not as clear, and investigators are in substantial disagreement on the length of time required to work through the painful loss experience and return to a normal life (15). In some cases, particularly among elderly widowers, the death of a significant other, especially a spouse, is the beginning of a downward spiral that may lead to the death of the survivor. For this reason, it is important to examine the bereavement process and identify physical characteristics, behavioral changes, and interpersonal and social changes of the survivors. Likewise, the special coping strategies that enable the bereaved to recover will give better understanding of this process.

Stages of Grief

Those who propose specific stages as a method for tracking the bereavement process have presented identifiable characteristics that many can follow. While these are useful in a general sense, caution must be taken when such information is applied to the individual case. These stages or conceptual models are only to be seen as guides. Careful assessment, along with specific probing, must be utilized before applying the labeled stage to a given survivor. Individuals may proceed along the suggested stages, they may get stuck or fixated in one phase, regress back to a former stage, skip part of the identified process entirely, or go through a period related to some intervening factor completely unique to their own situation and personal response. Professionals who assist the bereaved must proceed with caution when categorizing individuals into any particular stage. Survivor reaction to such assistance might cover a wide range—from a feeling of comfort that their responses are "normal," because others may feel the same way, to anger for being told how they should feel. The stages of grieving, then, should be seen as a useful way to group typical responses and not as specific to a given person. Survivors whose responses do not precisely fit the outlines of particular stages should not be seen as abnormal but merely as different. An abnormal or pathological response would be to become permanently disabled in some way and never recover. A few people do experience loss so intensely as to never develop coping skills, or their skills are so inept that they do not recover or do so with depleted physical and mental health.

Several researchers have proposed that grief work can be grouped into stages along a continuum on which one enters and exits the bereavement process. In general, the stage is defined as being the point during which the bereaved person most expresses the characteristics of the defined stage or point in development. The precise number of stages in this process varies by author from as low as three (12, 13) to as high as seven (14). Many of the definitions of the responses are similar.

The bereavement process can also be seen as a series of repeated grief experience (12). These waves or surges of emotion can come without warning and remind us that grieving continues for a long period. While the grief work can be put aside for a while, it is often continued at a later date. Three general stages of bereavement are described by Stephenson (12) to include reaction, disorganization and reorganization, and reorganization and recovery.

The **reaction** stage is the period of initial shock when news of the death is encountered. Shock is followed by numbness and a dazed lack of feeling. During this period, the absence of response allows the survivor to accomplish the necessary tasks associated with notifying other relatives and tending to the details of the funeral. To some extent, the initial reaction serves as a life-preserving buffer and may act to support the individual in emergency situations such as the death of a loved one who was in the car with you when an accident occurred. The shock and realization of such a situation could allow the survivor to achieve safety.

Another normal response during the reaction period includes bewilderment or trying to make some sense out of the loss. This is especially difficult when the loss is both unanticipated and defined as most inappropriate, as in the death of an infant. Once the loss is understood, a conscious or unconscious urge to recover the deceased follows. Crying out in sorrow over the lost person is not uncommon. The tension builds and the survivor gives in to the emotional overload of grief.

Anger is also a part of this reaction and may be directed at the dead for leaving the survivor behind or in such frustration. The grief-stricken person may blame God or an individual and by doing so relieve himself of guilt accompanying the loss. Recently bereaved parents may sense a failure of their responsibility to protect and care for a child. The need to blame someone else helps to assuage their own guilt at wondering if they could have done something to prevent the demise of their cherished offspring.

Hostility is another form of anger which may be expressed during the reaction phase. It is not usual for the hostility to be directed toward friends offering sympathy and support. It is, after all, they who are suggesting that the bereaved accept the loss when, in fact, he or she may not want to face the facts and reality of the death.

In the second stage—**disorganization and reorganization**—reality sets in, and the bereaved is disappointed that the loss cannot be recovered. Incapacitating despair may leave the individual with unfocused thoughts and inability to make sense out of old activities. Reasons or satisfaction for former actions may no longer exist, and they must be examined in light of their lack of meaning or painful association with the dead person. The bereaved may not be able to maintain organized patterns of activity and feel unsure of what to do with themselves.

The need to reevaluate actions and former patterns of living involves a process of internal reorganization. The characteristic loss of meaningful focus, helplessness, and uncertainty is often the result of feeling stripped of a part of the self. The bereaved may wish for someone to come and organize their lives. They may develop dependencies on those who offer help. The process of reorganization which emerges from such a painful and desperate emotional response is especially difficult because the grief-stricken person must dismantle the sense of former structure provided by the connectedness and activities surrounding the loved one. The feelings associated with this stage are complicated and often conflicting. To grieve is to pay respect to the dead. To give up grieving is to lose that respect and possibly feel guilty. To grieve is to live a tragic role. To give up grieving is to give up a position which offers us the respect of others. The bereaved may be especially overwhelmed by fearful feelings that a sense of identity is being lost or a sense of loosing one's mind.

In the **reorientation and recovery** stage, the person reorganizes the symbolic world and gives the deceased a new identity outside the world of the survivor. In giving the dead a new status, often in a new place such as heaven, the griever is enabled to continue in the old world. Funeral ceremonies are among those rites of passage that announce status changes of individuals. For the bereaved, the ceremony is for themselves as well as for the dead in that it signals the status change of both. Acceptance of the changes and the new perspectives on the world that are built during this stage are crucial to successful recovery. Grief becomes resolved when the individual is able to reintegrate with the world, interact openly with others, find new avenues for creative living, and take charge of life in an independent fashion.

Gorer (13) also described a similar three-stage response of bereaved individuals. The first few days, the bereaved experienced an initial shock along with loss of self-control, a decrease in energy, loss of motivation, bewilderment, disorientation, and loss of perspective. During this period, one is preoccupied with the activities of the funeral and the visitation of relatives and friends offering condolences. In the second stage of intense grief, common characteristics of the survivor included periodic crying and lack of understanding of the reality of death. This stage might last from several weeks to several months. At this time, the bereaved experiences the physiological symptoms associated with intense grieving—weight loss, difficulty sleeping, dreams in which the deceased person is present. Friends and family have concluded their sympathetic support, and the bereaved person is often alone to continue the grief work. In the final stage, the bereaved experience a gradual renewal of interest in life and acceptance of the reality of the death of the loved one, placing that reality in meaningful perspective with the survivor's life. The secondary symptoms of weight loss, intense dreams, and disturbing sleep patterns diminish and disappear.

Glick, Weiss, and Parkes (2) have described stages based upon their research. In the first few weeks, the widows surveyed experienced shock and disbelief, followed by weeping and crying out. For periods up to a year, the respondents continued to express a repeated review of events recalling how the death occurred. The recovery period generally occurred about a year after the initial bereavement.

Most stage theorists describe similar symptoms of shock, disbelief, periods of intense grief, anger directed toward the deceased and those who are sympathetic, guilt, withdrawal, disorganization, loneliness, reintegration, and some form of adjustment or acceptance. There are a few bereaved, however, who do not follow this pattern. Some experience unresolved grief and are never able to fully return to a normal pattern of living. These individuals may fall into several different categories. Some are those who experienced a sudden, unexpected, and inappropriate death (7, 10). Others include those who were in a relationship which involved considerable conflict. This type of grieving, reflecting a traumatic relationship, has been called the conflicted grief syndrome (10). Still others experience a chronic grief syndrome, manifested by those who had an excessively dependent relationship with the deceased and now feel incapable of surviving alone. As many as 12 to 15 percent of the surviving widows in one study were reported to have symptoms similar to clinical depression (16).

REACTIONS TO SPECIFIC DEATHS

Parental death. The most traumatic reactions appear to occur when the death is that of a spouse or a child. However, the most common type of bereavement for adults is that following the loss of a parent. The societal expectation is that death of parents will not be especially debilitating for adults. There is, in fact, some indication that parental death is associated with more thoughts of suicide, an increase in attempted suicide, and higher rates of clinical depression (17). Deaths of mothers appear to be more difficult for adult children to adjust to than deaths of fathers. This may be due to the mother's nurturing role and a feeling of greater closeness than felt toward the father. Another explanation might be that in most cases the father dies first, so when we lose the mother, we grieve more over her absence and the sense of having no parents left. Moreover, her death often provokes a resurgence of the feelings associated with the loss of the father (17). Generally, adult children are able to continue their own occupational and familial responsibilities and to recover from parental loss with minimal levels of disruption. For most, the dependent ties to their parents have long been dissipated, and they have been, for some years, involved in the demands of their own family. This means that a certain amount of emotional, if not physical, distance has already occurred between middle-aged children and their parents.

Sibling death. We do not know as much about adult reaction to the death of their siblings. We do know that sibs who no longer live near each other often visit and maintain lifelong influential relationships. Sibling rivalry may be continued throughout life and may cause guilt feelings upon the death of a brother or sister. Further, if the siblings are predisposed to the same genetic illnesses, a good deal of anxiety may occur as the survivor contemplates his own demise. Changes in the caretaker role of aging or ill parents may occur when the most responsible sibling dies. At the very least, the remaining sons and daughters are forced to reexamine their roles in the family structure (17).

Suicide. Over 27,000 people each year are reported to commit suicide in the United States. The number is considered to be a low estimate due to underreporting of the cause of death and the social stigma surrounding self-destruction. Many accidents, including drug overdoses and automobile accidents, are unreported suicides.

The relatives of suicide victims often must contend with special problems. If a note is left blaming someone for provoking the person to take his life, the reaction is even more difficult to resolve. At the least, there are feelings of rejection, abandonment, or inadequacies for not having realized the severity of the problems of the deceased or not having been able to save them. Some researchers (18) have noted a tendency for family survivors to search for a scapegoat to blame. This may allow an emotional escape of feelings of responsibility for the death.

Other bereavement reactions to suicide include creating a family myth or story about the nature of the death that can help the family better accept what has happened. In these cases, deaths are called accidents or illnesses. Another common reaction is fear that the same sort of "madness" that caused the family member to commit suicide may be prevalent in other family members. This fear may not be altogether unfounded. Research has shown that there is "a far higher than chance incidence of prior suicide in families of individuals who commit suicide" (17). Suicide survivors may need professional help in dealing with their loss. Because they often have had a conflict relationship with the deceased, more trauma and guilt may be felt than for those whose interaction with the deceased had been positive.

Ex-spouses. Very little is known about the reaction of former mates to the deaths of their ex-spouses. Grieving may occur even though the person's response may not be recognized by others. The bereavement associated with relationships that are not formally recognized by others is called **disenfranchised grief** (19). These relationships may include cohabitors, homosexuals, long-term lovers and mistresses and are characterized by lack of societal support and approval. The bereavement process for these individuals is further complicated by the clandestine nature of the relationship.

When a former mate dies after divorce, disenfranchised grief may occur, especially when spouses share friends and continue contacts because of children. To others, however, their relationship is over, even though, internally, a variety of strong emotions may persist. Many people react to divorce in much the same way they would to the death of their partner. One grieves over the failure of the marriage, the loss of the intimate relationship, the loss of contact of former in-laws, and the loss of one of the parents in the home for the children. The bereavement of divorce can be seen much like that following the death of a spouse with the major exception that little, if any, social support comes from friends and relatives. In a study comparing divorcees and widows, divorcees were more restricted in their relationships with others and had less favorable attitudes toward their spouses (20). While widows are given social support and sympathy, divorced women often feel discrimination and report a sense of alienation based upon the social stigma surrounding divorce. While widows are likely to sanctify their former husbands, no such illusions surround the feelings toward divorced husbands. In addition, widows often have fond memories to support their bereavement adjustment, while divorcees may see both the past and the present as grim.

It appears that if the ex-spouse has resolved the grief from the relationship in a normal period following the divorce, then the impact of the death of that former spouse will be minimal (19). However, if for various reasons a person fails to adjust to the grief associated with divorce, then apparently he or she will also mourn over the death of the former partner (4, 19). Among the difficulties revealed by former mates in one study were awkwardness or anger at the funeral, feelings of hostility in reaction to the sympathy expressed by family members toward the surviving current spouse, and enraged responses to newspaper obituaries of a husband which included the names of the children when the wife had custody.

CHANGES IN FAMILY CONFIGURATION

A death in the family almost always causes a change in the number and kinds of interactions among the surviving members. They suddenly realize that their responsibilities have changed. For the mother who has lost her husband and her children's father, a new role must be assumed as head of the household. She must be both parents and deal with her own grief while comforting her children. She must also continue patterns of kinship interaction with her husband's parents and her children's paternal grandparents.

The death of the last parent often places the oldest brother or sister at the head of the family structure to assist other family members in decision making or to serve as the family elder. Likewise, the death of a wife who is an only child may leave a middle-aged husband with responsibilities to two sets of aging parents who need a variety of assistance while his own adolescents need guidance. While most survivors move consciously into the new roles necessitated by the death of a relative, some find the situation oppressive and have difficulty coping.

Another type of bereavement reaction is characterized by the **absence of grief.** Daily life is carried on as though nothing is different. People exhibiting this response do not speak of the recent death experience and often cannot endure conversations that express sympathy. In such cases, the denial of the death is a way of avoiding the painful reality of their loss. This form of escape may be temporarily useful and assist the bereaved in reducing fears, give them time to think through decisions which must be made, and allow reality to creep in slowly (21). However, if grief is postponed too long, resolution is also put off and the bereaved are then unable to get on with living. For those who delay grieving for months or even years, it is common for physiological and psychological symptoms to intensify (17, 22). These symptoms may range from tenseness and short-tempered attitudes (23) to neurotic, psychotic, or even suicidal behavior (22). The elderly are particularly vulnerable to suicide as loneliness and social isolation increase upon the deaths of a spouse and friends (24, 25).

Loneliness and isolation. The older individual may become isolated as a variety of factors accumulate (26). The deaths of friends, siblings, or one's spouse can cause a significant decrease in available social partners. A drop in income, such as occurs in retirement, often changes social patterns—how often and where the retiree can go for recreation and leisure activities. A disease associated with aging can physically impair an elderly person so that driving is no longer possible or getting out of the house becomes difficult. Social situations can also expose one's frailties and prompt the elderly to withdraw to avoid embarrassment over incontinence or similar disorders. It is how such factors are evaluated and perceived as problems that make them sources of concern. How the older person identifies and utilizes resources, in order to keep the potential isolators from restricting his or her physical and social behavior, makes the difference in kind of lifestyle.

Resources to combat problems also change as one ages. Friends who can fill social time when a spouse dies also age and become infirm themselves. Funds set aside for retirement dwindle and the costs of living one's usual lifestyle increase along with rising medical costs. For those elderly who respond to isolating life events by disregarding personal appearance, overindulging in alcohol, or social withdrawal and isolation, the chances of being attractive to friends and new potential mates decrease. A downward spiral is likely to occur as the older individual struggles with the accumulating isolators.

In a study of 400 elders in Evanston, Illinois, Golant (27) found loneliness to be associated with several social factors. Lonely older people were more dissatisfied about how far their homes were from family and relatives, less likely to enjoy visits with their neighbors, more likely to be recently widowed, and less confident about having someone to give emotional support when they might need it. Those old people who saw their children infrequently, never, or who had no children were more likely to indicate they were lonely.

Friendships, a most important support structure in later life, become increasingly difficult to maintain. Many older people suffer the loss of friends through death and migratory retirement to sunbelt states. Infirmities of one's self and friends further complicate the continuity of friendships. The quality of the friendships change as some friends become forgetful or cannot maintain a reciprocal relationship. While reciprocity is a key ingredient of friendship, it is not necessary that all relationships carry a 50:50 exchange ratio. Friendships endure over time as mutual support structures. When the calamities of old age change the nature of the exchange, the initial reasons for the friendship fall away and only loyalties remain (28). It is the long and loyal friends that can offer the most comfort in the face of grief.

Providing help for isolated elders. The chances that elders will look for help for isolating conditions may depend upon several conditions. First, the older person is more likely to seek assistance if a physical disorder is painful and cannot be dismissed. Second, as mentioned earlier, isolators are cumulative, so the more isolated an individual already is, the less likely he will seek help. Third, the more available, known, and accepted the resources are, which could be of assistance to the elderly individual who needs help, the more likely he will use them. Fourth, if past experiences with seeking assistance have been negative or unhelpful, the older person is not likely to look for future help (26).

There is strong evidence that a variety of activities predict health and happiness among older individuals. The strongest predictors of better health and satisfaction among the individuals followed in the Duke longitudinal studies of normal aging (2) were continued leisure activities, secondary group activities, interaction with others, and the total accumulation of social activities.

IMPACT OF BEREAVEMENT ON HEALTH

A variety of the symptoms associated with bereavement have been noted in previous sections. The links of physiological, behavioral, cognitive, and perceptual disturbances and the stress of bereavement are not yet conclusive. However, a widely held hypothesis proposes that social relationships are important in regulating many of our biological and sociobehavioral responses. An examination of the research that supports this stance reveals several important connections between the loss of significant others and health.

A special committee for the National Institute of Mental Health (NIMH) reviewed the major literature on the impact of bereavement on health and concluded that men are more at risk for health problems following the death of their spouse than women (17). First, there is an increase in mortality for men under age 75, especially in the first year of bereavement. These mortality rates remain high for as long as six years following the death of their wives for men who remain unmarried. For women, mortality rates remain unchanged for the first year after the death of their husbands. There is some suggestion that the second year may be dangerous for women (17), but the results of research are inconclusive.

Suicide rates, which were tracked since the 1940s, show an increase in male suicide in the first year of bereavement both for men who have lost their wives as well as for men whose mothers have died. The increase of suicide among widows is slight. In addition, studies which have focused on the survivors of people who have committed suicide have shown a propensity for the surviving mates to also be susceptible to suicide (17). This may be due to homogamous mate selection, that is, that people with similar psychiatric makeups are drawn toward and marry each other.

A third imbalance between male and female survivors includes the fact that the risks of dying from accidents, cardiovascular disease, and even some infectious diseases such as influenza are greater for bereaved widowers. For widows, the death rates rise from cirrhosis of the liver (p. 39). The impact of the stress associated with the traumatic shock of the death of a loved one is not completely understood. However, there is some evidence that such experiences may have a long-range negative influence on the immune system.

Several other variables are important for their impact on both widows and widowers. For those who already use alcohol, tobacco, tranquilizers, or hypnotic medication, the likelihood of increased use or abusing these depressants is greater among the recently bereaved. Depression is a common symptom of bereavement and in up to 20 percent of the recently widowed may continue for up to a year or more. Risk factors are greatest among those who were already in poor physical condition, had low mental health, abused or overused alcohol and other substances, and had few social supports. The best protection from adverse effects caused by widowhood appear to be a strong social support system (real or perceived) and remarriage.

Changes in Marital Status

Of all life change events, changes in marital status have been noted to have the most impact on changes in health status (30). Such changes may include divorce, loss of a spouse, or remarriage. Older men are twice as likely to be married as older women with rates of 79 percent versus 40 percent respectively (31). Numerous studies have revealed that changes in marital status among the elderly have an especially pronounced effect on both health and life satisfaction (5, 33–35). It appears to be the *undesired* change from married to single status that causes changes in perceived health rather than married status per se. Those never married appear to have better health than the married and have higher levels of perceived health with fewer days ill in bed. The never-married also have higher educational levels which is also related to fewer days in bed with illnesses (34).

Widowhood also appears to affect perception of one's health. Half of the women over aged 65 are widows; there are over five times as many older widows as older widowers (31). It appears that, for many, health perception drops immediately upon widowhood (35–39). In addition, when examined by physicians, the objective, or real, health status of recent widows and widowers is also lower. Older women report more disabilities and physiological disorders than men (35). This may be due to the greater concentration of older women and to the better reporting of females (40). However, older women generally rate their overall health status as higher than do men (37, 39). Clearly, the loss of a spouse has a greater health impact on older men than on older women. Younger women have more difficulty coping than do older women (5).

In a study of over 7,000 low-income, aged, and disabled elderly who were followed over a 14-month interval, Fenwick and Barresi (34) found that the deterioration of health status occurs rather immediately after the loss of a spouse but tends to stabilize over time for those who have previously lost a mate. The widowed or single elderly in the study spent more time in institutions than those who had been married a long while, and males spent more time in hospitals than females.

In a longitudinal study of over 4,000 widowers aged 55 years and over, Parkes (32) found that over 200 died within the first six months of the death of their wives, a rate that was 40 percent above the mortality rate of married men their age. In that first six-month period, the highest increase in mortality was among those dying from coronary thrombosis and other arteriosclerotic and degenerative heart diseases. The second greatest increase was among those who had other heart and circulatory diseases. These two categories alone accounted for two-thirds of the increase in mortality rates among men in the first six months of bereavement. This has been called the "broken heart syndrome" and suggests that bereavement may act as an "aggravating or a precipitating factor in coronary thrombosis" but not necessarily the cause of death (32, 42–43).

Broken Heart Syndrome or Complex

Studies have found that a death in the family increases the probability of premature demise among the remaining members. Typically, these studies match and compare families who have suffered a bereavement during the past year with families who have not. The results generally reveal a mortality rate among surviving family members significantly greater than that observed among families who had not encountered a loss. Moreover, one of these investigations found that the death rate increased among those relatives closest to the deceased i.e., remaining spouses and children (43). The same study also revealed that a) the subsequent risk was significantly higher for males than for females, and b) if the death was sudden, accidental, or unanticipated, the death rate among the survivors doubled.

One explanation offered to account for the above findings again involves the notion of a "broken heart" syndrome and suggests that loneliness and grief can so overwhelm certain individuals as to fatally affect their hearts (41). The idea that severe grief can somehow damage the heart is actually an old one that can be dated to antiquity. It gained some scientific credence from evidence that survivors, usually a spouse, sometimes die rather unexpectedly following the loss of a mate. Autopsy reports would then reveal that the survivor had succumbed to some form of heart disease. Sometimes, the death of a spouse aggravates an already present heart condition in the survivor, leading to fatal result. Such instances add empirical support to our intuitive perception that the emotional and psychological consequences of loss and severe grief can affect both our ability and our will to live. Indeed, there is evidence of a psychological state termed the "giving up complex" (1). A person reaching this psychological state feels that he is no longer able to cope with a situation and then develops strong feelings of helplessness and hopelessness. At this point, he becomes unusually vulnerable to the onset of disease and even death. For example, if he is predisposed to diabetes, then the disease may appear during this moment of stress (42).

The phenomenon of the broken heart syndrome, while being increasingly recognized among the lay and scientific community alike, does not yield to a simple pattern of etiology (33). The most recent evidence suggests that people who die from a "broken heart" have reduced body defenses—a condition caused by their grief. In a study of men whose wives had died of breast cancer, it was found that they experienced a significant decline in the activity of lymphocytes (white blood cells involved in the body's disease-fighting system) (44). This decline occurred shortly after the wife's demise and failed to return to its former level even after a year had passed. While other studies have shown that bereaved persons feel sicker, spend more time in hospitals, and use alcohol, cigarettes, and tranquilizers more than persons who are not bereaved, such was not the case here. Rather, the subjects "did not report major or persistent changes in diet or activity levels or in the use of medications, alcohol, tobacco, or other drugs, and no significant changes in weight were noted" (p. 337).

Diminished lymphocyte activity, then, may be an important element in the biosocial chain of reactions to the bereavement process which influences the health of survivors. This finding adds to the accumulating evidence that immunity may be altered as a consequence of the bereavement experience and, thereby, contribute to subsequent morbidity and mortality. While it has not been established that bereavement can directly cause disease, the evidence suggests that loss reactions do contribute to the epidemiology of stress-related diseases. The processes by which this occurs are not yet well understood, but the idea that grief and a broken heart can cause premature death is gaining acceptance among the lay and scientific communities.

Other explanations offered to account for the increased mortality risk of surviving spouses can be summarized as follows (46). a) *Homogamy.* The idea is that "there is a tendency for the fit to marry the fit, and the unfit the unfit," with the latter situation producing a kind of marital association through disease; b) *Common infection.* This suggestion is made on the basis of some evidence that both the husband and the wife may succumb to the same infectious disease. This notion of mutual infection may have some validity, for example, in the case of tuberculosis, influenza, or pneumonia; c) *Joint unfavorable environment.* The suggestion here is that the unfavorable environment which led to the demise of one spouse may significantly influence the death of the other; d) *Loss of care.* This hypothesis is that, for a variety of reasons, the adaptation of the survivor may be more difficult for the husband, especially the older husband. Several researchers have suggested that the widower's ability to resist disease is impaired by the loss of care and attention formerly provided by his wife. Young, Benjamin, and Wallis (45), for example, speak of the widower becoming "malnourished" following the demise of his spouse. Kutner et al. (46) offer a similar explanation, noting that:

A lifetime of close association with a woman whose complementary activities form the basis of a home now requires the most basic revision for which the widower may be wholly unprepared. . . . The viniculum that is marriage is disengaged by death and the widower may find himself incapable of remaking his life into an integrated whole. (p. 63)

The older widower becomes vulnerable to demoralization and incapacitation in the absence of the socioemotional support provided by the former spouse; e) *The desolation effect.* In a related fashion, some researchers make a distinction between isolation and desolation, with the latter viewed as having the more deleterious consequences for the survivor (47). In general, isolation refers to the state of being separated from others, of being alone. Desolation, on the other hand, refers to feelings of abandonment and loneliness. Survivor adaptation, it is argued, is impeded by intense or prolonged states of desolation. These conditions of unaltered sadness and melancholy presumably have the consequence of diminishing the normal probabilities for survival. Perhaps it is for this reason that most societies have instituted rules and rituals designed to reintegrate bereaved persons and to assist them in making a satisfactory adjustment to their new status.

The above suggests that grief can carry with it the potential for early demise. However, as we have noted, research has consistently shown that the loss of a spouse is much more devastating to men that it is to women. That is to say, men whose wives have died are much more likely to die much earlier than men of the same age who are still married. One of the most recent studies indicates that the death of a husband, on the other hand, has little or no effect on the mortality rate of wives (48). It also noted a link between marriage and longevity by finding that remarriage increased a male's chances of living longer. The study involved a 12-year survey of more than 4,000 widowed people age 18 and above. For both sexes, the impact of spousal loss was slight during the first year. However, in the ensuing years, widowed men had a 28 percent greater mortality rate than their married male counterparts; between the ages of 55 and 65, this mortality rate was 60 percent higher.

How does one account for the higher mortality among widowers? Why are women less affected by the loss of a husband? The researchers speculate that "missing a spouse affects a man's quality of life in so many, many ways . . . that, even if he joins a club or some other social activity, something is always going to be missing—someone to pay attention to him, to go out with him" (49). They note that the effect of the wife's death on the husband appeared to reflect a chronic, long-term problem of being alone, rather than an immediate response to the death itself. Women, on the other hand, may simply have greater capacities for adapting to change. In other words, it may be "that the same physiological and psychological differences that give females greater longevity than males also act to make females more resistant to the stress of widowhood" (49, p. 809). In addition, it may be that women socialize other women into widowhood networks, and this has positive consequences (6).

Social factors may also play a significant role in the higher mortality risk of males and help explain their greater vulnerability to the stress of being a widower. For example, in one study that compared the critical problems confronting an aged, married, and widowed group, the widowers emerged as the most socially isolated subjects (50, 51). This was especially true among those who were older, relatively uneducated, and residing in a rural environment. Another factor that led to social isolation was poor health, which sometimes caused a widower to be confined to his home and, consequently, limited his social contacts. In addition, in comparison to other marital statuses, widowers were *least likely* to be living with children, to have a high degree of kin interaction or to be satisfied with extended family relationships, to receive from or give to children various forms of assistance, to have friends either inside or outside the community, or to be satisfied with their opportunities to be with close friends. Further, they were *least likely* to be church members or to attend church services or to belong to and participate in formal organizations or groups. Obviously, the cumulative consequences of these conditions would lead to an insufficient amount of stimulating and rewarding social interaction. Younger male survivors, on the other hand, usually are able to avoid these problems through remarriage.

Remarriage and Mortality Risk

Indeed, remarriage may have life-extending potentialities. For example, in the study cited earlier (52), in addition to finding that for both sexes, mortality rates were significantly higher for those who lived alone, they also found that, for most age ranges, the mortality rates among remarried widowers were significantly *lower* than the rates among married males (p. 805). Unfortunately, the causes for these differences have not been pinpointed. The researchers found some support for both the *selectivity hypothesis,* which argues that the healthy remarry and the sick do not, as well as for the *social support network hypothesis,* which argues that remarriage provides conditions for care and support that are effective in ameliorating the effects of bereavement and thereby reduces mortality risk.

It has long been known, of course, that sex differences in mortality consistently favor females. Indeed, the greater longevity of wives is one of the major factors underlying the growing population of widows in the United States (53, 54). One way that husbands might decrease this greater mortality risk, vis-a-vis wives, then, is to marry a younger woman.

BEREAVEMENT OVERLOAD

Older people often suffer from a succession of bereavement experiences. The many losses suffered as a result of aging—decreases in income, physical loss, social psychological losses—add to the bereavement experience. It is especially difficult for the older person to find substitutes for losses, particularly if it is the death of a middle-aged child, or the loss of their home and some of their cherished possessions due to decreased income. We have noted that some older people even grieve over social, economic, and physical restrictions such as not being able to get out as much as they had when they were younger. The body itself may be a source of grief. A stroke, for example, could leave them partially paralyzed.

The older person's grief work may never be completed due to multiple losses. If, as some authors have suggested, it takes a year or even two years to recover from the loss of a loved one, it may in contrast take an elderly person much longer, and, in fact, they may never recover from the death of a marriage partner of 40 years or more. The multiple losses of spouse, aging friends, associates, and sometimes middle-aged children can cause **bereavement overload.** This may prevent the person from "catching up" on their grief work and bringing normal closure to the bereavement process.

Reactions may include a variety of responses. For example, the elderly widower might try to find an appropriate replacement for the lost partner. Many widowers do this within a relatively short time after the death of their spouse. Others try to lose themselves in their work or some other activity. This may be difficult for those who are retired. They may choose just to take these emotional blows on the chin and just bear them. Still others may disengage and pass up chances to get reinvolved because of fear of losing significant others again. Some may have personality problems and other negative reactions including acute paranoia (55).

HELPING MOURNERS

More attention has been paid recently to ways to assist bereaved individuals in coping with their loss (2, 57). The ceremonies and visitation rituals following death help the bereaved person to examine the reality of their loss and to express their feelings about it (57, 58). Anxiety and fear are some of the normal feelings which may be revealed. Grieving would be facilitated by factors which promote security and offer a sense of safety while concepts that suggest uncertainties or danger make grieving more difficult. Positive suggestions of safe places, helpful or close people, and comfortable situations should be offered in conversations.

Recently bereaved people may find home to be the best and the worst of places. It represents both one's place of retreat and comfort as well as the continued reminder of the loved one lost who once lived there. Nevertheless, bereaved people should be encouraged to stay in their home and keep it if possible. Those who have felt that they couldn't cope in the home without the loved one often do worse in less familiar surroundings. A brief visit for a change of environment may help introduce some distance from the turmoil of coping with the memories in the familiar surroundings, but a permanent change is not beneficial early in the bereavement process.

Safe people who are known to be supportive should be mentioned in discussions with the bereaved. These may include family, friends, and others who may be assisting the survivor. Emotional support comes from those who are willing to be involved and actively protect the grieving individual, not from those whose only concerns are expressed as pity. Such expressions of pity may leave the bereaved feeling even more weak and insecure.

Likewise, safe situations to be recalled to the mourner are those shared happy times of the past. New situations to suggest should be those which are simple and clear cut and that do not tax the individual's emotional resources. A neighbor might suggest that the new widow or widower to come over for a visit when things are getting difficult or to call her to drop over for coffee. These suggestions offer both support and an escape route from excessive overwhelming feelings.

Some researchers have studied the actual types of statements made to bereaved individuals and whether they made them feel supported and understood, or alienated and hurt. Davidowitz and Myrick (56) analyzed statements from a small sample of "caring" persons and their impact on the survivors. They found that statements could be placed along a continuum encompassing facilitative and nonfacilitative categories. Some examples they give are:

Facilitative	Nonfacilitative
Come with us now.	He (God) had a purpose.
You're being very strong.	I know how you feel.
It's okay to be angry at God.	Time makes it easier.
It must be hard to accept.	You have to keep on going.
That must be very painful for you.	You're not the only one who suffers.

Tell me how you're feeling.	That's over now, let's not deal with it.
How can I be of help?	The living must go on.
Go ahead and grieve.	She has led a full life.

Somewhat surprisingly, they found that 80 percent of all the responses made by "caring persons" could be categorized as nonhelpful and low-facilitative in nature. Their analysis revealed that most people are, in fact, not very helpful in what they say to the bereaved. These results led them to suggest that people learn to focus on high facilitative responses as a means of providing supportive encounters.

> When caring people learn to make more facilitative responses they are helping to build a bridge to the bereaved and enabling them to gently cross from the depths of despair to the shores of understanding, acceptance, and personal growth. (56, p. 41)

CONCLUSION

The process of bereavement and its accompanying emotional, physical, and social responses is unique to each individual. While there are similarities in the grieving patterns, the symptoms may be so strong as to increase one's own mortality or relatively weak when the experience involves mourning a more distant relation. While we know the most about closer deaths, that is, those of a spouse or a child, other intimate relationships of parents, siblings, and less socially obvious relationships like those of ex-spouse or secret lover need further investigation.

The recovery from the shock of a loss to normal functioning may be relatively short—such as a few months to two years or may be much longer. A few never recover from a significant loss. Even those who do regain normal functioning may experience surges or waves of grief periodically. One's age and sex are closely tied to the potential recovery period with older male individuals having more difficulty. Sudden, unexpected deaths also lengthen the recovery period and may, as in the case of suicide, cause guilt or blame for survivors.

There are some ways that we can assist survivors. Positive and safe verbal statements are among the first most-needed responses. Suggestions or transportation to other sources of assistance are also helpful, especially for isolated or potentially isolated elderly. Understanding factors associated with grief and the responses of bereavement enriches the potential for living and enhances our own human interaction.

SUMMARY

Bereavement, or the process of reacting and coping with the death of a person who is very important to us, varies considerably by individual circumstances. We might begin to prepare for bereavement by the coping strategies developed to adjust to less significant losses in life, such as disappointments and failures in not meeting certain goals we have set for ourselves.

The closer the emotional relationship to the deceased, the more likely that intense grief will be felt upon the death of that person. Since conflicted relationships are also emotionally charged, a similar intense grief response often occurs upon the death of a person with whom there has been violent disagreements or ambivalent feelings. Likewise, the bereavement experience is less traumatic when the loss is a person with whom we are more distant, or who we think has lived a full and productive life, and even with those who have experienced a lingering but terminal illness that has allowed both the dying and the survivors to adjust to the impending death.

Several adjustments occur during the bereavement process. Major role shifts are often evident for survivors. Socialization or learning how to competently perform new roles may be facilitated by others who have had to make similar adjustments. There are usually more helpers to assist an older person adjust to widowhood than there are to help parents adjust to the death of a young child or to help a young wife adjust to the death of her husband. Sudden, unexpected death of loved ones appears to result in more trauma, a longer psychological adjustment period accompanied by depression, and even financial losses for many of the survivors.

Several researchers have described the grieving process by identifying certain stages that are passed through in recovering from loss. While individuals names, number, and length of the stages vary by author, the symptoms are quite similar. The initial responses are shock, numbness, and disbelief. These and subsequent symptoms are eventually followed by the desire to recover the lost person. Crying out or overt hostility is not uncommon. From feelings of disorientation and disorganization, the bereaved eventually begin to recover and reorient their lives in new patterns of living. Since individual responses to death are quite unique, it is often impractical and sometimes counterproductive to apply a given stage theory to any one person's bereavement experience. The survivor's grieving process may be assisted by ceremony, friends, and other relatives. While the individual time frame varies in the bereavement process, there are some who exhibit an **absence of grief** and hold all emotional response tightly within themselves. Other less normal responses include **unresolved grief** where the individual is never able to cope in a normal pattern, **conflicted grief** where the relationship between the survivor and the deceased was highly ambivalent, and **chronic grief** which may occur when the survivor was excessively dependent upon the deceased.

Reactions to the death of specific others may also be different. Parental death is often assumed to be less traumatic than the death of a child or a spouse because it usually comes at the time of an adult's life which is consumed with work and child-rearing activities. Deaths of mothers appear to have more impact than the deaths of fathers. This may be compounded by the usual loss of the father first and the mother's death being the final loss of both parents. While less is known about the reactions to the death of siblings, the usual rivalry between sibs could result in conflicted grief. Another form of anxiety may occur when sibs have similar genetic makeup and one dies of a particular disease. Reaction to the suicide of a family member is surrounded by feelings of failure, blame, abandonment, or guilt. Families often develop a story about the death and agree to call it an illness or disease. They may often find a scapegoat to blame for the suicide. Another specific death reaction, for which we have little information, is the death of someone we feel close to, but the relationship is not socially confirmed. The reaction to the death of a secret lover, be it a heterosexual or homosexual relationship or an ex-spouse with whom emotions are still entangled, has been called **disenfranchised grief**. This type of grief is felt but is especially awkward for the survivor to express, thereby blocking the needed support from others. The deaths of specific others in a given family have a notable impact on the structure or configuration of that family. Role responsibilities of survivors may shift significantly when the demise of the last parent forces another family member to assume the role of authority figure or when the death of a spouse makes a mother a single parent.

The elderly are especially vulnerable to loneliness and isolation upon the death of a spouse and the accumulated deaths of old friends and loved ones. Declines in income and physiologic state may further isolate the older person. Assistance to the isolated elderly may be welcomed if they have not already become too withdrawn, if they are in pain, if the aid is well known to them, and if they have had positive experiences with past requests for aid.

The impact of bereavement on health includes higher mortality risks from cardiovascular diseases or suicide, especially for older males, and increased incidences of accidents and infectious diseases. Widowhood changes both an individual's perceived and real health status. Deaths following the demise of an especially dear other, usually a spouse, have been attributed to the **broken heart syndrome**. Bereavement not only alters an already poor health condition but may, in fact, decrease the body's defenses against diseases, thereby making grief-stricken survivors particularly at risk. Supporting social factors—such as living with others or remarriage—that assist the bereaved in adjustment diminish the vulnerability of the widowed.

The inability to recover from one grief period before the death of additional significant others can cause **bereavement overload**. Losing a spouse, a dear friend, and a child within a narrow time frame may result in compounded grieving which is most difficult to conclude.

Recently, more attention has been given to assisting mourners to recognize and come to terms with their grief. Guidelines for such help include staying in familiar surroundings, talking about safe people, places, and relationships. It is also important to give positive facilitative responses that allow the bereaved to express the normal emotions surrounding grieving.

While there are still areas of bereavement which need to be investigated, the results of previous research give us an overview of both common and unusual responses to the death of loved ones. Such knowledge concerning the process of mourning is useful in understanding the personal reaction to loss and enhancing our interactions with the living.

REVIEW QUESTIONS

1. Describe examples of losses in the experience of living that may help prepare us for the loss of a loved one.
2. Explain why death of a beloved family member may leave many unprepared for significant role changes. What factors ease the role transition for widows?
3. Discuss at least three reasons why sudden, unexpected death can cause great turmoil in the lives of survivors.
4. Why must social scientists and helping professionals be wary of applying a specific stage theory of grief to a given individual? In your opinion, what is a more appropriate approach?
5. What is the most common death that adults in the United States are likely to

encounter? Under what circumstances might it be particularly difficult to adjust to this type of death?

6. Describe at least four ways that bereavement impacts on the health of individuals.
7. Compare the adjustment process of older widowers with that of older widows. What factors account for the differences and similarities?
8. Describe two different levels of support that you might offer a bereaved person who is close to you. On the personal level, discuss what kinds of support you might give that person. On the community level, explain where you would suggest that the individual gain other assistance.

REFERENCES

1. Engel, G. (1977). Emotional stress and sudden death. *Psychology Today, 11*, 114, 118, 153.
2. Glick, I. O., Weiss, R. S., & Parkes, M. (1974). Dealing With Loss, *The first year of bereavement*. New York: Wiley & Sons.
3. Fulton, R. (1970). Death, grief, and social recuperation, *Omega, 1*, 27.
4. Raphael, B. (1983). *The anatomy of bereavement*. New York: Basic Books.
5. Parkes, M. C. (1964). Effects of bereavement on physical and mental health: A study of the medical records of widows. *British Medical Journal, 2*, 274–279.
6. Blau, Z. S. (1981). Aging in a changing society (2nd ed.). New York: Franklin Watts.
7. Ball, J. F. (1977). Widows grief. The impact of age and mode of death. *Omega, 7*, 307–333.
8. Lehman, D. & Wortman, C. (1984–85). The impact of sudden loss. *The Institute for Social Research Newsletter*, p. 3, 7.
9. Lindemann, E. (1944). Symptomatology and management of acute grief. *American Journal of Psychiatry, 101*, 141–148.
10. Parkes, C. M., & Weiss, R. S. (1983). *Recovery from bereavement*. New York: Basic Books.
11. Smith, K. R. & Zick, C. D. (1986). The incidence of poverty among the recently widowed: Mediating factors in the life course. *Journal of Marriage and the Family, 48*, 619–630.
12. Stephenson, J. S. (1985). *Death, grief, and mourning*. New York: The Free Press.
13. Gorer, G. (1967). *Death, grief, and mourning*. Garden City, NJ: Doubleday.
14. Kavanaugh, R. E. (1974). *Facing death*. New York: Penguin Books.
15. Wass, H., & Myers, J. E. (1984). Death and dying: Issues for educational gerontologists. *Educational Gerontology, 10*, 65–81.
16. Clayton, P. J., & Darvish, H. S. (1979). Course of depressive symptoms following the stress of bereavement. In J. E. Barrett (Ed.), *Stress and mental disorder*. New York: Raven Press.
17. Osterweis, M., Solomon, F., & Green, M. (Eds.). (1964). *Bereavement: Reactions, consequences, and care*. Washington, DC: National Academy Press.
18. Lindemann, E., & Greer, I. M. (1953). A study of grief: Emotional response to suicide. *Pastoral Psychology, 4*, 9–13.
19. Doka, K. J. (1986). Loss upon loss: The impact of death after divorce. *Death Studies, 10*(5), 441–450.
20. Kitson, G. C., Lopata, H. Z., Holmes, W. M., & Meyering, S. M. (1980). Divorcees and widows: Similarities and differences. *American Journal of Orthopsychiatry, 50*(20), 291–301.
21. Horowitz, M. (1982). Psychological processes induced by illness in grief and loss. In T. Millon, C. Green, & R. Meagher (Eds.), *Handbook of Clinical Health Psychology*. New York: Plenum.
22. Aiken, L. R. (1985). *Dying, death, and bereavement*. Newton, MA: Allyn and Bacon.

23. Bowlby, J. (1980). Loss: Sadness and depression—attachment and loss (Vol. III). New York: Basic Books.

24. Bock, W., & Webber, I. (1972). Suicide among the elderly: Isolating widowhood and mitigating alternatives. *Journal of Marriage and the Family, 34*, 24-30.

25. Osgood, N. J. (1985). *Suicide in the elderly.* Rockville, MD: Aspen Systems.

26. Rathbone-McCuan, E. & Hashimi, J. (1982). *Isolated elders: Health and social intervention.* Rockville, MD: Aspen Systems.

27. Golant, S. M. (1984). *A place to grow old: The meaning of environment in old age.* New York: Columbia Press.

28. Matthews, S. H. (1986). *Friendships through the life course.* Beverly Hills, CA: Sage Publications.

29. Busse, E. W., & Maddox, G. L. (1985). The Duke longitudinal studies of normal aging: 1955-1980. New York: Springer.

30. Holmes, T. H., & Rahe, R. H. (1967). The social readjustment rating scale. *Journal of Psychosomatic Research, 11*, 213-218.

31. Fowles, D. G. Profile of older Americans: 1984. Washington, DC: American Association of Retired Persons and the Administration on Aging, U.S. Dept. of Health and Human Services.

32. Parkes, M. C. (1969). Broken heart: A statistical study of increased mortality among widowers. *British Medical Journal, 1*, 740-743.

33. Parkes, C. M. (1972). *Bereavement: Studies of grief in adult life.* New York: International Universities Press.

34. Fenwick, R., & Baresi, C. M. (1981). Health consequences of marital status change among the elderly: A comparison of cross-sectional and longitudinal analysis. *Journal of Health and Social Behavior, 22*, 106-116.

35. Ferraro, K. F. (1980). Self ratings of health among the old and the old old. *Journal of Health and Social Behavior, 21*, 337-383.

36. Ferraro, K. F. (1985-86). The effect of widowhood on the health status of older persons. *International Journal on Aging and Human Development, 21*(1), 9-25.

37. Ferraro, K., Mutran, E., & Barresi, C. M. (1984). Widowhood, health and friendship support in later life. *Journal of Health and Social Behavior, 25*, 246-259.

38. Thompson, L. W., Breckenridge, J. N., Gallagher, D., & Peterson, J. (1984). Effects of bereavement on self-perceptions of physical health in elderly widows and widowers. *Journal of Gerontology, 39*(1), 309-314.

39. Stoller, E. P. (1984). Self assessment of health by the elderly. *Journal of Health and Social Behavior, 25*, 260-269.

40. Verbrugge, L. M. (1985). Gender and health: An update on hypotheses and evidence. *Journal of Health and Social Behavior, 25*, 156-182.

41. Lynch, J. J. (1977). *The broken heart: The medical consequences of loneliness.* New York: Basic Books.

42. Broken heart syndrome. (1967, October 23).*Newsweek*, pp. 70, 92.

43. Rees, W. D., & Lutkins, S. G. (1967). Mortality of bereavement. *British Medical Journal, 4*, 13-16.

44. Schleifer, S. J., Keller, S. E., Camarino, M., Thornton, J. C., & Stein, M. (1983). Suppression of lymphocyte stimulation following bereavement. *Journal of the American Medical Association, 250*, 374-377.

45. Young, M., Benjamin, B., & Wallis, C. (1963). The mortality of widowers, *The Lancet*, August, 454-456.

46. Kutner, B., Fanshel, D., Togo, A. M., & Langner, T. S. (1956). Five-hundred over sixty. New York: Russell Sage Foundation.

47. Townsend, P. (1957). *The family life of old people.* London: Routledge and Kegan.
48. Helsing, K. J., Szklo, M., & Comstock, G. W. (1981). Factors associated with mortality after widowhood. *American Journal of Public Health, 71,* 802–809.
49. Greenberg, J. (1981, August). Marriage and mortality. *New York Times,* pp. 1A, 16A.
50. Berardo, F. M. (1968). Widowhood status in the United States: Perspective on a neglected aspect of the family life cycle. *The Family Coordinator: Journal of Education, Counseling, and Service, 17,* 191–203.
51. Berardo, F. M. (1970). Survivorship and social isolation: The case of the aged widower. *The Family Coordinator, 19*(1), 11–25.
52. Blair, S. N. et al. (1984). Physical fitness and incidence of hypertension in healthy normotensive men and women. *Journal of American Medical Association, 252,* 487–490.
53. Fridman, M., & Rosenman, R. H. (1974). *Type "A" behavior and your heart.* New York: Knopf.
54. Lazarus, R. S., & Cohen, J. B. (1977). Environmental stress. In I. Altman & J. F. Wohlwill (Eds.), *Human behavior and environment* (Vol. 2) (pp. 89–127). New York: Plenum.
55. Pathologic behavior in old age may be result of "bereavement overload." (1969, June 15). *Geriatric Focus, 8*(12), 2–3.
56. Davidowitz, M., & Myrick, R. D. (1984). Responding to the bereaved: An analysis of "helping" statements. *Research Record, 1,* 35–42.
57. Doka, K. J. (1984–85). Expectation of death, participation in funeral arrangements, and grief adjustment. *Omega, 15*(2), 119–129.
58. Clark, P., Siviski, R. W., & Weiner, R. (1986). Coping strategies of widowers in the first year. *Family Relations, 35*(3), 425–430.

14

Death and the Law

Sheryl Schroeder Scheible

While most people are somewhat reluctant to confront the details of their own inevitable deaths, they usually have at least general notions regarding how they would like their bodily remains treated and to whom they would like to give their specific belongings. They may also have concerns about assuring that certain family members or friends will be physically or financially provided for. In death, as in life, legal restrictions may pose obstacles to the fulfillment of a person's desires. Failure to plan for death may not only thwart a person's intentions but may cause considerable delay and expense for family members and other survivors. It is critical, therefore, to plan for the practical aspects of death and to make arrangements in a manner that will be enforceable under the constraints imposed by the law.

THE IMPORTANCE OF LEGAL COUNSEL

Most of the law which regulates the disposition of a person's body and property upon death is state law, not federal law, and considerable variation exists between the laws of different states. In general, the law of the state where a person lives at the time of death controls disposition of the body and of property, although real estate (land and the structures thereon) is governed by the law of the state where the property is located. Thus, the laws of several states may have an impact on a particular individual's planning, as well as the laws of the federal government, which are applied nationwide.

While general statements can be made regarding legal planning for death, it is important for an individual to seek legal advice in order to comply with the relevant law and to execute properly the necessary documents to assure that the plan can be implemented according to the individual's desires and without unnecessary complications. Estate planners have expertise in developing individualized plans and in foreseeing contingencies that might otherwise be overlooked. Once a plan has been drawn up, it should be reviewed periodically because changes in the law or changes in a person's family, employment, or financial circumstances may alter the effect of the plan.

DISPOSITION OF PROPERTY

The Probate Process

Upon death, a person's business affairs must be concluded; debts, taxes, funeral and administrative expenses must be paid; and the property owned at death must be distributed to others. The management, administration, and transfer functions are accomplished through the probate process under the supervision of a court. Property dealt with by the probate court is the decedent's estate and is administered by the decedent's personal representative.

The title of the personal representative is executor or executrix, if the person is named by the decedent in a will, and administrator or administratrix if appointed by the court. The personal representative may be required to deposit a sum of money as bond to assure the proper performance of the administrative duties. Those duties include inventorying and collecting assets; notifying parties with claims; paying debts, expenses, and taxes; winding up business affairs; arranging for the preparation of documents; and distributing the decedent's remaining property to those entitled to take it, then closing the estate (1, pp. 37–39). Generally, an attorney will be hired to assist in the estate administration, even when no unusual problems arise. The personal representative's commission and the attorney's fees generally are calculated on a percentage of the estate assets. These fees, along with court costs, make the probate process expensive as well as time consuming.

Intestacy: The Effect of Failing to Plan for Death

A person dying without a valid will is regarded as having died intestate. Partial intestacy occurs if a will disposes of only part of the decedent's property. Intestacy statutes in every state describe, in order of preference, those who are entitled to take the decedent's estate as the decedent's heirs, sometimes referred to as next-of-kin. Unless a person falls within an express category as an heir under the statute, he or she may not share in the intestate estate.

Intestacy statutes are drafted and enacted by a state's legislators, based on their assumptions of how a typical person would want his or her property distributed (p. 91). The details of these statutes vary considerably between states, but general patterns of heirship exist (2). A surviving spouse and children are preferred heirs. If a child of a decedent has predeceased his or her parent, that child's children or other descendents take the decedent's child's share as representatives of their parent. In the absence of descendents, some states allow a surviving spouse to take the entire estate, while others apportion the estate between the spouse and the decedent's parents, if living. When a person dies leaving no surviving descendents or spouse, the property passes to the decedent's ancestors and descendents of those ancestors. In most states, parties related to the decedent through his or her parents have superior rights to those related through a more distant ancestor.

Except for a surviving spouse, only parties related to a decedent through bloodlines or by legal adoption are considered heirs; persons related by marriage, such as in-laws, or by informal relationships, such as cohabitants, foster children, or friends, are excluded from the intestacy statutes. The statutes often prohibit inheritance by persons only distantly related to a decedent. When an intestate person leaves no one who qualifies as an heir under the state's intestacy statute, the estate "escheats" or passes to the state.

A person may be described as an heir under the intestacy statute and still not receive a portion of the decedent's estate. A child who receives a portion of a parent's property during the parent's lifetime, for example, may have the value of the lifetime gift charged against the share the child otherwise would receive through intestacy (3, pp. 716–725). Additionally, certain actions may prevent an heir from inheriting in some states, such as an heir's killing the decedent or an earlier abandonment of or failure to support a dependent spouse or child (1, pp. 120–126). Furthermore, heirs may be totally or partially disinherited by a valid will.

Wills

Subject to exceptions enacted by most states to protect certain family members, a person is free to direct that his or her property be transferred to anyone according to the terms of a formal document, the will. A will must be probated to be effective. In many states, it is a crime to withhold a will from probate.

Every state has statutory formalities, which, when strictly complied with, authorize distribution of the decedent's estate by will. Although the will's statutes, like the intestacy statutes, vary considerably among states, some states will recognize a will that was validly executed in another state when the will is offered for probate in its own courts, even if it would not have been valid had it been executed in the state of probate (2, §2–506). The strict, formal requirements of the will's statutes are intended to impress upon the writer of a will, the testator, the importance of the act in order to protect against fraud or other improper motives of others, and to provide evidence at probate that will assure that the document is in fact the testator's will, representing his or her intentions (4). A document that does not comply properly with the statutory formalities will have no legal effect and the estate will pass under the laws of intestacy.

In general, any adult of "sound mind" is permitted to dispose of his or her estate by will. A minimum mental capacity is imposed to ensure that persons writing wills have an appropriate appreciation of their actions, their property, and the parties to whom they wish their estates to pass (3, pp. 232–241). A will may be invalid if another person unduly influences the testator to the extent that the document does not represent the testator's true intentions. Persons who would be entitled to take the testator's estate in absence of a will are allowed to contest the validity of the will in an attempt to overturn it.

A formal will must be attested to and signed by at least two witnesses, who will be required to testify at probate that the formalities were properly complied with. A person who will benefit by the disposition of the estate through the will should not witness the document. Although in most states today a witness with a personal interest in the will does not render the will itself invalid, the witness will usually forfeit the gift to him or her in the will, at least to the extent that such gift exceeds the share the witness would take if the decedent had died intestate.

Although almost half the American states recognize handwritten, unwitnessed wills, known as "holographic" wills, attempts to leave one's property through such an instrument are generally considered risky for several reasons (p. 14). First, the requirements for a holographic will vary among those states which authorize them. Words that are part of a printed form or that have been typed, rather than written in the testator's own hand, may not be given effect or may render the entire instrument inoperative. Specific information such as the date or place of the writing may be required, and some states require that a holographic will be found in a particular location at the testator's death. Second, a controversy may arise as to whether the document was actually intended to be a will or was merely a statement of intentions, a memorandum for a later will, or another type of writing that will not have the effect of passing property at death. A third danger is that even though the courts consider a testator's intentions to be of primary importance in construing the terms of a will, either attested or holographic, legal words will be given their legal meanings and imprecise language may frustrate the testator's intentions. Because of the risks involved, it is advisable to avoid holographic and form wills and to seek professional legal assistance in order to tailor the will to the individual's wishes and to assure that it will have the desired legal effect.

A will is regarded as "ambulatory," in that it may be changed or revoked at any time before the testator's death, so long as the requisite mental capacity exists and the intention to revoke is present. Terms of a prior valid will may be changed, deleted, or added by a codicil, an additional or supplementary document that complies with the same formalities of the will's statute. The codicil leaves the earlier will intact except for the changes and avoids the expense of having an entirely new will executed. A later valid will may revoke an earlier will, if not expressly by its language, at least to the extent its terms are inconsistent with the earlier will. The most recent valid will controls disposition of the decedent's property.

A will or a codicil usually can be revoked by physical act as well. The state's wills statute describes the acts effective to revoke a will and other types of actions will be ineffective to constitute revocation (2, §2–507). The proper acts must be performed personally by the testator, or at his or her direction and in the testator's presence, and must be accompanied by an intention to revoke, not a mere mistaken belief regarding the legal effect of the action or the facts which prompted it (5).

A will that has not been revoked properly will be given legal effect at the testator's death. Even though the actual will itself may not exist, its terms may be proved by other competent evidence, usually a copy of the original will. The safest route to revoke a will is to execute a new will that expressly states that all previous wills are revoked (1, p. 241). In many states, once a will has been revoked either by subsequent written instrument or by physical act, it may not be revived. Thus, the will must be reexecuted in order to reinstate its terms.

In many states, certain events in the testator's life may cause an earlier will to be implicitly revoked, totally or in pertinent part. Commonly, these events include subsequent marriage, marriage followed by birth of a child, or divorce of the testator (1, pp. 260, 267–268). A person experiencing important family changes should, therefore, seek legal advice as to the status of his or her will and the advisability of executing a new will.

Other specific changes in the testator's property or intended beneficiaries may affect how a will disposes of his or her estate. For instance, if the testator attempts to dispose of specific items of property by will and those exact items are no longer owned by the testator at death because of sale, gift, destruction, or any other reason, the intended beneficiary of those items generally will not receive a substitution or replacement, such as the insurance proceeds for destroyed or lost items or an asset that was purchased by the testator in exchange for a specific article of property (3, pp. 741–748). Furthermore, the testator's estate may have insufficient assets to pay debts and to fulfill all gifts. Unless the will itself indicates which gifts should fail first, the state's specified order of abatement will control and the testator's preferred beneficiaries may receive a smaller share of the estate than the testator intended (1, pp. 374–375; 3, pp. 754–763). Additionally, gifts to certain beneficiaries, usually the testator's children, made during the testator's lifetime, may count against the share of the estate that the beneficiary receives (1, p. 381). Finally, if a beneficiary predeceases the testator, the gift is said to lapse, and the gift will be ineffective, unless the state has an antilapse statute that preserves the gift for the deceased beneficiary's children or other descendants (3, pp. 777–786).

Protecting Family Members

In general, a person is free to leave his or her property to whomever or whatever he or she pleases. Disposition may be made to relatives, nonrelatives, or organizations. The laws of most states, however, protect certain close family members from disinheritance. Eight states—Arizona, California, Idaho, Louisiana, Nevada, New Mexico, Texas, and Washington—provide spousal protection under what is known as community property law. Community property doctrine regards marriage as an economic partnership. Under community property law, each spouse acquires an equal undivided interest in certain property, labeled community property, obtained during the marriage. Each spouse may also hold separate property, typically assets owned before marriage and obtained by gift or inheritance during the marriage. On death, the surviving spouse is entitled to one-half of the community property, while the decedent spouse may dispose of the other half and all separate assets without regard to the spouse, although the spouse may be named as an heir under the state's intestacy statute (6, 7). In 1985, Wisconsin (8) became the first noncommunity property state to adopt the Uniform Marital Property Act (9), which affords a surviving spouse benefits comparable to those available under the community property system.

In other states, ownership of property generally is attributed to the spouse who earns the funds for its acquisition. On death, that spouse may dispose of his or her own property, creating the potential that the surviving spouse who was not employed outside the home may be left destitute. To protect against that possibility, in earlier times, most states permitted a widow to receive dower, a lifetime interest in certain real estate owned by her husband during their marriage, although, then, spouses were not considered heirs of the decedent. A surviving husband could receive a comparable, but not identical, interest known as curtesy from his deceased wife's estate. Today, most states include spouses as heirs of the decedent upon intestacy and have replaced dower and curtesy with a statutory elective share (10, pp. 540–542). The elective share allows a surviving spouse to demand a specified portion of the estate, often similar in size to the intestate share, if the spouse has been left a smaller portion or nothing by the decedent's will. Elective share statutes are premised on the idea of protecting dependent surviving spouses from being left destitute but are available to any surviving spouse without inquiry into the actual financial condition of that spouse (11, pp. 395–400). In some jurisdictions, additional protection is afforded the surviving spouse and, sometimes, minor children of the decedent in the form of entitlements to certain types of property, such as personal belongings and household articles, portions of the decedent's unpaid wages, rights to the family home, and support allotments from the estate during the probate process (1, pp. 391–394).

Unlike the preferential treatment afforded a surviving spouse, almost every state permits a testator to leave nothing to his or her children, regardless of their age or actual financial or physical dependency. Most states protect children from inadvertent disinheritance to some extent. However, statutory provisions allow specified children to demand a share equal to the portion the child would have received from the parent's estate upon the parent's intestacy when they are not expressly or intentionally omitted from the parent's will (12). Usually such statutes apply only to children who were born after the last will was executed or to those who were inadvertently omitted from the will. The statutes generally apply to the testator's children born out of wedlock and adopted children, as well as those children born of a legal marriage (2, §§2–109, 2–302). A child born alive to a decedent's spouse within nine lunar months of the testator's death is presumed to be the testator's child and receives the same inheritance rights as other children. The best practice is to acknowledge all the testator's children in the will and either specifically provide for or disinherit them (1, p. 448).

Gifts to minor children pose additional problems because it is often necessary for a guardian to be appointed by the court to manage, control, and account for the child's property until he or she becomes an adult. Gifts to an incompetent adult are treated similarly. Use of guardianships incurs further expense and administrative responsibility. Additionally, investment and use of the guardianship property, in addition to expenditure of funds, may be severely restricted (13). Alternatives to a guardianship may be achieved by careful legal planning. For instance, the testator may prefer to leave a gift directly to a child's living parent for the child's benefit or to establish a trust fund or other device to avoid the time, expense, and restrictions involved in a guardianship (14, pp. 231–236). Most states have enacted statutes authorizing relatively small gifts to be made directly to a minor's legal custodian for the child's benefit, without the appointment of a guardian (2, §5–103).

Will Substitutes

In order to avoid the expense and delay of the probate process, a person planning for the disposition of property upon death may desire to transfer many or most of his or her assets during life to keep them out of the probate estate (15). Under a variety of formats recognized by many states laws, it is possible and legal to make transfers which give possession and complete ownership rights to anther at the property owner's death, while allowing the owner to retain part or most of the benefits and control of the property until that time. Because such transfers, when effective, are functionally equivalent to transfers made by will, while avoiding the disadvantages of the probate process, they are commonly referred to as will substitutes.

The most common, and often the most ineffective, types of will substitutes attempted by lay persons are gifts and deeds (1, pp. 332–333). Promises to make gifts in the future are unenforceable (16, p. 77). Except under limited circumstances where death is imminent (pp. 130–131), gifts must be irrevocable and unconditional and must transfer full control of the object of the gift to the recipient at the time the gift is made (p. 77). Physical delivery of the object is generally necessary, evidencing an intention on the part of the donor to make a present gift (pp. 80–85). Although a completed and effective lifetime gift will remove the item from the donor's estate, the donor will not be able to enjoy the property during the remainder of his or her life.

Transfers of land and the structures located thereon require the delivery of a written deed. Unlike a will, a deed must have an immediate legal effect. A deed that is meant to become effective only at the owner's death will not transfer an interest, and the property will remain in the decedent's estate (1, pp. 332–333). An ineffective deed will not be construed to be a valid will. While deeds may permit the owner to retain use and possession of the property until death then immediately confer the right to possession to another party, precise legal language must be used (pp. 332–333). Many states do not permit revocable deeds and conditions on deed are limited. A present intention to transfer a legal interest in the property must be present, and the deed must be delivered to the recipient, another person, or at least placed outside of the original owner's control. Professional legal advice always should be obtained before attempting to transfer property by deed to avoid the will's statutes.

Another common form of will substitute is the transfer of property into a form of co-ownership known as a joint tenancy with right of survivorship. Under this legal arrangement, two or more parties are given equal rights to the property in question during their mutual lifetimes. When one party dies, that person's ownership rights dissolve, leaving nothing to pass through his or her probate estate; thus, the survivor's or survivors' interests automatically expand to include the remaining ownership rights. The last co-owner to survive becomes the complete owner of the entire property interest. The joint tenancy with right of survivorship is frequently created with respect to land but may be used for other types of property (14, pp. 46–48). Bank accounts, for example, may be established in the joint tenancy form. The drawback of a joint tenancy with right of survivorship is that the property owner gives equal access to the property to others during life in order to achieve the desired result at death (10, pp. 486–487). If the joint tenancy is terminated during life, each co-owner may be entitled to an immediate share of the property (p. 487).

Life insurance policies are commonly used as a form of legitimate will substitute (14, p. 108). Every state will uphold a contractual agreement between a policy owner and an insurance company to pay a designated amount of money to a specified beneficiary upon the death of the insured. Many varieties of life insurance exist, including those which give the insured considerable flexibility over the monetary value of the policy during his or her lifetime and the power to change beneficiaries before death (14, pp. 110–113). Money paid to a beneficiary of a life insurance policy does not become an asset of the insured's probate estate and, thus, may function as a valid will substitute.

Although insurance contracts to pay money to a designated beneficiary are liberally enforced in the United States, other types of contractual agreements to transfer property on a person's death are not so uniformly or easily enforceable. For example, a bank account opened in the owner's name designating that the account is "payable on death" to another is frequently invalidated (15, p. 9). Somewhat ironically, by use of slightly different language, a person may establish a savings account trust or "Totten trust," which accomplishes the same purpose and is valid in many states (17). Where recognized, a savings account trust affords the depositor full lifetime ownership and control of the funds and, on death, automatically transfers ownership to another without probate (17).

Probably the most effective and flexible method of avoiding probate is to establish a trust (14, pp. 169–170). Any type of property may be placed in a trust and the original owner, or settlor, of the trust may retain extensive use and control over the property during life. On the settlor's death, the trust property will be distributed to designated beneficiaries without becoming part of the probate estate. In a trust arrangement, the settlor transfers property to a trustee with directions regarding the management and distribution of the property. While the settlor may act as the trustee, it is more common that a third party, often an officer of a corporation or a bank, is named trustee. The trustee has a legal duty to use the trust property for the benefit of the beneficiaries and only under the terms provided in the trust instrument or imposed by the law (18, pp. 1, 6–7).

A settlor may expressly reserve the right to amend or revoke the trust, including the power to change or add beneficiaries (pp. 22–24). The trustee may be directed to distribute the trust property upon the settlor's death or may be instructed to continue management of the property and distribute designated portions of the income upon the occurrence of certain events. A trust may be useful to assure the continued property management and a source of income for minor children, the elderly, or the incapacitated (pp. 1–3). Several generations of beneficiaries may receive benefits of the trust before the trust ends and the property is finally distributed. The settlor can tailor the terms of the trust to suit individual desires and may give the trustee discretion to vary the management and distribution of the trust as contingencies arise. While private trusts are restricted in duration by law (pp. 56–59), trusts for recognized charitable purposes may continue indefinitely (pp. 388–390). Because of their flexibility, trusts are often considered the best method of retaining maximum control over a person's assets during life, while being able to pass property to beneficiaries at death without involving the probate process.

Trusts may also be created in a will or assets may be disposed of in a will into a previously created trust known as a pour-over trust. These types of trusts do not avoid probate, as the assets become a part of the estate, but are used primarily to afford professional management or postpone outright distribution of assets until sometime after the settlor's death (14, pp. 178–183).

The use of will substitutes that are enforceable is an effective way of legally circumventing the will's statute formalities and avoiding probate but may not be entirely effective to achieve other results. For example, most jurisdictions today will invalidate, or at least require an accounting for, certain lifetime transfers intended to defeat a surviving spouse's rights (19). Furthermore, contrary to popular belief, most lifetime transfers that otherwise act as valid will substitutes afford the decedent few, if any, tax benefits.

Taxes

Death taxes are imposed in two general forms: estate tax and inheritance tax. Estate taxes are imposed on the decedent's estate and are paid from the estate before the remaining assets are distributed to heirs or beneficiaries. Inheritance taxes are levied against individuals who receive property through inheritance (20, pp. 1–2). The purposes of these taxes are to raise revenue for the government and to restrict inheritance of great amounts of wealth (pp. 10–12).

The federal estate tax applies uniformly throughout this country, regardless of which state controls the probate of the decedent's estate. Since the Tax Reform Act of 1976 (21) and the Economic Recovery Tax Act of 1981 (22), which effect an essentially uniform tax on cumulative lifetime and death transfers, there is generally little tax advantage to transferring property before death, although limited amounts of yearly tax-free gifts are authorized. An advantage to lifetime transfer may exist, however, when property is expected to increase in value, since gift or estate taxes are assessed on the value of the asset at the time of transfer (20, pp. 313, 318; 23, §§2033, 2512). Lifetime transfers intended to act as will substitutes to avoid probate are taxed as estate assets when the creator of the devise retained any of many designated types of lifetime interests in the property, such as a personal benefit from the property or a right to control distribution to other beneficiaries (20, pp. 138–230).

Contrary to common belief, federal estate taxes should not greatly concern persons of moderate wealth. As of 1987, for example, only estates greater than $600,000, accounting for the value of lifetime gifts and after the allowance of various deductions, will be liable for federal estate tax (p. 7). An unlimited amount of property may be given to charity, thus avoiding federal estate taxation (23, §§2055, 2522). Similarly, an unlimited marital deduction allows a person to transfer property to a surviving spouse and avoid estate tax consequences (§§2056, 2523). The tax may not be avoided completely but will be deferred until the spouse's death, at which time any remaining property received from the first dying spouse will be taxable as part of the second spouse's estate. The advantage of the marital deduction is that taxation will be delayed, and if the remaining spouse has a smaller estate at death, the tax rate will be lower (20, pp. 373–416).

Although a recipient does not have to pay federal income tax on gifts and inheritances, most states have a tax on inheritances, either instead of or in addition to an estate tax imposed at the state level. While an individual receiving property is taxed by the state on the amount of the gift, usually the tax is paid by the decedent's personal representative from the recipient's share before distributing the gift. State death taxes, unlike their federal counterparts, may be significant even in the case of smaller estates. Persons closely related to the decedent may be taxed at a lower rate than more distant relatives or persons unrelated to the decedent (1, pp. 1058–1060). With regard to tax implications, estate planning is extremely complex and specialists continue to develop legal methods of avoiding the tax. Expert tax advice should be obtained in order to maximize tax savings.

DISPOSITION OF THE BODY

Funeral and Burial

Immediately after death, arrangements must be made for disposing of the body of the deceased. Family members and close friends may be emotionally unprepared to make quickly the numerous necessary decisions (24, p. 1). Such questions include whether the body will be buried or cremated, whether funeral home visitation will be desired, what type of casket will be used and whether it should be open or closed, what type of obituary should be published, whether to request that gifts be made to a specific charity in lieu of flowers, what type of religious or memorial service should be conducted and where the bodily remains will be laid finally to rest (24). Because these matters are intended primarily to comfort the survivors and allow them to pay their final respects (25, p. 901), it is appropriate for a person, in planning for his or her own death, to simplify the responsibilities of, and eliminate as much trauma as possible for, family and friends by considering such details during life. This can be at least partly accomplished by clarifying one's desires and leaving specific directions for disposing of one's body. Unless a person's close relatives agree with the plans, however, there is little certainty that the decedent's decisions or desires will be implemented.

Funeral and burial procedures and rites are largely a matter of religious and social custom (25). They are restricted, to some extent, by legal regulations designed to protect the public health and safety and to prevent acts likely to offend general notions of decency and propriety. The law further attempts to protect the survivors, in their often diminished emotional state caused by shock and mourning, from unfair or deceptive practices in businesses and industries which provide goods and services relating to death and disposition of the body (24).

American funeral and burial practices are largely a product of a religious and legal heritage developed in England. In early England, the ecclesiastical or church courts had authority over matters relating to death (26, p. 31). Proper services and burial were considered important to assure that the deceased would attain eternal peace (p. 31). Prior to burial, the body was regarded as the vessel of the now departed soul and, as such, was entitled to special care and respect. A churchyard burial was important, and the bodies of persons who were refused a Christian burial because of their lifetime failings were frequently donated to medical research (p. 31).

The courts in the United States rejected the English ecclesiastical law but formed the American law regarding the rights and duties related to dead bodies on basic principles similar to those established in England. Regardless of a decedent's religious beliefs, the courts in this country concluded that a person's body deserves extraordinary treatment (p. 31). The courts, however, experienced difficulty in formulating precise rules, as is illustrated by the language of an opinion of the Georgia Supreme Court in 1905:

> Death is unique. It is unlike aught else in its certainty and its incidents.
> A corpse in some respects is the strangest thing on earth. A man who
> but yesterday breathed and thought and walked among us has passed
> away. Something has gone. The body is left still and cold, and is all
> that is visible to mortal eye of the man we knew. Around it cling love
> and memory. Beyond it may reach hope. It must be laid away. And the

law—that rule of action which touches all human things—must touch also this thing of death. It is not surprising that the law relating to this mystery of what death leaves behind cannot be precisely brought within the letter of all the rules regarding corn, lumber and pig iron. And yet the body must be buried or disposed of. If buried, it must be carried to the place of burial. And the law, in its all-sufficiency, must furnish some rule, by legislative enactment or analogy, or based on some sound legal principal, by which to determine between the living questions of the disposition of the dead and the rights surrounding their bodies.(27)

The indefiniteness and uncertainty as to rights and duties regarding the body and its disposition remain apparent in the law today.

Power to Determine One's Own Disposition

Unlike the individual's relatively broad power to dispose of his or her property upon death, the right to control the disposition of his or her own body is considerably more limited. The decedent's body is not "property" in any conventional sense of the word and does not become part of the decedent's estate (26, p. 22). The right to control one's own body, like other legal rights, ends at death, and any remaining rights pass to other individuals. Therefore, any preferences or directions a person may have expressed, either orally or in writing, during life, related to funeral arrangements and burial or cremation, will be considered but will not be binding (26). Rather, the deceased's nearest relative, or next of kin— usually a spouse, child, parent or other household member, or in some cases, the decedent's personal representative—will be granted the right to arrange the details for the funeral and burial. Not only do the decedent's family members have a right to bury the deceased, but they have a corresponding duty to do so, in an expeditious and appropriate manner (28, p. 561). While the courts have stated that the individual's expressed intentions should be respected to the extent proper and reasonable, the law is equivocal as to how much weight to accord those intentions when they conflict with the wishes of the survivors (p. 562). Similarly, a decedent's directions that a nonrelative should decide on funeral and burial arrangements may be overridden by the surviving relatives. Few states have resolved the conflict by statute, and the court cases addressing the problem are often inconsistent (26).

Although a decedent cannot dispose of his or her body by will, directions or preferences expressed in a formal will may be accorded greater respect than oral or informally written instructions. Testamentary instructions regarding disposition of the body may be altered or revoked informally without compliance with the will's statute. Nevertheless, the formality inherent in execution of a will may be persuasive as to the strength of the deceased's wishes (28, p. 563). Because, typically, a will is not read prior to disposal of the decedent's remains, it is advisable for a person to give a copy of funeral and burial instructions to someone who is likely to be available when death occurs. To help assure that the directions will be followed, the spouse or other close relatives should be consulted, in an attempt to obtain concurrence (26).

The right of certain survivors to arrange for burial of the deceased is not only limited to some extent by the wishes of the decedent but also by what has been described as a "trust" (26). This trust requires that the body be disposed of properly and that it not be mishandled, desecrated, or sold. The survivors have a right to recover damages from a party who deliberately or negligently mistreats or improperly deals with the body (28, pp. 566–567).

Anatomical Gifts

Although a person's freedom to direct the disposition of his or her body is somewhat limited with respect to funeral and burial arrangements, greater, although not absolute, certainty exists that the decedent's wishes will be followed when the person desires to donate his or her body or its individual components for legitimate medical purposes. In the past, medical research and teaching depended on the bodies of prisoners and paupers and other bodies that were unclaimed (26). Although a shortage of corpses for these purposes has always existed, an increased demand far exceeding the supply has developed since medical technology has advanced in the area of organ transplantation (29).

Gifts of anatomical parts at death provide the primary source of transplant organs. During life, vital organs critical to survival may not be donated because of criminal prohibitions against suicide and homicide (30, p. 265). Even with respect to nonvital organs, legal problems exist regarding the donor's informed consent and the health risks to the donor resulting from surgical procedures (p. 265).

Although no obligation to donate organs has ever existed, the decedent's next of kin traditionally have been authorized to donate specific parts or the entire body of the deceased for transplantation, research, or medical education, at least when not contrary to the known wishes of the decedent. Organ donations, especially for transplantation, can help alleviate the family's sense of loss and can make the death seem less meaningless (31). Many types of organs, such as corneas, pituitary glands, and skin, can be stored in organ banks until needed (31). Many vital organs, such as livers, hearts, and kidneys, must be transplanted immediately to avoid tissue deterioration that could harm or even kill the recipient. Predeath authorization is, therefore, preferable in order to avoid delay. Until recently, however, the legal effects of such authorizations were unpredictable when a prospective donor's family members objected to the donation upon death.

By the early 1970s, all states had enacted some version of the Uniform Anatomical Gift Act (32). The Act permits a person's directions regarding anatomical gifts to be honored without intervention by the surviving family; in practice, however, a physician will generally refuse a donation when the family objects (30). The Act allows any adult to donate specific organs, prosthetic devices, or the entire body to any hospital, physician, medical or dental school, or storage facility. The donation may be utilized for medical or dental education, research, therapy, or transplant. The gift can be made broadly for any authorized purpose or may be limited to transplant to or therapy for a specified individual (32). Central registries exist for distribution of certain vital organs (31). A national computerized system, accessible to all hospitals, exists for matching organs with persons awaiting transplants.

The Uniform Act contemplates a short, simple form, which may be a separate document or included in a will, even if the will has not yet been probated (29). Most states provide forms on generally available documents such as driver's licenses and senior citizen's cards. Two witnesses are required. The donor must be competent at the time the instrument is executed, but mental capacity does not need to be proven at the death of the donor. The form need not be delivered to the recipient, but if it is delivered, additional formalities are necessary for revocation (32). Most of the widely distributed types of forms contain insufficient space for specific instructions, but sometimes include a provision to indicate that the person does *not* wish to make any anatomical gifts (29).

Although a 1967 Gallup Poll Survey indicated that 70 percent of Americans would be willing to donate organs after death (30, p. 266), only a minute proportion of the population has executed donor cards. For example, of approximately 170 kidney transplants performed at one teaching hospital, about 100 of those kidneys were removed from some 60 bodies, none of which carried a donor card (25, p. 265, fn. 23). Relatedly, many potential donors remain undiscovered and unutilized, as many hospitals, police personnel, or paramedics do not, as a matter of course, specifically look for donor cards due to the intrinsic medical nature and time constraints of their duties. Many prospective donations are thereby passed over. If the current organ shortage is to be alleviated, appropriate personnel must be instructed to conduct an immediate and thorough investigation to identify donors, and the public must be made aware of the simple procedure available for making an anatomical gift.

When an individual has not executed a donor card or the card cannot be found at death, the Act permits specified family members to consent to anatomical gifts absent a contrary expression of intention by the deceased prior to death. However, if those specified family members are unavailable, some states permit local officials to authorize donations (32). Unlike the execution of a donor card, little formality is required in obtaining the consent of the family member, who can authorize, without witnesses, by telephone, telegraph, or other recorded device (32). This provision has been criticized (25) for failing to protect adequately the rights of the deceased and the family, because truly informed consent may be unlikely or impossible to obtain when the request for donation must be made almost simultaneously with the notification of death (p. 893). If the request is made prior to death, the family's hope for recovery, however unrealistic, may be destroyed (30).

While the Act has had some effect on increasing the number of organs available for transplant, the demand continues greatly to surpass the supply. Automatic or routine removal as a normal course of action, without the consent of the donor or the survivors, is presently illegal, except when the donation decision falls upon local authorities. Furthermore, if only specified body parts have been donated, removal of additional organs is likewise forbidden. A reversal of the current law, involving compulsory removal of critical organs, has been advocated by some commentators (33) as a matter of policy giving the living priority over the dead. Mandatory and involuntary removal of anatomical parts may be an unjustified interference with the religious freedom and privacy rights of the survivors (30). Perhaps a more acceptable alternative would be to presume consent—absent objection by the deceased during life or by the surviving family, a practice followed in most European countries (30).

Anatomical gifts may take various forms. A person may donate some or all organs or the entire body. Only organs meeting necessary requirements of age and physical condition will be removed and nonstorable organs will be removed only if compatible donees are available.

Although practice varies among facilities, generally, when only certain organs are removed, the body is returned to the family (32, §7(a)), and traditional funeral services may be performed (31, p. 838). When remains are donated for research, some institutions cremate the remains and bury locally (25, p. 896) while others return the remains or ashes to the family if desired.

One concern that may inhibit persons otherwise willing to donate anatomical gifts from actually doing so is the uncertainty as to when death actually occurs (30), which is left undefined by the Act, and the related apprehension that medical professionals might not take all steps necessary to prevent death if awaiting an organ for transplant. To safeguard against this potential abuse, various statutory definitions of death have been adopted (34). Generally, death is declared when the brain has undergone irrevocable damage and no realistic possibility of recovery exists, as evidenced by cessation of cardiac, respiratory, and neural activity (34). As an additional assurance, the physician who pronounces death is prohibited from participating in an organ transplant from the deceased (30).

Termination of Treatment

The controversy regarding organ transplants and defining death in a manner satisfactory to the legal as well as to the medical profession has been further complicated in recent years by the issue of when life should be prolonged artificially by technological means. Delaying death once no likelihood of recovery exists, usually, financially and emotionally devastates the family, places an unnecessary burden on medical resources, and frequently conflicts with the wishes of the patient (34). Although no medical treatment can be authorized without the consent of the patient, a patient who is unconscious, mentally incapacitated, or a minor cannot legally refuse treatment or consent to withdrawal from life support systems already in operation. The general public has legitimate interests in preserving life, preventing suicide, assuring the integrity of the medical profession, and protecting the patient's family members (34). Individual privacy rights and freedom of choice may conflict with those public interests and give rise to a right to die, or "die with dignity," under certain circumstances (34).

To reconcile these often conflicting interests, an increasing number of states (36, as of 1986) have enacted a type of euthanasia legislation known as "right to die" or "death with dignity" acts. These laws permit a person to express, by means of a document or directive frequently referred to as a "living will," an intention to decline life-prolonging or extraordinary treatment when death is imminent. Organizations such as the Concern for Dying Educational Council and the Society for the Right to Die, as well as a number of churches, have drafted and disseminated living will documents that may be filed in states which have not enacted euthanasia laws. Although, without legislation, such documents are not legally binding, they may provide some assurance that a person's family and physicians would honor the formal expression of intent.

Right-to-die legislation varies considerably among the states as to whether the person must be terminally ill when the document is executed or if a healthy person may similarly authorize a directive (34). The laws generally require two witnesses who are unrelated to the person and who do not have conflicting interests, such as those that medical or hospital personnel or potential beneficiaries may have. The directive is revocable and, in some states, may be effective for a limited time only. Further variations in state right-to-die laws include the availability of sanctions on physicians who fail to comply with the living will or refuse to transfer the patient to a doctor who will effectuate the patient's intent; the application of the law to comatose, incompetent, or minor patients; and the availability of discontinuation of extraordinary treatment to pregnant women. The existence of such variation between state laws is especially problematic in cases where the document was executed in one state but the decision to terminate treatment must be made in another state with different legislation, such as when the patient had previously moved from the original state or had been transferred to a hospital elsewhere.

In addition to the fact that the laws vary extensively between states, a further major problem exists in the ambiguity of the language used in virtually all right-to-die laws. The laws frequently fail to resolve the questions of to what extent the directive will bind family members and what type of treatment should be considered extraordinary under particular circumstances, and, thus, when life-sustaining measures can be terminated (31). Some states require loss of all higher brain activity, others also require lack of spontaneous respiration and circulation (34, pp. 432–435). In 1984, the Uniform Determination of Death Act was promulgated (35). By 1986, 19 states and the District of Columbia had adopted the Act, which provides: "An individual who has sustained either (1) irreversible cessation of circulatory and respiratory functions, or (2) irreversible cessation of all functions of the entire brain, including the brain stem, is dead. A determination of death is to be made in accordance with acceptable medical standards" (35). Although this Uniform Act clarifies the definition of death to a certain extent, the Act probably still will be subject to varying interpretations and, thus, will not eliminate the numerous lawsuits and conflicting judgments. As an alternative to a living will, some states authorize a person to designate another to decide when medical treatment should be refused or terminated. Such authorizations may be in the form of a limited guardianship or a "durable power of attorney," which permits an agent to act as representative of another after loss of capacity occurs (1, p. 283).

In the absence of a statement of intention by the patient, expressed pursuant to legislation, a person risks criminal or civil liability, or both, for engaging in euthanasia (31). While the question of artificially prolonging life is essentially a medical and moral, not a legal, issue, legal guidelines are necessary to bridge the gap between law and medicine (34). In the past, decisions to refuse or withdraw medical treatment of an incapacitated adult or of a minor have been made on an *ad hoc* basis (31). Primary focus has been on determining what the individual most likely would choose if competent and whose judgment should be substituted for the individual patient's. Court action is generally necessary (36) and may involve a prolonged process. Some cases have held that a hospital ethics committee may substitute for a court review as a practical alternative in appropriate cases (37). Statutory authorization is preferable to protect the decision maker and the physician from liability based on the possibility that the patient might have recovered (31).

Health and Safety Regulations

The rights of the individual and the family members to dispose of the decedent's body may be further restricted when necessary to protect the public health, safety, or general welfare. State and local regulations often control the location and operation of funeral homes and mortuaries to ensure sanitation and to prevent the spread of contagious or infectious disease (38). Embalming may be mandated when the body will not be disposed of immediately and refrigeration is not available (24). Transporters of corpses may be regulated and, in extreme circumstances when a long delay is foreseen, the body may be buried at sea or where it is presently located (28). Funeral homes may be prohibited in residential areas or near hospitals in order to shield neighbors and patients from the constant reminder of death (38). Many localities require a certification of death to provide health data as well as to compile information for other vital statistics (39).

Local boards of health may require a burial permit and states or municipalities may restrict the sites of cemeteries (38). In some areas, crematory ashes may not be scattered over land or water (24). Once buried, a body may not be disinterred or exhumed except for extraordinary reasons and then only upon court order. The body may be disinterred by court order when necessary for evidence in a criminal case, such as to prove that a person accused of killing the decedent could not have done so in the manner alleged (28, p. 568). Less frequently, exhumation may be authorized in a private lawsuit; for instance, to prove cause of death in a suit brought on an insurance claim (28, pp. 568–569). Permission for disinterment or exhumation is less likely to be granted as the time from death elapses. Any disinterment or exhumation must be properly performed, both for health reasons and for respect for the sensitivities and rights of the family members (28). Unauthorized interference with the body or the gravesite may subject the violator both to criminal liability and to a suit for damages on behalf of the deceased's relatives (28).

Police Intervention

When a person dies of unnatural causes, by violence or accident, the body may be made available to the appropriate police authorities as evidence and for official record purposes. When the cause of death is uncertain or when there is reason to believe it was unnatural, the coroner or public medical examiner may be authorized to view the body and conduct an autopsy if necessary. Where criminal conduct or suicide is suspected or where the public health or welfare may be affected, an autopsy may be performed over the philosophical or religious beliefs of the deceased's family. The conditions under which an official autopsy may be demanded without consent of the survivors generally are prescribed by statute. Usually difficult or controversial diagnosis, settlement of a private dispute, or the advancement of scientific knowledge are insufficient reasons for ordering an involuntary autopsy (39).

The coroner is a public officer, usually elected but sometimes appointed, on the county level of government. Many localities require the coroner to be a licensed physician. The coroner's duties are fixed by statute and liability may arise for misbehavior, including conducting an autopsy in bad faith or engaging in transactions which would indicate a conflict of interest, such as selling funeral supplies (39).

If necessary, the coroner may call an inquest to determine if death resulted from criminal acts and to assist in prosecuting the person responsible. The inquest is a preliminary investigation, not a trial, but may involve calling in witnesses to testify in order for the coroner to decide whether to advise that a criminal action be brought. Some areas require a jury to hear the testimony, but examination of the body is performed outside the jury; the public may be excluded from the proceedings. The result of an inquest is a death certificate or other official report which relates to the cause of death and other relevant information, not a conclusion of guilt or innocence, although in some localities the coroner is authorized to issue warrants for arrest (39).

Regulation of the Funeral Industry

Because of its relationship to the general public welfare, the funeral industry is subject to regulation by state and local government and is supervised by state agencies. Undertakers and embalmers may be required to be licensed and may need to meet certain educational, training, and skill criteria (38). Funeral professionals may be subject to discipline for failure to comply with sanitation requirements, for unprofessional conduct or incompetency, or for unfair sales or pricing techniques (38). Solicitation of business may be prohibited and advertising may be limited or otherwise restricted. While funeral insurance or contracts for funeral services are legal, they are subject to regulation because of the potential for fraud, the uncertainty as to the time for performance, and the chance that the company might not exist at the time of death or that the survivors may be unaware of the existence of the plan (28).

The funeral industry provides merchandise and services to over 2 million American families a year at an average cost of about $2,400 (24). Often, persons arranging a funeral are emotionally distraught and must act in haste and are not initially concerned with the cost of what may be one of their most expensive lifetime purchases (p. 1). To protect the vulnerable public from overextending themselves financially because of sales pressure or deceptive or fraudulent business practices, the Bureau of Consumer Protection of the Federal Trade Commission began investigating the funeral industry in the early 1970s (p. 3). As a result of this investigation, federal regulations, collectively known as the "funeral rule," were enacted in 1984 (40). The rule requires full disclosure of costs related to funeral goods and services and requires the sale of individual items as an alternative to a complete package. Alternative prices of types of caskets and outer burial containers must be revealed, and the requirements imposed by both the law and the selected cemetery with regard to specific goods must be disclosed. Funeral providers may not make claims that expensive products are necessary for cremation. The provider must inform the consumer when embalming is not required by law and must make no inaccurate claims regarding any preservative effect of particular items (40). In instances where the funeral home arranges for providing and caring for flowers, preparing newspaper death notices, providing hearses and limosines, pallbearers, guest registers, or other such services (24, pp. 7–8), the individual costs must be disclosed and any rebates to or handling charges imposed by the funeral home must be revealed (40). By providing consumers with full information regarding alternatives and prices, purchasers of funeral goods and services can select only what they want and need (24, p. 2).

CONCLUSION

Effective planning for death can only be accomplished within the existing and often intricate legal structure. Only by becoming aware of and planning (in the context of the legal limitations on disposition of one's property and body) can a person feel reasonably secure that his or her wishes will be carried out and that family and friends will be provided for adequately, with minimal expense, delay, and distress. Relevant financial information should be compiled and adequate instructions should be left easily accessible to alleviate the unavoidable and necessary practical problems that arise on one's inevitable death.

REVIEW QUESTIONS

1. Why should the funeral industry be subject to greater governmental regulation than other businesses? (How do federal regulations protect the public from potential unfair practices in the funeral industry?)
2. What dangers are inherent in writing one's own will?
3. Intestacy scenarios are based on legislators' conceptions of how a typical person would want his or her property disposed of on death. How do the typical intestacy statues fail in this respect?
4. Why does the law restrict a person's disposition of his or her body to a greater extent than his or her property?
5. Discuss the alternatives to leaving a will and the advantages and disadvantages of various will substitutes.
6. Why does the law require wills to be drafted and executed with precision and formality?
7. Under what circumstances is the state likely to interfere with a family member's wishes regarding funeral arrangements and burial?
8. Discuss the pros and cons of adopting a legal presumption that all persons wish to donate anatomical gifts in the absence of specific instructions to the contrary.

REFERENCES

1. Dukeminier, J., & Johanson, S. M. (1983). *Wills, trusts, and estates* (3rd ed.). Boston: Little, Brown.
2. Uniform Probate Code, 8 U.L.A. 1 (1983).
3. Atkinson, T. E. (1953). *Law of wills* (2nd ed.). St. Paul, MN: West.
4. Gulliver, A. G., & Tilson, C. J. (1941). Classification of gratuitous transfers. *The Yale Law Journal, 51,* 1–39.
5. Palmer, G. E. (1971). Dependent relative revocation and its relation to relief for mistake. *Michigan Law Review, 69,* 989–1010.
6. DeFuniak, W. Q., & Vaughn, M. J. (1971). *Principles of community property* (2nd ed.). Tucson, AZ: University of Arizona Press.
7. McClanahan, W. S. (1982). *Community property in the United States.* Rochester, NY: Lawyers Co-operative.
8. 1983 Wis. Laws 186, §§8–20 (codified at Wis. Stat. 766).
9. Uniform Marital Property Act, 9A U.L.A. 21 (Supp. 1985).
10. Dukeminier, J. & Krier, J. E. (1981). *Property.* Boston: Little, Brown.
11. Phillips, H., & Robinson, J. W. (1983). *Pritchard on the law of will and administration of estates* (4th ed.) (Vols. 1–3). Charlottesville, VA: Michie.
12. Rein, J. E. (1979). A more rational system for the protection of family members against disinheritance: A critique of Washington's pretermitted child statute and other matters. *Gonzaga Law Review, 15,* 11–64.

13. Fratcher, W. F. (1960). Powers and duties of guardians of property. *Iowa Law Review, 45,* 264–335.

14. Lynn, R. J. (1983). *Introduction to estate planning* (3rd ed.). St. Paul, MN: West.

15. McGovern, W. M. (1972). The payable on death account and other will substitutes. *Northwestern University Law Review, 67,* 7–41.

16. Brown, R. A. (1975). In Raushenbush, W. B. (Ed.). *The law of personal property* (3rd ed.). Chicago: Callaghan & Company.

17. Wittebort, R. J. (1974). Savings account trusts: A critical examination. *Notre Dame Lawyer, 49,* 686–699.

18. Haskell, P. G. (1975). *Preface to the law of trusts.* Mineola, NY: Foundation Press.

19. Pherigo, B. J. (1979). Estate planning: Validity of *inter vivos* transfers which reduce or defeat the surviving spouse's statutory share in the decedent's estate. *Oklahoma Law Review, 32,* 837–853.

20. McNulty, J. K. (1983). *Federal gift and estate taxation* (3rd ed.). St. Paul, MN: West.

21. Tax Reform Act of 1976 (Pub. L. 94-455, 90 Stat. 1520).

22. Economic Recovery Tax Act of 1981 (Pub. L. 97-34, 95 Stat. 172).

23. Internal Revenue Code, 26 U.S.C. (1984).

24. Roybal, E. R. (1984). *A guide to funeral planning.* (Comm. Pub. No. 98–166). Washington, DC: U.S. Government Printing Office.

25. Quay, P. M. (1984). Utilizing the bodies of the dead. *St. Louis University Law Journal, 28,* 889–927.

26. Marshall, J. R. (1982). Testamentary rights of bodily disposition. *Law Notes, 18,* 31–36.

27. Louisville & N.R. Co. v. Wilson, 123 Ga. 62, 51 S.E. 24 (1905).

28. American Jurisprudence (2nd ed.) (Vol. 22) (1965). *Dead bodies.* Rochester, NY: Lawyers Co-operative, San Francisco: Bancroft-Whitney.

29. Crown, J. L. (1982). Anatomical gift form. *Probate and Property, 11,* 9–12.

30. Weissman, S. I. (1977). Why the Uniform Anatomical Gift Act has failed. *Trusts and Estates, 116,* 264–267, 281–282.

31. Crown, J. L. (1980). Last requests—the right to die and anatomical gifts. *Notre Dame Estate Planning Institute, 5,* 743–840.

32. Uniform Anatomical Gift Act, 8A U.L.A. 15 (1983).

33. Dukeminier, J. (1970). Supplying organs for transplantation. *Michigan Law Review, 68,* 811–866.

34. Janzen, P. S. (1984). Law at the edge of life: Issues of death and dying. *Hamline Law Review, 7,* 431–462.

35. Uniform Determination of Death Act, 12 U.L.A. 270 (Supp. 1986).

36. Superintendent of Belchertown State School v. Saikewicz, 373 Mass 728, 370 N.E.2d 417 (1977).

37. *In re* Quinlan, 70 N.J. 10, 355 A.2d 647, (*cert. denied*), 429 U.S. 922 (1976).

38. American Jurisprudence (2nd ed.) (Vol. 38) (1968). *Funeral directors and embalmers.* Rochester, NY: Lawyers Co-operative; San Francisco: Bancroft-Whitney.

39. American Jurisprudence (2nd ed.) (Vol. 18) (1985). *Coroners.* Rochester, NY: Lawyers Co-operative; San Francisco: Bancroft-Whitney.

40. Funeral Industry Practice (Funeral Rule), 16 C.F.R. §453 (1985).

Challenge: Meeting
the Issues of Death

15

The Right to Die:
Ethical and Medical Issues

Arthur Zucker

The goal of philosophy is to question. This can be maddening if it takes the form of a child's never ending series of "Why?" An infinite regress of why questions is not, however, the true mark of philosophy. Rather, the crux is to know just what needs questioning and to know just how to phrase the questions. Philosophy also must be prepared to recognize and accept an answer. Those who are questioned should be prepared to understand that philosophical analysis of necessity leads to surprise. Where there was simplicity, there will be complexity. Where there was certainty, there will be doubt. Where there were answers, there will be questions. Where there was justified action, there will be a call for more reasons and perhaps inaction. Words will no longer be clear. Concepts will be muddled before clarified. It is no wonder that some saw a good dose of hemlock as an antidote to the philosophical approach.

This chapter is not meant to be philosophy, except in the following sense. The question "Is there a right to euthanasia?" is put into readiness for philosophical sorts of answers. Concepts which traditionally appear in these discussions appear in this discussion. Arguments which traditionally appear in these discussions appear in this discussion. Questions usually asked are asked. But there are no answers in this chapter. Indeed, its structure might perplex a traditional philosopher. For what happens in this chapter is an organic unfolding of the terms, concepts, questions, issues, and arguments as they might actually appear and grow in their true homes—the medical contexts which make them all so intensely felt.

Very few of us look forward to dying. No matter what we may believe about what happens after death, we do know that once dead, our earthly options are ended. It is this lack of future potential that is probably responsible for the feeling that death is an evil—an evil to be avoided at just about any cost. Yet there are exceptions to this belief. Some people risk death in order to intensify their enjoyment of life. Some people risk death as part of a chosen profession. Still other people actually choose death rather than face the certain travails of life. The question "What counts as a good reason for choosing death?"—given that in general death is an evil—is the question at the heart of the issue of euthanasia. But it is not the only question at the heart of the euthanasia issue. For central to understanding euthanasia must be a delineation of the proper role of medicine as a profession *and* a characterization of the doctor-patient relationship.

Following the philosopher Wittgenstein, who emphasized how difficult it was to find definitions for fuzzy concepts, we shall begin with cases which exemplify the "problem of euthanasia."

I was called to the newborn nursery to see Baby C, whose father was a busy surgeon with three teen-aged children. The diagnoses of imperforate anus and microencephalus were obvious. Doctor C called me after being informed of the situation by the pediatrician. "I'm not going to sign that op permit," he said. When I didn't reply, he said, "What would you do, Doctor, if he were your baby?" "I wouldn't let him be operated on either," I replied. Palliative support only was provided, and the infant died 48 hours later (1).

Brother Fox was an alert and active 83-year-old priest when he was hospitalized for the surgical repair of an inguinal hernia. As the procedure was nearing its conclusion, Brother Fox suffered a cardiac arrest. In spite of [prompt treatment] Brother Fox sustained substantial brain damage. He became comatose and showed little signs of ever regaining a state of sapience or consciousness. . . . Father Eichner, who had known Brother Fox for many years, asked the hospital to discontinue the respirator (2).

A young, ex-marine pilot, who thrived on his good looks and athletic ability, was severely burned in a freak gasline accident. In that accident, his father, to whom he was very close, was killed. After a year of painful treatment for his burns, the young man was just as adamant as he was when first taken to the hospital: Please let me die. The pain of the treatment would in no way be compensated for by the low quality of life in store: little vision, little mobility, and very severe scarring.

An elderly man, dying of cancer of the jaw, asks for enough pain killer to be fatal. He sees no difference between being unconscious and pain free and being dead. Since these have become the only real options for him, he asks for a swifter death.

MORAL THEORY

Probably the easiest way to understand moral theory is by assuming that it is analogous to scientific theory. The analogy is not perfect, but it is, nonetheless, worth pursuing. Scientific theories are created by scientists to explain and to predict areas of interest. No one theory explains or predicts everything. Theorizing begins with a puzzle: Why do some things work the way they do? Why do some things look the way they do? Theorizing continues with a mix of categorizing (whales are really mammals), generalizing (all mammals have four-chambered hearts) and, finally, explaining. Predictions need not follow from explanations, although the hope is that when the explanation gets good enough, accurate predictions will be possible.

Moral theory follows similar paths. We start with a puzzle: When is ending a human life morally justifiable? We categorize: Why just human life? Is "euthanasia" very different from suicide as when a distraught medical student shoots himself? We often try to generalize: Treat each case differently. Never cause unnecessary pain and suffering. Finally, we do something analogous to scientific explanation. We offer the reasons from which our actions should follow: "I see, it would be wrong to let this patient die." Sometimes we can also do something like predict: We can judge that if in a certain set of circumstances, we would probably do X because Y.

A moral theory will do two other things: 1) It will provide us with characterizations of crucial terms: good, bad, right, wrong, fair, justice, etc. 2) It will also tell us something about human nature. Indeed, it should be a requirement for any good, moral theory that it contains, or in some way be accompanied by, a theory of human nature. The reason for this is relatively clear. A moral theory, if not meant to be totally descriptive, should not be impossible for people to put into practice. In other words, a moral theory which made it too difficult to be good would not be a very useful theory. Also, a moral theory which made it too easy to be good would be less than useful. Even so, a moral theory should allow for the possibility of "showing the way." That is, people should be given the opportunity to become better people.

There is another set of reasons which show why moral theory and a theory of human nature should go hand-in-hand. Understanding people's needs, desires, wants, goals, and motivations will be crucial if moral theory is to be more than mere description, i.e., if moral theory is to be applied to real circumstances. What is often called "applied ethics" does not stand to moral theory as pure science stands to technology. Rather, applied ethics is more like the correct application of a scientific law to a particular situation. To apply a scientific law, one needs to know that the initial and boundary conditions of the law have been met. Thus, the Hardy-Weinberg Law, $p^2 + 2pq + q^2 = 1$, cannot be applied unless:

- The rates of forward and backward mutation are equal
- The rates of immigration and emigration are equal
- There is random mating
- The population is (infinitely) large, and there is no measurable natural selection.

To apply part of a moral theory is to understand that the situation encountered, e.g., a terminal cancer patient asks to have chemotherapy withdrawn, is such that just this part of the moral theory (always act to alleviate suffering) does apply. Put another way, there must be ways to classify situations, e.g., this is a case of requested withdrawal of life-sustaining treatment by a competent adult.

But moral theory cannot tell us everything. Consider again the case of science. Although the initial and boundary conditions of a law may be stated in general terms by the theory, e.g., at temperature close to "room temperature," we got confirmation of the Wiedemann-Franz law. To know that any particular case is an instance of when we should expect this *law* to hold, we have to measure. The way the world really is at a given time cannot be part of the theory. So it is with moral theory. What this means is that we must bring something to the theory. What we bring to it is our already relatively finely honed knowledge about the world, including our sense of what is right and what is wrong. It is easy to see that this must be so.

Suppose we used theory and theory alone. As previously discussed, we could never be sure that we were applying it correctly unless we could test the results against something independent from what the theory allows as correct. This is really not a subtle point; we do it all the time. We argue by pointing out "obviously" absurd or contradictory consequences: How can you be for euthanasia but against capital punishment? It is a classic attempted refutation of a naive form of utilitarianism that justifies slavery that any moral theory which justifies slavery must be wrong.

What this points to is that there is something else that moral theory will do for us. It will allow us to put our house of moral intuitions in order. A moral theory will be in accord with our clearest judgments of right and wrong, e.g., Nazi concentration camps were evil. A moral theory will pick out the moral quandaries for us, e.g., when can killing be medically therapeutic? It will explain to us why these are the quandaries. A moral theory will, therefore, represent accurately our feelings about, or knowledge of, which problems are easy and which are difficult. Naturally, the moral theory of choice will help us decide how to act in moral quandaries. Since a powerful moral theory will come with a theory of human nature, we will also come to understand our moral feelings.

In this way, moral theory begins and ends with what we already know about right and wrong. This process where the starting data create a theory, which is validated by being in accord (once again) with the starting data, can be called "bootstrapping." With morals, it probably cannot be avoided.

PHYSICIAN OBLIGATION/ PATIENT EXPECTATION

With this very brief and general introduction, let us turn to the topic of euthanasia. A traditional four-fold distinction is almost always made at the beginning of every discussion of euthanasia. When a person asks for euthanasia, we refer to this as voluntary euthanasia in contrast to involuntary euthanasia. Perhaps some instances of capital punishment by lethal injections can be considered involuntary euthanasia. When the euthanasia involves a clear action, e.g., firing a shotgun at one's brother who has Alzheimer's disease, the euthanasia is classified as active. This is to be distinguished from less clear cases of direct action, e.g., writing the order on a patient's chart "No Code." This, in turn, can be distinguished from deciding (with or without the patient's consent) never even to begin treatment. These sorts of cases are classified as passive.

(In technical philosophical circles, there is something called action theory. The distinction between active and passive applied to human behavior is not easy to draw. Indeed, it hides a welter of confusion. For our purposes, we need only examine the active/passive distinction as follows.)

In a now classic article, James Rachels argues as follows. The distinction between active and passive euthanasia will not hold up to analysis. It is easy to show that morally the two are equivalent. He shows this by example. Consider Smith, who stands to gain a fortune should his six-year-old cousin die. Smith murders his cousin by drowning him while he is taking a bath. Now suppose that with the same plan, Smith enters the bathroom, but before he can do a thing, the little boy slips in the tub, hits his head, goes under the water, and drowns. Smith makes no attempt to save his cousin. Rachels claims that Smith is equally as immoral in both cases. Thus, the active/passive distinction fails to hold water (3).

K. D. Clouser, in a veiled reply, points out that what makes the case of a physician different from the case of the uncle is that it is clear that the uncle has a moral duty to save his nephew from drowning. It is precisely the fact that there is a clear duty to save that makes both styles of killing wrong. Often, in cases of euthanasia, it is not clear what the duty on the part of the physician is. It is in these sorts of cases where active (killing) and passive (letting die) may not be moral equivalents. If there is even the hint of a duty to save, then a clear action (to kill) almost certainly must be different from a passive (letting die) (4). A case will help make this point.

Consider an 83-year-old diabetic woman. The disease has been getting worse and worse. She is losing her vision to diabetic retinopathy and now one of her legs is gangrenous. He leg must be amputated, or she will die. When she enters the hospital, she is lucid and determined. She will die, i.e., she will refuse the option of surgery. Her life is getting more and more restricted by her disease and by the resulting circumstances. Moreover, she now will become even more of a burden on her son and daughter-in-law with whom she lives. Her son has mixed feelings about whether to respect his mother's wishes. The resident in charge of the case feels that she definitely has a moral and legal right to die. The attending physician believes that she has a right to die but not on his service, when her life can so easily be saved. It is not obvious that she should be allowed to die. It, therefore, cannot be the case that she should be killed, e.g., given an overdose of morphine. This particular case also shows that the moral standing of euthanasia is in part a function of how particular physicians view their duties and responsibilities.

Another case will illustrate even more clearly that the doctor's obligations are involved in deciding when and how physicians should hasten the deaths of their patients. Emma was a 64-year-old retired department store executive. She was suffering from the last stages of emphysema. Although the use of a ventilator had been put off as long as possible, it was felt that she now needed the ventilator. She agreed; she also agreed to a tracheotomy. However, this sort of existence soon depressed her. After a few weeks, she asked to be taken off the respirator. Her physician said that this would be her decision. Emma, who realized that her death off the ventilator would be difficult, asked her physician for "a drug or some-thing" to ease the discomfort. The physician refused.

The physician had no trouble withdrawing life sustaining-therapy (the respirator) but could not administer a drug to make the death "easy." He couldn't give the drug because it would be, in his mind, tantamount to killing her because it became clear that she wouldn't let herself die otherwise. (The physician was not punishing the woman. He agonized over his feelings. He wanted to give her the drug, but he just couldn't do it.) To this physician there was a real line between active and passive euthanasia—a line which he just could not cross. To him, anything that was clearly a killing could not be part of medicine. It did not matter that the killing would make dying easier. For this physician when the principles, "do not kill" and "alleviate suffering," clashed, the choice was clear. "Do not kill" took precedence even if it caused (resulted in) suffering. The clash of moral rules will almost always create problems.

Does a patient have a moral right to expect (no) treatment from a physician, with the intention that death would come sooner than if a traditional course of action were continued or begun? This question is different from: Is it fair to ask for such treatment from one's physician? This latter question is often more concerned with personal relationships since it may be fair to ask more of a trusted ally than from a professional who is personally a "stranger." The former question can be seen as a general question, the answer to which turns on the values of the medical profession. We turn now to a brief characterization of the medical profession and the concept of professionalism in general.

THE MEDICAL PROFESSION

Eliot Freidson has emphasized that professions make every effort to maintain ultimate control over their own work. "What is essential is control over the determination and evaluation of the technical knowledge used in the work. . . . Professions are granted this sort of status by society, which believes in the dignity and importance of the profession's work (5).

Freidson characterizes the medical profession in line with his general ideas. What is important for our purposes is Freidson's concept of the physician as "moral entrepreneur."

Clearly, neither medicine nor the physician may be characterized as passive. As a consulting rather than scholarly or scientific profession, medicine is committed to treating rather than merely defining and studying man's ills. It has a mission of active intervention guided by what, in whatever time and place it exists, it believes to be ill in the world. Furthermore, it is active in seeking out illness. The profession does treat the illnesses laymen take to it, but it also seeks to discover illness of which laymen may not even be aware. One of the greatest ambitions of the physician is to discover and describe a "new" disease or syndrome and to be immortalized by having his name used to identify the disease. Medicine, then, is oriented to seeking out and finding illness, which is to say that it seeks to create social meanings of illness where that meaning of interpretation was lacking before. And insofar as illness is defined as something bad—to be eradicated or contained—medicine plays the role of what Becker called the "moral entrepreneur." Medical activity leads to the creation of new rules defining deviance; medical practice seeks to enforce those rules by attracting and treating the newly defined deviant sick (6).

To maintain currency, physicians, therefore, must find disease, treat disease, eliminate disease. Every time a disease defeats a physician, the claim of special status rings more and more hollow. Since death in general can be seen as a clear defeat, it is easy to understand how physicians come to see the death of a patient—even when "inevitable"—as a threat and defeat. Death is seen as the enemy. On these grounds, saying to a physician, "Let me die" or "Kill me" is asking a great deal.

Even so, why shouldn't patients ask a great deal from their physicians? Isn't it possible that we all have a right to die as we see fit? This would be a general right. Isn't it possible that we should have the right to contract with our physician for an "easy death" when we decide that the time is right. Let us examine each of these questions in turn.

We each have a right to die as we see fit. This right would be a right to commit suicide whenever we deem it appropriate. Theoretically, it is easy to say that there is such a right. If there is such a right, then the rest of us are obligated, at least, not to interfere in the suicide attempts of others. Yet this just does not square with our reactions. We have suicide hotlines. We publicize, as heroes, police who risk their lives to prevent others from committing suicide. We often think after a suicide "What a waste!" If there is a right to suicide, it is probably a circumscribed right. That is, is the person contemplating suicide competent? If the person is competent, are the reasons really good enough to merit our noninterference? It is not clear that the right to privacy, given how we act toward others, extends to suicide without the previously mentioned riders.

The right to die when and how we please can be considered a legitimate part of the doctor-patient relationship. If the physician is in full charge of the relationship, then, of course, the patient cannot make the contract. The contract "I will let you die/I will kill you, if _____ " has to be offered by the physician. If the patient is in full control of the doctor-patient relationship, then clearly the choice belongs to the patient. There is a middle ground: negotiation. The doctor and the patient (and perhaps the patient's family) can decide together about how best to handle the patient's dying. Since rights and obligations usually go together as correlatives, it would be unfair to give all the rights to the physician or all the rights to the patient or to the patient's family. It would be unfair on the assumption that, in general, one shouldn't knowingly ask another to violate a strongly held moral principle. Yet even this straightforward claim is complicated by the professionalism of the physician in the following sense.

It may be that doctors ought to be willing to do what they find uncomfortable if requested by their patients. If a patient asks to be allowed to die/to be killed, and it is almost assuredly a request aimed at what the patient perceives as in his or her best interest, then as long as the physician is not likely to be harmed by the request, perhaps taking on the obligation to let a patient die is just one of the profession's unpleasant task. Professional obligations are often more difficult precisely because of the profession. Indeed, perhaps with the prestige of the profession may come some unpleasant responsibilities.

Sometimes in discussion of euthanasia the expression "death with dignity" occurs. Tacked onto rights talk, one gets "Isn't there a right to a death with dignity?" Dignity is probably a very idiosyncratic concept. To some people, dying is not dignified and that is the end of the matter. To others, getting undressed and being probed by physicians is the height of indignity. It is not at all clear that there is anything intrinsically undignified about being hooked to monitors, machines, intravenously delivered drugs, etc. Whatever indignity there is as a result of such treatment is related to the patient's not wanting the treatment or to having little chance of restoring the health (even for a short while) of the patient. Death with dignity is likely best filled out as a death in the style chosen (or negotiated for).

Usually, the indignity is a violation of a patient's desire to be left alone; a violation of autonomy or a violation of good sense, i.e., the patient's privacy is invaded by medical technology when there is not sufficient reason for believing that the gains, given the cost, would be chosen by the patient.

Opposed to death with dignity is another catch phrase, the sanctity of life. Sanctity of life is used to mean that each and every life has infinite importance and value and, therefore, that it is always wrong to take life or to hasten death. Embedded in this position is the idea that we do not have the moral authority to set the value of our lives. In a way, what this principle suggests is that we do not own our lives in any way analogous to the way that we own our cars and television sets. Cars can be trashed if they upset us enough. But our lives can't be snuffed out even for the (apparently) best reasons. A physician who held a sanctity-of-life principle would be opposed to all forms of euthanasia. It is important to recognize that the sanctity-of-life principle, while ruling out euthanasia as legitimate, does not imply that the physician is "in charge" of lives. It is rather that no one is "in charge" except to save and to prolong.

We have suggested that in our present sociomedical contexts, the question of the legitimacy of euthanasia cannot be separated from the doctor-patient relationship or from the concept of professional obligations.

Precisely what are the professional obligations of a physician? How do professional obligations differ from general moral obligations? The latter question is not particularly difficult to answer. We all have general moral obligations, whatever those general obligations may be. Some authors such as B. Gert view general obligations as primarily negative. He lists 10 "moral rules" which determine 10 general obligations. "Don't kill. Don't cause pain. Don't disable. Don't deprive of freedom or opportunity. Don't deprive of pleasure. Don't deceive. Keep promises. Don't cheat. Obey the law. Do your duty" (7). Notice that eight of these ten are framed in a negative fashion. John Stuart Mill, somewhat on the other hand, would see a general obligation to increase happiness (8). The main point to stress is that these obligations bind us all.

Professional obligations bind only those members of the profession in question. Firefighters have somewhat different obligations from lifeguards. Both are sworn to save lives in extreme situations, but, of course, the lifeguard may be afraid of climbing tall ladders, while the fireman may be afraid of the water. This may be obvious, but to lose sight of the concept would be a mistake, for professional obligations come to be felt each in their contexts as strongly, if not more so, than some general obligations.

MEDICAL SETTINGS

Professional obligations come to be discharged in special settings: at the place of a robbery, the ocean, in the medical clinic. These settings create a atmosphere which can inform and give feeling to the problematic aspects of acting on one's professional obligations. Examples are legion for issues surrounding the right to die.

The Emergency Room

The most traditional case discussed in the literature of medical ethics in this respect revolves about Jehovah's Witness patients asking that they not be given blood transfusions.

A 22-year-old unmarried woman was involved in a motor vehicle accident. On medical examination at the hospital to which she had been taken it was determined that she would die unless operated on for a ruptured spleen. It was further determined that the young woman would die unless blood was administered. Both the patient and her parents were Jehovah's Witnesses who did not believe in blood transfusions. The patient insists that she expressed her refusal to accept blood. The evidence indicates, however, that she was in shock on admittance to the hospital and that it was her mother who was adamant in her refusal to consent to the administration of blood. The mother even signed a release of liability of medical and hospital personnel. The patient did not execute a release; presumably, she could not. Her father could not be located.

The hospital, believing the death of a patient to be imminent, made application through its attorney for the appointment of a guardian for the young woman with directions to consent to transfusions as needed to save life. The judge, after a hearing, appointed a guardian with authority to consent to blood transfusions for the preservation of the life of the young woman. Of some interest is the fact that during the hearing, the woman's mother told the judge she thought she could obtain the services of a surgeon who would perform the splenectomy without a transfusion. The judge called this surgeon; he declined the case. Surgery was performed, blood was administered, and the young woman survived. This appellate procedure stemmed from patient's efforts to vacate the trial court's order. (John F. Kennedy Memorial Hospital vs. Delores Heston and Jane Heston,—A2d—, 1971). (9)

What this case points out is that the emergency room does not lend itself to a negotiated doctor-patient relationship. Indeed, it may be a place in medicine where the swift application of technology *should* take precedence over face-to-face interpersonal relations. The emergency room is "geared up" to save lives in traditional and expedient ways. Physicians in this setting are unlikely to pause in order to reflect on the right to die. Whether this is morally wrong is a question which can be addressed after the discussion of the professional-institutional reasons often cited against the general legitimization of euthanasia.

The Nursing Home

Elderly nursing home patients often feel abandoned. Many deteriorate mentally, as well as physically, sometimes due to their age and sometimes due to their (perceived) situations. Still others, of course, suffer from chronic and debilitating diseases such as Alzheimer's disease, diabetes, chronic obstructive lung disease, or severe arthritis. How long should such patients be kept alive primarily by utilizing advanced technology? Should the family of such patients have the primary say in the decision to "let die"? How trustworthy (competent) are such nursing home patients? If they say, "Let me die," is that enough to bind the staff? The question of competence merges into the question of when should extraordinary means be used to keep a patient alive. These two questions can be highlighted by a brief examination of the burn unit.

The Burn Unit

After initial stabilization, burn victims await the most recent treatments which promise success. There is a problem, however. Some victims have an extremely poor prognosis, given their age and degree of injury. Should everything be done for every patient no matter what, or should patients (along with family) be allowed to decide? Part of being competent is being able to understand that treatment holds out little hope of recovery. Part of the proper use of medical technology is understanding that when technology holds out little, if any, hope for recovery, there is little reason to use such technology. Just about the only reasons are a) the patient requests its use; b) it is there, so it is used; c) there are many surprises in medicine. In any case, when therapy is unlikely to help, its use can be considered extraordinary (remembering that the word "extraordinary" is reserved for cases of life and death or very severe, if not life-threatening, injuries). All treatment not extraordinary is ordinary.

There is a sliding scale in that today's extraordinary treatment may become ordinary. This happens in three ways: 1) the treatment, although remaining basically the same, improves, e.g., coronary artery bypass; 2) the treatment is used so much that it becomes too common to merit the term extraordinary, e.g., dialysis; 3) auxiliary modalities, when combined with the treatment, make its application much more successful, e.g., the use of cyclosporine. These changes show that saying a treatment is extraordinary is not strong general support for arguments about when to withhold treatment.

The Neonatal Intensive Care Unit

This may be the most emotion-laden place of all. Here we deal with families whose deepest hopes have been apparently lost through a trick of nature. From extreme prematurity to spina bifida and congenital heart defects, physicians have to deal with the lives of infants and the lives of the parents of those infants. We shall return to these cases in the second part of this chapter. For now, it should be noted that we have a clear example of where feelings and emotions in the parents run high. Should the physician step back and not let those feelings and emotions have an affect at all, or should a physician, perhaps to be humane, allow those feelings and emotions to enter into medical decision making? Is it even possible to stand back in a situation like this and not be affected? For moral theory, the question is this: Who has the better look at a moral question, someone totally involved or someone totally uninvolved? If we come to believe that total involvement will clearly confuse the issue, then we ask: Is the best moral view one that is as free as possible from emotion?

SUMMARY

In this part of the chapter we have characterized moral theory, suggesting that it bears similarities to scientific theory. With this analogy comes a view of what applied ethics might mean.

We have, in general, discussed classical approaches to understanding the issue of euthanasia or the right to die. Distinctions discussed were: voluntary vs. involuntary; active (killing) vs. passive (letting die). Two often used expressions, death with dignity and the sanctity of life, were discussed. The concepts of professionalism and professional obligations were analyzed.. Four special medical settings were used to highlight the concepts of professional obligations, extraordinary medical treatment, and the question: What is the best moral perspective on a difficult moral issue?

Notably missing so far is a discussion of quality of life. Since this concept may underlie much of the following analysis, we shall now turn to quality of life.

MEASURING LIFE

Quantity of life is rather clearly the opposition in the dichotomy to quality of life. Briefly, quantity of life can mean no more than "Is the organism living or not?" As we shall see in our discussion of the definition of death, this question is not always easy to resolve. Quality of life refers to the value of the life in question. For "value" we can substitute other similar terms: meaning, good, worth, etc. There are further questions to ask when asking "How valuable is this life?" a) Should someone or some group, other than the person whose life it is, be allowed to answer the question? If so, who should be allowed: family, friends, hospital committees, governmental agencies, society? b) Is the concept "quality of life" such that it even makes sense to think that another can truly answer the question? c) How "binding" is the answer, and does the degree of binding depend on who gave the answer? We shall introduce our discussion of paternalism within the context of quality-of-life decisions as they affect the right to die.

We turn now to a sampling of illustrative cases. These samples are not meant to be exhaustive.

INFANTS AND EUTHANASIA

These sorts of cases run the gamut from infants with Down's syndrome and life-threatening but correctible conditions such as duodenal atresia or tracheoesophageal fistula to cases of anencephalic infants. The various forms of spina bifida lie in the middle. Let us start with anencephaly.

Anencephaly means that the brain is almost totally absent. As physicians sometimes euphemistically say, "This condition is incompatible with life." We can add to this, "No matter what." These infants will die. Is there any benefit to keeping these children alive as long as possible? Why should it matter who or what is benefited? Isn't all life sacred and worth preserving (the sanctity-of-life principle)? How could one answer the question about the benefit of keeping an anencephalic infant alive as long as possible? This is a question worth pursuing because it leads so clearly to the issue involved with children: Who should speak for the rights of children?

The reasons usually given for extending the life of an anencephalic infant are a) to satisfy parental requests, b) because it is a special obligation on the medical profession, or c) an application of some version of the sanctity-of-life principle. A question worth addressing is, of course, what to do when parental demands conflict with professional obligations? This leads us to Baby Doe sorts of cases. Before raising the Baby Doe examples, a theoretical distinction is needed.

Sometimes we know what we ought to do, that is, know all the appropriate reasons for justifying a course of action. Yet, even in these cases, we sometimes do otherwise. In some instances, we fail to do our duty out of weakness of will. In other instances, we don't so much fail to do our duty as we decide to follow what we feel is right, although our feelings may conflict with our reason. Many acts of heroism are seen, in cooler moments, as foolish and certainly not morally obligatory. At the moment, however, there is (often reported) an intensely felt obligation to act. The distinction worth drawing, for medical contexts especially, is between professional obligations—rationally and unemotionally known—and felt obligations, which are perhaps nothing more than the responses felt because of a difficult situation. With this distinction and the previously made points, we can go on to the general question of infant euthanasia.

The easiest way to focus on the question of infant euthanasia is to use the case which has come to be known as Baby Doe. The case can be cited briefly. A child with Down's syndrome and tracheoesophageal (TE) fistula was born. TE fistula, if not corrected, is fatal; but it is easily corrected by surgery. The physicians at the hospital were divided; some recommended (to the parents) surgery, others did not. The parents opted for no surgery. The baby died. The Supreme Court of Indiana ruled that the parents were within their rights in making this decision (10).

What might be behind a decision to let such a baby die?

1. The parents were selfish. They just didn't want to spend the extra energy needed to raise a child who would be retarded. The parents might also have been embarrassed about not being able to produce a healthy, normal child. These sorts of reasons center on the parents. There is a suggestion that selfish reasons are never good reasons. "Selfish," as ordinarily used, is a bit vague. It may mean interested only in furthering one's interests even at the total expense of others. But selfish may mean choosing one's interest over the interests of others when reasonable. This latter sense of selfish leads to a second set of reasons for letting Baby Doe die.

2. The baby's potential life—her quality of life—just did not merit the sacrifices called for by the parents. By appealing to quality of life, we can understand how the parents might have felt—that they were actually helping the infant by letting her die. Here we see a danger. Can we judge the quality of life for another person? In this sort of case, the problem is intensified by the fact that we can't accurately predict the degree of retardation of the child. Even if we were sure that a *severely* retarded child was "better off dead" we could not use the reasoning behind that judgment to help us with Baby Doe.

Obviously, this sort of case is especially vexing because the infant cannot speak for herself and because she cannot defend her own interests. Indeed, it is tempting to argue that since the infant is so helpless, it is a sign of our humanity to use the sanctity-of-life approach. That is, given the helpless state of the infant, the only true moral attitude to take is a presumption for life.

Such a view may be in keeping with a physician's attitude toward the practice of medicine in general. However, such a view conflicts with the apparent moral and legal rights of parents to make decisions for their children. Imagining the pediatric intensive care unit, looking at the baby with the parents, we should be able to see the strength of the distinction between obligations and felt obligations. As physicians, we may know that the parents have the right to decide and that we have an obligation to give the parents unbiased information about the likely future of the child. On the other hand, we may *feel* that that child ought to be given a chance to live. Notice that it is only on the sanctity-of-life view that the infant *has* rights. On the other view, we are, at best, allowing the infant certain rights.

A question of style has to be addressed here. If the decision to let the baby die is made, then how should the baby be allowed to die? Should the baby be denied food and water? Should the baby be kept hydrated but denied food? It has been argued that it is more merciful to allow the baby to die quickly rather than slowly. In keeping with this line of reasoning, some authors have proposed that the most moral course of action would be to kill the baby outright. In this way, we would be as certain as possible that the baby never suffered as a result of the decision to let him/her die.

Infants with severe physical disabilities in their futures present as difficult a problem as children who are bound to be badly retarded. Our inclinations generally are such that we suppose that a reasonable mental life is worth having even at the expense of a poor physical existence. We will return to this point when we discuss the case of the injured sculptor. Children who, after life-saving surgery, can expect hydrocephaly, incontinence, and paralysis, albeit normal intelligence, present exquisite problems for their parents. In terms of quality of life, should such children be saved? Can anyone really make such a judgment? Are the parents the best or the worst parties to make the decision? Again, what is the proper role of the physician? Should physicians give only the facts and take care to give them neutrally, so that if there is a bias, it will not show? Or, should physicians give advice based on their knowledge and opinions?

It is crucial to see that if physicians probably cannot be perfectly neutral and if there is a reasonable likelihood that parents will be sensitive to the doctor's feelings, then it may be incumbent on physicians to make an effort to understand the parents so that whatever direction they give will not be covert. A close doctor-patient relationship will also undercut, what many doctors fear, the development of a dependency on the physician. "Anything you say, doctor." Naturally, some doctors and some patients thrive on this sort of relationship. Where that is so, it will, by definition, be part of (arise from) the doctor-patient relationship.

BRAIN DEATH
AND IRREVERSIBLE COMA

As was suggested in the previous section, we find lack of a mental life, especially total lack, to be such a detriment that it seems to lead inexorably to a decision to let die. Thus, it is not surprising that if we discover that the *entire* brain is dead, then we find the fact that the rest of the body can be supported not enough reason to begin or even to continue life support. This claim needs some emendations. We have to be quite convinced that the medical criteria for whole brain death are accurate and precise, and that, of course, they have been met. We also need consent from the patient or from the next of kin. Naturally, one cannot get consent from a patient whose brain is dead. However, there are situations where the patient made his/her wishes known. There are also cases where there was a known risk of brain damage and, therefore, the issue was specifically discussed with the patient.

Irreversible coma differs from brain death in that the criteria for whole brain death are not met. Rather criteria are met which indicate that the patient will never again regain what we understand as full consciousness. Often it is said that the patient is in a permanent vegetative state. What makes irreversible coma more troublesome than whole brain death is that such patients may have some mental states.

If science proceeded to the point where it was possible to say that only the part of the brain responsible for mental life was destroyed, then we might feel that such a patient was no longer a person. That is, as the expression "vegetative state" implies, there is a distinction between a person and a vegetable in that (presumably) the main difference is the possibility of self-consciousness, what has been called "mental life," in the person. Turnips and carrots may have some similarity in anatomical structure and physiological mechanism to humans. But the similarity (most likely) ends there. Just as "person" has a legal meaning, so it might be claimed, does it have a moral force? A person, by virtue of being a person, has certain rights and expectations. But when the biological basis of personhood is lost forever and there is no longer any possibility for a mental life, then we have not a person but a body. It is not at all clear that bodies, qua bodies, have or ought to have rights, e.g., to be kept "alive."

A problem has been skirted in this discussion. How can we decide that a body with no mental life is not worth life support? There are at least four ways. 1) It just may not be worth the effort—in solely economical terms. This may sound harsh. But in a world where not everything can be done at once, this sort of consideration cannot be postponed forever. 2) We can perform three sorts of thought experiments: (a) Would this patient, given what we know, want to continue in a vegetative state? (b) Would I want to continue in a vegetative state? and (c) Would anyone want to continue in a vegetative state? The three thought experiments require some further analysis.

Clearly (a) calls for a good doctor-patient relationship. Especially where the question was not specifically asked, the opinion of the physician will have to depend on information gleaned from knowledge of the patient (and family). Naturally, we are assuming that the physician has been asked something like "What should we do?" by the family, for it is their decision to make unless there are specific requests by the patient.

What I might want, whether I am physician, husband, father, or daughter, can be relevant only if I am reasonably certain that my desires, feelings, emotions, etc. are relatively like those of the patient. What anyone would want seems to have the advantage of being general. But this generality carries problems with it. Does "anyone" refer to the average person? Does anyone mean all people like the patient? Or does anyone mean any rational person? The last question brings with it all the difficulties of deciding what is the best characterization of rational.

The point of this philosophical diversion is this. Sometimes we are forced to make important judgments for other people. It is essential to understand the principles involved in making decisions for others. In other words, we have come to the issue of paternalism, an issue which many authors see as the central one for understanding many of the more difficult medical-ethical cases.

PATERNALISM

In general, how do we justify what we do for others when we aren't sure whether they want to be left alone by us or not? This question ranges from a forced

Caesarean in the interests of the fetus to withholding some frightening information from a patient about to undergo surgery. The middle ground is faced more often. When do we try to influence others even if they do not ask for help? Nozick defines paternalism as a *prima facie* infringement on liberty. In his *Anarchy, State and Utopia,* he says:

> My nonpaternalistic position holds that someone may choose (or permit another) to do to himself *anything* unless he has acquired an obligation to some third party not to do or allow it (11).

The rider is meant to show how to justify paternalism. The justification would include a discussion of obligations, both professional and general, and how they are acquired. In general, where liberty is restrained, the burden should be put on the restrainer to justify interference. Otherwise, morality would become the morality of the strong.

Gert give the following characterization of paternalism:

> A is acting paternalistically toward S if and only if A's behavior (correctly) indicated that A believes that (1) his action is for S's good; (2) he is qualified to act on S's behalf; (3) his action involves violating a moral rule (or will require him to do so) with regard to S; (4) S's good justifies him in acting on S's behalf independently of S's past, present, or immediately forthcoming (free, informed) consent; and (5) S believes (perhaps falsely) that he (S) generally knows what is for his own good (7).

We have already listed Gert's 10 moral rules. (See page 330.) Gert goes on to say:

> Being deprived of freedom is simply being deprived of an indefinite number of opportunities. Being deprived of an opportunity is simply being deprived of the freedom to do some particular thing. (7)

Gert offers the following as a justification for paternalistic intervention:

> (A necessary condition is that) it must also be true that the evils that would be prevented to S are so much greater than the evils, if any, that would be caused by the violation of the rule, that it would be irrational for S not to want to have the rule violated with regard to himself. But even this is not sufficient: To make it sufficient one must also be able to universally allow the violation of this rule in these circumstances, or, in somewhat more technical terminology, be able to publicly advocate this kind of violation. (12)

By offering a sufficient condition, Gert is trying to undercut the force of the following example. Consider a law school student, otherwise competent, who has not prepared for the Bar exam. The law student cheats and is caught. An argument which might be used by the student is that there is no question of competence (law grades attest to this) and that the cheating, if not found out, will hurt no one, whereas if reported, there will be harm done. Gert admits that this argument is relevant, but it is not enough. One must also be ready to advocate publicly that anyone like this student could cheat. In other words, we must consider the hypothetical consequences of allowing this moral rule (don't cheat) to be violated.

Publicly advocating an attitude does not necessarily require advocating it openly or "out loud." Publicly advocating resembles what some philosophers may have meant by universalizing, but the difference is significant enough to justify introducing the new phrase. One is publicly advocating, in my technical sense, when and only when one regards all rational men as potential listeners and believes that they all could accept the attitude being advocated. (7)

The attitude is "The rule (don't cheat) should be obeyed by all others with regard to those for whom they were concerned" (7).

Charles Fried, in his book *Right and Wrong*, argues that the norms of right and wrong spring ultimately from respect for persons. For Fried to break a moral rule (intentionally) is to deny the "personal status" of the victim. Where a moral rule is unintentionally broken, the effect, where public guidelines are concerned, is to demean personal status. Breaking a moral rule unwittingly merely, at best, excuses the breaker from blame (13).

What this discussion of paternalism shows is that our intuition about how to help make decisions for others was correct. We have to know those others well, and we have to be willing to put ourselves and others in the position of being acted on. (Remember that to be a patient in its root sense is to be someone acted on; someone who, by definition, is passive.) The upshot of the discussion is *NOT* that paternalism is always unjustified. The insight that sometimes paternalism is called for is found in the legal doctrine of therapeutic privilege: A physician may decide to cut corners—usually centering on consent—if the physician has good reason to believe that such action is definitely in the best interest of the patient. Again, we see how important a good doctor-patient relationship is, since the best support for acting on therapeutic privilege would come from such a relationship. Moreover, our examination of paternalism leads us to see that therapeutic privilege itself is underwritten by what Gert refers to as "publicly advocating." The physician who uses therapeutic privilege in a just fashion must also be ready to have therapeutic privilege used on him/her.

With even more technical philosophy on line, we can move on to our next set of cases.

EUTHANASIA IN ADULTS

Let us examine the category of terminal patients first. Obviously, we should settle on a characterization of terminal: A disease is terminal when cure is unlikely given the a) survival time of similar patients from time of diagnosis and b) research state of the art at the time of diagnosis. There is a relatively direct causal chain, so it can be established that death was due to the disease and that death occurred sooner than would have been expected or predicted if the disease had not been present (14).

We immediately have a further distinction. Some terminal patients are not near death. If they are not near death and if they have some "quality of life" ahead, should we—as physicians—accede to their request to be left to die? That is, suppose such a patient prefers no treatment, where treatment will extend life. Should a physician agree and do nothing else? Is it part of the professional or general moral obligation of a physician to make some effort to persuade this patient to undergo therapy? Is it (usually) the patient's legal right to refuse treatment? When treatment has already been started, then it is usually more difficult for the physician to stop treatment, when requested, without also attempting to change the patient's mind. Perhaps it should be easier to "give in" to the patient's wishes because at least he or she has tried.

Naturally, part of the decision will be the kind of dying in store for the individual. Life shortly after diagnoses and initiation of treatment may be acceptable, whereas the prognosis may hold in store a relatively long and painful death—even a short but intensely painful death is exceedingly unpleasant as one's inevitable future. Shouldn't it be the patient's right to decide that the pain of the dying just isn't worth the quality of life up until that time?

Is the best reason for euthanasia in these cases a) being terminal; b) the perception of unpleasantness and the pain that lies ahead; c) the actual unpleasantness and pain? If one chooses a) or b), then euthanasia would seem to be justified before the point of closeness of dying is reached. If one chooses c), then euthanasia, it would seem, would have to wait until the time of dying.

This sort of approach is made from the standpoint of evaluating reasons. It does not deal with the real issue of who should have the power and authority to make such decisions. By now we should realize that in medical settings the answer to the real question is: some negotiated settlement between the desires of the patient and the felt obligations of the physician and medical staff. In other words, the very concept of "best reason" tied to action presumes that the patient *should* ask and that the physician does or does not deliver, depending upon an objective analysis of the reasons for requesting euthanasia. Such a model will not stand the scrutiny of the real world.

Another way to put this issue into perspective is to reask: Where the quality of life of an individual is the central feature of a decision, should anyone even try to interfere or change, in any way, the decision made by that person? Even if the answer to this question is a resounding NO, does it follow that any doctor is obligated to allow any patient to die or to hasten death in any way? What are the sources of professional obligations? Are they primarily the physician and the profession, or do they stem from the desires of the patient and, therefore, in large part from the negotiated terms of the doctor-patient relationship? We approach these questions obliquely.

What of patients who are so unhappy with their physical conditions that, even though they are not terminal, they wish to die? Cases will help here, since this is a category not obvious to those outside the medical profession. Some patients have chronic diseases that get more and more debilitating, e.g., diabetes. As we saw, a patient with advancing diabetes might choose to die rather than to have life-saving surgery for a gangrenous leg. The thought of an even more crippling existence can be just too much. Other patients, often because of trauma, are forced to realize that to remain alive will be to accept a totally new lifestyle. For example, in the play (and movie) "Whose Life Is It Anyhow?" a young sculptor is injured in a car accident. Once vigorous, he now can move only his head. What lies ahead for him is a life of total dependence—certainly a life devoid of sculpting. Should he reject this "new" life before he actually gives it a try? What are the obligations of his physicians?

Instead of asking "Does he have a right to reject this new life?" we ask, "Should he reject the new life without giving it a try?" Isn't he giving up in the face of adversity and asking the medical profession to give up as well? On the other hand, is it the job of the medical profession to create moral fiber in such patients?

Applying the quality-of-life principle and assuming that it is a judgment to be made by the patient yields one answer: Let him die. Applying the sanctity-of-life principle that any life is inestimably precious and, therefore, to be saved at all costs, yields another answer: Don't let him die. These two ways of approaching the problem yield conflict, which is not surprising, since, in a sense, they are principles constructed in such a way that they must conflict.

There are other approaches. A cost-benefit analysis would give an answer. Flipping a coin would give another answer. The point of using two approaches which give conflicting results is to remind ourselves that moral problems often come from choices of principle and that those choices rarely lead to compromise, since principles are so often stated in absolutist terms. Loosening the concept of a moral principle to "other things equal, do X (or don't do Y)" helps, but only if we can clearly spell out the riders—"other things equal" or "within reason." For example, if we considered the principle, "Within reason, don't let mentally alert and physically stable patients die," would we apply it in this case? a) Is such a patient truly stable? b) Is such a rule really meant to apply to such severely injured patients? c) Can we ignore the rule when a mentally alert patient asks us? That is, isn't this patient too depressed to be considered competent? Obviously, a teenager who could no longer play tennis and asked to be allowed to die for that reason alone, would be rebuffed, but the sculptor and the burn victim (from the introduction) may have compelling reasons. The rules and the riders don't supply answers.

Is there a middle ground, a way to avoid choosing between the application of conflicting principles? Wouldn't it be at least rational to suggest to such a patient that a new life is worth a try? If it turns out to be as dismal as it now appears, then "letting die" can again be discussed as a live option. The importance of this strategy is that it shows to the patient that the medical profession can be supportive and not merely adversarial. While this strategy does not yield total control to the patient, neither does it emphasize what is often felt as a total lack of control. Indeed, some requests for euthanasia can easily be reinterpreted as requests for return of some self-control—a return of autonomy and, in this sense, dignity. The very offer may be enough to change an intended course of action. It may not, but at least it makes discussion real and more than just talk.

TERMINAL PATIENTS

The cases of terminal patients can be handled in a similar fashion. As long as there is a trustworthy doctor-patient relationship, there can be an agreement to the effect that if the dying becomes unbearable, especially due to pain, then the idea of "letting die" will be seriously considered. It should be clear, however, that this strategy will not satisfy someone who wants to die now or, at least, soon. Before dealing with "direct" killing, let us deal with the question of when, if ever, it is permissible to withhold food and water from a patient, since it will lead us to one approach to an answer about "direct killing."

In 1986, in New Jersey, a judge ruled that food and water could be withheld from a 31-year-old woman who had been in a vegetative state for six years. Her husband had petitioned the court for the right to stop "treatment." Withholding food and water, unlike stopping chemotherapy for cancer, will necessarily lead to death. Because of this, it can be held that withholding food and water is equivalent to active killing. Since active killing is never allowed, neither should the withdrawing of food and water. It may be that legally there is no difference between mechanical ventilation and "artificial" feeding. Still, there is a moral difference based on the inevitability of death when feeding is discontinued.

What has to be understood in evaluating this argument is that when life-sustaining treatment, e.g., a ventilator, is removed, one has every good reason to expect that death will ensue. Surprises occur. But surprises cannot be used to claim that the reasoning was fallacious or that one should never act on good reasons. For then, no action would ever be possible. Thus, the argument that withholding food and water is of a different moral ilk from withholding mechanical ventilation is, at best, a weak argument.

There is, however, another sort of argument to shore-up the claim that food and water must never be withheld or withdrawn. This argument turns on a characterization of medicine as a profession.

According to this line of reasoning, medicine's primary goal is to preserve life at all costs. Lives should be saved and bettered, if at all possible; but above all, lives must never be ended by interfering with the natural course of events. Since feeding is natural (as is breathing), it follows that just about any mechanical intervention is justified and may never be withdrawn once started. Indeed, they must also be started whenever available. Without the presumption that lives must be preserved, the trust which makes up the core of the doctor-patient relationship would be corroded to the point where medicine as a profession would be impossible. At least, without the idea of "preserve all lives" at its core, we would no longer recognize the profession of medicine.

Accompanying this line of argument is the claim that once we let certain patients die, it will be too easy to let certain other patients die until our reasons for "letting die" have less and less to do with the patient's perceived quality of life and more and more to do with our reasons for not wanting to deal with some patients. Some physicians use a variation of this argument to support the view that hospices should be kept separate from teaching hospitals. As it is, terminal patients are not the favorites of residents, for there is often little left to learn (about scientific medicine) from them. With a hospice handy, it would be all too easy to transfer these patients, thus leaving the residents even less able to deal with the interpersonal aspects of the dying. Moreover, the proper attitude for a teaching hospital is not resignation to fate but should be, instead, fight to the end—if the patient desires to fight. But where patients see the hospice at the end of the hall or on the next floor, the chances of fighting are dimmed.

Can we kill a patient directly? Here we are being told "no," and the reason has to do with the nature of the medical profession and its role in society. This complex line of reasoning is difficult to analyze. It turns on facts, e.g., how do residents in oncology really feel about patients near death? It turns on values, e.g., what is the proper attitude worth instilling in young physicians? It turns on a view of the goals of medicine as if those goals can be determined only by the practitioners. Although this pattern of reasoning should not be dismissed out of hand, it is clear that if patients have some say in what the goals of medicine should be, then much of the force of the above argument is lost. Again, we are reminded that medicine as a profession should grow out of an agreement between two parties. Once the doctor-patient relationship is opened to negotiation, then some physicians might be persuaded to kill and still others might find a different ground of agreement with the patient. The value of seeing the source of the disagreement and being willing to deal with the disagreement is that it is the only real way to ensure an open, nondogmatic approach, not only by the physician but also by the patient.

The perplexing questions surrounding euthanasia are certainly ones for moral philosophy. Yet it must be remembered that these perplexing questions grow out of personal relationships, out of deeply felt needs, desires, emotions, and fears. It would be easy to forget these factors while concentrating on the conceptual analysis of moral philosophy. The goal of this chapter was to redirect attention from philosophy and ideas to people with all their frailties.

VIRTUES AND ETHICS

An approach to ethical theory which recognizes the social nature of medicine and does not overly stress the use of moral principles is suggested by MacIntyre's *After Virtue*. He suggests that we ask, "What kind of a person do I want to be?" If we focus on any particular act, letting myself or another die, we should be able to see that these acts, and the reasons we give to justify them, are part of a larger picture made of our lifestyles and our constant fine-tuning of our character and its relationship to our lifestyle. In any particular moral quandary, we ask, "If I take this route now and then again in similar circumstances, what kind of a person will that make me?" One of the assumptions of this approach is that being moral is best understood as part of a larger becoming (more and more moral) a certain kind of person. As one does this, actions and reasons are incorporated into one's character. Being moral on this view is a skill akin to hitting a baseball or tying a bow. At first there are "rules" to follow. At first we concentrate on getting it right. But after practice and attention to result, we find the technique "internalized." We just tie the bow. We hit the ball.

Now imagine a third objective party watching my activities. That third party would be able to list the virtues which I exhibit as I go through life. Are those virtues, which make up my character, the virtues I want for myself? Are they the virtues I would want others around me to have?

SUMMARY: IS EUTHANASIA A RIGHT?

If X is right, then people with that right have another right: the right not to have their right to X interfered with. This right creates in the rest of us a duty not to interfere. On a different view, if X is a right, then those with that right have another right: the right to have help in exercising their right to X. This right creates in the rest of us a positive duty to help others exercise their rights. As if this weren't complex enough, some rights are probably more central than others. The right to park in my allotted parking space is not nearly as important as my right to be treated by, and not turned away from, an emergency room when I am bleeding to death.

Implicitly, this chapter has tried to show that one has to choose between the two pictures of rights given above. That done, one must also distinguish between the rights and duties which bind us all and those rights and duties which spring from professions, i.e., from special contexts. None of this can be abstracted from the fact that the context of "the right to die" is an exceedingly personal one. Its context demands attention to the human relations which make up the doctor-patient relationship.

None of this is satisfying if one sought a clear and easy answer. But to seek a clear and easy answer is only to ensure a dissatisfaction which is more likely to lead one astray than is the tortuous path to legitimate understanding.

REVIEW QUESTIONS

1. Why does a moral theory need to incorporate a philosophical or theoretical model of the nature of human behavior?
2. Discuss the issue of control in the doctor-patient relationship as it applies to the right to die.
3. Discuss the manner in which a physician's professional obligation may be contingent upon the particular medical setting in which he/she is operating.
4. How does the state of the art in medical technology determine "extraordinary" treatment? What effect does this have on the use of the issue of withholding treatment?
5. Discuss the concepts of duty as they pertain to the "rights" of human beings within the ethical context of life and death decisions.
6. What are the chief factors that must be considered when addressing the issue of euthanasia for the terminally ill adult patient?
7. Elaborate the core issue inherent in the incompatibility of the principles of "quality of life" and "sanctity of life."
8. Are the answers to moral questions to be defined in absolute terms. or are they to be tempered by situational variables?
9. In what way does the "duty to save" differentiate active from passive euthanasia? What potential problems are raised by this distinction?
10. What do you consider to be the major issues surrounding the question of "quality" vs. "quantity" of life?

REFERENCES

1. Shaw, A. (1973). Dilemmas of 'informed consent' in children. *New England Journal of Medicine, 289,* 880–885.
2. Reed, E. (1981). The case of Brother Fox. *Legal Aspects of Medical Practice, 9,* 1.
3. Rachels, J. (1975). Active and passive euthanasia. *New England Journal of Medicine, 292,* 78–80.
4. Clouser, K. D. (1977). Allowing for causing: Another look. *Annals of Internal Medicine, 87,* 622–625.
5. Freidson, E. (1973). *Profession of medicine* (p. 186). New York: Dodd, Meade and Co.
6. Freidson, E. (1973). *Profession of medicine* (p. 253). New York: Dodd, Meade and Co.
7. Gert, B. (1970). *The moral rules.* New York: Harper & Row.
8. Mill, J. S. (1961). Utilitarianism. In M. Cohen (Ed.), *The Philosophy of J. S. Mill* (321–398). New York: Modern Library.
9. Holman, E. J. (1972). Adult Jehovah's Witnesses and blood transfusions. *Journal of the American Medical Association, 219,* 273–274.

10. Holder, A. (1983). Parents, courts and refusal of treatment. *Journal of Pediatrics, 103*, 515–521.

11. Nozick, R. (1974). *Anarchy, state and utopia*, p. 58. New York: Basic Books.

12. Gert, B. and Culver, C. (1979). The justification of paternalism. *Ethics, 89*, 199–210.

13. Zucker, A. (1986). To the marriage of true minds: Some synergisms of ethics, law and medicine. *Death Studies 10*, 119–133.

14. Zucker, A. (1980). Terminal and safe. *Journal of Health Politics, Politics, Policy, and Law, 5*, 6–10.

Life Preservation:
Individual and Societal Contexts

Felix M. Berardo, Anthony J. La Greca,
and Donna H. Berardo

The pathogens that lessen one's life are ubiquitous (1). They are in our social-cultural and psychological world, just as much as they are in our physical world of microbiology and chemistry. If the pathogens are ubiquitous, so are those characteristics and attributes of all aspects of life that can promote longevity. This chapter is an explication of the salient positive and negative dimensions that help to account for why one person lives longer than another.

The topic of survivorship can be approached in a variety of ways ranging from manuals on mega-vitamin theories to highly technical compilations of life-expectancy tables done by demographers. We attempt to embrace both individual and societal contexts which significantly influence life potential. Several strategies are noted which can be implemented to strengthen our survival capability. It is important to emphasize that these strategies are *active*—the individual proceeds from a conscious posture of pursuing a longer life. Basically, these strategies for survival comprise those elements of death education that contribute to the art of living.

Death education and survivor education are complementary sides of the same coin. A primary objective of the former is to assist people in coming to grips with their feelings and attitudes toward death and the dying process. A major goal of the latter is to sensitize people to those attitudes, behaviors, and conditions which threaten their lives and decrease their longevity. Both death education and survivor education presume that through knowledge and the achievement of these goals, death will become less fearful and life will be more rewarding and enjoyable.

This chapter represents a condensed and revised version of earlier work by the authors (65).

INDIVIDUAL LIFESTYLES
AND SURVIVORSHIP

The Role of Habits, Attitudes, and Nutrition

The familiar saying that we are all "victims of habit" carries with it a great deal of truth. For some people, the chief threat to survival comes from personal habits whose deleterious effects are known but ignored. Smoking, excessive eating, drug abuse, and alcoholism are all examples of a person's involvement with his own "slow death," which has been defined as "a predictable event, coming sooner rather than later, because of some systematic habit which threatens or injures health" (2, p. 81). Regardless of the flood of public warnings, millions of people choose to disbelieve or ignore the fatal consequences of their own habits, and their continuation points toward a certain degree of active involvement in shortening their lives. This "death by installment" shows a person's cooperating posture with his/her own demise.

For example, the most common form of cancer in the United States is skin cancer. The sun is responsible for 95 percent of all skin cancer, with 500,000 cases reported each year. Melanoma, the most virulent and deadly skin cancer, also occurs through overexposure to the rays of the sun. And, it appears that skin cancers, in general, are developing at even younger ages, due to increased leisure time being spent outdoors.

Despite the above, and despite the fact that most people are now aware of the damaging effects of prolonged exposure to ultraviolet rays, millions continue to bake their bodies under the sun. Moreover, many are not aware that several common drugs, for example, tetracycline, some diuretics, and even oral contraceptives, increase their sensitivity to the sun which, in turn, increase their risk of skin cancer through overexposure. Artificial tanning machines are similarly dangerous and risky.

The knowledge and procedures necessary to avoid such risks are available. Avoiding overexposure in the first place is the first rule of survival. Using a broad spectrum sunscreen and having yearly medical examinations of the skin are all easy to do. With early detection, skin cancer is almost always curable.

Just as one can take precaution against skin cancer becoming a threat to life, so one can significantly reduce the risk of injury from auto accidents. Forty-seven percent of the annual 100,000 accidental deaths are due to motor vehicle accidents (3). Traffic safety experts agree that if drivers would simply "buckle up" before starting their engines, the probability of car deaths would be drastically reduced by as much as 30 percent (4). Seat belt installation in automobiles has failed to achieve its maximum potential for reducing the risk of premature mortality. People are still in the negative habit of not taking the simple forethought to "buckle up."

Cultural and Personal Attitudes

Over the past 15 years, there has been an accumulation of research documenting "that certain attitudes and behaviors can promote survival in a variety of conditions, can halt or slow disease processes, and can even prolong life" (5, p. 19). While the deleterious effects of negative habits are rather apparent, the more subtle aspects of other patterns of lifestyle are not. This can be illustrated by the less easily identifiable factors that contribute to greater social isolation and higher mortality risk among males in American society. Such factors are partly cultural in nature and pertain to sex-role definitions and expectations. They involve notions of "machismo" in the face of traumatic events. In Berardo's (6) study of older widowers, for example, he notes that:

> . . . society expects males to fend for themselves and avoid becoming dependent . . . his *awareness* of that expectation may lead to a certain hesitation or reluctance to ask for or seek assistance. Indeed, this awareness may sometimes make the widower feel compelled to sustain an image of self–sufficiency in the face of a burdensome existence.

Males and perhaps, in particular, older widowers become victims of the "masculine must be strong" ethic (7).

The expectation that men play a stoic, nonemotional role even in the face of crises can have other negative consequences. Some psychologists argue that this type of male frequently ignores his personal health, tends to take more risks in driving or sports, represses emotional expression, and often reacts to stress by overeating, drinking or smoking (8). By denying his vulnerability, he is pretending he is immortal. His body, of course, has no such illusions.

Four additionally important attitudes and behaviors that merit special discussion here are: 1) the ability of individuals to see themselves in a holistic manner; 2) the attention people must give to physical exercise to increase their survival; 3) the role played by our "paying attention" to the world around us; and 4) cynicism.

A HOLISTIC PERSPECTIVE

The trend toward holistic medicine is not "pop therapeutics." Biofeedback and certain meditation techniques such as yoga, for example, have been linked to being able to lower body temperature, and both Kent (9, p. 162) and Mann (10, p. 159) postulate that such ability when implemented may actually increase longevity. Twenty minutes a day of quiet meditation and reflection is an excellent means of "taking 10 steps backward" to help better understand the situations and tasks faced daily.

PHYSICAL EXERCISE

Not only does exercise help one both physically and psychologically, studies substantiate that such activity is life-saving. A major finding of one large-scale study was that physical exercise lengthens life and prevents heart disease and stroke (11). Other evidence for the crucial role of exercise continues to mount (12, 13). It is becoming increasingly clear that people who do not exercise are failing to take advantage of a significant means to prevent premature mortality.

PAYING ATTENTION

One's philosophy of life not only influences the quality and vitality of daily living, but may also contribute to longevity. In evaluating the lessons learned from the long, winding letters from her grandmother, who died at age 80, Cameron (14) concluded that "survival lies in sanity, and sanity lies in paying attention . . . success or failure, the facts of life really have little to do with its quality. The quality of life is in proportion, always, to the capacity for delight. The capacity for delight is the gift for paying attention" (p. 138). Moreover, the act of paying attention brings with it the reward of healing.

Cameron concluded that paying attention is an act of connection to all that is within our environment and that such connections give new meaning to life and enhance our ability to survive. She notes that it often takes some kind of pain to get people to pay attention to the discrete and precious moments of their existence. Pain forces us to reevaluate our circumstances, to appreciate the value of right now, and to look forward to each moment of each day.

CYNICISM

Studies designed to further specify the negative components of the widely publicized "Type A" personality point to a link between "cynicism" and increased risk of coronary disease (15). It's been found that patients who scored high on hostility were 50 percent more likely to have clogged arteries than those with low scores. In a related retrospective study (15), it was found that among 225 physicians tested 25 years earlier, those with high hostility scores had five times more heart disease than others who scored below the median. Further analysis of the hostility measure revealed that it was mostly tapping an attitude of mistrust, that is, cynicism. Mistrustful people often times produce "fight or flight" hormones that accelerate plaque buildup leading to a "hardening" of the arteries. If one seeks to strengthen one's survival potential, some modification of the cynical outlook appears essential.

Nutrition

Perhaps the area of nutritional behavior is one that is most illustrative of how cultural and personal attitudes affect survival. The relationship between nutrition and health is a complex one. Experts differ on the effects of nutrition, and there is controversy as to how far one can extrapolate relevant studies of animals to conclusions about humans. Good nutrition *per se* is not a guarantee of survivorship if a person has other negative habits, such as smoking, or is not able to cope with stress. Yet, a wide spectrum of government agencies, committees, and institutes has supported the need for a balanced nutritional intake from the four main food groups, as well as a diet that limits fat contents to one-third of the calories necessary for a particular weight group (11).

FATS AND CHOLESTEROL

One of the key factors regarding proper nutrition is that of limiting the intake of fats and cholesterol (9, 11, 16). High levels of cholesterol and the manner with which it travels through the blood have been related to heart disease by many medical researchers. For most Americans, careful diets can keep cholesterol under control, particularly the dangerous low-density-lipoprotein (LDL) cholesterol. Weight reduction and eating certain fiber foods, such as carrots, apples, oats, and soybeans, also help decrease cholesterol. Aerobic exercise can cut down the percentage of LDL cholesterol in the blood. While it can be stated unequivocally that too much cholesterol in the blood will cause atherosclerosis and heart attacks, we still don't know how much is too much. Consequently, people must by willing to devote time and energy toward understanding what cholesterol level is appropriate for them.

There are, of course, countless nutritional considerations that cannot be covered here (for example, the relationship between nutrition and its impact on the central nervous system or the pituitary system). Three conclusions can be stated regarding nutrition and longevity: 1) Nutrition greatly affects the onset of a host of pathologies, such as myocardial degeneration, cardiovascular diseases, and others (11, 16). 2) Proper nutrition can be a significant component of an overall approach to increase longevity (11). 3) In spite of the central importance that nutrition plays in enhancing our survivorship potential, few people in and out of the health care system give sufficient attention to understanding one's *personal* nutrition needs. While general knowledge regarding nutrition is being disseminated, precise recommendations may vary from individual to individual. What is more, a person's diet habits regarding balanced nutrition can never be evaluated in isolation from other central considerations. The person aware of survivorship implications questions the nutritional effects and interactions of each and every prescription drug prescribed by a physician. The person aware of life-threatening potentials seeks to understand the relationship between any disease or pathology and nutrition. Until each person seeks to understand and implement this and other precise information, one's life chances are diminished.

THE PSYCHOSOCIAL FACTORS IN SURVIVING STRESS

Modern health research has moved away from a narrow physiological/ biological/chemical model for explaining death. Nowhere is this more apparent than in the research examining the relationship between stress and survivorship. Stressors are ". . . *demands that tax or exceed the resources of the system* or, to put it in a slightly different way, demands to which there are not readily available or automatic adaptive responses. . . ." (17, p. 109). Stress can cause, as well as alter, the effect of disease (18). The brain's hypothalamus is affected by and controls the biochemical response of our body to stress. This response can be lethal. We now know that how one copes with stress can adversely affect the central nervous system, the cardiovascular system, and the immune system.

Wilding (18) reports that those who worked at the Kennedy Space Center in its pioneer days of the 1960s now have a 50 percent higher incidence of sudden death and cardiovascular disorders than the general population. He also reports on a group of students who, 25 years ago, were given tests to assess levels of anger and hostility. Today, those who had scored high on levels of anger and hostility are now afflicted with five times the rate of heart disease compared to those who had average anger and hostility scores. Also, those who had high scores are now dying at six times the expected death rate.

The effects on the immune system can also be profound. Researchers have found that the way a heavy smoker reacts to the pressure of life affects the risk of developing lung cancer. In a recent study, it was found that heavy smokers who coped well with stress did not develop lung cancer. Those who did not cope well with the same types of stress did develop lung cancer (18). Similarly, speculation has emerged that those who carry the AIDS virus may help to trigger its active destruction by not coping well with stress. If this is proven, it will help provide a vital linkage between stress and the deterioration of the immune system.

Psychosocial Dimensions of Stress

We know that potentially stressful situations are a common part of life. Six intervening psychosocial factors that influence the impact stress has on health and illness are: 1) childhood adaptation; 2) personality hardiness; 3) expectation of stress; 4) compartmentalization of stress; 5) social support networks; and 6) general environment.

CHILDHOOD ADAPTATION

Childhood experience of a highly distressful nature can affect the level of stress throughout one's life. Visintainer and Seligman (19) found that: 1) Early family conflicts increase one's chances of developing cancer as an adult; 2) Significant childhood events resulting in the loss of a loved one (death or divorce of parents) are experienced in a helpless manner by a child. This sense of helplessness may actually lead to a lessening of our adult immune systems and our ability to cope with adult pressure. Of course, the reverse may also be true. Early childhood experiences where one copes with stress (and can even have a sense of control over it) can protect people from disease later on.

PERSONALITY HARDINESS

Adult personality "hardiness" is composed of three major elements: 1) seeing stress as a challenge; 2) one's sense of commitment; and 3) one's sense of control (20, 21). Those who see stress as a challenge are more likely to be physically healthy compared to those who see it as a catastrophe. Kobasa, Hilker, and Maddi (22) found that such personality hardiness could allow one to be under great pressure and yet have a low occurrence of illness. However, there are extreme cases of those who are obsessed with stress as challenge. Excessive fearlessness can easily lead to a premature death when such "fearless" people do not respond to the fact that intense stress could be a signal to be very cautious (23).

A second component of the hardiness of personality entails a sense of *commitment*. By commitment, Kobasa (20) means that people seek to live a life of meaningful activity. They actively participate in their career/work setting as well as in interpersonal relationships. This high sense of commitment is correlated with the capability to deal with stress and to lead a healthier physical life.

However, if one had to select the single most important factor of personality hardiness related to mitigating the effects of stress, it is the matter of *control*. Control involves active measures a person takes to change, adjust to, or lessen the effects of stress (24, 25). People with a high sense of control significantly cope better with stress (26), and they are more likely to engage in behavior that promotes health (27). The evidence continues to mount that a sense of low control is itself related to negative consequences for health and can even lead to death (28, 29). Seeman and Seeman (24) found that a strong sense of control led to a person's: taking positive steps to maintain good health (e.g., exercise, moderate alcohol consumption); avoiding negative habits (e.g., smoking); being more optimistic about the early treatment of cancer; having higher ratings on one's self-reporting of general health; specifying a lower frequency of acute, and even chronic, illness; being better able to manage a response to illness (e.g., length of time staying in bed); and exhibiting less dependence on physicians.

If control is such an important factor, what does one do about life-threatening situations that are seemingly out of control? A fatal plane crash that will kill all on board is just that, fatal. There is nothing one can do to survive such incidents, except to assume a neurotic avoidance of never leaving the house to get on a plane. Yet, a recent plane fire in Cincinnati showed that several passengers could have been saved had they counted the number of rows of seats they were from exits; they would have been able to crawl to the rows containing the exits. This would have alleviated the effects of smoke that obscured their vision when they stood upright. The person in a hotel room passively increases his chance of death by not calculating how to exit in case of fire. In other words, there are strategies that one can routinely follow in anticipating an emergency. To not anticipate and implement such strategies is an indication that some people underestimate the control they could have in saving their own lives.

Perhaps the importance of control is nowhere more acutely felt than at moments of extreme emotional trauma. Such experiences can lead to the "sudden death syndrome," whereby people die as the result of emotional trauma. Sudden death can occur when people ". . . are confronted with events that are impossible to ignore, either because of their abrupt, unexpected, or dramatic quality, or because of their intensity, irreversibility, or persistence" (30, pp. 153–154). Engel found that the 275 sudden deaths he analyzed were due to one of four causes. 1) *The loss or disruption of a close human relationship:* Almost four out of ten in this category died within the first 14 days after the loss of a loved one or after a loved one was exposed to danger. A father was watching his two-year-old child in a wading pool, but his attention wandered, and he became distracted. His child fell in the pool and drowned. The father died moments later. A middle-aged woman witnessed a truck accident involving her husband, ran to his aid, collapsed, and died, even though her husband had not been injured.

2) *Moments of intensity:* The dramatic and intense nature of sudden emotional impact can even result in death when one is actually spared of life-threatening physical factors. That is, a person can come out of a major auto accident unhurt only to drop dead walking away from the accident in the realization of the intensity of the life-threatening incident just experienced. A journalist died while photographing the drama of a rescue attempt to save a boy from an ice flow near Niagara Falls.

3) *Moments of intensely felt failure or defeat:* Engel found that all 21 deaths due to this sense of failure dimension involved males. One was a 59-year-old college president who was forced out of his position. He died at the ceremony installing the new president.

4) *Time of intense joy or triumph:* In regard to 16 deaths at times of great joy, Engel gives the example of the middle-aged minister who was exhilarated about the opportunity to talk to the President over a radio call-in show. The minister had a fatal heart attack shortly after the conversation. In another case, an elderly man died of a coronary attack after winning the daily double.

Engel's four categories of sudden death underscore the significance of control as a component of survivorship. At times of trauma, we must call on one of our two basic emergency systems: quick motor activity (fight/flight) or inactivity and disengagement (a more passive acceptance of, or withdrawal from, the trauma). Since these systems are reciprocal, a person under severe distress or trauma must realize that the response chosen can contain elements of both emergency systems. The important matter is for the person to control that response.

EXPECTATION OF STRESS

Life is inherently filled with stress. However, the expectation of stress need not only be concerned with extreme trauma. Pines (26) reports on Kobasa's study of lawyers and does not find the expected relationship between stress and illness. She speculates that lawyers are socialized to see pressure as intrinsic to their careers. Therefore, attorneys might well internalize a notion that their best work is actually produced under stress, so there is not the same relationship between it and illness as there is for other occupational groups.

COMPARTMENTALIZATION

Even when one lives with a healthy expectation of stress, one must also learn how to compartmentalize that stress. The old adage of "leaving one's job at the office" and not taking it home is proper advice for longevity. Army captains, for example, were highly prone toward mental and physical illness (26). This can be attributed, in part, to the total institutional nature of the armed forces. An army captain, for example, cannot easily isolate his/her military career from the rest of life.

SOCIAL SUPPORT

Social support is related to one's coping with stress, but Pines emphasizes that: "The strength of these supports is closely tied in with one's personality and commitment" (26, p. 40). Strong, affirming social relationships help an individual under pressure to feel a sense of support and belonging, thereby diminishing the unsound effects of stress on survivorship.

The lack of strong social ties can greatly amplify the unhealthy effects of tension. As far back as 1942, Cannon (31) noted that one of the major causes of death from the ancient voodoo practices was the complete isolation a person experienced after a "hex" was placed on him. In a recent study in Israel, Pines (26) looked at the relative isolation of urban children at times of military bombings versus those children who experienced such bombings while living in the context of a kibbutz. During bombing attacks, children who lived in a kibbutz had less mental stress and anxiety from frequent bombings than did their urban counterparts who felt more isolated from others. During such attacks, children in the kibbutz were always assured of not having to be alone while no such assurance was available to children who lived in the cities.

However, one's motivation for seeking social ties may be an important factor in relation to stress. McClelland (32) found that some people sought social ties so as to satisfy a strong desire for power. Those who pursued social ties for this reason *and* were greatly inhibited about expressing this need for power were the most vulnerable to illness. At times of stress, such people feel an inner restraint that frustrates their ability to act. College students who sought social ties for affiliation purposes did not experience the same degree of severe illness under stress compared to their counterparts who were motivated by a need for power and were inhibited in expressing this need (26).

ENVIRONMENT

The concept of environment is quite all encompassing. Therefore, our immediate focus is on environment as it pertains to two important considerations: one's occupation/work setting and the life events one encounters. As far as occupation is concerned, our previous discussion of "control" is also relevant here. Wallis (33) reports on the research of Karasek, who found that:

> . . . people who have little control over their jobs, such as cooks, garment stitchers and assembly-line workers, have higher rates of heart disease than people who can dictate the pace and style of their work. (p. 52)

Most at risk are those whose occupations require great demands being made but allow the worker few decision-making powers (such as telephone operators, waiters, and cashiers). Low control in one's occupation appears to be so paramount that its negative effects on health are similar to those of smoking (34).

Significant life events also play a role to increase the effect of stress, thereby leading to possible changes in health. Research has focused on the extent to which Life Crisis Events (LCEs) impact on psychological and physical well-being. Although investigators distinguish among a wide range of such LCEs (35), perhaps the most crucial are loss of spouse or family member, divorce/separation, loss of job, retirement, change in status, major financial difficulty, and, of course, change in one's own health or that of a loved one.

For our purpose, we need emphasize only the following: First, both negative (e.g., loss of job) and positive (e.g., promotion at work) life events have the potential for affecting stress. Second, how one copes with life events influences the possible deterioration in life chances by adverse psychological and/or physical consequences. These can range from suicide to a propensity to be involved in auto accidents to a more subtle, yet direct, consequence on well-being, including depression, alcoholism, and cardiovascular problems (36). Third, as with any tension, the effect of LCEs is contingent on one's past experience of dealing with stress, as well as how one presently copes with stress. Therefore, survivorship is not so much affected by life events but rather by how one copes with and responds to these events.

Further Stress-Reduction Strategies

The above discussion underscores the linkage between stress and its resulting harm on health as well as the psychosocial factors that affect this linkage. Awareness of these psychosocial factors is instrumental for survivorship provided the individual acts on this awareness. Furthermore, there are specific behaviors and strategies that one can utilize to "short-circuit" the link between stress and disease, including the following (37):

1. *Development of Priorities.* Organization of time is an excellent strategy for controlling stress. A sense of priorities enables one to see pressure in perspective. Tension eminating from a low-priority matter is wasted emotional energy. Tension from high-priority matters can be effectively dealt with by focusing behavior to deal with and work through these situations.

2. *Stress Avoidance.* One way to prevent stress from being pathological is to avoid it. This is not a passive avoidance which can itself produce negative consequences. There are positive strategies one can utilize to circumvent situations that are stress provoking. Leave home for school ten minutes earlier to avoid heavy traffic. Bring a brown bag lunch to work to allow some quiet moments alone. The

key is to avoid stress where possible and to learn to invoke positive behaviors where it cannot be avoided.

3. *Get Away.* It is important to have a set time to relax and get one's mind off of stressful situations. On a daily basis, this can be going for a walk, unplugging the phone and television for quiet time alone or with the family. On a long-term basis, one must realize that getting out of town is sometimes essential to coping with stress for most people. Vacations must be a priority. Getting away for the weekend several times a year can be extremely therapeutic and life enhancing.

4. *Exercise.* Physical activity not only helps prevent heart disease and stroke, it also lessens the impact of stress. Such activity not only helps to get one's mind off stress, it also has a direct physiological consequence which mitigates the effect of stress. Research has shown that physical exercise helps the release of endorphins which are, quite literally, the body's opiates that help to reduce depression resulting from stress. Also, a positive self-image resulting from improved physical appearance helps to increase one's level of confidence and control in handling a variety of stressful situations.

5. *Expand Interpersonal Networks.* As already noted, developing friendships and maintaining close primary ties can be a very important influence for survivorship. This is especially true for coping with stress. Loners are more likely to suffer mental disease than nonloners and are more likely to die prematurely. By expanding one's interpersonal networks, one can enjoy the pleasant and therapeutic company of friends who can offer emotional support as well as sound advice.

6. *Proper Diet.* When a person is at one's proper weight, one usually has a better feeling about how one looks, thereby reducing a major source of stress—that of being under or overweight. However, a proper diet of balanced meals, fiber, protein, and low cholesterol also increases the positive effect that nutrition can have on the body chemistry. This body chemistry must be especially maintained under times of stress when one's immune system is especially susceptible to disease.

7. *Use of Relaxation and Biofeedback Techniques.* There are a variety of behaviors that can be done throughout the day to reduce the physiological ramifications of stress. These can often be done in one's home or office. By slowly deep-breathing and exhaling for five minutes, one can slow down the anxiety-provoked breathing rhythm produced by stress. By tightening one's muscles, then slowly relaxing them, tension can also be reduced. Daily meditation or time spent imagining a pleasant setting can produce a similar effect.

Although stress is a part of life, a person can control and prevent it from being an influence in the development of disease and other pathologies. It is this ability to cope with stress that is a hallmark for survivorship.

SOCIAL NETWORKS AND LIFE PRESERVATION

The importance of social support as it relates to survivorship cannot be overemphasized. There is growing evidence that people who are embedded in networks of social relationships exhibit the lowest mortality risk. Consensus is building in the scientific community that social ties play a critical role in the determination of health status.

Berkman and Syme (38) undertook a study in which the impact of a range of social ties and networks was examined in relation to mortality from all causes in a large sample of men and women between the ages of 30–69, who were followed over a nine-year period. They found that people who lacked social and community ties were more likely to die in the follow-up period than those with more extensive contacts. This association between social ties and mortality was independent of self-reported physical health status at the time of the initial survey, year of death, socioeconomic status, and health practices, such as smoking, alcoholic beverage consumption, obesity, physical activity, and utilization of preventive health services, as well as a cumulative index of health practices.

The investigators constructed a Social Network Index, which took into account not only the number of social ties a person had but also their relative importance. Analyses of the age and sex specific mortality rates from all causes for the Social Network Index revealed "a consistent pattern of increased mortality rates associated with each decrease in social connection" (38, p. 190). Even more significant is their finding that the relationship between social networks and mortality exists independently of many of the variables traditionally expected to be predictors of mortality. That is, they found this relationship to hold true independent of one's health status, social class, smoking status, obesity, alcoholic beverage consumption, and physical activity. The evidence from this study offers strong support for the argument that social and community ties significantly affect a person's life-expectancy potential: "that social factors may influence host resistance and affect vulnerability to disease in general" (38, p. 203).

The mechanisms by which social network embeddedness influences health status and subsequent mortality have yet to be specified. Berkman and Syme (38) found that social isolation was associated with overall mortality as well as specific causes of: ischemic heart disease, cancer, cerebrovascular and circulatory diseases, as well as diseases of the digestive and respiratory system, accidents, and suicides. They reason that there are probably several "pathways" that could lead from social isolation to illness. They suggest three such pathways:

> . . . One pathway might be through the use of health practices which may lead to poor health consequences . . . A second pathway may be through psychological responses to isolation such as depression or changed coping and appraisal processes. . . Another pathway might lead directly from social isolation to physiological changes in the body which increase general susceptibility to disease. (p. 202)

While any one of these pathways, or some combination of them, could lead to increased morbidity, the mechanisms by which they are capable of doing so, by which they are translated into such outcomes, remains far from clear.

Remarriage and Mortality Risk

Remarriage may have life-extending potentialities. For example, in the study (39) cited earlier, in addition to finding that, for both sexes, mortality rates were significantly higher for those who lived alone, they also found that, for most age ranges, the mortality rates among remarried widowers were significantly *lower* than the rates among married males (p. 805). Unfortunately, the causes for these differences have not been pinpointed. The researchers found some support for both the *selectivity hypothesis,* which argues that the healthy remarry and the sick do not, as well as for the *social support network hypothesis,* which argues that remarriage provides conditions for care and support that are effective in ameliorating the effects of bereavement and thereby reduces mortality risk (p. 808).

It has long been known, of course, that sex differences in mortality consistently favor females. Indeed, the greater longevity of wives is one of the major factors underlying the growing population of widows in the United States (40, 41). One way that husbands can decrease this greater mortality risk, vis-a-vis wives, is to marry a younger woman. Several studies have found that marriage to a younger wife is significantly related to a husband's longevity (42). Foster et al. (43), for example, examined national mortality and census data and found significant mortality differentials for husbands married to younger and older wives. Specifically, they found that men married to younger women have a lower mortality risk than men married to women of the same age or older. At least two possible explanations are advanced for the finding that marriage to a younger woman enhances the survivorship probabilities of men. "The first hypothesis is that healthier, wealthier, or more vigorous men select, or are selected by, younger women. The second hypothesis is that marriage to a younger woman is somehow psychologically, physiologically, or socially peculiarly beneficial" (p. 120). Unfortunately, the nature of their data did not allow the authors to test either of these alternatives.

We have seen evidence that remarriage has life-extending potentials, especially for males. In the case of older persons, however, courtship opportunities may be extremely limited unless they have unusual resources. Even with such resources, and even if the older person is successful in locating a potential mate, he or she may still have to overcome a cultural bias in American society that often discourages such unions. Such attitudes and negative sanctions can effectively restrain an individual from remarrying and even force the couple to marry in secret (44). With the dramatic growth in our aged population, such attitudes have apparently become more tolerant with a concomitant diminution of biases toward marriages among older persons.

From the discussion in this section, one major conclusion emerges: the maintenance of meaningful human contacts somehow prevents illness and leads to life extension. The absence or loss of such relationships, on the other hand, can be life threatening. For example, while much is made of the single lifestyle and its advantages, the research shows that people who live alone, regardless of age or sex, experience significantly higher death rates than those who are married or live with others. This is true for major causes of premature death, such as heart disease, automobile accidents, lung cancer, suicide, cirrhosis of the liver, and stroke (45). The evidence strongly suggests that a major contributing factor is isolation and associated loneliness, leading to the conclusion that "enduring human relationships—between children and parents, among friends, and, most importantly, between husbands and wives—are essential prerequisites for emotional and physical well-being. In fact, people without such intimate, long-lasting ties are more likely to suffer disabling disease and even premature death" (46, p. 182). Nonmarried status, per se, does not diminish life chances. If single people (especially the separated, divorced, and widowed) develop and maintain meaningful relationships, the positive quality of those relationships will be more influential than the mere fact that they are single.

The research cited in the previous pages points to the crucial role and, indeed, the necessity of significant others in our lives. Apparently, such people help directly in our efforts to cope with the stresses of daily living. It also suggests that the choice to live alone may inadvertently lead to increased vulnerability to serious medical and emotional problems. For example, the single, widowed, and divorced visit their physicians nearly twice as often as married persons, and they remain in hospitals nearly twice as long for similar medical problems (46). Thus, continuous and stable human intimacy seems to be an essential ingredient for the maintenance of good health.

THE SOCIETAL CONTEXT OF SURVIVORSHIP

Salient societal influences also affect life chances. These chances vary by regional patterns as well as an array of other aspects of our society. Race and social class have an influence on survivorship because of our society's differential sensitivity to members of those groups. Changes in technology and mores also impact on longevity and quality of life.

Region and Site of Habitation

Regional analysis shows strong relationships between where one lives and mortality rates (47). A general conclusion is that death rates are lower in areas west of the Mississippi. The highest mortality rates are found in the Southeast, especially ". . . from southern Louisiana to southeastern Virginia, in the Coastal Plain and Fall Line, but also including portions of the Piedmont in South Carolina" (pp. 43–44). This high death rate is officially conceptualized as "the enigma of the Southeast." The effects of the enigma are further amplified by the growing tendency for nonmetropolitan counties in Georgia and the Carolinas to have higher death rates than metropolitan areas for cardiovascular disease for white males and females and also for all causes of death for white males.

Another regional factor that is strongly related to death rates is that of living where mining is a major activity. Not only are death rates statistically higher in such areas, they are also higher for people in those regions whether they work in mines or not. Even women who do not work in mines suffer higher death rates than females in nonmining areas (47).

Except for mining areas, areas of high elevation tend to be associated with low death rates. Density continues to lose its importance in relation to mortality since metropolitan and nonmetropolitan areas are not significantly different for overall mortality rates. However, it should be noted that few metropolitan areas tend to have the lowest mortality rates. Also, cancer rates tend to be higher in more densely populated areas (pp. 47–57). These data on density may change if official compilations could be obtained by measuring density in terms of clustering and not merely people per square mile. This measurement may substantiate a trend that lowest death rates do, in fact, occur in nonmetropolitan areas.

There are some aspects of urban life in general that affect survivorship. Toufexis (48) reports on research that links the extremely high rate of heart disease in Moscow to smoking, alcoholism, and stress resulting from crowded urban living environments. In America, Schwirian and La Greca (49) studied Columbus,

Ohio, and found that social status levels and, more importantly, urban housing conditions adversely affect the crude death rate. Poor blacks of Detroit who lived in areas of high unemployment, crime, and poor housing also exhibited high incidences of hypertension (50). In addition, the highest mortality rates in Boston occurred in the black ghetto as well as in a working-class area of whites who bitterly opposed busing. Mortality rates in these "death zones" were elevated both for hypertension-related ailments like stroke and for all other causes of death (50).

Some of the negative aspects of urban life are out of the direct control of the individual. While one may write Congress, for example, to enact new antipollution laws, the more immediate presence of that pollution is beyond the control of the individual. Nevertheless, some sense of personal control is an essential element of coping with urban life. Rudolph (51) cites research which shows that excessive noise pollution was not as detrimental when people had the option of "turning off" that noise. Even when this option is never exercised, the knowledge that one could choose to do so was sufficient to alleviate much of its negative impact. Urbanites can implement hundreds of strategies to gain some control over their environment. They can plan alternate routes home to avoid delays from accidents; they can have preplanned strategies to put into place on days of snowstorms when transportation is problematic; they can choose indoor exercise activities on days of high air pollution. The important thing is for the urbanite to plan a variety of options for diverse situations. Such planning enables one to actively anticipate stressful and physically deleterious situations and to actively lessen the impact of such situations.

Technological and Social Change

Changes on the societal level have significant consequences for the length and quality of life. The Industrial Revolution and its resulting urbanization in America and Western Europe were corollaries to an increase in longevity and standard of living. The accompanying decline in birth rates diminished one of the chief threats to women since a high number of pregnancies increases their chances of premature death. By lowering the growth of population, industrialization and technological development allowed the benefits of modernization to be shared more abundantly than if birth rates had remained high.

Relatively "simple" technological changes and inventions can have far-reaching effects on survivorship if they can be accepted by the general population. For example, while auto industry representatives agree that automatically inflated air bags would reduce the risks of an accidental death, they have at the same time resisted installing them as standard equipment. Generally, they argue that the installation and maintenance is cost prohibitive and would affect sales. The controversy over air bags brings into sharp focus the conflict between economic values and those placed upon preserving human life.

The rapid evolution of complex and high-risk technologies in recent decades have brought with them a heightened catastrophic potential (52). Examples of this include nuclear power plants, nuclear weapons systems, recombinant DNA production, ships and trucks carrying highly toxic or explosive cargoes, and the accumulation of petrochemical toxic wastes and toxic discharges. These and other risky enterprises have the ability to either cripple, shorten the lives of, or actually kill large numbers of people in a single incident. Perrow (52) has argued that many modern technologies are characterized by an interactive complexity of components (people, parts, procedures) which, in his phrase, are "tightly coupled." This means that processes occur very quickly which cannot be stopped; accidents are inevitable, even "normal." Because failed parts cannot be isolated from other working parts, it becomes impossible to keep production going safely.

The accidents at the Three Mile Island nuclear plant in Pennsylvania in 1979 and the Chernobyl plant in the U.S.S.R. in 1986 are examples of the catastrophic potential of complex technological systems. To avoid life-threatening catastrophes or minimize their potential for causing widespread fatalities, we need to develop better management of such enterprises. This would include such improvements as better operator training, safer designs, more quality control, and more effective regulation. Without such improvements, the lives of large numbers of people will remain unnecessarily at risk.

Yet, we must also recognize that sophisticated technological and scientific changes can eradicate threats to life. The advances of medicine can now increase survivorship beyond levels ever thought possible. New medications, artificial hearts, and other advances help to promote both the quality of life and its duration. Interrelated with technological advances, however, is the willingness of society to expend the monetary resources to make such technology accessible to the general population.

Such medical advances also open the door to unanticipated consequences. The modern drugs developed to prolong life often can have side effects that actually destroy life. Surveys have shown that 10 to 18 percent of hospital patients develop reactions to drugs they receive. The mechanisms by which therapeutic drugs may cause death or disability include disturbance of body defense mechanisms, cell injury, imbalance of essential materials, genetic disturbances, chemical carcinogens, and change in microbial ecology (53, p. 259). A widely known example of such effects is thalidomide. As a sedative, this drug was to have enhanced the quality of life of pregnant women. Instead, it led to babies being born with severe limb distortions and other congenital anomalies.

The use of drugs and other health remedies that have dangerous side effects are justified, in part, by the fact that the benefits usually outweigh the risks. Yet, some pharmacologists claim that society is actually delinquent in monitoring drugs and health aids (54). It took the Food and Drug Administration (FDA) seven years to put warning labels on very low-calorie, liquid-protein diet products, even though it was common knowledge that over 60 people had died from these diets and countless others suffered severe negative consequences. In 1970, researchers had reported that cardiovascular problems occurred with the use of oral diabetes drugs. In spite of this fact, it took the FDA 14 years to mandate warnings about the drug. Graedon, a noted pharmacologist and consultant to the Federal Trade Commission, blames such delays on the bureaucracy of the FDA and the power of vested interests opposed to seeing products banned (54).

Similarly, modern diagnostic procedures in medicine also entail unintended consequences that threaten life. These procedures involve the puncturing of arteries, veins, and other organs. They also include the catheterization of the urinary tract, blood vessels, as well as biopsies of a very delicate manner. The major hazards of these procedures are mechanical trauma to tissues or organs, anoxia of brain or heart, embolism, spread of tumor cells, infection, drug reactions, and disabling anxiety (53, p. 260). One can postulate that the desire to prolong life (and the desire of doctors to cover all diagnostic avenues to avoid malpractice) results in more people being exposed to diagnostic and treatment procedures that are themselves life threatening. Thus, changes in medical technology expose one to latent risks from the treatment itself.

In the years ahead, we will see increased use of experimental laser techniques to remove the plaque that hardens arteries and the development of new and more effective ways to lower cholesterol. New machinery is being developed for heart and other organ transplants. The results, thus far, from these and similar efforts have been pronounced and encouraging. In the last 15 years, death rates have fallen 25 percent for heart disease and 40 percent for strokes. The average life expectancy continues to move upward—from 70.9 years in 1970 to 74.5 years today (55).

Other scientific applications affect survivorship in subtle and unexpected ways. A case in point is the massive amounts of antibiotics fed to farm animals in order to prevent the spread of bacterial infections (56). One positive side effect of these drugs is that they somehow accelerate animal growth as well. However, there is also the possibility that animal antibiotics eventually produce antibiotic-resistant germs in animals, which are then transferred to humans through meat and poultry products. Such germs were apparently responsible for a serious outbreak of gastrointestinal illness among a group of Minnesota residents who had eaten beef from a feed lot that had routinely added chlortetracycline to the animals' feed. Over the past decade, several countries have moved to limit the addition of certain drugs into animal feeds. In the United States, on the other hand, intensive lobbying by livestock breeders and pharmaceutical companies has blocked the passage of similar legislation in the Congress since it was first proposed by the Food and Drug Administration in 1977. It is worth noting that in 1983 alone, pharmaceutical companies sold more than $270 million worth of antibiotics to the feed industry (56).

A seemingly harmless trend in society can also affect survivorship. For example, approximately 20 percent of all homes now use wood burning for all or some of their heat (57). However, the rustic charm of wood-burning stoves masks the fact that such fires produce some of the carcinogens found in cigarette smoking. Not only do such carcinogens threaten the people in the home, but wood-burning stoves also pollute the air of the community. In cities like Portland, Oregon, Missoula, Montana, and Denver, Colorado, over one-half of the particulates (minute solids) in the winter air come from wood-burning stoves, not from autos or industrialized factories (57).

Also, general changes in societal mores and standards of living have a linkage of complex consequences on survivorship. The "sexual revolution" had dire results far beyond gonorrhea and syphilis—both treatable by drug therapy. New strains of syphilis and intestinal disorders that are immune to modern drug therapy have emerged because of frequent sexual contact. The increase in hepatitis in the 1970s brought death to many and a chronic debility to hundreds of thousands. Certain strains of herpes evolved with similar consequences. The appearance of AIDS (Acquired Immune Deficiency Syndrome) is the latest example of how changes in sexual mores seriously affect life chances. In 1979, the Centers for Disease Control in Atlanta classified 11 people as having AIDS. In 1980 it was 47; 260 in 1981; 994 in 1982; 2,719 in 1983; 5,331 in 1984; and over 6,000 new

AIDS cases were diagnosed in 1985. Each week 100–200 people die of AIDS in America. Over half the people who have been diagnosed with AIDS are now dead. There is no known cure.

Fluctuations in the economic life of our nation also affect survivorship. Researchers have found that in recent decades a certain increase in the unemployment rate is followed by a concomitant rise in the overall mortality rate. More specifically, they discovered that changes in the unemployment rate and other economic measures are strongly correlated with various indicators of medical or social pathology. These include mortality from cardiovascular and renal disease, the rate of first admissions to mental hospitals, the suicide rate, the rate of reported crime, and the homicide rate (58). Moreover, it appears that these effects continue for a considerable period (as long as 15 years later in some instances) after the initial economic shock.

Radical changes in the economy often widen the disparity between the living conditions of the upper and lower classes, especially the poor. It is not surprising, therefore, that rising rates of several of the most severe pathologies correlate with an increase in social inequality (59, p. 82). In other words, the life chances of the poor are much more sensitive to major shifts in the economy or to government policies which affect their economic well-being. The above research found, for example, that government-mandated *decreases* in AFDC (Aid for Dependent Children) payments were associated with an immediate rise in the infant mortality rate.

The social inequality of death and survivorship has long been noted by social analysts. Longitudinal data on a variety of countries reveal a persistent inverse relationship between parental social class and infant mortality. Such findings confirm that "the classic rule still prevails: Unfavorable social conditions increase prenatal and postnatal mortality. Mortality is lowest in the highest social class and increases more or less progressively with decreases in social class" (60, pp. 35–36).

Patterns of Survivorship in Contemporary America

With the above considerations in mind, the next questions to ask are: What are prevalence patterns of key factors of American society that affect survivorship, and what are the goals of our society to enhance the length and quality of life? Answers to these questions are perhaps best found in the 1983 *Prevention Profile* on the general state of health factors in America (55). It focuses on 15 areas in which health promotion and disease prevention measures might be expected to achieve further gains in health, and it lays out a set of broad national goals for improving the health of the American people in the decade of the 1980s. For each of these areas, it specifies the prevalence, goals, and strategies designed to reduce premature morbidity and mortality in the nation by minimizing or eliminating the risk factors in each of these areas.

While these 15 areas cannot be discussed in detail here, an inspection of what they emphasize is a good summary of the major considerations for living a longer life:

1. Reduce high blood pressure to reduce stroke and heart disease.
2. Lessen the prevalence of smoking—the largest preventable cause of premature death and illness.
3. Eliminate the use of cocaine and heroin and reduce alcohol abuse.

4. Reduce the number of cases of sexually transmitted diseases by education programs beginning at the junior high level.
5. Develop better vaccines and antibodies for infectious diseases.
6. Encourage Americans to eat less salt and fat and to reduce weight.
7. Mitigate the link between severe stress and inappropriate responses such as violent behavior (e.g., child abuse).
8. Prevent injuries from accidents in the work place and home.
9. Promote exercise and physical fitness in order to reduce hypertension and obesity.
10. Immunize the young and old from diseases that could easily be prevented through such immunization.
11. Increase awareness for women to receive prenatal care and to reduce America's infant mortality rate which is one of the highest for Western, developed nations.
12. Educate Americans on the benefits of, and means for, effective family planning.
13. Minimize exposure to radiation (e.g., excessive x-rays) and control the dumping of toxic agents.
14. Mandate and enforce strict occupational safety codes to eliminate illnesses and accidents associated with the work place.
15. Increase fluoridation and other preventive measures for the reduction of tooth decay.

Our discussion on the societal context of survivorship has shown that patterns of mortality are not randomly distributed. They reflect an array of factors that underscore the close link between societal conditions and their impact on the individual. Technological and social changes can be profound in promoting or threatening life chances. A societal commitment to health would be a significant impetus in achieving the overall goal that the government has established for reducing the risks of premature mortality.

SUMMARY AND CONCLUSION

We have stressed that the ability to achieve maximum life expectancy is a function of personal choices and societal incentives. Within either context, strategies can be invoked which result in a reduction of mortality and morbidity risks and, therefore, an increased survival rate. The emphasis has been not so much on death and dying as on the human potential for living.

A similar emphasis comes from the interdisciplinary fields of geriatric medicine and social gerontology. Fries and Crapo (61), for example, have noted how chronic diseases have emerged as the greatest health problem in society today. Such diseases evolve as we grow older, and they have become increasingly manifest with the growth of our aging population. The knowledge necessary for decreasing the probability of occurrence and the incremental growth of chronic disease is rapidly accumulating. It involves the identification of risk factors and the formulation of positive strategies designed to ensure longer-lasting good health.

Positive strategies for reducing "universal, chronic, incremental, accelerated loss of organ reserve" parallel those discussed earlier in this chapter: a) a routine program of aerobic exercise; b) avoidance of smoking and excessive alcohol use; c) proper diet and a reduction of obesity; d) mature coping with stress;

and e) maintenance of a strong sense of self-worth and confidence in being able to control many aspects of one's life (61, pp. 86–89). In most instances, the postponement of disease will require permanent changes in lifestyle in order to adhere to the above strategies. The elimination or avoidance of risk factors "requires personal choice, and the very process of making the choices may itself have positive health benefits" (p. 89).

Risk Taking

We have noted that attitudes play a significant role in defining our vulnerability to life-threatening situations and how we react to them. Indeed, in many instances one's basic attitudes toward life determine the kinds of risks people are willing to take. Daily newspapers and weekly magazines are filled with reports of persons who voluntarily place themselves in positions of heightened danger. This is especially the case with respect to certain recreational activities and sports; for example, jumping out of airplanes to skydive, whitewater kayaking, race car driving, scuba diving, motorcycle racing, and mountain climbing. Some people engage in such risk-taking activity primarily for the thrill of it. Others may do so because of the personal challenge these activities pose to their confidence and ability to overcome physical and emotional obstacles. Still others derive excitement and satisfaction *because* there is an element of risk and from successfully achieving the goal involved. The majority of participants acknowledge the dangers involved in these activities, and take the necessary precautions. But others are not so cautious and take on added risks that place their lives in jeopardy.

Some individuals treat danger with greater equanimity than others. For example, a person with a strong faith in the promises of a better life in the hereafter is apt to be less afraid of mortal peril than one who perceives death as the final extinction (62). An attitude of fatalism, which conditions people to accept passively whatever may befall them, can lower their guard against danger. If a person believes that we are mere pawns of fate, he or she is apt to be more susceptible to threats of injury or death. Often, such people attribute the outcome of life events to "luck." Trusting in luck, however, often leads people to take chances with their health by clinging to harmful habits, such as excessive drinking or smoking. Underlying this nonchalance is the fatalistic feeling that when "your number is up," there is nothing that you can do about it. This is reinforced by the human sense of uniqueness: If anybody can beat the odds, it's "you" (62). Of course, few gamblers ever stay in the win column!

No one, of course, would deny that luck sometimes plays a role in the course of our lives. We all know people who have avoided premature death through one or more unplanned but fortunate set of chance circumstances or events. Indeed, the excelsior of life would probably disappear if all risk were totally removed from daily living. People, for example, ordinarily would not forego a vacation abroad because of the possibility that the plane might crash. Nor would an avid sportsman decline an invitation to accompany friends on a deep sea fishing venture for fear of the boat sinking. "The point is that no one can expect to exist totally without risk; nor would any sane person want to. To live at all is to live a little dangerously; to live in the fullest sense of the word is to balance personal fulfillment against risk" (62). In order to enhance our potential for survival, however, we need to avoid creating additional and unnecessary danger to our daily endeavors. One must constantly ask whether the added risk is worth it. The reasonably prudent person seeks to always distinguish between the risks that are realistic and those that are reckless.

Changing or Modifying Habits

Survivorship, in large part, reflects the degree to which a person actively pursues the goals of self-knowledge and self-control. The achievement of these goals depends on how diligently one practices "self-watching" (63). Self-watching involves a conscious program of systematic self-surveillance in order to understand and change behavior which can be life-threatening. It also involves a preventive orientation designed to halt further development of dangerous habits. It needs to be emphasized, however, that modifying lifetime habits requires a high degree of commitment, motivation, and a plan of action in order to avoid relapses. Addictions or compulsions are basically strong habits which can be successfully modified or even unlearned if the proper strategies are consistently followed.

Evidence is accumulating that under proper regimens and conditions, bad habits can be permanently abandoned. Many people are, in fact, able to "kick the habit" on their own through sheer determination (24). Often, however, will power alone is insufficient to do the job. A greater degree of success can be achieved by combining positive motivation with participation in self-help groups or organizations, such as Alcoholics Anonymous, Smokenders, and Weightwatchers. Such groups are based upon the premise that most people need external support and assistance to break their bad habits. The success rate reported by such groups has been encouraging.

Societal incentives also have health consequences and, by implication, survival value. Indeed, it is often the case that a concerted effort at the national level is essential for minimizing the various risk factors which threaten good health. Without such a societal effort, the individual initiatives will have limited success. Thus, just as individuals can take action to increase the probability of long-term survival so can the society continually seek to promote longevity. Americans are becoming increasingly responsive to health information and are incorporating that information into life-saving risk assessment and risk management orientations. These orientations are, in turn, encouraged by the activities of a variety of local, state, and federal agencies and involve risk assessment, management, and the promotion of good health.

However, without some modification in individual behavior, the societal effort will have only limited success. Indeed the best hope for achieving increased survival may lie in the voluntary efforts derived from personal choice (61, pp. 130–131). We have noted that there is a countless array of options that individuals can take to increase their survival. Growing acceptance of the scientific evidence of a connection between such habits as smoking and certain health hazards often has a "ripple effect" in that it starts people thinking about their survivorship potential (64). The alteration of those habits of our lifestyles which have deleterious consequences for our health is becoming increasingly recognized as one of the major direct routes to a long and relatively risk-free existence. To be most effective, these changes must be accompanied by a concomitant shift in attitudes which support a rational and moderate approach to daily living. Aristotle was perhaps the first to write that enjoyment within the bounds of moderation leads to human advancement. That is no less true today.

REVIEW QUESTIONS

1. Discuss the notion that death education and survivor education are complementary sides of the same coin. Give examples.
2. What is meant by "death by installment?" Give examples.
3. It has been stated that one's philosophy of life not only influences the quality of life but may also contribute to longevity. Explain and illustrate the meaning of this statement.
4. Research suggests some connection between attitudes and mortality. In this connection, discuss the findings which relate cynicism and coronary disease.
5. Studies show that high levels of cholesterol are related to heart disease. Discuss the ways in which cholesterol levels can be brought under control.
6. This chapter presents six intervening psychosocial factors that influence the impact that stress has on health and illness. List and discuss them.
7. Engle's research on sudden deaths revealed that they are generally the result of one of four causes. Discuss each of these. Which one accounts for the majority of sudden deaths and which the least?
8. Discuss the general relationship between social networks and survivorship. What are the effects of remarriage on mortality risk?
9. This chapter stresses that salient societal influences can affect the life chances. Summarize the major dynamics of survivorship as related to a) region and site of habitation and b) technological and social change.
10. One of the more provocative dimensions of survivorship is that of "risk taking." Discuss this concept as it relates to one's vulnerability to life-threatening behavior.
11. You are to present a short talk on "changing or modifying habits to improve longevity." What are the major points that you would include in your talk, and what are the examples you would use to support what you say?

REFERENCES

1. Antonovsky, A. (1979). *Health, stress, and coping.* San Francisco: Jossey-Bass.
2. Cutter, F. (1974). Installment dying. In *Coming to terms with death.* Chicago: Nelson-Hall.
3. Accidental death toll in 1982. *Statistical Bulletin, 1982, 64,* 10–11.
4. National Institute on Aging. (1983, Nov.). *Age page: Safety belt sense.* (pp. 1–2). Washington, DC: U.S. Government Printing Office.
5. Brantner, J. P. (1971). Death and the self. In B. Green & D. P. Irish (Eds.), *Death education: Preparation for living* (pp. 15–27) Cambridge, MA: Schenkman Publishing.
6. Berardo, F. M. (1976). *Social adaptation to widowhood among a rural-urban aged population.* Washington Agricultural Experiment Station, Technical Bulletin 689. Pullman: Washington State University.
7. Cohen, J. F. (1979). Male roles in midlife. *The Family Coordinator, 28* 465–471.
8. Lipton, M. B. (1984, March 30). John Hopkins University, *Bottom Line, 5,* 1.
9. Kent, S. (1983). *The life extension revolution.* New York: Quill.
10. Mann, J. A. (1980). *Secrets of life extension.* Toronto: Bantam Books.
11. Pelletier, K. R. (1981). *Longevity: Fulfilling our biological potential.* New York: Dell Publishing.
12. Paffenbarger, R. S. (1984). A natural history of athleticism and cardiovascular health. *Journal of American Medical Association, 252,* 491–495.

13. Blair, S. N. et al. (1984). Physical fitness and incidence of hypertension in healthy normotensive men and women. *Journal of American Medical Association, 252,* 487–490.
14. Cameron, J. (1981). A few irresistible reasons for paying attention. *Vogue, 171,* 138.
15. Carey, J., & Bruno, M. (1984, September 10). Why cynicism can be fatal. *Newsweek,* p. 68.
16. Friedman, M., & Rosenman, R. H. (1974). *Type "A" behavior and your heart.* New York: Knopf.
17. Lazarus, R. S., & Cohen, J. B. (1977). Environmental stress. In I. Altman & J. F. Wohlwill (Eds.), *Human Behavior and Environment* (Vol. 2) (pp. 89–127). New York: Plenum.
18. Wilding, T. (1984). Is stress making you sick? *America's Health, 6,* 2–5.
19. Visintainer, M., & Seligman, M. (1983, July–August). The hope factor. *American Health,* pp. 58–61.
20. Kobasa, S. C. (1979). Stressful life events, personality, and health: An inquiry into hardiness. *Journal of Personality and Social Psychology, 37,* 1–11.
21. Kobasa, S. C., Maddi, S. R., & Kahn, S. (1982). Hardiness and health: A prospective study. *Journal of Personality and Social Psychology, 42,* 168–177.
22. Kobasa, S. C., Hilker, R. R. J., & Maddi, S. R. (1979). Who stays healthy under stress? *Journal of Occupational Medicine, 21,* 595–598.
23. Lykken, D. T. (1982). Fearlessness: Its carefree charm and deadly risks. *Psychology Today, 16,* 20–28.
24. Seeman, M., & Seeman, T. E. (1983). Health behavior and personal autonomy: A longitudinal study of the sense of control in illness. *Journal of Health and Social Behavior, 24,* 144–160.
25. Antonovsky, A. (1979). *Health, stress, and coping.* San Francisco: Jossey-Bass.
26. Pines, M. (1980). Psychological hardiness: The role of challenge in health. *Psychology Today, 14,* 34–44.
27. Strickland, B. R. (1978). Internal-External expectancies and health-related behaviors. *Journal of Consulting and Clinical Psychology, 46,* 1192–1211.
28. Seligman, M. E. P. (1975). *Helplessness.* San Francisco: Freeman.
29. Croog, S. H., & Levine, S. (1971). *The heart patient recovers.* New York: Human Science Press.
30. Engel, G. (1977). Emotional stress and sudden death. *Psychology Today, 11,* 114, 118, 153.
31. Cannon, W. B. (1942). Voodoo death. *American Anthropologist, 44*(2), 169–181.
32. McClelland, D. C. (1976). Cited in Serban, G. (Ed.), *Sources of stress in the drive for power.* New York: Plenum Press.
33. Wallis, C. (1983, June 6). Stress: Can we cope? *Time, 121*(23), pp. 48–54.
34. Nelson, B. (1983, April 15). Heart disease found prevalent among workers. *Gainesville Sun,* p. 11A.
35. Dohrenwend, B. S., Krasnoff, L., Askenasy, A., & Dohrenwend, B. P. (1978). Exemplification of a method for scaling life events: The PERI life events scale. *Journal of Health and Social Behavior, 19,* 205–229.
36. Isherwood, J. (1971). The study of life event stress. *New Zealand Psychologist, 10,* 71–79.
37. Stress without distress: How to cope. (1984). *America's Health, 6,* 6–7.
38. Berkman, L. F., & Syme, S. L. (1979). Social networks, host resistance, and mortality: A nine-year follow-up study of Alameda County residents. *American Journal of Epidemiology, 109,* 186–204.
39. Helsing, K. J., Szklo, M., & Comstock, G. W. (1981). Factors associated with mortality after widowhood. *American Journal of Public Health, 71,* 802–809.
40. Berardo, F. M. (1968). Widowhood status in the United States: Perspective on a neglected aspect of the family life cycle. *The Family Coordinator: Journal of Education, Counseling, and Service, 17,* 191–203.
41. Berardo, F. M. (1970). Survivorship and social isolation: The case of the aged widower. *The Family Coordinator: Journal of Education, Counseling, and Service, 19,* 11–25.

42. Fox, J., Bulusa, L., & Kinlen, L. (1979). Mortality and age differences in marriage. *Journal of Biosocial Science, 11*, 117–131.
43. Foster, D., Klinger-Vartabedian, L., & Wispe, L. (1984). Male longevity and age differences between spouses. *Journal of Gerontology, 39*, 117–120.
44. McKain, W. (1969). Retirement marriage. *Storrs Agricultural Experiment Station Monograph 3.* University of Connecticut, Storrs.
45. Lynch, J. J. (1978, October). Doctor's warning: Being single can be hazardous to your health. *Harper's Bazaar,* pp. 182–183.
46. Lynch, J. J. (1977). *The broken heart: The medical consequences of loneliness.* New York: Basic Books.
47. U. S. Department of Health and Human Services. (1980). *Geographic patterns in the risk of dying and associated factors ages 35–74 years.* Hyattsville, MD: National Center for Health Statistics.
48. Toufexis, A. (1983, November 28). Cardiology city, U.S.S.R. *Time,* p. 70.
49. Schwirian, K. P., & La Greca, A. J. (1971, December). An ecological analysis of urban mortality rates. *Social Science Quarterly,* December, 574–587.
50. Wallis, C. (1983, June 6). Stress: Can we cope? *Time,* pp. 48–54.
51. Rudolph, M. (1972, Dec.) City stress: Learning to live in condition red. *New York, 5,* 50–54.
52. Perrow, C. (1984). *Normal accidents: Living with high-risk technologies.* New York: Basic Books.
53. Ford, A. B. (1970). Casualties of our time. *Science, 167,* 256–263.
54. Graedon, J. (1984, July 13). FDA delays action while Americans buy dangerous drugs. *Gainesville Sun,* 9A.
55. Golden, P. M., Wilson, R. W., & Kavet, J. (1983). Prevention profile. In *Health, United States, 1983.* U.S. Department of Health and Human Services (DHHS Publication No. [PHS] 84-1232). Washington, DC: U.S. Government Printing Office.
56. Toufexis, A. (1984, September 24). Linking drugs to the dinner table. *Time,* p. 77.
57. Golden, F. (1984, January 16). Heat over wood burning. *Time,* p. 67.
58. Brenner, M. H. (1984). *Estimating the effects of economic change on national health and social well-being* (Publication No: SPRT 98-198). Washington, DC: U.S. Government Printing Office.
59. And the poor get sicker (1984, September). *Scientific American,* p. 82.
60. Goldscheider, C. The social inequality of death. In E. Shneidman (Ed.), *Death: Current perspectives* (3rd ed.). Palo Alto, CA: Mayfield.
61. Fries, J. F., & Crapo, L. M. (1981). *Vitality and aging: Implications of the rectangular curve.* San Francisco: W. H. Freeman.
62. Dealing with danger (1980, July). *The Royal Bank Newsletter, 61(6).*
63. Hodgson, R., & Miller, P. (1982). *Self-watching. Addiction, habits, compulsions: What to do about them.* New York: Facts on File.
64. Will, G. (1984, May 1). Social disease in America. *Gainseville Sun,* p. 5A.
65. Berardo, F. M. (Ed.). (1985). Survivorship: The other side of death and dying. *Death Studies, 9,* 1–76.

17

Threats to Global Survival

Harry H. Sisler and Hannelore Wass

In this chapter, we shall discuss global issues affecting human life—problems that carry the potential for massive loss of life, for catastrophic death. The most threatening include: nuclear war; accidents resulting from the malfunctioning of nuclear power generators; the effects of ecological change brought about by industrial activity, such as the devastation of forests by acid rain; the depletion of the protective blanket of ozone in the upper atmosphere that shields living beings from excessive ultraviolet radiation; the threat of catastrophic changes in world climate, resulting from the increasing concentration of carbon dioxide in the world's atmosphere; and the burgeoning problem of waste product disposal, both nuclear and otherwise.

We shall examine facts relating to these problems so that boundary conditions that control ameliorative action may be somewhat clarified. In particular, it will be important to see how these issues are interrelated and how applying "tunnel vision" to a single issue can result in grievous error. Solving these global problems is plainly necessary for the survival of humanity and is, perhaps, the ultimate challenge of our time.

INCREASE IN ENERGY DEMANDS OF WORLD POPULATION

Some of the life-threatening problems that plague human beings at the present time are closely related to the rapidly accelerating increase in the world's population and its associated expanding demands for manufactured goods and services. These and other factors have brought about a major growth in the demand for energy and, hence, a rapid increase in the production of electrical power with its concomitant expansion in the consumption of fossil fuels—coal, petroleum, and natural gas. Formed by plant and animal life of past geological eras, these fuels represent a store of solar energy received by the earth over the billions of years of the earth's history. During the past few decades, those resources have been expended at a phenomenal rate. This has not only created the pressures of the much discussed energy shortage of the past quarter century but has also led to some important life-threatening global problems. This issue is given perspective by the estimates of world population shown in Table 1 (1).

The trend of these data was supported by an Associated Press release (2) on July 7, 1986 which quoted Werner Fornos, President of the World Population Institute. Fornos' statement indicated that on that date, world population would reach the 5 billion mark, only 12 years after reaching the 4 billion level. Table 1 shows not only the large rise in world population but, in addition, indicates the rapid rise in the rate of increase. Thus, in the 19 centuries from A.D. 1 to A.D. 1900, world population increased only a bit more than five times whereas, in the 31 years between 1950 and 1982, the world's population more than tripled. Therefore, it is not surprising that problems relating to waste products of human activity should be approaching the critical stage. Among the more critical of these problems are those resulting from the fact that the burning of fossil fuels results in the emission of various substances into the earth's atmosphere which adversely affect the ecosystems on which life processes depend. The quantities of such pollutants are increasing at a rate that is frightening in its implications concerning global survival.

THE CARBON DIOXIDE PROBLEM

The Carbon Cycle

One problem that threatens to have global effects on the survival of human beings is the continuing increase in the combustion products of fossil fuels used in industry and in the home. To see how this comes about let us review briefly the relationship of atmospheric carbon dioxide to life processes in the plant and animal worlds.

Virtually all of the energy that supports living processes has its source in the sun. The mechanism by which this energy becomes available is known as photosynthesis. The green leaves of plants contain a blue pigment (chlorophyll) that catalyzes the reaction of carbon dioxide and water to form various carbohydrates such as glucose, starches, and sugars, and other products, and releases oxygen (3). The energy content of these compounds is greater than that of the water and carbon dioxide from which they were formed. This additional energy comes from the

TABLE 1   World Population

Year	Population
A.D. 1	300,000,000
1700	625,000,000
1900	1,600,000,000
1950	2,510,000,000
1982	4,845,000,000
2000 (projected)	6,127,000,000

sunlight which is absorbed by the green leaves. Thus, in photosynthesis, green plants take up carbon dioxide from the atmosphere and release oxygen thereto.

Opposing processes occur in the combustion of fossil fuels or in the metabolism of various food substances by animal organisms (e.g., the human body). In these processes, the fuel or food substance combines with oxygen to release carbon dioxide, water, and other products. Thus, oxygen is consumed, and carbon dioxide is released into the atmosphere. The combination of these two processes constitutes the carbon cycle in the environment. Since the combustion of fuel or the metabolism of food products results in the formation of products (carbon dioxide and water) that contain less energy than the fuel or food product plus oxygen, these processes release, rather than absorb, energy. This energy is available for life processes of the animal organism or for industrial or domestic processes utilizing the fuel.

The concentration of carbon dioxide in the atmosphere is a function of the balance between the opposing processes of the carbon cycle. Therefore, it is a function of the relative rates of photosynthesis and combustion of fuel or metabolism of food and other processes utilizing or emitting carbon dioxide (4, pp. 790–791), including the decay of plants and animals and their excreta, aided by bacterial action, returning carbon dioxide to the atmosphere.

The Carbon Dioxide Greenhouse Effect

Much of the radiant energy from the sun is in the ultraviolet sector of the electromagnetic spectrum. When this energy is absorbed at the earth's surface, the surface is warmed and radiates energy back into the atmosphere as heat or infrared rays. Carbon dioxide molecules are relatively transparent to ultraviolet radiation but tend to trap and return a significant amount of infrared radiation back to the earth. This action, analogous to that of the glass panes in a greenhouse, raises the temperature at the earth's surface (5). As the concentration of carbon dioxide in the earth's atmosphere increases, the temperature at the surface may be expected to increase. Indeed, this rise is already being detected.

The carbon dioxide level, as measured at the Mauna Loa Observatory in Hawaii, has been recorded for more than 20 years and has increased approximately 9 percent during that period (6, pp. 412, 414; 7). Predictions concerning the future concentrations of carbon dioxide in the atmosphere depend on a number of behavioral assumptions, including projections of population growth; the cutting of forests (which consume carbon dioxide and produce oxygen in the photosynthetic process); the magnitude of reforestation projects; and the per capita consumption of coal, petroleum, and natural gas. There are, of course, other factors that enter into the estimate. What fraction of the released carbon dioxide will remain in the atmosphere, and what fraction will be concentrated in the ocean? Through the greenhouse effect, climate will be changed. What effect will this have on the atmosphere-retained fraction? Also, we may expect that the increased concentration of carbon dioxide will accelerate the photosynthetic process and, thus, slow down the rate of accumulation of carbon dioxide in the atmosphere. It might also increase the overall growth patterns of the biosphere with both favorable and adverse consequences depending on the species and the ecosystem. Nevertheless, most agree that this trend is long-lasting and, in terms of century time scales, is irreversible. It is, therefore, of concern not only to the present generation but to future generations as well.

Climatic Response to the Greenhouse Effect

Estimation of the climatic response to the greenhouse effect is a complex problem and has been approached through computer modeling. These computer models must take into account the interplay—the positive and negative feedback— between various climatic factors. For example, raising the surface temperature will increase the rate of evaporation of water which will increase the water content of the atmosphere. Since the greenhouse effect of water vapor in the atmosphere is even greater than that of carbon dioxide, this factor will enhance the surface temperature rise that initially results from increase in carbon dioxide. There are numerous other such feedbacks necessitating complex mathematical models. However, most climatic models agree that a global carbon-dioxide induced temperature increase has already begun and will accelerate during the next quarter century (8). In a recent press release, Michael Oppenheimer (9), senior scientist for the Environmental Defense Fund, issued the following statement:

> The consequences of these changes (the green-house effect) can be estimated with computer models, and the results are troubling. The climate may be measurably warmer within 20 years and the global temperature will increase by about 6 °F by the middle of the next century. Washington, D.C. may experience as many as forty 100-degree days in some summers; six are now unusual. The sea level will rise as polar ice melts and the ocean expands. Beaches will erode while wetlands will largely disappear in New England and elsewhere. Coastal Louisiana and other low lying areas will become uninhabitable. Where will the people go? For instance, in South Asia, flooding from cyclones could kill thousands trapped on already marginal land.

Whereas estimates of regional effects of the carbon dioxide greenhouse effect require even more complex models, preliminary studies based on a few such models suggest the following: increased rainfall in subtropical rainbelts, lengthened growing seasons in the higher altitudes, drier midsummers in some mid- and high-latitude regions, increased rainfall at high- and mid-altitudes in the springtime, and more growing days per year but less moisture in the soil. Fiercer hurricanes with 40 to 50 percent more energy are also predicted. These predictions are, however, tentative and await the application of more precisely tuned models for their confirmation. Nevertheless, it is clear that such changes may have a major impact on the world's food supply, and, considering the already marginal character of that supply, the effects could, in the short term at least, be catastrophic. For example, at present, approximately three-fourths of the world's grain supply comes from the midwestern United States. If the productivity of this region is sharply reduced, the world food problem would be seriously intensified. Major effects, direct and indirect, on crop yields throughout the world may, reasonably, be expected. The potential for altering the range and concentration of various diseases and insect pests that affect the world fauna and flora is also of grave concern.

Perhaps even more startling is the fact that sea levels throughout the world will be altered as the average world temperature rises and a portion of the polar ice caps melt. If there were a deglaciation in Western Antarctica, a possibility over the next one to two centuries, sea levels throughout the world could rise some 16 feet. The catastrophic effects of such a rise on seashore populations throughout the world can be readily imagined.

The temperature rise in itself can be serious, even though the average increase is moderate, when the increases occur during the hot season in climates already characterized by high-temperature extremes. For example, in the southeastern United States during the abnormally hot summer of 1980, old, poor, and infirm people suffered unusually large rates of illness and death.

Societal Implications

It is clear that the results of the carbon dioxide greenhouse effect will modify sharply the economic, political, and geographic relationships that currently characterize our world. Some regions will be favored by the changes; others will be adversely affected in a major way. Whole seashore cities may be inundated; agricultural industry in certain areas may be wiped out; changes in environmental relationships may adversely affect the health of millions of people. On the other hand, regions that are presently unfavored may become the desirable parts of the globe as a result of the climatic change. This could very well bring about political upheavals that in themselves could be catastrophic, particularly since the climatic change will not respect international boundaries. How will the "loser" regions be recompensed? What sort of "tax" will the newly favored areas "pay" to enjoy their newfound favored status? Solving such problems will not be easy, particularly if the present rate of increase in world population continues. One comforting fact: The change will not occur overnight or in a catastrophic hour as with nuclear war. This, unfortunately, makes the change easier to ignore. Nevertheless, humankind will have an opportunity to adjust, even to modify the threatened changes provided that they exercise the vision and mutual concern to deal with the problems intelligently.

The bottom line in dealing with global problems such as that posed by the carbon dioxide effect is the global response of society to the challenge that the problems present. The response, to be effective, must be global or very nearly so. National boundaries do not extend into the upper atmosphere except perhaps with respect to flight plans for airplanes. Certainly, atmospheric pollutants are not restricted by the boundaries of the politically defined airspace of the various nations. Unfortunately, the international cooperation necessary to deal effectively with the problems described above is extremely difficult to achieve. Steps that have been and are being taken will be discussed after the problems of acid rain and ozone are considered.

ACID RAIN

Among other global issues related to atmospheric pollution—issues which carry the potential of major modifications of the environment and, hence, extensive harm to humanity—is that of acid rain. This term is applied to the growth in acidity of rainwater, resulting from the presence of increased quantities of sulfur dioxide and nitrogen oxides in the atmosphere. In the presence of air and water, these substances are converted slowly to strong, corrosive acids.

The problem of acid rain arises from the fact that most fossil fuels contain sulfur compounds in appreciable amounts. When these fuels are burned, sulfur dioxide is produced and, unless artificially removed, is discharged into the atmosphere. Coals containing less than 1 percent of sulfur are extremely rare. Nitrogen compounds are also present in many fossil fuels and oxides of nitrogen are produced in the burning process. In addition, when such fuels are burned in automobiles, nitrogen and oxygen from the atmosphere combine to form oxides of nitrogen.

As a result of these processes, the acidities of rainfall and the resultant lakes and streams in various parts of the world have increased alarmingly. In a 1983 report (10), the National Research Council listed a large area of eastern Canada and the United States as having rain and snow with substantially increased acidity. The problem is causing much concern in northern and central Europe. The effects of increased acidity on the ecosystems of lakes and streams can be severe. Aluminum dissolved from the soil by acid groundwater poisons fish in numerous lakes. Surges in high acidity occur in the spring when the snow accumulation of the winter melts and runs off, commonly with catastrophic effects on the ecosystems of the lake.

Perhaps of more general concern is the obvious effect of acid rain on the growth of trees (11, 12). The continued existence of some forests is in jeopardy. Damage to forests at higher elevations from the northeastern part of the United States to as far south as Georgia have been detected. Decreased thickness of annual growth rings on trees, not to mention actual dying of trees, is occurring. But the problem in the United States pales in comparison to that in West Germany (11). Within a period of only a few years, diseased trees in the Black Forest and surrounding areas have increased from only a few percent to an estimate exceeding 50 percent.

In addition, nitrogen oxides bring about the conversion of atmospheric oxygen to ozone, a substance that is itself highly toxic to plants and trees. Such effects have been noted in southern California vegetation for many years.

Acid rain also has a variety of direct effects on human health. Particularly notable among these is the increasing danger from metal poisoning arising from the corrosion of lead and copper plumbing and the accumulation of mercury and cadmium poisoning in foods from aquatic sources.

THE OZONE PROBLEM

Ozone (O_3) is a natural constituent of the earth's atmosphere since it is formed by the action of ultraviolet radiation from the sun on ordinary atmospheric oxygen (O_2). It is concentrated (up to about 27 percent by weight) in the upper atmosphere (15 to 25 km) (13, p. 488). Direct contact with ozone is extremely harmful to living organisms, but its existence in the upper layers of the atmosphere is essential to life on this planet for it absorbs ultraviolet radiation and reduces that component of the sun's emissions to a level tolerable to human beings and other living organisms (14). Thus, we need to protect the ozone concentration in the upper atmosphere but prevent its accumulation at lower levels where it will be in direct contact with living organisms. Ozone is formed by the interaction of various pollutants with oxygen in the air under the action of sunlight. Thus, it is a common impurity in the northern hemisphere during midsummer months. Ozone causes shortness of breath and coughing even in healthy people, if they are exercising, but has more serious effects on very young, old, or infirm people. It increases susceptibility to infection and is believed to cause premature aging of the lungs. It is a paradox that ozone is being produced near the surface of the earth, where it is harmful, at the same time that other human activities destroy ozone in the stratosphere, where it forms a shield that protects living organisms from harmful solar radiation.

Certain gases that are discharged into the atmosphere bring about the decomposition of ozone and result in the depletion of the ozone layer in the stratosphere. Quantitative assessment of the damage that would result from various stages of depletion of the ozone shield is difficult, but available information suggests that biological damage to the earth's ecosystem would be extremely severe. This is so because certain segments of ultraviolet emission from the sun, (UV-B), known to be biologically harmful, would be disproportionately enhanced by reduction in the ozone shield in the stratosphere (14, pp. 78–87). The effects would be similar over the entire globe but different for various living species. We know with certainty that ultraviolet radiation is fatal, or at least severely harmful, to most organisms. For example, ultraviolet light is used as a sterilizing agent in medical and other scientific operations. A comprehensive report by the Department of Transportation entitled "Impacts of Climatic Change on the Biosphere" states that "excessive UV-B radiation is decidedly detrimental for most organisms, including (human beings)" and, further, "Even current levels of solar UV-B irradiance can be linked with phenomena such as increased mutation rates, delay of cell division, depression of photosynthesis in phytoplankton, skin cancer in humans, cancer eye in certain cattle, and lethality of many lower organisms" (14, p. 83). There seems to be little question that reduction in the ozone layer would seriously increase the incidence of skin cancer. Of equal or greater concern is that an increase in the intensity of UV-B radiation could result in photophthalmia, or "snow blindness," a loss of sight lasting a number of days after each exposure (14, pp. 83–84). Further, if the ozone layer were depleted by 70 percent, incapacitating sunburn would occur in 10 minutes, and such depletions are predicted as a result of nuclear attack (p. 385). It has been suggested that the increase in ultraviolet radiation could raise the amounts of vitamin D in the skins of mammals to toxic levels. It is also believed that alteration in the ozone layer, either as to concentration of ozone or as to redistribution of the layer with respect to altitude, would have a substantial effect on the terrestrial energy balance and, hence, on global climate (6, p. 401).

During the past two decades, concern over the depletion of the ozone layer by two types of gases has occupied the attention of environmentalists: viz. oxides of nitrogen (by-product of the operation of internal combustion engines) and chlorofluorocarbons (commercially known as "Freons"). Certain Freons are used in mechanical refrigeration units and as the propellant gas in aerosol spray cans. Nitrogen oxides act as catalysts for the ozone-oxygen transformation, so their presence can appreciably affect the concentration of ozone in the atmosphere. As early as 1974, Molina and Rowland (15) stated that chlorofluorocarbons from spray cans can reach the stratosphere, release chlorine, and destroy ozone. They further noted that chlorofluorocarbons were being released into the atmosphere at an increasing rate and could eventually destroy 20 percent of the ozone layer. During the 1970s and early 1980s, a score of nations that produce chlorofluorocarbons had begun taking action to control chlorofluorocarbon emissions (6, p. 404). These include the United States, Sweden, the Netherlands, West Germany, the United Kingdom, and France. However, by 1979, the production of chlorofluorocarbons had dropped by only 20 percent (16). Increased nonaerosol use of chlorofluorocarbons, such as in refrigeration units, threatens to negate the reduction which results from control of the aerosol use.

AMELIORATIVE POLICIES TOWARD ATMOSPHERIC ISSUES

Thus far, we have pointed to three problems of atmospheric pollution that have the potential for massive effects on the people of the earth that are, in fact, life-and-death issues. The problem of determining appropriate ameliorative actions with respect to these issues is complex. Two of the issues, the carbon dioxide greenhouse effect and the depletion of the ozone layer, are global in scope. Societal response has associated with it all the problems of achieving effective cooperation between nations. The third of the issues, acid rain, is more regional in its effects but, nevertheless, the response crosses national boundaries and entails political difficulties similar to the other two. Furthermore, apparently logical responses to some problems of atmospheric pollution—such as the restriction of the use of fossil fuels, particularly coal—run afoul of the economic ambitions of third-world developing nations, not to mention the objectives of those who would seek to abolish, or at least greatly reduce, the use of nuclear power. Thus, solving problems by isolating them and dealing with each one individually is of doubtful applicability to global problems of atmospheric pollution. Further, in almost every case, the problem is not limited to scientific and geographic considerations but involves difficult economic and international political questions as well. The exercise of "tunnel vision" in confronting these issues can easily compound them rather than lead to solutions. Concerning the political aspects of the problem, an additional difficulty is that response to atmospheric pollution is long-term, whereas most political cycles (length of terms, etc.) are short-term.

Schneider and Thompson (6) list a variety of possible responses. These are classified under the headings mitigation, adaptation, and prevention. *Mitigative* responses include such actions as liming lakes and streams to neutralize excess acidity resulting from acid rain. Various practical and economic considerations reduce the attractiveness of this approach on a large scale. Extracting carbon dioxide from the atmosphere and pumping it into the deep ocean has been suggested (17), but this also has its difficulties for some of the carbon dioxide would eventually return to the atmosphere. Since green plants take up carbon dioxide in photosynthesis and release oxygen, reforestation has been suggested as an ameliorative procedure for the greenhouse effect.

Adaptive responses are those in which efforts are made to cause society to adjust to changes in the environment without attempting to mitigate or prevent the change. Such an approach seems unattractive except as a last resort. It is far better to seek to prevent or to mitigate the threatened environmental change, rather than to modify the biological characteristics of various living species including human beings. Of course, living species are continuously undergoing adaptive changes, but these take place on a much longer time scale than is contemplated (and needed) as a response to the global problems considered here.

A more hopeful approach, providing the problems of international cooperation can be solved, is to adopt *preventive* measures that reduce or prevent the pollution that causes the problem. A primary strategy to meet the problem of depletion of the ozone layer is the reduction or complete banning of all nonvital uses of chlorofluorocarbons. For this purpose, extensive research to increase the efficiency in the use of chlorofluorocarbons and to find nonoffensive alternative materials is needed. The United States has prohibited the use as propellants in aerosol cans of those particular chlorofluorocarbons that affect the ozone layer. The emission of nitrogen oxides from the engines of aircraft makes it essential to consider this factor in developing plans for new generations of aircraft. Present commercial jet aircraft, other than the supersonic Concorde, seldom fly high enough to penetrate the ozone layer. This consideration, along with others, is reflected in the policy of the United States in limiting access of the Concorde to continental United States airspace.

Other factors, such as the use of certain types of fertilizers, result in the emission of nitrogen compounds potentially harmful to the ozone layer. Technologies for limiting acid rain are presently available. Sulfur dioxide arises from the presence of sulfur compounds in fossil fuels. Switching to low-sulfur coal or oil is an obvious preventive measure. It becomes less attractive, however, in light of the fact that only one-fifth of the known reserves of petroleum in the world are low in sulfur. Much of the coal from the Appalachian region, as well as from the Midwest, has a high sulfur content. Methods are available for removing up to 90 percent of the sulfur from coal or for removing 80 to 90 percent of the sulfur dioxide from effluent furnace gases (6, p. 425). However, these processes are expensive. With respect to nitrogen oxides generated in coal-fired furnaces, improved furnace design and operation methods can reduce nitrogen oxide emission by 40 to 70 percent (6, p. 425). Engine design, changes in carburetion, and the use of catalytic converters on engine exhaust can appreciably reduce the production of nitrogen oxides, but more research is needed. Again, the cost is high. Cost estimates for emission-control programs in the United States alone range as high as US $20 billion per year (6, p. 425).

The most promising and most economic responses to the global threats posed by the pollution of the atmosphere are a worldwide program of energy conservation and of population control. Increasing energy efficiency can reduce atmospheric pollution, lead to increased energy independence, reduce the growth of the greenhouse effect, abate the increase in atmospheric acidity leading to acid rain, and reduce the risk of depletion of the ozone layer. Population control makes such ameliorative actions long-term in their effect. Combined with other preventive techniques such as those discussed above, conservation and population control can successfully respond to many of the critical global issues that face human society today.

To carry out such a program will be difficult, but the prize to be won by taking such a path is inestimable. It will provide the ultimate test of the capacity of the human race to achieve global survival.

NUCLEAR ISSUES

The global issues discussed thus far in this chapter are related mostly to ordinary chemical processes such as combustion. They involve the separation of atoms in various types of molecules and their recombination to form new types of molecules with the concurrent emission of energy. These changes occur by processes which involve only the outer peripheries of atoms and leave their nuclear cores and, hence, their elemental identities unchanged.

Nuclear processes involve changes that are much more deep seated. In nuclear reactions, the nuclei of the atoms are changed. The radiant energy from the sun and the stars come largely from nuclear processes in which the final result is the combination of hydrogen nuclei to form helium nuclei. Each of the resulting helium nuclei has a slightly lesser mass than the sum of the masses of the hydrogen nuclei from which it is formed. As indicated by the famous equation first stated early in this century by Albert Einstein ($E = mc^2$ where E is energy, m is mass, and c is the speed of light, a very large number), even this very small decrease in mass results in the liberation of enormous quantities of energy.

About half a century ago a process that held the promise of providing a practical source of usable energy was discovered. In 1939, Lise Meitner (4), discussing some experimental work of Otto Hahn and Fritz Strassman in which they had bombarded certain very heavy atoms with neutrons (atomic particles that carry no electrical charge), pointed out that the nuclei of these heavy atoms had broken into two lighter nuclei plus additional neutrons. Since these neutrons can, under favorable circumstances, cause additional heavy nuclei to break apart and give further neutrons which can, in turn, cause further breaking of the heavy nuclei, this process provided a path to a self-sustaining chain reaction (pp. 883–884). Since the products of this process, called *nuclear fission,* have less total mass than the starting materials, the process liberates enormous amounts of energy (4, pp. 177–179, 885–888).

Never before in the history of humankind has a scientific or technological development provided humanity with such an awesome potential for good and evil, for lifting the many burdens that oppress millions of people, or for destroying human civilization and the ecosystems of this planet. The alternative that the world's people now face is that of learning to live together or of dying together in nuclear holocaust. Let us look first at the positive alternative and consider some of the aspects of nuclear power.

Nuclear Power Production

Nuclear reactors are devices that control the fission of uranium (U235 and U233), or plutonium (Pu239) so that the energy of the fission process is released slowly and steadily instead of explosively as in the explosive devices discussed below. Conceptually, a nuclear reactor is a relatively simple device (4, pp. 889–890), but the safe operation of a nuclear reactor depends upon mechanisms that will automatically shut down the reactor if the system departs from acceptable safe operating conditions and, thus, prevent the system from going into runaway or explosive operation. It also depends upon the whole reactor system being enclosed in a confining shell. Should the reactor go out of control because of improper operation or mechanical failure, the shell should prevent the release of harmful radioactive isotopes and neutrons that are products of nuclear fission and gamma radiation, the very energetic, lethal radiation that accompanies the fission process. The operation of nuclear reactors in the United States has been relatively uneventful and, in those instances where operation mishaps have occurred, no harm has been done to the environment. However, concern that a catastrophic event might occur has slowed down the development of the nuclear power industry in the United States. The most widely publicized event in the United States was the accident at the Three Mile Island plant in Pennsylvania in 1979. Here, mechanical failure of control devices resulted in major damage to one of the nuclear operating units. There was no apparent harm to the surroundings. This, unfortunately, was not the case in the accident at the Chernobyl nuclear power facility in the Soviet Union in May 1986 in which a reactor went out of control, melted down, and burned. The result: Radioactive dust first spread over Scandinavia and Eastern Europe, then fell on a wide range of food and water supplies in dozens of countries (18). Four months after this accident a report by U.S.S.R. officials to the International Atomic Energy Agency in Vienna stated that the reactor meltdown had already resulted in 31 deaths and hundreds of casualties, and radioactive dust was still being released. Residents in neighboring communities were exposed to radiation 1,000 times more intense than was observed during the Three Mile Island incident in the United States. The report predicted that, ultimately, there will be more cancer deaths from Chernobyl than are predicted from the atomic explosions at Hiroshima and Nagasaki. About 100,000 deaths occurred from these latter two explosions, and between 500 and 1,000 are ultimately expected to die of radiation-induced cancer, whereas it has been predicted that 5,300 cancer deaths will result from the Chernobyl incident. The report also raised the possibility of continuing contamination of fish, vegetation, and housing up to dozens of miles from the plant. The report attributes the disaster to six major blunders by the operating personnel at the Soviet reactor, which made more serious the defects that the Soviet report indicated were characteristic of the design of the Chernobyl plant. It was indicated that these design deficiencies were known and had been pointed out to the Soviet engineers by foreign consultants at the time the plant was built (19).

In addition to the danger from nuclear explosions, the nuclear power industry presents another severe environmental problem, viz. the proper disposal of the waste products of the fission reaction. As stated above, nuclear fission involves the splitting of the nuclei of heavy atoms such as those of U235 into two lighter nuclei. There are many pathways this fission reaction may follow so that scores of different lighter nuclei are produced, many of which are radioactive and emit lethal radiation. One, strontium 90, requires 28 years for half of it to disintegrate. Chemically, it is similar to calcium, a constituent of milk, and, when ingested by dairy cattle, becomes concentrated in dairy products. Moreover, since calcium compounds are important constituents of bone structure, consumption of these dairy products by people results in the lethal strontium 90 being integrated into their bone structures from which it is not readily excreted. It is believed to be a cause of bone cancer. Every person in the world now has a measurable deposit of strontium 90 in his/her bone structure resulting from the atmospheric testing of nuclear explosives (see below) (14, p. 62).

Cesium 137, because of its chemical similarity to sodium and potassium, is a similarly dangerous product of nuclear fission. The growing accumulation of this isotope—carried by winds from the Chernobyl disaster into northern Europe—is slowly crippling the reindeer industry in Norway and Sweden. Reindeer meat harvested in this region is showing steadily increasing concentrations of cesium 137. Some believe that it may be a quarter century before it will be safe to eat reindeer meat from this locality. Similarly, Scandinavian sheep are showing cesium 137 concentrations far above acceptable values. Iodine 131, with properties similar to those of chlorine, is also a dangerous byproduct of nuclear fission. The International Atomic Energy Agency reports that levels of this isotope a month after the Chernobyl accident exceeded Soviet standards by as much as 10 times. Hundreds of square miles of Ukranian farmland and forests are expected to remain uninhabitable for up to four years. About 135,000 people have been evacuated from this area.

Many byproduct nuclei are long-lived; some of them require thousands of years for their radiation to decrease to one-half of its initial value. Thus, nuclear waste must be stored in a manner and location where for centuries to come it will not harm human beings nor interfere with their activities. It is not surprising that inhabitants of various locations throughout the world have not been enthusiastic about nuclear waste "dumps" being placed in their vicinities. Numerous highly original and exotic procedures for disposing of nuclear waste have been suggested including sealing the waste products into containers and propelling them into outer space. Present disposal procedures involve depth storage. For example, placement of nuclear waste in ancient salt beds far below the earth's surface is being considered. Satisfactory solutions to this problem are still being sought (20).

The problems associated with the nuclear power industry are not trivial for they carry with them the possibility of tremendous harm to people. However, it would be a grave error to write off nuclear power as unacceptable, for it has the potential of helping to solve the problems discussed earlier, notably the carbon dioxide greenhouse effect and the problem of acid rain. Moreover, it has the potential of greatly reducing the dependence of this and other countries on foreign fossil fuel supplies, thus lessening the pressures toward international conflict. The present (July, 1986) share of U.S. electrical energy generated by nuclear power plants is summarized in Table 2 (21). There are more than 100 nuclear power plants now operating in the United States. France has 44 nuclear power plants, and Sweden has a total of 12. It would seem that giving major attention to solving the problems associated with the nuclear power industry would be justified rather than arbitrarily seeking to abolish it given the major contribution that nuclear power is making to the energy needs of this country as well as to nations on other continents, and the intensification of acid rain problems and the greenhouse effect

TABLE 2   Electricity Generated by Nuclear Plants in U.S.A.

Region	Percent
New England	33.4
Middle Atlantic	24.2
South Atlantic	25.0
South Central	16.4
East North Central	16.0
West North Central	16.0
Mountain	0.5
Pacific	12.9

associated with the utilization of fossil fuels, as well as the expected depletion of supplies of those fuels of acceptable quality. A quotation from *Time* magazine (22) is worth noting with regard to this question:

> No commercial nuclear reactors have been ordered in the U.S. since 1978, a year before the Three Mile Island accident. In the aftermath of Chernobyl, moreover, the prospects for nuclear energy have become even bleaker. And yet, say many experts, there is no long-range alternative. The oil crisis has receded but is likely to become a problem again within decades. Coal is still plentiful, but its consequences—air pollution, acid rain and the threat of global warming caused by the greenhouse effect—will limit its use. (p. 60)

A new generation of reactors with much higher safety factors is under development. One of these, the modular high-temperature gas reactor, is designed so that if anything goes wrong, the reactor simply cools down (22). With respect to the possibility of making nuclear power reactors dependable and safe, one must note that 150 units of the U.S. Navy are propelled by nuclear engines and have a record of 3,000 ship-years of accident-free operation (23).

Nuclear Fusion

There is another type of energy-emitting nuclear process that enters into the consideration of the role of nuclear power in meeting the world's energy needs. This type of nuclear reaction, known as nuclear fusion, involves the combination of very light atomic nuclei, namely one, or more of the isotopes of hydrogen, to form the heavier nuclei of helium atoms.

As noted earlier in this chapter, nuclear processes such as these account for the energy released by the sun and stars. If such reactions could be carried out under controlled conditions so as to yield a steady flow of energy, they would provide an extremely attractive source of energy that would avoid most of the problems associated with nuclear fission power production. Nuclear fusion reactions have very few waste products, and the supply of fuel is virtually unlimited. However, though nuclear bombs deriving their energy from nuclear fusion reactions proceeding explosively have been developed, methods for carrying out such reactions under controlled, steady-flow conditions have not as yet been discovered.

The principal problem in developing power plants based on nuclear fusion reactions lies in the fact that temperatures of the order of tens of millions of degrees Celsius are required to start the fusion reaction. For this reason, these reactions are generally called thermonuclear reactions. Thus, the problem is to find a method of confinement of the nuclear reactions at a high enough temperature for nuclear fusion to proceed (4, p. 895). Such methods have not yet been developed, though some progress is being made. The rewards for solving this problem are so great that continued intensive effort toward achieving a solution is highly justified.

Nuclear Explosions

Of all the global issues that threaten human society, in fact the very existence of life on this planet, the one which most people would consider most threatening is that of nuclear war. The capacity to destroy that is intrinsic in nuclear bombs and the very large number of nuclear warheads stockpiled by the major powers are frightening and deserve the careful attention of every thinking person.

Explosions, either chemical or nuclear, occur when a rapid chain reaction is sustained. In naturally occurring uranium, the concentration of U235 is so low that the probability of a neutron striking a U235 nucleus rather than a nucleus of the much more abundant U238 (which does not undergo fission readily) is very small. Therefore, the extra neutrons produced in the event that a U235 nucleus does undergo fission are dissipated by being absorbed by the nonfissioning U238. Hence, there is no self-sustaining chain reaction. To be used as nuclear fuel, U235 must be separated at least in part from the U238 with which it occurs in nature. Because of·their small size, lack of electrical charge, and high velocity, product neutrons travel relatively large distances before interacting with another nucleus. Thus, if the piece of U235 is improperly shaped or its mass is too small, a chain reaction does not occur. The least amount of fissionable material that will produce a chain reaction is called the critical mass. An explosion is produced when two or more subcritical masses of fissionable material are rapidly brought together so as to produce a supercritical mass. The fissioning of only 50 kilograms of U235 or Pu239 has the same explosive yield as the detonation of 1 million tons (one mega-ton) of TNT (trinitrotoluene) (4, pp. 886–888).

Thermonuclear explosions are of a different type involving, as they do, the fusion of light nuclei to form heavier nuclei. Many fusion processes that involve the conversion of hydrogen-1 nuclei to helium-4 nuclei occur at relatively moder-ate rates (i.e., nonexplosively) under stellar conditions. However, as pointed out above (p. 381), initiation of fusion reactions requires temperatures of the order of tens of millions of degrees Celsius. Typically, thermonuclear (hydrogen) bombs are four-stage devices. The first stage involves a conventional explosion. In the second stage, the conventional explosion initiates a fission reaction which, in the third stage, raises the temperature to a point where the fusion reaction takes place. In the fourth stage, neutrons from the fusion reaction bring about additional fission in a surrounding shell of fissionable material. The only limit to the size of a thermonuclear weapon is the capacity of the earth to absorb the explosion. Ther-monuclear bombs have been exploded with energy outputs equivalent to the explo-sion of 60 million tons of TNT (4, pp. 894–895; 14, p. 46).

The Threat of Nuclear Warfare

It is impossible to adequately describe the potential for destruction incorpo-rated in the nuclear arsenals of the five nations that presently possess nuclear armaments. It is likewise difficult to imagine the devastation that would result if these nuclear arms were used in a full-scale war. Never before in the history of the world has so much destructive power resided at the fingertips of national leaders. In terms of its potential for megadeath, the issue of international peace in the nuclear age is without question the major global issue of our time. None of the problems discussed earlier in this chapter are so fraught with the possibilities of destruction of the human race, indeed of the ecosphere of the planet earth.

We shall in the remaining pages of this chapter examine the threat of nuclear warfare and consider some of the possible actions that individuals may take to reduce the likelihood of such a conflict occurring.

Nuclear Stockpiles

Five nations are known to have stockpiles of nuclear weapons. Estimates of the number of nuclear warheads possessed by these five nations are listed in Table 3 (24, p. 38). These various warheads are categorized according to seemingly specific and distinctive purposes. Strategic (long-range) weapons (approximately half of the total) are for attacking enemy homelands and include land-based missiles, submarine-launched missiles, and missiles to be launched from strategic bombers. The remaining warheads are usually classified as nonstrategic and are divided into such categories as battlefield nuclear weapons, tactical nuclear weapons, theater nuclear weapons, and sea-control nuclear weapons. Each military service and each geographic command has its own supply of nuclear weapons. The United States has nuclear weapons stores in more than half of the 50 states and in eight foreign countries: West Germany, the United Kingdom, Turkey, South Korea, the Netherlands, Greece, Belgium, and Italy. U.S. nuclear warheads are, thus, maintained in Europe and Asia and always are present on U.S. naval vessels in the Atlantic, Pacific, and Indian Oceans (25). The Soviet Union has a similar diversity of warheads and its warheads are similarly widely dispersed. It appears that Soviet nuclear missiles are in Poland, East Germany, Czechoslovakia, and Hungary (26, 27). Roughly half of the nuclear arsenal of U.S.S.R. is aimed at the United States. It is interesting to note that the only nuclear missiles directed toward the United States are part of the arsenal of the Soviet Union, whereas Great Britain, France, and China, as well as the United States, have missiles directed toward the Soviet Union (24, p. 39).

However, the bare statement of the number of nuclear warheads of the various powers does not convey the criticality of the issue. To evaluate the urgency of the problem, it is necessary to realize that most people live each day without appreciating how close to nuclear conflict we truly are. Every moment, at a multitude of locations in North America, Europe, and Asia, rockets bearing nuclear warheads are ready to be sent into orbits of destruction. At every minute of every hour, aircraft bearing nuclear warheads are in flight ready to release their death-dealing payloads. Undersea craft and surface vessels armed with nuclear weapons are constantly on patrol on and under the seas of our planet. All this is underlaid by a support structure of research laboratories, electronic networks, test sites, and many other facilities involving scores of countries that themselves are not nuclear powers (24, p. 2). An example of the extent to which the level of peacetime military preparedness has reached wartime dimensions is the fact that, on a typical day, military command centers in the United States must assess the nearly 2,000 flights that cross the boundaries of U.S. airspace to determine if the flight is civilian or involves a covert military operation. And this assessment must be made

TABLE 3 World Stockpile of Nuclear
Warheads by Nation as of 1984

Nation	No. of warheads
United States	26,000
Soviet Union	22,000–33,000
Great Britain	700
France	500
China	250–330

quickly and accurately. An incorrect assessment and the concomitant response could have horrendous consequences. Let us try to visualize some of the grim results if the "trigger" were pulled and nuclear conflict initiated.

The Results of Nuclear Battle

The explosion of a conventional bomb has only one directly destructive effect, namely the shock wave, though there may be other secondary results from the damage produced by the shock wave. Nuclear explosions produce many directly destructive results.

With the explosion of a nuclear bomb of any type, there is a simultaneous, intense emission of *gamma radiation*. Gamma radiation, like visible light waves, ultraviolet rays, infrared rays, microwave radiation, x-rays, and radio waves, is a form of electromagnetic radiation but of much higher energy than any of these and is extremely lethal in its effect on all forms of life. It is estimated that the detonation in the air of a one-megaton bomb, medium size in present-day nuclear armaments, would emit gamma radiation sufficient to kill all unprotected human beings within an area of six square miles (14, p. 17).

A second destructive effect of a nuclear explosion, virtually simultaneous with the emission of gamma radiation and resulting from the interaction of the gamma radiation with the molecules in the atmosphere, is the generation of an *electromagnetic pulse* of frightening power. In July 1962, a nuclear rocket explode at a point 248 miles above Johnson Atoll, 800 miles southwest of Hawaii. A second or so after the explosion, the Hawaiian Islands were affected with a multitude of electrical problems, electrical circuits blown, burglar alarms set off, power lines dead. A recent generation warhead exploded 250 miles above Iowa would cover the United States with an electromagnetic pulse strong enough to shut down all power and communications in the country (28). Though the pulse would be harmless in its direct action on human beings, the country would be thrown into complete confusion because of the lack of communication facilities. What happens to the ability of national leaders to respond to critical situations under these conditions? When such response is impossible, who will be in control of our own arsenals?

A third destructive effect results when the energy of the nuclear explosion is absorbed by the surrounding atmosphere. This creates a fireball that expands as a *thermal pulse*—a wave of intense heat and light vaporizing or burning everything in its path. This pulse can last for several seconds and, in the case of a one-megaton bomb, produce at least second-degree burns on living flesh at a distance of almost 10 miles (an area of nearly 300 square miles). The explosion of a 20-megaton bomb would produce this effect over an area of over 2,400 square miles.

A fourth destructive effect of a nuclear explosion is the *blast wave* that accompanies the expanding fireball. The blast wave from a one-megaton bomb can destroy or severely damage all ordinary buildings within a radius of about five miles. The blast from a 20-megaton explosion would have this result of a 12-mile radius.

Another destructive effect comes about from the fact that the nuclear blast, particularly if it was near the surface of the earth, would draw into its mushroom cloud many tons of dust and debris. These would be contaminated with the lethal fission products and spread over the earth, particularly down wind, usually in the form of a fine ash known as *radioactive fallout*. Explosions higher in the air produce much less fallout. The lethal effects of this fallout vary widely, depending on weather conditions. A report of the Congressional Office of Technology Assessment estimates that, under average conditions, a one-megaton ground explosion would spread lethal fallout over an area of more than 1,000 square miles (29).

The five effects, however, only represent the skeleton of the monster of nuclear destruction. Human life is destroyed not only by these primary, direct effects of nuclear explosions but is also obliterated by the destruction by massive nuclear explosions of the many systems, both natural and those made by human beings, on which organized society depends. The collapse of these support systems will cause the death of human beings just as certainly as if they had been at ground zero when an explosion occurred.

Life's most extensive and most irreplaceable support system is the earth itself, and a major nuclear conflict could gravely impair that system, even completely destroy its support function. As examples of such effects, consider the fact that it is highly probable that a major nuclear war could result in a major depletion of the ozone layer with the adverse results described earlier (p. 375). The complete disruption of the food supply chain would result in people dying of starvation. People in vast numbers would certainly die from exposure. The shortage of the absolute necessities of life would probably result in survivors killing each other fighting for what supplies remain. Major illnesses would probably run rampant through whatever population survived the nuclear battle. Especially grim is the prediction that the dust and smoke from a major nuclear conflict would so becloud the atmosphere for a long period of time that the average temperature at the earth's surface would be greatly reduced, and the long-term exposure to cold, dark, and radioactivity would pose a grave hazard to the survivors (30). Certainly, the world's food supply would be greatly reduced as a result of the catastrophic change in climate. This predicted climate change has been called *nuclear winter.*

What has been described in this section discusses the results of nuclear battle only as a pencil sketch compares to a completed painting. Such considerations should, however, cause human beings to direct major effort to developing a scenario for the future of society that does not include nuclear war. Comments relevant to this objective are the concern of the final section of this chapter.

Response to Nuclear Danger

The possibility of a natural end to life on this planet and, more often, the threat of destruction by extraterrestrial beings or supernatural powers have long been the subject of human concern as expressed in philosophical treatises, literary works of science fiction, and prophetic pronouncements. However, since the middle of the present century, as discussed earlier in this chapter, the threat of global death brought about the the earth's own inhabitants has burdened the minds of people throughout the world. Despite warnings at mid-century by political leaders and scientists involved in the creation of nuclear technology, more and more nuclear weapons with greater and greater sophistication and ever-increasing destructive power are continuously being added to the arsenals of major powers. Today, humanity has within its power the capability of destroying all life on the planet many times over, and this can be done within minutes. The frightening reality of this situation confronts us daily in the news media as we read about, see, or hear of progress, or lack of it, on agreements between the two superpowers concerning a bilateral freeze on nuclear testing, bans on further development of nuclear warheads, reduction in strategic nuclear weapons, and eventual total nuclear disarmament.

As citizens of a nation and inhabitants of the planet, we are not innocent of this threat, although many may be ignorant of frightening details outlined in earlier sections of this chapter. We may choose to disbelieve, but such disbelief requires elaborate mental maneuvering: It requires that we dismiss all sources of information concerning the situation to be in error, that we consider the political negotiations as childish games, and the people who are calling for action as alarmist doomsayers. We may also choose to believe that though some threat exists, it is minimal or at least manageable. We may ease our minds by assuming that a nuclear attack is unlikely and that, should it occur, an effective defense against it will protect us. We may put our trust in what has been euphemistically termed as a "peace shield" or "star wars" system defense, even though such a system has not yet been designed and, even in the minds of its most enthusiastic proponents, would be capable of protecting only a fraction of the world's population.

We may assume that we can safely survive nuclear war. This idea is fostered by elaborate civil defense plans to protect the population, assure continuity of government, and improve prospects for postwar recovery. The United States, Great Britain, and the Soviet Union have such plans. In the United States, for example, more than 3,000 localities are identified as high risk and designated for evacuation in the event of nuclear conflict. Half of these have developed complete "crisis relocation plans." Current plans call for 3,000 local "emergency operating centers." However, only 350 of these are operational, that is, can provide radioactive fallout protection, emergency power generation, a two-week supply of fuel, ventilation, water, and sanitation. There are 600 "protected" commercial broadcast stations. There are shelters for important government documents. There are even plans for postnuclear postal services (24, pp. 81–82). But there are more than 240 million people in the United States, only a tiny percentage of whom could gain access to shelters.

Moreover, these civil defenses are based on the erroneous belief that a nuclear war would be like other wars. How, for example, do the planners envision the successful evacuation of New York City under direct nuclear attack with a warning of only a few minutes? How could any kind of coordinated postattack action take place when electronic communication systems have been disabled by the electromagnetic pulse produced by a major nuclear explosion? Trusting in such plans is totally unrealistic.

There is also the attitude that nuclear war is like a natural disaster. This reinforces the belief that nuclear war is inevitable and at the same time reassures us that it is survivable. Both beliefs are self-deluding. The first leads to apathy, the second to false hope. These beliefs are also cognitively dissonant. Either attitude takes away the sense of urgent need for action now. Such attitudes make doing nothing an acceptable mode of response.

Accurate assessment of people's beliefs about the threat of nuclear war is difficult, but several opinion polls have sought such assessment. A 1981 Gallup poll (31) showed the following results: Asked the question as to their being more concerned that the United States would become involved in a major war with the Soviet Union than in a limited war such as that in Vietnam, 47 percent were more concerned about a major war, 25 percent about a limited war, and only 18 percent about neither. Ten percent did not know. Fifty percent thought that a major war between the United States and the Soviet Union would be an all-out nuclear conflict, 21 percent thought it would be limited, 16 percent thought it would be a conventional conflict, and 13 percent did not know. Thirty percent of those questioned considered a nuclear war between the two countries to be probable within the next 10 years. Forty-three percent thought if the Soviet Union attacked some nuclear bases with nuclear weapons the chances of living through it would be poor, 43 percent thought they were 50:50, and only 9 percent believed they were good. Surveys and other studies involving thoughts and feelings of older children and adolescents have also been carried out.

CHILDREN, ADOLESCENTS, AND THE NUCLEAR THREAT

Adolescents are more pessimistic about nuclear war than adults. A Gallup poll (32) of U.S. teenagers ages 13–17 and British teenagers ages 14–16 showed that about half of both groups believe that there will be a nuclear war. Only 10 percent of the teenagers in both nations believed that the chance of national survival would be good. A fair rating for survival was given by 17 percent of the British and 23 percent of the American group. Sixty-five percent of the American and 75 percent of the British teenagers rated the chance of national survival as poor. With respect to personal survival, British teenagers were more pessimistic than their American counterparts—82 percent and 66 percent, respectively, believed that the chance of personal survival was poor. Other surveys of American adolescents have found that more than half believe the likelihood of a nuclear war in their lifetimes to be high (33–36). A number of studies have addressed the question of worries and concerns about nuclear war. Goldenring and Doctor (33) asked American adolescents to list their greatest fears. They found that nuclear war was ranked among the four greatest fears by nearly 60 percent of the sample. Similar or even higher rankings and percentages were reported for adolescents in Canada, the Soviet Union, the United Kingdom, Sweden, Finland, the Netherlands, and New Zealand (37–41). Apparently, children in the United States and in other countries worry even more about nuclear war than do adolescents (33, 36, 37, 40).

There is increasing concern among professionals that the nuclear threat creates anxiety, anger, and a sense of helplessness in our young. Furthermore, it is suggested that the nuclear threat has a negative impact on young people's values, goals, outlook on life, and general orientation toward the future (42–45).

In view of the adversarial positions of the Soviet Union and the United States in world politics and the fact that these nations are the superpowers with respect to nuclear arms, it is important for us to know that apparently children and adolescents in the Soviet Union are as apprehensive concerning the threat of nuclear war as United States youth are. This is poignantly illustrated in a report by Moon (43). She writes:

During a recent trip to the Soviet Union I visited a seventh grade English class in Leningrad. At the end of the class the teacher urged her students to ask questions of their American visitor. A boy in thick glasses stood up and asked shyly but with great intensity, "Do children in America struggle for peace like we do?''. . . . When I came home I didn't think about this Russian boy until I went to a school in El Cerrito, California to talk to a group of seventh and eighth graders about my trip to the U.S.S.R. After I showed some slides, I asked if there were any questions. They sat quiet for a moment, blinking after the darkness, until a tall girl asked, "Do kids in Russia want peace as much as we do?" (p. 175)

ROLES FOR PARENTS

Studies also suggest that most parents do not discuss nuclear issues with their children (45). Yet, there is evidence that children and adolescents who were willing to express fears about the threat of nuclear war also had a sense of personal and social efficacy when confronted with serious problems, whereas the lack of expression of fear about nuclear war was associated with feelings of helplessness (46) This finding also supports the notion that expressing fear can be positive and is healthier than denying it (47). Thus, parents have an important role in encouraging their children to share their worries and concerns about nuclear war. In addition, responsible parents can assure their young, in a convincing manner, of their support for global peace and for a future for them and for generations to come.

Parents are the most significant persons in the lives of their children. They have a great impact on their children's attitudes and behaviors. Parents are important mediators in the socialization process. They can monitor their children's exposure to filmed and televised violence. They can select nonviolent games and toys for their children. In Sweden, it is illegal for toy manufacturers to produce toys related to nuclear war (48). Consider the many destructive video games American children play. On the other hand, many organizations and services concerned with the prevention of nuclear conflict have developed and are promoting toys, games (including computer games), and activities designed to teach cooperation and nonviolent conflict resolution (e.g., 49).

Parents can instill in their children values such as empathy, caring, sharing, and helping others. Friendship and cooperation are basic elements of domestic peace. They should also contribute to the foundation for peace at the global level. Ideally, parents should be active in working for peace and, thus, provide the best teaching possible, namely, by example. Children can do a number of things. They can write letters to congressional representatives or to the president. One organization (49, p. 15) has been founded solely for the purpose of national letter-writing campaigns for children. Doing something to promote peace, even if it is nothing more than writing a letter, is worthwhile. More active involvement such as pen friendships with students from other countries and participation in student-exchange programs or in peace-related efforts sponsored by churches or synagogues will make important contributions.

A ROLE FOR ADULTS

What can adults in general do? The enormity of destructive nuclear power in existence today is frightening. It can have the effect of deepening the individual's sense of powerlessness. What can one person do to save the earth? This question may be asked in cynicism, frustration, or helpless resignation. Fortunately, however, many people respond with action. Today, individuals can add their influence to one or more of the over 5,000 citizen's organizations in the United States that are seeking to influence this country's role in world politics (50). These are non-militant, nonviolent organizations with no subversive or illegal objectives, whose members are professionals, members of trades, church personnel, or simply concerned citizens. The joining together of these groups could be an even more powerful instrument for influencing national policy. For an outstanding and comprehensive analysis and presentation of ideas and options for resolving international conflicts and, thus, avoiding nuclear war, the reader is referred to Woito's 755-page book *To end war: A new approach to international conflict* (50).

Various philanthropic foundations regularly provide grants to scholars seeking to devise methods for avoiding nuclear war. The Carnegie Foundation of New York (51), for example, dispensed over $11 million in 1983 to a large number of universities to support studies in fields such as research analysis and dissemination to policy-making communities, public education, and American-Soviet relations.

It is important to remember the existence of international, nongovernmental organizations that seek to influence world social and political life, consisting of people of diverse national, religious, ideological persuasions, and other differences. These organizations focus on specific areas and have, in these areas, achieved considerable success. Examples include the International Red Cross, Amnesty International, the International Olympics Committee, and numerous others. Is the idea of an international nongovernmental organization to work for planetary survival so utopic? Even if the idea does seem utopic, are not the stakes too high to fail to do everything within our power and imagination?

The nature of the problem logically supports a global approach to its solution. Is it not feasible to consider the issues from a perspective that goes beyond national interest but does not threaten national security? Again, we have the record of many intergovernmental agencies: World Health Organization in Geneva, Switzerland; International Civic Aviation Organization in Montreal, Canada; World Bank and the International Monetary Fund in Washington, D.C.; World Food Program in Rome, Italy (50, pp. 135–138); and numerous others. It has been suggested that intergovernmental organizations can become instruments of world law. We have the Law of the Sea and the International Copyright Law, for example. Woito (50, p. 118) suggests that world peace might be achieved through world law that would supercede the authority of sovereign states but only in this respect. The establishment of world laws alone is no guarantee that all nations would honor them. Certain nations ignore or regularly break the International Law of the Sea, for instance. Such laws are only a first step toward international cooperation. Continuing debate and diplomacy are also needed, as well as mechanisms for enforcing such laws and making them operative.

Finally, as citizen members of a free electorate, we can use the ballot box to elect political leaders of our states and nation who show the best evidence of understanding the global problems of our time and have the courage and compassion to give top priority to their solution. There is reason for optimism. The knowledge of the nuclear threat that people are beginning to gain can cause them to use their influence, their creative problem-solving talents, their good will, and their concern for others in meeting this most significant challenge. Albert Einstein (52) said, "When we released the energy from the atom, everything changed except our way of thinking. Because of that, we drift toward unparalleled disaster. We shall require a substantially new manner of thinking if mankind is to survive."

We believe that humanity is beginning to make this change. The factual and detailed report of the Chernobyl nuclear plant disaster by Soviet representatives to the International Atomic Energy Agency in Vienna in August 1986 (19) indicates a growing efficacy of world opinion in influencing world affairs and offers a small ray of hope for the future of world cooperation in meeting global issues.

REVIEW QUESTIONS

1. What is meant by the greenhouse effect? In what ways does it constitute a threat to global survival?
2. Describe what is meant by acid rain. Show how suggestions for solving this problem are in conflict with some responses to the global threat constituted by possible màlfunctions of nuclear power plants. What steps would you propose to reduce the problem of acid rain?
3. Describe the protective function served by the ozone content of the upper atmosphere. How would the depletion of this "ozone layer" constitute a threat to global survival? Explain the current concern over this possibility.
4. What do you consider to be the principal problems associated with the use of nuclear power plants? List what you consider to be the principal reasons for continuing to develop nuclear power facilities. What reasons would you give for discontinuing nuclear power production? What action would you take?
5. It has been stated that every person in the world has a measurable deposit of strontium 90 in his/her skeletal framework. What is the source of this isotope? Why is its presence harmful? Large increases in the presence of this isotope in some sections of northern Europe resulted from the Chernobyl power plant explosion. How did this occur?
6. Discuss the five direct effects of the explosion of a nuclear bomb. Describe some of the important indirect effects of large scale nuclear war. What is meant by nuclear winter?
7. How effective would well-organized civil defense procedures be in protecting the world population in the event of large-scale nuclear conflict? What do you consider to be the most rational official response to the nuclear threat?
8. How can parents help their children to cope with nuclear concerns and to participate in peace-promoting activities appropriate to their developmental levels?
9. Describe activities in which individuals and citizens' and professional groups might engage in working toward reducing or eliminating the threat of nuclear war.

REFERENCES

1. 1986 World Almanac, pp. 501, 529.
2. Gainesville Sun (1986, July 7).
3. Encyclopedia Britannica (15th Ed.), 14, 366 (1979).
4. Sisler, H., Dresdner, R., & Mooney, W. (1980). Chemistry, a systematic approach. New York: Oxford University Press.
5. Trefil, J. (1987). The year in science: An overview. In Yearbook of science and the future. Chicago: Encyclopedia Britannica, Inc., 308–309.
6. Schneider, S., & Thompson, S. (1985). Future changes in the atmosphere. In R. Repetto, The global possible. New Haven, CT: Yale University Press.

7. Lovins, A., Lovins, L., Krause, F., & Bach, W. (1982). *Least-cost energy: Solving the CO_2 problem.* Andover, MA: Brick House.

8. Trefil, J. (1987). The year in science: An overview. *Yearbook of science and the future.* Chicago: Encyclopedia Britannica, Inc. 352.

9. Oppenheimer, M. (1986, July 5). Earth's becoming uninhabitable. *Gainesville Sun.*

10. National Research Council. (1983). *Acid deposition: Atmospheric processes in eastern North America* (Report of the Committee on Atmospheric Transport and Chemical Transformation in Acid Precipitation). Washington, DC: National Academy Press.

11. Abelson, P. (1984). Effects of SO_2 and NO_x emissions. *Science, 226,* p. 14.

12. Watt, K. Energy. (1985) *Yearbook of science and the future* (p. 321). Chicago: Encyclopedia Britannica.

13. Cotton, F., & Wilkinson, G. (1980). *Advanced inorganic chemistry.* New York: John Wiley.

14. Schell, J. (1982). *The fate of the earth.* New York: Avon.

15. Molina, M., & Rowland, F. (1974). Stratospheric sink for chlorofluoromethanes: Chlorine atomic-atalized destruction of ozone. *Nature, 249,* 810–812.

16. (1981) Environmental assessment of ozone layer depletion and its impact as of November 1980. Nairobi: UNEP.

17. Marchetti, C. (1977). On geoengineering the CO_2 problem. *Climatic Change, 1,* 59–68.

18. Greenwald, J. (1986). More fallout from Chernobyl. *Time 127* (20), 44–46.

19. Serrill, M. S. (1986). Anatomy of a Catastrophe. *Time 128* (9), 26–29.

20. Harrison, J. (1984). Disposal of radioactive wastes. *Science 226,* 11–14.

21. Energy Information Administration cited in the *Gainesville Sun,* July 13, 1986.

22. Lemonick, M. (1986, July 21). A Chernobyl-proof reactor? *Time, 128* (3), 60.

23. Rickover dead at 86. (1986). *Science News, 130* (2), 22.

24. Arkin, W., & Fieldhouse, R. (1985). *Nuclear battlefields.* Cambridge, MA: Ballinger.

25. Cochran, T., Arkin, W., & Hoenig, M. (1984). *Nuclear weapons databook: U.S. nuclear forces and capabilities* (Vol. 1). Cambridge, MA: Ballinger. Updated in Bulletin of the Atomic Scientists (Aug.–Sept., 1984).

26. Arkin, W., & Sands, J. (1984). The Soviet nuclear stockpile. In *Arms control today.* Cambridge, MA: Ballinger.

27. Cochran, T., Arkin, W., & Sands, J. (1986). *Nuclear weapons databook: Soviet nuclear weapons* (Vol. 3). Cambridge, MA: Ballinger.

28. Broad, W. (1983). The chaos factor. *Science 83, 4*(1), 41–49.

29. Congressional Office of Technology Assessment (1979). *The effects of nuclear war.*

30. Turco, R., Toon, O., Ackerman, T., Pollack, J., and Sagan, C. (1983). Nuclear winter: Global consequences of multiple nuclear explosions. *Science,* pp. 1283–1292.

31. Gallup poll on nuclear war. (1981, October 5). *Newsweek,* p. 35.

32. *Gainesville Sun* (1985, July 3).

33. Goldenring, J. M., & Doctor, R. (1981). California adolescents' concerns about the threat of nuclear war. In T. Solantaus, E. Chivian, M. Vartanyan, & S. Chivian (Eds). *Impact of the threat of nuclear war on children and adolescents* (pp. 112–133). Boston: International Physicians for the Prevention of Nuclear War.

34. Beardslee, W., & Mack, J. E. (1982). The impact on children and adolescents of nuclear development. In *Psychosocial Aspects of Nuclear Development, Task Force Report #20* (pp. 64–93). Washington, DC: American Psychiatric Association.

35. Blackwell, P. L., & Gessner, J. C. (1983). Fear and trembling: An inquiry into adolescent perceptions of living in the nuclear age. *Youth and Society, 15,* 237–255.

36. Stillion, J. M. (1986). Examining the shadow: Gifted children respond to the nuclear threat. *Death Studies, 10,* 27–44.

37. Sommers, E., Goldberg, S., Levinson, D., Ross, C., & LaCombe, S. (1981). Children's mental health and the threat of nuclear war: A Canadian pilot study. In T. Solantaus, E. Chivian, M. Vartanyan, & S. Chivian (Eds.), *Impact of the threat of nuclear war on children and adolescents* (pp. 61–98), Boston: International Physicians for the Prevention of Nuclear War.

38. Chivian, E., Mack, J. E., Waletsky, J. P., Lazaroff, C. L., Doctor, R., & Goldenring, J. (1985). Soviet children and the threat of nuclear war: A preliminary study. *American Journal of Orthopsychiatry, 55,* 484–502.

39. Holmborg, P. O., & Bergstrom, A. (1981). How Swedish teenagers think and feel concerning the nuclear threat. In T. Solantaus, E. Chivian, M. Vartanyan, & S. Chivian (Eds.), *Impact of the threat of nuclear war on children and adolescents* (pp. 170–180). Boston: International Physicians for the Prevention of Nuclear War.

40. Solantaus, T., Rimpela, M., & Taipale, V. (1984). The threat of war in the minds of 12–18 year olds in Finland. *Lancet,* 784–785.

41. Gray, B., & Valentine, J. J. (1981). Nuclear war: The knowledge and attitudes of New Zealand secondary school children. In T. Solantaus, E. Chivian, M. Vartanyan, & S. Chivian (Eds.), *Impact of the threat of nuclear war on children and adolescents.* Boston: International Physicians for the Prevention of Nuclear War.

42. Escalona, S. K. (1982). Growing up with the threat of nuclear war: Some indirect effects on personality development. *American Journal of Orthopsychiatry, 52,* 600–607.

43. Gould, B. B., Moon, S., & Van Hoorn, J. (Eds.). (1986). *Growing up scared? The psychological effect of the nuclear threat on children.* Berkeley, CA: Open Books.

44. Schwebel, M. (1982). Effects of the nuclear war threat on children and teenagers: Implications for professionals. *American Journal of Orthopsychiatry, 52,* 608–618.

45. Mack, J. E. (1986). Approaching the nuclear threat in clinical work with children and their families. In B. B. Gould, S. Moon, & J. Van Hoorn (Eds.), *Growing up scared? The psychological effect of the nuclear threat on children* (pp. 25–37). Berkeley, CA: Open Books.

46. Goldberg, S., Lacombe, S., Levinson, D., Ross Parker, K., Ross, C., & Sommers, F. (1985). Thinking about the threat of nuclear war: Relevance to mental health. *American Journal of Orthopsychiatry, 55,* 503–512.

47. Macy, J. (1983). *Despair and personal power in the nuclear age.* Philadelphia: New Society Publishers.

48. C. G. Wenestam (personal communication, 1985).

49. Meier, P., & McPherson, B. (1983). *Nuclear dangers: A resource guide for secondary school teachers.* Washington, DC: Nuclear Information and Resource Service. (See also *A resource guide for elementary school teachers*)

50. Woito, R. (1982). *To end war: A new approach to nuclear conflict.* New York: Pilgrim.

51. Carnegie Corporation of New York (1985). Reducing the risk of nuclear war: What can scholars do? *Carnegie Quarterly, 30,* 1–2.

52. Totten, S. (1983). A nuclear arms race unit for classroom teachers. *Social Education, 47,* 507.

Conclusion

18

Dying: Integrating the Facts

Hannelore Wass, Felix M. Berardo, and Robert A. Neimeyer

THE UBIQUITOUS CHARACTER OF THANATOLOGY

One of the editors to this volume asks students to list all the death-related topics they can think of. Students shortly observe that the list can be surprisingly lengthy. Indeed, the subject matter embraced by death studies is encyclopedic.

Countless acts of terrorism are daily killing innocent, unsuspecting, and unarmed persons on cruise ships, in airports, shopping centers, work places, on the streets, and in their homes. Political assassinations and assassination attempts have become almost commonplace, as have hostage-taking, torture, and murder. Unfortunately, social scientists, the growing field of terrorist investigators and analysts, and other professionals have, for obvious reasons, had difficulty in researching this aspect of violence.

Individual violence, homicide, is a topic that the reader will not find extensively explored in this volume. While we have fairly reliable statistics on rates, demographics, and other aspects of murderers and their victims, there are also widely varying explanations for the causes and dynamics of homicide. The death penalty, while not analyzed in the present text, is a controversial topic and the growing literature surrounding it speaks to a number of important thanatological issues related to the fundamental meaning of life and death.

The "near-death" experience is another topic we could have included in this volume. The investigation of this phenomenon is pursued by a relatively small group of researchers. Nevertheless, the subject has created widespread interest and captured the imagination of the general public. Moody's 1975 best seller, *Life after Life,* is probably responsible for this. Since its publication, at least six books have been published on the topic—all in the 1980s, three of them in one year. Even the professionals are fascinated by this topic, perhaps because it hovers between the edge of what we consider respectable science and those areas of study that deal with the more elusive phenomena in the realm of human experience. The data collected and reported thus far earn the right to be taken seriously; however, there are still many unanswered questions. More critically, the explanations and conclusions are not readily verifiable.

What all this says is that the subject matter of thanatology is ubiquitous. Indeed, that is one of its attractions. This means that much work remains to be done before the full potential of this new field is realized. That is the challenge that lies ahead. As McClure (1) has noted:

> Perhaps the most intriguing challenge posed by the subject is its reconstructive nature. Anyone who pretends to be a humanist, to be interested in intergenerational learning, to be concerned with problems of aging, to care at all about the segregation phenomenon of death, will find in this curriculum organizer a powerful engine. Education in death and dying is an agent of great promise for balancing the curriculum and making it a more complete approximation of life. Ultimately, it promises to add a richer appreciation for the value of existence. (p. 485).

THE NEED FOR DEATH EDUCATION

The intense and emotionally charged life and death scenarios described and analyzed by the contributors to this volume give additional urgency to the need for adequate death education. Thanatologists, of course, have long contended that such education provides positive preparation for both dying and living. Many have echoed the notion that confronting one's own mortality and that of others is essential for developing the mature perspective necessary for making decisions about crucial life and death events (2, p. 388). Still others see learning about death and dying as an avenue to achieving an understanding of the human condition within broader social contexts. As Morgan noted, "Death education relates not only to death itself but to our feelings about ourselves and nature and the universe we live in. It has to do with our values and ideals, the way we relate to one another and the kind of world we are building. Thoughtfully pursued, it can deepen the quality of our lives and of our relationships" (3, p. 3). Whether those exposed to death education ultimately achieve these or many other goals espoused by its proponents is, of course, difficult if not impossible to determine. Nevertheless, one can predict with some certainty that, given the increasing biomedical and sociocultural complexities that impinge on human survival, the pressure for widespread and formalized death education will be sustained. If this is true, then it may prove useful at this point to look at the status of death education today and make some observations about the direction it seems to be taking.

STATUS OF DEATH EDUCATION

It was recognized from the beginning of the so-called death-awareness movement (4) that death education would need to perform a significant function if it were to become something more than a specialized curiosity at the fringes of established scientific disciplines. If thanatology were to move beyond the parochial and passing fadism, both on the part of professionals and the general public, education would be the social agent to accomplish that critical transcendence (5).

Education occurs in many forms and levels of sophistication, intensity, and extensiveness—from the occasional information exchange of a single datum with the general public to a systematic and highly structured curriculum of academic study and clinical experience (6–8). In addition, it deals not merely with generating knowledge and disseminating it but with fundamental issues involving attitudes toward life itself (1–3). As several authors in this volume have aptly demonstrated, attitudes and learning are intricately related in ways that can either prolong living or hasten dying.

Death Education for the Public

Education assumes that changes in attitudes and behavior are readily accomplished through the acquisition of knowledge. The facts all too often belie that assumption. In the past few decades, the public has become increasingly health conscious. Through the mass media as well as through schools and pervasive networks of informal communication, we are familiar with the requirements for living a long and relatively illness-free existence. However, the evidence is clear that, despite this knowledge, large segments of the population cling to dangerous habits, attitudes, and life-threatening behaviors. Certain chapters in this book present a virtual litany of such behaviors which serve to endanger individual, societal, and even global survival.

There is reason to question whether public attitudes and the general outlook on death have significantly changed. With all the admittedly greater permissiveness for open discussion of formerly taboo topics, we may have merely achieved what Kastenbaum terms "a more sophisticated level of denial." We still observe too many occasions that reveal the level of death avoidance that was exhibited 20 years ago. One can still observe an almost absolute taboo on the word "death" in most of our nursing homes and in many hospitals. Not long ago one of us visited a friend in a hospital in a large city. While near the nursing station, the supervisor was overheard saying to a young man, apparently a new intern, "Death and dying are dirty words in our facility. I won't have you using them while you are with us. Our patients expire. Is that clear?" We are reminded of Geoffrey Gorer who wrote "death is viewed as pornographic" but that was over two decades ago (9)! We like to think that the denial of death has significantly diminished, but such instances make us less than certain.

Consider Fulton's findings of diminished mourning by adult children and the decrease in ceremonial grief expressions throughout society. Are these manifestations of death denial (10)? Fulton and others have observed that, frequently, children are kept from attending funerals, so they may not even learn the *forms* of our rituals. Television gives minimal attention to such rituals. In a recent study of over 1,500 commercial television programs aired on prime-time and weekday afternoons, there were about 300 incidents of one or multiple deaths, four-fifths of them caused by violence. However, grief reactions were portrayed in less than 10 percent of these instances, and only nine funerals were shown (11).

There are other signs of denial by society and by those who shape its attitudes. We have stockpiled enough nuclear warheads to destroy all life on this planet several times over. The awesome implications of that fact are quickly removed from the stream of consciousness perhaps because they are too terrible to ponder. This too is a form of denial. New euphemisms are created that allow us to avoid the anxiety provoked by direct recognition of the threat of annihilation by nuclear weapons. What's more comforting than the thought of "star wars?" It's a magic phrase. We picture ourselves sitting in a movie or at home watching extra-terrestrial homing vehicles, rocket pods, smart rockets, pellets, and other yet-to-be-invented weapons do their devastating work far out in space. Even more comforting and benign is the more recently created euphemism "peace shield." This concept removes our thinking even further from the horrendous effects of nuclear war.

Perhaps worse than minimizing the consequences of the widespread use of such weapons is an attitude of apathy. Adolescents and young adults often believe that the world will end by nuclear war and that it could happen anytime. Not too long ago the students at Brown University demonstrated their awareness of that threat with a referendum requesting that the administration stockpile cyanide pills for their use if such a war occurred. Robert Coles, the Harvard psychiatrist, reports the reaction of a blue collar worker who said, "These spoiled rich kids. Everyone else is going to suffer a slow death, and they want a quick way out" (12). At this point in time, we are led to conclude that public enlightenment concerning death and death-related issues still falls short of the mark.

Death Education for Elementary School Children

Despite dedicated efforts by many individuals, and a sizable literature outlining rationale, goals, subject matter, and methods of teaching, death education has not yet received wide acceptance at the elementary school level. The available survey data suggest that a small proportion of the elementary school teachers deal with the subject in any planned way (13). How death-related crises are handled in the schools seems at present to be related more to the teacher's personality, rapport with children, comfort with the topic, and degree of empathy than to any special preparation.

As a consequence, teachers and school officials often are not well prepared to handle a death-related crisis. When one occurs, nurses, counselors, or professors from nearby colleges or universities are called upon to handle these situations. The following occurrence is illustrative:

Susie is in the first grade. One morning she stood before her classmates during "show and tell." She had nothing to show but something very important to tell. She said, "My brother Jamie died." The teacher was completely unprepared, and her response was silence. She pretended that she hadn't heard and motioned to another child. But Susie was determined. She repeated, more loudly, "My brother Jamie died." Now all the children heard. They looked expectantly to the teacher, then to Susie, then back to the teacher. But the teacher appeared to be petrified. By now Susie demanded that the teacher "pay attention" to what she had to say. She screamed the statement at her teacher who promptly came to life for now she was on familiar ground. She took Susie by the hand and said firmly, "We do not shout in the classroom," and then she walked her out of the room. What unintended lessons do we teach our children when adults are traumatized and ineffectual when death invades the classroom?

Death Education for High School Students

More noticeable success can be perceived at the high school level (14). University health educators have been the single most successful group in bringing death education into high schools. Most college texts in health education now include materials on this topic. One survey indicates that in the state of New York, 14 percent of the health educators in high schools teach a unit on death and another 64 percent incorporate the subject into another unit (15). However, one needs to remember that in the United States health is an important value. Thus, dealing with death can provide a powerful stimulus for students to keep themselves alive through healthy living.

Less death education is occurring in the biological and social sciences, in the humanities, or in the practically oriented courses such as home economics and family development. On the other hand, it is probably safe to say that death is the subject of many individual projects and informal class discussions as well as field trips to funeral homes or cemeteries in many high schools. While such activities are a piecemeal approach to death education, they are important steps forward. We hope that students, eventually, will have the opportunity to examine significant life issues through a structured program on death education. Death education has the potential for enhancing their abilities to cherish life; to improve the quality of their relationships with family, friends, and peers; to help them to focus more sharply on their goals and priorities; and, simply, to live more fully each day. All these life-enhancing effects have been reported by adults and children who have been close to death or otherwise confronted it in a profound way.

Death Education for College Students

A decade ago, Cummins (16) reported survey data which suggested that 1,000 undergraduate courses in death and dying were being offered in four-year degree-granting colleges and universities in the United States. Today, that figure has probably tripled. The subject matter has been increasingly incorporated into the community college curriculum. The death and dying classes are popular and are taught in a variety of disciplines, including sociology, psychology, religion, anthropology, and the humanities. Today, courses in death education have become generally accepted in our colleges and universities. It was, in fact, at this level that the early instruction on death and dying was initiated. Unfortunately, there are no data available to determine the quality of instruction.

Reaffirming the Goals of Death Education

The advocates of death education have made some noticeable, if modest, progress in overcoming some of the problems cited in previous sections. Death education has evolved into a recognized professional field. It may be amorphous and there may be problems having to do with territorial rights vis-a-vis other disciplines. Nonetheless, there are a growing number of dedicated and committed death educators who are actively engaged in legitimizing this new profession.

At least two professional organizations are currently working toward improving and promoting the field of death education: the Association for Death

Education and Counseling and the International Work Group on Death, Dying, and Bereavement. Both have stepped up their efforts to develop principles and standards, and one has initiated a certification process. These activities are an important beginning toward achieving quality control in death education. However, standards and certification are effective only to the extent that the institutions or agencies employing death educators require and recognize them. This has yet to be fully accomplished. Moreover, death education has to become an acknowledged subspecialty within the professional community. In addition, its practitioners need to become visible and make their case before the general public. This will also enable them to discover the major sources of resistance to their acceptance and to clarify the major concerns of the opposition. Consideration of these concerns can result in a critical reexamination of the goals and objectives of death education and the evidence that supports them.

The leaders in the death-awareness movement have a vision of death education for all. They have long established and reaffirmed various sets of goals. Three general goals apply across all educational levels. Knott (2) defines them as follows: information sharing, values' clarification, and coping behaviors. The first goal concerns the dissemination of relevant data in the field of thanatology: a variety of theoretical and empirical information; statements on attitudes toward death, bereavement, and mourning; demographics; and medical and ethical issues surrounding the definition of death. Knott sees the second goal as the examination and clarification of one's personal values relating to the many vital decision-making opportunities involving what might be called "deathstyle," more commonly termed "lifestyle," that includes considering the death-influencing alternatives in one's manner of living, social issues such as the threats of global catastrophe, holocaust, violence in its many forms, and self-destructive behaviors. Knott views the third goal, coping behaviors, as a series of skills aimed at solving problems for and giving help to oneself, relatives, friends, or clients and notes their particular importance at the present time—a time in which there is a lack of appropriate sociocultural norms with respect to death (2, pp. 389–390).

INTEGRATING THANATOLOGY INTO ESTABLISHED DISCIPLINES

As a society, we have managed, to a large degree, to segregate death from our everyday lives and turned the tasks related to the dying and the deceased over to specialists. However, the fact is that death does not exist in splendid isolation. Likewise, the field of thanatology cannot exist in a vacuum if it hopes to grow and become a viable area of inquiry and education. As with other new areas of study, there is an initial tendency to focus exclusively on its arena of concern. Eventually, there comes a point where that arena needs to be expanded and embraced by a broader context.

We are reminded of the emphasis on black studies that grew out of the civil rights movement as it related to racial inequalities. Suddenly, scholars were pouring over archival records to identify the contributions made by blacks in literature, history, and science. All material was packaged into courses and introduced into various curricula as special offerings. The problem was that, after an initial curiosity, few students other than blacks enrolled in these courses. Though these courses undoubtedly contributed to our understanding of black culture and perhaps increased the pride of black students, they probably did not reach the majority of the student population. It was eventually recognized that in order to accomplish that goal, black contributions would have to be included into the broader disciplines of history, literature, and the sciences. We see a similar need for mainstreaming the thanatological contributions i.e., integrating them into appropriate disciplines and professional fields. For example, anxiety is a major topic in psychology; hence, the knowledge concerning death anxiety can be assimilated by that field. Similarly, the subject of the dying experience, including the theoretical models of psychosocial coping as well as the existing research data, should be an integral part of the curricula of nursing, medicine, social work, counseling psychology, etc. The demographics of death and how they relate to widowhood can be incorporated into social gerontology and geriatrics. At present, however, the degree of thanatological knowledge that filters into other disciplines and fields is a poor facsimile of what is available.

The obverse should also be the case: Thanatologists should draw more heavily on the theories and data in the mainstream disciplines. For example, there is a rich literature on the experiences of separation and loss in marriage and family research, some of which has been utilized to explore thanatological issues. A great deal more of this sort of cross-fertilization is needed. Otherwise, much death research will remain unconnected with the more established relevant fields and consequently have unnecessarily limited impact.

LOTS OF QUESTIONS—NO EASY SOLUTIONS

The death-awareness movement and the formalized system of death education that its proponents advocate inevitably raises difficult questions, controversial issues, and debates that often challenge traditional assumptions. Illustrative here are the critical issues surrounding euthanasia. Until very recently, decisions concerning terminal care were generally assumed to be within the sole province of the medical profession. However, dramatic innovations in medical technology along with significant advances in public health have created circumstances which allow that view to be challenged and have provoked complex medical, ethical, legal, and social issues involved in prolonging or terminating life.

Controversial cases surrounding the "right to die" continue to emerge despite the fact that nearly four-fifths of our states have legislated "natural death" or "living will" laws designed to humanize and rationalize euthanasia. Wass (17) has noted several current and unresolved problems in this area.

1. *Language.* The language of the laws is frequently ambiguous. For example, many fail to address questions related to patients who are minors or mentally incompetent adults.

2. *Ideological.* Various individuals or groups file law suits against physicians, nurses, and even family members for practicing or not practicing euthanasia. They represent a spectrum of ideological positions concerning the right to die. Often, adherents of these positions select or reject scientific evidence on the basis of whether it supports their particular beliefs and values. Consequently, efforts to achieve compromise or agreement typically fall victim to ideological fervor.

3. *Definitional.* Consensus on the definition of death remains elusive. "How can you settle the issue of whether or not to let a terminally ill person with extremely poor prognosis die when we do not agree when a person is dead or on the criteria by which to determine that it is so?" (17, p. vi). The definitional problem has real and critical implications, legal and otherwise, for example, with respect to the removal and transplantation of human organs. It is neither a small nor "nitpicking" matter and encompasses an extensive list of life and death situations. Examples such as the following recently reported incident dramatically highlight the problem. A wife had told her husband that if she ever became so ill that only machines could keep her alive, she would prefer that he pull the plug. She subsequently suffered a cerebral hemorrhage and fell into a coma. After she had remained comatose for nearly a month and a half, her husband asked a judge to order the physicians to let her die. The judge felt it was too soon to make such a decision and denied the request. Shortly thereafter, the wife regained consciousness and would eventually be discharged from the hospital. Her husband is quoted as saying, "I guess we've muddied the waters surrounding the question of a person's right to die" (18, p. 35). Indeed, it needs to be stressed that "the decision of when the human spirit is gone, when to turn off the machines, is a moral as well as a medical and legal problem" (19, p. 35). Therefore, it is essential that the "dialogue regarding the criteria for the determination of death must continue, and the public must be kept informed to a greater extent than ever before" (p. 49).

4. *Abortion.* Consensus on when life begins is equally elusive and is at the heart of the death-related controversy over abortion. Despite the 1973 Supreme Court ruling upholding the woman's prerogative in this matter, ideological battles continue to rage between the "right-to-life" individuals and organizations and those who support freedom of choice. During the 1980s, the intensity of emotions concerning this issue erupted into direct attacks on and several bombings of clinics providing abortion counseling and services.

The battle has spilled over into the related issue of whether or not to withhold treatment from severely imperiled, multiply handicapped newborns. "The issue of treating severely life-threatened neonates is further compounded by the rapid developments in medical technology. Today, it is technically possible to maintain prematurely born fetuses at 24 weeks gestation weighing 400 grams, with a 10 percent chance of survival. Where to draw the line is a critical question. And another is who has the right to decide: the doctor; the parents; the fetus; the federal government? There are no categorical answers" (17, p. viii).

5. *Economics.* Keeping humans alive, whether they be a fetus or an adult with a life-threatening illness, can be extremely expensive. This often leads to tortuous dilemmas and a clash of values. Some hold to a position of "life at any cost" while others accept death as an alternative when the situation becomes economically unbearable. The current concern over the treatment of AIDS (acquired immune deficiency syndrome) victims is illustrative. Treatment for one person can run into the hundreds of thousands of dollars. Many question the expenditure of such sums on patients who will ultimately die for lack of a cure. This particular debate is exacerbated by moral judgments related to sexual preferences and activities, as well as by considerable misinformation about the disease itself. Are financial costs and moral judgments to serve at the primary bases for proceeding with or denying treatment?

Biomedical advances will continue to provoke a variety of old and new ethical and legal questions and personal dilemmas related to death. A case in point is the recent breakthrough regarding the detection of Huntington's disease—an inherited, untreatable, and fatal brain disorder. Children with a Huntington's parent have a 50 percent probability of contracting the disease, which causes progressive dementia and loss of body control. Until recently, there was no way of detecting whether progeny would develop the disease. In 1986, however, a chromosomal test was devised which does just that. People who test positive will have to live with the grim certainty of that knowledge. Consequently, some may choose to resolve this dilemma by electing not to take the test. For an unknown number of individuals, this may, in fact, be the best choice. Studies have revealed that people who know they are at risk often have a high rate of depression and behavioral disorders. Moreover, one-fourth of those who are diagnosed with early symptoms of the disease attempt suicide. In such instances, a little knowledge may be a dangerous thing.

The test raises difficult ethical and legal questions with practical implications. Employers and insurance companies, for example, may decide to require the test for people at risk. It may become difficult to safeguard the right of certain people not to know—for instance, a husband with a family history of the disease whose pregnant wife decides to test the unborn fetus for the gene. If the fetus has Huntington's, then you know the at-risk parent also has it (20, p. 80). Clearly, resolutions to the dilemmas raised by such circumstances will not be easily achieved.

Indeed, contemporary thanatological discourse can be characterized by what appears to be an endless string of provocative issues generated by an expanding technological capacity. The implications can be staggering.

> Mario and Elsa Rio, millionaires, were killed in an air crash. There is nothing extraordinary about this, except that they left two frozen embryos in an Australian laboratory for eventual implantation in Mrs. Rio's womb. The legal question raised was whether these embryos can inherit the estate. The more basic question, however, was whether they should be implanted in another womb or be destroyed. Do frozen embryos have the moral, if not the legal, right to life? Does anyone own them? These and other questions are perplexing. Answers now given point at the vexing paradoxes in our values both as individuals and as a society. On one hand, we may consider human life as infinitely precious, to be cherished and preserved, in which a 10 percent chance of fetal survival is worth all the resources it requires. On the other hand, life is also held to be cheap. We demonstrate this on a large scale when we fail to enforce public safety laws so that numerous deaths occur and more are threatened by toxic/ radioactive material in the air, soil, and water; with hazardous occupational environments; and less than vigorous action against substance abuse. (17, p. viii)

The conflicting and competing value systems depicted here and throughout this volume often become the focal point of controversy and help us to understand why death-related issues do not easily lend themselves to quick and simple solutions.

Despite the above complexities, it is important to note that preserving life and improving the quality of human existence remain core values and goals around which there exists widespread consensus. As a result, one can find examples where medical technology is utilized to reflect those ends. For instance, in the 1980s, medicine and law worked together to insure that brain dead, comatose, pregnant women were sustained by respirators until their babies could be delivered. As of this writing, at least a dozen babies had been delivered under such circumstances, thus establishing a firm precedent for the practice to be continued.

Similarly, research involving fetal-cell implants, in which cells obtained from aborted human fetuses are used to develop new therapies, is aimed at enhancing the life chances of people suffering from a variety of ailments, including diabetes, brain disease, head injuries, leukemia, stroke, and paralysis. Again, experiments utilizing fetal cells raises difficult medical and legal questions (21, pp. 68–69). However, few would fail to support the general goal of searching for treatments for those suffering from severe, incurable diseases.

Such cases lend some balance to a literature heavily weighted toward issues of dying and death by stressing survivorship and the quality of life. As the authors of one of the chapters in this volume have noted, survivor education and death education are, after all, two sides of the same coin.

REFERENCES

1. McClure, J. W. (1974). Death education. *Phi Delta Kappan,* 483–485.
2. Knott, J. E. (1979). Death education for all. In H. Wass (Ed.), *Dying: Facing the Facts* (pp. 385–403). Washington, DC: Hemisphere.
3. Morgan, E. (1977). *A manual of death education and simple burial* (8th ed.). Burnsville, NC: Celo Press.
4. Pine, V. R. (1977). A socio-historical portrait of death education. *Death Education, 1,* 57–84.
5. Pine, V. R. (1986). The age of maturity for death education: A sociohistorical portrait of the era 1976–1985. *Death Studies, 10,* 209–231.
6. Leviton, D. (1977). The scope of death education. *Death Education, 1,* 41–56.
7. Wass, H., Corr, C. A., Pacholski, R. A., & Sanders, C. M. (1980). *Death education: An annotated resource guide.* Washington, DC: Hemisphere.
8. Wass, H., Corr, C. A., Pacholski, R. A., & Forfar, C. S. (1985). *Death education II: An annotated resource guide.* Washington, DC: Hemisphere.
9. Gorer, G. (1965). *Death, grief and mourning in contemporary Britain.* London: Cresset.
10. Fulton, R. (1987). The many faces of grief. *Death Studies, 11,* 243–256.
11. Wass, H. (1985). Depiction of death, grief, and funerals on national television. *Research Record, 2,* 81–82.
12. Who's afraid of the bomb? (1984, October 29). *Time,* p. 78.
13. Croskery, B. F. (1979). *Death education: Attitudes of teachers, school board members and clergy.* Palo Alto, CA: R&E Research Associates.
14. Crase, D. (1982). The many faces of death education. *Death Education, 6,* 391–393.
15. Cappiello, L. A., & Troyer, R. E. (1979). A study of the role of health educators in teaching about death and dying. *Journal of School Health, 49,* 397–399.
16. V. Cummins. (Personal communication, 1983).
17. Wass, H. (1986). Editorial. *Death Studies, 10*(1), iii-xiii.

18. Back from the dead. (1986, October 6). *Time*, p. 35.
19. Hendin, D. (1973). *Death as a fact of life*. New York: Norton.
20. Levine, J. (1986, October 20). Do they really want to know? *Time*, p. 80.
21. McAuliffe, K. (1986, November 3). A startling fount of healing. *U.S. News & World Report*, pp. 68–70.

Appendixes

Appendixes

Appendix A: For Further Reading

Allen, N. H. (1980). *Homicide: Perspectives on prevention.* New York: Human Sciences Press.

Amato, J. A. (1985). *Death book: Terrors, consolations, contradictions, and paradoxes.* Peoria, IL: Ellis Press.

American Psychiatric Association Task Force Report 20 (1982). *Psychosocial aspects of nuclear developments.* Washington, DC: Author.

Anthony, S. (1972). *The discovery of death in childhood and after.* New York: Basic Books.

Ariès, P. (1981). *The hour of our death.* New York: Knopf.

Arkin, W. M., & Fieldhouse, R. W. (1985). *Nuclear battlefields.* Cambridge, MA: Ballinger.

Becker, E. (1973). *The denial of death.* New York: Free Press.

Benoliel, J. Q. (Ed.). (1982). *Death education for the health professional.* Washington, DC: Hemisphere.

Bluebond-Langner, M. (1978). *The private worlds of dying children.* Princeton: Princeton University Press.

Bracken, P. (1983). *The command and control of nuclear forces.* New Haven: Yale University Press.

Brim, O. E., Freeman, H. E., Levine, S., & Scotch, N. A. (Eds.). (1970). *The dying patient.* New York: Russell Sage.

Carse, J. P. (1980). *Death and existence.* New York: John Wiley & Sons.

Charmaz, K. (1980). *The social reality of death.* Reading, MA: Addison-Wesley.

Choron, J. (1978). *Death and Western thought.* New York: Collier.

Corr, C. A., & Corr, D. M. (Eds.). (1985). *Hospice approaches to pediatric care.* New York: Springer.

Corr, C. A., & McNeil, J. N. (Eds.). (1986). *Adolescence and death.* New York: Springer.

Curran, D. K. (1987). *Adolescent suicidal behavior.* Washington, DC: Hemisphere.

Degner, L. F., & Beaton, J. I. (1987). *Life-death decisions in health care.* Washington, DC: Hemisphere.

Davidson, G. W. (1978). *The hospice: Development and administration.* Washington, DC: Hemisphere.

Davidson, G. W. (1984). *Understanding mourning: A guide for those who grieve.* Minneapolis: Augsburg.

Davidson, G. W. (Ed.). (1985). *The hospice: Development and administration* (2nd ed.). Washington, DC: Hemisphere.

Doudera, A. E., & Peters, J. D. (Eds.). (1982). *Legal and ethical aspects of treating critically and terminally ill patients.* Ann Arbor, MI: AUPHA Press.

DuBois, P. M. (1980). *The hospice way of death.* New York: Human Sciences Press.

Elder, G. H., Jr., (Ed.). (1985). *Life course dynamics.* Ithaca, NY: Cornell University Press.

Epting, F. R., & Neimeyer, R. A. (Eds.). (1984). *Personal meanings of death: Applications of personal construct theory to clinical practice.* Washington, DC: Hemisphere.

Farberow, N. L. (Ed.). (1980). *The many faces of suicide: Indirect self-destructive behavior.* New York: McGraw-Hill.

Farrell, J. J. (1980). *Inventing the American way of death.* Philadelphia: Temple University Press.

Feifel, H. (Ed.). (1959). *The meaning of death.* New York: McGraw-Hill.

Feifel, H. (Ed.). (1977). *New meanings of death.* New York: McGraw-Hill.

Feigenberg, L. (1980). *Terminal care: Friendship contracts with dying cancer patients.* New York: Brunner/Mazel.

Fulton, R. (Ed.). (1976). *Death and identity.* Revised edition. Bowie, MD: The Charles Press.

Garfield, C. A. (Ed.). (1978). *Psychosocial care of the dying.* New York: McGraw-Hill.

Glaser, B. G., & Strauss, A. L. (Eds.). (1968). *Time for dying.* Chicago: Aldine.

Grollman, E. A. (1976). *Talking about death: A dialogue between parent and child.* Boston: Beacon.

Harris, J. (1985). *The value of life.* Boston: Routledge & Kegan Paul.

Harron, F. (1983). *Health and human values: A guide to making your own decisions.* New Haven: Yale University Press.

Hatton, C. L., & Valente, S. M. (1984). *Suicide: Assessment and intervention* (2nd ed.). New York: Appleton-Century-Crofts.

Illich, I. (1976). *Medical Nemesis.* New York: Bantam.

Jacobs, J. (1982). *The moral justification of suicide.* Springfield, IL: Charles C Thomas.

Kalish, R. A., & Reynolds, D. K. (1976). *Death and ethnicity: A psychocultural study.* Los Angeles: University of Southern California Press.

Kalish, R. A. (1985). *Death, grief, and caring relationships* (2nd ed.). Monterey, CA: Brooks/Cole.

Kass, L. R. (1985). *Toward a more natural science: Biology and human affairs.* New York: Free Press.

Kastenbaum, R., & Aisenberg, R. (1972). *The psychology of death.* New York: Springer.

Kastenbaum, R. (1977). *Death, society and human experience.* St. Louis: Mosby.
Koff, T. H. (1980). *Hospice: A caring community.* Cambridge, MA: Winthrop.
Korein, J. (Ed.). (1978). *Brain death: Interrelated medical and social issues.* New York: New York Academy of Sciences.
Kübler-Ross, E. (1969). *On death and dying.* New York: Macmillan.
Kushner, H. S. (1981). *When bad things happen to good people.* New York: Schocken.
Ladd, J. (Ed.). (1979). *Ethical issues relating to life and death.* New York: Oxford University Press.
La Grand, L. E. (1986). *Coping with separation and loss as a young adult.* Springfield, IL: Charles C Thomas.
Lamb, D. (1985). *Death, brain death, and ethics.* Albany: SUNY Press.
Lepp, I. (1968). *Death and its mysteries.* Toronto: Macmillan.
LeShan, E. (1976). *Learning to say good-by: When a parent dies.* New York: Macmillan.
Lifton, R. J. (1979). *The broken connection.* New York: Simon & Schuster.
Lifton, R. J., & Falk, R. (1982). *Indefensible weapons: The psychological case against nuclearism.* New York: Basic Books.
Lonetto, R. (1980). *Children's conceptions of death.* New York: Springer.
Lynch, J. J. (1977). *The broken heart: The medical consequences of loneliness.* New York: Basic Books.
Mack, A. (Ed.). *Death in American experience.* New York: Schocken.
Maris, R. W. (1981). *Pathways to suicide: A survey of self-destructive behaviors.* Baltimore, MD: The Johns Hopkins University Press.
Martocchio, B. C. (1980). *Living while dying.* Bowie, MD: Robert J. Brady.
McIntire, M., & Angle, C. (1980). *Suicide attempts in children and youth.* New York: Harper & Row.
McIntosh, J. L. (1985). *Research on suicide: A bibliography.* Westport, CT: Greenwood Press.
Munley, A. (1983). *The hospice alternative: A new context for death and dying.* New York: Basic Books.
Neale, R. E. (1973). *The art of dying.* New York: Harper & Row.
Osterweis, M., Solomon, F., & Green, M. (Eds.). (1984). *Bereavement: Reactions, consequences, and care.* Washington, DC: National Academy Press.
Parkes, C. M., & Weiss, R. S. (1983). *Recovery from bereavement.* New York: Basic Books.
Pattison, E. M. (1977). *The experience of dying.* Englewood Cliffs, NJ: Prentice-Hall.
Peppers, L. G., & Knapp, R. J. (1980). *Motherhood and mourning: Perinatal death.* New York: Praeger.
Pine, V. R. (1975). *Caretaker of the dead: The American funeral director.* New York: Halsted.
Population Reports, AIDS—A public health crisis (1986). Series L. Population Information Program. Baltimore, MD: The Johns Hopkins University.
President's Commission for the Study of Ethical Problems in Medicine and Biomedical and Behavioral Research (1983). *Deciding to forego life-sustaining treatment: Ethical, medical and legal issues in treatment decisions.* Washington, DC: U.S. Government Printing Office.
President's Commission for the Study of Ethical Problems in Medicine and Biomedical and Behavioral Research (1981). *Defining death: Medical, legal and*

clinical issues in the definition of death. Washington, DC: U.S. Government Printing Office.

Quint, J. C. (1967). *The nurse and the dying patient.* New York: Macmillan.

Ramsey, P. (1970). *The patient as person.* New Haven, CT: Yale University Press.

Ramsey, P. (1978). *Ethics at the edges of life.* New Haven, CT: Yale University Press.

Rando, T. A. (Ed.). (1986). *Loss and anticipatory grief.* Lexington, MA: Lexington Books.

Rando, T. A. (Ed.). (1986). *Parental loss of a child.* Champaign, IL: Research Press.

Raphael, B. (1983). *The anatomy of bereavement.* New York: Basic Books.

Regan, T. (Ed.). (1980). *Matters of life and death.* Philadelphia: Temple University Press.

Repetto, R. (Ed.). (1985). *The global possible: Resources, development, and the new century.* New Haven, CT: Yale University Press.

Reynolds, D. K., & Farberow, N. L. (1981). *The family shadow: Sources of suicide and schizophrenia.* Berkeley: University of California Press.

Rifkin, J., & Howard, T. (1980). *Entropy: A new world view.* New York: Bantam.

Ring, K. (1982). *Life at death: A scientific investigation of the near-death experience.* New York: Quill.

Rosen, H. (1986). *Unspoken grief: Coping with childhood sibling loss.* Lexington, MA: D. C. Heath.

Rosenblatt, P. D., Walsh, R. P., & Jackson, D. A. (1976). *Grief and mourning in cross-cultural perspective.* Minneapolis: HRAF Press.

Rosenblatt, P. C., Walsh, R. P., & Jackson, D. A. (1976). *Grief and mourning in cross-cultural perspective.* Minneapolis: HRAF Press.

Rowe, D. (1982). *The construction of life and death.* New York: John Wiley & Sons.

Saunders, C. (Ed.). (1978). *The management of terminal disease.* London: Edward Arnold.

Saunders, C., Summers, D. H., & Teller, N. (1981). *Hospice: The living idea.* London: Edward Arnold.

Schell, J. (1982). *The fate of the earth.* New York: Avon.

Self, D. (Ed.). (1977). *Philosophy and public policy.* Norfolk, VA: Teagle and Little.

Shaw, M. W., & Doudera, A. E. (Eds.). (1983). *Defining human life.* Ann Arbor, MI: AUPHA Press.

Shneidman, E. S. (1974). *Deaths of man.* New York: Penguin Books.

Shneidman, E. (Ed.). (1976). *Suicidology: Contemporary developments.* New York: Grune & Stratton.

Shneidman, E. (1982). *Voices of death.* New York: Bantam.

Spicker, S. F. (Ed.). (1978). *Organism, medicine and metaphysics.* Boston: D. Reidel.

Stannard, D. E. (1977). *The Puritan way of death: A study in religion, culture, and social change.* New York: Oxford University Press.

Stephenson, J. S. (1985). *Death, grief, and mourning: Individual and social realities.* New York: The Free Press.

Stillion, J. M. (Ed.). (1984). Suicide: Practical, developmental, and speculative issues. *Death Education, 8,* Supplement.

Stillion, J. M. (1985). *Death and the sexes: An examination of differential longevity, attitudes, behaviors, and coping skills.* Washington, DC: Hemisphere.

Stoddard, S. (1978). *The hospice movement.* New York: Stein and Day.

Strauss, A. L. (1975). *Chronic illness and the quality of life.* St. Louis: Mosby.

Sudnow, D. (1967). *Passing on: The social organization of dying.* Englewood Cliffs, NJ: Prentice-Hall.

Turnbull, R. (Ed.). (1986). *Terminal care.* Washington, DC: Hemisphere.

Twycross, R., & Ventafridda, V. (Eds.). (1980). *The continuing care of the cancer patient.* Oxford: Pergamon.

Vachon, M. L. S. (1987). *Occupational stress in the care of the critically ill, the dying, and the bereaved.* Washington, DC: Hemisphere.

Veatch, R. M. (1976). *Death, dying and the biological revolution.* New Haven, CT: Yale University Press.

Vladek, B. C. (1980). *Unloving care: The nursing home tragedy.* New York: Basic Books.

Walker, A. E. (1985). *Cerebral death.* Baltimore, MD: Urban & Schwarzenberg.

Wass, H., Corr, C. A., Pacholski, R. A., & Sanders, C. M. (1980). *Death education: An annotated resource guide.* Washington, DC: Hemisphere.

Wass, H., & Corr, C. A. (Eds.). (1984). *Childhood and death.* Washington, DC: Hemisphere.

Wass, H., & Corr, C. A. (Eds.). (1984). *Helping children cope with death: Guidelines and resources* (2nd ed.). Washington, DC: Hemisphere.

Wass, H., Corr, C. A., Pacholski, R. A., & Forfar, C. S. (1985). *Death education II: An annotated resource guide.* Washington, DC: Hemisphere.

Weisman, A. (1972). *On dying and denying.* New York: Behavioral Publications.

Weisman, A. (1979). *Coping with cancer.* New York: McGraw-Hill.

Weisman, A. D. (1984). *The coping capacity: On the nature of being mortal.* New York: Human Sciences Press.

Wilkes, E. (Ed.). (1982). *The dying patient: The management of incurable and terminal illness.* Ridgewood, NJ: George A. Bogden and Son.

Woito, R. (1982). *To end war: A new approach to international conflict.* New York: Pilgrim Press.

Worden, J. W. (1982). *Grief counseling and grief therapy: A handbook for the mental health practitioner.* New York: Springer.

Zinner, E. S. (Ed.). (1985). *Coping with death on campus.* San Francisco: Jossey-Bass.

Appendix B: Audiovisual Resources and Organizations

AUDIOVISUAL RESOURCES

Dying and Care of the Dying

Childhood cancer: A day at a time. Videocassette, color, 59 min. Filmmakers Library, Inc., 133 East 58th St., Suite 703A, New York, NY 10022.

Death of a gandy dander. 16 mm film, color, 26 min. Learning Corporation of America, 1350 Avenue of the Americas, New York, NY 10019.

Going to the edge. Videocassette, color, 33 min. Media Library, University of Michigan Medical Center, R4440 Kresge I., Ann Arbor, MI 48109-0518.

Gramp: A man ages and dies. Film strip and audiocassette, black and white, 20 min. Sunburst Communications, 39 Washington Ave., Pleasantville, NY 10570.

Jocelyn. 16 mm film or videocassete, color, 28 min. Filmmakers Library, Inc., 133 East 58th St., Suite 703A, New York, NY 10022.

Peege. 16 mm film, color, 28 min. Phoenix Films, 470 Park Ave. South, New York, NY 10016.

Further details concerning these audiovisual resources as well as additional ones can be found in Wass, H., Corr, C. A., Pacholski, R. A., & Sanders, C. M. (1980). *Death education: An annotated resource guide.* Washington, DC: Hemisphere; Wass, H., Corr, C. A., Pacholski, R. A., & Forfar, C. S. (1985). *Death education II: An annotated resource guide.* Washington, DC: Hemisphere; and the Media Exchange section of *Death Studies* (formerly *Death Education*), a bimonthly international journal.

For a more extensive list of organizations and information, see Wass, H., Corr, C. A., Pacholski, R. A., & Sanders, C. M. (1980). *Death education: An annotated resource guide.* Washington, DC: Hemisphere; and Wass, H., Corr, C. A., Pacholski, R. A., & Forfar, C. S. (1985). *Death education II: An annotated resource guide.* Washington, DC: Hemisphere.

Planting things I won't see flower. 16mm film, color, 26 min. United Methodist Film Service, 1525 McGavock St., Nashville, TN 37203.

Softfire. 16mm film or videocassette, color, 19 min. Centre Productions, 1327 Spruce St., Suite 3, Boulder, CO 80302.

Terminal cancer: The hospice approach to pain (Part I).. Videocassette, color, 19 min. Network for Continuing Medical Education, 15 Columbus Circle, New York, NY 10023.

Terminal cancer: The hospice approach to the family (Part II). Videocassette, color, 19 min. Network for Continuing Medical Education, 15 Columbus Circle, New York, NY 10023.

The Rothe tape. Videocassette, color, 30 min. Department of Pastoral Care, Shands Teaching Hospital, Box J-323, Gainesville, FL 32611.

To expect to die: A film about living. Videocassette, color, 59 min. Public Television Library Video Programs Service, 475 L'Enfant Plaza, S.W., Washington, DC 20024.

Walk me to the water: Three people in their time of dying. 16mm film or videocassette, black and white, 28 min. John Seakwood, Box 126, Mountain Road, New Lebanon, NY 12125.

Weekend. 16mm film, color, 10 min. Mass Media Associates, 225 South Main St., P.O. Box 427, Stewartstown, PA 17363.

Suicide

But Jack was a good driver (1974). 16mm film, color, 15 min. McGraw-Hill Films, 1221 Avenue of the Americas, New York, NY 10020.

Suicide. (Originally made for general television audience), 16mm film or videocassette, color, 25 min. Films, Inc., 8124 N. Central Park, Skokie, IL 60076 (for rentals); Films, Inc., 733 Green Bay Rd., Wilmette, IL 60091 (for purchase).

Teen suicide: Who, why and how you can prevent it. Four filmstrips and audiocassettes or videocassettes, color, 45 min. Guidance Associates, Communications Park, Box 3000, Mount Kisco, NY 10549-9989.

The threat of suicide. Videocassette, color, 27 min. Network for Continuing Medical Education, 15 Columbus Circle, New York, NY 10023.

Ethical Issues

A dignified exit (1981). 16mm film, color, 26 min. Filmmakers Library, 133 East 58th St., Suite 703A, New York, NY 10022.

Born dying. 16mm film or videocassette, color, 20 min. Research Press, Box 31779, Champaign, IL 61821.

Code gray: Ethical dilemmas in nursing. 16mm film or videocassette, color, 28 min. Fanlight Productions, 47 Halifax St., Boston, MA 02130.

Dax's case (1984). 16mm film or videocassette, color, 60 min. Concern for Dying: An Educational Council, 250 West 57th St., New York, NY 10107.

Hard choices: Death and dying. One of six programs aired on PBS in 1981. Videocassette, color, 60 min. University of Washington, Instructional Media Services, 23 Kane Hall, DG10, Seattle, WA 98195.

No heroic measures (1986). 16mm film or videocassette, color, 22 min. Carle Medical Communications, 510 West Main St., Urbana, IL 61801.

The last right. 16mm film or videocassette, color, 29 min. New Dimension Films, 85895 Lorane Highway, Eugene, OR 97405.

The right to die (1985). 16mm film or videocassette, color, 19 min. Carle Medical Communications, 510 West Main St., Urbana, IL 61801.

Bereavement and Grief

But he was only seventeen. Filmstrip and audiotape, color, 22 min. Sunburst Communications, 39 Washington Ave., Pleasantville, NY 10507.

Death of the wished-for child. 16mm film, color, 28 min. O.G.R. Service Corporation, P.O. Box 3586, Springfield, IL 62708.

Footsteps on the ceiling. 16mm film or videocassette, color, 8 min. Phoenix Films, 470 Park Ave., South, New York, NY 10016.

One in 350: Sudden infant death. 16mm film, black and white, 30 min. National Sudden Infant Death Syndrome Foundation, 310 South Michigan Ave., Chicago, IL 60604.

The compassionate friends. Filmstrip and audiotape. The Compassionate Friends, P.O. Box 1347, Oak Brook, IL 60521.

The life that's left. 16mm film or videocassette, color, 29 min. Great Plains National Instructional Television Library, P.O. Box 80669, Lincoln, NE 68501.

The pitch of grief (1985). Videocassette, color, 30 min. Fanlight Productions, 47 Halifax St., Boston, MA 02130.

With his playclothes on. 16mm filmstrip and audiotape, color, 47 min. O.G.R. Service Corporation, P.O. Box 3586, Springfield, IL 62708.

ORGANIZATIONS

American Association of Suicidology, 2459 S. Ash, Denver, CO 80222.

American Cancer Society, National Headquarters, 777 3rd Ave., New York, NY 10017.

American Hospital Association, 840 N. Lake Shore Dr., Chicago, IL 60611.

American Medical Association, 535 Dearborn St., Chicago, IL 60610.

Association for Death Education and Counseling, Inc., 2211 Arthur Ave., Lakewood, OH 44107.

Concern for Dying—An Educational Council, 250 West 57th St., New York, NY 10107 (concerned primarily with the living will, death with dignity, and other patients' rights).

Cancer Information Service, National Cancer Institute, Bethesda, MD 20014 (1-800-492-6600).

Candlelighters Foundation, 123 C St., S.E., Washington, DC 20003 (self-help organization for families with dying children).

International Association for Near-Death Studies, Box U-20, University of Connecticut, Storrs, CT 06268.

International Workgroup on Death, Dying and Bereavement, Secretariat King's College, 266 Epworth Ave., London, Ontario, Canada N6A 2M3.

Leukemia Society of America, 211 East 43rd St., New York, NY 10017.

Make Today Count, P.O. Box 303, Burlington, IA 52601 (self-help organization for persons with life-threatening illnesses and their families).

National Citizens' Coalition for Nursing Home Reform, 1424 16th St., N.W., Room 204, Washington, DC 20036.

National Hospice Organization, 1901 North Fort Myer Drive, Suite 902, Arlington, VA 22209.

National Right to Life Committee, Suite 341, National Press Building, 529 14th St., N.W., Washington, DC 20045.

National Self-Help Clearinghouse. Graduate School and University Center, City University of New York, 33 West 42nd St., Room 1227, New York, NY 10036.

National Sudden Infant Death Syndrome Foundation, 8240 Professional Place, Suite 205, Landover, MD 20785.

Society for the Right to Die, 250 West 57th St., New York, NY 10019.

The Compassionate Friends. P.O. Box 1347, Oak Brook, IL 60521 (self-help organization for bereaved parents).

Appendix C: Documents

THE OATH OF HIPPOCRATES
(460–359 B.C.)

I swear by Apollo, the physician, and Aesculapius and health and all-heal and all the Gods and Goddesses that, according to my ability and judgment, I will keep this oath and stipulation:

To reckon him who taught me this art equally dear to me as my parents, to share my substance with him and relieve his necessities if required; to regard his offspring as on the same footing with my own brothers, and to teach them this art if they should wish to learn it, without fee or stipulation, and that by precept, lecture and every other mode of instruction, I will impart a knowledge of the art to my own sons and to those of my teachers, and to disciples bound by a stipulation and oath, according to the law of medicine, but to none others.

I will follow that method of treatment which, according to my ability and judgment, I consider for the benefit of my patients, and abstain from whatever is deleterious and mischievous. I will give no deadly medicine to anyone if asked, nor suggest such counsel; furthermore, I will not give to a woman an instrument to produce abortion.

With purity and with holiness I will pass my life and practice my art. I will not cut a person who is suffering from a stone, but will leave this to be done by practitioners of this work. Into whatever houses I enter I will go into them for the benefit of the sick and will abstain from every voluntary act of mischief and corruption; and further from the seduction of females or males, bond or free.

Whatever, in connection with my professional practice, or not in connection with it, I may see or hear in the lives of men which ought not to be spoken abroad I will not divulge, as reckoning that all such should be kept secret.

While I continue to keep this oath unviolated may it be granted to me to enjoy life and the practice of the art, respected by all men at all times but should I trespass and violate this oath, may the reverse be my lot.

PRINCIPLES OF MEDICAL ETHICS
American Medical Association

The medical profession has long subscribed to a body of ethical statements developed primarily for the benefit of the patient. As a member of this profession, a physician must recognize responsibility not only to patients, but also to society, to other health professionals, and to self. The following Principles adopted by the American Medical Association are not laws, but standards of conduct which define the essentials of honorable behavior for the physician.

I. A physician shall be dedicated to providing competent medical service with compassion and respect for human dignity.

II. A physician shall deal honestly with patients and colleagues, and strive to expose those physicians deficient in character or competence, or who engage in fraud or deception.

III. A physician shall respect the law and also recognize a responsibility to seek changes in these requirements which are contrary to the best interests of the patient.

IV. A physician shall respect the rights of patients, of colleagues, and of other health professionals, and shall safeguard patient confidences within the constraints of the law.

V. A physician shall continue to study, apply and advance scientific knowledge, make relevant information available to patients, colleagues, and the public, obtain consultation, and use the talents of other health professionals when indicated.

VI. A physician shall, in the provision of appropriate patient care, except in emergencies, be free to choose whom to serve, with whom to associate, and the environment in which to provide medical services.

VII. A physician shall recognize a responsibility to participate in activities contributing to an improved community.

Adopted by AMA House of Delegates at annual meeting. July 22, 1980.
Reprinted by permission of the American Medical Association.

CODE FOR NURSES
American Nurses Association

The Code for Nurses is based on belief about the nature of individuals, nursing, health, and society. Recipients and providers of nursing services are viewed as individuals and groups who possess basic rights and responsibilities and whose values and circumstances command respect at all times. Nursing encompasses the promotion and restoration of health, the prevention of illness, and the alleviation of suffering. The statements of the Code and their interpretation provide guidance for conduct and relationships in carrying out nursing responsibilities consistent with the ethical obligations of the profession and quality in nursing care.

1. The nurse provides services with respect for human dignity and the uniqueness of the client unrestricted by considerations of social or economic status, personal attributes, or the nature of health problems.
2. The nurse safeguards the client's right to privacy by judiciously protecting information of a confidential nature.
3. The nurse acts to safeguard the client and the public when health care and safety are affected by the incompetent, unethical, or illegal practice of any person.
4. The nurse assumes responsibility and accountability for individual nursing judgments and actions.
5. The nurse maintains competence in nursing.
6. The nurse exercises informed judgment and uses individual competence and qualifications as criteria in seeking consultation, accepting responsibilities, and delegating nursing activities to others.
7. The nurse participates in activities that contribute to the ongoing development of the profession's body of knowledge.
8. The nurse participates in the profession's efforts to implement and improve standards of nursing.
9. The nurse participates in the profession's efforts to establish and maintain conditions of employment conducive to high-quality nursing care.
10. The nurse participates in the profession's effort to protect the public from misinformation and misrepresentation and to maintain the integrity of nursing.
11. The nurse collaborates with members of the health professions and other citizens in promoting community and national efforts to meet the health needs of the public.

Reprinted with permission. American Nurses Association.

A PATIENT'S BILL OF RIGHTS
American Hospital Association

The American Hospital Association Board of Trustees' Committee on Health Care for the Disadvantaged, which has been a consistent advocate on behalf of consumers of health care services, developed the Statement on a Patient's Bill of Rights, which was approved by the AHA House of Delegates February 6, 1973. The statement was published in several forms, one of which was the S74 leaflet in the Association's S series.

The American Hospital Association presents a Patient's Bill of Rights with the expectation that observance of these rights will contribute to more effective patient care and greater satisfaction for the patient, his physician, and the hospital organization. Further, the Association presents these rights in the expectation that they will be supported by the hospital on behalf of its patients, as an integral part of the healing process. It is recognized that a personal relationship between the physician and the patient is essential for the provision of proper medical care. The traditional physician-patient relationship takes on a new dimension when care is rendered within an organizational structure. Legal precedent has established that the institution itself also has a responsibility to the patient. It is in recognition of these factors that these rights are affirmed.

1. The patient has the right to considerate and respectful care.
2. The patient has the right to obtain from his physician complete current information concerning his diagnosis, treatment, and prognosis in terms the patient can be reasonably expected to understand. When it is not medically advisable to give such information to the patient, the information should be made available to an appropriate person in his behalf. He has the right to know, by name, the physician responsible for coordinating his care.
3. The patient has the right to receive from his physician information necessary to give informed consent prior to the start of any procedure and/or treatment. Except in emergencies, such information for informed consent should include but not necessarily be limited to the specific procedure and/or treatment, the medically significant risks involved, and the probable duration of incapacitation. Where medically significant alternatives for care or treatment exist, or when the patients requests information concerning medical alternatives, the patient has the right to such information. The patient also has the right to know the name of the person responsible for the procedures and/or treatment.
4. The patient has the right to refuse treatment to the extent permitted by law and to be informed of the medical consequences of his action.
5. The patient has the right to every consideration of his privacy concerning his own medical care program. Case discussion, consultation, examination, and treatment are confidential and should be conducted discreetly. Those not directly involved in his care must have the permission of the patient to be present.

6. The patient has the right to expect that all communications and records pertaining to his care should be treated as confidential.

7. The patient has the right to expect that within its capacity a hospital must make reasonable response to the request of a patient for services. The hospital must provide evaluation, service, and/or referral as indicated by the urgency of the case. When medically permissible, a patient may be transferred to another facility only after he has received complete information and explanation concerning the needs for and alternatives to such a transfer. The institution to which the patient is to be transferred must first have accepted the patient for transfer.

8. The patient has the right to obtain information as to any relationship of his hospital to other health care and educational institutions insofar as his care is concerned. The patient has the right to obtain information as to the existence of any professional relationship among individuals, by name, who are treating him.

9. The patient has the right to be advised if the hospital proposes to engage in or perform human experimentation affecting his care or treatment. The patient has the right to refuse to participate in such research projects.

10. The patient has the right to expect reasonable continuity of care. He has the right to know in advance what appointment times and physicians are available and where. The patient has the right to expect that the hospital will provide a mechanism whereby he is informed by his physician or a delegate of the physician of the patient's continuing health care requirements following discharge.

11. The patient has the right to examine and receive an explanation of his bill regardless of source of payment.

12. The patient has the right to know what hospital rules and regulations apply to his conduct as a patient.

No catalog of rights can guarantee for the patient the kind of treatment he has a right to expect. A hospital has many functions to perform, including the prevention and treatment of disease, the education of both health professionals and patients, and the conduct of clinical research. All these activities must be conducted with an overriding concern for the patient, and, above all, the recognition of his dignity as a human being. Success in achieving this recognition assures success in the defense of the rights of the patient.

MODEL BILLS

The following Model Bill was drafted at Yale Law School in a 1978 Legislative Services Project sponsored by the Society for the Right to Die. The use of * and ** is to indicate alternatives.

While the Model Bill in its original form permitted the naming of a proxy as one of the "personal directions" that could be added, the Society has added suggested modifications to include specific provision for the appointment of a proxy.

MEDICAL TREATMENT DECISION ACT

1. Purpose. The Legislature finds that adult persons have the fundamental right to control the decision relating to the rendering of their own medical care, including the decision to have life-sustaining procedures withheld or withdrawn in instances of a terminal condition.

In order that the rights of patients may be respected even after they are no longer able to participate actively in decisions about themselves, the Legislature herby declares that the laws of the State of _____ shall recognize the right of an adult person to make a written declaration instructing his or her physician to withhold or withdraw life-sustaining procedures in the event of a terminal condition. It further provides for a proxy appointment, naming another to accept or refuse medical treatment if the appointer is incapable of making such decisions.

2. Definitions. The following definitions shall govern the construction of this act:

(a) "Attending physician" means the physician selected by, or assigned to, the patient who has primary responsibility for the treatment and care of the patient.

(b) "Declaration" means a witnessed document in writing, voluntarily executed by the declarant in accordance with the requirements of Section 3 of this act.

(c) "Life-sustaining procedure" means any medical procedure or intervention which, when applied to a qualified patient, would serve only to prolong the dying process and where, in the judgement of the attending physician, death will occur whether or not such procedures are utilized. "Life-sustaining procedure" shall not include the administration of medication or the performance of any medical procedure deemed necessary to provide comfort care.

(d) "Qualified patient" means a patient who has executed a declaration in accordance with this act and who has been diagnosed and certified in writing to be afflicted with a terminal condition by two physicians who have personally examined the patient, one of whom shall be the attending physician.

3. Execution of Declaration. Any adult person may execute a declaration directing the withholding or withdrawal of life-sustaining procedures in a terminal condition. The declaration shall be signed by the declarant in the presence of two subscribing witnesses at least 18 years of age *(who are not) **(no more than one of whom may be) related to the declarant by blood or marriage, entitled to any portion of the estate of the declarant according to the laws of intestate succession of the State of _____ or under any will of the declarant or codicil thereto, or directly financially responsible for the declarant's medical care.

It shall be the responsibility of declarant to provide for notification to his or her attending physician of the existence of the declaration. An attending physician

Reprinted by permission of Concern for Dying.

who is so notified shall make the declaration, or a copy of the declaration, a part of the declarant's medical records.

The declarant may appoint an agent, or proxy, who will act on behalf of the declarant if, in the judgment of the attending physician, the declarant is incapable of making decisions to accept or refuse medical treatment, and such incapacity is due to illness or injury.

The declaration shall be substantially in the following form, but in addition may include other specific directions. Should any of the other specific directions be held to be invalid, such invalidity shall not affect other directions of the declaration which can be given effect without the invalid direction, and to this end the directions in the declaration are severable.

DECLARATION

Declaration made this _____ day of _____ (month, year).
I, _____ , being of sound mind, willfully and voluntarily make known my desire that my dying shall not be artificially prolonged under the circumstances set forth below, and do herby declare:

If at any time I should have an incurable injury, disease, or illness certified to be a terminal condition by two physicians who have personally examined me, one of whom shall be my attending physician, and the physicians have determined that my death will occur whether or not life-sustaining procedures are utilized and where the application of life-sustaining procedures would serve only to artificially prolong the dying process, I direct that such procedures be withheld or withdrawn, and that I be permitted to die naturally with only the administration of medication or the performance of any medical procedure deemed necessary to provide me with comfort care.

In the absence of my ability to give directions regarding the use of such life-sustaining procedures, it is my intention that this declaration shall be honored by my family and physician(s) as the final expression of my legal right to refuse medical or surgical treatment and accept the consequences from such refusal.

I understand the full import of this declaration and I am emotionally and mentally competent to make this declaration.

Signed _____

City, County and State of Residence _____

The declarant has been personally known to me and I believe him or her to be of sound mind.

Witness _____

Witness _____

Designation Clause (optional)*

Should I become comatose, incompetent or otherwise mentally or physically incapable of communication, I authorize _____ , presently residing at _____ , to make treatment decisions on my behalf in accordance with my Living Will Declaration. I have discussed my wishes concerning terminal care with this person, and I trust his/her judgment on my behalf.

Signed _____ Date _____

Witness _____   Witness _____

*If I have not designated a proxy as provided above, I understand that my Living Will Declaration shall nevertheless be given effect should the appropriate circumstances arise.

4. Revocation. A declaration may be revoked at any time by the declarant, without regard to his or her mental state or competency, by any of the following methods:

(a) By being canceled, defaced, obliterated, or burnt, torn, or otherwise destroyed by the declarant or by some person in his or her presence and by his or her direction.

(b) By a written revocation of the declarant expressing his or her intent to revoke, signed and dated by the declarant. The attending physician shall record in the patient's medical record the time and date when he or she received notification of the written revocation.

(c) By a verbal expression by the declarant of his or her intent to revoke the declaration. Such revocation shall become effective upon communication to the attending physician by the declarant or by a person who is reasonably believed to be acting on behalf of the declarant. The attending physician shall record in the patient's medical record the time, date and place of the revocation and the time, date and place, if different, of when he or she received notification of the revocation.

5. Physician's Responsibility: Written Certification. An attending physician who has been notified of the existence of a declaration executed under this act shall, without delay after the diagnosis of a terminal condition of the declarant, take the necessary steps to provide for written certification and confirmation of the declarant's terminal condition, so that declarant may be deemed to be a qualified patient, as defined in Section 2(d) of this act.

An attending physician who fails to comply with this section shall be deemed to have refused to comply with the declaration and shall be liable as specified in Section 7(a).

6. Physician's Responsibility and Immunities. The desires of a qualified patient who is competent shall at all times supersede the effect of the declaration.

If the qualified patient is incompetent at the time of the decision to withhold or withdraw life-sustaining procedures, a declaration executed in accordance with

Section 3 of this act is presumed to be valid. For the purpose of this act, a physician of health care facility may presume in the absence of actual notice to the contrary that an individual who executed a declaration was of sound mind when it was executed. The fact of an individual's having executed a declaration shall not be considered as an indication of a declarant's mental incompetency. *(Age of itself shall not be a bar to a determination of competency.)

In the absence of actual notice of the revocation of the declaration, none of the following, when acting in accordance with the requirements of this act, shall be subject to civil liability therefrom, unless negligent, or shall be guilty of any criminal act or of unprofessional conduct:

(a) A physician or health facility which causes the withholding or withdrawal of life-sustaining procedures from a qualified patient.

(b) A licensed health professional, acting under the direction of a physician, who participates in the withholding or withdrawal of life-sustaining procedures.

7. Penalties. (a) An attending physician who refuses to comply with the declaration of a qualified patient pursuant to this act shall make the necessary arrangements to effect the transfer of the qualified patient to another physician who will effectuate the declaration of the qualified patient. An attending physician who fails to comply with the declaration of a qualified patient or to make the necessary arrangements to effect the transfer shall be civilly liable

(b) Any person who willfully conceals, cancels, defaces, obliterates, or damages the declaration of another without such declarant's consent or who falsifies or forges a revocation of the declaration of another shall be civilly liable.

(c) Any person who falsifies or forges the declaration of another, or willfully conceals or withholds personal knowledge of a revocation as provided in Section 4, with the intent to cause a withholding or withdrawal of life-sustaining procedures contrary to the wishes of the declarant, and thereby, because of such act, directly causes life-sustaining procedures to be withheld or withdrawn and death to thereby be hastened, shall be subject to prosecution for unlawful homicide.

8. General Provisions. (a) The withholding or withdrawal of life-sustaining procedures from a qualified patient in accordance with the provisions of this act shall not, for any purpose, constitute a suicide.

(b) The making of a declaration pursuant to Section 3 shall not affect in any manner the sale, procurement, or issuance of any policy of life insurance, nor shall it be deemed to modify the terms of an existing policy of life insurance. No policy of life insurance shall be legally impaired or invalidated in any manner by the withholding or withdrawal of life-sustaining procedures from an insured qualified patient, notwithstanding any term of the policy to the contrary.

(c) No physician, health facility, or other health provider, and no health care service plan, insurer issuing disability insurance, self-insured employee welfare benefit plan, or non-profit hospital plan, shall require any person to execute a declaration as a condition for being insured for, or receiving, health care services.

(d) Nothing in this act shall impair or supersede any legal right or legal responsibility which any person may have to effect the withholding or withdrawal of life-sustaining procedures in any lawful manner. In such respect the provisions of this act are cumulative.

(e) This act shall create no presumption concerning the intention of an individual who has not executed a declaration to consent to the use or withholding of life-sustaining procedures in the event of a terminal condition.

(f) If any provisions of this act or the application thereof to any person or circumstances is held invalid, such invalidity shall not affect other provisions or applications of the act which can be given effect without the invalid provision or application, and to this end the provisions of the act are severable.

THE RIGHT TO REFUSE TREATMENT: A MODEL ACT

Legal Advisors Committee,* Concern for Dying

Introduction

The most important right that patients possess is the right of self-determination, the right to make the ultimate decision concerning what will or will not be done to their bodies.[1] The right, embodied in the informed consent doctrine, has a critical and essential corollary: the right to refuse treatment.[2] Unless the right to refuse treatment is honored, the right of self-determination degenerates into a "right" to agree with one's physician.

Courts have recently declared that both the common law[3] and the United States Constitution[4] protect an individual's right to refuse medical treatment. These decisions might be seen as arguments against legislation that would reaffirm and enhance this right since such legislation might be viewed as either unnecessary or undesirable and confusing. On the other hand, cases continue to recur in which individuals are treated despite their competent objections or withdrawal of consent.[5,6] And although courts universally recognize the patient's right to refuse treatment, they have differed in their enunciation of the proper standards to be followed in implementing this right.[3,4,7] We believe the centrality of the right to refuse treatment makes its periodic reaffirmation appropriate, and a clear articulation of its applicability in particular contexts is a proper subject for legislation.

Living Will and Natural Death Statutes

To help promote the right of self-determination by preventing unwanted heroic medical interventions, many commentators have proposed, and 12 states and the District of Columbia have adopted, so-called "living will" or "natural death" statutes.[8]** The primary purpose of these statues is to provide competent individuals with a mechanism to set forth in a document, called a "living will," what they do and do not want done to them in case they become mentally incompetent and require medical intervention to keep them alive.

The rationale is that, with the advent of more effective medical technology, patients may have their lives prolonged painfully, expensively, fruitlessly, and against their wills. By signing a prior statement, the patient hopes to avoid a technological imperative which commands that that which can be done, must be done, and instead keep some control over his or her medical treatment.

Although specific provisions of these statutes vary, a typical statute allows patients to direct the withholding or withdrawal of medical treatment in the event the patient becomes terminally ill. Most current "living will" statutes basically permit physicians to honor a terminally ill patient's directive not to be treated if the physician agrees that treatment is not indicated. This, of course, can be done in the

*The Legal Advisors Committee of Concern for Dying consists of George J. Annas, JD, MPH, Chairman: J. Dinsmore Adams, JD; Leonard Glantz, JD: Jane Greenlaw, RN, JD; Jay Healey, JD; Barbara Katz, JD; John Robertson, JD; Richard Stanley Scott, JD, MD; Margaret A. Somerville, AuA (Pharm), LLB, DCL; C. Dickerman Williams, JD; Kenneth Wing, JD, MPH.

**As of this writing 38 states in the country have passed "Right to die" legislation, Eds.

Reprinted by permission of Concern for Dying.

absence of any statute;[2,9-11] and the current statutes do not so much enhance patients' rights as they enhance provider privileges (i.e., physicians typically are granted immunity if they follow a patient's directive, but are not required to follow it if they do not want to).[12-20]

Previous Model Acts

Model statutes suggested by other commentators have been of three basic kinds: 1) syntheses of the best features of existing legislation and proposals;[21-23] 2) proposals to extend the right to refuse treatment to nonterminally ill patients;[24] and 3) proposals to permit the individual to designate another person to make the treatment decisions when the individual is unable to make them.[25,26] We believe all of these efforts are laudatory, and have attempted to incorporate in our own model the best of each current proposal. However, we also believe it is time to move beyond the limitations of "living will" and "natural death" legislation, and propose a model that incorporates all the features necessary in what might be considered "second generation" legislation. Such legislation:

- should not be restricted to the terminally ill, but should apply to all competent adults and mature minors;
- should not limit the types of treatment an individual can refuse (e.g., to "extraordinary" treatment) but should apply to all medical interventions;
- should permit individuals to designate another person to act on their behalf and set forth the criteria under which the designated person is to make decisions;
- should require health care providers to follow the patient's wishes and provide sanctions for those who do not do so;
- should require health care providers to continue to provide palliative care to patients who refuse other interventions.

The Model Legislation

The specific provisions of our proposal are set forth in the Appendix to this article. Many of the sections are self-explanatory, but some merit additional comment. No specific form or document is included because we believe the individual's wishes will be more likely to be set forth if their own words are used.

It should be stressed initially that the right being reaffirmed is the right to refuse treatment implicit in any meaningful concept of individual liberty. Living will statutes on the other hand, usually rely on a vaguely articulated "right to die" which has no legal pedigree. We include both adults and mature minors in the purview of the Act because we believe minors who understand the nature and consequences of their actions should not be forced to undergo medical treatment against their will.

Competence

The definitions seek to clarify the scope of the right by including all "competent" individuals who can understand the nature and consequences of their decisions. Thus while mature minors and previously competent individuals are included, individuals who have never been competent or who did not express their wishes while competent are not within the scope of the proposal. The competent person's understanding must be attested to by two adult witnesses at the time a written declaration is executed, or be determined at the time of an oral refusal. While the Act's definition of competence is consistent with the law of most states on this subject, hospitals may wish to develop objective criteria, procedures, and documentation requirements to assess competency accurately.

The competence standard used is a functional one, based on the individual's ability to give informed consent. It rejects any notion that a patient's decision must be consistent with the "medically rational choice" as defined by the physician. Competence is *the* crucial issue, since a lack of competence, or even the questioning of an individual's competence, deprives the individual of the power to make treatment decisions.

For example, in *Lane v. Candura*, a 77-year-old woman refused to permit amputation of her gangrenous leg. Her physician believed that this decision, which would lead to her death, was medically irrational, and that Mrs. Candura was incompetent.[27] As is often the case, Mrs. Candura's competence was not questioned at any time when she agreed to undergo recommended surgical procedures. The court noted that Candura's occasional fluctuations in mental lucidity did not affect her basic ability to understand what the doctor wanted to do and what would happen if he didn't: she knew that the doctor wanted to amputate her leg, and that she believed she would otherwise die. The court also clarified that the competent patient's decision must be respected even when, as in this case, physicians or others consider it unfortunate, medically irrational, or misguided. Using these principles, the court refused to appoint a guardian for Mrs. Candura since she had exhibited a reasonable appreciation of the issues surrounding the treatment refusal. Other courts have validated a competence definition substantially identical to the one used in this Act.[2,28-31]

The proposed Act aims at protecting the autonomy of not only terminally ill patients, but those who are not terminally ill as well. If we do not raise our sensitivity regarding respect for the nonterminal patient's right to autonomy, it is extremely unlikely that the rights of terminal patients will be respected. The Act also applies to patients like Karen Ann Quinlan who, while in a hopeless, persistent vegetative state, do not suffer from an underlying, terminal illness.

Designating a Proxy

The President's Commission for the Study of Ethical Problems in Medicine has recently noted that "by combining a proxy directive with specific instructions, an individual could control both the content and the process of decision-making about care in case of incapacity.[32] Concern for Dying's Act incorporates this suggestion by permitting the declarant to both define what interventions are refused, and to name an authorized individual to make decisions consistent with the declarant's desires as expressed in the declaration. Thirty-seven states currently have durable power of attorney laws that arguably permit such a designation, provided that the individual gives specific authorization regarding medical treatment. However, these statutes were passed long before living wills became an issue, and although we believe courts should honor medical decisions made by a proxy named under a durable power of attorney statute, there have been no reported cases on this issue to date.[32,33]

There is not time limit to the validity of declarations, just as there is no time limit on ordinary wills or on donations made under Uniform Anatomical Gift Acts. The primary protection regarding the authenticity of the wishes of a person is the requirement for two witnesses to certify that they believe the person understood what he was signing and did it voluntarily. We have not restricted the individuals who can be either witnesses or authorized persons (e.g., the attending physician or relatives who might benefit under a will are not excluded because we think this unnecessarily implies bad faith on the part of categories of individuals and unnecessarily restricts the autonomy of a person to choose his own proxy and witnesses). Further, criminal penalties exist for falsification and forgery, and, if a physician or relative wants to harm the declarant, there are much easier ways to do it than by utilizing this mechanism. A second protection for the declarant is that revocation of a declaration is made easy. But the intent to revoke must be specific. Merely signing a blanket hospital admissions form that "consents" to whatever treatment physicians at the hospital wish to render is insufficient indication of revocation of a declaration.

Responsibility of Providers

The Model Act further clarifies that refusal of treatment does not terminate the physician-patient relationship, and that a physician who declines to follow the patient's wishes must transfer the patient to a physician who will. The Act recognizes that some providers may have different belief or value systems from the people they care for as patients, and attempts to establish a realistic procedure which allows the ethical views of both parties to be respected. However, the Act also recognizes that the patient is most immediately affected by failure to carry out a treatment-refusal decision, since the patient's own future and quality of life are at stake. Consequently, when a patient's directive and provider's views differ, the patient's directive must prevail over the physician's views on the rare occasions where transfer is impossible.

Providers who follow the procedures outlined in this Act are relieved of liability pursuant to any civil, criminal, or administrative action. However, providers who abandon their patients or refuse to comply with valid declarations are subject to sanctions. They may face civil actions including charges of negligence and battery. Administrative sanctions may include license revocation, suspension, or other disciplinary action by the state board of professional registration.

Other sections of the Act make it clear that this method of refusing treatment is not exclusive, but in addition to any other methods recognized by law; that the refusal of treatment is not suicide; that a treatment refusal does not affect any insurance policy; and that regardless of refusals, palliative care must be given unless specifically refused by the patient himself.

Summary

In summary, this model Right to Refuse Treatment Act clearly enunciates the competent person's right to refuse treatment, does not limit the exercise of this right to terminally ill patients or to extraordinary or heroic measures, and provides a mechanism by which a competent person can declare his or her intentions concerning treatment in the event of future incompetence, and can name another person to enforce this declaration.

The Act is designed to promote autonomy and respect for persons, by enhancing the individual's right to accept or reject medical treatments recommended by health care providers. It protects all competent persons, and incompetent persons who executed a declaration while they were competent. It provides that individuals may execute a written, signed declaration setting forth their intentions on treatment and refusal decisions and permits them to designate authorized individuals to make treatment decisions on their behalf, should they become incompetent in the future. The Act expresses, upholds, and clarifies recognized patient rights to autonomy and inviolability, recognition of which accords with the ethics of the medical profession; shields complying physicians, witnesses, and authorized persons acting in good faith, from liability; and provides sanctions for those who violate its provisions.

It has been almost three-quarters of a century since Judge Benjamin Cardozo wrote, regarding medical that, "Every human being of adult years has a right to determine what shall be done with his own body."[34] Today's medical care would be incomprehensible to a physician practicing when these words were written. Nonetheless, medicine's success in radically improving its ability to prolong life has made the right of self-determination an even more vital principle. By proposing this Act, the Legal Advisors of Concern for Dying reaffirm the right to self-determination in the hope that the discussion fostered will enhance the liberty of all citizens.

References

1. Annas GJ, Glantz LH, Katz BF: Informed Consent to Human Experimentation: The Subject's Dilemma. Cambridge, MA: Ballinger, 1977.
2. Cantor NL: A patient's decision to decline life-saving medical treatment: bodily integrity versus the preservation of life. Rut L Rev 1973; 26:228–264.
3. In re Eichner, 52 N.Y. 2d 363 (1983).
4. Belchertown v. Saikewicz, 370 N.E.2d 417 (Ma. 1977).
5. Satz v. Perlmutter, 363 So. 2d 160 (Fla. Dist. Ct. App. 1978), affirmed, 379 So. 2d 359 (Fla. 1980).
6. William James Foster v. Wallace W. Tourtellotte, Dist. Ct. Order CV 81-5046-RMT (Mx), U.S. Dist. Ct. Central Dist. California (Nov. 16, 1981) (Takasugi, J).
7. In re Quinlan, 70 N.J. 10, 355 A.2d 647 (1976).
8. Alabama Code secs. 22-8A-1 to 22-8A-10 (Supp. 1981); Arkansas Stat. Ann. secs. 82-3801-.3804 (Supp. 1981); California Health and Safety Code secs. 7185-7195 (Deering Supp. 1982): District of Columbia Code secs. 6-2421 to 2430 (Supp. 1982); Delaware Code Ann. tit. 16, secs. 2501-2509 (1982); Idaho Code secs. 39-4501 to 4508 (Supp. 1982); Kansas Stat. Ann. secs. 65-28.101 to 65-28.109 (Supp. 1981); Nevada Rev. Stat. secs. 449.540-.690 (1979); New Mexico Stat. Ann. secs. 24-7-1 to 24-7-11 (1981); North Carolina Gen Stat. secs. 90-320 to 90-322 (1981); Oregon Rev. Stat. secs. 97.050-.090 (1981); Texas-Rev. Civ. Stat. Ann. art. 4590h secs. 1-11 (Vernon 1982); 18 Vermont Stat. Ann. secs. 5251-5262 (1982); Washington Rev. Code Ann. 70.122.010-70.122.905 (West 1982).
9. Dickens B: The right to natural death. McGill Law J 1981; 26:847–879.
10. Keyserlingk EW: Sanctity of Life or Quality of Life. Ottawa, CN: Law Reform Comm. of Canada, 1981.
11. Law Reform Commission of Canada: Euthanasia, Aiding Suicide, and Cessation of Treatment (Working Paper 28). Ottawa, CN: Law Reform Comm. of Canada, 1982.

12. Kutner L: Due process of euthanasia: the living will, a proposal. Ind. Law J 1969; 44:539–554.
13. Annas GJ, Glantz LH, Katz BF: The Rights of Doctors, Nurses, and Allied Health Professionals. Cambridge, MA: Ballinger, 1981.
14. Stephenson: The right to die: A proposal for natural death legislation. U Cin Law Rev 1980; 49:228–243.
15. Beraldo: Give me liberty and give me death: the right to die and the California Natural Death Act. Santa Clara Law Rev 1980; 20:971–991.
16. Walters: The Kansas Natural Death Act. Washburn Law J 1980; 19:519–535.
17. Kutner: The living will: coping with the historical event of death. Baylor Law Rev 1975; 27:39–63.
18. Hand C: Death with dignity and the terminally ill: the need for legislative action. Nova Law Rev 1980; 4:257–269.
19. Kite: The right to die a natural death and the living will. Tex Tech Law Rev 1982; 13:99–128.
20. Havens: In re living will. Nova Law J 1981; 5:446–470.
21. Yale Law School model bill. NY: Society for the Right to Die, Legislative Handbook 1981; 23–26.
22. Kaplan RP: Euthanasia legislation: A survey and a model act. Am J Law & Med 1976; 2:41–99.
23. Stephenson S: The right to die: a proposal for natural death legislation. U Conn Law Rev 1980; 49:228–243.
24. Grisez G, Boyle JM: Life and Death with Liberty and Justice. Notre Dame: U of Notre Dame Press 1979; 109–120.
25. Veatch R: Death, Dying and the Biological Revolution. New Haven, CT: Yale U Press 1976; 199–201.
26. Relman AS: Michigan's Sensible Living Will. N Engl J Med 1979; 300:270–271.
27. Lane v. Candura, 6 Mass. App. 377, 376 N.E. 2d 1232 (1978).
28. In re Osborne, 294 A. 2d 372 (D.C. 1972).
29. In re Melido, 88 Misc. 2d 974, 390 N.Y.S. 2d 523 (1976).
30. In re Yetter, 62 Pa. D. & C. 2d 619 (1973).
31. Doudera AE, Peters JD (eds): Legal and Ethical Aspects of Treating Critically and Terminally Ill Patients. Ann Arbor, MI: AUPHA Press, 182.
32. President's Commission for the Study of Etical Problems in Medicine and Biomedical and Behavioral Research: Making Health Care Divisions, Vol One, Washington, DC: U.S. Govt Printing Office, 1982; 155–160.
33. Legal problems of the aged and infirm—the durable power of attorney—Planned protective services and the living will. Real Property, Probate and Trust J 1978; 13:1–42.
34. Scholendorf v. Society of New York Hospitals, 211 N.Y. 125,129 (1914).

Appendix:
Right to Refuse Treatment Act

SECTION 1. DEFINITIONS

"Competent person" shall mean an individual who is able to understand and appreciate the nature and consequences of a decision to accept or refuse treatment.

"Declaration" shall mean a written statement executed according to the provisions of this Act which sets forth the declarant's intentions with respect to medical procedures, treatment or nontreatment, and may include the declarant's intentions concerning palliative care.

"Declarant" shall mean an individual who executes a declaration under the provisions of this Act.

"Health care provider" shall mean a person, facility or institution licensed or authorized to provide health care.

"Incompetent person" shall mean a person who is unable to understand and appreciate the nature and consequences of a decision to accept or refuse treatment.

"Medical procedure or treatment" shall mean any action taken by a physician or health care provider designed to diagnose, assess, or treat a disease, illness, or injury. These include, but are not limited to, surgery, drugs, transfusions, mechanical ventilation, dialysis, resuscitation, artificial feeding, and any other medical act designed for diagnosis, assessment or treatment.

"Palliative care" shall mean any measure taken by a physician or health care provider designed primarily to maintain the patient's comfort. These include, but are not limited to, sedatives and pain-killing drugs; non-artificial, oral feeding; suction; hydration; and hygienic care.

"Physician" shall mean any physician responsible for the declarant's care.

SECTION 2.

A competent person has the right to refuse any medical procedure or treatment, and any palliative care measure.

SECTION 3.

A competent person may execute a declaration directing the withholding or withdrawal of any medical procedure or treatment or any palliative care measure, which is in use or may be used in the future in the person's medical care or treatment, even if continuance of the medical procedure or treatment could prevent or postpone the person's death from being caused by the person's disease, illness or injury. The declaration shall be in writing, dated and signed by the declarant in the presence of two adult witnesses. The two witnesses must sign the declaration, and by their signatures indicate they believe the declarant's execution of the declaration was understanding and voluntary.

SECTION 4.

If a person is unable to sign a declaration due to a physical impairment, the person may execute a declaration by communicating agreement after the declaration has been read to the person in the presence of the two adult witnesses. The two witnesses must sign the declaration, and by their signatures indicate the person is physically impaired so as to be unable to sign the declaration, that the person understands the declaration's terms, and that the person voluntarily agrees to the terms of the declaration.

SECTION 5.

A declarant shall have the right to appoint in the declaration a person authorized to order the administration, withholding, or withdrawal of medical procedures and treatment in the event that the declarant becomes incompetent. A person so authorized shall have the power to enforce the provisions of the declaration and shall be bound to exercise this authority consistent with the declaration and the authorized person's best judgment as to the actual desires and preferences of the declarant. No palliative care measure may be withheld by an authorized person unless explicitly provided for in the declaration. Physicians and health care providers caring for incompetent declarants shall provide such authorized persons all medical information which would be available to the declarant if the declarant were competent.

SECTION 6.

Any declarant may revoke a declaration by destroying or defacing it, executing a written revocation, making an oral revocation, or by any other act evidencing the declarant's specific intent to revoke the declaration.

SECTION 7.

A competent person who orders the withholding or withdrawal of treatment shall receive appropriate palliative care unless it is expressly stated by the person orally or through a declaration that the person refuses palliative care.

SECTION 8.

This act shall not impair or supersede a person's legal right to direct the withholding or withdrawal of medical treatment or procedures in any other manner recognized by law.

SECTION 9.

No person shall require anyone to execute a declaration as a condition of enrollment, continuation, or receipt of benefits for disability, life, health or any other type of insurance. The withdrawal or withholding of medical procedures or treatment pursuant to the provisions of this Act shall not affect the validity of any insurance policy, and shall not constitute suicide.

SECTION 10.

This act shall create no presumption concerning the intention of a person who has failed to execute a declaration. The fact that a person has failed to execute a declaration shall not constitute evidence of that person's intent concerning treatment or nontreatment.

SECTION 11.

A declaration made pursuant to this Act, an oral refusal by a person, or a refusal of medical procedures or treatment through an authorized person, shall be binding on all physicians and health care providers caring for the declarant.

SECTION 12.

A physician who fails to comply with a written or oral declaration and to make necessary arrangements to transfer the declarant to another physician who will effectuate the declaration shall be subject to civil liability and professional disciplinary action, including license revocation or suspension. When acting in good faith to effectuate the terms of a declaration or when following the direction of an authorized person appointed in a declaration under Section 5, no physician or health care provider will be liable in any civil, criminal, or administrative action for withholding or withdrawing any medical procedure, treatment, or palliative care measure. When acting in good faith, no witness to a declaration, or person authorized to make treatment decisions under Section 5, shall be liable in any civil, criminal, or administrative action.

SECTION 13.

A person found guilty of willfully concealing a declaration, or falsifying or forging a revocation of a declaration, shall be subject to criminal prosecution for a misdemeanor [the class or type of misdemeanor is left to the determination of individual state legislatures].

SECTION 14.

Any person who falsifies or forges a declaration, or who willfully conceals or withholds information concerning the revocation of a declaration, with the intent to cause a withholding or withdrawal of life-sustaining procedures from a person, and who thereby causes life-sustaining procedures to be withheld or withdrawn and death to be hastened, shall be subject to criminal prosecution for a felony [the class or type of felony is left to the determination of individual state legislatures].

SECTION 15.

If any provision or application of this Act is held invalid, this invalidity shall not affect other provisions or applications of the Act which can be given effect without the invalid provision or application, and to this end the provisions of this Act are severable.

RECOMMENDATION OF A UNIFORM DETERMINATION OF DEATH ACT

Section 1. [Determination of Death.] An individual who has sustained either (1) irreversible cessation of circulatory and respiratory functions, or (2) irreversible cessation of all functions of the entire brain, including the brain stem, is dead. A determination of death must be made in accordance with accepted medical standards.

Section 2. [Uniformity of Construction and Application.] This Act shall be applied and construed to effectuate its general purpose to make uniform the law with respect to the subject of this Act among states enacting it.

Section 3. [Short Title.] This Act may be cited as the Uniform Determination of Death Act.

The adoption of this text for the statute in all jurisdictions in the United States was approved by the following groups, agencies, and organizations:

Commissioners on Uniform State Laws (July/August 1980)
American Medical Association (October 1980)
The President's Commission for the Study of Ethical Problems in Medicine and
    Biomedical and Behavioral Research (November 1980)
American Bar Association (February 1981)

UNIFORM ANATOMICAL GIFT ACT*

"An act authorizing the gift of all or part of a human body after death for specified purposes."

Section 1. (Definitions)

(a) "Bank or storage facility" means a facility licensed, accredited or approved under the laws of any state for storage of human bodies or parts thereof.

(b) "Decedent" means a deceased individual and includes a stillborn infant or fetus.

(c) "Donor" means an individual who makes a gift of all or part of his body.

(d) "Hospital" means a hospital licensed, accredited or approved under the laws of any state and includes a hospital operated by the United States government, a state or a subdivision thereof, although not required to be licensed under state laws.

(e) "Part" includes organs, tissues, eyes, bones, arteries, blood, other fluids and other portions of a human body, and "part" includes "parts."

(f) "Person" means an individual, corporation, government or governmental subdivision or agency, business trust, estate, trust, partnership or association or any other legal entity.

(g) "Physician" or "surgeon" means a physician or surgeon licensed or authorized to practice under the laws of any state.

*Note. Copy of final draft as approved on July 30, 1968, by the National Conference of Commissioners on Uniform State Laws. Reprinted with permission from The Uniform Anatomical Gift Act, the Journal of the American Medical Association, vol. 206, p. 2501ff., Dec. 9, 1968.

(h) "State" includes any state, district, commonwealth, territory, insular possession, and any other area subject to the legislative authority of the United States of America.

Section 2. (Persons Who May Execute an Anatomical Gift)

(a) Any individual of sound mind and 18 years of age or more may give all or any part of his body for any purposes specified in section 3, the gift to take effect upon death.

(b) Any of the following persons, in order of priority stated, when persons in prior classes are not available at the time of death, and in the absence of actual notice of contrary indications by the decedent, or actual notice of opposition by a member of the same or a prior class, may give all or any part of the decedent's body for any purposes specified in section 3.

1. the spouse,
2. an adult son or daughter,
3. either parent,
4. an adult brother or sister,
5. a guardian of the person of the decedent at the time of his death,
6. any other person authorized or under obligation to dispose of the body.

(c) If the donee has actual notice of contrary indications by the decedent, or that a gift by a member of a class is opposed by a member of the same or a prior class, the donee shall not accept the gift. The persons authorized by subsection (b) may make the gift after death or immediately before death.

(d) A gift of all or part of a body authorizes any examination necessary to assure medical acceptability of the gift for the purposes intended.

(e) The rights of the donee created by the gift are paramount to the rights of others except as provided by section 7(d).

Section 3. (Persons Who May Become Donees, and Purposes for which Anatomical Gifts May Be Made)

The following persons may become donees of gifts of bodies or parts thereof for the purposes stated:

(a) any hospital, surgeon, or physician, for medical or dental education, research, advancement of medical or dental science, therapy or transplantation; or

(b) any accredited medical or dental school, college or university for education, research, advancement of medical of dental science or therapy; or transplantation; or

(c) any bank or storage facility for medical or dental education, research, advancement of medical or dental science, therapy or transplantation; or

(d) any specified individual for therapy or transplantation needed by him.

Section 4. (Manner of Executing Anatomical Gifts)

(a) A gift of all or part of the body under section 2(a) may be made by a will. The gift becomes effective upon the death of the testator without waiting for probate. If the will is not probated, or if it is declared invalid for testamentary purposes, the gift, to the extent that it has been acted upon in good faith, is nevertheless valid and effective.

(b) A gift of all or part of the body under section 2(a) may also be made by document other than a will. The gift becomes effective upon the death of the donor. The document, which may be a card designed to be carried on the person, must be signed by the donor, in the presence of 2 witnesses who must sign the document in his presence. If the donor cannot sign, the document may be signed for him at his direction and in his presence, and in the presence of 2 witnesses who must sign the document in his presence. Delivery of the document of gift during the donor's lifetime is not necessary to make the gift valid.

(c) The gift may be made to a specified donee or without specifying a donee. If the latter, the gift may be accepted by the attending physician as donee upon or following death. If the gift is made to a specified donee who is not available at the time and place of death, the attending physician upon or following death, in the absence of any expressed indication that the donor desired otherwise, may accept the gift as donee. The physician who becomes a donee under this subsection shall not participate in the procedures for removing or transplanting a part.

(d) Notwithstanding section 7(b), the donor may designate in his will, card or other document of gift the surgeon or physician to carry out the appropriate procedures. In the absence of a designation, or if the designee is not available, the donee or other person authorized to accept the gift may employ or authorize any surgeon or physician for the purpose.

(e) Any gift by a person designed in section 2(b) shall be made by a document signed by him, or made by his telegraphic, recorded telephonic or other recorded message.

Section 5. (Delivery of Document of Gift)

If the gift is made by the donor to a specified donee, the will, card, or other document, or an executed copy thereof, may be delivered to the donee to expedite the appropriate procedures immediately after death, but delivery is not necessary to the validity of the gift. The will, card or other document, or an executed copy thereof, may be deposited in any hospital, bank or storage facility or registry office that accepts them for safekeeping or for facilitation of procedures after death. On request of any interested party upon or after the donor's death, the person in possession shall produce the document for examination.

Section 6. (Amendment or Revocation of the Gift)

(a) If the will, card or other document or executed copy thereof has been delivered to a specified donee, the donor may amend or revoke the gift by:

1. the execution and delivery to the donee of a signed statement, or
2. an oral statement made in the presence of 2 persons and communicated to the donee, or
3. a statement during a terminal illness or injury addressed to an attending physician and communicated to the donee, or
4. a signed card or document found on his person or in his effects.

(b) Any document of gift which has not been delivered to the donee may be revoked by the donor in the manner set out in subsection (a) or by destruction, cancellation, or mutilation of the document and all executed copies thereof.

(c) Any gift made by a will may also be amended or revoked in the manner provided for amendment or revocation of wills, or as provided in subsection (a).

Section 7. (Rights and Duties at Death)

(a) The donee may accept or reject the gift. If the donee accepts a gift of the entire body, he may, subject to the terms of the gift, authorize embalming and the use of the body in funeral services. If the gift is a part of the body, the donee upon the death of the donor and prior to embalming, shall cause the part to be removed without unnecessary mutilation. After removal of the part, custody of the remainder of the body vests in the surviving spouse, next of kin or other persons under obligation to dispose of the body.

(b) The time of death shall be determined by a physician who attends the donor at his death, or, if none, the physician who certifies the death. This physician shall not participate in the procedures for removing or transplanting a part.

(c) A person who acts in good faith in accord with the terms of this Act, or under the anatomical gift laws of another state (or a foreign country) is not liable for damages in any civil action or subject to prosecution in any criminal proceedings for his act.

(d) The provisions of this Act are subject to the laws of the state prescribing powers and duties with respect to autopsies.

Section 8. (Uniformity of Interpretation)

This act shall be so construed as to effectuate its general purpose to make uniform the law of those states which enact it.

Section 9. (Short Title)

This Act may be cited as the Uniform Anatomical Gift Act.

Department of Health and Rehabilitative Services
DIVISION OF HEALTH
BUREAU OF VITAL STATISTICS

CERTIFICATE OF DEATH
FLORIDA

STATE FILE NO. _____

REGISTRAR'S NO. _____

TYPE, OR PRINT IN
PERMANENT INK
SEE HANDBOOK FOR
INSTRUCTIONS

DECEASED

DECEASED — NAME
FIRST | MIDDLE | LAST
1.

SEX
2.

DATE OF DEATH (MONTH, DAY, YEAR)
3.

RACE WHITE, NEGRO, AMERICAN INDIAN, ETC. (SPECIFY)
4.

AGE — LAST BIRTHDAY (YEARS)
5a.

UNDER 1 YEAR
MOS. | DAYS
5b.

UNDER 1 DAY
HOURS | MIN.
5c.

DATE OF BIRTH (MONTH, DAY, YEAR)
6.

CITY, TOWN, OR LOCATION OF DEATH
7b.

INSIDE CITY LIMITS (SPECIFY YES OR NO)
7c.

COUNTY OF DEATH
7a.

HOSPITAL OR OTHER INSTITUTION — NAME (IF NOT IN EITHER, GIVE STREET AND NUMBER)
7d.

STATE OF BIRTH (IF NOT IN U.S.A., NAME COUNTRY)
8.

CITIZEN OF WHAT COUNTRY
9.

MARRIED, NEVER MARRIED, WIDOWED, DIVORCED (SPECIFY)
10.

SURVIVING SPOUSE (IF WIFE, GIVE MAIDEN NAME)
11.

SOCIAL SECURITY NUMBER
12.

USUAL OCCUPATION (GIVE KIND OF WORK DONE DURING MOST OF WORKING LIFE, EVEN IF RETIRED)
13a.

KIND OF BUSINESS OR INDUSTRY
13b.

USUAL RESIDENCE WHERE DECEASED LIVED. IF DEATH OCCURRED IN INSTITUTION, GIVE RESIDENCE BEFORE ADMISSION.

RESIDENCE — STATE
14a.

COUNTY
14b.

CITY, TOWN, OR LOCATION
14c.

INSIDE CITY LIMITS (SPECIFY YES OR NO)
14d.

STREET AND NUMBER
14e.

PARENTS

FATHER — NAME
FIRST | MIDDLE | LAST
15.

MOTHER — MAIDEN NAME
FIRST | MIDDLE | LAST
16.

INFORMANT — NAME
17a.

MAILING ADDRESS (STREET OR R.F.D. NO., CITY OR TOWN, STATE, ZIP)
17b.

442

PART I. DEATH WAS CAUSED BY: [ENTER ONLY ONE CAUSE PER LINE FOR (a), (b), AND (c)]

18.

IMMEDIATE CAUSE

(a)

DUE TO, OR AS A CONSEQUENCE OF:

CONDITIONS, IF ANY,
WHICH GAVE RISE TO
IMMEDIATE CAUSE (a),
STATING THE UNDER-
LYING CAUSE LAST

(b)

DUE TO, OR AS A CONSEQUENCE OF:

(c)

PART II. OTHER SIGNIFICANT CONDITIONS: CONDITIONS CONTRIBUTING TO DEATH BUT NOT RELATED TO CAUSE GIVEN IN PART I (a)

APPROXIMATE INTERVAL
BETWEEN ONSET AND DEATH

AUTOPSY (YES OR NO)
19a.

IF YES WERE FINDINGS CON-
SIDERED IN DETERMINING CAUSE
OF DEATH
19b.

CAUSE

(Probably) ACCIDENT, SUICIDE OR
HOMICIDE; OR UNDETERMINED
(Specify)
20a.

DATE OF INJURY (MONTH, DAY, YEAR)
20b.

HOUR
20c.
M.

HOW INJURY OCCURRED (ENTER NATURE OF INJURY IN PART I OR PART II, ITEM 18)
20d.
M.

INJURY AT WORK
(SPECIFY YES OR NO)
20e.

PLACE OF INJURY AT HOME, FARM, STREET, FACTORY,
OFFICE BLDG., ETC. (SPECIFY)
20f.

LOCATION (STREET OR R.F.D. NO., CITY OR TOWN, STATE)
20g.

CERTIFIER

CERTIFICATION—
PHYSICIAN:
I ATTENDED THE
21a. DECEASED FROM

MONTH   DAY   YEAR
TO
21b.

MONTH   DAY   YEAR

AND LAST SAW HIM/HER ALIVE ON
MONTH   DAY   YEAR
21c.

I DID/DID NOT VIEW THE
BODY AFTER DEATH.
21d.

DEATH OCCURRED AT THE PLACE, ON THE
DATE, AND, TO THE BES
OF MY KNOWLEDGE, DU
TO THE CAUSE(S) STATED
(HOUR)
21e.
M.

CERTIFICATION—MEDICAL EXAMINER OR CORONER: ON THE BASIS OF THE
EXAMINATION OF THE BODY AND/OR THE INVESTIGATION, IN MY OPINION,
DEATH OCCURRED ON THE DATE AND DUE TO THE CAUSE(S) STATED.
22a.

THE DECEDENT WAS PRONOUNCED DEAD
MONTH   DAY   YEAR
22b.
M.

HOUR OF DEATH

CERTIFIER—NAME (TYPE OR PRINT)
22c.

SIGNATURE
23b.

DATE SIGNED (MONTH, DAY, YEAR)
23c.

MAILING ADDRESS—CERTIFIER
23d.

STREET OR R.F.D. NO.

CITY OR TOWN

DEGREE OR TITLE

STATE   ZIP

BURIAL

BURIAL, CREMATION, REMOVAL
(SPECIFY)
24a.

CEMETERY OR CREMATORY—NAME
24b.

LOCATION
24c.

CITY OR TOWN   STATE

DATE (MONTH, DAY, YEAR)
24d.

FUNERAL HOME—NAME AND ADDRESS (STREET OR R.F.D. NO., CITY OR TOWN, STATE, ZIP)
25a.

FUNERAL DIRECTOR—SIGNATURE
25b.

REGISTRAR—SIGNATURE
26a.

DATE RECEIVED BY LOCAL REGISTRAR
26b.

V. S. #612
Rev. 1970

443

PERMIT FOR POSTMORTEM EXAMINATION

Must Be Completed in Duplicate

Date _____

Name of deceased _____ Hosp. No. _____
First　　　　Middle　　　Last

Date and time of death _____ A.M.
_____ P.M.
Month　　　Day　　　Year　　　Hour

1. I hereby authorize any qualified member of the Staff of Physicians of the Hospital, to perform an autopsy upon the body of the above named, at such place as the hospital or physician may designate. My relation to the deceased being that of _____

2. I know of no survivor of the deceased who is closer kin than I to authorize this post mortem examination.

3. The postmortem examination here authorized may be either complete or partial and such parts of the body may be removed as may be necessary for subsequent study in order to accomplish its purpose. If the nature and extent of this examination or the right to remove parts of the body are to be limited in any way, these limitations must be clearly stated below. In the absence of any stated limitations, it is to be understood that the physician by whom the operation is performed, is hereby permitted to examine any portion of the body that, in his opinion, should be examined, including organs within the chest, abdomen, skull and extremities.

4. I further authorize him to have present at the post mortem examination such persons as he may deem proper.

Limitations (if any) _____

Signed _____

_____ (Witness)

_____ (Witness)

THE FLORIDA LAW GOVERNING THE AUTHORIZATION OF AN AUTOPSY

872.04 Autopsies: consent required, exception.

(1) Unless otherwise authorized by statute, no autopsy shall be performed without the written consent of the spouse, nearest relative or, if no such next of kin can be found, the person who has assumed custody of the body for purposes of burial; where two or more persons assume custody of the body for such purposes, then the consent of any one of them shall be sufficient to authorize the autopsy.

(2) Any such written consent may be given by telegram, and any telegram purporting to have been sent by a person authorized to give such consent will be presumed to have been sent by such person.

(3) If after diligent search and inquiry it is established by the chief law enforcement officer having jurisdiction through his examination of missing persons records and other inquiry that no person can be found who can authorize an autopsy as herein provided, then after reasonable time, any person licensed to practice medicine under chapter 458 or osteopathic medicine under chapter 459, and whose practice involves the usual performance of autopsies, may conduct an autopsy on the remains for purposes of confirming medical diagnosis and suspected communicable diseases, without written consent, and no cause of action will be brought against such physician for performance of such autopsy. A reasonable time for purposes of this provision shall be not less than forty-eight hours or more than seventy-two hours after death.

CLINICAL INFORMATION AND DIAGNOSES

Date _____

_____

_____

_____

_____

_____

_____

_____ M.D.

NOTE: Pertinent clinical information and
diagnoses must be entered if admission,
progress and terminal notes are incomplete
in patient's clinical chart or emergency
room record has insufficient information.

INSTRUCTIONS FOR RELEASE OF BODY

Date _____

I hereby authorize the General Hospital to release the body of _____

_____ to _____
(name and location of funeral home)

_____

Signed _____

_____ (Witness)

_____ (Witness)

FUNERAL DIRECTORS RECEIPT FOR BODY

This is to certify that I have removed the body of _____

from the Hospital, this _____ day of _____ 19 _____

at _____ A.M.
P.M.

(Witness) _____ Signed _____

Address _____

POSTMORTEM EXAMINATION
OF THE BODY

8/25/86

The body is that of a well-developed, well-nourished white male which appears its recorded age of 60 years. It measures approximately 67½ " in length. It is received clothed in the following: navy pants, white T-shirt, white underpants, black shoes, and white socks. A white metal watch is present on the left wrist. Rigor is well developed in all major muscle groups; livor is violaceous and present on posterior dependent surfaces. A tattoo is present on the extensor surface of the right forearm. The external examination is otherwise unremarkable.

The pleural surfaces are smooth and glistening. The right lung weighs 570 g. and the left lung 450 g. The lungs are generally subcrepitant to palpation; serial sections are without localizing lesions. Anthracotic pigment is identified in the pulmonary parenchyma and hilar lymph nodes. The heart weighs 425 g. The epicardial and pericardial surfaces are smooth and glistening. The posterior wall of the left ventrical is thinned, mottled and softened. These changes also focally extend into the posterior right ventricle. The myocardium is otherwise reddish-brown and without evidence of recent or remote injury. The endocardium is smooth and glistening. The cardiac valves are physiologic. The coronary arteries show proximal calcific arteriosclerosis with 75% occlusion of the left anterior descending and 90% occlusion of both the circumflex branch of the left coronary artery and proximal right coronary artery. The aorta and its major branches show generalized calcific atherosclerosis most marked at vascular orifices and bifurcations. There is an early atherosclerotic aneurysm of the abdominal aorta located below the renal arteries without involvement of the iliac bifurcation. The aneurysm measures approximately 3.5 cm in internal diameter and is partially filled with laminated thrombus. The peritoneal surfaces are smooth and glistening. The liver weighs 1575 g. The capsule is smooth and glistening and the hepatic parenchyma has the normal firm consistency. Cut sections of liver are dark brown, homogeneous, and without focal defects. The extrahepatic biliary tree is patent. The gallbladder contains a small amount of dark green bile. The esophagus is unremarkable. The stomach contains approximately 400 cc of yellowish-tan liquid with small bits of partially digested unrecognizable foodstuffs. The stomach and remainder of the gastrointestinal tract are otherwise unremarkable. The spleen weighs 50 g. The capsule is pearly-gray and wrinkled, and the parenchyma is dark purple and without focal defects. The pancreas weighs 175 g. and is of the usual contours and consistency. The right and left adrenals are intact and unremarkable. The right kidney weighs 175 g. and the left kidney 200 g. The capsules strip, with some difficulty, to reveal finely granular cortical surfaces. The cortices are somewhat thinned with an average width of 4 to 5 mm. The cortices and medullae are well demarcated and otherwise unremarkable. The renal vessels, pelvocalyceal systems, and ureters are unremarkable. The urinary bladder contains approximately 3 cc of pale yellow transparent urine and is otherwise without gross abnormality. The remainder of the genitourinary tract is likewise unremarkable.

The neck organs are free of trauma or obstruction. The scalp, calvarium, and base of skull are free of recent notable injury. The brain weighs 1325 g. There is no blood in the extradural, subdural, subarachnoid, or intracerebral spaces. The cerebral hemispheres are symmetric without evidence of mass displacement. The circle of Willis is intact. Serial coronal sections through the brain are otherwise unremarkable.

Microscopic Examination

Sections of the following structures are taken for microscopic examination at the time of autopsy: thyroid, lungs, heart, coronary arteries, aorta, liver, spleen, kidneys, adrenals, pancrease, prostate, and brain. All are without significant histopathologic abnormality except for the following which are specifically commented on. Multiple sections of both lungs show generalized mucus plugging of proximal and distal airways. Peribronchial and peribronchiolar basement membrane thickening is noted throughout. Hypertrophy of subepithelial mucus glands and moderate centrilobular emphysema are also apparent. Myocardium exhibits patchy interstitial fibrosis with extensive wavy fiber change. Edema, acute inflammation, and neovascularization are not identified. Sections of both coronary arteries show generalized severe calcific arteriosclerosis with up to 95 percent occlusion of the left coronary artery and focal complete occlusion of the right coronary artery. Sections of distal aorta show severe calcific atherosclerosis with secondary thinning of the vascular wall and aneurysm formation. Said abdominal aortic aneurysm contains atherosclerotic debris and laminated thrombus. Both kidneys show focal cortical hyaline obliteration of glomeruli. Postmortem autolysis is noted in the pancreas.

Autopsy Findings

1. Myocardial infarction, acute, posterior right and left ventricles
2. Myocardial infarction, remote, posterior left ventricle
3. Calcific arteriosclerosis, proximal coronary arteries, severe
4. Calcific atherosclerosis, generalized, with early aneurysm formation, infrarenal abdominal aorta
5. Arterionephrosclerosis, generalized, moderate
6. Chronic obstructive pulmonary disease, with generalized mucus plugging of proximal and distal airways
7. Centrilobular emphysema, generalized, moderate

Cause of death: Acute myocardial infarction associated with chronic obstructive pulmonary disease (history of perimortem acute asthmatic attack)

Manner of death: Natural.

_____ , M.D.

OFFICE OF THE MEDICAL EXAMINER

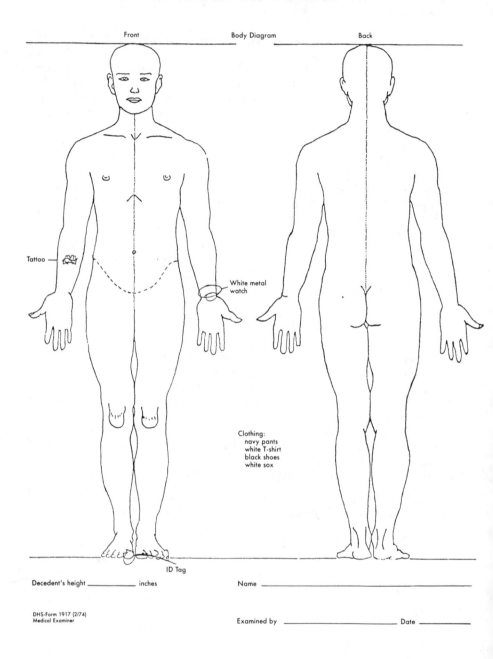

Front   Body Diagram   Back

Tattoo

White metal
watch

Clothing:
    navy pants
    white T-shirt
    black shoes
    white sox

ID Tag

Decedent's height _____ inches   Name _____

DHS-Form 1917 (2/74)
Medical Examiner   Examined by _____ Date _____

Appendix D: Literary Works, Visual Arts, and Musical Selections

LITERARY WORKS

Dying

Alsop, S. (1973). *Stay of execution.* Philadelphia: Lippincott.

Bryant, W. C. (1976). Thanatopsis. In R. Ellman (Ed.), *The new Oxford book of American verse.* New York: Oxford University Press.

Craven, M. (1973). *I heard the owl call my name.* New York: Dell.

Cummings, E. E. (1944). Who's most afraid of death? Thou. In E. E. Cummings, *Complete poems: 1913–1962.* New York: Harcourt, Brace, Jovanovich.

de Beauvoir, S. (1972). *A very easy death.* New York: Warner.

Emerson, R. W. (1976). Terminus. In R. Ellman (Ed.), *The new Oxford book of American verse.* New York: Oxford University Press.

Goethe, J. W. von. (1939). The Erl-King (Sir Walter Scott, trans.). In M. V. Doren (Ed.), *An anthology of world poetry.* New York: Halcyon House.

Gunther, J. (1965). *Death be not proud.* New York: Harper & Row.

Hesse, H. (1932). *Death and the lover.* New York: Signet.

Jury, M., & Jury, D. (1976). *Gramp: A man ages and dies.* New York: Grossman.

Lawrence, D. H. (1933). The ship of death. In V. de Sola Pinto & F. W. Roberts (Eds.), *The complete poems of D. H. Lawrence.* New York: The Viking Press.

Lund, D. (1974). *Eric.* New York: Dell.

McMurtry, L. (1976). *Terms of endearment.* New York: New American Library.

de Montaigne, M. (1965). That to philosophize is to learn to die. In *The complete essays of Montaigne.* Palo Alto: Stanford University Press.

Morris, J. (1971). *Brian Piccolo: A short season.* New York: Dell.

Rosenthal, T. (1973). *How could I not be among you?* New York: George Braziller.

Silkin, J. (1973). Death of a son. In P. Larkin (Ed.), *The Oxford book of twentieth century English verse*. Oxford: Clarendon.

Spark, M. (1961). *Memento mori*. New York: Penguin.

Thomas, D. (1974). Do not go gentle into that good night. In D. Thomas, *Collected poems*. New York: New Directions Books.

Tolstoy, L. (1960). *The death of Ivan Ilych and other stories*. New York: New American Library.

War

Bly, R. (1975). Driving through Minnesota during the Hanoi bombings. In A. W. Allison et al. (Eds.), *The Norton anthology of poetry. Revised*. New York: Norton.

Crane, S. (1951). *The red badge of courage*. New York: Modern Library.

Freud, S. C. (1915/1959). Thoughts for the times on war and death. *Collected papers* (Vol. 4). New York: Basic Books.

Hardy, T. (1978). The man he killed. In J. Gibson (Ed.), *The complete poems of Thomas Hardy*. New York: Macmillan.

Heller, J. (1955). *Catch-22*. New York: Dell.

Hemingway, E. (1929). *A farewell to arms*. New York: Charles Scribners.

Mailer, N. (1948). *The naked and the dead*. New York: Rinehart.

Mason, R. (1983). *Chickenhawk*. New York: Penguin.

Owen, W. (1963). Anthem for doomed youth. In C. D. Lewis (Ed.), *The collected poems of Wilfred Owen*. New York: New Directions Books.

Remarque, E. M. (1967). *All quiet on the western front*. Greenwich, CN: Fawcett.

Shapiro, K. (1944). Elegy for a dead soldier. In *Poems: 1940–1953*. New York: Random House.

Spender, S. (1973). Two armies. In P. Larkin (Ed.), *The Oxford book of twentieth century English verse*. Oxford: Clarendon.

Suicide

Alvarez, A. C. (1972). *The savage god: A study of suicide*. New York: Random House.

Dickinson, E. (1960). He scanned it—staggered. (1062). In T. H. Johnson (Ed.), *The complete poems of Emily Dickinson*. Boston: Little, Brown.

Dickinson, E. (1960). What if I say I shall not wait! (277). In T. H. Johnson (Ed.), *The complete poems of Emily Dickinson*. Boston: Little, Brown.

Plath, S. (1975). Ariel. In A. W. Allison et al. (Eds.), *The Norton anthology of poetry. Revised*. New York: Norton.

Plath, S. (1975). Lady Lazarus. In A. W. Allison et al. (Eds.), *The Norton anthology of poetry. Revised*. New York: Norton.

Plath, S. (1971). *The bell jar*. New York: Harper & Row.

Shakespeare, W. (1938). *Romeo and Juliet*. In *The works of William Shakespeare* (1938). New York: Oxford University Press.

Wertenbaker, L. (1957). *Death of a man*. Boston: Beacon Press.

Surviving and Mourning

Agee, J. (1965). *A death in the family.* New York: Avon.
Bantock, G. (1973). Dirge. In P. Larkin (Ed.), *The Oxford book of twentieth century English verse.* Oxford: Clarendon Press.
Bronte, E. (1941). Remembrance. In C. W. Hatfield (Ed.), *Complete poems of Emily Jane Bronte.* New York: Columbia University Press.
De La Mare, W. (1975). Away. In A. W. Allison et al. (Eds.), *The Norton anthology of poetry. Revised.* New York: Norton.
Frank, A. (1952). *The diary of a young girl.* New York: Doubleday.
Frost, R. (1964). In a disused graveyard. In L. Untermeyer (Ed.), *Robert Frost's poems.* New York: Washington Square Press.
Gibran, K. (1950). Parting. In *A tear and a smile.* New York: Knopf.
Holy Bible, *The book of Job.*
Lewis, C. S. (1961). *A grief observed.* New York: Bantam.
Lifton, R. J. (1968). *Death in life: Survivors of Hiroshima.* New York: Random House.
Ondaatje, M. (1975). We're at the graveyard. In A. W. Allison et al. (Eds.), *The Norton anthology of poetry. Revised.* New York: Norton.
Poe, E. A. (1978). Annabel Lee. In N. Sullivan (Ed.), *The treasury of American poetry.* Garden City, NY: Doubleday.
Pudney, J. (1973). Missing. In P. Larkin (Ed.), *The Oxford book of twentieth century English verse.* Oxford: Clarendon Press.
Rilke, R. M. (1940). The song of the waif. In R. M. Rilke, *Selected poems.* With English translations by C. F. MacIntire. Berkeley: University of California Press.
Romain, J. (1944). *The death of a nobody.* New York: Knopf.
St. Vincent Millay, E. (1928). Dirge without music. In *The buck in the snow and other poems.* New York: Harper & Row.
Schiff, H. S. (1977). *The bereaved parent.* New York: Penguin.
Sexton, A. (1961). A curse against elegies. In A. Sexton, *All my pretty ones.* Boston: Houghton Mifflin.
Thomas, D. (1946). Elegy (unfinished). In D. Thomas, *Collected poems.* New York: New Directions Books.
Whitman, W. (1976). When lilacs last in the dooryard bloom'd. In R. Ellman (Ed.), *The new Oxford book of American verse.* New York: Oxford University Press.

Immortality

Blake, W. (1975). Eternity. In A. W. Allison et al. (Eds.), *The Norton anthology of poetry. Revised.* New York: Norton.
Coward, N. (1942). *Blythe spirit.* Garden City, NY: Doubleday.
Dickinson, E. (1960). Because I could not stop for death. (712). T. H. Johnson (Ed.), *The complete poems of Emily Dickinson.* Boston: Little, Brown.
Donne, J. (1975). From holy sonnets (Death be not proud). In A. W. Allison et al. (Eds.), *The Norton anthology of poetry. Revised.* New York: Norton.
Eliot, T. S. (1952) *Murder in the cathedral.* New York: Harcourt, Brace.

Ehrlich, M. (1975). *The reincarnation of Peter Proud.* New York: Bantam.

Evans-Wentz, W. Y. (Ed.). (1960). *The Tibetan book of the dead.* New York: Oxford University Press.

Goethe, J. W. von (1979). *Faust* (George Madison Priest, Trans.). Franklin Center, PA: The Franklin Library.

Gunn, J. (1962). *The immortals.* New York: Simon & Schuster.

Harrington, A. (1969). *The immortalist.* New York: Random House.

Heinlein, R. (1958). *Methuselah's children.* New York: New American Library.

Holy Bible, *Psalms 23, 27, 68, 139.*

Holy Bible, *Isaiah 24-27.*

Holy Bible, *The gospel according to St. John.*

Holy Bible, *The first epistle of Paul to the Corinthians, 15.*

MacLeish, A. The snowflake which is now and hence forever. In A. W. Allison et al. (Eds.), *The Norton anthology of poetry. Revised.* New York: Norton.

Sartre, J. P. (1956). *Being and nothingness* (Hazel Barnes, Trans.). New York: Philosophical Library.

Tennyson, A. (1975). Crossing the bar. In A. W. Allison et al. (Eds.), *The Norton anthology of poetry. Revised.* New York: Norton.

Thomas, D. (1946). And death shall have no dominion. In D. Thomas, *Collected poems.* New York: New Directions Books.

Thomas, D. (1946). The force that through green fuse drives the flower. In D. Thomas, *Collected poems.* New York: New Directions Books.

Tillich, P. (1957). *The dynamics of faith.* New York: Harper & Row.

Books for Children

Abbot, S. (1972). *The old dog.* (G. Mocniak, illus.). New York: Coward. Fiction. Ages 8-10.

Blue, R. (1976). *Grandma didn't wave back.* New York: Dell. Nonfiction. Ages 7-11.

Brown, M. W. (1965). *The dead bird.* Reading, MA: Addison-Wesley. Fiction. Preschool to age 8.

Cleaver, V., & Cleaver, B. (1970). *Grover.* Philadelphia: Lippincott. Fiction. Ages 9 and above.

Coburn, J. (1967). *Anne and the sand dobbies.* New York: Seabury. Fiction. Ages 8-12.

Cohen, B. (1974). *Thank you, Jackie Robinson.* New York: Lothrop. Fiction. Ages 8-11.

Cunningham, J. (1970). *Burnish me bright.* New York: Pantheon. Fiction. Ages 10-14.

De Paola, T. (1973). *Nana upstairs and Nana downstairs.* New York: Putnam's. Fiction. Preschool to 7.

Dobrin, A. (1971). *Scat!* New York: Four Winds. Fiction. Ages 6-9.

Farley, C. (1975). *The garden is doing fine.* New York: Atheneum. Fiction. Ages 6-8.

Fassler, J. (1971). *My grandpa died today.* (S. Kranz, Illus.). New York: Human Sciences. Fiction. Preschool to 8.

Greene, C. C. (1976). *Beat the turtle drum.* New York: Viking. Fiction. Ages 9-13.

Kantrowitz, M. (1973). *When Violet died.* New York: Parents' Magazine Press. Fiction. Preschool to 8.

Lundgren, M. (1972). *Matt's grandfather.* (A. Pyk, Trans.; F. Hald, Illus.). New York: Putnam's. Fiction. Ages 6–8.

Miles, M. (1971). *Annie and the old one.* Boston: Little, Brown. Fiction. Ages 8–12.

Norris, G. B. (1973). *The friendship hedge* (D. Payson, Illus.). New York: Dutton. Ages 6–9.

Orgel, D. (1971). *Mulberry music.* New York: Harper & Row. Fiction. Ages 8–12.

Shotwell, L. R. (1967). *Adam bookout.* New York: Viking. Fiction. Ages 12 and above.

Slote, A. (1973). *Hang tough, Paul Mather.* Philadelphia: Lippincott. Fiction. Ages 9–12.

Smith, D. B. (1973). *A taste of blackberries.* New York: Crowell. Fiction. Preschool to 6.

White, E. B. (1952). *Charlotte's web.* New York: Harper & Row. Fiction. Ages 8–11.

Note. A more extensive annotated list is found in Wass, H., Corr, C. A., Pacholski, R. W., & Forfar, C. S. (1985). *Death education II: An annotated resource guide.* Washington, DC: Hemisphere.

VISUAL ARTS

Bernini, Gian Lorenzo. *Tomb of Pope Urban VIII, 1628–1647,* St. Peter's, Vatican, Rome

Bruegel, Peter, the Elder, *The Triumph of Death, 1560–64,* Prado Museum, Madrid

Chagall, Marc, *The Gate to the Cemetery, 1917.* Collection Mme. Meyer-Chagall, Bern

Courbet, Gustave, *Burial at Ornans, 1849,* Louvre, Paris

Delacroix, Eugene, *Dante and Virgil in Hell, 1822,* Louvre, Paris

Delacroix, Eugene, *Massacre at Chios, 1824,* Louvre, Paris

Van Dyck, Anthony, *The Deposition, 1634,* Alte Pinokothek, Munich

El Greco, *Laocoon, c. 1610,* National Gallery of Art, Washington, D.C.

Friedrich, Caspar David, *Cemetery of a Monastery in the Snow, 1819,* National-Galerie, Berlin

Gaugin, Paul, *Mahana No Atua (Day of the God), 1894,* Art Institute, Chicago

Giotto, *Pieta (Lamentations), 1305–1306,* Fresco, Arena Chapel, Padua

van Gogh, Vincent, *Wheatfield with Crows,* July, 1980, Vincent van Gogh Foundation, Amsterdam

Goya, Francesco, *Executions of the Third of May 1808, 1808,* Prado, Madrid

Hofmann, Hans, *Memoria in Aeternum, 1962,* Museum of Modern Art, New York

Holbein, Hans, the Younger, *Todestanz (Dance of Death), 1515,* (woodcut). Prints available in most major museums

Klee, Paul, *Heavenly and Earthly Time, 1927.* Museum of Art, Philadelphia

Manet, Edouard, *The Shooting of the Emperor Maximilian, 1867,* Städtische Kunsthalle, Mannheim
Michelangelo, *Last Judgment, 1534–1541,* Fresco, Sistine Chapel, Vatican, Rome
Michelangelo, *Pieta, 1498–1500,* Marble sculpture, St. Peter's, Vatican, Rome
Munch, Edvard, *Death in the Sick Chamber, 1892,* National Gallery, Oslo
Oseberg Burial Ship, c. 825. University Museum of Antiquities, Oslo
Rattner, Abraham, *The Valley of Dry Bones, 1953–1956,* The Downtown Gallery, New York
Rembrandt von Ryn, *The Descent from the Cross, 1651,* National Gallery of Art, Washington, D.C.
Rodin, Auguste, *Gates of Hell, 1880–1917,* Sculpture, Rodin Museum, Philadelphia
Rouault, George, *This Will Be The Last Time, Little Father!, 1927,* Museum of Modern Art, New York
Uelsmann, Jerry N., *Silver Meditations, 1975,* Photographic Art. Dobbs Ferry, New York: Morgan and Morgan (selections; most photographs are untitled)

MUSICAL SELECTIONS

Dance of Death/Dies Irae

Berlioz, Hector, from Symphonie Fantastique; 4th mvt: *March to the gallows;* 5th mvt: *Dream of a witch's sabbath,* 1830.
Liszt, Franz, *Totentanz,* 1853; *Mephisto Waltz,* 1881.
Rachmaninof, Syergyey, *Isle of the dead,* 1907 (inspired by Arnold Böcklin's painting of the same name).
Saint-Saëns, Camille, *Danse macabre,* 1874.

Requiems/Oratorios/Other Classical Memorial Music

Bach, Johann Sebastian: A number of his cantatas, e.g., *A dialogue between Jesus and the soul; God's time is best; Funeral ode; Passion according to St. Matthew,* 1729; *Ascension oratorio,* 1735.
Beethoven, Ludwig van, in Symphonia No. 3 (Eroica) *Funeral march,* 1804.
Berlioz, Hector, *Grand messe des morts,* 1837.
Brahms, Johannes, *Funeral hymn,* 1958; *German requiem,* 1868.
Britten, Benjamin, *War requiem,* 1961.
Copland, Aaron, *A Lincoln portrait* (for narrator and orchestra), 1942.
Händel, George Frideric, *Funeral anthem for Queen Caroline,* 1737; *The Messiah,* 1741.
Mahler, Gustav, *Kindertotenlieder* (songs on the death of children), 1909.
Mozart, Wolfgang Amadeus, *Requiem,* 1791 (on his deathbed).
Schoenberg, Arnold, *A survivor from Warsaw,* 1947 (cantata).
Schubert, Franz, *Der Erlkönig* (the Erlking), song, 1815, the poem of the same title by Goethe.
Schutz, Heinrich, *Resurrection or*ätorio; Easter oratorio, 1623.

Strauss, Richard, *Tod und Verkl*ärung (Death and Transfiguration), 1889 (symphonic poem); *Four last songs*, 1948.
Stravinsky, Igor, Mass, 1948; *In memoriam Dylan Thomas*, 1954; *Eulogy for J.F.K.*, 1964; *Requiem canticles*, 1966.
Tchaikovsky, Peter Ilych, *Romeo and Juliet* (overture), final version 1880.
Verdi, Guiseppe, *Requiem*, 1874 (in memory of Manzoni).

Operas

Berlioz, Hector, *La damnation of Faust*, 1893.
Donizetti, Gaetano, *Lucia di Lammermoor*, 1835.
Gounod, Charles, *Faust*, 1859.
Gounod, Charles, *Romeo and Juliette*, 1867.
Mozart, Wolfgang Amadeus, *Don Giovanni* (Don Juan), 1787.
Puccini, Giacomo, *La Boheme*, 1896.
Puccini, Giacomo, *Madame butterfly*, 1904.
Saint-Saëns, Camille, *Samson and Delilah*, 1877.
Thomar, Ambrose, *Hamlet*, 1868.
Verdi, Guiseppe, *Macbeth*, 1847.
Verdi, Guiseppe, *Aida*, 1871.
Verdi, Guiseppe, *Othello*, 1887.
Wagner, Richard, *Der Fliegende Holl*änder (The Flying Dutchman), 1843.
Wagner, Richard, *Tristan and Isolde*, 1865.

Popular Songs/Spirituals/Blues

American girl, Tom Petty, 1983.
American pie, Don McLean.
Bookends theme, Paul Simon and Art Garfunkel, 1970.
Bridge over troubled water, Paul Simon and Art Garfunkel, 1969.
But I might die tonight, Cat Stevens, 1970.
Deep river, 1917 (based on a traditional black-American spiritual as early as 1875 arranged by Henry Thacker Burleigh).
Do space men pass dead souls on their way to the moon?, J. S. Bach and Linda Grossman, 1973.
Don't bury me before I'm dead, Johnnie Paycheck, 1983.
Fire and rain, James Taylor, 1971.
Give peace a chance, John Lennon, 1970.
Hello in there, John Prine, 1971.
Nightshift, The Commodores, 1985.
Ode to Billy Joe, Bobby Gentry, 1967.
Poems, prayers and promises, John Denver, 1971.
Pride in the name of love, U-2, 1985.
Save the life of my child, Paul Simon and Art Garfunkel, 1970.
Someone's knocking at the door, Paul McCartney, 1978.
Swing low, sweet chariot, 1917 (based on a traditional black-American spiritual as early as 1872 arranged by Henry Thacker Burleigh).
Vincent, Don McLean.
When the saints go marching in, 1896 (words by Katharine E. Purvis; music by James M. Black).

Where have all the flowers gone?, Peter, Paul, and Mary, 1962.
Will the circle be unbroken?, Joan Baez, 1969.

References

Arnold, D. (1983). *The new Oxford companion to music.* New York: Oxford University Press.

Gilder, E., & Port, J. G. (1978). *The dictionary of composers and their music.* New York: Paddington.

Mondadori, A. (Ed.). (1978). *The Simon and Schuster book of the opera: A complete reference guide—1957 to the present.* New York: Simon and Schuster.

Mordden, E. (1980). *A guide for orchestral music.* New York: Oxford University Press.

Note: For bibliographies of death-related music in 20 different classes of music including folk songs, popular music, and rock and roll (over 100 entries). See, Pacholski, R. A. (1986). Death themes in music: Resources and research opportunities for death educators. *Death Studies, 10*, 239–263.

Appendix E: Personal Death Awareness Exercises and Other Activities Concerning My Death

INTRODUCTION

Many thanatologists believe that the ability to acknowledge one's own mortality is beneficial in a variety of ways. We endorse this view. For this reason we present the material in this section. It is illustrative rather than comprehensive or even representative. We have successfully used these exercises and suggested these activities in our classes and in workshops and seminars with widely divergent audiences.

It is difficult to trace the originators of the exercises. We find that some textbooks and many training packages for various professional groups and lay persons contain exercises for which no credit lines are given, so it appears that these exercises are public. Nonetheless, we think that two primary sources should be recognized. One is Edwin Shneidman's extensive questionnaire "You and Death" published in a survey of the readers of the magazine *Psychology Today* (August, 1970, pp. 67–72). The other is the now out-of-print book by J. William Worden and William Proctor, *PDA*: Breaking Free of Fear to Live a Better Life Now, *Personal Death Awareness* (1976, Englewood Cliffs, NJ: Prentice-Hall). Some of the exercises below are adapted from these sources, a few are from colleagues, and the others are our own.

We give brief instructions only where we deem it necessary. The exercises can be done with small groups, dyads, or by individuals. Some activities suggested here have practical utility.

HISTORY OF MY PERSONAL DEATH EXPERIENCES

1. The first death I experienced was the death of . . . .
2. I was . . . . old.

3. I remember that I felt . . . .

4. The things that frightened me most were . . . .

5. I was most curious about . . . .

6. The first funeral I attended was . . . .

7. The most interesting thing about the funeral was . . . .

8. The scariest thing about the funeral was . . . .

9. My first personal acquaintance of my own age who died was . . . .

10. I remember feeling . . . .
11. I lost my first close relative when I was . . . . years old.
12. This relative was my . . . .
13. This loss was especially significant because . . . .

14. The most recent death of a loved one that I experienced was that of . . . . who died . . . . ago.
15. This loss affected me greatly because . . . .

16. At age . . . . I personally came close to death when . . . .

17. This experience had a great impact on me because . . . .

FEARS ABOUT MY DYING

What frightens me about my own dying is:

_____ losing control
_____ losing my intellectual capacities
_____ being left alone
_____ being a burden
_____ that my death will not be witnessed
_____ being looked down upon
_____ the pain
_____ getting weak
_____ that I will be hooked to machines and gadgets
_____ being emotionally overwhelmed
_____ not knowing what's going on
_____ getting inadequate medical care
_____ being declared dead when I'm still alive
_____ being buried alive
_____ being isolated from others
_____ that I will die of cancer

_____ looking ugly
_____ the grief I would cause my relatives and friends
_____ dying too slowly
_____ not being able to die calmly
_____ dying too soon
_____ that I will be too weak to say goodbye to my loved ones
_____ that the nurses will not realize when it happens
_____ being in agony
_____ that I may act disgracefully
_____ that I will die in a fire
_____ that I will suffocate
_____ that I will be murdered

FEARS ABOUT MY BODY AFTERWARDS

I dread the thought that my body will

_____ decay
_____ never be found
_____ be confused with another
_____ be left in the morgue
_____ be cremated
_____ be embalmed
_____ be dug up
_____ be displayed
_____ look disgusting
_____ be eaten by worms
_____ be mutilated
_____ be invaded by maggots

MY FEARS ABOUT WHAT HAPPENS AFTERWARDS

I am afraid that

_____ there may be no life after death
_____ I may go to hell
_____ I may have to be in purgatory
_____ Heaven may not be what I expect
_____ I may have to be with others I disliked on earth
_____ I may not get a new body
_____ my spirit may be trapped in my body
_____ my spirit may have to hover near my body
_____ my spirit may be lost in the universe
_____ my spirit may frighten my loved ones
_____ my spirit may have to travel forever
_____ my spirit may never find peace
_____ I may be conscious but in utter darkness

MY FEARS ABOUT MY LOVED ONES AND OTHERS AFTER MY DEATH

I fear that

_____ my loved ones will not be able to cope without me
_____ my loved ones will suffer many years of grief
_____ my loved ones will become physically or emotionally ill
_____ my loved ones will lose their will to live
_____ my loved ones will fight over my possessions
_____ my loved ones will not cherish what I leave them and what I cherished
_____ my loved ones will sell my treasures
_____ very few people will attend my funeral
_____ it will rain on the day of my funeral
_____ there will be a tornado/hurricane/snow storm/electrical storm on the day of my funeral
_____ my loved ones will not talk about me much
_____ my loved ones will not feel much grief
_____ my loved ones will soon forget me
_____ few people will miss me
_____ my loved ones and friends will remember the bad things about me
_____ some may be glad I'm dead
_____ my friends will laugh and have fun without giving me a thought
_____ there will be nothing that reminds people that I once existed

MY VIEWS AND BELIEFS ABOUT DEATH

_____ I firmly believe in life after death
_____ I believe there is a God who is concerned about me as an individual
_____ I wish there were life after death but I don't believe there is
_____ I am not interested in life after death
_____ I believe there is a supreme power or principle
_____ I think death is a kind of peaceful rest, an endless sleep
_____ I believe that after death we return to simple substances and may later take on another form
_____ I believe that after death our spirits join with a cosmic consciousness

MY GOALS AND VALUES

1. Here are three things that would be said about me if I died tomorrow:
   a.
   b.
   c.
2. Assuming that I will not die tomorrow, and that I will have time to change things in my life, here are three things that I would most like to have said about me if I died later.

a.

b.

c.

3. My Lifeline

   Instructions: Draw a line on a sheet of paper. Pretend that this line represents your life span. Mark the beginning of the line with your date of birth. Mark a point on the line at which you presently are. Put down your age. Now mark the end of your life line with the year in which you imagine you will die. Now look at the life time that has already passed and compare it with the projected time you have yet to live. Make a list of all the things you want to do and all the things you want to accomplish. Then rank-order them. The purpose of this exercise is to help people to clarify their goals and priorities.

OTHER ACTIVITIES

1. Prepare a Living Will.

   Instructions. Find out if your home state has a law concerning the right to die. Obtain a copy of that law. Consider if you want to exercise this right. If so, fill out the form and file it with your physician. Give copies to your family. Tell your friends. If your state has no such law, fill out the Living Will below.

2. Make a draft of a last will and testament.

3. If you wish, fill out organ and/or body donation forms or a uniform donor card.

4. Write a farewell letter to a loved one. In doing so pretend that you are terminally ill and have only a short time to life. Give your letter to your loved one if you think he or she can handle it.

5. Prearrange your funeral with the funeral home of your choice. Discuss your wishes and plans with your next of kin.

6. Plan your funeral/memorial service. Discuss your wishes with your next of kin.

7. Write your own eulogy.

8. Write your own obituary using the following form as a guide.

LIVING WILL DECLARATION

To My Family, Doctors, and All Those Concerned with My Care

I, _____ , being of sound mind, make this statement as a directive to be followed if for any reason I become unable to participate in decisions regarding my medical care.

I direct that life-sustaining procedures should be withheld or withdrawn if I have an illness, disease or injury, or experience extreme mental deterioration, such that there is no reasonable expectation of recovering or regaining a meaningful quality of life.

These life-sustaining procedures that may be withheld or withdrawn include, but are not limited to:

SURGERY   ANTIBIOTICS   CARDIAC RESUSCITATION
RESPIRATORY SUPPORT   ARTIFICIALLY ADMINISTERED FEEDING AND FLUIDS

I further direct that treatment be limited to comfort measures only, even if they shorten my life.

You may delete any provision above by drawing a line through it and adding your initials.

Other personal instructions:

These directions express my legal right to refuse treatment. Therefore, I expect my family, doctors, and all those concerned with my care to regard themselves as legally and morally bound to act in accord with my wishes, and in so doing to be free from any liability for having followed my directions.

Signed _____ Date _____

Witness _____ Witness _____

PROXY DESIGNATION CLAUSE

If you wish, you may use this section to designate someone to make treatment decisions if you are unable to do so. Your Living Will Declaration will be in effect even if you have not designated a proxy.

I authorize the following person to implement my Living Will Declaration by accepting, refusing and/or making decisions about treatment and hospitalization:

Name _____

Address _____

If the person I have named above is unable to act on my behalf, I authorize the following person to do so:

Name _____

Address _____

I have discussed my wishes with these persons and trust their judgment on my behalf.

Signed _____ Date _____

Witness _____ Witness _____

Reprinted by permission of the Society for the Right to Die, 250 W. 59th St., New York, NY 10107.

MY OBITUARY

_____ died today at the age of _____ .
          Your full name

A native of _____ he/she died _____
                    Your birthplace   The cause of your death

_____ . He/she is survived by _____
                                                                    Who in your family will

_____ . Details of the funeral are as follow:
          survive you

_____

_____

_____

_____

_____

_____

_____

_____

1. What was the most difficult part of writing your obituary?
2. How do you feel right now?

tense	anxious	calm	strange	hopeless	interested
amused	angry	bored	depressed	happy	conflicted
sick	helpless	tired	frightened	neutral	_____
glad to be alive		hostile	silly	desperate	_____
					Other?

(circle the words that best describe your feelings)

Index